Lineberger

Lu...

Fo.. 45

D1204463

STRABO

II

LCL 50

STRABO

GEOGRAPHY

BOOKS 3–5

WITH AN ENGLISH TRANSLATION BY

HORACE LEONARD JONES

HARVARD UNIVERSITY PRESS
CAMBRIDGE, MASSACHUSETTS
LONDON, ENGLAND

First published 1923
Reprinted 1949, 1960, 1969, 1988, 1999

LOEB CLASSICAL LIBRARY® is a registered trademark
of the President and Fellows of Harvard College

ISBN 0-674-99056-0

Printed in Great Britain by St Edmundsbury Press Ltd,
Bury St Edmunds, Suffolk, on acid-free paper.
Bound by Hunter & Foulis Ltd, Edinburgh, Scotland.

CONTENTS

LIST OF THE BOOKS OF
THE GEOGRAPHY OF STRABO

Showing their place in the volumes of this
edition and in the edition of Casaubon of 1620

LIST OF THE BOOKS

THE
GEOGRAPHY OF STRABO

BOOK III

ΣΤΡΑΒΩΝΟΣ ΓΕΩΓΡΑΦΙΚΩΝ

Γ

I

1. Ἀποδεδωκόσι δ' ἡμῖν τὸν πρῶτον τύπον τῆς γεωγραφίας οἰκεῖός ἐστιν ὁ ἐφεξῆς λόγος περὶ τῶν καθ' ἕκαστα· καὶ γὰρ ὑπεσχόμεθα οὕτως, καὶ δοκεῖ μέχρι νῦν ὀρθῶς ἡ πραγματεία μεμερίσθαι. ἀρκτέον δὲ πάλιν ἀπὸ τῆς Εὐρώπης καὶ τῶν μερῶν αὐτῆς τούτων ἀφ' ὧνπερ καὶ πρότερον, κατὰ τὰς αὐτὰς αἰτίας.

2. Πρῶτον δὲ μέρος αὐτῆς ἐστι τὸ ἑσπέριον, C 137 ὡς ἔφαμεν, ἡ Ἰβηρία. ταύτης δὴ τὸ μὲν πλέον οἰκεῖται φαύλως· ὄρη γὰρ καὶ δρυμοὺς καὶ πεδία λεπτὴν ἔχοντα γῆν, οὐδὲ ταύτην ὁμαλῶς εὔυδρον, οἰκοῦσι τὴν πολλήν· ἡ δὲ πρόσβορρος ψυχρά τέ ἐστι τελέως πρὸς τῇ τραχύτητι καὶ παρωκεανῖτις, προσειληφυῖα τὸ ἄμικτον κἀνεπίπλεκτον τοῖς ἄλλοις, ὥσθ' ὑπερβάλλει τῇ μοχθηρίᾳ τῆς οἰκήσεως. ταῦτα μὲν δὴ τὰ μέρη τοιαῦτα, ἡ δὲ νότιος πᾶσα εὐδαίμων σχεδόν τι, καὶ διαφερόντως ἡ ἔξω

---

[1] See 2 5. 4.   [2] See 2. 5. 26.

2

THE GEOGRAPHY OF STRABO

BOOK III

I

1. Now that I have given the first general outline of geography, it is proper for me to discuss next the several parts of the inhabited world; indeed, I have promised to do so,[1] and I think that thus far my treatise has been correctly apportioned. But I must begin again with Europe and with those parts of Europe with which I began at first,[2] and for the same reasons.

2. As I was saying, the first part of Europe is the western, namely, Iberia. Now of Iberia the larger part affords but poor means of livelihood; for most of the inhabited country consists of mountains, forests, and plains whose soil is thin—and even that not uniformly well-watered. And Northern Iberia, in addition to its ruggedness, not only is extremely cold, but lies next to the ocean, and thus has acquired its characteristic of inhospitality and aversion to intercourse with other countries; consequently, it is an exceedingly wretched place to live in. Such, then, is the character of the northern parts; but almost the whole of Southern Iberia is fertile, particularly the region outside the Pillars. This

3

Στηλῶν· ἔσται δὲ δῆλον ἐν τοῖς καθ' ἕκαστα, ὑπογράψασιν ἡμῖν πρότερον τό τε σχῆμα καὶ τὸ μέγεθος.

3. Ἔοικε γὰρ βύρσῃ τεταμένῃ κατὰ μῆκος μὲν ἀπὸ τῆς ἑσπέρας ἐπὶ τὴν ἕω, τὰ πρόσθια ἐχούσῃ μέρη πρὸς τῇ ἕῳ, κατὰ πλάτος δ' ἀπὸ τῶν ἄρκτων πρὸς νότον. ἔχει δὲ σταδίων ἑξακισχιλίων ὁμοῦ τὸ μῆκος, πλάτος δὲ πεντακισχιλίων τὸ μέγιστον, ἔστι δ' ὅπου πολὺ ἔλαττον τῶν τρισχιλίων, καὶ μάλιστα πρὸς τῇ Πυρήνῃ τῇ ποιούσῃ τὴν ἑώαν πλευράν. ὄρος γὰρ διηνεκὲς ἀπὸ νότου πρὸς βορρᾶν τεταμένον ὁρίζει τὴν Κελτικὴν ἀπὸ τῆς Ἰβηρίας. οὔσης δὲ καὶ τῆς Κελτικῆς ἀνωμάλου τὸ πλάτος καὶ τῆς Ἰβηρίας, τὸ στενώτατον τοῦ πλάτους ἑκατέρας ἀπὸ τῆς ἡμετέρας θαλάττης ἐπὶ τὸν ὠκεανόν ἐστι τὸ τῇ Πυρήνῃ πλησιάζον μάλιστα, ἐφ' ἑκάτερον αὐτῆς τὸ μέρος, καὶ ποιοῦν κόλπους, τοὺς μὲν ἐπὶ τῷ ὠκεανῷ, τοὺς δὲ ἐπὶ τῇ καθ' ἡμᾶς θαλάττῃ· μείζους δὲ τοὺς Κελτικούς, οὓς δὴ καὶ Γαλατικοὺς καλοῦσι, στενώτερον τὸν ἰσθμὸν ποιοῦντας παρὰ τὸν[1] Ἰβηρικόν. καὶ δὴ τὸ μὲν ἑῷον πλευρὸν τῆς Ἰβηρίας ἡ Πυρήνη ποιεῖ, τὸ δὲ νότιον ἥ τε καθ' ἡμᾶς θάλαττα ἀπὸ τῆς Πυρήνης μέχρι Στηλῶν, καὶ ἡ ἐκτὸς τὸ ἐξῆς μέχρι τοῦ Ἱεροῦ καλουμένου ἀκρωτηρίου· τρίτον ἐστὶ τὸ ἑσπέριον πλευρὸν παράλληλόν πως τῇ

---

[1] τόν, Corais from sec. man. in B, for τό.

---

[1] According to Strabo, there were two "Galatic" ("Celtic") gulfs, the one "looking towards the north and Britain" (2. 5. 28), and the other on the Mediterranean side; that is, respectively, the Gulf of Gascogne, in its extent on the French side of the Pyrenees, and the Gulf of

will become clear in the course of my detailed description of Iberia. But first I must briefly describe its shape and give its dimensions.

3. Iberia is like an ox-hide extending in length from west to east, its fore-parts toward the east, and in breadth from north to south. It is six thousand stadia in length all told, and five thousand stadia in its greatest breadth; though in some places it is much less than three thousand in breadth, particularly near the Pyrenees, which form its eastern side. That is, an unbroken chain of mountains, stretching from south to north, forms the boundary line between Celtica and Iberia; and since Celtica, as well as Iberia, varies in breadth, the part of each country that is narrowest in breadth between Our Sea and the ocean is that which lies nearest to the Pyrenees, on either side of those mountains, and forms gulfs both at the ocean and at Our Sea. The Celtic gulfs, however, which are also called Galatic, are larger, and the isthmus which they form is narrower as compared with that of Iberia.[1] So the eastern side of Iberia is formed by the Pyrenees; the southern side is formed in part by Our Sea, from the Pyrenees to the Pillars, and from that point on by the ocean, up to what is called the Sacred Cape[2]; the third is the western side, which

Lyon. The latter, however, comprised within itself the two "Galatic" gulfs (4. 1. 6.) here mentioned as "larger"; that is, "larger" than the two gulfs on the Iberian side of the Pyrenees, which Strabo does not name (see small map inserted in Map III in this volume). The fact is, however, that the shortest distance across Spain, say from San Sebastian to Tarragona, is shorter than that across France, say from Bayonne to Narbonne.

[2] Cape St. Vincent.

Πυρήνη, τὸ ἀπὸ τοῦ Ἱεροῦ ἀκρωτηρίου μέχρι
τῆς πρὸς Ἀρτάβροις ἄκρας, ἣν καλοῦσι Νέριον·
τέταρτον δὲ τὸ ἐνθένδε μέχρι τῶν βορείων ἄκρων
τῆς Πυρήνης.

4. Ἀναλαβόντες δὲ λέγωμεν τὰ καθ' ἕκαστα,
ἀπὸ τοῦ Ἱεροῦ ἀκρωτηρίου ἀρξάμενοι. τοῦτο δέ
ἐστι τὸ δυτικώτατον, οὐ τῆς Εὐρώπης μόνον, ἀλλὰ
καὶ τῆς οἰκουμένης ἁπάσης σημεῖον· περατοῦται
μὲν γὰρ ὑπὸ τῶν δυεῖν ἠπείρων ἡ οἰκουμένη πρὸς
δύσιν τοῖς τε τῆς Εὐρώπης ἄκροις καὶ τοῖς πρώτοις
τῆς Λιβύης, ὧν τὰ μὲν Ἴβηρες ἔχουσι, τὰ δὲ
Μαυρούσιοι, προΰχει δὲ τὰ Ἰβηρικὰ ὅσον χιλίοις
καὶ πεντακοσίοις σταδίοις κατὰ τὸ λεχθὲν ἀκρωτήριον. καὶ δὴ καὶ τὴν προσεχῆ τούτῳ χώραν τῇ
Λατίνῃ φωνῇ καλοῦσι Κούνεον, σφῆνα σημαίνειν
βουλόμενοι. αὐτὸ δὲ τὸ ἄκρον καὶ προπεπτωκὸς
εἰς τὴν θάλατταν Ἀρτεμίδωρος εἰκάζει πλοίῳ,
C 138 γενόμενος, φησίν, ἐν τῷ τόπῳ, προσλαμβάνειν δὲ
τῷ σχήματι νησίδια τρία, τὸ μὲν ἐμβόλου τάξιν
ἔχον, τὰ δὲ ἐπωτίδων, ἐφόρμους ἔχοντα μετρίους.
Ἡρακλέους δ' οὔθ'[1] ἱερὸν ἐνταῦθα δείκνυσθαι
(ψεύσασθαι δὲ τοῦτο Ἔφορον), οὔτε βωμόν, οὐδ'
ἄλλου τῶν θεῶν, ἀλλὰ λίθους συγκεῖσθαι τρεῖς
ἢ τέτταρας κατὰ πολλοὺς τόπους, οὓς ὑπὸ τῶν
ἀφικνουμένων στρέφεσθαι κατά τι πάτριον καὶ

---

[1] οὔθ', Kramer, for θ'; so the later editors.

---

[1] Cape Finisterre.

is approximately parallel to the Pyrenees and extends from the Sacred Cape to that Cape of the Artabrians which is called Nerium [1]; and the fourth side extends from Cape Nerium up to the northern headlands of the Pyrenees.

4. But, to resume, let me describe Iberia in detail, beginning with the Sacred Cape. This cape is the most westerly point, not only of Europe, but of the whole inhabited world ; for, whereas the inhabited world comes to an end in the west with the two continents (in the one case, at the headlands of Europe, and in the other, at the extremities of Libya, of which regions the Iberians occupy the one, and the Maurusians the other), the headlands of Iberia project at the aforementioned cape about fifteen hundred stadia beyond those of Libya. Moreover, the country adjacent to this cape they call in the Latin language "Cuneus," meaning thereby to indicate its wedge-shape. But as for the cape itself, which projects into the sea, Artemidorus (who visited the place, as he says) likens it to a ship ; and he says that three little islands help to give it this shape, one of these islands occupying the position of a ship's beak, and the other two, which have fairly good places of anchorage, occupying the position of cat-heads. But as for Heracles, he says, there is neither a temple of his to be seen on the cape (as Ephorus wrongly states), nor an altar to him, or to any other god either, but only stones [2] in many spots, lying in groups of three or four, which in accordance with a native custom are

---

[2] "Rocking Stones." They were so nicely poised on their points that they could be rocked or turned with merely a slight force.

μεταφέρεσθαι σπονδοποιησαμένων·[1] θύειν δ' οὐκ
εἶναι νόμιμον, οὐδὲ νύκτωρ ἐπιβαίνειν[2] τοῦ τόπου,
θεοὺς φασκόντων κατέχειν αὐτὸν ἐν τῷ τότε
χρόνῳ, ἀλλὰ τοὺς ἐπὶ θέαν ἥκοντας ἐν κώμῃ
πλησίον νυκτερεύειν, εἶτ' ἐπιβαίνειν ἡμέρας, ὕδωρ
ἐπιφερομένους διὰ τὴν ἀνυδρίαν.

5. Ταῦτα μὲν οὖν οὕτως ἔχειν ἐγχωρεῖ, καὶ δεῖ
πιστεύειν· ἃ δὲ τοῖς πολλοῖς καὶ χυδαίοις ὁμοίως
εἴρηκεν, οὐ πάνυ. λέγειν γὰρ δή φησι Ποσειδώνιος τοὺς πολλούς, μείζω δύνειν τὸν ἥλιον ἐν
τῇ παρωκεανίτιδι καὶ μετὰ ψόφου παραπλησίως
ὡσανεὶ σίζοντος τοῦ πελάγους κατὰ σβέσιν αὐτοῦ
διὰ τὸ ἐμπίπτειν εἰς τὸν βυθόν. ψεῦδος δ' εἶναι
καὶ τοῦτο καὶ τὸ παραχρῆμα νύκτα ἀκολουθεῖν
μετὰ τὴν δύσιν· οὐ γὰρ παραχρῆμα, μικρὸν δ'
ὕστερον, καθάπερ καὶ ἐν τοῖς ἄλλοις πελάγεσι
τοῖς μεγάλοις. ὅπου μὲν γὰρ εἰς ὄρη δύεται,
πλείω τὸν μετὰ δύσιν χρόνον τῆς ἡμέρας συμβαίνειν ἐκ τοῦ παραφωτισμοῦ, ἐκεῖ δὲ πλείω μὲν
οὐκ ἐπακολουθεῖν, μὴ μέντοι μηδὲ παραχρῆμα
συνάπτειν τὸ σκότος, καθάπερ καὶ ἐν τοῖς μεγάλοις πεδίοις. τὴν δὲ τοῦ μεγέθους φαντασίαν
αὔξεσθαι μὲν ὁμοίως κατά τε τὰς δύσεις καὶ τὰς
ἀνατολὰς ἐν τοῖς πελάγεσι διὰ τὸ τὰς ἀναθυ-

---

[1] σπονδοποιησαμένων, Corais, for ψευδοποιησαμένων; generally followed.
[2] ἐπιβαίνειν, conj. of Meineke, for ἐπιβάλλειν; generally
followed.

---

[1] That is, to the original position; but the Greek word
might mean "transferred" to other spots. Hübner (Pauly-

turned round by those who visit the place, and then, after the pouring of a libation, are moved back again.[1] And it is not lawful, he adds, to offer sacrifice there, nor, at night, even to set foot on the place, because the gods, the people say, occupy it at that time; but those who come to see the place spend the night in a neighbouring village, and then enter the place by day, taking water with them, for there is no water there.

5. Now these assertions of Artemidorus are allowable, and we should believe them; but the stories which he has told in agreement with the common crowd of people are by no means to be believed. For example, it is a general saying among the people, according to Poseidonius, that in the regions along the coast of the ocean the sun is larger when it sets, and that it sets with a noise much as if the sea were sizzling to extinguish it because of its falling into the depths. But, says Poseidonius, this is false, as also the statement that night follows instantly upon sunset; for night does not come on instantly, but after a slight interval, just as it does on the coasts of the other large seas. For in regions where the sun sets behind mountains, he says, the daylight lasts a longer time after sunset, as a result of the indirect light; but on the sea-coasts no considerable interval ensues, albeit the darkness does not come on instantly, either, any more than it does on the great plains. And, he says, the visual impression of the size of the sun increases alike both at sunset and sunrise on the seas, because at those times a greater amount of vapour rises

Wissowa, *Real-Encyclopädie*, vol. iv, 1908) thinks the stones "apparently were carried away" by the visitors.

μιασεις πλείους ἐκ τῶν ὑγρῶν ἀναφέρεσθαι· διὰ
δὲ τούτων ὡς δι᾽ ὑάλων[1] κλωμένην τὴν ὄψιν
πλατυτέρας δέχεσθαι τὰς φαντασίας, καθάπερ
καὶ διὰ νέφους ξηροῦ καὶ λεπτοῦ βλέπουσαν
δυόμενον ἢ ἀνατέλλοντα τὸν ἥλιον ἢ τὴν σελή-
νην, ἡνίκα καὶ ἐνερευθὲς φαίνεσθαι τὸ ἄστρον.
τὸ δὲ ψεῦδος ἐλέγξαι φησὶ τριάκονθ᾽ ἡμέρας
διατρίψας ἐν Γαδείροις καὶ τηρήσας τὰς δύσεις.
ὁ δέ γε Ἀρτεμίδωρος ἑκατονταπλασιόνα φησὶ
δύεσθαι τὸν ἥλιον, καὶ αὐτίκα νύκτα καταλαμ-
βάνειν. ὡς μὲν οὖν αὐτὸς εἶδε τοῦτο ἐν τῷ Ἱερῷ
ἀκρωτηρίῳ, οὐχ ὑποληπτέον, προσέχοντας τῇ
ἀποφάσει αὐτοῦ, ἔφη γὰρ νύκτωρ μηδένα ἐπι-
βαίνειν· ὥστ᾽ οὐδὲ δυομένου ἡλίου οὐδεὶς ἂν
ἐπιβαίνοι, εἴπερ εὐθὺς ἡ νὺξ καταλαμβάνει. ἀλλ᾽
οὐδ᾽ ἐν ἄλλῳ τόπῳ τῆς παρωκεανίτιδος· καὶ γὰρ
τὰ Γάδειρα ἐπὶ τῷ ὠκεανῷ, καὶ ὁ Ποσειδώνιος
ἀντιμαρτυρεῖ καὶ ἄλλοι πλείους.

6. Τῆς δὲ συνεχοῦς τῷ Ἱερῷ ἀκρωτηρίῳ παρα-
C 139 λίας ἡ μέν ἐστιν ἀρχὴ τοῦ ἑσπερίου πλευροῦ τῆς
Ἰβηρίας μέχρι τῆς ἐκβολῆς τοῦ Τάγου ποταμοῦ,
ἡ δὲ τοῦ νοτίου μέχρι ἄλλου ποταμοῦ τοῦ Ἄνα
καὶ τῆς ἐκβολῆς αὐτοῦ. φέρεται δ᾽ ἀπὸ τῶν
ἑῴων μερῶν ἑκάτερος· ἀλλ᾽ ὁ μὲν ἐπ᾽ εὐθείας εἰς
τὴν ἑσπέραν ἐκδίδωσι πολὺ μείζων ὢν θατέρου,
ὁ δ᾽ Ἄνας πρὸς νότον ἐπιστρέφει, τὴν μεσοπο-

---

1 ὑάλων, I. Voss, for αὐλῶν; so Schneider, Groskurd,
Meineke, Forbiger, and Tardieu.

---

[1] A globe filled with water, apparently.
[2] We should say "refracted." Empedocles (quoted by
Aristotle, *De Sensu et Sensili*, chap. 2) advanced the theory

from the water; that is, the visual rays, in passing through this vapour as through a lens,[1] are
broken,[2] and therefore the visual impression is
magnified, just as it is when the setting or the rising
sun, or moon, is seen through a dry, thin cloud, at
which time the heavenly body also appears somewhat ruddy. He convinced himself, he says, of the
falsity of the above assertions during his stay of
thirty days in Gades, when he observed the settings
of the sun. Nevertheless, Artemidorus says that
the sun sets a hundred times larger than usual, and
that night comes on immediately! However, if we
look closely at his declaration, we are obliged to
assume that he did not himself see this phenomenon
at the Sacred Cape, for he states that no one sets
foot on the place by night; and hence no one could
set foot on it while the sun was setting, either, if
it be true that night comes on immediately. Neither,
in fact, did he see it at any other point on the ocean-
coast, for Gades also is on the ocean, and Poseidonius
and several others bear witness against him.

6. The coastline adjacent to the Sacred Cape, on
the west, is the beginning of the western side of
Iberia as far as the mouth of the Tagus River, and,
on the south, the beginning of the southern side as
far as another river, the Anas, and its mouth. Both
rivers flow from the eastern regions; but the Tagus,
which is a much larger stream than the other, flows
straight westward to its mouth, whereas the Anas
turns south, and marks off a boundary of the inter-
fluvial region, which is inhabited for the most part

that the visual rays emanate from the eyes, but Aristotle
(*l. c.*) controverted it. See also Plato, *Timaeus*, 45 c and
46 B; and Seneca, *Quaestiones Naturales*, 1. 6.

ταμίαν ἀφορίζων, ἣν Κελτικοὶ νέμονται τὸ πλέον,
καὶ τῶν Λυσιτανῶν τινες ἐκ τῆς περαίας τοῦ
Τάγου μετοικισθέντες ὑπὸ Ῥωμαίων· ἐν δὲ τοῖς
ἄνω μέρεσι καὶ Καρπητανοὶ καὶ Ὠρητανοὶ καὶ
Οὐεττώνων συχνοὶ νέμονται. αὕτη μὲν οὖν ἡ
χώρα μετρίως ἐστὶν εὐδαίμων, ἡ δ' ἐφεξῆς πρὸς
ἕω κειμένη καὶ νότον ὑπερβολὴν οὐκ ἀπολείπει
πρὸς ἅπασαν κρινομένη τὴν οἰκουμένην ἀρετῆς
χάριν καὶ τῶν ἐκ γῆς καὶ θαλάττης ἀγαθῶν.
αὕτη δ' ἐστίν ἣν ὁ Βαῖτις διαρρεῖ ποταμός, ἀπὸ
τῶν αὐτῶν μερῶν τὴν ἀρχὴν ἔχων ἀφ' ὧνπερ καὶ
ὁ Ἄνας καὶ ὁ Τάγος, μέσος πως ἀμφοῖν τούτων
ὑπάρχων κατὰ μέγεθος· παραπλησίως μέντοι τῷ
Ἄνᾳ κατ' ἀρχὰς ἐπὶ τὴν ἑσπέραν ῥυεὶς εἶτ'
ἐπιστρέφει πρὸς νότον καὶ κατὰ τὴν αὐτὴν ἐκδίδωσι τούτῳ παραλίαν. καλοῦσι δ' ἀπὸ μὲν τοῦ
ποταμοῦ Βαιτικήν, ἀπὸ δὲ τῶν ἐνοικούντων Τουρ-
δητανίαν· τοὺς δ' ἐνοικοῦντας Τουρδητανούς τε
καὶ Τουρδούλους προσαγορεύουσιν, οἱ μὲν τοὺς
αὐτοὺς νομίζοντες, οἱ δ' ἑτέρους· ὧν ἐστι καὶ
Πολύβιος, συνοίκους φήσας τοῖς Τουρδητανοῖς
πρὸς ἄρκτον τοὺς Τουρδούλους· νυνὶ δ' ἐν αὐτοῖς
οὐδεὶς φαίνεται διορισμός. σοφώτατοι δ' ἐξετά-
ζονται τῶν Ἰβήρων οὗτοι, καὶ γραμματικῇ χρῶνται, καὶ τῆς παλαιᾶς μνήμης ἔχουσι συγγράμματα
καὶ ποιήματα καὶ νόμους ἐμμέτρους ἑξακισχιλίων
ἐτῶν,[1] ὥς φασι· καὶ οἱ ἄλλοι δ' Ἴβηρες χρῶνται
γραμματικῇ, οὐ μιᾷ δ' ἰδέα, οὐδὲ γὰρ γλώττῃ μιᾷ.
τείνει δὲ ἡ χώρα αὕτη, ἡ ἐντὸς τοῦ Ἄνα, πρὸς ἕω

---

[1] Paulmier de Grentemesnil conj. ἐπῶν for ἐτῶν; Meineke
following. Cp. Caesar Bell. Gall. 6. 14.

by Celtic peoples, and by certain of the Lusitanians who were transplanted thither by the Romans from the other side of the Tagus. But in the regions farther inland dwell Carpetanians, Oretanians, and large numbers of Vettonians. This country, to be sure, has only a moderately happy lot, but that which lies next to it on the east and south takes pre-eminence in comparison with the entire inhabited world in respect of fertility and of the goodly products of land and sea. This is the country through which the Baetis flows, which rises in the same districts as both the Anas and the Tagus, and in size is about midway between the other two rivers. Like the Anas, however, it at first flows towards the west, and then turns south, and empties on the same coast as the Anas. They call the country Baetica after the river, and also Turdetania after the inhabitants; yet they call the inhabitants both Turdetanians and Turdulians, some believing that they are the same people, others that they are different. Among the latter is Polybius, for he states that the Turdulians are neighbours of the Turdetanians on the north; but at the present time there is no distinction to be seen among them. The Turdetanians are ranked as the wisest of the Iberians; and they make use of an alphabet, and possess records of their ancient history, poems, and laws written in verse that are six thousand years old,[1] as they assert. And also the other Iberians use an alphabet, though not letters of one and the same character, for their speech is not one and the same, either. Now Turdetania, the country this side the

---

[1] Some think the text should be emended to read "six thousand verses in length."

μὲν μέχρι τῆς Ὠρητανίας, πρὸς νότον δὲ μέχρι
τῆς παραλίας τῆς ἀπὸ τῶν ἐκβολῶν τοῦ Ἄνα
μέχρι Στηλῶν. ἀνάγκη δὲ διὰ πλειόνων περὶ
αὐτῆς εἰπεῖν καὶ τῶν σύνεγγυς τόπων, ὅσα συν-
τείνει πρὸς τὸ μαθεῖν τὴν εὐφυΐαν τῶν τόπων καὶ
τὴν εὐδαιμονίαν.

7. Τῆς δὲ παραλίας ταύτης, εἰς ἣν ὅ τε Βαῖτις
καὶ ὁ Ἄνας ἐκδίδωσι, καὶ τῶν ἐσχάτων τῆς
Μαυρουσίας εἰς τὸ μεταξὺ ἐμπῖπτον τὸ Ἀτλαν-
τικὸν πέλαγος ποιεῖ τὸν κατὰ Στήλας πορθμόν,
καθ' ὃν ἡ ἐντὸς θάλαττα συνάπτει τῇ ἐκτός.
ἐνταῦθα δὴ ὄρος ἐστὶ τῶν Ἰβήρων τῶν καλουμένων Βαστητανῶν, οὓς καὶ Βαστούλους καλοῦσιν, ἡ Κάλπη, τῇ περιοχῇ μὲν οὐ μέγα, τῷ δ'
ὕψει μέγα καὶ ὄρθιον, ὥστε πόρρωθεν νησοειδὲς
C 140 φαίνεσθαι. ἐκπλέουσιν οὖν ἐκ τῆς ἡμετέρας
θαλάττης εἰς τὴν ἔξω δεξιόν ἐστι τοῦτο, καὶ πρὸς
αὐτῷ[1] Κάλπη πόλις, ἐν τετταράκοντα σταδίοις,
ἀξιόλογος καὶ παλαιά, ναύσταθμόν ποτε γενομένη
τῶν Ἰβήρων. ἔνιοι δὲ καὶ Ἡρακλέους κτίσμα
λέγουσιν αὐτήν, ὧν ἐστι καὶ Τιμοσθένης, ὅς φησι
καὶ Ἡρακλείαν ὀνομάζεσθαι τὸ παλαιόν, δείκνυ-
σθαί τε μέγαν περίβολον καὶ νεωσοίκους.

8. Εἶτα Μενλαρία, ταριχείας ἔχουσα, καὶ μετὰ
ταῦτα Βελὼν πόλις καὶ ποταμός. ἐντεῦθεν οἱ
διάπλοι μάλιστά εἰσιν εἰς Τίγγιν τῆς Μαυρουσίας

---

[1] αὐτῷ, Jones, for αὐτό.

---

[1] Previous editors have unnecessarily emended Calpe to
Carteia. Ancient writers, in describing the highway on the
coast from Malaga to Gades, thought of Calpe and its
close neighbour, Carteia, as a single halting-place. In the

Anas, stretches eastward as far as Oretania, and southward as far as the coastline that extends from the mouths of the Anas to the Pillars. But I must describe it and the regions that are close to it at greater length, telling all that contributes to our knowledge of their natural advantages and happy lot.

7. Between this stretch of coastline, on which both the Baetis and the Anas empty, and the limits of Maurusia, the Atlantic Ocean breaks in and thus forms the strait at the Pillars, and by this strait the interior sea connects with the exterior sea. Now at this strait there is a mountain belonging to those Iberians that are called Bastetanians, who are also called Bastulians; I mean Calpe, which, although its circumference is not great, rises to so great a height and is so steep that from a distance it looks like an island. So when you sail from Our Sea into the exterior sea, you have this mountain on your right hand; and near it, within a distance of forty stadia, is the city Calpe,[1] an important and ancient city, which was once a naval station of the Iberians. And some further say that it was founded by Heracles, among whom is Timosthenes, who says that in ancient times it was also called Heracleia, and that its great city-walls and its docks are still to be seen.

8. Then comes Menlaria, with its establishments for salting fish; and next, the city and river of Belon. It is from Belon that people generally take ship for the passage across to Tingis in Maurusia; and at Belon there are trading-places and establish-

Antonine Itinerary (*Itin. Prov. Ant. Aug.* 406. 3) the halting-place is called "Calpe Carteia."

καὶ ἐμπόρια καὶ ταριχεῖαι. ἦν δὲ καὶ Ζῆλις τῆς
Τίγγιος ἀστυγείτων, ἀλλὰ μετῴκισαν ταύτην εἰς
τὴν περαίαν Ῥωμαῖοι, καὶ ἐκ τῆς Τίγγιος προσλα-
βόντες τινάς· ἔπεμψαν δὲ καὶ παρ' ἑαυτῶν ἐποίκους, καὶ ὠνόμασαν Ἰουλίαν Ἰοζαν τὴν πόλιν.
εἶτα Γάδειρα, πορθμῷ στενῷ διειργομένη νῆσος
ἀπὸ τῆς Τουρδητανίας, διέχουσα τῆς Κάλπης
περὶ ἑπτακοσίους καὶ πεντήκοντα σταδίους, οἱ
δὲ ὀκτακοσίους φασίν. ἔστι δ' ἡ νῆσος αὕτη
τἆλλα μὲν οὐθὲν διαφέρουσα τῶν ἄλλων, ἀνδρείᾳ
δὲ τῶν ἐνοικούντων τῇ περὶ τὰς ναυτιλίας καὶ
φιλίᾳ πρὸς Ῥωμαίους τοσαύτην ἐπίδοσιν εἰς
πᾶσαν εὐτυχίαν ἔσχεν, ὥστε, καίπερ ἐσχάτῃ
ἱδρυμένη τῆς γῆς, ὀνομαστοτάτη τῶν ἁπασῶν
ἐστιν. ἀλλὰ περὶ μὲν ταύτης ἐροῦμεν ὅταν καὶ
περὶ τῶν ἄλλων νήσων λέγωμεν.

9. Ἐφεξῆς δ' ἐστὶν ὁ Μενεσθέως καλούμενος
λιμὴν καὶ ἡ κατὰ Ἄσταν ἀνάχυσις καὶ Νάβρισσαν.[1] λέγονται δὲ ἀναχύσεις αἱ πληρούμεναι
τῇ θαλάττῃ κοιλάδες ἐν ταῖς πλημμυρίσι καὶ
ποταμῶν δίκην ἀνάπλους εἰς τὴν μεσόγαιαν ἔχουσαι καὶ τὰς ἐπ' αὐταῖς πόλεις. εἶτ' εὐθὺς αἱ
ἐκβολαὶ τοῦ Βαίτιος διχῇ σχιζόμεναι· ἡ δὲ ἀπο-
λαμβανομένη νῆσος ὑπὸ τῶν στομάτων ἑκατόν,
ὡς δ' ἔνιοι, καὶ πλειόνων σταδίων ἀφορίζει παραλίαν. ἐνταῦθα δέ που καὶ τὸ μαντεῖον τοῦ
Μενεσθέως ἐστί, καὶ ὁ τοῦ Καιπίωνος ἵδρυται
πύργος ἐπὶ πέτρας ἀμφικλύστου, θαυμασίως κατεσκευασμένος, ὥσπερ ὁ Φάρος, τῆς τῶν πλοϊζο-
μένων σωτηρίας χάριν· ἥ τε γὰρ ἐκβαλλομένη

---

[1] Νάβρισσαν, Corais, for ἀνάβρασις; so subsequent editors.

ments for salting fish. There used to be a city of
Zelis, also, a neighbour of Tingis, but the Romans
transplanted it to the opposite coast of Iberia, taking
along some of the inhabitants of Tingis; and they
also sent some of their own people thither as
colonists and named the city "Julia Ioza." Then
comes Gades, an island separated from Turdetania
by a narrow strait, and distant from Calpe about
seven hundred and fifty stadia (though some say
eight hundred). This island does not differ at all
from the others except that, because of the daring
of its inhabitants as sailors, and because of their
friendship for the Romans, it has made such advances
in every kind of prosperity that, although situated
at the extremity of the earth, it is the most famous
of them all. But I shall tell about Gades when I
discuss the other islands.

9. Next in order comes what is called the Port
of Menestheus, and then the estuary at Asta and
Nabrissa. (The name of estuaries is given to hollows
that are covered by the sea at the high tides, and,
like rivers, afford waterways into the interior and to
the cities on their shores.) Then immediately comes
the outlet of the Baetis, which has a twofold division;
and the island that is enclosed by the two mouths
has a coastal boundary of one hundred stadia, or, as
some say, still more than that. Hereabouts is the
oracle of Menestheus; and also the tower of Caepio,
which is situated upon a rock that is washed on
all sides by the waves, and, like the Pharos tower,[1]
is a marvellous structure built for the sake of the
safety of mariners; for not only do the alluvial

---

[1] See 1. 2. 23 and 17. 1. 9.

χοῦς ὑπὸ τοῦ ποταμοῦ βραχέα ποιεῖ, καὶ χοιρα-
δώδης ἐστὶν ὁ πρὸ αὐτοῦ τόπος, ὥστε δεῖ σημείου
τινὸς ἐπιφανοῦς. ἐντεῦθεν δ' ὁ τοῦ Βαίτιος
ἀνάπλους ἐστὶ καὶ πόλις Ἔβουρα καὶ τὸ τῆς
Φωσφόρου ἱερόν, ἣν καλοῦσι Λούκεμ Δουβίαμ·
εἶθ' οἱ τῶν ἀναχύσεων τῶν ἄλλων ἀνάπλοι· καὶ
μετὰ ταῦτα ὁ Ἄνας ποταμός, δίστομος καὶ οὗτος,
καὶ ὁ ἐξ αὐτῶν ἀνάπλους· εἶθ' ὕστατον τὸ Ἱερὸν
ἀκρωτήριον, διέχον τῶν Γαδείρων ἐλάττους ἢ
δισχιλίους σταδίους· τινὲς δ' ἀπὸ μὲν τοῦ Ἱεροῦ
ἀκρωτηρίου ἐπὶ τὸ τοῦ Ἄνα στόμα ἑξήκοντα
μίλιά φασιν, ἐντεῦθεν δ' ἐπὶ τὸ τοῦ Βαίτιος
C 141 στόμα ἑκατόν, εἶτα εἰς Γάδειρα ἑβδομήκοντα.

II

1. Τῆς δ' οὖν ἐντὸς τοῦ Ἄνα παραλίας ὑπερ-
κεῖσθαι συμβαίνει τὴν Τουρδητανίαν, ἣν ὁ Βαῖτις
διαρρεῖ ποταμός. ἀφορίζει δὲ αὐτὴν πρὸς μὲν
τὴν ἑσπέραν καὶ ἄρκτον ὁ Ἄνας ποταμός, πρὸς
δὲ τὴν ἕω Καρπητανῶν τέ τινες καὶ Ὠρητανοί,
πρὸς νότον δὲ Βαστητανῶν οἱ μεταξὺ τῆς Κάλπης
καὶ τῶν Γαδείρων στενὴν νεμόμενοι παραλίαν, καὶ
ἡ ἑξῆς θάλαττα μέχρι Ἄνα. καὶ οἱ Βαστητανοὶ
δέ, οὓς εἶπον, τῇ Τουρδητανίᾳ πρόσκεινται καὶ οἱ
ἔξω τοῦ Ἄνα, καὶ οἱ πολλοὶ τῶν προσχώρων.
μέγεθος δ' οὐ πλεῖόν ἐστι τῆς χώρας ταύτης ἐπὶ
μῆκος καὶ πλάτος ἢ δισχίλιοι στάδιοι, πόλεις δ'

---

[1] That is, Artemis Phosphorus ("Light-bringer.")
[2] Strabo refers to the Roman mile, which was equal to
eight stadia.

deposits that are discharged by the river form shallows, but the region in front of it is full of reefs, so that there is need of a conspicuous beacon. Thence is the waterway up the Baetis, and the city of Ebura, and the shrine of Phosphorus,[1] which they call "Lux Dubia." Then come the waterways up the other estuaries; and after that the Anas River, which also has two mouths, and the waterway from both mouths into the interior. Then, finally, comes the Sacred Cape, which is less than two thousand stadia distant from Gades. Some, however, say that the distance from the Sacred Cape to the mouth of the Anas is sixty miles, and thence to the mouth of the Baetis, a hundred, and then, to Gades, seventy.[2]

II

1. At all events, it is above the coast this side the Anas that Turdetania lies, and through it flows the Baetis River. And its boundary is marked off on the west and north by the Anas River, on the east by a part of Carpetania and by Oretania, and on the south by those of the Bastetanians who occupy a narrow stretch of coast between Calpe and Gades and by the sea next to that stretch as far as the Anas. But these Bastetanians of whom I have just spoken also belong to Turdetania, and so do those Bastetanians beyond the Anas, and most of its immediate neighbours. The extent of this country is not more than two thousand stadia, that is, in length or breadth,[3] but it contains a surpassing

---

[3] Strabo means *geographical* "length" and "breadth," as defined in 2. 1. 32.

ὑπερβάλλουσαι τὸ πλῆθος, καὶ γὰρ διακοσίας
φασί. γνωριμώταται δὲ αἱ ἐπὶ τοῖς ποταμοῖς
ἱδρυμέναι καὶ ταῖς ἀναχύσεσι καὶ τῇ θαλάττῃ διὰ
τὰς χρείας. πλεῖστον δ' ἥ τε Κόρδυβα ηὔξηται,
Μαρκέλλου κτίσμα, καὶ δόξῃ καὶ δυνάμει, καὶ
ἡ τῶν Γαδιτανῶν πόλις, ἡ μὲν διὰ τὰς ναυτιλίας
καὶ διὰ τὸ προσθέσθαι Ῥωμαίοις κατὰ συμμα-
χίας, ἡ δὲ χώρας ἀρετῇ καὶ μεγέθει, προσλαμβά-
νοντος καὶ τοῦ ποταμοῦ Βαίτιος μέγα μέρος·
ᾤκησάν τε ἐξ ἀρχῆς Ῥωμαίων τε καὶ τῶν ἐπιχωρίων ἄνδρες ἐπίλεκτοι· καὶ δὴ καὶ πρώτην
ἀποικίαν ταύτην εἰς τούσδε τοὺς τόπους ἔστειλαν
Ῥωμαῖοι. μετὰ δὲ ταύτην καὶ τὴν τῶν Γαδιτανῶν ἡ μὲν Ἴσπαλις ἐπιφανής, καὶ αὐτὴ ἄποικος
Ῥωμαίων, νυνὶ δὲ τὸ μὲν ἐμπόριον συμμένει, τῇ
τιμῇ δὲ καὶ τῷ ἐποικῆσαι νεωστὶ τοὺς Καίσαρος
στρατιώτας ἡ Βαῖτις ὑπερέχει, καίπερ οὐ συνοι-
κουμένη λαμπρῶς.

2. Μετὰ δὲ ταύτας Ἰτάλικα καὶ Ἴλιπα ἐπὶ τῷ
Βαίτι, Ἄστιγις δ' ἀπωτέρω καὶ Κάρμων καὶ
Ὀβούλκων· ἔτι δὲ ἐν αἷς οἱ Πομπηίου παῖδες
κατεπολεμήθησαν, Μοῦνδα καὶ Ἀτέγουα καὶ Οὔρ-
σων καὶ Τοῦκκις καὶ Οὐλία καὶ Αἴγουα· ἅπασαι

---

[1] The Turdetanian city of Baetis cannot be identified.
C. Muller proposes to read Asidigis, *i. e.* Asido (now Medina
Sidonia), citing the "Asido surnamed Caesariana" of Pliny
(*Nat. Hist.* 3. 1. 3). Hübner (Pauly-Wissowa, *Real-Encyclo-*

number of cities—as many, indeed, as two hundred, it is said. The best known are those situated on the rivers, on the estuaries, and on the sea; and this is due to their commercial intercourse. But the two that have grown most in fame and in power are Corduba, which was founded by Marcellus, and the city of the Gaditanians: the latter, because of its maritime commerce and because it associated itself with the Romans as an ally; the former because of the excellence of its soil and the extent of its territory, though the Baetis River has also contributed in great measure to its growth; and it has been inhabited from the beginning by picked men of the Romans and of the native Iberians; what is more, the first colony which the Romans sent to these regions was that to Corduba. After Corduba and the city of the Gaditanians, Hispalis, itself also a colony of the Romans, is most famous, and still remains the trade-centre of the district; yet, in the matter of distinction, that is, in the fact that the soldiers of Caesar have recently colonised it, Baetis[1] ranks higher, albeit a city not notable for its population.

2. After these cities come Italica and Ilipa, both near the Baetis River; and Astigis, farther away from the river, and Carmo, and Obulco, and, besides these, the cities in which the sons of Pompey were defeated, namely, Munda, Ategua, Urso, Tuccis, Ulia, and Aegua[2]; and all of these

---

pädie, ii. 2764) says, "Undoubtedly Italica is meant," but the manner in which Italica is introduced below makes this seem inprobable.

[2] The city of Aegua, in Turdetania, is otherwise unknown. Escua is probably the correct reading.

δ' αὗται Κορδύβης οὐκ ἄπωθεν. τρόπον δέ τινα
μητρόπολις κατέστη τοῦ τόπου τούτου Μοῦνδα·
διέχει δὲ Καρτηίας ἡ Μοῦνδα σταδίους χιλίους[1]
καὶ τετρακοσίους, εἰς ἣν ἔφυγεν ἡττηθεὶς ὁ Γναῖος·
εἶτ' ἐκπλεύσας ἔνθεν καὶ ἐκβὰς ἔς τινα ὑπερκειμένην θαλάττης ὀρεινὴν διεφθάρη. ὁ δ' ἀδελφὸς
αὐτοῦ Σέξτος ἐκ Κορδύβης σωθεὶς καὶ μικρὸν ἐν
τοῖς Ἴβηρσι πολεμήσας χρόνον ὕστερον Σικελίαν
ἀπέστησεν, εἶτ' ἐκπεσὼν ἐνθένδε εἰς τὴν Ἀσίαν
ἁλοὺς ὑπὸ τῶν Ἀντωνίου στρατηγῶν ἐν Μιλήτῳ
κατέστρεψε τὸν βίον. ἐν δὲ τοῖς Κελτικοῖς Κονί-
στοργίς ἐστι γνωριμωτάτη· ἐπὶ δὲ ταῖς ἀναχύσεσιν
ἡ Ἄστα, εἰς ἣν οἱ τὸ νῦν Γαδιτανοὶ συνίασι μάλιστα, ὑπερκειμένην τοῦ ἐπινείου τῆς νήσου σταδίους
οὐ πολὺ πλείους τῶν ἑκατόν.

3. Παροικεῖται δὲ ὑπὸ πλείστων ὁ Βαῖτις, καὶ
ἀναπλεῖται σχεδόν τι ἐπὶ χιλίους καὶ διακοσίους
C 142 σταδίους ἐκ θαλάττης μέχρι Κορδύβης καὶ τῶν
μικρὸν ἐπάνω τόπων. καὶ δὴ καὶ ἐξείργασται
περιττῶς ἥ τε παραποταμία καὶ τὰ ἐν τῷ ποταμῷ
νησίδια. πρόσεστι δὲ καὶ τὸ τῆς ὄψεως τερπνόν,

___

[1] χιλίους, the reading of A, adopted by Casaubon instead
of ἑξακισχιλίους (BCl).

___

[1] Hübner (Pauly-Wissowa, iii. 1618; iv. 1223) would
delete Munda, thus making apply to Corduba the reference
to "the capital city" (Ptolemaeus 2. 4. 9), and to the distance
of "four hundred stadia from Carteia" (Caesar, Bell. Hisp.
32. 5, makes the distance from Carteia to Corduba one
hundred and seventy miles, i e. one thousand three hundred
and sixty stadia). But according to Strabo's text Munda
was a city near Corduba, and must not be identified with
the Monda of to-day (four hundred and forty stadia from
Carteia).

22

cities are not far from Corduba. In a way, Munda[1]
has become the capital city of this region. Munda[1]
is one thousand four hundred stadia distant from
Carteia, whither Gnaeus fled after his defeat[2]; he
sailed away from there, and disembarked into a
certain mountainous region overlooking the sea,
where he was put to death. But his brother Sextus
escaped from Corduba, carried on war for a short
time in Iberia, and later on caused Sicily to revolt;
then, driven out of Sicily into Asia, he was captured
by the generals of Antony, and ended his life at
Miletus.[3] In the country of the Celti,[4] Conistorgis
is the best known city; but on the estuaries Asta
is the best known, where the Gaditanians[5] of to-day
usually hold their assemblies, and it is situated not
much more than one hundred stadia beyond the
seaport of the island.

3. The Baetis has a large population along its
shores, and is navigable for approximately one
thousand two hundred stadia from the sea up to
Corduba and the regions a little higher up. Furthermore, the land along the river, and the little islands
in the river, are exceedingly well cultivated. And
besides that, there is the charm of the scenery, for

[2] Caesar's defeat of Gnaeus Pompey at the battle of Munda
took place in March, 45 B.C.

[3] According to Dio Cassius (49. 18), Sextus was captured,
and, apparently, executed at Midaeium (a city in Phrygia
Epictetus); but Appian (*Civil Wars*, 5. 144) says that he
was executed at Miletus.

[4] The Iberian Celts, who lived in what is now Southern
Portugal.

[5] Pliny (*Nat. Hist.* 3. 1. 3) says that there were four
jurisdictions in Baetica, those of Gades, Corduba, Astigis,
and Hispalis.

ἄλσεσι καὶ ταῖς ἄλλαις φυτουργίαις ἐκπεπονη·
μένων τῶν χωρίων. μέχρι μὲν οὖν Ἱσπάλιος
ὁλκάσιν ἀξιολόγοις ὁ ἀνάπλους ἐστὶν ἐπὶ σταδίους οὐ πολὺ λείποντας τῶν πεντακοσίων, ἐπὶ
δὲ τὰς ἄνω πόλεις μέχρι Ἰλίπας ταῖς ἐλάττοσι,
μέχρι δὲ Κορδύβης τοῖς ποταμίοις σκάφεσι, πη-
κτοῖς μὲν τὰ νῦν, τὸ παλαιὸν δὲ καὶ μονοξύλοις·
τὸ δ' ἄνω τὸ ἐπὶ Κασταλῶνος¹ οὐκ ἔστι πλόϊμον·
παράλληλοι δέ τινες ῥάχεις ὀρῶν παρατείνουσι τῷ
ποταμῷ, μᾶλλόν τε καὶ ἧττον αὐτῷ συνάπτουσαι,
πρὸς βορρᾶν, μετάλλων πλήρεις. πλεῖστος δ' ἐστὶν
ἄργυρος ἐν τοῖς κατὰ Ἰλίπαν τόποις καὶ τοῖς κατὰ
Σισάπωνα, τόν τε παλαιὸν λεγόμενον καὶ τὸν νέον·
κατὰ δὲ τὰς Κωτίνας λεγομένας χαλκός τε ἅμα
γεννᾶται καὶ χρυσός. ἐν ἀριστερᾷ μὲν οὖν ἐστι
τοῖς ἀναπλέουσι τὰ ὄρη ταῦτα, ἐν δεξιᾷ δὲ πεδίον
μέγα καὶ ὑψηλὸν καὶ εὔκαρπον καὶ μεγαλόδενδρον
καὶ εὔβοτον. ἔχει δὲ καὶ ὁ Ἄνας ἀνάπλουν,²
οὔτε δὲ τηλικούτοις σκάφεσιν, οὔτ' ἐπὶ τοσοῦτον.
ὑπέρκειται δὲ καὶ αὐτοῦ³ μεταλλείας ἔχοντα ὄρη,
καθήκει δὲ ταῦτα πρὸς τὸν Τάγον. τὰ μὲν οὖν
τὰς μεταλλείας ἔχοντα χωρία ἀνάγκη τραχέα τε
εἶναι καὶ παράλυπρα, οἷάπερ καὶ τὰ τῇ Καρπη-
τανίᾳ συνάπτοντα, καὶ ἔτι μᾶλλον τοῖς Κελτίβηρσι. τοιαύτη δὲ καὶ ἡ Βαιτουρία, ξηρὰ ἔχουσα
πεδία τὰ παρήκοντα τῷ Ἄνᾳ.

¹ Κασταλῶνος, Kramer, for Κλαστῶνος.
² ὁ Ἄνας ἀνάπλουν, Kramer, from the conj. of Casaubon,
for ᾗόνας ὁ ἀνάπλους ; editors following.
³ αὐτοῦ (τοῦ, AC, τά, Bl), Meineke.

---

¹ Cotinae is not elsewhere referred to, and cannot be

the farms are fully improved with groves and gardens of the various plants. Now, up to Hispalis, the river is navigable for merchant-vessels of considerable size, that is, for a distance not much short of five hundred stadia; to the cities higher up the stream as far as Ilipa, for the smaller merchant vessels; and, as far as Corduba, for the river-boats (at the present time these are builded boats, whereas in antiquity they were merely dugout canoes); but above Corduba, in the direction of Castalo, the river is not navigable. On the north, there are some mountain-ridges which extend parallel to the river, approaching it closely, sometimes more so, sometimes less, and they are full of mines. Silver, however, is the most plentiful in the regions about Ilipa, and in those about Sisapo—I mean what is called the Old Sisapo as well as the New Sisapo; and at the place called Cotinae[1] both copper and gold are mined at the same time. Now on your left, as you sail up the river, are these mountains, while on your right is a large plain, high, very productive, with lofty trees, and affording good pasturage. The Anas also is navigable, though neither for such large vessels nor for so great a distance. Beyond the Anas, too, lie mountains that contain ores, and these mountains reach down to the Tagus River. Now the regions which contain ores are necessarily rugged as well as rather poor in soil, precisely as are the regions that join Carpetania, and still more so those that join Celtiberia. And such is the nature of Baeturia also, which contains arid plains that stretch along the Anas.

identified. Du Thiel conjectures Constantia, about twenty miles from Almaden.

4. Αὐτὴ δ᾿ ἡ Τουρδητανία θαυμαστῶς εὐτυχεῖ·
παμφόρου δ᾿ οὔσης αὐτῆς, ὡσαύτως δὲ καὶ πολυ-
φόρου, διπλασιάζεται τὰ εὐτυχήματα ταῦτα τῷ
ἐκκομισμῷ· τὸ γὰρ περιττεῦον τῶν καρπῶν
ἀπεμπολεῖται ῥᾳδίως τῷ πλήθει τῶν ναυκληριῶν.
ποιοῦσι δὲ τοῦτο οἵ τε ποταμοὶ καὶ αἱ ἀναχύσεις,
ὡς εἶπον, ἐμφερεῖς τοῖς ποταμοῖς οὖσαι καὶ ἀνα-
πλεόμεναι παραπλησίως ἐκ θαλάττης οὐ μικροῖς
μόνον, ἀλλὰ καὶ μεγάλοις σκάφεσιν εἰς τὰς ἐν τῇ
μεσογαίᾳ πόλεις. ἅπασα γάρ ἐστι πεδιὰς ἡ ὑπὲρ
τῆς παραλίας ἐπὶ πολὺ τῆς μεταξὺ τοῦ τε Ἱεροῦ
ἀκρωτηρίου καὶ Στηλῶν. ἐνταῦθα δὲ πολλαχοῦ
κοιλάδες εἰς τὴν μεσόγαιαν ἐκ τῆς θαλάττης ἀνέχουσι, φάραγξι μετρίαις ἢ καὶ ῥείθροις ἐοικυῖαι
ποταμίοις, ἐκτεταμέναι ἐπὶ πολλοὺς σταδίους·
ταύτας δὲ πληροῦσιν αἱ τῆς θαλάττης ἐπιβάσεις
κατὰ τὰς πλημμυρίδας, ὥστ᾿ ἀναπλεῖσθαι μηδὲν
ἧττον ἢ τοὺς ποταμούς, ἀλλὰ καὶ βέλτιον· τοῖς
C 143 γὰρ κατάπλοις ἔοικε τοῖς ποταμίοις, ἀντικόπτον-
τος μὲν οὐδενός, ἐπουρίζοντος δὲ τοῦ πελάγους
καθάπερ τοῦ ποταμίου ῥεύματος διὰ τὴν πλημμυ-
ρίδα. αἱ δ᾿ ἐπιβάσεις μείζους εἰσὶν ἐνταῦθα ἢ ἐν
τοῖς ἄλλοις τόποις, ὅτι εἰς πόρον συνωθουμένη
στενὸν ἡ θάλαττα ἐκ μεγάλου πελάγους, ὃν ἡ
Μαυρουσία ποιεῖ πρὸς τὴν Ἰβηρίαν, ἀνακοπὰς
λαμβάνει, καὶ φέρεται πρὸς τὰ εἴκοντα μέρη τῆς
γῆς εὐπετῶς. ἔνιαι μὲν οὖν τῶν τοιούτων κοιλάδων κενοῦνται κατὰ τὰς ἀμπώτεις, τινὰς δ᾿ οὐ
παντάπασιν ἐπιλείπει τὸ ὕδωρ, ἔνιαι δὲ καὶ νήσους

26

4. Turdetania itself is marvellously blessed by nature; and while it produces all things, and likewise great quantities of them, these blessings are doubled by the facilities of exportation; for its surplus products are bartered off with ease because of the large number of the merchant vessels. This is made possible by the rivers, and by the estuaries as well, which, as I have said,[1] resemble rivers, and, like rivers, are navigable inland from the sea, not only for small boats but also for large ones, to the cities of the interior. For the whole country beyond the seaboard that lies between the Sacred Cape and the Pillars is a plain for a considerable distance inland. And here, at a large number of places, are inlets which run up from the sea into the interior, resembling moderate-sized ravines or simply river-beds, and extending for many stadia; and these inlets are filled by the overflows of the sea at the flood-tides, so that one can sail inland thereon as readily as on the rivers—in fact, better, for it is like sailing down the rivers, not only because there is no opposing current, but because, on account of the flood-tide, the sea wafts you onwards just as the river-current does. And the overflows are greater on this coast than in the other regions, because the sea, coming from the great ocean, is compressed into the narrow strait which Maurusia forms with Iberia, there meets resistance, and then easily rushes to those parts of the land that yield to it. Now, while a number of the inlets of this kind are emptied at the ebb-tides (though some of them do not become wholly dry), yet a number of them enclose islands

[1] 3. 1. 9.

ἀπολαμβάνουσιν ἐν ἑαυταῖς. τοιαῦται μὲν οὖν
εἰσιν αἱ ἀναχύσεις αἱ μεταξὺ τοῦ τε Ἱεροῦ ἀκρωτηρίου καὶ τῶν Στηλῶν, ἐπίδοσιν ἔχουσαι σφοδρο-
τέραν παρὰ τὰς ἐν τοῖς ἄλλοις τόποις· ἡ τοιαύτη
δ᾽ ἐπίδοσις ἔχει μέν τι καὶ πλεονέκτημα πρὸς τὰς
χρείας τῶν πλοϊζομένων· πλείους γὰρ καὶ μείζους
ποιεῖ τὰς ἀναχύσεις, πολλάκις καὶ ἐπὶ ὀκτὼ σταδίους ἀναπλεομένας, ὥστε τρόπον τινὰ πᾶσαν
πλωτὴν παρέχεται τὴν γῆν καὶ εὐπετῆ πρός τε
τὰς ἐξαγωγὰς τῶν φορτίων καὶ τὰς εἰσαγωγάς.
ἔχει δέ τι καὶ ὀχληρόν· αἱ γὰρ ἐν τοῖς ποταμοῖς
ναυτιλίαι¹ διὰ τὴν σφοδρότητα τῆς πλημμυρίδος
ἰσχυρότερον τῇ ῥύσει² τῶν ποταμῶν ἀντιπνέ-
ουσαν³ κίνδυνον οὐ μικρὸν ταῖς ναυκληρίαις ἐπι-
φέρουσι, κατακομιζομέναις τε ὁμοίως καὶ ἀνακο-
μιζομέναις. αἱ δὲ ἀμπώτεις ἐν ταῖς ἀναχύσεσίν
εἰσι βλαβεραί· ταῖς γὰρ πλημμυρίσιν ἀνὰ λόγον
καὶ αὐταὶ παροξύνονται, διά τε τὸ τάχος καὶ ἐπὶ
ξηρᾶς πολλάκις ἐγκατέλιπον τὴν ναῦν. τά τε
βοσκήματα εἰς τὰς νήσους διαβαίνοντα τὰς πρὸ
τῶν ποταμῶν ἢ⁴ πρὸ τῶν ἀναχύσεων τοτὲ μὲν
οὖν καὶ ἐπεκλύσθη, τοτὲ δὲ ἀπελήφθη, βιαζόμενα
δ᾽ ἐπανελθεῖν οὐκ ἴσχυσεν, ἀλλὰ διεφθάρη· τὰς
δὲ βοῦς φασι καὶ τετηρηκυίας τὸ συμβαῖνον περι-
μένειν τὴν ἀναχώρησιν τῆς θαλάττης, καὶ τότε
ἀπαίρειν εἰς τὴν ἤπειρον.

5. Καταμαθόντες δ᾽ οὖν τὴν φύσιν τῶν τόπων

¹ αἱ, before διά, Corais deletes.
² ῥύσει, Siebenkees, for φύσει; so subsequent editors.
³ ἀντιπνέουσαν, Corais, for ἀντιπνέουσαι; so Kramer, Forbiger, and Meineke.
⁴ ἤ, Jones inserts.

28

within themselves. Such, then, are the estuaries between the Sacred Cape and the Pillars, for they have an excessive rise of tide as compared with those in the other regions. A rise of tide like this affords a certain advantage to be utilised by sailors, namely, the estuaries are made more numerous and larger, oftentimes being navigable even for a distance of eight [1] stadia; so that, after a fashion, it renders the whole country navigable and convenient both for exporting and importing merchandise. And yet it also affords a certain annoyance; for, on account of the vehemence of the flood-tides, which press with superior force against the current of the rivers, navigation on the rivers is attended by no small danger to the vessels, alike in their descent and ascent. But in the case of the estuaries the ebb-tides too are harmful; for the ebb-tides too grow violent in proportion to the strength of the flood-tides, and on account of their swiftness have oftentimes even left the ship stranded on dry land. Again, the cattle which cross over to the islands that lie off the rivers or the estuaries have at times actually been engulfed; at other times they have merely been cut off, and in their struggle to get back to the land lacked the strength to do so, and perished. But the cows, they say, are by observation actually aware of what happens, wait for the retirement of the sea, and then make off for the mainland.

5. At any rate, it was because the people had

[1] "Eight," the reading of the MSS. cannot be right (cf. **3. 3. 1**). Penzel, followed by Corais, proposes eight hundred, and Groskurd, followed by Forbiger and Tardieu, proposes one hundred.

οἱ ἄνθρωποι καὶ τὰς ἀναχύσεις ὁμοίως ὑπουργεῖν
τοῖς ποταμοῖς δυναμένας πόλεις ἔκτισαν ἐπ' αὐτῶν
καὶ ἄλλας κατοικίας, καθάπερ ἐπὶ τῶν ποταμῶν.
τούτων δ' ἐστὶν ἥ τε Ἄστα καὶ Νάβρισσα καὶ Ὄνο-
βα καὶ Ὀσσόνοβα καὶ Μαίνοβα καὶ ἄλλαι πλείους.
προσλαμβάνουσι δὲ καὶ διώρυγες ἔσθ' ὅπου γεγο-
νυῖαι τῷ πολλαχόθεν εἶναι καὶ πολλαχόσε τὴν κο-
μιδὴν καὶ πρὸς ἀλλήλους καὶ πρὸς τοὺς ἔξω. καὶ αἱ
σύρροιαι δὲ ὡσαύτως ὠφελοῦσι κατὰ τὰς ἐπὶ πολὺ
πλήμας, διαχεομένας ἐπὶ[1] τῶν διειργόντων ἰσθμῶν
τοὺς πόρους καὶ πλωτοὺς ἀπεργαζομένας,[2] ὥστε
πορθμεύεσθαι καὶ ἐκ τῶν ποταμῶν εἰς τὰς ἀναχύσεις κἀκεῖθεν δεῦρο. ἅπασα δ' ἡ ἐμπορία πρὸς
τὴν Ἰταλίαν ἐστὶ καὶ τὴν Ῥώμην, ἔχουσα τὸν
C 144 πλοῦν μέχρι τῶν Στηλῶν ἀγαθόν, πλὴν εἴ τίς
ἐστι περὶ τὸν πορθμὸν δυσκολία, καὶ τὸν πε-
λάγιον τὸν ἐν τῇ καθ' ἡμᾶς θαλάττῃ. διὰ γὰρ
εὐδίου κλίματος οἱ δρόμοι συντελοῦνται, καὶ μάλιστα τῷ πελαγίζοντι· τοῦτο δὲ πρόσφορόν ἐστι
ταῖς ἐμπορικαῖς ὁλκάσιν. ἔχουσι δὲ καὶ οἱ ἄνεμοι
τάξιν οἱ πελάγιοι. πρόσεστι δὲ καὶ ἡ νῦν εἰρήνη,
τῶν ληστηρίων καταλυθέντων, ὥσθ' ἡ σύμπασα
ὑπάρχει ῥᾳστώνη τοῖς πλοϊζομένοις. ἴδιον δέ τι
φησι Ποσειδώνιος τηρῆσαι κατὰ τὸν ἀνάπλουν
τὸν ἐκ τῆς Ἰβηρίας, ὅτι οἱ Εὖροι κατ' ἐκεῖνο τὸ
πέλαγος ἕως τοῦ Σαρδῴου κόλπου πνέοιεν ἐτησίαι·

---

[1] διαχεομένας ἐπί, Meineke, for διειργομένας ὑπό; Forbiger,
and Tardieu, following.

[2] καὶ πλωτοὺς ἀπεργαζομένας, Meineke, and Müller-Dübner,

learned the character of these regions and that the estuaries could subserve the same purpose as the rivers, that they built cities and other settlements on their banks, just as on the rivers. Among these cities are Asta, Nabrissa, Onoba, Ossonoba, Maenoba, and several others. Again, canals that have been dug in a number of places are an additional aid, since many are the points thereon from which and to which the people carry on their traffic, not only with one another but also with the outside world. And further, the meetings of the waters when the flood-tides reach far inland are likewise helpful, for the waters pour across over the isthmuses that separate the waterways, thus rendering the isthmuses navigable also; so that one can cross over by boat from the rivers into the estuaries and from the estuaries into the rivers. But all the foreign trade of the country is carried on with Italy and Rome, since the voyage as far as the Pillars is good, except, perhaps, for a certain difficulty in passing the strait, and also the voyage on the high seas of Our Sea. For the sea-routes all pass through a zone of fair weather, particularly if the sailor keeps to the high seas; and this fact is advantageous to the merchant-freighters. And further, the winds on the high seas are regular. Added to that, too, is the present peace, because all piracy has been broken up, and hence the sailors feel wholly at ease. Poseidonius says that he observed a peculiar circumstance on his return voyage from Iberia, namely, that the east winds on that sea, as far as the Gulf of Sardinia, blew at a fixed time each

---

for καὶ πλωτὸν ἀπεργαζομένων (ABC) and πλωτοὺς ἀπεργαζόμεναι (l).

διὸ καὶ τρισὶ μησὶν εἰς Ἰταλίαν καταραι μόλις
παραδιενεχθεὶς [1] περί τε τὰς Γυμνησίας νήσους
καὶ περὶ Σαρδόνα καὶ τὰ ἄλλα ἀπαντικρὺ τούτων
μέρη τῆς Λιβύης.

6. Ἐξάγεται δ' ἐκ τῆς Τουρδητανίας σιτός τε
καὶ οἶνος πολὺς καὶ ἔλαιον οὐ πολὺ μόνον, ἀλλὰ
καὶ κάλλιστον· καὶ κηρὸς δὲ καὶ μέλι καὶ πίττα
ἐξάγεται καὶ κόκκος πολλὴ καὶ μίλτος οὐ χείρων
τῆς Σινωπικῆς γῆς τά τε ναυπήγια συνιστᾶσιν
αὐτόθι ἐξ ἐπιχωρίας ὕλης, ἅλες τε ὀρυκτοὶ παρ'
αὐτοῖς εἰσι καὶ ποταμῶν ἁλμυρῶν ῥεύματα οὐκ
ὀλίγα, οὐκ ὀλίγη δὲ οὐδὲ ἐκ τῶν ὄψων ταριχεία
οὐκ ἔνθεν μόνον, ἀλλὰ καὶ ἐκ τῆς ἄλλης τῆς ἐκτὸς
Στηλῶν παραλίας, οὐ χείρων τῆς Ποντικῆς. πολλὴ
δὲ καὶ ἐσθὴς πρότερον ἤρχετο, νῦν δὲ ἔρια μᾶλλον
τῶν κοραξῶν. καὶ ὑπερβολή τίς ἐστι τοῦ κάλ-
λους· ταλαντιαίους γοῦν ὠνοῦνται τοὺς κριοὺς εἰς
τὰς ὀχείας. ὑπερβολὴ δὲ καὶ τῶν λεπτῶν ὑφα-
σμάτων, ἅπερ οἱ Σαλακιῆται [2] κατασκευάζουσιν.
ἄφθονος δὲ καὶ βοσκημάτων ἀφθονία παντοίων
καὶ κυνηγεσίων. τῶν δ' ὀλεθρίων θηρίων σπάνις
πλὴν τῶν γεωρύχων λαγιδέων, οὓς ἔνιοι λεβηρίδας
προσαγορεύουσι· λυμαίνονται γὰρ καὶ φυτὰ καὶ

[1] παραδιενεχθείς, Kramer, for γὰρ διενεχθείς; so Meineke.
[2] Σαλακιῆται, Harduin, for Σαλτιῆται; so Groskurd, Forbiger, Tardieu, and C. Müller.

[1] Poseidonius was near enough to Libya on this trip to see
a number of apes on the shore (17. 3. 4).
[2] A crimson dye-stuff obtained from the dried bodies of
the female scale-insects of the genus *Kermes ilicis*. The
species referred to by Strabo feeds on the *Quercus coccifera*,
a dwarf-oak, and is very common in the Mediterranean
countries.

year; and that this was why he barely reached Italy even in three months; for he was driven out of his course in both directions, not only near to the Gymnesian Islands and Sardinia, but also to the different parts of Libya [1] opposite to these islands.

6. There are exported from Turdetania large quantities of grain and wine, and also olive oil, not only in large quantities, but also of best quality. And further, wax, honey, and pitch are exported from there, and large quantities of kermes,[2] and ruddle [3] which is not inferior to the Sinopean earth. And they build their ships there out of native timber; and they have salt quarries in their country, and not a few streams of salt water; and not unimportant, either, is the fish-salting industry that is carried on, not only from this county, but also from the rest of the seaboard outside the Pillars; and the product is not inferior to that of the Pontus. Formerly much cloth came from Turdetania, but now, wool, rather of the raven-black sort.[4] And it is surpassingly beautiful; at all events, the rams are bought for breeding purposes at a talent apiece. Surpassing, too, are the delicate fabrics which are woven by the people of Salacia.[5] Turdetania also has a great abundance of cattle of all kinds, and of game. But there are scarcely any destructive animals, except the burrowing hares, by some called "peelers"; for they damage both plants and seeds by eating the

[3] As in 12. 2. 10, Strabo uses " miltos" ("ruddle") as a general term in comparing, as sources of dyes, Spanish cinnabar (red mercuric sulphide) and Sinopean "red earth."

[4] Cp. 12. 8. 16.

[5] Alcacer-do-Sal. Pliny (*Nat. Hist.* 8. 7) also refers to the fabrics woven in this Lusitanian town.

σπέρματα ῥιζοφαγοῦντες· καὶ τοῦτο συμβαίνει καθ' ὅλην τὴν Ἰβηρίαν σχεδόν, διατείνει δὲ καὶ μέχρι Μασσαλίας, ὀχλεῖ δὲ καὶ τὰς νήσους. οἱ δὲ τὰς Γυμνησίας οἰκοῦντες λέγονται πρεσβεύσασθαί ποτε πρὸς Ῥωμαίους κατὰ χώρας αἴτησιν· ἐκβάλλεσθαι γὰρ ὑπὸ τῶν ζῴων τούτων, ἀντέχειν μὴ δυνάμενοι διὰ τὸ πλῆθος. πρὸς μὲν οὖν τὸν τοσοῦτον ἴσως πόλεμον, ὃς οὐκ ἀεὶ συμβαίνει, φθορᾷ[1] δέ τινι λοιμικῇ, καθάπερ ὄφεων καὶ μυῶν τῶν ἀρουραίων, χρεία τῆς τοσαύτης ἐπικουρίας, πρὸς δὲ τὸ μέτριον ἐξεύρηνται πλείους θῆραι· καὶ δὴ καὶ γαλᾶς ἀγρίας, ἃς ἡ Λιβύη φέρει, τρέφουσιν ἐπίτηδες, ἃς φιμώσαντες παριᾶσιν εἰς τὰς ὀπάς· αἱ δ' ἐξέλκουσιν ἔξω τοῖς ὄνυξιν, οὓς ἂν καταλάβωσιν, ἢ φεύγειν ἀναγκάζουσιν εἰς τὴν ἐπιφάνειαν, ἐκπεσόντας δὲ θηρεύουσιν οἱ ἐφεστῶτες. τὴν δὲ ἀφθονίαν τῶν ἐκκομιζομένων ἐκ τῆς Τουρδητανίας ἐμφανίζει τὸ μέγεθος καὶ τὸ πλῆθος τῶν ναυκληρίων· ὁλκάδες γὰρ μέγισται παρὰ τούτων πλέουσιν εἰς Δικαιαρχείαν καὶ τὰ Ὤστια, τῆς Ῥώμης ἐπίνειον· τὸ δὲ πλῆθος μικροῦ δεῖν ἐνάμιλλον τοῖς Λιβυκοῖς.[2]

7. Τοιαύτης δὲ τῆς μεσογαίας οὔσης τῆς ἐν τῇ Τουρδητανίᾳ, καὶ τὴν παράλιον ἐνάμιλλον εὕροι τις ἂν τοῖς ἐκ θαλάττης ἀγαθοῖς. τά τε γὰρ ὀστρεώδη πάντα καὶ κογχοειδῆ καὶ τοῖς πλήθεσιν ὑπερβάλλει καὶ τοῖς μεγέθεσι καθόλου κατὰ τὴν ἔξω θάλατταν πᾶσαν, ἐνταῦθα δὲ διαφερόντως,

---

[1] φθορᾷ, Jones, for φθόρον. Meineke, Forbiger and others emend to φορᾷ. Cp. Aristotle, *Hist. An.* 6. 37 (μυῶν . . . ἡ φθορά).

roots. This pest occurs throughout almost the whole of Iberia, and extends even as far as Massilia, and infests the islands as well. The inhabitants of the Gymnesian Islands, it is said, once sent an embassy to Rome to ask for a new place of abode, for they were being driven out by these animals, because they could not hold out against them on account of their great numbers. Now perhaps such a remedy is needed against so great a warfare (which is not always the case, but only when there is some destructive plague like that of snakes or field-mice),[1] but, against the moderate pest, several methods of hunting have been discovered; more than that, they make a point of breeding Libyan ferrets, which they muzzle and send into the holes. The ferrets with their claws drag outside all the rabbits they catch, or else force them to flee into the open, where men, stationed at the hole, catch them as they are driven out. The abundance of the exports of Turdetania is indicated by the size and the number of the ships; for merchant-men of the greatest size sail from this country to Dicaearchia, and to Ostia, the seaport of Rome; and their number very nearly rivals that of the Libyan ships.

7. Although the interior of Turdetania is so productive, it will be found that the seaboard vies with it in its goodly products from the sea. For the various kinds of oysters as well as mussels are in general surpassing, both in their number and in their size, along the whole of the exterior sea; but

---

[1] See 3. 4. 18. and foot-note.

---

[2] ἐκπολλαπλασιασιος, after Λιβυκοῖς, deleted by *l*; and so the editors in general.

ἅτε καὶ τῶν πλημμυρίδων καὶ τῶν ἀμπώτεων
ἐνταῦθα αὐξομένων, ἃς εἰκὸς αἰτίας εἶναι καὶ τοῦ
πλήθους καὶ τοῦ μεγέθους διὰ τὴν γυμνασίαν.
ὡς δ' αὕτως ἔχει καὶ περὶ τῶν κητέων ἁπάντων,
ὀρύγων τε καὶ φαλαινῶν καὶ φυσητήρων, ὧν ἀνα-
φυσησάντων φαίνεταί τις νεφώδους ὄψις κίονος
τοῖς πόρρωθεν ἀφορῶσι· καὶ οἱ γόγγροι δὲ ἀπο-
θηριοῦνται, πολὺ τῶν παρ' ἡμῖν ὑπερβεβλημένοι
κατὰ τὸ μέγεθος, καὶ αἱ σμύραιναι καὶ ἄλλα πλείω
τῶν τοιούτων ὄψων. ἐν δὲ Καρτηίᾳ κήρυκας
δεκακοτύλους καὶ πορφύρας φασίν· ἐν δὲ τοῖς
ἐξωτέροις τόποις καὶ μείζους ὀγδοήκοντα μνῶν
τὴν σμύραιναν καὶ τὸν γόγγρον, ταλαντιαῖον δὲ
τὸν πολύποδα, διπήχεις δὲ τὰς τευθίδας καὶ τὰ
παραπλήσια. πολὺς δὲ καὶ ὁ θύννος συνελαύνεται
δεῦρο ἀπὸ τῆς ἄλλης [1] τῆς ἔξωθεν παραλίας [2]
πίων καὶ παχύς. τρέφεται δὲ βαλάνῳ δρυΐνῃ
φυομένῃ κατὰ τῆς θαλάττης χαμαιζήλῳ τινὶ παντάπασιν, ἁδρότατον δ' ἐκφερούσῃ καρπόν. ἥπερ
καὶ ἐν τῇ γῇ φύεται πολλὴ κατὰ τὴν Ἰβηρίαν,
ῥίζας μὲν ἔχουσα μεγάλας ὡς ἂν τελείας δρυός,
ἐξαιρομένη δὲ θάμνου ταπεινῆς ἧττον· τοσοῦτον
δ' ἐκφέρει καρπόν, ὥστε μετὰ τὴν ἀκμὴν πλήρη
τὴν παραλίαν [3] εἶναι τήν τε ἐντὸς καὶ τὴν ἐκτὸς

---

[1] ἄλλης, Kramer, for ἀλέης; so generally the editors.
Casaubon reads ἀλέης, Groskurd, ἀλέας. Probably the con-
text should be emended to suit ἀλέας (cp. Aristotle, *Hist.
An.* 8. 19, and Athenaeus 7. 63, 301 E).

[2] παραλίας, Casaubon, for παλαιᾶς; so all editors.

[3] Apparently βαλάνου has fallen out after παραλίαν.
Groskurd, Forbiger, and Meineke so read.

especially so here, inasmuch as the flood-tides and the ebb-tides have increased power here, and these tides, it is reasonable to suppose, are, on account of the exercise they give, responsible both for the number and the size of them. So it is, in the same way, with respect to all the cetaceans: narwhals, "phalaenae"[1] and spouting-whales; when these spout, the distant observer seems to see a cloud-like pillar. And further, the conger-eels become monsters, far exceeding in size those of Our Sea; and so do the lampreys and several other edible fish of the kind. And at Carteia, it is said, there are shells of trumpet-fish and purple-fish which hold ten cotylae,[2] and in the regions farther out to sea the lamprey and the conger-eel weigh even more than eighty minae,[3] the sea-polypus a talent,[4] the cuttle-fish are two cubits long—and other things in like proportion. Again, large numbers of plump, fat tunny-fish congregate hither from the other coast, namely, that outside the Pillars. And they feed on the acorns of a certain very stunted oak that grows at the bottom of the sea and produces very large fruit.[5] This oak also grows in abundance on the dry land, in Iberia; and although its roots are large like those of a full-grown oak, yet it does not grow as high as a low bush. But the sea-oak brings forth so much fruit that, after the ripening, the seacoast,

---

[1] The typical genus of whalebone whales called by the Romans "balaenae," which is the term still used by zoologists.   [2] About five pints
[3] About eighty pounds.   [4] About sixty pounds.
[5] Apparently the *Quercus coccifera* (see note on " Kermes " 3. 2. 6.) is meant, but so far as is known no shrub or tree-like plant grows in salt water.

37

Στηλῶν, ἣν ἐκβάλλουσιν αἱ πλῆμαι· ἡ δ᾽ ἐντὸς
Στηλῶν ἐλάττων ἀεὶ καὶ μᾶλλον εὑρίσκεται. λέγει
δ᾽ ὁ Πολύβιος καὶ μέχρι τῆς Λατίνης ἐκπίπτειν
τὴν βάλανον ταύτην, εἰ μὴ ἄρα, φησί, καὶ ἡ Σαρδὼ
φέρει καὶ ἡ πλησιόχωρος ταύτῃ. καὶ οἱ θύννοι
δ᾽ ὅσῳ πλέον συνεγγίζουσι ταῖς Στήλαις ἔξωθεν
φερόμενοι, τοσῷδ᾽ ἰσχναίνονται πλέον,[1] τῆς τροφῆς
ἐπιλειπούσης· εἶναί τε ἄρα[2] θαλάττιον ὗν τὸ
ζῷον τοῦτο· ἥδεσθαι γὰρ τῇ βαλάνῳ καὶ πιαίνε-
σθαι διαφερόντως ἀπ᾽ αὐτῆς, φορᾶς τε τῆς βαλάνου
γενομένης, φορὰν καὶ τῶν θύννων εἶναι.

8. Τοσούτοις δὲ τῆς προειρημένης χώρας ἀγα-
C 146 θοῖς κεχορηγημένης, οὐχ ἥκιστα, ἀλλὰ καὶ μάλιστα
ἀποδέξαιτ᾽ ἄν τις καὶ θαυμάσειε τὸ περὶ τὰς
μεταλλείας εὐφυές· ἅπασα μὲν γὰρ μεστὴ τῶν
τοιούτων ἐστὶν ἡ τῶν Ἰβήρων χώρα, οὐ πᾶσα δ᾽
εὔκαρπος οὐδ᾽ εὐδαίμων οὕτως, καὶ μάλιστα ἡ
τῶν μετάλλων εὐποροῦσα. σπάνιον δ᾽ ἐν ἀμφοτέροις εὐτυχεῖν· σπάνιον δὲ καὶ τὸ τὴν αὐτὴν ἐν
ὀλίγῳ χωρίῳ παντοίοις πληθύνειν μετάλλοις. ἡ
δὲ[3] Τουρδητανία καὶ ἡ προσεχὴς αὐτῇ λόγον οὐ-
δένα ἄξιον καταλείπει περὶ τῆνδε τὴν ἀρετὴν τοῖς
ἐπαινεῖν βουλομένοις. οὔτε γὰρ χρυσός, οὔτ᾽[4]
ἄργυρος, οὐδὲ δὴ χαλκός, οὐδὲ σίδηρος οὐδαμοῦ τῆς
γῆς οὔτε τοσοῦτος οὔθ᾽ οὕτως ἀγαθὸς ἐξήτασται
γεννώμενος μέχρι νῦν. ὁ δὲ χρυσὸς οὐ μεταλ-
λεύεται μόνον, ἀλλὰ καὶ σύρεται· καταφέρουσι
δ᾽ οἱ ποταμοὶ καὶ οἱ χείμαρροι τὴν χρυσῖτιν ἄμ-

[1] πλέον, Corais, for πλεῖον; Kramer, and Meineke,
following. [2] τε ἄρα, Tyrwhitt, for παρά.
[3] δέ, for τε; so the old reading (before Kramer), and so
Meineke. [4] οὔτ᾽, Jones, for οὐκ.

both inside and outside the Pillars, is covered with the acorns, for they are cast ashore by the tides. However, those inside the Pillars are always smaller, and are to be found in greater quantities. Polybius tells us that the sea casts these acorns ashore even as far as Latium, unless perhaps, says he, also Sardinia and the neighbouring land produce them. And further, the nearer the tunny-fish approach the Pillars, in coming from the exterior sea, the leaner they become, since their food fails them. This creature, says Polybius, is therefore a sea-hog, for it is fond of the acorn and gets exceedingly fat on it; and whenever the sea-oak has produced a large crop of acorns, there is also a large crop of tunny-fish.

8. Now, although the aforesaid country has been endowed with so many good things, still one might welcome and admire, not least of all, but even most of all, its natural richness in metals. For the whole country of the Iberians is full of metals, although not all of it is so rich in fruit, or so fertile either, and in particular that part of it which is well supplied with metals. It is rare for a country to be fortunate in both respects, and it is also rare for the same country to have within a small area an abundance of all kinds of metals. But as for Turdetania and the territory adjoining it, there is no worthy word of praise left to him who wishes to praise their excellence in this respect. Up to the present moment, in fact, neither gold, nor silver, nor yet copper, nor iron, has been found anywhere in the world, in a natural state, either in such quantity or of such good quality. And the gold is not only mined, but is also washed down; that is, the gold-bearing sand is carried down by the rivers and the torrents, although it is often found in

μον, πολλαχοῦ καὶ ἐν τοῖς ἀνύδροις τόποις οὖσαν,
ἀλλ' ἐκεῖ μὲν ἀφανής ἐστιν, ἐν δὲ τοῖς ἐπικλύστοις
ἀπολάμπει τὸ τοῦ χρυσοῦ ψῆγμα· καὶ τοὺς ἀνύ-
δρους δὲ φορητῷ ἐπικλύζοντες ὕδατι στιλπνὸν
ποιοῦσι τὸ ψῆγμα, καὶ φρέατα δ' ὀρύσσοντες καὶ
ἄλλας τέχνας ἐπινοοῦντες πλύσει τῆς ἄμμου τὸν
χρυσὸν ἐκλαμβάνουσι, καὶ πλείω τῶν χρυσωρυ-
χείων ἐστὶ νῦν τὰ χρυσοπλύσια προσαγορευό-
μενα. ἀξιοῦσι δὲ Γαλάται ἴσα[1] παρ' ἑαυτοῖς εἶναι
τὰ μέταλλα τά τε[2] ἐν τῷ Κεμμένῳ ὄρει καὶ τὰ
ὑπ' αὐτῇ κείμενα τῇ Πυρήνῃ· τὸ μέντοι πλέον[3]
τἀντεῦθεν εὐδοκιμεῖ. ἐν δὲ τοῖς ψήγμασι τοῦ
χρυσίου φασὶν εὑρίσκεσθαί ποτε καὶ ἡμιλιτριαίας
βώλους, ἃς καλοῦσι πάλας, μικρᾶς καθάρσεως
δεομένας. φασὶ δὲ καὶ λίθων σχιζομένων εὑρί-
σκειν βωλάρια θηλαῖς ὅμοια· ἐκ δὲ τοῦ χρυσοῦ
ἑψομένου καὶ καθαιρομένου στυπτηριώδει τινὶ γῇ
τὸ κάθαρμα ἤλεκτρον εἶναι· πάλιν δὲ τούτου
καθεψομένου, μίγμα ἔχοντος ἀργύρου καὶ χρυσοῦ,
τὸν μὲν ἄργυρον ἀποκαίεσθαι, τὸν δὲ χρυσὸν
ὑπομένειν· εὐδιάχυτος γὰρ ὁ τύπος καὶ λιθώδης·
διὰ τοῦτο καὶ τῷ ἀχύρῳ τήκεται μᾶλλον ὁ χρυσός,
ὅτι ἡ φλόξ, μαλακὴ οὖσα, συμμέτρως ἔχει πρὸς
τὸ εἶκον καὶ διαχεόμενον ῥᾳδίως, ὁ δὲ ἄνθραξ
ἐπαναλίσκει πολύ, ὑπερτήκων τῇ σφοδρότητι καὶ

---

[1] ἴσα, Madvig, for τά.
[2] τά τε, before ἐν, the insertion of l, and the editors.
[3] πλέον, Meineke, for πλεῖον.

---

[1] The Gauls.   See 4. 4. 2.   [2] The Cevennes.
[3] Apparently a native Iberian word.   Cp. Pliny, *Nat. Hist.*
33. 21.

the waterless districts also; but in these districts it cannot be seen, whereas in the flooded districts the gold-dust glitters. Besides, they flood the waterless districts by conducting water thither, and thus they make the gold-dust glitter; and they also get the gold out by digging pits, and by inventing other means for washing the sand; and the so-called "gold-washeries" are now more numerous than the gold-mines. The Galatae [1] hold that their own mines, both those in the Cemmenus [2] Mountains and those situated at the foot of the Pyrenees themselves, are equal to those of Turdetania; the metals from the latter, however, are held in greater esteem. And in the gold-dust, they say, nuggets weighing as much as half a pound are sometimes found, which are called "palae," [3] and they need but little refining. They further say that when stones are split they find in them small nuggets resembling nipples, and when the gold is smelted and refined by means of a sort of styptic earth [4] the residuum thereof is "electrum"; [5] and, again, that when this electrum, which contains a mixture of silver and gold, is smelted, the silver is burned away, while the gold remains. For the alloy-type is easily fused and stone-like. [6] For this reason, too, the gold is preferably melted with chaff-fire, because the flame, on account of its softness, is suitable to a substance that yields and fuses easily; but the charcoal-fire consumes much of it because, owing to its intensity, it

[4] Containing alum and vitriol.

[5] Electrum is defined by Pliny (*Nat. Hist.* 33. 23) as consisting of one part of silver to four parts of gold.

[6] In fact, the alloy is more easily fused, and harder, than either of the constituent metals.

ἐξαίρων. ἐν δὲ τοῖς ῥείθροις[1] σύρεται καὶ πλύνεται πλησίον ἐν σκάφαις, ἢ ὀρύττεται φρέαρ, ἡ
δὲ ἀνενεχθεῖσα γῆ πλύνεται. τὰς δὲ τοῦ ἀργύρου
καμίνους ποιοῦσιν ὑψηλάς, ὥστε τὴν ἐκ τῶν
βώλων λιγνὺν μετέωρον ἐξαίρεσθαι· βαρεῖα γάρ
ἐστι καὶ ὀλέθριος. τῶν δὲ χαλκουργείων τινὰ
καλεῖται χρυσεῖα, ἐξ ὧν τεκμαίρονται χρυσὸν ἐξ
αὐτῶν ὀρύττεσθαι πρότερον.

9. Ποσειδώνιος δέ, τὸ πλῆθος τῶν μετάλλων
C 147 ἐπαινῶν καὶ τὴν ἀρετήν, οὐκ ἀπέχεται τῆς συνή-
θους ῥητορείας, ἀλλὰ συνενθουσιᾷ ταῖς ὑπερ-
βολαῖς. οὐ γὰρ ἀπιστεῖν τῷ μύθῳ φησίν, ὅτι τῶν
δρυμῶν ποτε ἐμπρησθέντων ἡ γῆ τακεῖσα, ἅτε
ἀργυρῖτις καὶ χρυσῖτις, εἰς τὴν ἐπιφάνειαν ἐξέζεσε
διὰ τὸ πᾶν ὄρος καὶ πάντα βουνὸν ὕλην εἶναι
νομίσματος ὑπό τινος ἀφθόνου τύχης σεσωρευ-
μένην. καθόλου δ' ἂν εἶπε, φησίν, ἰδών τις τοὺς
τόπους, θησαυροὺς εἶναι φύσεως ἀενάους ἢ τα-
μιεῖον ἡγεμονίας ἀνέκλειπτον· οὐ γὰρ πλουσία
μόνον, ἀλλὰ καὶ ὑπόπλουτος ἦν, φησίν, ἡ χώρα,
καὶ παρ' ἐκείνοις ὡς ἀληθῶς τὸν ὑποχθόνιον τόπον
οὐχ ὁ Ἅδης, ἀλλ' ὁ Πλούτων κατοικεῖ. τοιαῦτα
μὲν οὖν ἐν ὡραίῳ[2] σχήματι εἴρηκε περὶ τούτων,
ὡς ἂν ἐκ μετάλλου καὶ αὐτὸς πολλῷ χρώμενος
τῷ λόγῳ. τὴν δ' ἐπιμέλειαν φράζων τὴν τῶν
μεταλλευόντων παρατίθησι τὸ τοῦ Φαληρέως,
ὅτι φησὶν ἐκεῖνος ἐπὶ τῶν Ἀττικῶν ἀργυρείων

---

[1] ῥείθροις, for ἐρύθροις; a correction of Corais, from a
conjecture of Casaubon.
[2] ὡραίῳ, for οὐρανῷ (ABC), ὁραίῳ (l); so the editors.

---

[1] In the word-play here Pluto is identified (as often) with
Plutus, the god of riches.

over-melts the gold and carries it off as vapour. The soil is carried along in the streams, and is washed near by in troughs; or else a pit is dug, and the soil that has been accumulated is there washed. They build their silver-smelting furnaces with high chimneys, so that the gas from the ore may be carried high into the air; for it is heavy and deadly. Some of the copper-mines are called gold-mines, and from this fact it is inferred that in former times gold was mined from them.

9. Poseidonius, in praising the quantity and the excellence of these ores, does not abstain from his usual rhetorical speech; indeed, he enthusiastically concurs with the extravagant stories told; for example, he does not discredit the story, he says, that, when on a time the forests had been burned, the soil, since it was composed of silver and gold ores, melted and boiled out over the surface, because, as he says, every mountain and every hill is bullion heaped up there by some prodigal fortune. And, in general, he says, anyone who had seen these regions would declare that they are everlasting storehouses of nature, or a never-failing treasury of an empire. For the country was, he adds, not only rich, but also rich down below; and with the Turdetanians it is verily Pluto,[1] and not Hades, who inhabits the region down below. Such, then, are the flowery utterances of Poseidonius on this subject—himself drawing much of his language from a mine, as it were. Again, in speaking of the industry of the miners, he cites the statement of Demetrius of Phalerum. Demetrius, he says, states in reference to the Attic silver-mines,[2]

[1] The silver-mines of Laurium.

οὕτω συντόνως ὀρύττειν τοὺς ἀνθρώπους, ὡς ἂν
προσδοκώντων αὐτὸν ἀνάξειν τὸν Πλούτωνα· καὶ
τούτων οὖν ἐμφανίζει παραπλησίαν τὴν σπουδὴν
καὶ τὴν φιλεργίαν, σκολιὰς τεμνόντων καὶ βαθείας
τὰς σύριγγας, καὶ πρὸς τοὺς ἐν αὐταῖς ἀπαν-
τῶντας ποταμοὺς πολλάκις τοῖς Αἰγυπτίοις ἀναντλούντων[1] κοχλίαις. τὸν δ' ὅλον[2] οὐ ταὐτὸν
εἶναι τούτοις ποτὲ καὶ τοῖς Ἀττικοῖς, ἀλλ' ἐκείνοις
μὲν αἰνίγματι ἐοικέναι τὴν μεταλλείαν· ὅσα μὲν
γὰρ ἀνέλαβον[3] φησίν, οὐκ ἔλαβον, ὅσα δὲ εἶχον,
ἀπέβαλον· τούτοις δ' ὑπεράγαν λυσιτελῆ, τοῖς
μὲν χαλκουργοῖς τέταρτον μέρος ἐξάγουσι τῆς
γῆς τὸν χαλκόν, τῶν δ' ἀργυρευόντων τισὶν[4]
ἰδιωτῶν ἐν τρισὶν ἡμέραις Εὐβοϊκὸν τάλαντον
ἐξαίρουσι. τὸν δὲ καττίτερον οὐκ ἐπιπολῆς εὑρίσκεσθαί φησιν, ὡς τοὺς ἱστορικοὺς θρυλεῖν, ἀλλ'
ὀρύττεσθαι· γεννᾶσθαι δ' ἔν τε τοῖς ὑπὲρ τοὺς
Λυσιτανοὺς βαρβάροις καὶ ἐν ταῖς Καττιτερίσι
νήσοις, καὶ ἐκ τῶν Βρεττανικῶν δὲ εἰς τὴν Μασσαλίαν κομίζεσθαι. ἐν δὲ τοῖς Ἀρτάβροις, οἳ τῆς
Λυσιτανίας ὕστατοι πρὸς ἄρκτον καὶ δύσιν εἰσίν,
ἐξανθεῖν φησιν τὴν γῆν ἀργυρίῳ, καττιτέρῳ,
χρυσίῳ λευκῷ (ἀργυρομιγὲς γάρ ἐστι), τὴν δὲ γῆν

---

[1] ἀναντλούντων, Corais, for ἀνατλοῦντα; so the editors.
[2] τὸν δ' ὅλον, conj. of Scaliger, for τὸν δόλον. But perhaps,
τὸν δ' ἄθλον (C. Müller), which is generally accepted, is right ;
or τὸν θόλον. (Meineke's conj.).
[3] Meineke and others emend ἀνέλαβον to ἔμελλον, the word
of Athenaeus (6. 23).
[4] τισίν, Corais, for τῶν; so the editors in general.

---

[1] Archimedes' screw. Another method was that of divert-
ing the water by subterranean trenches (Diod. Sic. 5. 37.)

that the people dig as strenuously as if they expected to bring up Pluto himself. So Poseidonius implies that the energy and industry of the Turdetanian miners is similar, since they cut their shafts aslant and deep, and, as regards the streams that meet them in the shafts, oftentimes draw them off with the Egyptian screw.[1] However, the whole affair, he says, is never the same for these miners as for the Attic miners; indeed, for the latter, mining is like a riddle: "What they took up," he says, "they did not take, yet what they had, they lost";[2] but, for the Turdetanians, mining is profitable beyond measure, since one-fourth of the ore brought out by their copper-workers is pure copper, while some of their private adventurers who search for silver pick up within three days a Euboean talent[3] of silver. Tin, however, is not found there on the surface of the ground, he says, as the historians continually repeat, but is dug up; and it is produced both in the country of the barbarians who live beyond Lusitania, and in the Cassiterides Islands; and tin is brought to Massilia from the British Islands also. But among the Artabrians, who live farthest on the north-west of Lusitania, the soil "effloresces," he says, with silver, tin, and "white gold" (for it is mixed with silver). This soil, however, he adds, is

---

[2] This riddle was said to have been propounded to Homer by some fishermen after they had had bad luck. They sat on the sand with their small catch, and became covered with vermin. The fish they abandoned, but the vermin they could neither abandon nor catch. Demetrius, Poseidonius, Diodorus Siculus (5. 37), Athenaeus (6. 23), and Strabo apply the riddle to Attica's loss of invested capital when the revenues from her mines failed.

[3] About fifty-seven and one-half pounds avoirdupois.

ταύτην φέρειν τοὺς ποταμούς· τὴν δὲ σκαλίσι τὰς γυναῖκας διαμώσας πλύνειν ἐν ἠθητηρίοις πλεκτοῖς εἰς κίστην.[1] οὗτος μὲν περὶ τῶν μετάλλων τοιαῦτ᾽ εἴρηκε.

10. Πολύβιος δέ, τῶν περὶ Καρχηδόνα Νέαν ἀργυρείων μνησθείς, μέγιστα μὲν εἶναί φησι, διέχειν δὲ τῆς πόλεως ὅσον εἴκοσι σταδίους, περιειληφότα κύκλον τετρακοσίων σταδίων, ὅπου τέτταρας μυριάδας ἀνθρώπων μένειν τῶν ἐργαζομένων, ἀναφέροντας τότε τῷ δήμῳ τῶν Ῥωμαίων καθ᾽ ἑκάστην ἡμέραν δισμυρίας καὶ πεντακισχιλίας δραχμάς. τὴν δὲ κατεργασίαν τὴν μὲν ἄλλην ἐῶ (μακρὰ γάρ ἐστι), τὴν δὲ συρτὴν βῶλον τὴν ἀργυρῖτίν φησι κόπτεσθαι καὶ κοσκίνοις εἰς ὕδωρ διαρτᾶσθαι,[2] κόπτεσθαι δὲ πάλιν τὰς ὑποστάσεις, καὶ πάλιν διηθουμένας ἀποχεομένων τῶν ὑδάτων κόπτεσθαι· τὴν δὲ πέμπτην ὑπόστασιν χωνευθεῖσαν, ἀποχυθέντος τοῦ μολύβδου, καθαρὸν τὸν ἄργυρον ἐξάγειν. ἔστι δὲ καὶ νῦν τὰ ἀργυρεῖα, οὐ μέντοι δημόσια, οὔτε ἐνταῦθα οὔτε ἐν τοῖς ἄλλοις τόποις, ἀλλ᾽ εἰς ἰδιωτικὰς μετέστασαν κτήσεις· τὰ δὲ χρυσεῖα δημοσιεύεται τὰ πλείω. ἐν δὲ καὶ Κασταλῶνι καὶ ἄλλοις τόποις ἴδιόν ἐστι μέταλλον ὀρυκτοῦ μολύβδου· παραμέμικται δέ τι καὶ τούτῳ τοῦ ἀργύρου μικρόν, οὐχ ὥστε λυσιτελεῖν ἀποκαθαίρειν αὐτόν.

[1] εἰς κίστην, Kramer, for ἐπιπιστην (AC), ἐπὶ κίστην (B); so the editors in general.

[2] Casaubon emends διαρτᾶσθαι to διαττᾶσθαι; all later editors following.

[1] This simple method (now called "jigging") of separating the mineral from the light refuse is still in use. The sieve is

brought by the streams; and the women scrape it up with shovels and wash it in sieves woven basket-like. Such, then, is what Poseidonius has said about the mines.

10. Polybius, in mentioning the silver-mines of New Carthage, says that they are very large; that they are distant from the city about twenty stadia and embrace an area four hundred stadia in circuit; and that forty thousand workmen stay there, who (in his time) bring into the Roman exchequer a daily revenue of twenty-five thousand drachmae. But as for the processes of the work, I omit all he says about it (for it is a long story) except what he says of the silver-bearing ore that is carried along in the streams, namely, that it is crushed and by means of sieves disengaged in water; [1] then the sediment is again crushed, and again strained through (the waters meantime being poured off), and crushed; then the fifth sediment is smelted, and, after the lead has been poured off, yields the pure silver. The silver-mines are still being worked at the present time; they are not state-property, however, either at New Carthage or anywhere else, but have passed over to private ownership. But the majority of the gold-mines are state-property. Both in Castalo and elsewhere there is a special metal of mined lead; this, too, has a slight quantity of silver mixed with it, though not enough to make the refining of it profitable.

shaken up and down under water, and by gravity the heavier substance goes through the sieve to the bottom, the lighter forming a layer on top, which is scraped off. The Greek phrase (translated literally above) is syncopated, as is the further description of the process.

11. Οὐ πολὺ δ' ἄπωθεν τοῦ Κασταλῶνός ἐστι καὶ τὸ ὄρος, ἐξ οὗ ῥεῖν φασι τὸν Βαῖτιν, ὃ καλοῦσιν Ἀργυροῦν διὰ τὰ ἀργυρεῖα τὰ ἐν αὐτῷ. Πολύβιος δὲ καὶ τὸν Ἄναν καὶ τοῦτον ἐκ τῆς Κελτιβηρίας ῥεῖν φησι, διέχοντας ἀλλήλων ὅσον ἐννακοσίους σταδίους· αὐξηθέντες γὰρ οἱ Κελτίβηρες ἐποίησαν καὶ τὴν πλησιόχωρον πᾶσαν ὁμώνυμον ἑαυτοῖς. ἐοίκασι δ' οἱ παλαιοὶ καλεῖν τὸν Βαῖτιν Ταρτησσόν, τὰ δὲ Γάδειρα καὶ τὰς πρὸς αὐτὴν νήσους Ἐρύθειαν· διόπερ οὕτως εἰπεῖν ὑπολαμβάνουσι Στησίχορον περὶ τοῦ Γηρυόνος βουκόλου, διότι γεννηθείη

σχεδὸν ἀντιπέρας κλεινᾶς Ἐρυθείας
Ταρτησσοῦ ποταμοῦ παρὰ παγὰς ἀπείρονας
ἀργυρορίζους,
ἐν κευθμῶνι πέτρας.[1]

δυεῖν δὲ οὐσῶν ἐκβολῶν τοῦ ποταμοῦ, πόλιν ἐν τῷ μεταξὺ χώρῳ κατοικεῖσθαι πρότερόν φασιν, ἣν καλεῖσθαι Ταρτησσόν, ὁμώνυμον τῷ ποταμῷ, καὶ τὴν χώραν Ταρτησσίδα, ἣν νῦν Τουρδοῦλοι νέμονται. καὶ Ἐρατοσθένης δὲ τὴν συνεχῆ τῇ Κάλπῃ Ταρτησσίδα καλεῖσθαί φησι, καὶ Ἐρύθειαν νῆσον εὐδαίμονα. πρὸς ὃν Ἀρτεμίδωρος ἀντιλέγων καὶ ταῦτα ψευδῶς λέγεσθαί φησι ὑπ' αὐτοῦ, καθάπερ καὶ τὸ ἀπὸ Γαδείρων ἐπὶ τὸ Ἱερὸν ἀκρωτήριον διάστημα ἀπέχειν ἡμερῶν πέντε πλοῦν, οὐ πλειόνων ὄντων ἢ χιλίων καὶ ἑπτακοσίων σταδίων, καὶ τὸ τὰς ἀμπώτεις μέχρι δεῦρο περατοῦσθαι ἀντὶ τοῦ κύκλῳ περὶ πᾶσαν τὴν οἰκουμένην συμβαίνειν, καὶ τὸ τὰ προσαρκτικὰ

[1] See Bergk's re-arrangement of the words, *Poet. Lyr.* iii. 208.

11. Not very far from Castalo is also the mountain in which the Baetis is said to rise; it is called "Silver Mountain" on account of the silver-mines that are in it. According to Polybius, however, both this river and the Anas, though distant from each other as much as nine hundred stadia, rise in Celtiberia; for, as a result of their growth in power, the Celtiberians caused the whole neighbouring country to have the same name as their own. The ancients seem to have called the Baetis River "Tartessus"; and to have called Gades and the adjoining islands "Erytheia"; and this is supposed to be the reason why Stesichorus spoke as he did about the neat-herd [1] of Geryon, namely, that he was born "about opposite famous Erytheia, beside the unlimited, silver-rooted springs of the river Tartessus, in a cavern of a cliff." Since the river had two mouths, a city was planted on the intervening territory in former times, it is said,—a city which was called "Tartessus," after the name of the river; and the country, which is now occupied by Turdulians, was called "Tartessis." Further, Eratosthenes says that the country adjoining Calpe is called "Tartessis," and that Erytheia is called "Blest Isle." Eratosthenes is contradicted by Artemidorus, who says that this is another false statement of Eratosthenes, like his statement that the distance from Gades to the Sacred Cape is a five days' sail (although it is not more than one thousand seven hundred stadia), and his statement that the tides come to an end at the Sacred Cape (although the tides take place round the whole circuit of the inhabited world), and his state-

---

[1] Eurytion.

μέρη τῆς Ἰβηρίας εὐπαροδώτερα εἶναι πρὸς τὴν
Κελτικὴν ἢ κατὰ τὸν ὠκεανὸν πλέουσι, καὶ ὅσα
δὴ ἄλλα εἴρηκε Πυθέᾳ πιστεύσας, δι' ἀλαζονείαν.

C 149   12. Ὁ δὲ ποιητής, πολύφωνός τις ὢν καὶ
πολυΐστωρ, δίδωσιν ἀφορμὰς ὡς οὐδὲ τούτων
ἀνήκοός ἐστι τῶν τόπων, εἴ τις ὀρθῶς συλλο-
γίζεσθαι βούλοιτο ἀπ' ἀμφοῖν, τῶν τε χεῖρον
λεγομένων περὶ αὐτῶν, καὶ τῶν ἄμεινον καὶ ἀλη-
θέστερον. χεῖρον μέν, ὅτι πρὸς δύσιν ἐσχάτη
ἤκουεν αὕτη, ὅπου, καθάπερ αὐτός φησιν, εἰς τὸν
ὠκεανὸν ἐμπίπτει

λαμπρὸν φάος ἠελίοιο,
ἕλκον νύκτα μέλαιναν ἐπὶ ζείδωρον ἄρουραν.
(Il. 8. 485)

ἡ δὲ νὺξ ὅτι δύσφημον καὶ τῷ Ἅδῃ πλησιάζον
δῆλον, ὁ δὲ Ἅδης τῷ Ταρτάρῳ. εἰκάζοι οὖν[1] ἄν
τις ἀκούοντα[2] περὶ Ταρτησσοῦ τὸν Τάρταρον
ἐκεῖθεν παρονομάσαι τὸν ἔσχατον τῶν ὑποχθονίων
τόπων, προσθεῖναι δὲ καὶ μῦθον, τὸ ποιητικὸν
σώζοντα. καθάπερ καὶ τοὺς Κιμμερίους εἰδὼς
ἐν βορείοις καὶ ζοφεροῖς[3] οἰκήσαντας τόποις τοῖς
κατὰ τὸν Βόσπορον ἵδρυσεν αὐτοὺς πρὸς τῷ
Ἅδῃ, τάχα καὶ κατά τι κοινὸν τῶν Ἰώνων ἔχθος
πρὸς τὸ φῦλον τοῦτο· καὶ γὰρ καθ' Ὅμηρον ἢ
μικρὸν πρὸ αὐτοῦ λέγουσι τὴν τῶν Κιμμερίων

---

[1] οὖν, Groskurd inserts, after εἰκάζοι.
[2] ἀκούοντα, Kramer, for ἀκούων τά; Müller-Dübner, and
Meineke, following.
[3] ζοφεροῖς, Corais, for ζεφύροις; so the editors.

---

[1] Cp. 1. 4. 3–5, 2. 4. 1 and 3. 4. 4.

ment that the northerly parts of Iberia afford an easier passage to Celtica than if you sail thither by the ocean; and, in fact, every other statement which he has made in reliance upon Pytheas,[1] on account of the latter's false pretensions.

12. The poet,[2] man of many voices, so to speak, and of wide information, affords us grounds for the argument that even these regions were not unheard of by him, if one were only willing to argue scientifically from both statements that are made about these regions, not only from the worse, but also from the better and more truthful. Worse, namely, the statement that Tartessus was known by hearsay[3] as "farthermost in the west," where, as the poet himself says, falls into Oceanus "the sun's bright light, drawing black night over earth, the grain-giver." Now, that night is a thing of evil omen and associated with Hades, is obvious; also that Hades is associated with Tartarus. Accordingly, one might reasonably suppose that Homer, because he heard about Tartessus, named the farthermost of the nether-regions Tartarus after Tartessis, with a slight alteration of letters; and that he also added a mythical element, thus conserving the creative quality of poetry. Just as the poet, because he knew that the Cimmerians had taken their abode in northern and gloomy regions about the Bosporus, settled them in the neighbourhood of Hades, though perhaps he did it also in accordance with a certain common hatred of the Ionians for this tribe (indeed, it was in the time of Homer, or shortly before his time, they say, that that Cimmerian invasion which reached as far

[2] Homer.　　　　[3] In Homer's time.

ἔφοδον γενέσθαι τὴν μέχρι τῆς Αἰολίδος καὶ τῆς
Ἰωνίας. ταῖς δὲ Κυανέαις ἐποίησε παραπλησίως
τὰς Πλαγκτάς, ἀεὶ τοὺς μύθους ἀπό τινων ἱστο-
ριῶν ἐνάγων. χαλεπὰς γάρ τινας μυθεύει πέτρας,
καθάπερ τὰς Κυανέας φασίν, ἐξ οὗ καὶ Συμπλη-
γάδες καλοῦνται· διόπερ καὶ τὸν Ἰάσονος παρέ-
θηκε δι᾽ αὐτῶν πλοῦν. καὶ ὁ κατὰ τὰς Στήλας
δὲ πορθμὸς καὶ ὁ κατὰ Σικελίαν ὑπηγόρευον αὐτῷ
τὸν περὶ τῶν Πλαγκτῶν μῦθον. πρὸς μὲν δὴ τὸ
χεῖρον ἀπὸ τῆς τοῦ Ταρτάρου μυθοποιίας αἰνίτ-
τοιτό τις ἂν τὴν τῶν τόπων μνήμην τῶν περὶ
Ταρτησσόν.

13. Πρὸς δὲ τὸ βέλτιον ἐκ τούτων· ἥ τε γὰρ
Ἡρακλέους στρατεία μέχρι δεῦρο προελθοῦσα καὶ
τῶν Φοινίκων ὑπέγραφεν αὐτῷ πλοῦτόν τινα καὶ
ῥαθυμίαν τῶν ἀνθρώπων. οὗτοι γὰρ Φοίνιξιν
οὕτως ἐγένοντο σφόδρα ὑποχείριοι, ὥστε τὰς
πλείους τῶν ἐν τῇ Τουρδητανίᾳ πόλεων καὶ τῶν
πλησίον τόπων ὑπ᾽ ἐκείνων νῦν οἰκεῖσθαι. καὶ ἡ
τοῦ Ὀδυσσέως δὲ στρατεία δοκεῖ μοι δεῦρο γενη-
θεῖσα καὶ ἱστορηθεῖσα ὑπ᾽ αὐτοῦ παραδοῦναι
πρόφασιν· ὥστε καὶ -ην Ὀδύσσειαν, καθάπερ
καὶ τὴν Ἰλιάδα, ἀπὸ τῶν συμβάντων μεταγαγεῖν
εἰς ποίησιν καὶ τὴν συνήθη τοῖς ποιηταῖς μυθο-
ποιίαν. οὐ γὰρ μόνον οἱ κατὰ τὴν Ἰταλίαν καὶ
Σικελίαν τόποι καὶ ἄλλοι τινὲς τῶν τοιούτων
σημεῖα ὑπογράφουσιν, ἀλλὰ καὶ ἐν τῇ Ἰβηρίᾳ
Ὀδύσσεια πόλις δείκνυται καὶ Ἀθηνᾶς ἱερὸν καὶ

---

[1] *Odyssey* 12. 61 ; 23. 327.

as Aeolis and Ionia took place). Again, the poet modelled his "Planctae"[1] after the "Cyaneae," always bringing in his myths from some historical fact or other. For example, he tells a mythical story of certain rocks that are dangerous, just as they say the Cyaneae are (from which fact the Cyaneae are also called "Symplegades"), and this is the reason why he cited Jason's voyage through them. But both the strait at the Pillars and that at Sicily suggested to him the myth about the Planctae. As regards that worse statement, therefore, one might get a hint from the mythical invention of Tartarus that Homer had in mind the regions about Tartessus.

13. As regards the better, on the other hand, one might get hints from the following: In the first place, the expeditions of Heracles and of the Phoenicians, since they both reached as far as Iberia, suggested to Homer that the people of Iberia were in some way rich, and led a life of ease. Indeed, these people became so utterly subject to the Phoenicians that the greater number of the cities in Turdetania and of the neighbouring places are now inhabited by the Phoenicians. Secondly, the expedition of Odysseus, as it seems to me, since it actually had been made to Iberia, and since Homer had learned about it through inquiry, gave him an historical pretext; and so he also transferred the *Odyssey*, just as he had already transferred the *Iliad*, from the domain of historical fact to that of creative art, and to that of mythical invention so familiar to the poets. For not only do the regions about Italy and Sicily and certain other regions betray signs of such facts, but in Iberia also a city of Odysseia is to be seen, and a temple of

ἄλλα μυρία ἴχνη τῆς τε ἐκείνου πλάνης, καὶ
ἄλλων τῶν ἐκ τοῦ Τρωικοῦ πολέμου γενομένων
καὶ ἐπ᾽ ἴσης κακωσάντων τούς τε πολεμηθέντας
C 150 καὶ τοὺς ἑλόντας τὴν Τροίαν (καὶ γὰρ οὗτοι
Καδμείαν νίκην ἐτύγχανον ἠρμένοι), τῶν τε οἴκων
κατεφθαρμένων, καὶ τῶν λαφύρων ὀλίγων εἰς
ἕκαστον ἐληλυθότων, συνέβη τοῖς περιλειφθεῖσιν
ἀπελθοῦσιν[1] ἐκ τῶν κινδύνων κατὰ λῃστείας
τρέπεσθαι καὶ τοῖς Ἕλλησι, τοῖς μὲν διὰ τὸ ἐκ-
πεπορθῆσθαι, τοῖς δὲ διὰ τὴν αἰσχύνην, ἑκάστου
προλαβόντος

αἰσχρόν τοι δηρόν τε μένειν
ἄνευ τῶν οἰκείων,

κενεόν τε νέεσθαι
(Il. 2. 298)

παρ᾽ αὐτοὺς πάλιν. ἥ τε τοῦ Αἰνείου παραδέ-
δοται πλάνη καὶ Ἀντήνορος καὶ ἡ τῶν Ἐνετῶν·
ὡσαύτως καὶ ἡ Διομήδους τε καὶ Μενελάου καὶ
Ὀδυσσέως καὶ ἄλλων πλειόνων. ὁ τοίνυν ποιητὴς
τὰς τοσαύτας στρατείας ἐπὶ τὰ ἔσχατα τῆς
Ἰβηρίας ἱστορηκώς, πυνθανόμενος δὲ καὶ πλοῦτον
καὶ τὰς ἄλλας ἀρετάς (οἱ γὰρ Φοίνικες ἐδήλουν
τοῦτο), ἐνταῦθα τὸν τῶν εὐσεβῶν ἔπλασε χῶρον
καὶ τὸ Ἠλύσιον πεδίον, οὗ φησιν ὁ Πρωτεὺς
ἀποικήσειν τὸν Μενέλαον·

ἀλλά σ᾽ ἐς Ἠλύσιον πεδίον καὶ πείρατα γαίης
ἀθάνατοι πέμψουσιν, ὅθι ξανθὸς Ῥαδάμανθυς,
τῇ περ ῥηίστη βιοτὴ πέλει ἀνθρώποισιν·
οὐ νιφετὸς οὔτ᾽ ἄρ χειμὼν πολὺς οὐδέ ποτ᾽
ὄμβρος,

54

Athene, and countless other traces, not only of the wanderings of Odysseus, but also of other wanderings which took place thither after the Trojan War and afflicted the capturers of Troy quite as much as it did the vanquished [1] (for the capturers, as it happened, carried off only a Cadmean victory [2]). And since the Trojan homes were in ruins, and the booty that came to each Greek was but small, the result was that the surviving Trojans, after having escaped from the perils of the war, turned to acts of piracy, as did also the Greeks; the Trojans, because their city was now in utter ruins; the Greeks, for shame, since every Greek took it for granted that it was "verily shameful to wait long" far from his kindred "and then" back to them "empty-handed go." Thirdly, the wanderings of Aeneas are a traditional fact, as also those of Antenor, and those of the Henetians; [3] similarly, also, those of Diomedes, Menelaus, Odysseus, and several others. So then, the poet, informed through his inquiries of so many expeditions to the outermost parts of Iberia, and learning by hearsay about the wealth and the other good attributes of the country (for the Phoenicians were making these facts known), in fancy placed the abode of the blest there, and also the Elysian Plain, where Proteus says Menelaus will go and make his home: "But the deathless gods will escort thee to the Elysian Plain and the ends of the earth, where is Rhadamanthys of the fair hair, where life is easiest. No snow is there, nor yet great storm, nor ever any

[1] Cp. 1. 3. 2, vol. I, pp. 177–179.
[2] Alluding to the myth of Cadmus and the dragon's teeth.
[3] *Iliad* 2. 852.

---

[1] ἀπελθοῦσιν, Kramer, for ἀπειθοῦσιν (ACl), ἀπιοῦσιν (B); so the editors.

ἀλλ' αἰεὶ Ζεφύροιο λιγὺ πνείοντος ἀήτας
Ὠκεανὸς ἀνίησιν ἀναψύχειν ἀνθρώπους.

(Od. 4. 563)

τό τε γὰρ εὐάερον καὶ τὸ εὔπνουν τοῦ Ζεφύρου
ταύτης ἐστὶ τῆς χώρας οἰκεῖον, ἑσπερίου τε καὶ
ἀλεεινῆς οὔσης, τό τε ἐπὶ τοῖς πέρασι τῆς γῆς,
ἐφ' οἷς καὶ τὸν Ἅδην μεμυθεῦσθαί φαμεν. ὅ τε
Ῥαδάμανθυς παρατεθεὶς ὑπογράφει τὸν πλησίον
τῷ Μίνῳ τόπον, περὶ οὗ φησιν.

ἔνθ' ἤτοι Μίνωα ἴδον Διὸς ἀγλαὸν υἱόν,
χρύσεον σκῆπτρον ἔχοντα, θεμιστεύοντα νέ-
κυσσι.

(Od. 11. 568)

καὶ οἱ μετὰ ταῦτα δὲ ποιηταὶ παραπλήσια θρυ-
λοῦσι, τήν τε ἐπὶ τὰς Γηρυόνου βόας στρατείαν
καὶ τὴν ἐπὶ τὰ μῆλα τῶν Ἑσπερίδων τὰ χρύσεα
ὡσαύτως στρατείαν, καὶ Μακάρων τινὰς νήσους
κατονομάζοντες, ἃς καὶ νῦν δεικνυμένας ἴσμεν οὐ
πολὺ ἄπωθεν τῶν ἄκρων τῆς Μαυρουσίας τῶν
ἀντικειμένων τοῖς Γαδείροις.

14. Τοὺς δὲ Φοίνικας λέγω μηνυτάς· καὶ τῆς
Ἰβηρίας καὶ τῆς Λιβύης τὴν ἀρίστην οὗτοι κατέσχον πρὸ τῆς ἡλικίας τῆς Ὁμήρου καὶ διετέλεσαν
κύριοι τῶν τόπων ὄντες, μέχρις οὗ Ῥωμαῖοι κατ-
C 151 έλυσαν αὐτῶν τὴν ἡγεμονίαν. τοῦ δ' Ἰβηρικοῦ
πλούτου καὶ ταῦτα μαρτύρια· Καρχηδόνιοι μετὰ
τοῦ Βάρκα στρατεύσαντες κατέλαβον, ὥς φασιν
οἱ συγγραφεῖς, φάτναις ἀργυραῖς καὶ πίθοις χρωμένους τοὺς ἐν τῇ Τουρδητανίᾳ. ὑπολάβοι δ' ἄν
τις ἐκ τῆς πολλῆς εὐδαιμονίας καὶ Μακραίωνας

56

rain; but always Oceanus sendeth forth the breezes of clear-blowing Zephyrus." For both the pure air and the gentle breezes of Zephyrus properly belong to this country, since the country is not only in the west but also warm; and the phrase "at the ends of the earth" properly belongs to it, where Hades has been "mythically placed," as we say. And Homer's citing of Rhadamanthys suggests the region that is near Minos, concerning whom he says: "There it was I saw Minos, glorious son of Zeus, holding a golden sceptre, rendering decisions to the dead." Furthermore, the poets who came after Homer keep dinning into our ears similar stories: the expedition of Heracles in quest of the kine of Geryon and likewise the expedition which he made in quest of the golden apples of the Hesperides—even calling by name certain Isles of the Blest, which, as we know, are still now pointed out, not very far from the headlands of Maurusia that lie opposite to Gades.

14. The Phoenicians, I say, were the informants of Homer; and these people occupied the best of Iberia and Libya before the age of Homer, and continued to be masters of those regions until the Romans broke up their empire. The wealth of Iberia is further evidenced by the following facts: the Carthaginians who, along with Barcas, made a campaign against Iberia found the people in Turdetania, as the historians tell us, using silver feeding-troughs and wine-jars. And one might assume that it was from their great prosperity that the people there got the additional name of "Macraeones," [1]

---

[1] "Long-livers."

ὀνομασθῆναι τοὺς ἐνθάδε ἀνθρώπους, καὶ μάλιστα τοὺς ἡγεμόνας, καὶ διὰ τοῦτο Ἀνακρέοντα μὲν οὕτως εἰπεῖν·

> Ἔγωγ' οὔτ' ἂν Ἀμαλθίης
> βουλοίμην κέρας οὔτ' ἔτεα
> πεντήκοντά τε καὶ ἑκατόν
> Ταρτησσοῦ βασιλεῦσαι·
>
> (*Frag.* 8, Bergk)

Ἡρόδοτον δὲ καὶ τὸ ὄνομα τοῦ βασιλέως κατα-γράψαι, καλέσαντα Ἀργανθώνιον· ἢ γὰρ οὕτω δέξαιτ' ἄν τις ἢ ἴσον τούτῳ τὸ[1] Ἀνακρέοντος, ἢ κοινότερον οὔτε Ταρτησσοῦ πολὺν χρόνον βασι-λεῦσαι. ἔνιοι δὲ Ταρτησσὸν τὴν νῦν Καρτηίαν προσαγορεύουσι.[2]

15. Τῇ δὲ τῆς χώρας εὐδαιμονίᾳ καὶ τὸ ἥμερον καὶ τὸ πολιτικὸν συνηκολούθησε τοῖς Τουρδη-τανοῖς· καὶ τοῖς Κελτικοῖς δὲ διὰ τὴν γειτνίασιν, ὡς εἴρηκε Πολύβιος, ἢ[3] διὰ τὴν συγγένειαν, ἀλλ' ἐκείνοις μὲν ἧττον· τὰ πολλὰ γὰρ κωμηδὸν ζῶσιν. οἱ μέντοι Τουρδητανοί, καὶ μάλιστα οἱ περὶ τὸν Βαῖτιν, τελέως εἰς τὸν Ῥωμαίων μεταβέβληνται τρόπον, οὐδὲ τῆς διαλέκτου τῆς σφετέρας ἔτι με-μνημένοι. Λατῖνοί τε οἱ πλεῖστοι γεγόνασι, καὶ ἐποίκους εἰλήφασι Ῥωμαίους, ὥστε μικρὸν ἀπέ-

---

[1] τό, Siebenkees and Corais insert, from the conj. of Tyrwhitt.
[2] Meineke (followed by Forbiger and Tardieu) regards ἢ γὰρ . . . προσαγορεύουσι as a marginal gloss and unwar-rantedly omits it from the text.
[3] ἤ, Jones inserts.

---

[1] The sacred she-goat which suckled Zeus in his infancy. For gratitude Zeus placed her among the constellations.

and particularly the chieftains; and that this is why Anacreon said as follows: "I, for my part, should neither wish the horn of Amaltheia,[1] nor to be king of Tartessus for one hundred and fifty years"; and why Herodotus recorded even the name of the king, whom he called Arganthonius.[2] For one might either take the phrase of Anacreon literally or as meaning "a time equal to the king's," or else in a more general way, "nor to be king of Tartessus for a long time." Some, however, call Tartessus the Carteia of to-day.[3]

15. Along with the happy lot of their country, the qualities of both gentleness and civility have come to the Turditanians; and to the Celtic peoples, too, on account of their being neighbours to the Turdetanians, as Polybius has said, or else on account of their kinship; but less so the Celtic peoples, because for the most part they live in mere villages. The Turdetanians, however, and particularly those that live about the Baetis, have completely changed over to the Roman mode of life, not even remembering their own language any more. And most of them have become Latins,[4] and they have received Romans

---

Her horns gushed, one with nectar and the other with ambrosia. The "horn of Amaltheia" became proverbial for the cornucopia inexhaustible.

[2] "Silver Locks" is a fair equivalent of the Greek word. Herodotus says he reigned eighty years and lived one hundred and twenty (l. 163).

[3] Strabo's thought reverts to § 11 above. Cp. Pliny (*Nat. Hist.* 3. 3), who speaks of "Carteia, called by the Greeks Tartessus."

[4] That is, they acquired the so-called "Latin rights of citizenship," which comprehended more than "foreign rights" but less than "Roman rights." Cp. 4. 1. 12.

χουσι τοῦ πάντες εἶναι Ῥωμαῖοι. αἵ τε νῦν
συνῳκισμέναι πόλεις, ἥ τε ἐν τοῖς Κελτικοῖς Παξ-
αυγούστα καὶ ἡ ἐν τοῖς Τουρδούλοις Αὐγούστα
Ἡμερίτα καὶ ἡ περὶ τοὺς Κελτίβηρας Καισαραυ-
γούστα καὶ ἄλλαι ἔνιαι κατοικίαι τὴν μεταβολὴν
τῶν λεχθεισῶν πολιτειῶν ἐμφανίζουσι. καὶ δὴ
τῶν Ἰβήρων ὅσοι ταύτης εἰσὶ τῆς ἰδέας τογᾶτοι[1]
λέγονται· ἐν δὲ τούτοις εἰσὶ καὶ οἱ Κελτίβηρες οἱ
πάντων νομισθέντες ποτὲ θηριωδέστατοι. ταῦτα
μὲν περὶ τούτων.

III

1. Ἀπὸ δὲ τοῦ Ἱεροῦ πάλιν ἀκρωτηρίου τὴν ἀρχὴν λαμβάνουσιν ἐπὶ θάτερον μέρος τῆς παραλίας,
τὸ πρὸς τὸν Τάγον, κόλπος ἐστίν· ἔπειτα ἄκρα τὸ
Βαρβάριον καὶ αἱ τοῦ Τάγου ἐκβολαὶ πλησίον,
ἐφ' ἃς εὐθυπλοίᾳ[2] στάδιοι εἰσὶ δέκα·[3] ἐνταῦθα δὲ
καὶ ἀναχύσεις, ὧν μία ἐπὶ πλείους ἢ τετρακοσίους

---

[1] τογᾶτοι, Kramer, for στολάτοι ; Müller-Dübner, Forbiger,
Tardieu, and Meineke, following (the accent being Meineke's) ;
moor read στολάται ἢ τογάτοι. Cp. 3. 4. 20 ; and Dio Cassius,
46. 55, ἐκαλεῖτο δὲ ἐκείνη (i.e. Gallia Narbonensis) μὲν τογᾶτα,
ὅτι τε εἰρηνικωτέρα παρὰ τὰς ἄλλας ἐδόκει εἶναι καὶ ὅτι καὶ τῇ
ἐσθῆτι τῇ Ῥωμαικῇ τῇ ἀστικῇ ἐχρῶντο ἤδη.

[2] εὐθυπλοίᾳ, Corais, for εὐθύπλοιαι ; editors following.

[3] For δέκα Corais (followed by Groskurd, and Forbiger)
writes διακόσιοι (σ') or διακόσιοι δέκα (σ'ι'), omitting the δ'
(MSS.) before εἰσι. C. Müller (followed by Tardieu), conjectures ͵α (χίλιοι) for δ' and writes as follows : στάδιοι χίλιοι·
εἰσὶ δὲ καὶ ἐνταῖθα κ.τ.λ. But the problem is further complicated
by Strabo's later reference to a "tower," which indicates
that several words have fallen out of the text—probably
after εὐθυπλοίᾳ.

as colonists, so that they are not far from being all Romans. And the present jointly-settled cities, Pax Augusta in the Celtic country, Augusta Emerita in the country of the Turdulians, Caesar-Augusta near Celtiberia, and some other settlements, manifest the change to the aforesaid civil modes of life. Moreover, all those Iberians who belong to this class are called "Togati."[1] And among these are the Celtiberians, who were once regarded the most brutish of all. So much for the Turditanians.

III

1. Now if we again begin at the Sacred Cape, following the coast in the other direction, namely, towards the Tagus River, there is first a gulf, then a promontory, Barbarium, and near it the mouths of the Tagus; and the distance to these mouths in a direct voyage is ten[2] stadia. Here, too, there are estuaries; one of them extends inland from the

---

[1] The MSS. are nearly unanimous in support of "Stolati," "wearers of the stola," but this was a matrons' garment at Rome. Cp. 3. 4. 20. Again, Dio Cassius (see note on opposite page), in speaking of Gallia Narbonensis, says that it was called "Gallia Togata," both because it was reputed to be more peaceable than the others and because the people there were already (43 B.C.) wearing the Roman garb.

[2] As the MSS. stand, "ten" cannot be right. Strabo probably wrote "two hundred" (or "two hundred and ten"), if he meant *from Barbarium ;* or "one thousand," if *from the Sacred Cape.* The latter seems more likely, for it is inconceivable that Strabo would leave out the distance from the Sacred Cape to Barbarium and thus break his otherwise continuous circuit of distances extending all the way from the Trophies of Pompey (3. 4. 1.) to Cape Nerium. See critical note on opposite page.

σταδίους ἀπὸ τοῦ λεχθέντος πύργου, καθ᾽ ἣν
ὑδρεύονται ἐπὶ Σαλάκειαν.[1] ὁ δὲ Τάγος καὶ τὸ
πλάτος ἔχει τοῦ στόματος εἴκοσί που σταδίων
καὶ τὸ βάθος μέγα, ὥστε μυριαγωγοῖς ἀναπλεῖσθαι. δύο δ᾽ ἀναχύσεις ἐν τοῖς ὑπερκειμένοις
C 152 ποιεῖται πεδίοις, ὅταν αἱ πλῆμαι γίνωνται, ὥστε
πελαγίζειν μὲν ἐπὶ ἑκατὸν καὶ πεντήκοντα σταδίους καὶ ποιεῖν πλωτὸν τὸ πεδίον, ἐν δὲ τῇ ἐπάνω
ἀναχύσει καὶ νῆσον ἀπολαμβάνειν ὅσον τριάκοντα
σταδίων τὸ μῆκος, πλάτος δὲ μικρὸν ἀπολεῖπον
τοῦ μήκους, εὐαλσὲς[2] καὶ εὐάμπελον. κεῖται δ᾽
ἡ νῆσος κατὰ Μόρωνα πόλιν εὖ[3] κειμένην ἐν ὄρει
τοῦ ποταμοῦ πλησίον, ἀφεστῶσαν τῆς θαλάττης
ὅσον πεντακοσίους σταδίους, ἔχουσαν δὲ καὶ
χώραν ἀγαθὴν τὴν πέριξ καὶ τοὺς ἀνάπλους εὐπε-
τεῖς μέχρι μὲν πολλοῦ καὶ μεγάλοις σκάφεσι, τὸ
δὲ λοιπὸν τοῖς ποταμίοις· καὶ ὑπὲρ τὸν Μόρωνα
δ᾽ ἔτι μακρότερος ἀνάπλους ἐστί· ταύτῃ δὲ τῇ
πόλει Βροῦτος ὁ Καλλαϊκὸς προσαγορευθεὶς
ὁρμητηρίῳ χρώμενος ἐπολέμησε πρὸς τοὺς Λυσιτανοὺς καὶ κατέστρεψε τούτους. τοῖς δὲ τοῦ
ποταμοῦ κλείθροις[4] ἐπετείχισε[5] τὴν Ὀλυσιπῶνα,

---

[1] ἐπὶ Σαλάκειαν, C. Müller, for εἶπον λακεια; so Tardieu.
[2] εὐαλσές, conj. of Casaubon, for εὐαλτές; so most editors.
[3] κατὰ Μόρωνα πόλιν εὖ, Corais, from the conj. of Casaubon, for κατὰ λόγον ἀπολιπεῖν; so Forbiger, Müller-Dübner, Tardieu, and Meineke.
[4] κλείθροις, conj. of Meineke, for πλίθροις.
[5] ἐπετείχισε, Casaubon, for ἐπεχείρησε; so Kramer, Müller-Dübner, and Meineke.

afore-mentioned tower[1] for more than four hundred
stadia, and along this estuary the country is watered
as far as Salacia.[2] Now the Tagus not only has a
width of about twenty stadia at its mouth, but its
depth is so great that very large merchant-ships can
ascend it. And when the flood-tides come on, it
forms two estuaries in the plains that lie above it, so
that it forms a sea for a distance of one hundred and
fifty stadia, and renders the plain navigable, and also,
in the upper estuary, encloses an island about thirty
stadia in length, and in breadth a trifle short of the
length—an island with fine groves and vines. The
island is situated opposite Moron,[3] a city happily
situated on a mountain near the river, at a distance
of about five hundred stadia from the sea. And
further, not only is the country round about the city
rich, but the voyages thither are easy—even for
large ships a considerable part of the way, though
only for the river-boats the rest of the way. And
beyond Moron, also, the river is navigable for a still
greater distance. This city Brutus, surnamed
Callaicus,[4] used as a base of operations when he
warred against the Lusitanians and brought these
people under subjection. And, to command the bar[5]
of the river, he fortified Olysipo, in order that the

---

[1] Strabo seems previously to have referred to a tower (on
Barbarium?); but if so, the words have fallen out of the
manuscripts.

[2] The Greek text is corrupt, but it seems certain that
Strabo wrote " Salacia " here. It is about 400 stadia from
Barbarium. Cp. Ptolemaeus 2. 5.

[3] Now Al-Merim.

[4] D. Junius Brutus was thus surnamed from his subjection
of the Callaicans, 136 B.C.

[5] The narrows at Lisbon.

ἵν᾽[1] ἔχοι τοὺς ἀνάπλους ἐλευθέρους καὶ τὰς ἀνα
κομιδὰς τῶν ἐπιτηδείων, ὥστε καὶ τῶν περὶ τὸν
Τάγον πόλεων αὗται κράτισται. πολύϊχθυς δ᾽ ὁ
ποταμὸς καὶ ὀστρέων πλήρης. ῥεῖ δ᾽ ἔχων τὰς
ἀρχὰς ἐκ Κελτιβήρων διὰ Οὐεττώνων καὶ Καρπη
τανῶν καὶ Λυσιτανῶν ἐπὶ δύσιν ἰσημερινήν, μέχρι
ποσοῦ παράλληλος ὢν τῷ τε Ἄνᾳ καὶ τῷ Βαίτι,
μετὰ δὲ ταῦτα ἀφιστάμενος ἐκείνων, ἀποκλινόντων
πρὸς τὴν νότιον παραλίαν.

2. Οἱ δὲ ὑπερκείμενοι τῶν λεχθέντων ὀρῶν Ὠρη
τανοὶ μέν εἰσι νοτιώτατοι καὶ μέχρι τῆς παραλίας
διήκοντες ἐκ μέρους τῆς ἐντὸς Στηλῶν. Καρπη
τανοὶ δὲ μετὰ τούτους πρὸς ἄρκτους, εἶτα Οὐέτ
τωνες καὶ Οὐακκαῖοι, δι᾽ ὧν ὁ Δούριος ῥεῖ, κατ᾽
Ἀκούτειαν[2] πόλιν τῶν Οὐακκαίων ἔχων διάβασιν.
Καλλαϊκοὶ δ᾽ ὕστατοι, τῆς ὀρεινῆς ἐπέχοντες
πολλήν· διὸ καὶ δυσμαχώτατοι ὄντες τῷ τε κατα
πολεμήσαντι τοὺς Λυσιτανοὺς αὐτοὶ παρέσχον τὴν
ἐπωνυμίαν, καὶ νῦν ἤδη τοὺς πλείστους τῶν Λυσι
τανῶν Καλλαϊκοὺς καλεῖσθαι παρεσκεύασαν. τῆς
μὲν οὖν Ὠρητανίας κρατιστεύουσά ἐστι πόλις
Κασταλών, καὶ Ὠρία.

3. Τοῦ δὲ Τάγου τὰ πρὸς ἄρκτον ἡ Λυσιτανία
ἐστὶ μέγιστον τῶν Ἰβηρικῶν ἐθνῶν καὶ πλείστοις
χρόνοις ὑπὸ Ῥωμαίων πολεμηθέν. περιέχει δὲ
τῆς χώρας ταύτης τὸ μὲν νότιον πλευρὸν ὁ Τάγος,

---

[1] Ὀλυσιπῶνα, Kramer, for ὅλοσιν, retaining the ὡς ἄν (after
ὅλοσιν in the MSS.) ; but Meineke reads as above.

[2] Ἀκούτειαν, conj. of Kramer, for Ἀκόντιαν; so Meineke,
and Tardieu.

voyages inland and the importation of provisions might be unimpeded; so that among the cities about the Tagus these are strongest. The Tagus abounds in fish, and is full of oysters. It rises in Celtiberia, and flows through Vettonia, Carpetania, and Lusitania, towards the equinoctial west,[1] up to a certain point being parallel to both the Anas and the Baetis, but after that diverging from those rivers, since they bend off towards the southern seaboard.

2. Now of the peoples situated beyond the mountains mentioned above,[2] the Oretanians are most southerly, and their territory reaches as far as the seacoast in part of the country this side of the Pillars; the Carpetanians are next after these on the north; then the Vettonians and the Vaccaeans, through whose territory the Durius River flows, which affords a crossing at Acutia, a city of the Vaccaeans; and last, the Callaicans, who occupy a very considerable part of the mountainous country. For this reason, since they were very hard to fight with, the Callaicans themselves have not only furnished the surname for the man who defeated the Lusitanians but they have also brought it about that now, already, the most of the Lusitanians are called Callaicans. Now as for Oretania, its city of Castalo is very powerful, and so is Oria.[3]

3. And yet the country north of the Tagus, Lusitania, is the greatest of the Iberian nations, and is the nation against which the Romans waged war for the longest times. The boundaries of this country are: on the southern side, the Tagus; on the

---

[1] Literally, the sunset at the equinox.   [2] 3. 2. 3.
[3] Identical, apparently, with Nuestra Senora de Oreto, near Granatula.

τὸ δ' ἑσπέριον καὶ τὸ ἀρκτικὸν ὁ ὠκεανός, τὸ
δ' ἑωθινὸν οἵ τε Καρπητανοὶ καὶ οἱ Οὐέττωνες
καὶ Οὐακκαῖοι καὶ Καλλαϊκοί, τὰ γνώριμα ἔθνη·
τἆλλα δὲ οὐκ ἄξιον ὀνομάζειν διὰ τὴν μικρότητα
καὶ τὴν ἀδοξίαν· ὑπεναντίως δὲ τοῖς νῦν ἔνιοι καὶ
τούτους Λυσιτανοὺς ὀνομάζουσιν. ὅμοροι δ' εἰσὶν
ἐκ τοῦ πρὸς ἔω μέρους οἱ μὲν Καλλαϊκοὶ τῷ τῶν
Ἀστούρων ἔθνει καὶ τοῖς Κελτίβηρσιν,[1] οἱ δ'
C 153   ἄλλοι τοῖς Κελτίβηρσι. τὸ μὲν οὖν μῆκος μέχρι
Νερίου[2] τρισχιλίων σταδίων, τὸ δὲ πλάτος πολὺ
ἔλαττον, ὃ ποιεῖ τὸ ἑωθινὸν πλευρὸν εἰς τὴν ἀντι-
κειμένην παραλίαν. ὑψηλὸν δ' ἐστὶ τὸ ἑωθινὸν
καὶ τραχύ, ἡ δὲ ὑποκειμένη χώρα πεδιὰς πᾶσα
καὶ μέχρι θαλάττης πλὴν ὀλίγων ὀρῶν οὐ μεγά-
λων· ᾗ δὴ καὶ τὸν Ἀριστοτέλη φησὶν ὁ Ποσειδώνιος οὐκ ὀρθῶς αἰτιᾶσθαι τὴν παραλίαν καὶ τὴν
Μαυρουσίαν τῶν πλημμυρίδων καὶ τῶν ἀμπώ-
τεων· παλιρροεῖν γὰρ φάναι τὴν θάλατταν διὰ τὸ
τὰς ἄκρας ὑψηλάς τε καὶ τραχείας εἶναι, δεχομέ-
νας τε τὸ κῦμα σκληρῶς καὶ ἀνταποδιδούσας τῇ
ἴσῃ βίᾳ·[3] τἀναντία γὰρ θινώδεις εἶναι καὶ ταπεινὰς
τὰς πλείστας ὀρθῶς λέγων.

4. Ἡ δ' οὖν χώρα, περὶ ἧς λέγομεν, εὐδαίμων
τέ ἐστι καὶ διαρρεῖται ποταμοῖς μεγάλοις τε καὶ
μικροῖς, ἅπασιν ἐκ τῶν ἑωθινῶν μερῶν, παραλ-
λήλοις τῷ Τάγῳ· ἔχουσι δὲ καὶ ἀνάπλους οἱ πλείους
καὶ ψῆγμα τοῦ χρυσοῦ πλεῖστον. γνωριμώτατοι δὲ
τῶν ποταμῶν ἐφεξῆς τῷ Τάγῳ Μούνδας, ἀνάπλους

---

[1] Κελτίβηρσιν, Groskurd, for Ἴβηρσιν ; so the other editors.
[2] μέχρι Νερίου, C. Müller, for μυρίων καί ; so Tardieu.
[3] τῇ ἴσῃ βίᾳ, T. G. Tucker, for τῇ Ἰβηρίᾳ.

western and northern, the ocean; and on the eastern,
the countries of the Carpetanians, Vettonians, Vaccaeans, and Callaicans, the well-known tribes; it is
not worth while to name the rest, because of their
smallness and lack of repute. Contrary to the men
of to-day, however, some call also these peoples
Lusitanians. These four peoples, in the eastern part
of their countries, have common boundaries, thus:
the Callaicans, with the tribe of the Asturians and
with the Celtiberians, but the others with only the
Celtiberians. Now the length of Lusitania to Cape
Nerium is three thousand stadia, but its breadth,
which is formed between its eastern side and the
coast-line that lies opposite thereto, is much less.
The eastern side is high and rough, but the country
that lies below is all plain even to the sea, except a
few mountains of no great magnitude. And this, of
course, is why Poseidonius says that Aristotle is
incorrect in making the coast-line [1] and Maurusia the
cause of the flood-tides and the ebb-tides; whom he
quotes as saying that the sea ebbs and flows on
account of the fact that the coast-lands are both
high and rugged, which not only receive the waves
roughly but give them back with equal violence.
For on the contrary, Poseidonius correctly says, the
coast-lands are for the most part sandy and low.

4. At all events, the country of which I am
speaking is fertile, and it is also traversed by rivers
both large and small, all of them flowing from the
eastern parts and parallel to the Tagus; most of them
offer voyages inland and contain very great quantities
of gold-dust as well. Best known of the rivers
immediately after the Tagus are the Mundas, which

---

[1] Of Iberia.

ἔχων μικρούς, καὶ Οὐακούα ὡσαύτως· μετὰ δὲ
τούτους Δούριος μακρόθεν τε ῥέων παρὰ Νομαντίαν
καὶ πολλὰς ἄλλας τῶν Κελτιβήρων καὶ Οὐακκαίων
κατοικίας, μεγάλοις τ' ἀναπλεόμενος σκάφεσιν
ἐπὶ ὀκτακοσίους σχεδόν τι σταδίους. εἶτ' ἄλλοι
ποταμοί· καὶ μετὰ τούτους ὁ τῆς Λήθης, ὅν τινες
Λιμαίαν, οἱ δὲ Βελιῶνα καλοῦσι· καὶ οὗτος δ' ἐκ
Κελτιβήρων καὶ Οὐακκαίων ῥεῖ, καὶ ὁ μετ' αὐτὸν
Βαῖνις (οἱ δὲ Μίνιόν φασι) πολὺ μέγιστος τῶν
ἐν Λυσιτανίᾳ ποταμῶν, ἐπὶ ὀκτακοσίους καὶ αὐτὸς
ἀναπλεόμενος σταδίους. Ποσειδώνιος δὲ ἐκ Καντάβρων καὶ αὐτὸν ῥεῖν φησι· πρόκειται δὲ τῆς
ἐκβολῆς αὐτοῦ νῆσος καὶ χηλαὶ δύο ὅρμους ἔχουσαι. ἐπαινεῖν δ' ἄξιον τὴν φύσιν, ὅτι τὰς ὄχθας
ὑψηλὰς ἔχουσιν οἱ ποταμοὶ καὶ ἱκανὰς δέχεσθαι
τοῖς ῥείθροις τὴν θάλατταν πλημμυροῦσαν, ὥστε
μὴ ὑπερχεῖσθαι, μηδ' ἐπιπολάζειν ἐν τοῖς πεδίοις.
τῆς μὲν οὖν Βρούτου στρατείας ὅρος οὗτος, περαιτέρω δ' εἰσὶν ἄλλοι πλείους ποταμοὶ παράλληλοι
τοῖς λεχθεῖσιν.

5. Ὕστατοι δ' οἰκοῦσιν Ἄρταβροι περὶ τὴν
ἄκραν, ἣ καλεῖται Νέριον, ἣ καὶ τῆς ἑσπερίου
πλευρᾶς καὶ τῆς βορείου πέρας ἐστί. περιοικοῦσι
δ' αὐτὴν Κελτικοί, συγγενεῖς τῶν ἐπὶ τῷ Ἄνᾳ.
καὶ γὰρ τούτους καὶ Τουρδούλους στρατεύσαντας
ἐκεῖσε στασιάσαι φασὶ μετὰ τὴν διάβασιν τοῦ
Λιμαία ποταμοῦ· πρὸς δὲ τῇ στάσει καὶ ἀποβολῆς
τοῦ ἡγεμόνος γενομένης, καταμεῖναι σκεδασθέντας

---

[1] "Forgetfulness."
[2] "Belion" is probably an Iberian corruption, or cognate,
of the Latin "Oblivio."

offers short voyages inland, and likewise the Vacua. After these two is the Durius, which, coming from afar, flows by Numantia and many other settlements of the Celtiberians and Vaccaeans, and is navigable for large boats for a distance of about eight hundred stadia inland. Then come other rivers. And after these the River of Lethe,[1] which by some persons is called Limaeas, but by others Belion;[2] and this river, too, rises in the country of the Celtiberians and the Vaccaeans, as also does the river that comes after it, namely the Baenis (others say "Minius"), which is by far the greatest of the rivers in Lusitania—itself, also, being navigable inland for eight hundred stadia. Poseidonius, however, says that the Baenis rises in Cantabria. Off its mouth lies an island, and two breakwaters which afford anchorage for vessels. The nature of these rivers deserves praise, because the banks which they have are high, and adequate to receive within their channels the sea at high tide without overflowing or spreading over the plains. Now this river was the limit of Brutus' campaign, though farther on there are several other rivers, parallel to those mentioned.

5. Last of all come the Artabrians, who live in the neighbourhood of the cape called Nerium, which is the end of both the western and the northern side of Iberia. But the country round about the cape itself is inhabited by Celtic people, kinsmen of those on the Anas; for these people and the Turdulians made an expedition thither and then had a quarrel, it is said, after they had crossed the Limaeas River; and when, in addition to the quarrel, the Celtic peoples also suffered the loss of their chieftain, they scattered and stayed there; and it was from this

69

αὐτόθι· ἐκ τούτου δὲ καὶ τὸν ποταμὸν Λήθης
C 154 ἀγορευθῆναι. ἔχουσι δὲ οἱ Ἄρταβροι πόλεις
συχνὰς ἐν κόλπῳ συνοικουμένας, ὃν οἱ πλέοντες
καὶ χρώμενοι τοῖς τόποις Ἀρτάβρων λιμένα προσ-
αγορεύουσιν· οἱ δὲ νῦν τοὺς Ἀρτάβρους Ἀρο-
τρέβας καλοῦσιν. ἔθνη μὲν οὖν περὶ τριάκοντα[1]
τὴν χώραν νέμεται τὴν μεταξὺ Τάγου καὶ τῶν
Ἀρτάβρων, εὐδαίμονος δὲ τῆς χώρας ὑπαρχούσης
κατά τε καρποὺς καὶ βοσκήματα καὶ τὸ τοῦ χρυσοῦ καὶ ἀργύρου καὶ τῶν παραπλησίων πλῆθος,
ὅμως οἱ πλείους αὐτῶν, τὸν ἀπὸ τῆς γῆς ἀφέντες
βίον, ἐν λῃστηρίοις διετέλουν καὶ συνεχεῖ πολέμῳ
πρός τε ἀλλήλους καὶ τοὺς ὁμόρους αὐτοῖς δια-
βαίνοντες τὸν Τάγον, ἕως ἔπαυσαν αὐτοὺς Ῥωμαῖοι,
ταπεινώσαντες καὶ κώμας ποιήσαντες τὰς πόλεις
αὐτῶν τὰς πλείστας, ἐνίας δὲ καὶ συνοικίζοντες
βέλτιον· ἦρχον δὲ τῆς ἀνομίας ταύτης οἱ ὀρεινοί,
καθάπερ εἰκός· λυπρὰν γὰρ νεμόμενοι καὶ μικρὰ
κεκτημένοι τῶν ἀλλοτρίων ἐπεθύμουν. οἱ δὲ
ἀμυνόμενοι τούτους ἄκυροι τῶν ἰδίων ἔργων κα-
θίσταντο ἐξ ἀνάγκης, ὥστ' ἀντὶ τοῦ γεωργεῖν
ἐπολέμουν καὶ οὗτοι, καὶ συνέβαινε τὴν χώραν
ἀμελουμένην στεῖραν οὖσαν τῶν ἐμφύτων ἀγαθῶν
οἰκεῖσθαι ὑπὸ λῃστῶν.

6. Τοὺς δ' οὖν Λυσιτανούς φασιν ἐνεδρευτικούς,
ἐξερευνητικούς, ὀξεῖς, κούφους, εὐεξελίκτους· ἀσπί-
διον δ' αὐτοὺς δίπουν ἔχειν τὴν διάμετρον, κοῖλον

---

[1] Cl, and B.(after a correction), read πεντήκοντα; Groskurd
following.

---

[1] Some of the MSS. read "fifty." Pliny (4. 35) says there
are "forty-six peoples" in Lusitania, but his Lusitania

circumstance that the Limaeas was also called the River of Lethe. The Artabrians have many thickly-peopled cities on that gulf which the sailors who frequent those parts call the Harbour of the Artabrians. The men of to-day, however, call the Artabrians Arotrebians. Now about thirty [1] different tribes occupy the country between the Tagus and the Artabrians, and although the country was blest in fruits, in cattle, and in the abundance of its gold and silver and similar metals, still, most of the people had ceased to gain their livelihood from the earth, and were spending their time in brigandage and in continuous warfare both with each other and with their neighbours across the Tagus, until they were stopped by the Romans, who humbled them and reduced most of their cities to mere villages, though they improved some of their cities by adding colonies thereto. It was the mountaineers who began this lawlessness, as was likely to be the case; for, since they occupied sorry land and possessed but little property, they coveted what belonged to the others. And the latter, in defending themselves against the mountaineers, were necessarily rendered powerless over their private estates, so that they, too, began to engage in war instead of farming; and the result was that the country, neglected because it was barren of planted products, became the home only of brigands.

6. At any rate, the Lusitanians, it is said, are given to laying ambush, given to spying out, are quick, nimble, and good at deploying troops. They have a small shield two feet in diameter, concave

comprehends more territory than that of Strabo. Ptolemaeus (2. 5) gives a list of fifty-seven cities as belonging to Lusitania.

εἰς τὸ πρόσθεν, τελαμῶσιν ἐξηρτημένον (οὔτε γὰρ
πόρπακας οὔτ᾽ ἀντιλαβὰς ἔχει). παραξιφὶς πρὸς
τούτοις ἢ κοπίς· λινοθώρακες οἱ πλείους· σπάνιοι
δὲ ἀλυσιδωτοῖς χρῶνται καὶ τριλοφίαις, οἱ δ᾽ ἄλλοι νευρίνοις κράνεσιν· οἱ πεζοὶ δὲ καὶ κνημῖδας
ἔχουσιν, ἀκόντια δ᾽ ἕκαστος πλείω· τινὲς δὲ καὶ
δόρατι χρῶνται. ἐπιδορατίδες δὲ χάλκεαι. ἐνίους
δὲ τῶν προσοικούντων τῷ Δουρίῳ ποταμῷ Λα-
κωνικῶς διάγειν φασίν, ἀλειπτηρίοις χρωμένους
δὶς καὶ πυρίαις ἐκ λίθων διαπύρων, ψυχρολου-
τροῦντας καὶ μονοτροφοῦντας καθαρίως καὶ λιτῶς.
θυτικοὶ δ᾽ εἰσὶ Λυσιτανοί, τά τε σπλάγχνα ἐπι-
βλέπουσιν, οὐκ ἐκτέμνοντες· προσεπιβλέπουσι δὲ
καὶ τὰς ἐν τῇ πλευρᾷ φλέβας, καὶ ψηλαφῶντες δὲ
τεκμαίρονται. σπλαγχνεύονται δὲ καὶ δι᾽ ἀνθρώπων αἰχμαλώτων, καλύπτοντες σάγοις· εἶθ᾽
ὅταν πληγῇ ὑπὸ τὰ σπλάγχνα ὑπὸ τοῦ ἱερο-
σκόπου, μαντεύονται πρῶτον ἐκ τοῦ πτώματος·
τῶν δ᾽ ἁλόντων τὰς χεῖρας ἀποκόπτοντες τὰς
δεξιὰς ἀνατιθέασιν.

7. Ἅπαντες δ᾽ οἱ ὄρειοι λιτοί, ὑδροπόται,
χαμαιεῦναι, βαθεῖαν κατακεχυμένοι τὴν κόμην
γυναικῶν δίκην· μιτρωσάμενοι δὲ τὰ μέτωπα
C 155 μάχονται. τραγοφαγοῦσι δὲ μάλιστα, καὶ τῷ
Ἄρει τράγον θύουσι καὶ τοὺς αἰχμαλώτους καὶ

---

[1] Not "eating only one kind of food" (Stephanus'
Thesaurus, Liddell and Scott, and elsewhere). Athenaeus
(2. 21) quotes Phylarchus as saying that "the Iberians
always eat only one meal a day." Cp. also Xen. *Cyropaedia*
8. 8. 9. See the translator's note in *Classical Quarterly*,
London, April, 1917, pp. 132–134.

in front, and suspended from the shoulder by means
of thongs (for it has neither arm-rings nor handles).
Besides these shields they have a dirk or a butcher's-
knife. Most of them wear linen cuirasses; a few
wear chain-wrought cuirasses and helmets with
three crests, but the rest wear helmets made of
sinews. The foot-soldiers wear greaves also, and
each soldier has several javelins; and some also make
use of spears, and the spears have bronze heads.
Now some of the peoples that dwell next to the
Durius River live, it is said, after the manner of the
Laconians—using anointing-rooms twice a day and
taking baths in vapours that rise from heated stones,
bathing in cold water, and eating only one meal
a day;[1] and that in a cleanly[2] and simple way.
The Lusitanians are given to offering sacrifices, and
they inspect the vitals, without cutting them out.
Besides, they also inspect the veins on the side of the
victim; and they divine by the tokens of touch, too.
They prophesy through means of the vitals of human
beings also, prisoners of war, whom they first cover
with coarse cloaks, and then, when the victim has
been struck beneath the vitals by the diviner, they
draw their first auguries from the fall of the victim.
And they cut off the right hands of their captives
and set them up as an offering to the gods.

7. All the mountaineers lead a simple life, are
water-drinkers, sleep on the ground, and let their
hair stream down in thick masses after the manner
of women, though before going into battle they bind
their hair about the forehead. They eat goat's-meat
mostly, and to Ares they sacrifice a he-goat and also

[2] Cp. Diodorus Siculus, 5. 33, where the cleanly habits of
the Celtiberians are similarly spoken of.

ἵππους· ποιοῦσι δὲ καὶ ἑκατόμβας ἑκάστου γένους
Ἑλληνικῶς, ὡς καὶ Πίνδαρός φησι

πάντα θύειν ἑκατόν.

τελοῦσι δὲ καὶ ἀγῶνας γυμνικοὺς καὶ ὁπλιτικοὺς
καὶ ἱππικούς, πυγμῇ καὶ δρόμῳ καὶ διακροβολισμῷ
καὶ τῇ σπειρηδὸν μάχῃ. οἱ δ᾿ ὄρειοι τὰ δύο μέρη
τοῦ ἔτους δρυοβαλάνῳ χρῶνται, ξηράναντες καὶ
κόψαντες, εἶτα ἀλέσαντες καὶ ἀρτοποιησάμενοι,
ὥστ᾿ ἀποτίθεσθαι εἰς χρόνον. χρῶνται δὲ καὶ
ζύθει· οἴνου¹ δὲ σπανίζονται· τὸν δὲ γενόμενον
ταχὺ ἀναλίσκουσι κατευωχούμενοι μετὰ τῶν συγ-
γενῶν· ἀντ᾿ ἐλαίου δὲ βουτύρῳ χρῶνται· καθή-
μενοί τε δειπνοῦσι, περὶ τοὺς τοίχους καθέδρας
οἰκοδομητὰς ἔχοντες, προκάθηνται δὲ καθ᾿ ἡλικίαν
καὶ τιμήν. περιφορητὸν δὲ τὸ δεῖπνον, καὶ παρὰ
πότον ὀρχοῦνται πρὸς αὐλὸν καὶ σάλπιγγα χο-
ρεύοντες, ἀλλὰ καὶ ἀναλλόμενοι καὶ ὀκλάζοντες·
ἐν Βαστητανίᾳ δὲ καὶ γυναῖκες ἀναμὶξ ἀνδράσι
ἀντιλαμβανόμεναι² τῶν χειρῶν. μελανείμονες
ἅπαντες, τὸ πλέον ἐν σάγοις, ἐν οἷσπερ καὶ στι-
βαδοκοιτοῦσι. κηρίνοις δὲ ἀγγείοις χρῶνται,
καθάπερ καὶ οἱ Κελτοί. αἱ γυναῖκες δ᾿ ἐν ἐνδύμασι
καὶ ἀνθιναῖς ἐσθήσεσι διάγουσιν. ἀντὶ δὲ νομίσματος οἵ γε³ λίαν ἐν βάθει φορτίων ἀμοιβῇ
χρῶνται, ἢ τοῦ ἀργυροῦ ἐλάσματος ἀποτέμνοντες
διδόασι. τοὺς δὲ θανατουμένους καταπετροῦσι,

¹ οἴνου, Jones, for οἴνῳ. Cp. ὧν τοῖς σπανιζομένοις 2. 5. 26.
² ἀνδράσι ἀντιλαμβανόμεναι, Groskurd, for ἀντὶ προσαντιλαμ-
βανόμεναι; so Forbiger and Meineke.
³ οἵ γε, Groskurd, for οἱ δέ.

¹ Athenaeus gives a rather full description of the Celtic
banquet (4. 36), but he says nothing of waxen vessels. The

the prisoners and horses; and they also offer heca-
tombs of each kind, after the Greek fashion—as
Pindar himself says, " to sacrifice a hundred of every
kind." They also hold contests, for light-armed
and heavy-armed soldiers and cavalry, in boxing, in
running, in skirmishing, and in fighting by squads.
And the mountaineers, for two-thirds of the year,
eat acorns, which they have first dried and crushed,
and then ground up and made into a bread that may
be stored away for a long time. They also drink
beer; but they are scarce of wine, and what wine
they have made they speedily drink up in merry
feastings with their kinsfolk; and instead of olive-
oil they use butter. Again, they dine sitting down,
for they have stationary seats builded around the
walls of the room, though they seat themselves
forward according to age and rank. The dinner
is passed round, and amid their cups they dance
to flute and trumpet, dancing in chorus, but also
leaping up and crouching low. But in Bastetania
women too dance promiscuously with men, taking
hold of their hands. All the men dress in black,
for the most part in coarse cloaks, in which they
sleep, on their beds of litter. And they use waxen
vessels, just as the Celts do.[1] But the women
always go clad in long mantles and gay-coloured
gowns. Instead of coined money the people, at
least those who live deep in the interior, employ
barter, or else they cut off pieces from beaten silver
metal and pass them as money. Those who are
condemned to death they hurl from precipices; and

editors have variously emended the Greek word for
"waxen": to "wooden," "earthen," "plaited," and
"made of horns." But see the translator's note in *Classical
Quarterly*, London, April, 1917, pp. 132–134.

τοὺς δὲ πατραλοίας ἔξω τῶν ὁρῶν ἢ τῶν ποταμῶν
καταλεύουσι. γαμοῦσι δ' ὥσπερ οἱ Ἕλληνες· τοὺς
δὲ ἀρρώστους, ὥσπερ οἱ Αἰγύπτιοι[1] τὸ παλαιόν,
προτιθέασιν εἰς τὰς ὁδοὺς τοῖς πεπειραμένοις τοῦ
πάθους ὑποθήκης χάριν. διφθερίνοις τε πλοίοις
ἐχρῶντο ἕως ἐπὶ Βρούτου διὰ τὰς πλημμυρίδας
καὶ τὰ τενάγη, νυνὶ δὲ καὶ τὰ μονόξυλα ἤδη
σπάνια. ἅλες πορφυροῖ, τριφθέντες δὲ λευκοί.
ἔστι δὲ τῶν ὀρείων ὁ βίος οὗτος, ὥσπερ ἔφην,
λέγω τοὺς τὴν βόρειον πλευρὰν ἀφορίζοντας τῆς
Ἰβηρίας, Καλλαϊκοὺς καὶ Ἄστουρας καὶ Καντάβρους μέχρι Οὐασκώνων καὶ τῆς Πυρήνης· ὁμοει-
δεῖς γὰρ ἁπάντων οἱ βίοι. ὀκνῶ δὲ τοῖς ὀνόμασι
πλεονάζειν, φεύγων τὸ ἀηδὲς τῆς γραφῆς, εἰ μή
τινι πρὸς ἡδονῆς ἐστιν ἀκούειν Πλευταύρους καὶ
Βαρδυήτας καὶ Ἀλλότριγας καὶ ἄλλα χείρω καὶ
ἀσημότερα τούτων ὀνόματα.

8. Τὸ δὲ δυσήμερον καὶ ἀγριῶδες οὐκ ἐκ τοῦ
πολεμεῖν συμβέβηκε μόνον, ἀλλὰ καὶ διὰ τὸν
ἐκτοπισμόν· καὶ γὰρ ὁ πλοῦς ἐπ' αὐτοὺς μακρὸς
καὶ αἱ ὁδοί, δυσεπίμικτοι δ' ὄντες ἀποβεβλήκασι
C 156 τὸ κοινωνικὸν καὶ τὸ φιλάνθρωπον. ἧττον δὲ
νῦν τοῦτο πάσχουσι διὰ τὴν εἰρήνην καὶ τὴν τῶν
Ῥωμαίων ἐπιδημίαν· ὅσοις δ' ἧττον τοῦτο συμ-

---

[1] Kramer conjectures Ἀσσύριοι for Αἰγύπτιοι, citing Herodotus 1. 197 and Strabo 16. 1. 20. So read Forbiger, Müller-
Dübner, and Meineke.

[1] Since this custom was followed by the Assyrians (Herodotus 1. 197 and Strabo 16. 1. 20), and since there is no other
account of such a practice among the Egyptians, some of the
editors have presumed to emend the text, perhaps rightly.

the parricides they stone to death out beyond their
mountains or their rivers. They marry in the same
way as the Greeks. Their sick they expose upon
the streets, in the same way as the Egyptians[1] did
in ancient times, for the sake of their getting sug-
gestions from those who have experienced the
disease. Again, up to the time of Brutus[2] they
used boats of tanned leather on account of the flood-
tides and the shoal-waters, but now, already, even
the dug-out canoes are rare. Their rock-salt is red,
but when crushed it is white. Now this, as I was
saying, is the mode of life of the mountaineers, I
mean those whose boundaries mark off the northern
side of Iberia, namely, the Callaicans, the Asturians,
and the Cantabrians, as far as the Vasconians and the
Pyrenees; for the modes of life of all of them are
of like character. I shrink from giving too many of
the names, shunning the unpleasant task of writing
them down—unless it comports with the pleasure
of some one to hear "Pleutaurans," "Bardyetans,"
"Allotrigans," and other names still less pleasing
and of less significance than these.

8. The quality of intractability and wildness in
these peoples has not resulted solely from their
engaging in warfare, but also from their remoteness; for the trip to their country, whether by sea
or by land, is long, and since they are difficult to
communicate with, they have lost the instinct of
sociability and humanity. They have this feeling
of intractability and wildness to a less extent now,
however, because of the peace and of the sojourns
of the Romans among them. But wherever such

[2] See footnote 4, page 63.

βαίνει, χαλεπώτεροί εἰσι καὶ θηριωδέστεροι.
τοιαύτης δ' οὔσης καὶ ἀπὸ τῶν τόπων λυπρότητος
ἐνίοις, καὶ τῶν ὀρείων [1] εἰκὸς ἐπιτείνεσθαι τὴν
τοιαύτην ἀτοπίαν. ἀλλὰ νῦν, ὡς εἶπον, πέπαυται
πολεμοῦντα πάντα· τούς τε γὰρ συνέχοντας ἔτι
νῦν μάλιστα τὰ ληστήρια Καντάβρους καὶ τοὺς
γειτονεύοντας αὐτοῖς κατέλυσεν ὁ Σεβαστὸς Καῖσαρ, καὶ ἀντὶ τοῦ πορθεῖν τοὺς τῶν Ῥωμαίων
συμμάχους στρατεύουσι νῦν ὑπὲρ τῶν Ῥωμαίων
οἵ τε Κωνιακοὶ καὶ οἱ πρὸς ταῖς πηγαῖς τοῦ
Ἴβηρος οἰκοῦντες Πληντούισοι. ὅ τ' ἐκεῖνον
διαδεξάμενος Τιβέριος, τριῶν ταγμάτων στρατιωτικὸν ἐπιστήσας τοῖς τόποις, τὸ ἀποδειχθὲν ὑπὸ
τοῦ Σεβαστοῦ Καίσαρος, οὐ μόνον εἰρηνικούς,
ἀλλὰ καὶ πολιτικοὺς ἤδη τινὰς αὐτῶν ἀπεργα-
σάμενος τυγχάνει.

IV

1. Λοιπὴ δ' ἐστὶ τῆς Ἰβηρίας ἥ τε ἀπὸ Στηλῶν
μέχρι τῆς Πυρήνης καθ' ἡμᾶς παραλία καὶ ἡ
ταύτης ὑπερκειμένη μεσόγαια πᾶσα τὸ μὲν πλάτος ἀνώμαλος, τὸ δὲ μῆκος μικρῷ πλειόνων ἢ
τετρακισχιλίων σταδίων, τὸ δὲ τῆς παραλίας ἔτι [2]
πλεῖον καὶ δισχιλίοις σταδίοις εἴρηται. φασὶ δὲ
ἀπὸ μὲν Κάλπης, τοῦ κατὰ Στήλας ὄρους, ἐπὶ
Καρχηδόνα Νέαν δισχιλίους καὶ διακοσίους στα-
δίους· οἰκεῖσθαι δὲ τὴν ᾐόνα ταύτην ὑπὸ Βαστητανῶν, οὓς καὶ Βαστούλους καλοῦσιν, ἐκ μέρους

---

[1] ὀρείων, Jones, for ὀρῶν (cp. ὀρείων 3. 3. 7).
[2] ἔτι, Groskurd, for ἐπί.

sojourns are rarer the people are harder to deal with and more brutish; and if some are so disagreeable merely as the result of the remoteness of their regions, it is likely that those who live in the mountains are still more outlandish. But now, as I have said, they have wholly ceased carrying on war; for both the Cantabrians (who still to-day more than the rest keep together their bands of robbers) and their neighbours have been subdued by Augustus Caesar; and instead of plundering the allies of the Romans, both the Coniacans [1] and the Plentuisans,[2] who live near the source of the Iberus, now take the field for the Romans. Further, Tiberius, his successor, has set over these regions an army of three legions (the army already appointed by Augustus Caesar), and it so happens that he already has rendered some of the peoples not only peaceable but civilised as well.

IV

1. There remains of Iberia the seaboard of Our Sea from the Pillars to the Pyrenees Mountains, and also the whole of the interior above it, which is unequal in breadth but slightly more than four thousand stadia in length, though the length of the seaboard has been given as still greater than that by as much as two thousand stadia. They say that the distance from Calpe, the mountain near the Pillars, to New Carthage is two thousand two hundred stadia; and this coast is inhabited by Bastetanians, who are also called Bastulians, and,

[1] Possibly a corruption for "Coniscans," whom Strabo mentions later on as being a Cantabrian tribe (3. 4. 12).

[2] A people otherwise unknown.

δὲ καὶ ὑπὸ Ὠρητανῶν. ἐντεῦθεν δ' ἐπὶ τὸν Ἴβηρα
ἄλλους τοσούτους σχεδόν τι· ταύτην δ' ἔχειν
Ἐδητανούς. ἐντὸς δὲ τοῦ Ἴβηρος μέχρι Πυρήνης
καὶ τῶν Πομπηίου ἀναθημάτων χιλίους καὶ
ἑξακοσίους· οἰκεῖν δὲ Ἐδητανῶν τε ὀλίγους καὶ
λοιπὸν τοὺς προσαγορευομένους Ἰνδικήτας, μεμε-
ρισμένους τέτραχα.

2. Κατὰ μέρος δὲ ἀπὸ Κάλπης ἀρξαμένοις
ῥάχις ἐστὶν ὀρεινὴ τῆς Βαστητανίας καὶ τῶν
Ὠρητανῶν, δασεῖαν ὕλην ἔχουσα καὶ μεγαλόδενδρον, διορίζουσα τὴν παραλίαν ἀπὸ τῆς μεσογαίας. πολλαχοῦ δὲ κἀνταῦθά ἐστι χρυσεῖα καὶ
ἄλλα μέταλλα. πόλις δ' ἐστὶν ἐν τῇ παραλίᾳ
ταύτῃ πρώτη Μάλακα, ἴσον διέχουσα τῆς Κάλπης,
ὅσον καὶ τὰ Γάδειρα· ἐμπόριον δ' ἐστὶ νῦν [1] τοῖς
ἐν τῇ περαίᾳ Νομάσι,[2] καὶ ταριχείας δὲ ἔχει μεγάλας. ταύτην τινὲς τῇ Μαινάκῃ τὴν αὐτὴν
νομίζουσιν, ἣν ὑστάτην τῶν Φωκαϊκῶν πόλεων
πρὸς δύσει κειμένην παρειλήφαμεν, οὐκ ἔστι δέ·
ἀλλ' ἐκείνη μὲν ἀπωτέρω τῆς Κάλπης ἐστί, κατε-
σκαμμένη, τὰ δ' ἴχνη σώζουσα Ἑλληνικῆς πόλεως,
ἡ δὲ Μάλακα πλησίον μᾶλλον, Φοινικικὴ τῷ
σχήματι. ἐφεξῆς δ' ἐστὶν ἡ τῶν Ἐξιτανῶν πόλις,
ἐξ ἧς καὶ τὰ ταρίχη ἐπωνύμως λέγεται.

3. Μετὰ ταύτην Ἄβδηρα, Φοινίκων κτίσμα
C 157 καὶ αὐτή. ὑπὲρ δὲ τῶν τόπων ἐν τῇ ὀρεινῇ δεί-

---

[1] ἐστὶ νῦν, A. Miller, for ἐστὶν ἐν; A. Vogel approving.
[2] Νομάσι, Tyrwhitt, for the corrupt σαίμασι; so Groskurd,
and Meineke.

---

[1] These Trophies were set up near what is now La Junquera.
Cp. Sallust, *Hist. Frag.* 4. 29 (Dietsch).

in part, by Oretanians also; thence to the Iberus is another distance of about the same number of stadia, and this coast is occupied by Edetanians; and thence, this side the Iberus, to the Pyrenees and the Trophies of Pompey [1] is a coast of sixteen hundred stadia, which is inhabited by a few of the Edetanians, and also, for the rest of the way, by the peoples called Indicetans, who have been divided into four tribes.

2. In detail: if we begin from Calpe, we have a mountain-chain belonging to Bastetania and to the Oretanians, which has dense forests of tall trees, and separates the coast from the interior. Here also, in many places, there are mines of gold and other metals. The first city on this coastline is Malaca, which is as far distant from Calpe as Gades is; it is now an emporium for the Nomads on the opposite coast,[2] and it also has great establishments for salting fish. Some regard Malaca as identical with Maenaca,[3] which, as we have been taught, lies farthest of the Phocaean cities in the west; but this is not true. On the contrary, the city of Maenaca is farther away from Calpe, and is now in ruins (though it still preserves the traces of a Greek city), whereas Malaca is nearer, and bears the stamp of a Phoenician city. Next thereafter comes the city [4] of the Exitanians, after which the salted fish take their trade name.

3. After this city comes Abdera, which is itself a place founded by the Phoenicians. Beyond the regions in question, in the mountain country,

---

[2] Of Africa.

[3] The present site of Almunecar.

[4] The name of the city was "Sex" according to Ptolemaeus (2. 4. 7), "Hexi" according to Pomponius Mela (2. 6).

κυυται Ὀδύσσεια καὶ τὸ ἱερὸν τῆς Ἀθηνᾶς ἐν αὐτῇ, ὡς Ποσειδώνιός τε εἴρηκε καὶ Ἀρτεμίδωρος καὶ Ἀσκληπιάδης ὁ Μυρλεανός, ἀνὴρ ἐν τῇ Τουρδητανίᾳ παιδεύσας τὰ γραμματικὰ καὶ περιήγησίν τινα τῶν ἐθνῶν ἐκδεδωκὼς τῶν ταύτῃ. οὗτος δέ φησιν ὑπομνήματα τῆς πλάνης τῆς Ὀδυσσέως ἐν τῷ ἱερῷ τῆς Ἀθηνᾶς ἀσπίδας προσπεπατταλεῦσθαι καὶ ἀκροστόλια. ἐν Καλλαϊκοῖς δὲ τῶν μετὰ Τεύκρου στρατευσάντων τινὰς οἰκῆσαι, καὶ ὑπάρξαι πόλεις αὐτόθι, τὴν μὲν καλουμένην Ἕλληνες, τὴν δὲ Ἀμφίλοχοι, ὡς καὶ τοῦ Ἀμφιλόχου τελευτήσαντος δεῦρο καὶ τῶν συνόντων πλανηθέντων μέχρι τῆς μεσογαίας. καὶ τῶν μεθ᾽ Ἡρακλέους δέ τινας καὶ τῶν ἀπὸ Μεσσήνης ἱστορῆσθαί φησιν ἐποικῆσαι τὴν Ἰβηρίαν, τῆς δὲ Κανταβρίας μέρος τι κατασχεῖν Λάκωνας καὶ οὗτός φησι καὶ ἄλλοι. ἐνταῦθα δὲ καὶ Ὠψικέλλαν[1] πόλιν Ὀκέλα[1] κτίσμα λέγουσι τοῦ μετὰ Ἀντήνορος καὶ τῶν παίδων αὐτοῦ διαβάντος εἰς τὴν Ἰταλίαν. καὶ ἐν τῇ Λιβύῃ δὲ πεπιστεύκασί τινες, τοῖς τῶν Γαδειριτῶν ἐμπόροις προσέχοντες, ὡς καὶ Ἀρτεμίδωρος εἴρηκεν, ὅτι οἱ ὑπὲρ τῆς Μαυρουσίας οἰκοῦντες πρὸς τοῖς ἑσπερίοις Αἰθίοψι Λωτοφάγοι καλοῦνται σιτούμενοι λωτόν, πόαν τινὰ καὶ ῥίζαν, οὐ δεόμενοι δὲ ποτοῦ, οὐδὲ ἔχοντες διὰ τὴν ἀνυδρίαν, διατείνοντες καὶ μέχρι τῶν ὑπὲρ τῆς Κυρήνης τόπων. ἄλλοι τε πάλιν

---

[1] Siebenkees is probably right in emending Ὠψικέλλα to Ὠκέλλαν and Ὀκέλα to Ὠκέλλα; so, in general, the later editors read. Strabo apparently has in mind the Ὀκέλλον (or Ὀκέλον) of Ptolemaeus (2. 5. 7); cp. the *Ocelenses* of Pliny (4. 35).

Odysseia is to be seen, and in it the temple of
Athene, as has been stated by Poseidonius, Artemidorus, and Asclepiades the Myrlean, a man who
taught grammar in Turdetania and has published an
account of the tribes of that region. According to
Asclepiades, shields and ships' beaks have been
nailed up in the temple of Athene as memorials of
the wanderings of Odysseus; and some of those who
made the expedition with Teucer lived in Callaicia,
and there were once two cities there, of which one
was called Hellenes,[1] and the other, Amphilochi;[2]
for not only did Amphilochus die at the place, but
his companions wandered as far as the interior of the
country.   And, he further says, history tells us that
some of the companions of Heracles and of the
emigrants from Messene colonised Iberia. As for
Cantabria, a part of it was seized and held by the
Laconians, according to both Asclepiades and others.
Here, too, they mention a city Opsicella, founded by
Ocelas, who in company with Antenor and his
children crossed over to Italy.   Furthermore, in the
case of Libya, some have believed, giving heed to
the merchants of Gades (as Artemidorus has already
stated), that the people who live beyond Maurusia
next to the Western Ethiopians are called Lotus-
eaters because they feed on lotus (a sort of plant
and root) and do not need drink, or have any, either,
since there is no water in their entire country,
although it stretches even as far as the regions of
Cyrene.   And there is still another people called

---

[1] Named after Hellen, the eponymous hero of the
Hellenes.

[2] Named after Amphilochus. Cp. 14. 4. 3.

καλοῦνται Λωτοφάγοι, τὴν ἑτέραν οἰκοῦντες τῶν πρὸ τῆς μικρᾶς Σύρτεως νήσων, τὴν Μήνιγγα.

4. Οὐ δὴ θαυμάζοι τις ἂν οὔτε τοῦ ποιητοῦ τὰ περὶ τὴν Ὀδυσσέως πλάνην μυθογραφήσαντος τοῦτον τὸν τρόπον ὥστ᾿ ἔξω Στηλῶν ἐν τῷ Ἀτλαντικῷ πελάγει τὰ πολλὰ διαθέσθαι τῶν λεγομένων περὶ αὐτοῦ (τὰ γὰρ ἱστορούμενα ἐγγὺς ἦν, καὶ τοῖς τόποις καὶ τοῖς ἄλλοις τῶν ὑπ᾿ ἐκείνου πεπλασμένων, ὥστε οὐκ ἀπίθανον ἐποίει τὸ πλάσμα), οὔτ᾿ εἴ τινες αὐταῖς τε ταύταις ταῖς ἱστορίαις πιστεύσαντες καὶ τῇ πολυμαθίᾳ τοῦ ποιητοῦ καὶ πρὸς ἐπιστημονικὰς ὑποθέσεις ἔτρεψαν τὴν Ὁμήρου ποίησιν, καθάπερ Κράτης τε ὁ Μαλλώτης ἐποίησε καὶ ἄλλοι τινές. οἱ δ᾿ οὕτως ἀγροίκως ἐδέξαντο τὴν ἐπιχείρησιν τὴν τοιαύτην ὥστε οὐ μόνον τὸν ποιητὴν σκαπανέως ἢ θεριστοῦ δίκην ἐκ πάσης τῆς τοιαύτης ἐπιστήμης ἐξέβαλον, ἀλλὰ καὶ τοὺς ἁψαμένους τῆς τοιαύτης πραγματείας μαινομένους ὑπέλαβον· συνηγορίαν δὲ ἢ ἐπανόρθωσιν ἤ τι τοιοῦτον ἕτερον εἰς τὰ λεχθέντα ὑπ᾿ ἐκείνων εἰσενεγκεῖν οὐκ ἐθάρρησεν

C 158   οὔτε τῶν γραμματικῶν οὔτε τῶν περὶ τὰ μαθήματα δεινῶν οὐδείς. καίτοι ἐμοί γε δοκεῖ δυνατὸν εἶναι καὶ συνηγορῆσαι πολλοῖς τῶν λεχθέντων καὶ εἰς ἐπανόρθωσιν ἄγειν καὶ μάλιστα εἰς ταῦτα, ὅσα Πυθέας παρεκρούσατο τοὺς πιστεύσαντας αὐτῷ κατὰ ἄγνοιαν τῶν τε ἑσπερίων τόπων καὶ τῶν προσβόρρων τῶν παρὰ τὸν ὠκεανόν. ἀλλὰ ταῦτα μὲν ἐάσθω, λόγον ἔχοντα ἴδιον καὶ μακρόν.

---

[1] See 2. 5. 20.   [2] Homer.
[3] That is, Crates and others.

Lotus-eaters, who dwell in one of the two islands off the Lesser Syrtis, I mean Meninx.[1]

4. So no one could be surprised if, in the first place, the poet[2] has written his mythical account of the wanderings of Odysseus in such a way as to set most of his stories of Odysseus in the Atlantic Sea beyond the Pillars of Heracles (for the stories he told were so closely related to the facts, both in respect of places and of everything else created by his fancy, that he rendered his fiction not unplausible); nor surprised if, in the second place, some men, having believed in these stories themselves and also in the wide learning of the poet, have actually turned the poetry of Homer to their use as a basis of scientific investigations, as has been done by Crates of Mallos and certain others as well. Other men, however, have greeted all attempts of that sort with such ferocity that they not only have cast out the poet, as though he were a mere ditch-digger or harvest-labourer, from the whole field of scientific knowledge of this kind, but also have supposed to be madmen all who have taken in hand such a task as that; but as for introducing any defence, or revision, or anything else of the kind, for the assertions of those men,[3] no one either among the grammarians or the scientific experts has ventured to do so. And yet, to me at least, it seems to be possible not only to defend many of their assertions, but to bring them under revision, and in particular all those wherein Pytheas has led astray those men who, in ignorance both of the regions in the west and of those in the north along the ocean, have believed him. But let us pass by these matters, since they involve a special and lengthy discussion.

5. Τῆς δὲ τῶν Ἑλλήνων πλάνης εἰς τὰ βάρβαρα ἔθνη νομίζοι τις ἂν αἴτιον τὸ διεσπάσθαι κατὰ μέρη μικρὰ καὶ δυναστείας ἐπιπλοκὴν οὐκ ἐχούσας πρὸς ἀλλήλους κατ' αὐθάδειαν, ὥστε ἐκ τούτου πρὸς τοὺς ἐπιόντας ἔξωθεν ἀσθενεῖς εἶναι· τοῦτο δὲ τὸ αὔθαδες ἐν δὴ[1] τοῖς Ἴβηρσι μάλιστα ἐπέτεινε, προσλαβοῦσι καὶ τὸ πανοῦργον φύσει καὶ τὸ μὴ ἁπλοῦν· ἐπιθετικοὶ[2] γὰρ καὶ λῃστρικοὶ τοῖς βίοις ἐγένοντο τὰ μικρὰ τολμῶντες, μεγάλοις δ' οὐκ ἐπιβαλλόμενοι διὰ τὸ μεγάλας μὴ κατασκευάζεσθαι δυνάμεις καὶ κοινωνίας. εἰ γὰρ δὴ συνασπίζειν ἐβούλοντο ἀλλήλοις, οὔτε Καρχηδονίοις ὑπῆρξεν ἂν καταστρέψασθαι ἐπελθοῦσι τὴν πλείστην αὐτῶν ἐκ περιουσίας, καὶ ἔτι πρότερον Τυρίοις, εἶτα Κελτοῖς, οἳ νῦν Κελτίβηρες καὶ Βήρωνες καλοῦνται, οὔτε τῷ λῃστῇ Οὐριάθῳ καὶ Σερτωρίῳ μετὰ ταῦτα καὶ εἴ τινες ἕτεροι δυναστείας ἐπεθύμησαν μείζονος. Ῥωμαῖοί τε τῷ κατὰ μέρη πρὸς τοὺς Ἴβηρας πολεμεῖν καθ' ἑκάστην διὰ ταύτην τὴν δυναστείαν πολύν τινα διετέλεσαν χρόνον, ἄλλοτ' ἄλλους καταστρεφόμενοι τέως, ἕως ἅπαντας ὑποχειρίους ἔλαβον διακοσιοστῷ σχεδόν τι ἔτει ἢ μακρότερον. ἐπάνειμι δὲ ἐπὶ τὴν περιήγησιν.

6. Μετὰ τοίνυν Ἄβδηρά ἐστι Καρχηδὼν ἡ Νέα, κτίσμα Ἀσδρούβα, τοῦ διαδεξαμένου Βάρκαν

---

[1] δή, Meineke. for δέ.
[2] ἐπιθετικοί, Corais, for ἐπίθετοι; so the later editors.

5. Now the wanderings of the Greeks to the barbarian nations might be regarded as caused by the fact that the latter had become split up into petty divisions and sovereignties which, on the strength of their self-sufficiency, had no intercourse with one another; and hence, as a result, they were powerless against the invaders from abroad. This spirit of self-sufficiency, among the Iberians I mean, was particularly intense, since by nature they had already received both the quality of knavery and that of insincerity. For by their modes of life they became inclined to attack and to rob, venturing only upon petty undertakings, and never throwing themselves into large ones, because they would not establish large forces and confederations. For surely, if they had been willing to be shield-fellows with one another, it would not have been possible, in the first place, for the Carthaginians to overrun and subdue the most of their country by superiority of forces, or in still earlier times for the Tyrians to do so, or after that, for those Celti who are now called Celtiberians and Veronians; nor, in the second place, later on, for the brigand Viriathus, or for Sertorius, or for any others who may have coveted wider dominion. And the Romans, since they carried on merely a piecemeal war against the Iberians, attacking each territory separately, spent some considerable time in acquiring dominion here, subjecting first one group and then another, until, after about two hundred years or longer, they got them all under control. But I return to my geographical description.

6. After Abdera, then, comes New Carthage, which was founded by Hasdrubal, the successor of

τὸν Ἀννίβα πατέρα, κρατίστη πολὺ τῶν ταύτῃ
πόλεων· καὶ γὰρ ἐρυμνότητι καὶ τείχει κατεσκευ-
ασμένῳ καλῶς καὶ λιμέσι καὶ λίμνῃ κεκόσμηται
καὶ τοῖς τῶν ἀργυρίων μετάλλοις, περὶ ὧν εἰρή-
καμεν· κἀνταῦθα δὲ καὶ ἐν τοῖς πλησίον τόποις
πολλὴ ἡ ταριχεία· καὶ ἔστι τοῦτο μεῖζον ἐμπόριον
τῶν μὲν ἐκ θαλάττης τοῖς ἐν τῇ μεσογαίᾳ, τῶν δ'
ἐκεῖθεν τοῖς ἔξω πᾶσιν. ἡ δ' ἐνθένδε μέχρι τοῦ
Ἴβηρος παραλία κατὰ μέσον πως τὸ διάστημα
ἔχει τὸν Σούκρωνα ποταμὸν καὶ τὴν ἐκβολὴν
αὐτοῦ καὶ πόλιν ὁμώνυμον· ῥεῖ δὲ ἐκ τοῦ συνεχοῦς
ὄρους τῇ ὑπερκειμένῃ ῥάχει τῆς τε Μαλάκας
καὶ τῶν περὶ Καρχηδόνα [1] τόπων, περατὸς πεζῇ,
C 159   παράλληλος δέ πως τῷ Ἴβηρι, μικρὸν δὲ διέχει
τῆς Καρχηδόνος ἧττον ἢ τοῦ Ἴβηρος. μεταξὺ
μὲν οὖν τοῦ Σούκρωνος καὶ τῆς Καρχηδόνος τρία
πολίχνια Μασσαλιωτῶν εἰσιν οὐ πολὺ ἄπωθεν
τοῦ ποταμοῦ· τούτων δ' ἐστὶ γνωριμώτατον τὸ
Ἡμεροσκοπεῖον, ἔχον ἐπὶ τῇ ἄκρᾳ τῆς Ἐφεσίας
Ἀρτέμιδος ἱερὸν σφόδρα τιμώμενον, ᾧ ἐχρήσατο
Σερτώριος ὁρμητηρίῳ κατὰ θάλατταν· ἐρυμνὸν γάρ
ἐστι καὶ λῃστρικόν, κάτοπτον δὲ ἐκ πολλοῦ τοῖς
προσπλέουσι, καλεῖται δὲ Διάνιον, οἷον Ἀρτεμίσιον, ἔχον σιδηρεῖα εὐφυῆ πλησίον καὶ νησίδια,
Πλανησίαν καὶ Πλουμβαρίαν, καὶ λιμνοθάλατταν
ὑπερκειμένην, ἔχουσαν κύκλον [2] σταδίων τετρα-

---

[1] ὑπερκειμένων before τόπων, Xylander omits; so the later editors.
[2] κύκλον, Casaubon, for ἐν κύκλῳ.

---

[1] That is, colonised from Marseilles.

Barcas, the father of Hannibal. **New Carthage is**
by far the most powerful of all the cities in this
country, for it is adorned by secure fortifications,
by walls handsomely built, by harbours, by a lake,
and by the silver mines of which I have spoken.
And here, as well as at the places near by, the fish-
salting industry is large. Furthermore, New Carthage
is a rather important emporium, not only of the
imports from the sea for the inhabitants of the
interior, but also of the exports from the interior
for all the outside world. On the coast from New
Carthage up to the Iberus, about midway between
these two points, are the Sucro River and its mouth,
and a city with the same name as the river. The
river rises in the mountain which connects with the
mountain-chain that lies beyond Malaca and the
regions about New Carthage; it can be waded,
runs about parallel to the Iberus, and is slightly less
distant from New Carthage than from the Iberus.
Now between the Sucro River and New Carthage,
not far from the river, there are three small
Massiliote[1] cities. Of these, the best known is
Hemeroscopeium,[2] a place held in very great esteem,
since it has on its promontory a temple of the
Ephesian Artemis; and it was used by Sertorius
as a naval base. For it is a natural stronghold and
adapted to piracy, and is visible at a considerable
distance to the approaching sailors. It is also called
"Dianium," the equivalent[3] of "Artemisium"; it
has iron mines with fine deposits near by, and small
islands, Planesia and Plumbaria, and above it a lagoon
of salt-water four hundred stadia in circuit. Next,

---

[2] The word means "Day-watch."
[3] That is, in Greek.

STRABO

κοσίων. εἶθ' ἡ τοῦ Ἡρακλέους νῆσος ἤδη πρὸς
Καρχηδόνι, ἣν καλοῦσι Σκομβραρίαν[1] ἀπὸ τῶν
ἁλισκομένων σκόμβρων, ἐξ ὧν τὸ ἄριστον σκευ-
άζεται γάρον· εἴκοσι δὲ διέχει σταδίους καὶ τέτταρας τῆς Καρχηδόνος. πάλιν δ' ἐπὶ θάτερα τοῦ
Σούκρωνος ἰόντι ἐπὶ τὴν ἐκβολὴν τοῦ Ἴβηρος
Σάγουντον, κτίσμα Ζακυνθίων, ἣν Ἀννίβας κατα-
σκάψας παρὰ τὰ συγκείμενα πρὸς Ῥωμαίους τὸν
δεύτερον αὐτοῖς ἐξῆψε πόλεμον πρὸς Καρχηδο-
νίους. πλησίον δὲ πόλεις εἰσὶ Χερρόνησός τε καὶ
Ὀλέαστρον καὶ Καρταλίας· ἐπ' αὐτῇ δὲ τῇ δια-
βάσει τοῦ Ἴβηρος Δέρτωσσα κατοικία. ῥεῖ δὲ ὁ
Ἴβηρ, ἀπὸ Κανταβρων ἔχων τὰς ἀρχάς, ἐπὶ
μεσημβρίαν διὰ πολλοῦ πεδίου παράλληλος τοῖς
Πυρηναίοις ὄρεσι.

7. Μεταξὺ δὲ τῶν τοῦ Ἴβηρος ἐκτροπῶν καὶ
τῶν ἄκρων τῆς Πυρήνης, ἐφ' ὧν ἵδρυται τὰ ἀναθήματα τοῦ Πομπηίου, πρώτη Ταρράκων ἐστὶ
πόλις, ἀλίμενος μέν, ἐν κόλπῳ δὲ ἱδρυμένη καὶ
κατεσκευασμένη τοῖς ἄλλοις ἱκανῶς, καὶ οὐχ
ἧττον εὐανδροῦσα νυνὶ τῆς Καρχηδόνος. πρὸς
γὰρ τὰς τῶν ἡγεμόνων ἐπιδημίας εὐφυῶς ἔχει,
καὶ ἔστιν ὥσπερ μητρόπολις οὐ τῆς ἐντὸς Ἴβηρος
μόνον, ἀλλὰ καὶ τῆς ἐκτὸς τῆς πολλῆς. αἵ τε
Γυμνήσιαι νῆσοι προκείμεναι πλησίον καὶ ἡ
Ἔβυσος, ἀξιόλογοι νῆσοι, τὴν θέσιν εὔκαιρον
τῆς πόλεως ὑπαγορεύουσιν. Ἐρατοσθένης δὲ
καὶ ναύσταθμον ἔχειν φησὶν αὐτήν, οὐδὲ ἀγκυρο-
βολίοις σφόδρα εὐτυχοῦσαν, ὡς ἀντιλέγων εἴρηκεν
Ἀρτεμίδωρος.

[1] Σκομβραρίαν, Xylander, for Σκομβροαρίαν; so generally the
editors.

and quite near to New Carthage, comes the Island of Heracles, which they call Scombraria, from the scomber-fish caught there, from which the best fish-sauce is prepared. It is twenty-four stadia distant from New Carthage. And again, on the other side of the Sucro, as you go towards the mouth of the Iberus, is Saguntum, founded by Zacynthians, which Hannibal destroyed despite his treaty with the Romans, thereby kindling the second war against the Carthaginians. Near Saguntum are the cities of Cherronesus, Oleastrum, and Cartalias; and at the very crossing of the Iberus is the settlement of Dertossa. The course of the Iberus, which rises in Cantabria, is southwards through a great plain and parallel to the Pyrenees Mountains.

7. Between where the Iberus turns out seaward and the heights of the Pyrenees, on which are situated the Trophies set up by Pompey, the first city is Tarraco. It has no harbour, indeed, but it is situated on a bay and is adequately supplied with all other advantages; and at present it is not less populous than New Carthage. Indeed, it is naturally suited for the residence of the Prefects, and is a metropolis, as it were, not only of the country this side the Iberus, but also of the greater part of the country beyond the Iberus. And the Gymnesian Islands, which lie near by off the coast, and Ebusus,[1] all noteworthy islands, suggest that the position of the city is a happy one. Eratosthenes says that the city has also a roadstead, although, as Artemidorus, contradicting him, has already stated, it is not particularly blessed even with places of anchorage.

[1] Elsewhere (3. 5. 1.), Strabo spells the word Ἔβουσος (MSS. Ἄβουσος).

8. Καὶ ἡ σύμπασα δ' ἀπὸ Στηλῶν σπανίζεται
λιμέσι μέχρι δεῦρο, ἐντεῦθεν δ' ἤδη τὰ ἐξῆς εὐλίμενα καὶ χώρα ἀγαθὴ τῶν τε Λεητανῶν καὶ
Λαρτολαιητῶν καὶ ἄλλων τοιούτων μέχρι Ἐμπορίου. αὐτὸ δ' ἐστὶ Μασσαλιωτῶν κτίσμα, ὅσον
διακοσίους[1] διέχον τῆς Πυρήνης σταδίους καὶ
τῶν μεθορίων τῆς Ἰβηρίας πρὸς τὴν Κελτικήν·
καὶ αὕτη δ' ἐστὶ πᾶσα ἀγαθὴ καὶ εὐλίμενος.
C 160 ἐνταῦθα δ' ἐστὶ καὶ ἡ Ῥόδος,[2] πολίχνιον Ἐμπο-
ριτῶν, τινὲς δὲ κτίσμα Ῥοδίων φασί· κἀνταῦθα
δὲ καὶ ἐν τῷ Ἐμπορίῳ τὴν Ἄρτεμιν τὴν Ἐφεσίαν
τιμῶσιν, ἐροῦμεν δὲ τὴν αἰτίαν ἐν τοῖς περὶ Μασσαλίαν. ᾤκουν δ'[3] οἱ Ἐμπορῖται πρότερον νησίον
τι προκείμενον, ὃ νῦν καλεῖται Παλαιὰ πόλις, νῦν
δ' οἰκοῦσιν ἐν τῇ ἠπείρῳ. δίπολις δ' ἐστί, τείχει
διωρισμένη, πρότερον τῶν Ἰνδικητῶν τινας προσ-
οίκους ἔχουσα, οἳ, καίπερ ἰδίᾳ πολιτευόμενοι,
κοινὸν ὅμως περίβολον ἔχειν ἐβούλοντο πρὸς τοὺς
Ἕλληνας ἀσφαλείας χάριν, διπλοῦν δὲ τοῦτον,
τείχει μέσῳ διωρισμένον· τῷ χρόνῳ δ' εἰς ταὐτὸ
πολίτευμα συνῆλθον μικτόν τι ἔκ τε βαρβάρων
καὶ Ἑλληνικῶν νομίμων, ὅπερ καὶ ἐπ' ἄλλων
πολλῶν συνέβη.

9. Ῥεῖ δὲ καὶ ποταμὸς πλησίον, ἐκ τῆς Πυρήνης

---

[1] διακοσίους, Groskurd, and Corais, for τετρακισχιλίους.
[2] Ῥόδος (as in 14. 2. 10), Casaubon, for Ῥοδόπη; so
Siebenkees, Corais, Forbiger, and C. Müller. Meineke
reads Ῥόδη, following the spelling of Ptolemaeus.
[3] δ', Meineke inserts.

---

[1] The MSS. read 4000 stadia, which is, of course, corrupt.
Strabo has already given only 1600 stadia (§ 1 above) as the
distance from the Iberus to the Pyrenees. The emendations
of the editors run from 4 to 400 stadia.

8. Further, the whole coastline from the Pillars to Tarraco has few harbours, but from Tarraco on, all the way to Emporium, the coasts have fine harbours, and the country is fertile, both that of the Leëtanians and the Lartolaeëtans, and of other such peoples. Emporium was founded by the people of Massilia; it is about two hundred [1] stadia distant from the Pyrenees and from the common boundary between Iberia and Celtica, and this coast too, all of it, is fertile and has good harbours. Here, too, is Rhodus, a small town belonging to the Emporitans, though some say it was founded by Rhodians. Both in Rhodus and in Emporium they worship Artemis of the Ephesians, and I shall tell the reason for this in my account of Massilia. [2] The Emporitans formerly lived on a little island off the shore, which is now called Old City, [3] but they now live on the mainland. And their city is a double one, for it has been divided into two cities by a wall, because, in former times, the city had for neighbours some of the Indicetans, who, although they maintained a government of their own, wished, for the sake of security, to have a common wall of circumvallation with the Greeks, with the enclosure in two parts— for it has been divided by a wall through the centre; but in the course of time the two peoples united under the same constitution, which was a mixture of both Barbarian and Greek laws—a thing which has taken place in the case of many other peoples.

9. There is a river that flows near by, [4] which has

[2] 4. 1. 4–5.
[3] The isle of Medas, near the mouth of the Ter River.
[4] The Clodianus, now the insignificant Muga (cp. Ptolemaeus 2. 6. 19 and Mela 2. 89).

ἔχων τὰς ἀρχάς, ἡ δὲ ἐκβολὴ λιμήν ἐστι τοῖς
Ἐμπορίταις. λινουργοὶ δὲ ἱκανῶς οἱ Ἐμπορῖται·
χώραν δὲ τὴν μεσόγαιαν ἔχουσι, τὴν μὲν ἀγαθήν,
τὴν δὲ σπαρτοφόρον τῆς ἀχρηστοτέρας καὶ ἐλείας
σχοίνου, καλοῦσι δὲ Ἰουγκάριον πεδίον· τινὲς δὲ
καὶ τῶν τῆς Πυρήνης ἄκρων νέμονται μέχρι τῶν
ἀναθημάτων τοῦ Πομπηίου, δι' ὧν βαδίζουσιν εἰς
τὴν ἔξω καλουμένην Ἰβηρίαν ἐκ τῆς Ἰταλίας, καὶ
μάλιστα τὴν Βαιτικήν. αὕτη δ' ἡ ὁδὸς ποτὲ μὲν
πλησιάζει τῇ θαλάττῃ, ποτὲ δ' ἀφέστηκε, καὶ μάλιστα ἐν τοῖς πρὸς ἑσπέραν μέρεσι. φέρεται δὲ
ἐπὶ Ταρράκωνα, ἀπό τε τῶν ἀναθημάτων τοῦ
Πομπηίου διὰ τοῦ Ἰουγκαρίου πεδίου καὶ Βετέρων[1] καὶ τοῦ Μαραθῶνος καλουμένου πεδίου τῇ
Λατίνῃ γλώττῃ, φύοντος πολὺ τὸ μάραθον· ἐκ δὲ
τοῦ Ταρράκωνος ἐπὶ τὸν πόρον τοῦ Ἴβηρος κατὰ
Δέρτωσσαν πόλιν· ἐντεῦθεν διὰ Σαγούντου καὶ
Σετάβιος πόλεως ἐνεχθεῖσα κατὰ μικρὸν ἀφίσταται τῆς θαλάττης καὶ συνάπτει τῷ Σπαρταρίῳ,
ὡς ἂν Σχοινοῦντι, καλουμένῳ πεδίῳ· τοῦτο δ' ἐστὶ
μέγα καὶ ἄνυδρον, τὴν σχοινοπλοκικὴν φύον
σπάρτον, ἐξαγωγὴν ἔχουσαν εἰς πάντα τόπον, καὶ
μάλιστα εἰς τὴν Ἰταλίαν. πρότερον μὲν οὖν διὰ
μέσου τοῦ πεδίου καὶ Ἐγελάστας συνέβαινεν εἶναι
τὴν ὁδόν, χαλεπὴν καὶ πολλήν, νυνὶ δὲ ἐπὶ τὰ πρὸς

---

[1] Βετέρων, Wesseling, Meineke, for Βεττέρων ; so C. Müller,
Tardieu, and L. Kayser.

---

[1] The Romans called it " Campus Iuncarius," from Iuncus,
"rush." Cp. etymologically Eng. "junk."

[2] "Colony of Veterans": the Praetorium mentioned by
Antoninus (Itin. p. 398); exact site unknown, perhaps
Vidreras.

its source in the Pyrenees; and its outlet serves as
a port for the Emporitans. The Emporitans are
quite skilful in flax-working. As for the inland
territory which they hold, one part of it is fertile,
while the other produces the spart of the rather
useless, or rush, variety; it is called "Juncarian"
Plain.[1] But some of the Emporitans occupy even
some of the heights of the Pyrenees, as far as the
Trophies that were set up by Pompey, past which
runs the road from Italy to what is called "Farther"
Iberia, and in particular to Baetica. This road sometimes approaches the sea, though sometimes it stands
off at a distance from the sea, and particularly in the
regions on the west. It runs towards Tarraco from
the Trophies that were set up by Pompey, through
the Juncarian Plain and through Veteres [2] and what
in the Latin tongue is called Fennel Plain, because
it produces so much fennel.[3] From Tarraco it runs
towards the passage of the Iberus at the city of
Dertossa; thence, after passing through Saguntum
and the city of Setabis, it gradually departs from
the sea and joins what is called the Spartarian—or,
as we should say, "Rush"—Plain.[4] This plain is
large and has no water, but produces the kind of
spart that is suitable for twisting into ropes, and is
therefore exported to all regions, and particularly
to Italy. Now formerly the road must have passed
through the centre of this plain and through Egelasta, a road rough and long, but at the present day

---

[3] Literally, the Greek is: "Plain of Marathon, . . .
marathon." Strabo avoids transliterating "Fenicularius"
(the term actually used by the Romans) into Greek.
  [4] The Romans called it "Campus Spartarius."

θαλάττῃ μέρη πεποιήκασιν αὐτήν, ἐπιψαύουσαν
μόνον τοῦ Σχοινοῦντος, εἰς ταὐτὸ δὲ τείνουσαν
τῇ προτέρᾳ, τὰ περὶ Κασταλῶνα καὶ Ὀβούλκωνα, δι᾽ ὧν εἴς τε Κορδύβην καὶ εἰς Γάδειρα ἡ
ὁδός, τὰ μέγιστα τῶν ἐμπορίων. διέχει δὲ τῆς
Κορδύβης ἡ Ὀβούλκων περὶ τριακοσίους σταδίους.
φασὶ δ᾽ οἱ συγγραφεῖς, ἐλθεῖν Καίσαρα ἐκ Ῥώμης
ἑπτὰ καὶ εἴκοσιν ἡμέραις εἰς τὴν Ὀβούλκωνα καὶ
τὸ στρατόπεδον τὸ ἐνταῦθα, ἡνίκα ἔμελλε συνάπτειν εἰς τὸν περὶ τὴν Μοῦνδαν πόλεμον.

10. Ἡ μὲν δὴ παραλία πᾶσα ἡ ἀπὸ Στηλῶν
μέχρι τῆς μεθορίας τῆς Ἰβήρων καὶ Κελτῶν τοιαύτη. ἡ δ᾽ ὑπερκειμένη μεσόγαια, λέγω δὲ τὴν
ἐντὸς τῶν τε Πυρηναίων ὀρῶν καὶ τῆς προσαρκτίου
πλευρᾶς μέχρις Ἀστύρων, δυεῖν μάλιστα ὄρεσι
διορίζεται. τούτων δὲ τὸ μὲν παράλληλόν ἐστι
τῇ Πυρήνῃ, τὴν ἀρχὴν ἀπὸ τῶν Καντάβρων ἔχον,
τελευτὴν δ᾽ ἐπὶ τὴν καθ᾽ ἡμᾶς θάλατταν· καλοῦσι
δὲ τοῦτο Ἰδουβέδαν· ἕτερον δ᾽ ἀπὸ τοῦ μέσου
διῆκον ἐπὶ τὴν δύσιν, ἐκκλῖνον δὲ πρὸς νότον καὶ
τὴν ἀπὸ Στηλῶν παραλίαν· ὃ κατ᾽ ἀρχὰς μὲν
γεώλοφόν ἐστι καὶ ψιλόν, διέξεισι δὲ τὸ καλούμενον Σπαρτάριον πεδίον, εἶτα συνάπτει τῷ δρυμῷ
τῷ ὑπερκειμένῳ τῆς τε Καρχηδονίας καὶ τῶν
περὶ τὴν Μάλακαν τόπων· καλεῖται δὲ Ὀροσπέδα.
μεταξὺ μὲν δὴ τῆς Πυρήνης καὶ τῆς Ἰδουβέδας ὁ
Ἴβηρ ῥεῖ ποταμός, παράλληλος τοῖς ὄρεσιν ἀμφοτέροις, πληρούμενος ἐκ τῶν ἐντεῦθεν καταφε-
ρομένων ποταμῶν καὶ τῶν ἄλλων ὑδάτων. ἐπὶ δὲ
τῷ Ἴβηρι πόλις ἐστὶ Καισαραυγοῦστα καλουμένη
καὶ Κέλσα κατοικία τις, ἔχουσα γεφύρας λιθίνης

they have made it run towards the coastal regions,
merely touching upon the Rush Plain, yet leading
to the same place as did the former road, namely,
to the regions round about Castalo and Obulco; and
through these cities the road runs to Corduba and
Gades, the greatest of the trading-places. The
distance from Corduba to Obulco is about three
hundred stadia. The historians say that Caesar went
from Rome to Obulco and the camp there in twenty-
seven days, when he was about to engage in the
battle near Munda.

10. Such, then, is the character of the whole seaboard from the Pillars up to the common boundary
of Iberia and Celtica. The interior country that lies
beyond the seaboard (I mean the country enclosed
by the Pyrenees Mountains and the northerly side
of Iberia as far as Asturia) is divided by two
mountain-ranges, speaking roughly. Of these mountains, one is parallel to the Pyrenees, beginning in
Cantabria and ending at Our Sea (they call this
mountain Idubeda); whereas the other, beginning
at the centre of the first one, stretches towards the
west, though it inclines towards the south and the
coastline that runs from the Pillars. This latter
mountain is at first a mere hill and bare of trees,
and passes through the so-called Spartarian Plain;
then it joins the forest that lies beyond both New
Carthage and the regions round about Malaca; it is
called Orospeda. It is between the Pyrenees and
Idubeda, then, that the Iberus River flows, which is
parallel with both mountains and is filled by the
rivers and the other waters that pour down from
them. On the Iberus is a city called Caesar Augusta;
also Celsa, a colonial settlement, where there is a

διάβασιν. συνοικεῖται δὲ ὑπὸ πλειόνων ἐθνῶν ἡ
χώρα, γνωριμωτάτου δὲ τοῦ τῶν Ἰακκητανῶν λεγομένου. τοῦτο δ᾽ ἀρξάμενον ἀπὸ τῆς παρωρείας¹
τῆς κατὰ τὴν Πυρήνην εἰς τὰ πεδία πλατύνεται
καὶ συνάπτει τοῖς περὶ Ἰλέρδαν καὶ Ὄσκαν² χωρίοις, τοῖς τῶν Ἰλεργετῶν οὐ πολὺ ἄπωθεν τοῦ
Ἴβηρος. ἐν δὲ ταῖς πόλεσι ταύταις ἐπολέμει τὸ
τελευταῖον Σερτώριος καὶ ἐν Καλαγούρι Οὐασκώνων πόλει καὶ τῆς παραλίας ἐν Ταρράκωνι καὶ ἐν
τῷ Ἡμεροσκοπείῳ μετὰ τὴν ἐκ Κελτιβήρων ἔκ-
πτωσιν, ἐτελεύτα δ᾽ ἐν Ὄσκα.³ κἀν Ἰλέρδα⁴
ὕστερον Ἀφράνιος καὶ Πετρήιος οἱ τοῦ Πομπηίου
στρατηγοὶ κατεπολεμήθησαν ὑπὸ Καίσαρος τοῦ
θεοῦ. διέχει δὲ ἡ Ἰλέρδα τοῦ μὲν Ἴβηρος ὡς ἐπὶ
δύσιν ἰόντι σταδίους ἑκατὸν ἑξήκοντα, Ταρράκωνος δὲ πρὸς νότον περὶ τετρακοσίους ἑξήκοντα,
πρὸς ἄρκτον δὲ Ὄσκας πεντακοσίους τεσσαράκοντα. διὰ τούτων δὲ τῶν χωρίων⁵ ἡ ἐκ Ταρράκωνος ἐπὶ τοὺς ἐσχάτους ἐπὶ τῷ ὠκεανῷ Οὐάσκω-
νας τοὺς κατὰ Πομπέλωνα⁶ καὶ τὴν ἐπ᾽ αὐτῷ τῷ
ὠκεανῷ Οἰασῶνα⁷ πόλιν ὁδός ἐστι σταδίων δισχιλίων τετρακοσίων, πρὸς αὐτὰ τὰ τῆς Ἀκουιτανίας
ὅρια καὶ τῆς Ἰβηρίας. Ἰακκητανοὶ δ᾽ εἰσὶν ἐν οἷς

¹ παρωρείας, Kramer, for παρορίας; so the other editors.
² Ὄσκαν, Casaubon, for the corrupt Ἰλέοσκαν; so the other
editors.
³ δ᾽ ἐν Ὄσκᾳ, conj. of Puteanus, for δὲ νόσῳ; so the editors.
⁴ κἀν Ἰλέρδᾳ, Meineke, for καὶ Ἰλέρδαν.
⁵ χωρίων, Groskurd, for ὁρῶν.
⁶ Πομπέλωνα, Xylander, for the corrupt Πομβιαίλωνα; so
the editors.
⁷ Οἰασῶνα, Casaubon, for Οἰδασούνα (or Οἰασούνα); so, in
general, the editors. Cp. Ptolemaeus 2. 6. 10. and Mela
3. 1. 10.

stone bridge across the river. This country is jointly
settled by several tribes, though the best known is
what is called the tribe of the Iaccetanians. Their
country begins at the foothills of the Pyrenees and
then broadens out over the plains and joins the districts round about Ilerda and Osca, that is, the districts
which belong to the Ilergetans, not very far from the
Iberus. It was in these two cities, and in Calaguris
(a city of the Vasconians), and in the two cities of
Tarraco and Hemeroscopeium on the coast, that
Sertorius fought his last battles after his expulsion
from Celtiberia; but it was at Osca that he came to
his end.[1] And it was in Ilerda that Afranius and
Petreius, the generals of Pompey, were defeated in
battle later on by the Deified Caesar.[2] Ilerda is
distant from the Iberus one hundred and sixty stadia,
to a man travelling approximately towards the west;
from Tarraco, on the south, about four hundred and
sixty stadia; from Osca, on the north, five hundred
and forty stadia. Through these districts runs the
road from Tarraco to those outermost Vasconians on
the ocean who live about Pompelo, and about the
city of Oeaso, which is at the ocean itself—a road
of two thousand four hundred stadia, reaching to
the very frontier of Aquitania and Iberia. Iaccetania

---

[1] The Greek MSS. all read "of disease" instead of "at
Osca." The emendation is certainly right, since we know
that Sertorius was assassinated at Osca (cp. Velleius Pater-
culus 2. 30, and Plutarch's *Life of Sertorius*).

[2] Literally, "the god": Strabo's attempt to translate the
Latin adjective "divus" ("divine," hence "deified") into
Greek. The epithet "divus" was regularly applied to
the *deceased* emperors; here, of course, Julius Caesar is
meant.

τότε μὲν Σερτώριος ἐπολέμει πρὸς Πομπήιον, ὕστερον δ' ὁ τοῦ Πομπηίου υἱὸς Σέξτος πρὸς τοὺς Καίσαρος στρατηγούς. ὑπέρκειται δὲ τῆς Ἰακκη-
τανίας πρὸς ἄρκτον τὸ τῶν Οὐασκώνων ἔθνος, ἐν
ᾧ πόλις Πομπέλων, ὡς ἂν Πομπηιόπολις.

11. Αὐτῆς δὲ τῆς Πυρήνης τὸ μὲν Ἰβηρικὸν
πλευρὸν εὔδενδρόν ἐστι παντοδαπῆς ὕλης καὶ τῆς
C 162 ἀειθαλοῦς, τὸ δὲ Κελτικὸν ψιλόν, τὰ δὲ μέσα
περιέχει καλῶς οἰκεῖσθαι δυναμένους αὐλῶνας.
ἔχουσι δ' αὐτοὺς Κερρητανοὶ τὸ πλέον, τοῦ Ἰβηρικοῦ φυλοῦ, παρ' οἷς πέρναι διάφοροι συντίθενται
ταῖς Κανταβρικαῖς[1] ἐνάμιλλοι, πρόσοδον οὐ μικρὰν τοῖς ἀνθρώποις παρέχουσαι.

12. Ὑπερβάλλοντι δὲ τὴν Ἰδουβέδαν ἡ Κελτι-
βηρία παραχρῆμα πολλὴ καὶ ἀνώμαλος· τὸ μὲν
πλέον αὐτῆς ἐστι τραχὺ καὶ ποταμόκλυστον· διὰ
γὰρ τούτων ὅ τε Ἄνας φέρεται καὶ ὁ Τάγος καὶ
οἱ ἐφεξῆς ποταμοὶ οἱ πλείους οἱ ἐπὶ τὴν ἑσπερίαν
θάλατταν καταφερόμενοι, τὴν ἀρχὴν ἔχοντες ἐκ
τῆς Κελτιβηρίας·[2] ὧν ὁ Δούριος φέρεται παρὰ τὴν
Νομαντίαν καὶ τὴν Σεργουντίαν, ὁ δὲ Βαῖτις ἐκ
τῆς Ὀροσπέδας τὰς ἀρχὰς ἔχων διὰ τῆς Ὠρητανίας εἰς τὴν Βαιτικὴν ῥεῖ. οἰκοῦσι δ' ἐκ μὲν τῶν
πρὸς ἄρκτον μερῶν τοῖς Κελτίβηρσι Βήρωνες,
Καντάβροις ὅμοροι τοῖς Κονίσκοις, καὶ αὐτοὶ τοῦ
Κελτικοῦ στόλου γεγονότες, ὧν ἐστι πόλις Οὐαρία
κατὰ τὴν τοῦ Ἴβηρος διάβασιν κειμένη. συν-

---

1 Κανταβρικαῖς, conj. of Xylander, for the corrupt Κανθαρι-
καῖς ; so, in general, the editors ; but C. Müller, Καλαγουρι-
καῖς. and Tardieu, Κιβυρατικαῖς. Cp. Athenaeus 14. 75, where
in quoting this sentence from Strabo the reading of the MSS.
is ταῖς Κουρικαῖς.

is the country where not only Sertorius carried on
war in his day against Pompey, but also, later on,
Sextus, the son of Pompey, against the generals of
Caesar. It is beyond Iaccetania, towards the north,
that the tribe of the Vasconians is situated, where
there is a city Pompelo or, as one might say,
Pompeiopolis.

11. As for the Pyrenees themselves, the Iberian
side is well-wooded with trees of every kind
and with evergreens; whereas the Celtic side is
bare, although the central portions of it encompass
glens that are capable of affording a good livelihood.
These glens are occupied mostly by Carretanians,
of the Iberian stock; and among these people excellent hams are cured, rivalling those of Cantabria,
and affording the people no small revenue.

12. Crossing over the Idubeda Mountain, you are
at once in Celtiberia, a large and uneven country.
The greater part of it in fact is rugged and river-
washed; for it is through these regions that the
Anas flows, and also the Tagus, and the several
rivers next to them, which, rising in Celtiberia, flow
down to the western sea. Among these are the
Durius, which flows past Numantia and Serguntia,
and the Baetis, which, rising in the Orospeda, flows
through Oretania into Baetica. Now, in the first
place, the parts to the north of the Celtiberians are
the home of the Veronians, neighbours of the Cantabrian Coniscans, and they too [1] have their origin
in the Celtic expedition; they have a city, Varia,
situated at the crossing of the Iberus; and their

<hr>

[1] Cp. 3. 3. 5.

[2] Κελτιβηρίας, Casaubon, and Siebenkees, for Ἰβηρίας; so the
others.

εχείς δ' εἰσὶ καὶ Βαρδυήταις, οὓς οἱ νῦν Βαρδύλους
καλοῦσιν. ἐκ δὲ τοῦ ἐσπερίου τῶν τε Ἀστύρων
τινὲς καὶ τῶν Καλλαϊκῶν καὶ Οὐακκαίων, ἔτι δ'
Οὐεττώνων καὶ Καρπητανῶν. ἐκ δὲ τῶν νοτίων
Ὠρητανοί τε καὶ ὅσοι ἄλλοι τὴν Ὀροσπέδαν οἰκοῦσι Βαστητανῶν τε καὶ Ἐδητανῶν· πρὸς ἔω δὲ
Ἰδουβέδα.

13. Αὐτῶν τε τῶν Κελτιβήρων εἰς τέτταρα
μέρη διηρημένων, οἱ κράτιστοι μάλιστα πρὸς ἔω
εἰσὶ καὶ πρὸς νότον οἱ Ἀρουάκοι, συνάπτοντες
Καρπητανοῖς καὶ ταῖς τοῦ Τάγου πηγαῖς· πόλις
δ' αὐτῶν ὀνομαστοτάτη Νομαντία. ἔδειξαν δὲ
τὴν ἀρετὴν τῷ Κελτιβηρικῷ πολέμῳ τῷ πρὸς
Ῥωμαίους, εἰκοσαετεῖ γενομένῳ· πολλὰ γὰρ στρα-
τεύματα σὺν ἡγεμόσιν ἐφθάρη, τὸ δὲ τελευταῖον
οἱ Νομαντῖνοι πολιορκούμενοι διεκαρτέρησαν πλὴν
ὀλίγων τῶν ἐνδόντων τὸ τεῖχος. καὶ οἱ Λούσωνες
δὲ ἑῷοί εἰσι, συνάπτοντες καὶ αὐτοὶ ταῖς τοῦ
Τάγου πηγαῖς. τῶν δ' Ἀρουάκων ἐστὶ καὶ Σεγήδα
πόλις καὶ Παλλαντία. διέχει δὲ Νομαντία τῆς
Καισαραυγούστας, ἣν ἔφαμεν ἐπὶ τῷ Ἴβηρι ἱδρῦσθαι, σταδίους ἐπὶ ὀκτακοσίους. καὶ Σεγοβρίγα
δ' ἐστὶ τῶν Κελτιβήρων πόλις καὶ Βίλβιλις, περὶ
ἃς Μέτελλος καὶ Σερτώριος ἐπολέμησαν. Πολύβιος δὲ τὰ τῶν Οὐακκαίων καὶ τῶν Κελτιβήρων
ἔθνη καὶ χωρία διεξιὼν συλλέγει ταῖς ἄλλαις πόλεσι καὶ Σεγεσάμαν καὶ Ἰντερκατίαν. φησὶ δὲ

territory also runs contiguous to that of the Bardyetans, whom the men of to-day call Bardulians.
Secondly, the parts on the western side are the
home of some of the Asturians, Callaicans, and
Vaccaeans, and also of the Vettonians and Carpetanians. Thirdly, the southern parts are the home,
not only of the Oretanians, but of all other tribes
of those Bastetanians and Edetanians that live on
the Orospeda. And fourthly, on the east lies the
Idubeda.

13. Again, of the four divisions into which the
Celtiberians have been separated, the most powerful,
generally speaking, are the Arvacans, who live on
the east and south, where their territory joins
Carpetania and the sources of the Tagus; and they
have a city of very great renown, Numantia. They
gave proof of their valour in the Celtiberian War
against the Romans, which lasted for twenty years;
indeed, many armies, officers and all, were destroyed
by them, and at the last the Numantians, when
besieged, endured till death, except a few who
surrendered the fortress. The Lusonians, likewise,
live in the east, and their territory, too, joins the
sources of the Tagus. The cities of Segeda and
Pallantia both belong to the Arvacans. The distance of Numantia from Caesar Augusta, which
latter, as I was saying, is situated on the Iberus, is
as much as eight hundred stadia. The cities of
Segobriga and Bilbilis both belong to the Celtiberians, and it is near these cities that Metellus
and Sertorius had their war. Polybius, in detailing
the tribes and districts of the Vaccaeans and the
Celtiberians, includes with the rest of the cities both
Segesama and Intercatia. Poseidonius says that

Ποσειδώνιος Μάρκον Μάρκελλον πράξασθαι φόρον ἐκ τῆς Κελτιβηρίας τάλαντα ἑξακόσια· ἐξ οὗ τεκμαίρεσθαι πάρεστιν ὅτι καὶ πολλοὶ ἦσαν οἱ Κελτίβηρες καὶ χρημάτων εὐποροῦντες, καίπερ οἰκοῦντες χώραν παράλυπρον. Πολυβίου δ' εἰπόντος τριακοσίας αὐτῶν καταλῦσαι πόλεις Τιβέριον Γράκχον, κωμῳδῶν φησι τοῦτο τῷ Γράκχῳ χαρίσασθαι τὸν ἄνδρα, τοὺς πύργους καλοῦντα πόλεις, ὥσπερ ἐν ταῖς θριαμβικαῖς πομπαῖς. καὶ ἴσως οὐκ ἄπιστον τοῦτο λέγει· καὶ γὰρ οἱ στρατηγοὶ καὶ οἱ συγγραφεῖς ῥαδίως ἐπὶ τοῦτο φέρονται τὸ ψεῦσμα, καλλωπίζοντες τὰς πράξεις. ἐπεὶ καὶ οἱ φάσκοντες πλείους ἢ χιλίας τὰς τῶν Ἰβήρων ὑπάρξαι πόλεις ἐπὶ τοῦτο φέρεσθαί μοι δοκοῦσι, τὰς μεγάλας κώμας πόλεις ὀνομάζοντες. οὔτε γὰρ ἡ τῆς χώρας φύσις πόλεων ἐπιδεκτικὴ πολλῶν ἐστι διὰ τὴν λυπρότητα ἢ διὰ τὸν ἐκτοπισμὸν καὶ τὸ ἀνήμερον, οὔθ' οἱ βίοι καὶ πράξεις αὐτῶν (ἔξω τῶν κατὰ τὴν παραλίαν τὴν καθ' ἡμᾶς) ὑπαγορεύουσι τοιοῦτον οὐδέν· ἄγριοι γὰρ οἱ κατὰ κώμας οἰκοῦντες· τοιοῦτοι δ' οἱ πολλοὶ τῶν Ἰβήρων· αἱ δὲ πόλεις ἡμεροῦσιν οὐδ' αὐταὶ[1] ῥαδίως ὅταν πλεονάζῃ τὸ τὰς ὕλας ἐπὶ κακῷ τῶν πλησίον οἰκοῦν.

14. Μετὰ δὲ τοὺς Κελτίβηρας πρὸς νότον εἰσὶν οἱ τὸ ὄρος οἰκοῦντες τὴν Ὀροσπέδαν καὶ τὴν περὶ τὸν Σούκρωνα χώραν Ἐδητανοὶ[2] μέχρι Καρχηδόνος, καὶ Βαστητανοὶ καὶ Ὠρητανοὶ σχεδὸν δέ τι καὶ μέχρι Μαλάκας.

---

[1] αὐταί, Cobet restores, for αὖται ; so Forbiger, and Müller-Dübner.
[2] Ἐδητανοί, Kramer, for Σιδητανοί ; so the editors in general.

Marcus Marcellus exacted a tribute of six hundred talents from Celtiberia, from which it may be inferred that the Celtiberians were rich as well as numerous, albeit the country they live in is rather poor. But because Polybius went on to say that Tiberius Gracchus destroyed three hundred cities in Celtiberia, Poseidonius makes fun of him, saying that the man did this merely to gratify Gracchus, for he called the towers cities just as they do in the triumphal processions. And perhaps this remark of Poseidonius is not to be discredited, for not only generals but historians as well are easily led to indulge in such falsification as this, in trying to embellish the deeds they describe. In fact, even those who assert that there are more than one thousand cities in Iberia seem to me to be led to do so by calling the big villages cities; for, in the first place, the country is naturally not capable, on account of the poverty of its soil or else on account of the remoteness or wildness of it, of containing many cities, and, secondly, the modes of life and the activities of the inhabitants (apart from those who live on the seaboard of Our Sea) do not suggest anything of the kind; for those who live in villages are wild (and such are most of the Iberians), and even the cities themselves cannot easily tame their inhabitants when these are outnumbered by the folk that live in the forests for the purpose of working mischief upon their neighbours.

14. Next after the Celtiberians, on the south, are the people who live in the Orospeda Mountain and in the country round about the Sucro River, namely, the Edetanians, who extend as far as New Carthage; and then the Bastetanians and the Oretanians, who extend almost as far as Malaca.

15. Πελτασταὶ δ' ἅπαντες, ὡς εἰπεῖν, ὑπῆρξαν οἱ Ἴβηρες καὶ κοῦφοι κατὰ τὸν ὁπλισμὸν διὰ τὰς λῃστείας, οἵους ἔφαμεν τοὺς Λυσιτανούς, ἀκοντίῳ καὶ σφενδόνῃ καὶ μαχαίρᾳ χρώμενοι· ταῖς δὲ πεζαῖς δυνάμεσι παρεμέμικτο καὶ ἱππεία, δεδιδαγμένων ἵππων ὀρειβατεῖν καὶ κατοκλάζεσθαι ῥᾳδίως ἀπὸ προστάγματος, ὅτε τούτου δέοι. φέρει δ' ἡ Ἰβηρία δορκάδας πολλὰς καὶ ἵππους ἀγρίους. ἔστι δ' ὅπου καὶ αἱ λίμναι πληθύουσιν· ὄρνεις δὲ κύκνοι καὶ τὰ παραπλήσια, πολλαὶ δὲ καὶ ὠτίδες· κάστορας φέρουσι μὲν οἱ ποταμοί, τὸ δὲ καστόριον οὐκ ἔχει τὴν αὐτὴν δύναμιν τῷ Ποντικῷ· ἴδιον γὰρ τῷ Ποντικῷ πάρεστι τὸ φαρμακῶδες, καθάπερ ἄλλοις πολλοῖς. ἐπεί, φησὶν ὁ Ποσειδώνιος, καὶ ὁ Κύπριος χαλκὸς μόνος φέρει τὴν καδμείαν λίθον καὶ τὸ χαλκανθὲς καὶ τὸ σπόδιον. ἴδιον δ' εὕρηκεν[1] Ἰβηρίᾳ ὁ Ποσειδώνιος καὶ τὸ τὰς κορώνας μελαίνας εἶναι καὶ τὸ τοὺς ἵππους τῶν Κελτιβήρων ὑποψάρους ὄντας, ἐπειδὰν εἰς τὴν ἔξω μεταχθῶσιν Ἰβηρίαν, μεταβάλλειν τὴν χρόαν. ἐοικέναι δὲ τοῖς Παρθικοῖς, καὶ γὰρ ταχεῖς εἶναι καὶ εὐδρόμους μᾶλλον τῶν ἄλλων.

16. Καὶ τῶν ῥιζῶν τῶν εἰς βαφὴν χρησίμων πλῆθος. ἐλαίας δὲ πέρι καὶ ἀμπέλου καὶ συκῆς καὶ τῶν παραπλησίων φυτῶν ἡ καθ' ἡμᾶς Ἰβηρικὴ παραλία πάντων εὐπορεῖ, συχνὴ δὲ καὶ τῶν ἐκτός. ἡ μὲν παρωκεανῖτις ἡ πρόσβορρος ἀμοιρεῖ διὰ τὰ ψύχη, ἡ δ' ἄλλη τὸ πλέον διὰ τὴν ὀλιγωρίαν τῶν

C 164

---

[1] ἐν, before Ἰβηρίᾳ, Meineke deletes.

---

[1] 3. 3. 6.   [2] That is, on the Atlantic side.

15. The Iberians were once, virtually all of them, peltasts, and wore light armour on account of their brigand life (as I said [1] of the Lusitanians), using javelin, sling, and dirk. And intermingled with their forces of infantry was a force of cavalry, for their horses were trained to climb mountains, and, whenever there was need for it, to kneel down promptly at the word of command. Iberia produces many deer and wild horses. In places, also, its marshes teem with life; and there are birds, swans and the like; and also bustards in great numbers. As for beavers, the rivers produce them, but the castor from these beavers does not have the same efficacy as that from the beavers of the Pontus; for the medicinal quality of the castor from the Pontus is peculiar to it, as is the case with qualities in many other things. For instance, says Poseidonius, the copper of Cyprus is the only copper which produces calamine and chalcanthite and spodium. And it is peculiar to Iberia, according to Poseidonius, that the crows are black there and also that the slightly dappled horses of Celtiberia change their colour when they are brought over to Farther Iberia. The Celtiberian horses are like those of Parthia, he says, for not only are they faster but they are also smoother runners than the other horses.

16. Iberia also produces quantities of those roots that are useful for dyeing. As for olive-trees, grape-vines, fig-trees, and the similar plants, the Iberian coast on Our Sea is richly supplied with them all, as is also a great part of the outer coasts.[2] But the ocean-coast on the north has none on account of the cold, and, for the most part, the rest of the ocean-coast has none on account of the slovenly

ἀνθρώπων καὶ τὸ μὴ πρὸς διαγωγήν, ἀλλὰ μᾶλλον πρὸς ἀνάγκην καὶ ὁρμὴν θηριώδη μετὰ ἔθους
φαύλου ζῆν· εἰ μή τις οἴεται πρὸς διαγωγὴν ζῆν
τοὺς οὔρῳ λουομένους ἐν δεξαμεναῖς παλαιουμένῳ
καὶ τοὺς ὀδόντας σμηχομένους καὶ αὐτοὺς καὶ τὰς
γυναῖκας αὐτῶν, καθάπερ τοὺς Καντάβρους φασὶ
καὶ τοὺς ὁμόρους αὐτοῖς. καὶ τοῦτο δὲ καὶ τὸ
χαμευνεῖν κοινόν ἐστι τοῖς Ἴβηρσι πρὸς τοὺς
Κελτούς. ἔνιοι δὲ τοὺς Καλλαϊκοὺς ἀθέους φασί,
τοὺς δὲ Κελτίβηρας καὶ τοὺς προσβόρρους τῶν
ὁμόρων αὐτοῖς ἀνωνύμῳ τινὶ θεῷ θύειν [1] ταῖς
πανσελήνοις νύκτωρ πρὸ τῶν πυλῶν, πανοικίους
τε χορεύειν καὶ παννυχίζειν. τοὺς δὲ Οὐέττωνας,
ὅτε πρῶτον εἰς τὸ τῶν Ῥωμαίων παρῆλθον στρατόπεδον, ἰδόντας τῶν ταξιαρχῶν τινας ἀνακάμ-
πτοντας ἐν ταῖς ὁδοῖς περιπάτου χάριν, μανίαν
ὑπολαβόντας, ἡγεῖσθαι τὴν ὁδὸν αὐτοῖς ἐπὶ τὰς
σκηνάς, ὡς δέον ἢ μένειν καθ' ἡσυχίαν ἱδρυθέντας
ἢ μάχεσθαι.

17. Τῆς δὲ βαρβαρικῆς ἰδέας καὶ τὸν τῶν
γυναικῶν ἐνίων κόσμον θείη τις ἄν, ὃν εἴρηκεν
Ἀρτεμίδωρος· ὅπου μὲν γὰρ περιτραχήλια σιδηρᾶ
φορεῖν αὐτάς φησιν, ἔχοντα κόρακας καμπτομένους ὑπὲρ κορυφῆς καὶ προπίπτοντας πρὸ τοῦ
μετώπου πολύ, κατὰ τούτων δὲ τῶν κοράκων, ὅτε
βούλονται, κατασπᾶν τὸ κάλυμμα, ὥστε ἐμπε-
τασθὲν σκιάδιον τῷ προσώπῳ παρέχειν, καὶ
νομίζειν κόσμον· ὅπου δὲ τυμπάνιον περικεῖσθαι,

---

[1] θύειν, Corais inserts ; so the other editors.

---

[1] See Catullus, 39. 19.
[2] Literally, "a little kettle-drum."

character of the people and the fact that they live on a low moral plane—that is, they have regard, not for rational living, but rather for satisfying their physical needs and bestial instincts—unless some one thinks those men have regard for rational living who bathe with urine which they have aged in cisterns, and wash their teeth with it, both they and their wives, as the Cantabrians and the neighbouring peoples are said to do.[1] But both this custom and that of sleeping on the ground the Iberians share with the Celts. Some say the Callaicans have no god, but the Celtiberians and their neighbours on the north offer sacrifice to a nameless god at the seasons of the full moon, by night, in front of the doors of their houses, and whole households dance in chorus and keep it up all night. The Vettonians, when they visited the camp of the Romans for the first time, upon seeing some of the officers promenading up and down the streets merely for the sake of walking around, supposed they were crazy and proceeded to lead the way for them to the tents, thinking they should either remain quietly seated or else be fighting.

17. One might also class as barbaric in character the ornaments of some of the women, of which Artemidorus has told us. In some places, he says, they wear round their necks iron collars which have curved rods that bend overhead and project far in front of their foreheads; and at will they draw their veil down over these curved rods, so that the veil, thus spread out, furnishes a sunshade for the face; and all this they consider an ornament. In other places, he says, the women wear round their heads a "tympanium,"[2] rounded to the back of the head,

πρὸς μὲν τῷ ἰνίῳ περιφερές, καὶ σφίγγον τὴν
κεφαλὴν μέχρι τῶν παρωτίδων, εἰς ὕψος δὲ καὶ
πλάτος ἐξυπτιασμένον κατ᾽ ὀλίγον· ἄλλας δὲ τὰ
προκόμια ψιλοῦν ἐπὶ τοσοῦτον ὥστ᾽ ἀποστίλβειν
τοῦ μετώπου μᾶλλον· τὰς δ᾽ ὅσον ποδιαῖον τὸ
ὕψος ἐπιθεμένας στυλίσκον περιπλέκειν αὐτῷ
τὴν χαίτην, εἶτα καλύπτρᾳ μελαίνῃ περιστέλλειν.
πρὸς δὲ τῇ ἀληθείᾳ τῇ τοιαύτῃ πολλὰ καὶ ἑώραται
καὶ μεμύθευται περὶ πάντων κοινῇ τῶν Ἰβηρικῶν
ἐθνῶν, διαφερόντως δὲ τῶν προσβόρρων, οὐ μόνον
τὰ πρὸς ἀνδρείαν ἀλλὰ καὶ τὰ πρὸς ὠμότητα
καὶ ἀπόνοιαν θηριώδη· καὶ γὰρ τέκνα μητέρες
ἔκτειναν πρὶν ἁλῶναι κατὰ τὸν πόλεμον τὸν ἐν
Καντάβροις, καὶ παιδίον δὲ δεδεμένων αἰχμαλώτων τῶν γονέων καὶ ἀδελφῶν ἔκτεινε πάντας,
κελεύσαντος τοῦ πατρός, σιδήρου κυριεῦσαν, γυνὴ
δὲ τοὺς συναλόντας· κληθεὶς δέ τις εἰς μεθυσκο-
C 165 μένους ἔβαλεν αὐτὸν εἰς πυράν. κοινὰ δὲ καὶ
ταῦτα πρὸς τὰ Κελτικὰ ἔθνη καὶ τὰ Θρᾴκια καὶ
Σκυθικά, κοινὰ δὲ καὶ τὰ πρὸς ἀνδρείαν τήν τε

---

[1] That is, the cap, which fits closely the back of the head,
gradually spreads out from the head at the top and sides
(that is, at the front, all the way from ear to ear) and thus
forms a sort of sun-bonnet (cp. Tozer, *Selections from Strabo*,
p. 104). The whole head-dress suggests the shape of a kettle-
drum, and hence the name. But the Greek here is so incom-
plete and obscure that Artemidorus may have meant either
(1) a cylindrical head-dress, which, as it rises to its top,
gradually spreads out in breadth (the head-dress worn at
Constantinople in the Byzantine Empire and also called in
Greek "tympanium"), or (2) a sort of turban, which covers
and fits the hair tightly and spreads out over the top and
round the head—just such an improvised head-dress as the

and, as far as the ear-lobes, binding the head tightly, but gradually turned back at the top and sides;[1] and other women keep the hair stripped[2] from the forepart of the head so closely that it glistens more than the forehead does; and still other women put a rod about a foot high on the head, twist the hair round the rod, and then drape it with a black veil. And besides the true reports of this sort, many other things have not only been seen but also narrated with fictitious additions about all the Iberian tribes in common, but especially the northerners— I mean not only the stories relating to their courage but also those relating to their ferocity and bestial insensibility.[3] For instance, at the time of the Cantabrian War[4] mothers killed their children before being taken captive; and even a small boy, whose parents and brothers were in fetters as captives of war, gained possession of a sword and, at the command of his father, killed them all; and a woman killed all her fellow captives; and a certain Cantabrian, upon being summoned into the presence of drunken men,[5] threw himself upon a pyre. But these traits too are shared in common by them with the Celtic as also with the Thracian and Scythian tribes; and

negro working-women in the Southern States of America often wear to-day.

[2] Apparently not by cutting, but by plucking or by some destructive agent (cp. Theophrastus, *Hist. Plant.* 9. 20. 3).

[3] That is "insensibility to suffering," or, perhaps better, "contempt for suffering." The same trait is again mentioned by Strabo in § 18.

[4] The Cantabrians were subjugated by Augustus in 25 B.C., but they had to be reconquered (by Agrippa) in 19 B.C. Cp. "Cantabrum indoctum iuga ferre nostra" (Horace, *Carmina,* 2. 6. 2).

[5] His Roman captors, apparently.

τῶν ἀνδρῶν καὶ τὴν τῶν γυναικῶν· γεωργοῦσιν
γὰρ[1] αὗται, τεκοῦσαί τε διακονοῦσι τοῖς ἀνδράσιν,
ἐκείνους ἀνθ' ἑαυτῶν κατακλίνασαι· ἔν τε τοῖς
ἔργοις πολλάκις λοχεύονται[2] καὶ λούουσι καὶ
σπαργανοῦσιν, ἀποκλίνασαι πρός τι ῥεῖθρον. ἐν
δὲ τῇ Λιγυστικῇ φησιν ὁ Ποσειδώνιος διηγήσασθαι
τὸν ξένον ἑαυτῷ Χαρμόλεων, Μασσαλιώτην ἄνδρα,
ὅτι μισθώσαιτο ἄνδρας ὁμοῦ καὶ γυναῖκας ἐπὶ
σκαφητόν, ὠδίνασα δὲ μία τῶν γυναικῶν ἀπέλθοι
ἀπὸ τοῦ ἔργου πλησίον, τεκοῦσα δ' ἐπανέλθοι ἐπὶ
τοὔργον αὐτίκα, ὅπως μὴ ἀπολέσειε τὸν μισθόν·
αὐτὸς δὲ ἐπιπόνως ἰδὼν ἐργαζομένην, οὐκ εἰδὼς
τὴν αἰτίαν πρότερον ὀψὲ μάθοι καὶ ἀφείη, δοὺς
τὸν μισθόν· ἡ δ' ἐκκομίσασα τὸ νήπιον πρός τι
κρηνίον, λούσασα καὶ σπαργανώσασα οἷς εἶχε
διασώσειεν οἴκαδε.

18. Οὐκ ἴδιον δὲ τῶν Ἰβήρων οὐδὲ τοῦτο,
σύνδυο ἐφ' ἵππων κομίζεσθαι, κατὰ δὲ τὰς μάχας
τὸν ἕτερον πεζὸν ἀγωνίζεσθαι. οὐδὲ τὸ τῶν μυῶν
πλῆθος ἴδιον, ἀφ' οὗ καὶ λοιμικαὶ νόσοι πολλάκις
ἠκολούθησαν. συνέβη δ' ἐν τῇ Κανταβρίᾳ τοῦτο
τοῖς Ῥωμαίοις, ὥστε, καὶ μισθοὺς ἄρνυσθαι μυο-
θηροῦντας πρὸς μέτρον ἀποδειχθέν, διεσώζοντο
μόλις· προσελάμβανε δὲ καὶ ἄλλων σπάνις καὶ

---

[1] γάρ, Jones inserts.
[2] λοχεύονται Piccolo, for αὐταί; Groskurd and Meineke
conj. τίκτουσι.

---

[1] A custom still in vogue among several primitive peoples
(see article in *Encyc. Brit.* under "Couvade").
[2] The "field-mice" referred to in 3. 2. 6. The Greek word
"mus" may refer to any member of the Muridæ family;
here, presumably, to some sort of rat.

in common also the traits relating to courage—I mean the courage of women as well as of men. For example, these women till the soil, and when they have given birth to a child they put their husbands to bed instead of going to bed themselves and minister to them;[1] and while at work in the fields, oftentimes, they turn aside to some brook, give birth to a child, and bathe and swaddle it. Poseidonius says that in Liguria his host, Charmoleon, a man of Massilia, narrated to him how he had hired men and women together for ditch-digging; and how one of the women, upon being seized with the pangs of childbirth, went aside from her work to a place near by, and, after having given birth to her child, came back to her work at once in order not to lose her pay; and how he himself saw that she was doing her work painfully, but was not aware of the cause till late in the day, when he learned it and sent her away with her wages; and she carried the infant out to a little spring, bathed it, swaddled it with what she had, and brought it safely home.

18. Nor yet is the following custom peculiar to the Iberians alone: they ride double on horseback, though in the time of battle one of the two fights on foot; nor the especially great number of the mice,[2] from which pestilential diseases have often ensued. This was so much the case for the Romans in Cantabria that, although a proclamation was made that mice-catchers would gain bounties graded in proportion to the number caught, the Romans could barely come through with their lives; and, besides the plague, there was a scarcity, not only of other stuffs, but of grain too; and only with difficulty could they

σίτου· ἐπεσιτίζοντο δὲ ἐκ τῆς Ἀκυιτανίας χαλεπῶς διὰ τὰς δυσχωρίας. τῆς δ᾽ ἀπονοίας καὶ
τοῦτο λέγεται τῆς Καντάβρων, ὅτι ἁλόντες τινές,
ἀναπεπηγότες ἐπὶ τῶν σταυρῶν, ἐπαιώνιζον. τὰ
μὲν οὖν τοιαῦτα τῶν ἠθῶν ἀγριότητός τινος παρα-
δείγματ᾽ ἂν εἴη· τὰ δὲ τοιαῦτα ἧττον μὲν ἴσως
πολιτικά, οὐ θηριώδη δέ, οἷον τὸ παρὰ τοῖς Καντάβροις τοὺς ἄνδρας διδόναι ταῖς γυναιξὶ προῖκα,
τὸ τὰς θυγατέρας κληρονόμους ἀπολείπεσθαι, τούς
τε ἀδελφοὺς ὑπὸ τούτων ἐκδίδοσθαι γυναιξίν.
ἔχει γάρ τινα γυναικοκρατίαν. τοῦτο δ᾽ οὐ πάνυ
πολιτικόν. Ἰβηρικὸν δὲ καὶ τὸ ἐν ἔθει παρατί-
θεσθαι τοξικόν, ὃ συντιθέασιν ἐκ βοτάνης σελίνῳ
προσομοίας ἄπονον, ὥστ᾽ ἔχειν ἐν ἑτοίμῳ πρὸς
τὰ ἀβούλητα, καὶ τὸ κατασπένδειν αὐτούς, οἷς
ἂν προσθῶνται, ὥστε ἀποθνήσκειν αὐτοὺς ὑπὲρ
αὐτῶν.

---

[1] See footnote 3, p. 111.

[2] Apparently one of the wild members of the parsley
family (Apiaceæ), *i.e.* fool's parsley (*Aethusa cynapium*),
poison hemlock (*Conium maculatum*), or water hemlock
(*Cicuta maculata*); more likely, poison hemlock. But perhaps the herb should be identified with that deadly Sardinian
herb which Pausanias (10. 17) says is "like parsley," namely,
celery-leaved, or marsh, crowfoot (*Ranunculus sceleratus*;
see Dioscurides, *de Mat. Med.* 2. 206), and called by the
Greeks "wild parsley." This Sardinian herb produced a
convulsive laughter, with a drawing down of the angles of
the mouth (Solinus, *Collect. Rarum Memor* 4. 4., Mommsen's
ed., p. 51), and ended fatally, with the proverbial "Sardonic
smile" (Pausanias, l.c.) on the victim's face.

[3] The Celtiberians deemed it an unholy act for a "devoted"

get supplies out of Aquitania on account of the rough roads. As for the insensibility[1] of the Cantabrians, this instance is also told, namely, that when some captive Cantabrians had been nailed on their crosses they proceeded to sing their paean of victory. Now such traits as these would indicate a certain savageness; and yet there are other things which, although not marks of civilisation perhaps, are not brutish; for instance, it is the custom among the Cantabrians for the husbands to give dowries to their wives, for the daughters to be left as heirs, and the brothers to be married off by their sisters. The custom involves, in fact, a sort of woman-rule—but this is not at all a mark of civilisation. It is also an Iberian custom habitually to keep at hand a poison, which is made by them out of an herb that is nearly like parsley and painless,[2] so as to have it in readiness for any untoward eventuality; and it is an Iberian custom, too, to devote their lives to whomever they attach themselves, even to the point of dying for them.[3]

person to survive his master (Valerius Maximus 2. 6. 11). Thousands of Iberians were " devoted " to Sertorius (Plutarch *Sertorius* 14); Valerius Maximus (7. 6) gives an account of the revolting acts they committed in their loyalty to Sertorius in the defence of Calaguris; and Henry Swinburne (*Travels through Spain in 1775 and 1776*, Ninth Letter) quotes from the annals of Catalonia the following epitaph to them: " Hic multae quae se manibus   Q. Sertorii turmae, et terrae Mortalium omnium parenti Devovere, dum, eo sublato,   Superesse taederet et fortiter   Pugnando invicem cecidere,   Morte ad praesens optata jacent.   Valete posteri." And Adiatunnus, king of the Sotiates in Aquitania, had 600 " devoted " men, who, in the Celtic language, were called " soldurii," according to Caesar (*Bell. Gall.* 3. 22) or, according to Athenaeus (6. 54), " siloduri," which word, Athenaeus says, means in Greek " men under a vow."

19. Τινὲς μὲν οὖν εἰς τέτταρα μέρη διῃρῆσθαί φασι τὴν χώραν ταύτην, καθάπερ εἴπομεν, ἄλλοι δὲ πενταμερῆ λέγουσιν. οὐκ ἔστι δὲ τἀκριβὲς ἐν τούτοις ἀποδιδόναι διὰ τὰς μεταβολὰς καὶ τὴν C 166 ἀδοξίαν τῶν τόπων. ἐν γὰρ τοῖς γνωρίμοις καὶ ἐνδόξοις αἵ τε μεταναστάσεις γνώριμοι καὶ οἱ μερισμοὶ τῆς χώρας καὶ αἱ μεταβολαὶ τῶν ὀνομάτων καὶ εἴ τι ἄλλο παραπλήσιον· θρυλεῖται γὰρ ὑπὸ πολλῶν, καὶ μάλιστα τῶν Ἑλλήνων, οἳ λαλίστατοι πάντων γεγόνασι. ὅσα δὲ καὶ βάρβαρα καὶ ἐκτετοπισμένα καὶ μικρόχωρα καὶ διεσπασμένα, τούτων ὑπομνήματα οὔτ᾽ ἀσφαλῆ ἐστιν οὔτε πολλά· ὅσα δὲ δὴ πόρρω τῶν Ἑλλήνων ἐπιτείνει τὴν ἄγνοιαν. οἱ δὲ τῶν Ῥωμαίων συγγραφεῖς μιμοῦνται μὲν τοὺς Ἕλληνας, ἀλλ᾽ οὐκ ἐπὶ πολύ· καὶ γὰρ ἃ λέγουσι παρὰ τῶν Ἑλλήνων μεταφέρουσιν, ἐξ ἑαυτῶν δ᾽ οὐ πολὺ μὲν προσφέρονται τὸ φιλείδημον,[1] ὥσθ᾽, ὁπόταν ἔλλειψις γένηται παρ᾽ ἐκείνων, οὐκ ἔστι πολὺ τὸ ἀναπληρούμενον ὑπὸ τῶν ἑτέρων, ἄλλως τε καὶ τῶν ὀνομάτων, ὅσα ἐνδοξότατα, τῶν πλείστων ὄντων Ἑλληνικῶν. ἐπεὶ καὶ Ἰβηρίαν ὑπὸ μὲν τῶν προτέρων καλεῖσθαι πᾶσαν τὴν ἔξω τοῦ Ῥωδανοῦ

[1] Some MSS. read φιλέκδημον. Strabo may have written both words here, as in l. 2. 29. So Corais.

19. Now although some assert that this country[1] has been divided into four divisions, as I have already stated,[2] others say it has five divisions. But it is impossible, in this case, for us to represent a division that is scientifically accurate, because of the changes which have taken place and the disrepute of the regions. For it is only in the case of the well-known and reputable regions that the migrations, the divisions of the country, the changes in the names, and everything else of that kind, are well known. Indeed, our ears are filled with these things by many, and particularly by the Greeks, who have come to be the most talkative of all men. But as for all the nations that are barbarian and remote, as well as small in territory and split up,[3] their records are neither safe to go by nor numerous; and as for all the nations, of course, that are far off from the Greeks, our ignorance is still greater. Now although the Roman historians are imitators of the Greeks, they do not carry their imitation very far; for what they relate they merely translate from the Greeks, while the fondness for knowledge that they of themselves bring to their histories is inconsiderable; hence, whenever the Greeks leave gaps, all the filling in that is done by the other set of writers is inconsiderable—especially since most of the very famous names are Greek. Take, for example, even Iberia: the historians of former times, it is said, give the name of Iberia to all the country beyond the Rhodanus and that isthmus which is

---

[1] Celtiberia. [2] See 3. 4. 13.
[3] *I.e.*, as in 3. 4. 5, "into petty divisions and sovereignties."

καὶ τοῦ ἰσθμοῦ τοῦ ὑπὸ τῶν Γαλατικῶν κόλπων
σφιγγομένου, οἱ δὲ νῦν ὅριον αὐτῆς τίθενται τὴν
Πυρήνην, συνωνύμως τε τὴν αὐτὴν Ἰβηρίαν λέγουσι
καὶ Ἰσπανίαν· μόνην δ᾽[1] ἐκάλουν τὴν ἐντὸς τοῦ
Ἴβηρος, οἱ δ᾽ ἔτι πρότερον αὐτοὺς τούτους Ἰγλῆ-
τας, οὐ πολλὴν χώραν νεμομένους, ὥς φησιν
Ἀσκληπιάδης ὁ Μυρλεανός. Ῥωμαῖοι δὲ τὴν
σύμπασαν καλέσαντες συνωνύμως[2] Ἰβηρίαν τε
καὶ Ἰσπανίαν τὸ μὲν αὐτῆς μέρος εἶπον τὴν ἐκτός,
τὸ δὲ ἕτερον τὴν ἐντός· ἄλλοτε δ᾽ ἄλλως διαιροῦσι,
πρὸς τοὺς καιροὺς πολιτευόμενοι.

20. Νυνὶ δέ, τῶν ἐπαρχιῶν τῶν μὲν ἀποδει-
χθεισῶν τῷ δήμῳ τε καὶ τῇ συγκλήτῳ τῶν δὲ
τῷ ἡγεμόνι τῶν Ῥωμαίων, ἡ μὲν Βαιτικὴ πρόσ-

---

[1] δ᾽, Jones inserts.

[2] συνωνύμως, Meineke, for ὁμωνύμως; so Forbiger, Tardieu,
and C. Müller.

---

[1] They could have used "Iberia" thus only in a general
sense for "Hesperia," it seems. Very little was known of
the interior of the country until the second century B.C.,
and at that time, according to Polybius (3. 37), it was only
the country along the Mediterranean south of the Pyrenees
as far as Gibraltar that was called "Iberia," while the
country along the "outer sea" had no general name. The
chronology of Strabo here is obscure; and, so far as we
know, Hecataeus (b. about 540 B.C.) is the first Greek to
speak of "Iberia," and, after him, Herodotus (1. 163).
Later on, Eratosthenes (276-194 B.C.) is the first to dis-
tinguish Iberia from Celtica (3. 2. 11), of which hitherto
Iberia had been regarded as only a part; yet, if we accept
Polybius, "Iberia" did not come to include all the Spanish
peninsula, and hence equal "Hispania," until late in the
second century B.C.

[2] On the doubtful origin and meaning of "Iberia" and
"Hispania," see Burke-Hume, A History of Spain, vol. i,
p. 2, n. 4, and p. 14, n. 1.

[3] That is, between the Iberus and the Pyrenees.

[4] Between the Iberus and the Pyrenees.

comprised between the two Galatic gulfs,[1] whereas the historians of to-day set the Pyrenees as the limit of Iberia and speak synonymously of this same country as "Iberia" and "Hispania";[2] but they used to give the name of "Iberia" solely to the country this side the Iberus,[3] although the historians still before that called the inhabitants of this very country[4] "Igletes,"[5] who occupy no large territory, as Asclepiades the Myrlean says. But though the Romans called the country as a whole both "Iberia" and "Hispania" synonymously, they spoke of one division of it as "Farther" and of the other as "Hither"; at different times, however, they divide the country in different ways, suiting their government of the country to the requirements of the times.[6]

20. At the present time, now that some of the provinces have been declared the property of the people and the senate, and the others that of the Roman emperor, Baetica belongs to the people;[7]

---

[5] But Herodorus (fl. about 400 B.C.), according to Stephanus Byzantinus (s. 'Iβήριαι), places the "Igletes," or "Gletes," north of the Cynetes, that is, in south-western Iberia.

[6] There was no permanent boundary between Hither and Farther Spain. At first the boundary was the Iberus; Polybius makes it start at a point near Saguntum; after him, even Almeria in Murcia was made the starting-point; and at one time the capital of Hither Spain was New Carthage, though Augustus changed it to Tarraco. At first Hither Spain was merely the north-east corner; then, for a great part of the first and second centuries B.C., it was roughly bounded, let us say (cp. Burke-Hume, *op. cit.* p. 16, n. 2), by a line running through the modern Almeria, Saragossa and Gerona; and by the time of Julius Caesar, it comprised most of the peninsula except Baetica and Lusitania.

[7] The portion belonging to the emperor consisted of such parts of the country as required military defence. Baetica, now being the most civilised and peaceable, naturally fell to the people. Cp. 17. 3. 25.

κεῖται τῷ δήμῳ, καὶ πέμπεται στρατηγὸς ἐπ'
αὐτὴν ἔχων ταμίαν τε καὶ πρεσβευτήν· ὅριον δ'
αὐτῆς τεθείκασι πρὸς ἠῶ πλησίον Κασταλῶνος
ἡ δὲ λοιπὴ Καίσαρός ἐστι· πέμπονται δ' ἀπ'
αὐτοῦ δύο πρεσβευταί, στρατηγικός τε καὶ
ὑπατικός, ὁ μὲν στρατηγικός, ἔχων σὺν αὐτῷ
πρεσβευτήν, δικαιοδοτήσων Λυσιτανοῖς τοῖς πα-
ρακειμένοις τῇ Βαιτικῇ καὶ διατείνουσι μέχρι τοῦ
Δουρίου ποταμοῦ καὶ τῶν ἐκβολῶν αὐτοῦ· καλοῦσι γὰρ οὕτω τὴν χώραν ταύτην ἰδίως ἐν τῷ
παρόντι· ἐνταῦθα δ' ἐστὶ καὶ ἡ Αὐγούστα Ἠμε-
ρίτα. ἡ δὲ[1] λοιπή, αὕτη δ' ἐστὶν ἡ πλείστη τῆς
Ἰβηρίας, ὑπὸ τῷ ὑπατικῷ ἡγεμόνι, στρατιάν τε
ἔχοντι ἀξιόλογον τριῶν που ταγμάτων καὶ
πρεσβευτὰς τρεῖς· ὧν ὁ μέν, δύο ἔχων τάγματα,
παραφρουρεῖ τὴν πέραν τοῦ Δουρίου πᾶσαν ἐπὶ
τὰς ἄρκτους, ἣν οἱ μὲν πρότερον Λυσιτανοὺς ἔλε-
C 167 γον, οἱ δὲ νῦν Καλλαϊκοὺς καλοῦσι· συνάπτει δὲ
τούτοις τὰ προσάρκτια ὄρη μετὰ τῶν Ἀστύρων
καὶ τῶν Καντάβρων. ῥεῖ δὲ διὰ τῶν Ἀστύρων
Μέλσος ποταμός, καὶ μικρὸν ἀπωτέρω πόλις
Νοῖγα, καὶ πλησίον ἐκ τοῦ ὠκεανοῦ ἀνάχυσις,
ὁρίζουσα τοὺς Ἄστυρας ἀπὸ τῶν Καντάβρων.
τὴν δ' ἐξῆς παρόρειον[2] μέχρι Πυρήνης ὁ δεύτερος
τῶν πρεσβευτῶν μετὰ τοῦ ἑτέρου τάγματος. ἐπι-
σκοπεῖ δὲ ὁ τρίτος τὴν μεσόγαιαν, συνέχει δὲ τὰ

---

[1] δέ, Corais inserts.
[2] τὴν . . . παρόρειον, Kramer, for τῆς . . . παρόριον; so
Meineke, Forbiger, and Müller-Dübner.

and to govern it they send a praetor, who has under him both a quaestor and a legatus; its boundary, though, on the east, has been set in the neighbourhood of Castalo. But all the rest of Iberia is Caesar's; and he sends thither two legati, praetorian and consular respectively; the praetorian legatus, who has with him a legatus of his own, being sent to administer justice to those Lusitanians whose country is situated alongside Baetica and extends as far as the Durius River and its outlets (indeed, at the present time they apply the name Lusitania specifically to this country); and here, too, is the city of Augusta Emerita. The remainder of Caesar's territory (and this is the most of Iberia) is under the consular governor,[1] who has under him, not only a noteworthy army of, I should say, three legions, but also three legati. One of the three, with two legions, guards the frontier of the whole country beyond the Durius to the north: the inhabitants of this country were spoken of by the people of former times as Lusitanians, but by the people of to-day they are called Callaicans. Adjoining this country are the northerly mountains, together with the Asturians and the Cantabrians. The River Melsus flows through Asturia; a little farther on is the city of Noega; and near Noega there is an estuary from the ocean, which estuary is a boundary between the Asturians and the Cantabrians. The country next thereafter, along the mountains as far as the Pyrenees, is guarded by the second of the three legati and the other legion. The third legatus oversees the interior, and also conserves the interests

---

[1] Called above "the consular legatus."

τῶν τογάτων[1] ἤδη λεγομένων ὡς ἂν εἰρηνικῶν
καὶ εἰς τὸ ἥμερον καὶ τὸν Ἰταλικὸν τύπον μετα-
κειμένων ἐν τῇ τηβεννικῇ ἐσθῆτι. οὗτοι δ᾽ εἰσὶν
οἱ Κελτίβηρες καὶ οἱ τοῦ Ἴβηρος πλησίον ἑκατέρωθεν οἰκοῦντες μέχρι τῶν πρὸς θαλάττῃ μερῶν.
αὐτὸς δὲ ὁ ἡγεμὼν διαχειμάζει μὲν ἐν τοῖς ἐπι-
θαλαττιαίοις μέρεσι καὶ μάλιστα τῇ Καρχηδόνι
καὶ τῇ Ταρράκωνι δικαιοδοτῶν, θέρους δὲ περίει-
σιν, ἐφορῶν ἀεί τινα τῶν δεομένων ἐπανορθώσεως.
εἰσὶ δὲ καὶ ἐπίτροποι τοῦ Καίσαρος, ἱππικοὶ
ἄνδρες, οἱ διανέμοντες τὰ χρήματα τοῖς στρατιώ-
ταις εἰς τὴν διοίκησιν τοῦ βίου.

V

1. Τῶν δὲ προκειμένων νήσων τῆς Ἰβηρίας τὰς
μὲν Πιτυούσσας δύο καὶ τὰς Γυμνησίας δύο (ἃς
καλοῦσι καὶ Βαλιαρίδας) προκεῖσθαι συμβαίνει
τῆς μεταξὺ Ταρράκωνος καὶ Σούκρωνος παραλίας,
ἐφ᾽ ἧς ἵδρυται τὸ Σάγουντον· εἰσὶ δὲ καὶ πελάγιαι,
μᾶλλον δ᾽[2] αἱ Πιτυοῦσσαι[3] πρὸς ἑσπέραν κεκλι-
μέναι τῶν Γυμνησίων. καλεῖται δ᾽ αὐτῶν ἡ μὲν

---

[1] τογάτων, Kramer and Meineke insert after τῶν (others
after λεγομένων).
[2] δ᾽, Jones inserts.
[3] καί, before πρός, Spengel deletes.

---

[1] Cp. 3. 2. 15, and footnote.
[2] Diodorus Siculus (5. 17) says the islands were "by

of those peoples who are already called " Togati " [1]
(or, as you might say, " peaceably inclined "), and
have become transformed, clad in their toga-robe, to
their present gentleness of disposition and their
Italian mode of life ; these latter are the Celtiberians and the peoples that live near them on both
sides of the Iberus as far as the regions next to the
sea. As for the governor himself, he passes his
winters administering justice in the regions by the
sea, and especially in New Carthage and Tarraco,
while in the summer-time he goes the rounds of
his province, always making an inspection of some
of the things that require rectification. Caesar also
has procurators there, of the equestrian rank, who
distribute among the soldiers everything that is
necessary for the maintenance of their lives.

V

1. Of the islands which lie off Iberia, the two
Pityussae, and the two Gymnesiae (which are also
called the Baliarides),[2] lie off the stretch of coast
that is between Tarraco and Sucro, whereon
Saguntum is situated ; they are also out in the open
sea, all of them, although the Pityussae have a
greater inclination [3] to the west than the Gymnesiae.

the Greeks called 'Gymnesiae,' on account of the fact that
the inhabitants went ' unclad ' ($\gamma\upsilon\mu\nu\upsilon\grave{\upsilon}s$ $\tau\hat{\eta}s$ $\dot{\epsilon}\sigma\theta\hat{\eta}\tau\upsilon s$) in the
summer-time " (so Livy, Epit. 60), " but by the natives and
the Romans 'Baliarides,' from the fact that they hurl
($\beta\dot{\alpha}\lambda\lambda\epsilon\iota\nu$) big stones with their slings the best of all mankind "
(so Livy, l.c., who adds, " or else from Baleus, the com-
panion of Hercules "). Strabo elsewhere (14. 2. 10) makes
Baliarides of Phoenician origin.
    [3] Cp. vol. i, page 101, and footnote 1.

Ἔβουσος, πόλιν ἔχουσα ὁμώνυμον· κύκλος δὲ
τῆς νήσου τετρακόσιοι στάδιοι, παρώμαλος τὸ
πλάτος καὶ τὸ μῆκος· ἡ δὲ Ὀφιοῦσσα ἔρημος καὶ
πολὺ ἐλάττων ταύτης πλησίον κειμένη. τῶν δὲ
Γυμνησίων ἡ μὲν μείζων ἔχει δύο πόλεις, Πάλμαν
καὶ Πολεντίαν, τὴν μὲν πρὸς ἕω κειμένην, τὴν
Πολεντίαν, τὴν δ᾽ ἑτέραν πρὸς δύσιν. μῆκος δὲ
τῆς νήσου μικρὸν ἀπολεῖπον τῶν ἑξακοσίων
σταδίων, πλάτος δὲ διακοσίων, Ἀρτεμίδωρος δὲ
διπλάσιον εἴρηκε καὶ τὸ πλάτος καὶ τὸ μῆκος.
ἡ δ᾽ ἐλάττων ὡς διακοσίους [1] ἑβδομήκοντα τῆς
Πολεντίας διέχει σταδίους· κατὰ μέγεθος μὲν
οὖν πολὺ τῆς μείζονος ἀπολείπεται, κατὰ δὲ τὴν
ἀρετὴν οὐδὲν αὐτῆς χείρων ἐστίν· ἄμφω γὰρ
εὐδαίμονες καὶ εὐλίμενοι, χοιραδώδεις δὲ κατὰ τὰ
στόματα, ὥστε δεῖν προσοχῆς τοῖς εἰσπλέουσι·
διὰ δὲ τὴν ἀρετὴν τῶν τόπων καὶ οἱ κατοικοῦντες
εἰρηναῖοι, καθάπερ καὶ οἱ κατὰ τὴν Ἔβουσον.
κακούργων δέ τινων ὀλίγων κοινωνίας συστησα-
μένων πρὸς τοὺς ἐν τοῖς πελάγεσι λῃστάς, διε-
βλήθησαν ἅπαντες, καὶ διέβη Μέτελλος ἐπ᾽
αὐτοὺς ὁ Βαλιαρικὸς προσαγορευθείς, ὅστις καὶ
τὰς πόλεις ἔκτισε. διὰ δὲ τὴν αὐτὴν ἀρετὴν ἐπι-
βουλευόμενοι, καίπερ εἰρηναῖοι ὄντες, ὅμως σφεν-
δονῆται ἄριστοι λέγονται· καὶ τοῦτ᾽ ἤσκησαν, ὥς
C 168   φασι, διαφερόντως, ἐξ ὅτου Φοίνικες κατέσχον

---

[1] διακοσίους (σ′), Corais inserts; so Groskurd, Kramer,
Forbiger, and Meineke. Cp. Pliny (3. 11) who says "30
miles."

Now one of the Pityussae is called Ebusus, and it has a city of the same name; the circuit of the island is four hundred stadia, with the breadth and the length about equal. The other island, Ophiussa, which lies near Ebusus, is desert and much smaller. Of the Gymnesiae, the larger has two cities, Palma and Polentia, one of which, Polentia, is situated in the eastern part of the island, and the other in the western. The length of the island falls but little short of six hundred stadia, and the breadth but little short of two hundred—although Artemidorus has stated the length and breadth at double these figures. The smaller of the two is about two hundred and seventy stadia distant from Polentia. Now although it falls far short of the larger island in size, it is in no respect inferior thereto in the excellence of its soil; for both are blessed with fertility, and also have good harbours, though the harbours are full of reefs at the entrances, so that there is need of vigilance on the part of those who sail in. And it is on account of the fertility of these regions that the inhabitants are peaceable, as is also the case with the people on the island of Ebusus. But merely because a few criminals among them had formed partnerships with the pirates of the high seas, they were all cast into disrepute, and an over-sea expedition was made against them by Metellus, surnamed Balearicus, who is the man that founded their cities. On account of the same fertility of their islands, however, the inhabitants are ever the object of plots, albeit they are peaceable; still they are spoken of as the best of slingers. And this art they have practised assiduously, so it is said, ever since the Phoenicians took possession

τὰς νήσους. οὗτοι δὲ καὶ ἐνδῦσαι λέγονται
πρῶτοι τοὺς ἀνθρώπους χιτῶνας πλατυσήμους·
ἄζωστοι δ' ἐπὶ τοὺς ἀγῶνας ἐξήεσαν, αἰγίδα περὶ
τῇ χειρὶ ἔχοντες ἢ πεπυρακτωμένον ἀκόντιον
(σπάνιον δὲ καὶ λελογχωμένον σιδήρῳ μικρῷ),
σφενδόνας δὲ περὶ τῇ κεφαλῇ τρεῖς (μελαγκρανίνας,[1] σχοίνου εἶδος, ἐξ οὗ πλέκεται τὰ σχοινία·
καὶ Φιλητᾶς γε ἐν Ἑρμηνείᾳ·[2]

λευγαλέος δὲ χιτὼν πεπινωμένος· ἀμφὶ δ' ἀραιὴ
  ἰξὺς εἰλεῖται κόμμα μελαγκράνινον,[3]

ὡς σχοίνῳ ἐζωσμένου) μελαγκρανίνας[4] ἢ τριχίνας
ἢ νευρίνας· τὴν μὲν μακρόκωλον πρὸς τὰς μακρο-
βολίας, τὴν δὲ βραχύκωλον πρὸς τὰς ἐν βραχεῖ
βολάς, τὴν δὲ μέσην πρὸς τὰς μέσας. ἠσκοῦντο
δ' ἐκ παίδων οὕτως ταῖς σφενδόναις, ὥστ' οὐδ'
ἄλλως τοῖς παισὶν ἄρτον ἐδίδοσαν ἄνευ τοῦ τῇ
σφενδόνῃ[5] τυχεῖν. διόπερ ὁ Μέτελλος, προσπλέων
πρὸς τὰς νήσους, δέρρεις ἔτεινεν ὑπὲρ τῶν κατα-
στρωμάτων σκέπην πρὸς τὰς σφενδόνας. εἰσή-
γαγε δὲ ἐποίκους τρισχιλίους τῶν ἐκ τῆς Ἰβηρίας
Ῥωμαίων.

2. Πρὸς δὲ τῇ εὐκαρπίᾳ τῆς γῆς καὶ τὸ μηδὲν

---

[1] μελαγκρανίνας, Kramer, for μελαγκραίνας ; so Meineke.
[2] Tyrwhitt conjectures Ἑρμῇ ἐλεγείᾳ for Ἑρμηνείᾳ.
[3] μελαγκράνινον, Kramer, for μελαγκραίνον ; so Meineke.
[4] μελαγκρανίνας, Kramer, for μελαγκραίνας ; so Meineke.
[5] τῇ σφενδόνῃ, Casaubon, for the corrupt τῆς σφενδόνης of
the MSS.

---

[1] That is, for a shield.
[2] But cp. Diodorus Siculus, who says (5. 18) : "Their
equipment for fighting is three slings (so also Florus 3. 8 =
1. 43 in Rossbach's ed.) ; and, of these, they keep one round
the head, another round the belly, and a third in the hands."

of the islands. And the Phoenicians are also spoken of as the first to clothe the people there in tunics with a broad border; but the people used to go forth to their fights without a girdle on—with only a goat-skin, wrapped round the arm,[1] or with a javelin that had been hardened in the fire (though in rare cases it was also pointed with a small iron tip), and with three slings worn round the head,[2] of black-tufted rush (that is, a species of rope-rush, out of which the ropes are woven; and Philetas, too, in his "Hermeneia"[3] says, "Sorry his tunic befouled with dirt; and round about him his slender waist is entwined with a strip of black-tufted rush," meaning a man girdled with a rush-rope), of black-tufted rush, I say, or of hair or of sinews: the sling with the long straps for the long shots, the one with the short straps for the shots at short range, and the medium sling for the medium shots. And their training in the use of slings used to be such, from childhood up, that they would not so much as give bread to their children unless they first hit it with the sling.[4] This is why Metellus, when he was approaching the islands from the sea, stretched hides above the decks as a protection against the slings. And he brought thither as colonists three thousand of the Romans who were in Iberia.

2. In addition to the fruitfulness of the soil, there

[3] The works of Philetas of Cos are lost. This "Hermeneia," meaning "Interpretation" (?), is otherwise unknown. The reference may be to a poem of Philetas which, according to Parthenius (*Erotica* 2), was entitled "Hermes." However, the entire reference has every appearance of being merely a gloss on "black-tufted rush," as was first suggested by Casaubon.

[4] So Diodorus 5. 18 and Florus 3. 8.

τῶν σινομένων θηρίων εὑρίσκεσθαι ῥᾳδίως ἐνταῦθα
πρόσεστιν· οὐδὲ γὰρ τοὺς λαγιδεῖς ἐπιχωρίους
εἶναί φασιν, ἀλλὰ κομισθέντων ἐκ τῆς περαίας
ὑπό τινος ἄρρενος καὶ θηλείας γενέσθαι τὴν ἐπι-
γονήν· ἡ τοσαύτη κατ᾽ ἀρχὰς ὑπῆρχεν, ὥστε καὶ
οἴκους ἀνατρέπειν ἐκ τῆς ὑπονομῆς καὶ δένδρα,
καὶ ἐπὶ τοὺς Ῥωμαίους, ὥσπερ εἶπον, ἀναγκα-
σθῆναι καταφυγεῖν τοὺς ἀνθρώπους. νῦν μέντοι
τὸ εὐμεταχείριστον τῆς θήρας ἐπικρατεῖν οὐκ ἐᾷ
τὴν βλάβην, ἀλλὰ λυσιτελῶς οἱ ἔχοντες καρ-
ποῦνται τὴν γῆν. αὗται μὲν οὖν ἐντὸς στηλῶν
τῶν Ἡρακλείων καλουμένων.

3. Πρὸς αὐταῖς δὲ δύο νησίδια, ὧν θάτερον
Ἥρας νῆσον ὀνομάζουσι· καὶ δή τινες καὶ ταύτας
Στήλας καλοῦσιν. ἔξω δὲ Στηλῶν τὰ Γάδειρα,
περὶ ὧν τοσοῦτον μόνον εἰρήκαμεν, ὅτι τῆς Κάλπης διέχει περὶ ἑπτακοσίους καὶ πεντήκοντα
σταδίους (τῆς δὲ ἐκβολῆς τοῦ Βαίτιδος πλησίον
ἵδρυται), πλείους δ᾽ εἰσὶ λόγοι περὶ αὐτῆς. οὗτοι
γάρ εἰσιν οἱ ἄνδρες οἱ τὰ πλεῖστα καὶ μέγιστα
ναυκλήρια στέλλοντες εἴς τε τὴν καθ᾽ ἡμᾶς θάλατταν καὶ τὴν ἐκτός, οὔτε μεγάλην οἰκοῦντες
νῆσον οὔτε τῆς περαίας νεμόμενοι πολλὴν οὔτ᾽

---

[1] 3. 2. 6.

[2] "The Pillars" was used in various senses in ancient
times (cp. § 5 below), but the more common conception in
Strabo's time appears to have been that of Calpe (the Rock
of Gibraltar) and Abilyx (Ximiera, *i.e.* "Ape Mountain," in
Africa). The two isles here referred to as near the Pillars
cannot be identified ; there are no islands in the strait at
Calpe. Scymnus (142–145) puts the Pillar-isles near Maenaca
(now Almunecar), but he says nothing about "Hera's
Island." Perhaps the isles at Trafalgar—a cape, called by
Mela (2. 6. 9) the Promontory of Juno, on which there was

is also the fact that no injurious animal can easily be found in the Gymnesiae. For even the rabbits there, it is said, are not native, but the stock sprang from a male and female brought over by some person from the opposite mainland; and this stock was, for a fact, so numerous at first, that they even overturned houses and trees by burrowing beneath them, and that, as I have said,[1] the people were forced to have recourse to the Romans. At present, however, the ease with which the rabbits are caught prevents the pest from prevailing; indeed, the landholders reap profitable crops from the soil. Now these islands are this side of what are called the Pillars of Heracles.

3. Close to the Pillars there are two isles, one of which they call Hera's Island; moreover, there are some who call also these isles the Pillars.[2] Gades, however, is outside the Pillars. Concerning Gades I have said only thus much, that it is about seven hundred and fifty stadia distant from Calpe [3] (that is, it is situated near the outlet of the Baetis), but there is more to be said about it than the others. For example, here live the men who fit out the most and largest merchant-vessels, both for Our Sea and the outer sea, although, in the first place, it is no large island they live in, and, secondly, they do not occupy much of the continent opposite the island, and, thirdly, they are not well-off in the

a temple of Hera (Ptolemaeus 2. 4. 5)—were once regarded as the Pillars. From this, as Gosselin and Groskurd think, the Promontory of Juno became confused with Calpe; hence a Hera's Island at Calpe, and also, Groskurd adds, the invention of a corresponding isle at Abilyx. Cp. the reference to Artemidorus in § 5 below, and see the discussion of Bérard, *Les Phéniciens et l'Odyssée*, vol. i, pp. 264 ff.   [3] 3. 1. 8.

ἄλλων εὐποροῦντες νήσων, ἀλλὰ πλέον οἰκοῦντες
τὴν θάλατταν, ὀλίγοι δ' οἰκουροῦντες ἢ ἐν Ῥώμῃ
C 169 διατρίβοντες. ἐπεὶ πλήθει γε οὐδεμιᾶς ἂν ἀπολείπεσθαι δόξειε τῶν ἔξω Ῥώμης πόλεω· · ἤκουσα
γοῦν ἐν μιᾷ τῶν καθ' ἡμᾶς τιμήσεων πεντακοσίους
ἄνδρας τιμηθέντας ἱππικοὺς Γαδιτανούς, ὅσους
οὐδένας οὐδὲ τῶν Ἰταλιωτῶν πλὴν τῶν Πα-
ταουίνων. τοσοῦτοι δ' ὄντες νῆσον ἔχουσιν οὐ
πολὺ μείζονα τῶν ἑκατὸν σταδίων τὸ μῆκος,
πλάτος δ' ἔσθ' ὅπου καὶ σταδιαῖον. πόλιν δὲ
κατ' ἀρχὰς μὲν ᾤκουν παντάπασι μικράν, προσ-
έκτισε δ' αὐτοῖς Βάλβος Γαδιτανὸς ὁ θριαμβεύσας
ἄλλην, ἣν Νέαν καλοῦσι· τὴν δ' ἐξ ἀμφοῖν Δίδυ-
μην, οὐ πλειόνων εἴκοσι σταδίων οὖσαν τὴν περί-
μετρον, οὐδὲ ταύτην στενοχωρουμένην· ὀλίγοι γὰρ
οἰκουροῦσιν ἐν αὐτῇ διὰ τὸ πάντας θαλαττεύειν
τὸ πλέον, τοὺς δὲ καὶ τὴν περαίαν οἰκεῖν καὶ
μάλιστα τὴν ἐπὶ τῆς προκειμένης νησῖδος διὰ τὴν
εὐφυΐαν, ἣν ὥσπερ ἀντίπολιν πεποιήκασι τῇ
Διδύμῃ, χαίροντες τῷ τόπῳ. ὀλίγοι δὲ κατὰ
σύγκρισιν καὶ ταύτην οἰκοῦσι καὶ τὸ ἐπίνειον ὃ
κατεσκεύασεν αὐτοῖς Βάλβος ἐν τῇ περαίᾳ τῆς
ἠπείρου. κεῖται δ' ἐπὶ τῶν ἑσπερίων τῆς νήσου
μερῶν ἡ πόλις, προσεχὲς δ' αὐτῇ τελευταῖόν ἐστι

---

[1] Cp. 5. 1. 7.
[2] In 19 B.C., for his victory over the Garamantes and other
African peoples.
[3] "New" (City).   [4] "Twin" (City).
[5] Hardly the islet of Trocadero, Tozer thinks (*Selections*,
p. 110), although the description of the islet by Pliny (4. 36)
might suit Trocadero. Both Gosselin and Tozer conjecture
that the islet here mentioned by Strabo has disappeared, or
rather that all that is left of it is the dangerous reef of rocks
off Cadiz to the north.

possession of other islands; indeed, they live mostly on the sea, though a mere few keep at home or else while away their time at Rome. In population, however, Gades does not fall short, it would seem, of any of the cities except Rome; at any rate I have heard that in one of the censuses of our own time there were five hundred men assessed as Gaditanian Knights—a number not equalled even in the case of the Italian cities except Patavium.[1] But though the Gaditanians are so numerous, they occupy an island not much larger than a hundred stadia in length, and in places merely a stadium in breadth. As for their city, the one they lived in at first was very small indeed, but Balbus of Gades, who gained the honour of a triumph,[2] founded another for them, which they call "Nea"[3]; and the city which is composed of the two they call "Didyme,"[4] although it is not more than twenty stadia in circuit, and even at that not crowded. For only a few stay at home in the city, because in general they are all at sea, though some live on the continent opposite the island, and also, in particular, on account of its natural advantages, on the islet that lies off Gades;[5] and because they take delight in its geographical position they have made the islet a rival city, as it were, to Didyme.[4] Only a few, however, comparatively speaking, live either on the islet or in the harbour-town[6] which was constructed for them by Balbus on the opposite coast of the mainland. The city of Gades is situated on the westerly parts of the island; and next to it, at the extremity of

[6] The Portus Gaditanus of the Romans, now known as Puerto Real.

τὸ Κρόνιον πρὸς τῇ νησῖδι· τὸ δ' Ἡράκλειον ἐπὶ
θάτερα τέτραπται[1] πρὸς ἕω, καθ' ὃ δὴ μάλιστα
τῇ ἠπείρῳ τυγχάνει συνάπτουσα ἡ νῆσος ὅσον
σταδιαῖον πορθμὸν ἀπολείπουσα. καὶ λέγουσι
μὲν διέχειν τῆς πόλεως δώδεκα μίλια τὸ ἱερόν,
ἴσον ποιοῦντες τὸν τῶν ἄθλων καὶ τὸν τῶν μιλίων
ἀριθμόν· ἔστι δὲ μεῖζον καὶ σχεδόν τι τοσοῦτον
ὅσον ἐστὶ τὸ τοῦ μήκους τῆς νήσου· μῆκος δ' ἐστὶ
τῆς νήσου τὸ ἀπὸ τῆς δύσεως ἐπὶ τὴν ἀνατολήν.

4. Ἐρύθειαν δὲ τὰ Γάδειρα ἔοικε λέγειν ὁ
Φερεκύδης, ἐν ᾗ τὰ περὶ τὸν Γηρυόνην μυθεύουσιν.
ἄλλοι δὲ τὴν παραβεβλημένην ταύτῃ τῇ πόλει
νῆσον, πορθμῷ σταδιαίῳ διειργομένην, τὸ εὔβοτον
ὁρῶντες, ὅτι τῶν νεμομένων αὐτόθι προβάτων τὸ
γάλα ὀρὸν οὐ ποιεῖ. τυροποιοῦσί τε πολλῷ
ὕδατι μίξαντες διὰ τὴν πιότητα, ἐν πεντήκοντά
τε ἡμέραις πνίγεται τὸ ζῷον, εἰ μή τις ἀποσχάζοι
τι τοῦ αἵματος. ξηρὰ δέ ἐστιν ἣν νέμωνται βο-
τάνην, ἀλλὰ πιαίνει σφόδρα· τεκμαίρονται δ' ἐκ
τούτου[2] πεπλάσθαι τὸν μῦθον τὸν περὶ τὰ βουκό-
λια τοῦ Γηρυόνου. κοινῇ μέντοι συνῴκισται πᾶς
ὁ αἰγιαλός.

---

[1] τά, before πρός, Jones deletes.
[2] τούτου, from the margin of o, for τοῦ (ABC*l*); so the
other editors.

---

[1] This strait is now called the River of St. Peter.
[2] Roman miles.   [3] Of Heracles.
[4] Strabo means the longitudinal distance between the two
extremities of the island.   For his definition of "length,"
see 2. 1. 32 (vol. i, p. 321).   Strabo thought that the length

the island and near the islet, is the temple of Cronus; but the temple of Heracles is situated on the other side, facing towards the east, just where the island runs, it so happens, most closely to the mainland, thus leaving a strait of only about a stadium in width.[1] And they say that the temple is twelve miles [2] distant from the city, thus making the number of the miles equal to that of the Labours ; [3] yet the distance is greater than that and amounts to almost as much as the length of the island ; and the length of the island is that from the west to the east.[4]

4. By " Erytheia," in which the myth-writers place the adventures of Geryon, Pherecydes seems to mean Gades.[5] Others, however, think that Erytheia is the island that lies parallel to this city and is separated from it by a strait of a stadium in width,[6] that is, in view of the fine pasturage there, because the milk of the flocks that pasture there yields no whey. And when they make cheese they first mix the milk with a large amount of water, on account of the fat in the milk. Further, the animals choke to death within fifty days, unless you open a vein and bleed them. The grass upon which they graze is dry, but it makes them very fat; and it is from this fact, it is inferred, that the myth about the cattle of Geryon has been fabricated. The whole of the coast, however, is peopled jointly.[7]

of the island ran about east and west, but it really runs about north-north-west to south-south-east.

[5] Cp. 3. 2. 11.   [6] Cp. Pliny 4. 36.

[7] That is, by both Tyrians and Iberians. We are left to assume that the interior of the island was peopled by Tyrians alone.

5. Περὶ δὲ τῆς κτίσεως τῶν Γαδείρων τοιαῦτα
λέγοντες μέμνηνται Γαδιτανοὶ χρησμοῦ τινος, ὃν
γενέσθαι φασὶ Τυρίοις κελεύοντα ἐπὶ τὰς Ἡρακλέους στήλας ἀποικίαν πέμψαι· τοὺς δὲ πεμφθέν-
τας κατασκοπῆς χάριν, ἐπειδὴ κατὰ τὸν πορθμὸν
ἐγένοντο τὸν κατὰ τὴν Κάλπην, νομίσαντας τέρ-
μονας εἶναι τῆς οἰκουμένης καὶ τῆς Ἡρακλέους
στρατείας τὰ ἄκρα τὰ[1] ποιοῦντα τὸν πορθμόν,
C 170 ταῦτα δ᾽ αὐτὰ καὶ Στήλας ὀνομάζειν τὸ λόγιον,
κατασχεῖν εἴς τι χωρίον ἐντὸς τῶν στενῶν, ἐν ᾧ
νῦν ἐστιν ἡ τῶν Ἐξιτανῶν πόλις· ἐνταῦθα δὲ
θύσαντας, μὴ γενομένων καλῶν τῶν ἱερείων, ἀνα-
κάμψαι πάλιν. χρόνῳ δ᾽ ὕστερον τοὺς πεμφθέν-
τας προελθεῖν ἔξω τοῦ πορθμοῦ περὶ χιλίους
καὶ πεντακοσίους σταδίους εἰς νῆσον Ἡρακλέους
ἱεράν, κειμένην κατὰ πόλιν Ὀνόβαν τῆς Ἰβηρίας,
καὶ νομίσαντας ἐνταῦθα εἶναι τὰς Στήλας θῦσαι
τῷ θεῷ, μὴ γενομένων δὲ πάλιν καλῶν τῶν
ἱερείων, ἐπανελθεῖν οἴκαδε. τῷ δὲ τρίτῳ στόλῳ
τοὺς ἀφικομένους Γάδειρα κτίσαι καὶ ἱδρύσασθαι
τὸ ἱερὸν ἐπὶ τοῖς ἑῴοις τῆς νήσου τὴν δὲ πόλιν
ἐπὶ τοῖς ἑσπερίοις. διὰ δὲ τοῦτο τοὺς μὲν δοκεῖν
τὰ ἄκρα τοῦ πορθμοῦ τὰς Στήλας εἶναι, τοὺς δὲ
τὰ Γάδειρα, τοὺς δ᾽ ἔτι πορρώτερον τῶν Γαδείρων
ἔξω προκεῖσθαι. ἔνιοι δὲ Στήλας ὑπέλαβον τὴν
Κάλπην καὶ τὴν Ἀβίλυκα, τὸ ἀντικείμενον ὄρος

---

[1] τά, Corais inserts before ποιοῦντα.

---

[1] In speaking of the Pillars or the Strait, Strabo always
means "east of" by "inside" and "west of" by "outside."
[2] Gosselin would emend to "five hundred," thus making
the limit of the second expedition the cape of Trafalgar and

5. In telling stories of the following sort about the founding of Gades, the Gaditanians recall a certain oracle, which was actually given, they say, to the Tyrians, ordering them to send a colony to the Pillars of Heracles: The men who were sent for the sake of spying out the region, so the story goes, believed, when they got near to the strait at Calpe, that the two capes which formed the strait were ends of the inhabited world and of Heracles' expedition, and that the capes themselves were what the oracle called "Pillars"; and they therefore landed at a place inside[1] the narrows, namely, where the city of the Exitanians now is; and there they offered sacrifice, but since the sacrifices did not prove favourable they turned homeward again; but the men who were sent at a later period went on outside the strait, about fifteen hundred stadia,[2] to an island sacred to Heracles, situated near the city of Onoba in Iberia, and believing that this was where the Pillars were they offered sacrifice to the god, but since again the sacrifices did not prove favourable they went back home; but the men who arrived on the third expedition founded Gades, and placed the temple in the eastern part of the island but the city in the western. For this reason some are of the opinion that the capes at the strait are the Pillars; others, Gades; and others that they lie on ahead still farther outside the strait than Gades. Again, some have supposed that Calpe and Abilyx are the Pillars, Abilyx being that mountain in Libya

its islets, which are 250 stadia east of Gades, since Gades is 750 stadia (3. 1. 8) from Calpe. But Onoba (Huelva), near which this unidentified island is, is near the mouth of the Odiel River, sixty miles west of Gades.

ἐκ τῆς Λιβύης, ὅ φησιν Ἐρατοσθένης ἐν τῷ Με-
ταγωνίῳ, Νομαδικῷ ἔθνει, ἱδρῦσθαι· οἱ δὲ τὰς
πλησίον ἑκατέρου νησῖδας, ὧν τὴν ἑτέραν Ἥρας
νῆσον ὀνομάζουσιν. Ἀρτεμίδωρος δὲ τὴν μὲν τῆς
Ἥρας νῆσον καὶ ἱερὸν λέγει αὐτῆς, ἄλλην δέ
φησιν εἶναί τινα, οὐδ᾿ Ἀβίλυκα ὄρος οὐδὲ Με-
ταγώνιον ἔθνος. καὶ τὰς Πλαγκτὰς καὶ τὰς
Συμπληγάδας ἐνθάδε μεταφέρουσί τινες, ταύτας
εἶναι νομίζοντες Στήλας, ἃς Πίνδαρος καλεῖ πύλας
Γαδειρίδας, εἰς ταύτας ὑστάτας ἀφῖχθαι φάσκων
τὸν Ἡρακλέα. καὶ Δικαίαρχος δὲ καὶ Ἐρατοσθένης καὶ Πολύβιος καὶ οἱ πλεῖστοι τῶν Ἑλλήνων περὶ τὸν πορθμὸν ἀποφαίνουσι τὰς Στήλας.
οἱ δὲ Ἴβηρες καὶ Λίβυες ἐν Γαδείροις εἶναί φασιν,
οὐδὲν γὰρ ἐοικέναι στήλαις τὰ περὶ τὸν πορθμόν.
οἱ δὲ τὰς ἐν τῷ Ἡρακλείῳ τῷ ἐν Γαδείροις χαλ-
κᾶς ὀκταπήχεις, ἐν αἷς ἀναγέγραπται τὸ ἀνάλωμα τῆς κατασκευῆς τοῦ ἱεροῦ, ταύτας λέγεσθαί
φασιν· ἐφ᾿ ἃς ἐρχόμενοι οἱ τελέσαντες τὸν πλοῦν
καὶ θύοντες τῷ Ἡρακλεῖ διαβοηθῆναι παρεσκεύασαν, ὡς τοῦτ᾿ εἶναι καὶ γῆς καὶ θαλάττης τὸ
πέρας. τοῦτον δ᾿ εἶναι πιθανώτατον καὶ Ποσειδώνιος ἡγεῖται τὸν λόγον, τὸν δὲ χρησμὸν καὶ
τοὺς πολλοὺς ἀποστόλους ψεῦσμα Φοινικικόν.
περὶ μὲν οὖν τῶν ἀποστόλων τί ἄν τις διισχυρί-
σαιτο πρὸς ἔλεγχον ἢ πίστιν, οὐδετέρως παρά-
λογον ὄν[1]; τὸ δὲ τὰς νησῖδας ἢ τὰ ὄρη μὴ φάσκειν

---

[1] ὄν, Kramer inserts, from Casaubon's conj. ; so Meineke.

[1] The passage referred to is otherwise unknown to us.
[2] That is, the account that associates the Pillars of
Heracles with the bronze pillars.

opposite Calpe which is situated, according to Eratosthenes, in Metagonium, country of a nomadic tribe; while others have supposed that the isles near each mountain, one of which they call Hera's Island, are the Pillars. Artemidorus speaks of Hera's Island and her temple, and he says there is a second isle, yet he does not speak of Mount Abilyx or of a Metagonian tribe. There are some who transfer hither both the Planctae and the Symplegades, because they believe these rocks to be the pillars which Pindar calls the "gates of Gades" when he asserts that they are the farthermost limits reached by Heracles.[1] And Dicaearchus, too, and Eratosthenes and Polybius and most of the Greeks represent the Pillars as in the neighbourhood of the strait. But the Iberians and Libyans say that the Pillars are in Gades, for the regions in the neighbourhood of the strait in no respect, they say, resemble pillars. Others say that it is the bronze pillars of eight cubits in the temple of Heracles in Gades, whereon is inscribed the expense incurred in the construction of the temple, that are called the Pillars; and those people who have ended their voyage with visiting these pillars and sacrificing to Heracles have had it noisily spread abroad that this is the end of both land and sea. Poseidonius, too, believes this to be the most plausible account of the matter,[2] but that the oracle and the many expeditions from Tyre are a Phoenician lie.[3] Now, concerning the expeditions, what could one affirm with confidence as to their falsity or trustworthiness when neither of the two opinions is contrary to reason? But to deny that the isles or

[3] Cp. the proverbial "Punic faith."

ἐοικέναι στήλαις, ἀλλὰ ζητεῖν ἐπὶ τῶν κυρίως
λεγομένων στηλῶν τοὺς τῆς οἰκουμένης ὅρους ἢ
τῆς στρατείας τῆς Ἡρακλέους ἔχει μέν τινα νοῦν·
C 171 ἔθος γὰρ παλαιὸν ὑπῆρχε τὸ τίθεσθαι τοιούτους
ὅρους, καθάπερ οἱ Ῥηγῖνοι τὴν στυλίδα ἔθεσαν
τὴν ἐπὶ τῷ Πορθμῷ κειμένην, πυργίον τι, καὶ ὁ
τοῦ Πελώρου λεγόμενος πύργος ἀντίκειται ταύτῃ
τῇ στυλίδι· καὶ οἱ Φιλαίνων λεγόμενοι βωμοὶ
κατὰ μέσην που τὴν μεταξὺ τῶν Σύρτεων γῆν·
καὶ ἐπὶ τῷ ἰσθμῷ τῷ Κορινθιακῷ μνημονεύεται
στήλη τις ἱδρυμένη πρότερον, ἣν ἔστησαν κοινῇ
οἱ τὴν Ἀττικὴν σὺν τῇ Μεγαρίδι κατασχόντες
Ἴωνες, ἐξελαθέντες ἐκ τῆς Πελοποννήσου, καὶ οἱ
κατασχόντες τὴν Πελοπόννησον, ἐπιγράψαντες
ἐπὶ μὲν τοῦ πρὸς τῇ Μεγαρίδι μέρους,

τάδ' οὐχὶ Πελοπόννησος, ἀλλ' Ἰωνία,

ἐκ δὲ θατέρου,

τάδ' ἐστὶ Πελοπόννησος, οὐκ Ἰωνία.

Ἀλέξανδρος δὲ τῆς Ἰνδικῆς στρατείας ὅρια βωμοὺς
ἔθετο ἐν τοῖς τόποις εἰς οὓς ὑστάτους ἀφίκετο
τῶν πρὸς ταῖς ἀνατολαῖς Ἰνδῶν, μιμούμενος τὸν
Ἡρακλέα καὶ τὸν Διόνυσον. ἦν μὲν δὴ τὸ ἔθος
τοῦτο.

---

¹ See 6. 15.　　² See 1. 1. 17.
³ See 17. 3. 20, where Strabo gives the place a different
position, namely, on the coast of the Greater Syrtis, *i. e.* on
the Gulf of Sidra. These altars were said to have been
erected at the boundary between the Carthaginian Empire
and Cyrenaica by the Carthaginian in honour of the two
Philaeni brothers, who, in order to settle the boundary
favourably for Carthage, had given themselves up to be

the mountains resemble pillars, and to search for the limits of the inhabited world or of the expedition of Heracles at Pillars that were properly so called, is indeed a sensible thing to do; for it was a custom in early times to set up landmarks like that. For instance, the people of Rhegium set up the column—a sort of small tower—which stands at the strait;[1] and opposite this column there stands what is called the Tower of Pelorus.[2] And in the land about midway between the Syrtes there stand what are called the Altars of the Philaeni.[3] And mention is made of a pillar placed in former times on the Isthmus of Corinth, which was set up in common by those Ionians who, after their expulsion from the Peloponnesus, got possession of Attica together with Megaris, and by the peoples[4] who got possession of the Peloponnesus; they inscribed on the side of the pillar which faced Megaris, "This is not the Peloponnesus, but Ionia," on the other, "This is the Peloponnesus, not Ionia."[5] Again, Alexander set up altars,[6] as limits of his Indian Expedition, in the farthermost regions reached by him in Eastern India, thus imitating Heracles and Dionysus. So then, this custom was indeed in existence.

buried alive in the sand at the boundary (Sallust *Jugurtha* 79). Pliny (5. 4) says that the altars were of sand, thus implying that the altars were merely the sand-heaps over the two bodies.

[4] The Aeolians and Dorians (see 8. 1. 2).

[5] Plutarch (*Theseus* 25) also quotes the couplet, and says that the pillar was set up by Theseus. Strabo gives a fuller account in 9. 1. 6-7.

[6] Alexander set up twelve altars in honour of the twelve gods (Diodorus Siculus 17. 95).

6. Ἀλλὰ καὶ τοὺς τόπους εἰκός ἐστι μετα-
λαμβάνειν τὴν αὐτὴν προσηγορίαν, καὶ μάλιστα
ἐπειδὰν ὁ χρόνος διαφθείρῃ τοὺς τεθέντας ὅρους.
οὐ γὰρ νῦν οἱ Φιλαίνων βωμοὶ μένουσιν, ἀλλ᾽ ὁ
τόπος μετείληφε τὴν προσηγορίαν· οὐδὲ ἐν τῇ
Ἰνδικῇ στήλας φασὶν ὁραθῆναι κειμένας οὔθ᾽
Ἡρακλέους οὔτε Διονύσου, καὶ λεγομένων μέντοι
καὶ δεικνυμένων τῶν τόπων τινῶν οἱ Μακεδόνες
ἐπίστευον τούτους εἶναι στήλας ἐν οἷς τι σημεῖον
εὕρισκον ἢ τῶν περὶ τὸν Διόνυσον ἱστορουμένων
ἢ τῶν περὶ τὸν Ἡρακλέα. κἀνταῦθα δὴ τοὺς μὲν
πρώτους οὐκ ἂν ἀπιστήσαι τις ὅροις χρήσασθαι
χειροκμήτοις τισί, βωμοῖς ἢ πύργοις ἢ στυλίσιν,
ἐπὶ τῶν τόπων εἰς οὓς ὑστάτους ἧκον τοὺς ἐπιφα-
νεστάτους (ἐπιφανέστατοι δὲ οἱ πορθμοὶ καὶ τὰ
ἐπικείμενα ὄρη καὶ αἱ νησῖδες πρὸς τὸ ἀποδηλοῦν
ἐσχατιάς τε καὶ ἀρχὰς τόπων), ἐκλιπόντων δὲ
τῶν χειροκμήτων ὑπομνημάτων μετενεχθῆναι τοὔνομα εἰς τοὺς τόπους, εἴτε τὰς νησῖδάς τις βούλεται λέγειν εἴτε τὰς ἄκρας τὰς ποιούσας τὸν
πορθμόν. τοῦτο γὰρ ἤδη διορίσασθαι χαλεπόν,
ποτέροις χρὴ προσάψαι τὴν ἐπίκλησιν, διὰ τὸ
ἀμφοτέροις ἐοικέναι τὰς Στήλας. λέγω δὲ ἐοικέναι, διότι ἐν τοῖς τοιούτοις ἵδρυνται τόποις οἳ
σαφῶς τὰς ἐσχατιὰς ὑπαγορεύουσι, καθ᾽ ὃ καὶ
στόμα εἴρηται ὁ πορθμὸς καὶ οὗτος καὶ ἄλλοι
πλείους· τὸ δὲ στόμα πρὸς μὲν εἴσπλουν ἀρχή
ἐστι, πρὸς δὲ ἔκπλουν ἔσχατον. τὰ οὖν ἐπὶ τῷ
στόματι νησίδια, ἔχοντα τὸ εὐπερίγραφόν τε καὶ

---

[1] On the occasion of Alexander's Indian campaign.
[2] Specifically Strabo has in mind Calpe and Abilyx.

6. More than that, it is reasonable for the place where a landmark is to take on the same appellation, and especially after time has once destroyed the landmark that has been set up. For instance, the Altars of the Philaeni no longer remain, yet the place has taken on the appellation. In India, too, there are no pillars, it is said, either of Heracles or of Dionysus to be seen standing, and, of course, when certain of the places there were spoken of or pointed out to the Macedonians,[1] they believed to be Pillars those places only in which they found some sign of the stories told about Dionysus or of those about Heracles. So, in the case of Gades, too, one might not disbelieve that the first visitors used, so to speak, "hand-wrought" landmarks—altars or towers or pillars—setting them up in the most conspicuous of the farthermost places they came to (and the most conspicuous places for denoting both the ends and beginnings of regions are the straits, the mountains there situated,[2] and the isles), and that when the hand-wrought monuments had disappeared, their name was transferred to the places—whether you mean thereby the isles, or the capes that form the strait. For this is a distinction now hard to make —I mean to which of the two we should attach the appellation—because the term "Pillars" suits both. I say "suits" because both are situated in places of a sort that clearly suggest the ends; and it is on the strength of this fact that the strait has been called a "mouth,"—not only this strait, but several others as well: that is, as you sail in, the mouth is the beginning, and, as you sail out, the end. Accordingly, it would not be foolish for one to liken to pillars the isles at the mouth, since they have

σημειῶδες, οὐ φαύλως στήλαις ἀπεικάζοι τις ἄν·
ὡς δ' αὔτως καὶ τὰ ὄρη τὰ ἐπικείμενα τῷ πορθμῷ
καὶ ἐξοχήν τινα τοιαύτην ἐμφαίνοντα οἴαν αἱ
C 172 στυλίδες ἢ αἱ στῆλαι· καὶ ὁ Πίνδαρος οὕτως
ἂν ὀρθῶς λέγοι πύλας Γαδειρίδας, εἰ ἐπὶ τοῦ
στόματος νοοῖντο αἱ στῆλαι· πύλαις γὰρ ἔοικε
τὰ στόματα. τὰ δὲ Γάδειρα οὐκ ἐν τοιούτοις
ἵδρυται τόποις ὥστε ἀποδηλοῦν ἐσχατιάν, ἀλλ'
ἐν μέσῃ πως κεῖται μεγάλῃ παραλίᾳ κολπώδει.
τὸ δὲ ἐπ' αὐτὰς ἀναφέρειν τὰς ἐν τῷ Ἡρακλείῳ
στήλας τῷ ἐνθάδε ἧττον εὔλογον, ὡς ἐμοὶ φαίνε-
ται· οὐ γὰρ ἐμπόρων ἀλλ' ἡγεμόνων μᾶλλον ἀρξάντων τοῦ ὀνόματος τούτου κρατῆσαι πιθανὸν
τὴν δόξαν, καθάπερ καὶ ἐπὶ τῶν Ἰνδικῶν στηλῶν. ἄλλως τε καὶ ἡ ἐπιγραφή, ἥν φασιν,[1] οὐκ
ἀφίδρυμα ἱερὸν δηλοῦσα, ἀλλὰ ἀναλώματος
κεφάλαιον, ἀντιμαρτυρεῖ τῷ λόγῳ· τὰς γὰρ
Ἡρακλείους στήλας μνημεῖα εἶναι δεῖ τῆς ἐκείνου
μεγαλουργίας, οὐ τῆς Φοινίκων δαπάνης.

7. Φησὶ δὲ ὁ Πολύβιος κρήνην ἐν τῷ Ἡρακλείῳ
τῷ ἐν Γαδείροις εἶναι, βαθμῶν ὀλίγων κατάβασιν
ἔχουσαν εἰς τὸ ὕδωρ πότιμον, ἣν ταῖς παλιρροίαις
τῆς θαλάττης ἀντιπαθεῖν, κατὰ μὲν τὰς πλήμας
ἐκλείπουσαν, κατὰ δὲ τὰς ἀμπώτεις πληρουμένην.
αἰτιᾶται δ' ὅτι τὸ πνεῦμα τὸ ἐκ τοῦ βάθους εἰς

---

[1] φασιν, Corais, for φησιν; so subsequent editors.

---

[1] On the bronze pillars (§ 5).
[2] That is, the dedication to Heracles of a reproduction
(in bronze) of the original pillars, with a record of his
achievements.

the attributes of being both sharp of outline and
conspicuous as signs; and so, in the same way, it
would not be foolish to liken to pillars the mountains that are situated at the strait, since they
present just such a prominent appearance as do
columns or pillars. And in this way Pindar would
be right in speaking of the "gates of Gades," if the
pillars were conceived of as at the mouth; for the
mouths of straits are like gates. But Gades is not
situated in such a geographical position as to denote
an end; rather it lies at about the centre of a long
coastline that forms a bay. And the argument that
refers those pillars which are in the temple of Heracles
at Gades to the Pillars of Heracles is less reasonable
still, as it appears to me. For it is plausible that
the fame of the name "Pillars of Heracles" prevailed
because the name originated, not with merchants,
but rather with commanders, just as in the case of
the Indian pillars; and besides that, "the inscription"[1] which they speak of, since it does not set
forth the dedication of a reproduction[2] but instead
a summary of expense, bears witness against the
argument; for the Heracleian pillars should be re-
minders of Heracles' mighty doings, not of the
expenses of the Phoenicians.

7. Polybius says that there is a spring in the
Heracleium[3] at Gades, with a descent of only a few
steps to the water (which is good to drink), and
that the spring behaves inversely to the flux and
reflux of the sea, since it fails at the time of the
flood-tides and fills up at the time of the ebb-tides.
And he alleges as the cause of this that the air

---

[3] The Heracleium includes both the temple and the sacred
precinct of Heracles (cp. § 9 below).

τὴν ἐπιφάνειαν τῆς γῆς ἐκπῖπτον, καλυφθείσης
μὲν αὐτῆς ὑπὸ τοῦ κύματος κατὰ τὰς ἐπιβάσεις
τῆς θαλάττης, εἴργεται τῶν οἰκείων τοιούτων
ἐξόδων, ἀναστρέψαν δὲ εἰς τὸ ἐντὸς ἐμφράττει
τοὺς τῆς πηγῆς πόρους καὶ ποιεῖ λειψυδρίαν,
γυμνωθείσης δὲ πάλιν, εὐθυπορῆσαν ἐλευθεροῖ
τὰς φλέβας τῆς πηγῆς, ὥστ' ἀναβλύειν εὐπόρως.
Ἀρτεμίδωρος δὲ ἀντειπὼν τούτῳ καὶ ἅμα παρ'
αὑτοῦ τινα θεὶς αἰτίαν, μνησθεὶς δὲ καὶ τῆς Σιλα-
νοῦ δόξης τοῦ συγγραφέως, οὔ μοι δοκεῖ μνήμης
ἄξια εἰπεῖν, ὡς ἂν ἰδιώτης περὶ ταῦτα καὶ αὐτὸς
καὶ Σιλανός. Ποσειδώνιος δὲ ψευδῆ λέγων τὴν
ἱστορίαν εἶναι ταύτην δύο φησὶ εἶναι φρέατα ἐν
τῷ Ἡρακλείῳ καὶ τρίτον ἐν τῇ πόλει· τῶν δ'
ἐν τῷ Ἡρακλείῳ τὸ μὲν μικρότερον ὑδρευομένων
συνεχῶς αὐθωρὸν καὶ ἐκλείπειν, καὶ διαλειπόντων
τῆς ὑδρείας πληροῦσθαι πάλιν· τὸ δὲ μεῖζον δι'
ὅλης τῆς ἡμέρας τὴν ὑδρείαν ἔχον, μειούμενον
μέντοι, καθάπερ καὶ τἆλλα φρέατα πάντα, νύκτωρ πληροῦσθαι, μηκέτι ὑδρευομένων· ἐπειδὴ δὲ
συμπίπτει κατὰ τὸν τῆς συμπληρώσεως καιρὸν
ἡ ἄμπωτις πολλάκις, πεπιστεῦσθαι καινῶς[1] ὑπὸ
τῶν ἐγχωρίων τὴν ἀντιπάθειαν.[2] ὅτι μὲν οὖν ἡ
ἱστορία πεπίστευται καὶ οὗτος εἴρηκε καὶ ἡμεῖς
ἐν τοῖς παραδόξοις θρυλουμένην παρειλήφαμεν.

---

[1] Casaubon and subsequent editors emend καινῶς to
κενῶς.

[2] ἀντιπάθειαν, Xylander, for ἀντίπλοιαν; so subsequent
editors.

---

[1] Polybius has said that there was "a spring in the Heracleium"; Poseidonius says "two wells"; but Pliny (2. 100)
says, "At Gades, which is very near the temple of Heracles,

which is expelled from the depths of the earth to the surface, if the surface be covered by the waters at the time of the overflows of the sea, is shut off from its proper exits there, and turning back into the interior blocks up the passages of the spring and thus causes a failure of water, whereas if the surface be bared of the waters again the air passes straight forward and thus sets free the veins of the spring, so that it gushes forth abundantly. As for Artemidorus, although he speaks out against Polybius and at the same time puts forth a cause of his own, and also recalls the opinion of Silanus the historian, he does not seem to me to have stated anything worth recording, since both he himself and Silanus are, you might say, laymen with respect to these matters. But Poseidonius, although he calls the story of this spring false, says that there are two wells[1] in the Heracleium and a third in the city; and, of the two wells in the Heracleium, if you draw water continuously from the smaller it actually fails in the same hour, and if you leave off drawing the water, it fills up again; whereas you may draw water all day long from the larger (though it is diminished thereby, of course, just as all other wells are), and it fills up by night if you no longer draw from it, but since the ebb-tide often occurs at the particular time of the well's fullness, the natives have believed anew in the inverse-behaviour. Now not only has Poseidonius told us that the story has been believed, but I too, since it is told over and over again among the paradoxes,[2] have been taught the story. And I

there is a spring, enclosed like a well," to which he ascribes the phenomenon of the inverse-behaviour.

[2] The paradoxes constituted an important part of the teachings of the Stoics; and Strabo was a Stoic.

STRABO

C 173 ἠκούομεν δὲ καὶ φρέατα εἶναι, τὰ μὲν πρὸ τῆς
πόλεως ἐν τοῖς κήποις τὰ δὲ ἐντός, διὰ δὲ τὴν
μοχθηρίαν τοῦ ὕδατος κατὰ τὴν πόλιν δεξαμενὰς
ἐπιπολάζειν τοῦ λακκαίου ὕδατος· εἰ μέντοι καὶ
τούτων τι τῶν φρεάτων ἐπιδείκνυται τὴν τῆς
ἀντιπαθείας ὑπόνοιαν, οὐκ ἴσμεν. τὰς δ' αἰτίας,
εἴπερ συμβαίνει ταῦτα οὕτως, ὡς ἐν χαλεποῖς
ἀποδέχεσθαι δεῖ. εἰκὸς μὲν γὰρ οὕτως ἔχειν ὡς
ὁ Πολύβιός φησιν· εἰκὸς δὲ καὶ τῶν φλεβῶν τινας
τῶν πηγαίων νοτισθείσας ἔξωθεν χαυνοῦσθαι καὶ
παρέκχυσιν εἰς τὰ πλάγια μᾶλλον διδόναι τοῖς
ὕδασιν ἢ ἀναθλίβειν κατὰ τὸ ἀρχαῖον ῥεῖθρον
εἰς τὴν κρήνην (νοτίζεσθαι δ' ἀναγκαῖον, ἐπικλύ-
σαντος τοῦ κύματος). εἰ δ', ὥσπερ Ἀθηνόδωρός
φησιν, εἰσπνοῇ τε καὶ ἐκπνοῇ τὸ συμβαῖνον περὶ
τὰς πλημμυρίδας καὶ περὶ τὰς ἀμπώτεις ἔοικεν,
εἶναι ἄν τινα τῶν ῥεόντων ὑδάτων, ἃ κατ' ἄλλους
μὲν πόρους ἔχει τὴν ἔκρυσιν κατὰ φύσιν εἰς τὴν
ἐπιφάνειαν, ὧν δὴ τὰ στόματα πηγὰς καὶ κρήνας
καλοῦμεν, κατ' ἄλλους δὲ πόρους συνέλκεται πρὸς
τὸ τῆς θαλάττης βάθος· καὶ συνεξαίροντα μὲν
ἐκείνην, ὥστε πλημμυρεῖν, ὅταν οἷον ἡ ἐκπνοὴ
γίνηται, τὸ οἰκεῖον ἀπολείπει ῥεῖθρον, πάλιν δ'
ἀναχωρεῖ πρὸς τὸ οἰκεῖον ῥεῖθρον ὅταν κἀκείνη
λάβῃ τὴν ἀναχώρησιν.

8. Οὐκ οἶδα δὲ πῶς κατ' ἄλλα δεινοὺς ἀποφαίνων ὁ Ποσειδώνιος τοὺς Φοίνικας, ἐνταῦθα

---

[1] Strabo considered Athenodorus and Poseidonius the best
authorities on the ocean and the tides (1. 1. 9). He has
already compared the sea to animated beings (1. 3. 8). And
it was a popular doctrine among the Greek and Roman
philosophers that the universe was an animal; and in this
way they accounted for the tides (Pomponius Mela 3. 1).

have been hearing that there are still other wells,
some in the gardens in front of the city, and others
within the city, but that on account of the impurity
of the water reservoirs of cistern-water are prevalent
in the city. Whether, however, any of these wells
proves the truth of the supposition of the inverse-
behaviour, I do not know. But as for the causes
alleged—if it be true that the case is as reported—
we should, regarding the problem as a difficult one,
welcome them. For it is reasonable to suppose that
the cause is what Polybius says it is; and it is
reasonable to suppose also that some of the veins
of the spring, if soaked from the outside, become
relaxed and thus afford their water an outflow at
the sides, instead of forcing it up along the old
channel into the spring (the veins are of necessity
soaked when the tidal wave has washed over the
land). Yet if, as Athenodorus says, the case with
the flood-tides and with the ebb-tides is like in-
halation and exhalation,[1] then, of the flowing
waters, he says, there might be some which by
certain passages (whose mouths, of course, we call
fountains or springs) naturally have their outflow
to the surface, and by certain other passages are
drawn in together to the depths of the sea; that
is, in helping raise the sea[2] to flood-tide when the
exhalation, as it were, takes place, they abandon
their proper channel, and then retreat to their
proper channel again when the sea itself takes its
retreat.

8. I do not know how Poseidonius, who in other
instances has represented the Phoenicians as clever

[2] See the argument of Strato the physicist and the discussion of Strabo in 1. 3. 4-5.

μωρίαν μᾶλλον ἢ δριμύτητα αὐτῶν κατέγνωκεν.
ἡμέρα μὲν γὰρ καὶ νὺξ τῇ τοῦ ἡλίου περιφορᾷ[1]
μετρεῖται, τοτὲ μὲν ὑπὸ γῆς ὄντος, τοτὲ δὲ ὑπὲρ
γῆς φαινομένου· φησὶ δὲ τὴν τοῦ ὠκεανοῦ κίνησιν
ὑπέχειν ἀστροειδῆ περίοδον, τὴν μὲν ἡμερήσιον
ἀποδιδοῦσαν, τὴν δὲ μηνιαίαν, τὴν δ' ἐνιαυσιαίαν
συμπαθῶς τῇ σελήνῃ. ὅταν γὰρ αὕτη ζῳδίου μέγεθος ὑπερέχῃ τοῦ ὁρίζοντος, ἄρχεσθαι διοιδεῖν[2]
τὴν θάλατταν καὶ ἐπιβαίνειν τῆς γῆς αἰσθητῶς
μέχρι μεσουρανήσεως· ἐκκλίναντος δὲ τοῦ ἄστρου,
πάλιν ἀναχωρεῖν τὸ πέλαγος κατ' ὀλίγον, ἕως ἂν
ζῴδιον ὑπερέχῃ τῆς δύσεως ἡ σελήνη· εἶτα μένειν
τοσοῦτον ἐν τῇ αὐτῇ καταστάσει χρόνον ὅσον ἡ
σελήνη συνάπτει πρὸς αὐτὴν τὴν δύσιν, καὶ ἔτι
μᾶλλον τοσοῦτον ὅσον κινηθεῖσα ὑπὸ γῆς ζῴδιον
ἀπόσχοι ἂν τοῦ ὁρίζοντος· εἶτ' ἐπιβαίνειν πάλιν
ἕως τοῦ ὑπὸ γῆν μεσουρανήματος· εἶτ' ἀναχωρεῖν
ἕως ἂν πρὸς τὰς ἀνατολὰς περιχωρήσασα ἡ σελήνη
ζῴδιον τοῦ ὁρίζοντος ἀπόσχῃ· μένειν δὲ μέχρις ἂν
C 174 ζῴδιον ὑπὲρ γῆς μετεωρισθῇ, καὶ πάλιν ἐπιβαίνειν.
ταύτην μὲν εἶναι λέγει τὴν ἡμερήσιον περίοδον·
τὴν δὲ μηνιαίαν, ὅτι μέγισται μὲν αἱ παλίρροιαι
γίγνονται περὶ τὰς συνόδους, εἶτα μειοῦνται μέχρι
διχοτόμου· πάλιν δ' αὔξονται μέχρι πανσελήνου,
καὶ μειοῦνται πάλιν ἕως διχοτόμου φθινάδος· εἶθ'

---

[1] τῇ ... περιφορᾷ, Corais, for ἡ ... περιφορά; so the
subsequent editors.
[2] διοιδεῖν, the reading of the Epitome, for δεῖν ABCE*l*.

---

[1] That is, 30°.
[2] That is, when the sun and moon meet or pass each other
in the same degree of the zodiac; and hence at the time
of the new moon.

people, can here charge them with foolishness
rather than shrewdness. In the first place, a day
and night is measured by the revolution of the sun,
which, at one time, is below the earth, but, at
another, shines above the earth. And yet Poseidonius says that the movement of the ocean is
subject to periods like those of the heavenly bodies,
since, behaving in accord with the moon, the movement exhibits first the diurnal, secondly the monthly,
and thirdly the yearly period; for when the moon
rises above the horizon to the extent of a zodiacal
sign,[1] the sea begins to swell, and perceptibly invades the land until the moon is in the meridian;
but when the heavenly body has begun to decline,
the sea retreats again, little by little, until the moon
rises a zodiacal sign above her setting; then remains
stationary until such time as the moon reaches the
setting itself, and, still more than that, until such
time as the moon, moving on below the earth,
should be a sign distant from the horizon; then
invades the land again until the moon reaches the
meridian below the earth; then retreats until the
moon, moving round towards her risings, is a sign
distant from the horizon; but remains stationary
again until the moon is elevated a sign above
the earth, and then it again invades the land.
This, he continues, is the diurnal period. As for
the monthly period, he says the flux and reflux become greatest about the time of the conjunction,[2]
and then diminish until the half-moon;[3] and, again,
they increase until the full moon and diminish again
until the waning half-moon;[4] and then, until the

[3] The first quarter.   [4] The third quarter.

ἕως τῶν συνόδων αἱ αὐξήσεις, πλεονάζειν δὲ καὶ
χρόνῳ καὶ τάχει τὰς αὐξήσεις. τὰς δ' ἐνιαυσιαίας
παρὰ τῶν ἐν Γαδείροις πυθέσθαι φησί, λεγόντων
ὡς κατὰ θερινὰς τροπὰς μάλιστα αὔξοιντο καὶ αἱ
ἀναχωρήσεις καὶ αἱ ἐπιβάσεις. εἰκάζει δ' αὐτὸς
ἀπὸ τῶν τροπῶν μειοῦσθαι μὲν ἕως ἰσημερίας,
αὔξεσθαι δὲ ἕως χειμερινῶν τροπῶν, εἶτα μειοῦσθαι μέχρι ἐαρινῆς ἰσημερίας, εἶτ' αὔξεσθαι μέχρι
θερινῶν τροπῶν. τῶν δὲ περιόδων τούτων οὐσῶν
καθ' ἐκάστην ἡμέραν καὶ νύκτα, τὸν συνάμφω
χρόνον δὶς μὲν ἐπιβαινούσης τῆς θαλάττης, δὶς
δὲ ἀναχωρούσης, τεταγμένως δὲ καὶ τῶν ἡμερησίων
χρόνων καὶ τῶν νυκτερινῶν, πῶς οἷόν τε πολλάκις
μὲν συμβαίνειν κατὰ τὰς ἀμπώτεις τὴν πλήρωσιν
τοῦ φρέατος, μὴ πολλάκις δὲ τὴν λειψυδρίαν; ἢ
πολλάκις μέν, μὴ ἰσάκις δέ; ἢ καὶ ἰσάκις[1] μέν,
τοὺς δὲ Γαδειρίτας ταῦτα μὲν μὴ ἱκανοὺς γενέσθαι
τηρῆσαι τὰ καθ' ἡμέραν γινόμενα, τὰς δ' ἐνιαυσίους περιόδους ἐκ τῶν ἅπαξ συμβαινόντων κατ'
ἔτος τηρῆσαι;[2] ἀλλὰ μὴν ὅτι γε πιστεύει αὐτοῖς,
δῆλον ἐξ ὧν καὶ προσεικάζει γίνεσθαι[3] τὰς μειώ-
σεις καὶ πάλιν αὐξήσεις ἀπὸ τροπῶν ἐπὶ τροπάς
τε ἑτέρας κἀκεῖθεν πάλιν ἐπανόδους. καὶ μὴν

---

[1] δέ, before μέν, Meineke omits.
[2] τὰ καθ' ἡμέραν γινόμενα, after τηρῆσαι, Corais and the others omit.
[3] γίνεσθαι, Corais, for γενέσθαι; the subsequent editors following.

---

[1] That is, from the time of the third quarter on to that of the new moon, the interval of time between high-tide and high-tide (or low-tide and low-tide) increases, the same being also true of the velocity.

conjunction, the increases take place again, and the increases are further increased in respect both to duration and to speed.[1] As for the annual periods, he says that he learned of them from the people at Gades, who told him that both the retreat and the invasion grew greatest at the time of the summer solstice. And from this he himself surmises that they are diminished from that solstice up to the equinox,[2] increased up to the winter solstice, then diminished up to the spring equinox, and then increased up to the summer solstice. But if these periods repeat themselves every separate day and night, the sea invading the land twice and also retreating twice during the combined time of day and night, in regular order both within the day-time and within the night-time, how is it possible for the filling up of the well to occur "often" at the time of the ebb-tides[3] but for the failure not also to occur often? or often, but not equally often? or even equally often indeed, but for the people of Gades to have been incapable of observing these phenomena that were taking place every day, and yet to have been capable of observing the annual periods from what occurred only once a year? Furthermore, that Poseidonius really believes these people, is clear from the surmise which he adds to their story, namely, that the diminutions, and, in turn, the increases, take place from one solstice on to the other, and also that recurrences take place from the latter solstice back to the former. Moreover, that other

---

[2] The autumnal equinox.
[3] This assertion is attributed by Strabo to Poseidonius, not to the Phoenicians (cp. § 7 above).

οὐδὲ ἐκεῖνο εἰκός, ὅτι τηρητικοὶ ὄντες τὰ μὲν συμβαίνοντα οὐκ εἶδον, τοῖς δὲ μὴ συμβαίνουσιν ἐπίστευσαν.

9. Φησὶ δ᾽ οὖν Σέλευκον τὸν ἀπὸ τῆς Ἐρυθρᾶς θαλάττης καὶ ἀνωμαλίαν τινὰ ἐν τούτοις καὶ ὁμαλότητα λέγειν κατὰ τὰς τῶν ζῳδίων διαφοράς· ἐν μὲν γὰρ τοῖς ἰσημερινοῖς ζῳδίοις τῆς σελήνης οὔσης ὁμαλίζειν τὰ πάθη, ἐν δὲ τοῖς τροπικοῖς ἀνωμαλίαν εἶναι, καὶ πλήθει καὶ τάχει, τῶν δ᾽ ἄλλων ἑκάστῳ κατὰ τοὺς συνεγγισμοὺς εἶναι τὴν ἀναλογίαν. αὐτὸς δὲ κατὰ τὰς θερινὰς τροπὰς περὶ τὴν πανσέληνόν φησιν ἐν τῷ Ἡρακλείῳ γενόμενος τῷ ἐν Γαδείροις πλείους ἡμέρας μὴ δύνασθαι συνεῖναι τὰς ἐνιαυσίους διαφοράς. περὶ μέντοι τὴν σύνοδον ἐκείνου τοῦ μηνὸς τηρῆσαι μεγάλην παραλλαγὴν ἐν Ἰλίπᾳ τῆς τοῦ Βαίτιος ἀνακοπῆς παρὰ τὰς ἔμπροσθεν, ἐν αἷς οὐδὲ ἕως ἡμίσους τὰς
C 175   ὄχθας ἔβρεχε· τότε δ᾽ ὑπερχεῖσθαι τὸ ὕδωρ ὥσθ᾽ ὑδρεύεσθαι τοὺς στρατιώτας αὐτόθι (διέχει δ᾽

---

[1] At the beginning of § 8 Strabo sets out, rather captiously, to prove inconsistency and injustice on the part of Poseidonius. The latter had accused the Phoenicians (the people of Gades) of having the foolish notion about the "reverse-behaviour," of being incapable of seeing the daily phenomena, and of believing in things that did not occur; nevertheless, Strabo means, Poseidonius bases his own remarks about the tides upon what he had learned from the people of Gades, for example, that "the retreat and the invasion grew greatest at the time of the summer solstice." Of course, Strabo denies neither Poseidonius' account of the tides, nor the relation that Poseidonius says exists between the tides and the motion of the moon, both of which, so far as they go, are substantially correct. Cp. Pliny, 2. 99.

[2] The Chaldaean astronomer (1. 1. 9. and 16. 1. 6).

supposition of Poseidonius is not reasonable either, namely, that, although they were an observant people, they did not see the phenomena that occurred and yet believed in the things that did not occur.[1]

9. Be that as it may, he says that Seleucus—the Seleucus[2] from the region of the Erythraean Sea—speaks of a certain irregularity in these phenomena, or regularity, according to the differences of the signs of the zodiac; that is, if the moon is in the equinoctial signs, the behaviour of the tides is regular, but, in the solstitial signs, irregular, in respect both to amount and to speed, while, in each of the other signs, the relation[3] is in proportion to the nearness of the moon's approach.[4] But although he himself spent several days in the Heracleium at Gades at the summer solstice, about the time of the full moon, as he says, he was unable to discern those annual differences in the tides; about the time of the conjunction, however, during that month, he observed at Ilipa a great variation in the back-water of the Baetis, that is, as compared with the previous variations, in the course of which the water did not wet the banks so much as half-way up, whereas at the time in question the water overflowed to such an extent that the soldiers[5] got their supply of water on the spot (and Ilipa is about

[3] That is, the comparative regularity or irregularity of the tides.

[4] That is, to the equinoctial or the solstitial signs. It is clear from this passage that Seleucus had solved the law which governs the diurnal inequality of the tide in the Indian Ocean.

[5] That is, the Roman soldiers who were stationed at Ilipa.

Ἰλίπα τῆς θαλάττης περὶ ἑπτακοσίους σταδίους)·
τῶν δ' ἐπὶ θαλάττῃ πεδίων καὶ ἐπὶ τριάκοντα
σταδίους εἰς βάθος καλυπτομένων ὑπὸ τῆς πλημμυρίδος ὥστε καὶ νήσους ἀπολαμβάνεσθαι, τὸ τῆς
κρηπῖδος ὕψος τῆς τε τοῦ νεὼ τοῦ ἐν τῷ Ἡρακλείῳ
καὶ τῆς τοῦ χώματος ὃ τοῦ λιμένος πρόκειται τοῦ
ἐν Γαδείροις, οὐδ' ἐπὶ δέκα πήχεις καλυπτόμενον
ἀναμετρῆσαί φησι· κἂν προσθῇ δέ τις τὸ διπλάσιον τούτου κατὰ τὰς γενομένας ποτὲ παραυξή-
σεις, οὕτω παρασχεῖν ἂν τὴν ἔμφασιν, ἣν ἐν τοῖς
πεδίοις παρέχεται τὸ μέγεθος τῆς πλημμυρίδος.
τοῦτο μὲν δὴ τὸ πάθος κοινὸν ἱστορεῖται κατὰ
πᾶσαν τὴν κύκλῳ παρωκεανῖτιν, τὸ δὲ τοῦ Ἴβηρος
ποταμοῦ καινὸν καὶ ἴδιον, φησὶν οὗτος· πλημμυρεῖν
γὰρ ἔσθ' ὅπου τε, καὶ χωρὶς ὄμβρων καὶ χιόνων,
ἐπειδὰν τὰ βόρεια πνεύματα πλεονάσῃ, αἰτίαν δ'
εἶναι τὴν λίμνην δι' ἧς ῥεῖ· συνεκβάλλεσθαι γὰρ
τὸ λιμναῖον ὑπὸ τῶν ἀνέμων.

10. Ἱστορεῖ δὲ καὶ δένδρον ἐν Γαδείροις ὄζους
ἔχον καμπτομένους εἰς ἔδαφος, πολλάκις δὲ φύλλα
ξιφοειδῆ πηχυαῖα τὸ μῆκος, πλάτος δὲ τετρα-
δάκτυλα. περὶ δὲ Νέαν Καρχηδόνα δένδρον ἐξ
ἀκάνθης φλοιὸν ἀφιέναι, ἐξ οὗ ὑφάσματα γίνεται
κάλλιστα. τῷ μὲν οὖν ἐν Γαδείροις καὶ ἡμεῖς
οἴδαμεν[1] ὅμοιον ἐν Αἰγύπτῳ κατὰ τὴν τῶν κλά-

---

[1] Corais, Cobet, and Vogel would follow the reading of B and h : εἴδομεν.

---

[1] Some of the MSS. read "fifty."
[2] See 3. 2. 4. [3] Perhaps the *Dracaena Draco*.
[4] Strabo apparently means the fibre ("bark") in the leaf-sheaths ("thorns") of the European dwarf fan-palm

seven hundred stadia distant from the sea). And, he continues, although the plains near the sea were covered as far as thirty[1] stadia inland, to such a depth that islands were enclosed by the flood-tide,[2] still the altitude of the foundations, both the foundation of the temple in the Heracleïum and that of the mole which lies in front of the port of Gades, was, by his own measurement, as he says, not covered as high up as ten cubits; and further, if one should add the double of this figure for the additional increases which at times have taken place, one might thus present to the imagination the aspect which is produced in the plains by the magnitude of the flood-tide. This behaviour of the tides, then, according to his account, is general along the whole circuit of the ocean-coast, whereas the behaviour of the Iberus River is "novel, and peculiar," he says, to that river, namely: it floods the country in some places, even independently of rains or snows, when the north winds blow to excess; and the lake through which the river flows is the cause of this, since the lake-water is by the winds driven out of the lake along with the river-water.

10. Poseidonius also tells of a tree[3] in Gades which has branches that bend to the ground, and often-times has leaves (they are sword-like) a cubit in length but only four fingers in breadth. And near New Carthage, he says, there is a tree whose thorns yield a bark[4] out of which most beautiful woven stuffs are made. Now I too know a tree[5] in Egypt which is like that in Gades so far as the bending

(*Chamaerops humilis*). This fibre is called "African hair," and a fabric like haircloth is still made from it.

[5] Clearly a tree of the genus *Salix* (willow family).

δων κατάκαμψιν, τοῖς δὲ φύλλοις ἀνόμοιον, οὐδὲ καρπὸν ἔχον· τοῦτο δ' ἔχειν φησί. τὰ δ' ἀκάνθινα ὑφαίνεται καὶ ἐν Καππαδοκίᾳ, φέρει δ' οὐδὲν δένδρον τὴν ἄκανθαν, ἐξ ἧς ὁ φλοιός, ἀλλὰ χαμαίζηλος ἡ βοτάνη. τῷ δὲ δένδρῳ τῷ ἐν Γαδείροις καὶ τοῦτο προσιστόρηται, ὅτι κλάδου μὲν ἀποκλωμένου γάλα ῥεῖ, ῥίζης δὲ τεμνομένης μιλτῶδες ὑγρὸν ἀναφέρεται. τοσαῦτα καὶ περὶ Γαδείρων.

11. Αἱ δὲ Καττιτερίδες δέκα μέν εἰσι, κεῖνται δ' ἐγγὺς ἀλλήλων, πρὸς ἄρκτον ἀπὸ τοῦ τῶν Ἀρτάβρων λιμένος πελάγιαι· μία δ' αὐτῶν ἔρημός ἐστι, τὰς δ' ἄλλας οἰκοῦσιν ἄνθρωποι μελάγχλαινοι, ποδήρεις ἐνδεδυκότες τοὺς χιτῶνας, ἐζωσμένοι περὶ τὰ στέρνα, μετὰ ῥάβδων περιπατοῦντες, ὅμοιοι ταῖς τραγικαῖς Ποιναῖς· ζῶσι δ' ἀπὸ βοσκημάτων νομαδικῶς τὸ πλέον. μέταλλα δὲ ἔχοντες καττιτέρου καὶ μολύβδου κέραμον ἀντὶ τούτων καὶ τῶν δερμάτων διαλλάττονται καὶ ἅλας καὶ χαλκώματα πρὸς τοὺς ἐμπόρους. πρότερον μὲν οὖν Φοίνικες μόνοι τὴν ἐμπορίαν ἔστελλον ταύτην ἐκ τῶν Γαδείρων, κρύπτοντες ἅπασι τὸν πλοῦν· τῶν δὲ Ῥωμαίων ἐπακολουθούντων ναυκλήρῳ τινί, C 176 ὅπως καὶ αὐτοὶ γνοῖεν τὰ ἐμπόρια, φθόνῳ ὁ ναύκληρος ἑκὼν εἰς τέναγος ἐξέβαλε τὴν ναῦν, ἐπαγαγὼν δ' εἰς τὸν αὐτὸν ὄλεθρον καὶ τοὺς ἑπομένους, αὐτὸς ἐσώθη διὰ ναυαγίου καὶ ἀπέλαβε δημοσίᾳ τὴν τιμὴν ὧν ἀπέβαλε φορτίων. οἱ Ῥωμαῖοι δὲ ὅμως πειρώμενοι πολλάκις ἐξέμαθον τὸν πλοῦν·

down of the branches is concerned, but unlike it in respect to the leaves and also in that it has no fruit (he says the tree in Gades has fruit). Thorn-stuffs are woven in Cappadocia also; it is no tree, however, that produces the bark-yielding thorn, but only a sort of herb that keeps close to the ground. In regard to the tree at Gades, this additional circumstance is told: if a branch is broken, milk flows from it, while if a root is cut, a red liquid oozes forth. Concerning Gades, then, I have said enough.

11. The Cassiterides are ten in number, and they lie near each other in the high sea to the north of the port of the Artabrians. One of them is desert, but the rest are inhabited by people who wear black cloaks, go clad in tunics that reach to their feet, wear belts around their breasts, walk around with canes, and resemble the goddesses of Vengeance in tragedies. They live off their herds, leading for the most part a nomadic life. As they have mines of tin and lead, they give these metals and the hides from their cattle to the sea-traders in exchange for pottery, salt and copper utensils. Now in former times it was the Phoenicians alone who carried on this commerce (that is, from Gades), for they kept the voyage hidden from every one else. And when once the Romans were closely following a certain ship-captain in order that they too might learn the markets in question, out of jealousy the ship-captain purposely drove his ship out of its course into shoal water; and after he had lured the followers into the same ruin, he himself escaped by a piece of wreckage and received from the State the value of the cargo he had lost. Still, by trying many times, the Romans learned all about the

ἐπειδὴ δὲ καὶ Πόπλιος Κράσσος διαβὰς ἐπ' αὐτοὺς ἔγνω τὰ μέταλλα ἐκ μικροῦ βάθους ὀρυττό-
μενα καὶ τοὺς ἄνδρας εἰρηναίους, ἐκ περιουσίας
ἤδη τὴν θάλατταν ἐργάζεσθαι ταύτην τοῖς ἐθέλου-
σιν ἐπέδειξε, καίπερ οὖσαν πλείω τῆς διειργούσης[1]
τὴν Βρεττανικήν. καὶ περὶ μὲν Ἰβηρίας καὶ τῶν
προκειμένων νήσων ταῦτα.

[1] εἰς, before τήν, Corais deletes; so subsequent editors.

voyage After Publius Crassus crossed over to these
people and saw that the metals were being dug
from only a slight depth, and that the men there
were peaceable, he forthwith laid abundant information before all who wished to traffic over this sea,
albeit a wider sea than that which separates Britain
from the continent. So much, then, for Iberia and
the islands that lie off its coast.

BOOK IV

Δ´

I

1. Ἐφεξῆς δ᾽ ἐστὶν ἡ ὑπὲρ τῶν Ἄλπεων Κελτική.
ταύτης δὲ καὶ τὸ σχῆμα ὑπογέγραπται πρότερον
τυπωδῶς καὶ τὸ μέγεθος· νυνὶ δὲ λεκτέον τὰ καθ᾽
ἕκαστα. οἱ μὲν δὴ τριχῆ διῄρουν, Ἀκυϊτανοὺς
καὶ Βέλγας καλοῦντες καὶ Κέλτας· τοὺς μὲν Ἀκυϊτανοὺς τελέως ἐξηλλαγμένους οὐ τῇ γλώττῃ μόνον,
ἀλλὰ καὶ τοῖς σώμασιν, ἐμφερεῖς Ἴβηρσι μᾶλλον
ἢ Γαλάταις· τοὺς δὲ λοιποὺς Γαλατικοὺς μὲν τὴν
ὄψιν, ὁμογλώττους δ᾽ οὐ πάντας, ἀλλ᾽ ἐνίους μικρὸν παραλλάττοντας ταῖς γλώτταις, καὶ αἱ πολιτεῖαι[1] δὲ καὶ οἱ βίοι μικρὸν ἐξηλλαγμένοι εἰσίν.
Ἀκυϊτανοὺς μὲν οὖν καὶ Κέλτας ἔλεγον τοὺς πρὸς
τῇ Πυρήνῃ, διωρισμένους τῷ Κεμμένῳ ὄρει. εἴρηται γὰρ ὅτι τὴν Κελτικὴν ταύτην ἀπὸ μὲν τῆς
C 177 δύσεως ὁρίζει τὰ Πυρηναῖα ὄρη, προσαπτόμενα
τῆς ἑκατέρωθεν θαλάττης, τῆς τε ἐντὸς καὶ τῆς
ἐκτός· ἀπὸ δὲ τῶν ἀνατολῶν ὁ Ῥῆνος, παράλληλος
ὢν τῇ Πυρήνῃ. τὰ δ᾽ ἀπὸ τῶν ἄρκτων καὶ τῆς
μεσημβρίας, τὰ μὲν ὁ ὠκεανὸς περιείληφεν, ἀρξά-

---

[1] αἱ πολιτεῖαι, Jones, for πολιτεία.

---

[1] That is, after Iberia.
[2] The "Transalpine Gaul" of the Romans.
[3] 2. 5. 28 and 3. 1. 3.

BOOK IV

I

1. Next, in order,[1] comes Transalpine Celtica.[2] I have already [3] indicated roughly both the shape and the size of this country; but now I must speak of it in detail. Some, as we know, have divided it into three parts, calling its inhabitants Aquitani, Belgae, and Celtae.[4] The Aquitani, they said, are wholly different, not only in respect to their language but also in respect to their physique—more like the Iberians than the Galatae; while the rest of the inhabitants are Galatic in appearance, although not all speak the same language, but some make slight variations in their languages. Furthermore, their governments and their modes of life are slightly different. Now by "Aquitani" and "Celtae" they meant the two peoples (separated from each other by the Cemmenus Mountain) who live next to the Pyrenees; for, as has already been said,[5] this Celtica is bounded on the west by the Pyrenees Mountains, which join the sea on either side, that is, both the inner and the outer sea; on the east, by the River Rhenus, which is parallel to the Pyrenees; as for the parts on the north and the south, those on the north are surrounded by the ocean (beginning at the

---

[4] See 4. 1. 14 for the distinction between "Celtae" and "Celti."   [5] 2. 5. 28.

μενος ἀπὸ τῶν βορείων ἄκρων τῆς Πυρήνης, μέχρι
τῶν ἐκβολῶν τοῦ Ῥήνου, τὰ δ' ἐξ ἐναντίας ἡ κατὰ
Μασσαλίαν καὶ Νάρβωνα θάλαττα καὶ αἱ Ἄλπεις
ἀπὸ τῆς Λιγυστικῆς ἀρξάμεναι μέχρι τῶν πηγῶν
τοῦ Ῥήνου. τῇ δὲ Πυρήνῃ πρὸς ὀρθὰς ἦκται
Κέμμενον ὄρος διὰ μέσων τῶν πεδίων, καὶ παύεται
κατὰ μέσα πλησίον Λουγδούνου, περὶ δισχιλίους
ἐκταθὲν σταδίους. Ἀκυϊτανοὺς μὲν τοίνυν ἔλεγον
τοὺς τὰ βόρεια τῆς Πυρήνης μέρη κατέχοντας καὶ
ἀπὸ[1] τῆς Κεμμένης μέχρι πρὸς τὸν ὠκεανὸν τὰ
ἐντὸς Γαρούνα ποταμοῦ, Κέλτας δὲ τοὺς ἐπὶ θάτερα
μέρη καθήκοντας καὶ τὴν κατὰ Μασσαλίαν καὶ
Νάρβωνα θάλατταν, ἁπτομένους δὲ καὶ τῶν Ἀλπεινῶν ὀρῶν ἐνίων, Βέλγας δ' ἔλεγον τοὺς λοιπούς τε
τῶν παρωκεανιτῶν μέχρι τῶν ἐκβολῶν τοῦ Ῥήνου
καί τινας τῶν παροικούντων τὸν Ῥῆνον καὶ τὰς
Ἄλπεις. οὕτω δὲ καὶ ὁ Θεὸς Καῖσαρ ἐν τοῖς
ὑπομνήμασιν εὕρηκεν. ὁ δὲ Σεβαστὸς Καῖσαρ τε-
τραχῇ διελὼν τοὺς μὲν Κέλτας τῆς Ναρβωνίτιδος
ἐπαρχίας ἀπέφηνεν, Ἀκυϊτανοὺς δ' οὕσπερ κἀκεῖ-
νος, προσέθηκε δὲ τετταρεσκαίδεκα ἔθνη τῶν μεταξὺ τοῦ Γαρούνα καὶ τοῦ Λείγηρος ποταμοῦ
νεμομένων· τὴν δὲ λοιπὴν διελὼν δίχα τὴν μὲν
Λουγδούνῳ προσώρισε μέχρι τῶν ἄνω μερῶν τοῦ

[1] ἀπό, Jones inserts.

---

[1] Cp. 2. 5. 28.   [2] Lyon.

northern headlands of the Pyrenees) as far as the
mouths of the Rhenus, while those on the opposite
side are surrounded by the sea that is about Massilia
and Narbo, and by the Alps (beginning at Liguria)
as far as the sources of the Rhenus.   The Cemmenus
Mountain has been drawn at right angles to the
Pyrenees, through the midst of the plains; and it
comes to an end about the centre of these plains,[1]
near Lugdunum,[2] with an extent of about two
thousand stadia.   So, then, by "Aquitani" they
meant the people who occupy the northern parts of
the Pyrenees and, from the country of the Cemmenus
on to the ocean, the parts this side the Garumna
River; by "Celtae" they meant the people whose
territory extends in the other direction—down to
the sea that is about Massilia and Narbo—and also
joins some of the Alpine Mountains; and by "Belgae" they meant the rest of the people who live
beside the ocean as far as the mouths of the Rhenus
and also some of the people who live beside the
Rhenus and the Alps.   Thus the Deified Caesar, also,
has put it in his "Commentaries."[3]   Augustus
Caesar, however, divided Transalpine Celtica into
four parts: the Celtae he designated as belonging
to the province of Narbonitis;[4] the Aquitani he designated as the former Caesar had already done,
although he added to them fourteen tribes of the
peoples who dwell between the Garumna and the
Liger Rivers; the rest of the country he divided
into two parts: one part he included within the
boundaries of Lugdunum as far as the upper districts

[3] For a technical discussion of Strabo's description of Gaul,
the reader is referred to *Cäsarstudien*, by A. Klotz, 1910,
pp. 57–135.   [4] Provincia Narbonensis.

Ῥήνου, τὴν δὲ τοῖς Βέλγαις. ὅσα μὲν οὖν φυσι-
κῶς διώρισται δεῖ λέγειν τὸν γεωγράφον καὶ ὅσα
ἐθνικῶς, ὅταν[1] ᾖ καὶ μνήμης ἄξια, ὅσα δ' οἱ ἡγεμόνες πρὸς τοὺς καιροὺς πολιτευόμενοι διατάτ-
τουσι ποικίλως, ἀρκεῖ κἂν ἐν κεφαλαίῳ τις εἴπῃ,
τοῦ δ' ἀκριβοῦς ἄλλοις παραχωρητέον.

2. Ἅπασα μὲν οὖν ἐστιν αὕτη ποταμοῖς κατάρ-
ρυτος ἡ χώρα, τοῖς μὲν ἐκ τῶν Ἄλπεων καταφε-
ρομένοις, τοῖς δ' ἐκ τοῦ Κεμμένου καὶ τῆς Πυρήνης,
καὶ τοῖς μὲν εἰς τὸν ὠκεανὸν ἐκβάλλουσι, τοῖς δὲ
εἰς τὴν ἡμετέραν θάλατταν. δι' ὧν δὲ φέρονται
χωρίων, πεδία ἐστὶ τὰ πλεῖστα καὶ γεωλοφίαι
διάρρους ἔχουσαι πλωτούς. οὕτως δ' εὐφυῶς ἴσχει
τὰ ῥεῖθρα πρὸς ἄλληλα ὥστ' ἐξ ἑκατέρας τῆς
θαλάττης εἰς ἑκατέραν κατακομίζεσθαι, πορευ-
ομένων τῶν φορτίων ἐπ' ὀλίγον καὶ διὰ πεδίων
εὐμαρῶς, τὸ δὲ πλέον τοῖς ποταμοῖς, τοῖς μὲν
ἀναγομένων, τοῖς δὲ καταγομένων. ἔχει δέ τι
πλεονέκτημα πρὸς τοῦτο ὁ Ῥοδανός· καὶ γὰρ πολλαχόθεν ἐστὶ σύρρους, ὥσπερ εἴρηται, καὶ συνάπτει
πρὸς τὴν ἡμετέραν θάλατταν, κρείττω τῆς ἐκτὸς
οὖσαν, καὶ διὰ χώρας διέξεισι τῆς εὐδαιμονεστάτης
C 178 τῶν ταύτῃ. τοὺς γὰρ αὐτοὺς ἐκφέρει καρποὺς ἡ
Ναρβωνῖτις ἅπασα οὖσπερ ἡ Ἰταλία. προϊόντι
δ' ἐπὶ τὰς ἄρκτους καὶ τὸ Κέμμενον, ὄρος ἡ μὲν
ἐλαιόφυτος καὶ συκοφόρος ἐκλείπει, τἆλλα δὲ
φύεται. καὶ ἡ ἄμπελος δὲ προϊοῦσιν οὐ ῥᾳδίως

---

[1] ὅταν, Kramer, for ὅ τι ἄν.

---

[1] Gallia Lugdunensis. [2] Gallia Belgica.
[3] Not by Strabo, although he again mentions this in § 14
below.

of the Rhenus,[1] while the other he included within the boundaries of the Belgae.[2] Now although the geographer should tell of all the physical and ethnic distinctions which have been made, whenever they are worth recording, yet, as for the diversified political divisions which are made by the rulers (for they suit their government to the particular times), it is sufficient if one state them merely in a summary way; and the scientific treatment of them should be left to others.

2. Now the whole of this country is watered by rivers: some of them flow down from the Alps, the others from the Cemmenus and the Pyrenees; and some of them are discharged into the ocean, the others into Our Sea. Further, the districts through which they flow are plains, for the most part, and hilly lands with navigable water-courses. The river-beds are by nature so well situated with reference to one another that there is transportation from either sea into the other; for the cargoes are transported only a short distance by land, with an easy transit through plains, but most of the way they are carried on the rivers—on some into the interior, on the others to the sea. The Rhodanus offers an advantage in this regard; for not only is it a stream of many tributaries, as has been stated,[3] but it also connects with Our Sea, which is better than the outer sea, and traverses a country which is the most favoured of all in that part of the world. For example, the same fruits are produced by the whole of the province of Narbonitis as by Italy. As you proceed towards the north and the Cemmenus Mountain, the olive-planted and fig-bearing land indeed ceases, but the other things still grow. Also the vine, as

τελεσφορεῖ· ἡ δ' ἄλλη πᾶσα σῖτον φέρει πολὺν
καὶ κέγχρον καὶ βάλανον καὶ βοσκήματα παντοῖα,
ἀργὸν δ' αὐτῆς οὐδέν, πλὴν εἴ τι ἕλεσι κεκώλυται
καὶ δρυμοῖς· καίτοι καὶ τοῦτο συνοικεῖται, πολυ-
ανθρωπίᾳ μᾶλλον ἢ ἐπιμελείᾳ. καὶ γὰρ τοκάδες αἱ
γυναῖκες καὶ τρέφειν ἀγαθαί, οἱ δ' ἄνδρες μαχηταὶ
μᾶλλον ἢ γεωργοί· νῦν δ' ἀναγκάζονται γεωργεῖν,
καταθέμενοι τὰ ὅπλα. κοινῇ μὲν οὖν ταῦτα λέγομεν περὶ πάσης τῆς ἐκτὸς Κελτικῆς, περὶ δὲ τῶν
τεταρτημορίων ἑκάστου διαλαβόντες λέγωμεν νυνί,
μεμνημένοι τυπωδῶς, καὶ πρῶτον περὶ τῆς Ναρβωνίτιδος.

3. Ταύτης δὲ τὸ σχῆμα παραλληλόγραμμόν
πώς ἐστιν, ἐκ μὲν τῆς ἑσπέρας γραφόμενον τῇ
Πυρήνῃ, πρὸς δὲ τὰς ἄρκτους τῷ Κεμμένῳ· τὰς
δὲ λοιπάς, τὴν μὲν νότιον ἡ θάλαττα ποιεῖ μεταξὺ
Πυρήνης καὶ Μασσαλίας, τὴν δ' ἑωθινὴν αἱ Ἄλπεις
ἐκ μέρους, καὶ τὸ μεταξὺ διάστημα τῶν Ἄλπεων
ἐπ' εὐθείας αὐταῖς ληφθὲν καὶ τῶν ὑπωρειῶν τοῦ
Κεμμένου τῶν καθηκουσῶν ἐπὶ τὸν Ῥοδανὸν καὶ
ποιουσῶν ὀρθὴν γωνίαν πρὸς τὴν λεχθεῖσαν ἀπὸ
τῶν Ἄλπεων εὐθεῖαν. τῷ δὲ νοτίῳ πρόσκειται
παρὰ τὸ λεχθὲν σχῆμα ἡ ἐφεξῆς παραλία ἣν
ἔχουσιν οἵ τε Μασσαλιῶται καὶ οἱ Σάλλυες μέχρι
Λιγύων ἐπὶ τὰ πρὸς Ἰταλίαν μέρη καὶ τὸν Οὐᾶρον
ποταμόν. οὗτος δ' ἐστὶν ὡς εἶπον πρότερον, ὅριον
τῆς Ναρβωνίτιδος, καὶ τῆς Ἰταλίας· ὑπάρχει δὲ

---

[1] Cp. 4. 4. 3.
[2] Ulterior Gallia, that is, Transalpine Gaul.
[3] After Massilia.
[4] But there is no previous mention of the Varus River to
be found in any of the MSS. of Strabo.

you thus proceed, does not easily bring its fruit to
maturity. All the rest of the country produces
grain in large quantities, and millet, and nuts, and
all kinds of live stock. And none of the country is
untilled except parts where tilling is precluded by
swamps and woods. Yet these parts too are thickly
peopled—more because of the largeness of the population[1] than because of the industry of the people ;
for the women are not only prolific, but good nurses
as well, while the men are fighters rather than
farmers. But at the present time they are compelled
to till the soil, now that they have laid down their
arms. However, although I am here speaking only
in a general way of the whole of outer Celtica,[2] let
me now take each of the fourth parts separately and
tell about them, describing them only in rough outline. And first, Narbonitis.

3. The figure of Narbonitis is approximately a
parallelogram, since, on the west, it is traced by the
Pyrenees, and, on the north, by the Cemmenus ; as
for the remaining sides, the southern is formed by
the sea between the Pyrenees and Massilia, the
eastern by the Alps, partly, and also by the intervening distance (taken in a straight line with the
Alps) between the Alps and those foot-hills of the
Cemmenus that reach down to the Rhodanus and
form a right angle with the aforesaid straight line
from the Alps. To the southern part there belongs
an addition to the aforesaid figure, I mean the seaboard that follows next[3] which is inhabited by the
Massiliotes and the Sallyes, as far as the Ligures, to
those parts that lie towards Italy and to the Varus
River. This river is, as I stated before,[4] the boundary
between this Province and Italy. It is only a small

θέρους μὲν μικρός, χειμῶνος δὲ καὶ μέχρι ἑπτὰ
σταδίων πλατυνόμενος. ἐντεῦθεν μὲν οὖν ἡ παραλία παρατείνει μέχρι τοῦ ἱεροῦ τῆς Πυρηναίας
Ἀφροδίτης· καὶ τοῦτο δ' ἐστὶν ὅριον ταύτης τε
τῆς ἐπαρχίας καὶ τῆς Ἰβηρικῆς· ἔνιοι δὲ τὸν τόπον
ἐν ᾧ ἐστι τὰ Πομπηίου τρόπαια ὅριον Ἰβηρίας
ἀποφαίνουσι καὶ τῆς Κελτικῆς. ἔστι δ' ἔνθεν μὲν
εἰς Νάρβωνα μίλια ἑξήκοντα τρία, ἐκεῖθεν δὲ εἰς
Νέμαυσον ὀγδοήκοντα ὀκτώ, ἐκ Νεμαύσου δὲ διὰ
Οὐγέρνου καὶ Ταρούσκωνος εἰς τὰ θερμὰ ὕδατα τὰ
Σέξτια καλούμενα, ἅπερ πλησίον Μασσαλίας
ἐστί, πεντήκοντα τρία, ἐντεῦθεν δὲ εἰς Ἀντίπολιν
καὶ τὸν Οὐᾶρον ποταμὸν ἑβδομήκοντα τρία, ὥστε
τὰ σύμπαντα γίνεται μίλια διακόσια ἑβδομήκοντα
ἑπτά. ἔνιοι δ' ἀπὸ τοῦ Ἀφροδισίου μέχρι τοῦ
Οὐάρου σταδίους ἀνέγραψαν δισχιλίους ἑξακοσίους, οἱ δὲ καὶ διακοσίους προστιθέασιν. οὐ γὰρ
ὁμολογεῖται περὶ τῶν διαστημάτων. κατὰ δὲ τὴν
ἑτέραν ὁδὸν τὴν διὰ Οὐοκοντίων καὶ τῆς Κοττίου
C 179 μέχρι μὲν Οὐγέρνου καὶ Ταρούσκωνος κοινὴ ὁδὸς
ἡ ἀπὸ Νεμαύσου, ἐντεῦθεν δὲ ἐπὶ μὲν τοὺς Οὐοκοντίων ὅρους καὶ τὴν ἀρχὴν τῆς ἀναβάσεως τῶν
Ἄλπεων διὰ Δρουεντία καὶ Καβαλλίωνος μίλια
ἑξήκοντα τρία· πάλιν δ' ἐντεῦθεν ἐπὶ τοὺς ἑτέρους
ὅρους τῶν Οὐοκοντίων πρὸς τὴν Κοττίου μίλια
ἑκατὸν ἑνὸς δέοντα[1] ἐπ' Ἐβρόδουνον κώμην· εἶτ'
ἄλλα τοσαῦτα[2] διὰ Βριγαντίου κώμης καὶ Σκιγγομάγου καὶ τῆς τῶν Ἄλπεων ὑπερθέσεως ἐπὶ
Ὤκελον, τὸ πέρας τῆς Κοττίου γῆς· καὶ ἡ ἀπὸ

---

[1] εἰς, after δέοντα, Corais deletes; so the later editors.
[2] ἄλλα τοσαῦτα, Kramer, for ἄλλοι τοσοῦτοι; so the later editors.

river in summer, but in winter it broadens out to a breadth of as much as seven stadia. Now from this river the seaboard extends as far as the temple of the Pyrenaean Aphrodite. This temple, moreover, marks the boundary between the province of Narbonitis and the Iberian country, although some represent the place where the Trophies of Pompey are as marking the boundary between Iberia and Celtica. The distance thence to Narbo is sixty-three miles, from here to Nemausus [1] eighty-eight, from Nemausus through Ugernum and Tarusco to the hot waters that are called "Sextian," [2] which are near Massilia, fifty-three, and thence to Antipolis and the Varus River seventy-three; so that the sum total amounts to two hundred and seventy-seven miles. Some, however, have recorded the distance from the temple of Aphrodite on to the Varus River as two thousand six hundred stadia, while others add two hundred more; for there is disagreement with respect to the distances. But if you go by the other road—that leads through the country of the Vocontii and that of Cottius: from Nemausus the road is identical with the former road as far as Ugernum and Tarusco, but thence it runs across the Druentia River and through Caballio sixty-three miles to the frontiers of the Vocontii and the beginning of the ascent of the Alps; and thence, again, ninety-nine miles to the other frontiers of the Vocontii, at the country of Cottius, to the village of Ebrodunum; then, another ninety-nine through the village of Brigantium and Scingomagus and the pass that leads over the Alps to Ocelum, the end of the land of Cottius.

---

[1] Now Nîmes.   [2] "Aquae Sextiae," now Aix.

Σκιγγομάγου δὲ ἤδη Ἰταλία λέγεται· ἔστι δὲ ἐνθένδε ἐπὶ Ὠκελον μίλια εἴκοσι ὀκτώ.

4. Κτίσμα δ' ἐστὶ Φωκαιέων ἡ Μασσαλία, κεῖται δ' ἐπὶ χωρίου πετρώδους· ὑποπέπτωκε δ' αὐτῆς ὁ λιμὴν θεατροειδεῖ πέτρᾳ, βλεπούσῃ πρὸς νότον. τετείχισται δὲ καὶ αὐτὴ καλῶς καὶ ἡ πόλις σύμπασα, μέγεθος ἔχουσα ἀξιόλογον. ἐν δὲ τῇ ἄκρᾳ τὸ Ἐφέσιον ἵδρυται καὶ τὸ τοῦ Δελφινίου Ἀπόλλωνος ἱερόν· τοῦτο μὲν κοινὸν Ἰώνων ἁπάντων, τὸ δὲ Ἐφέσιον τῆς Ἀρτέμιδός ἐστι νεὼς τῆς Ἐφεσίας. ἀπαίρουσι γὰρ τοῖς Φωκαιεῦσιν ἐκ τῆς οἰκείας λόγιον ἐκπεσεῖν φασιν, ἡγεμόνι χρήσασθαι τοῦ πλοῦ παρὰ τῆς Ἐφεσίας Ἀρτέμιδος λαβοῦσι· τοὺς μὲν δή, προσαχθέντας τῇ Ἐφέσῳ, ζητεῖν ὅντινα τρόπον ἐκ τῆς θεοῦ πορίσαιντο τὸ προσταχθέν. Ἀρισταρχῃ δὲ τῶν ἐντίμων σφόδρα γυναικῶν παραστῆναι κατ' ὄναρ τὴν θεὸν καὶ κελεῦσαι συναπαίρειν τοῖς Φωκαιεῦσιν, ἀφίδρυμά τι τῶν ἱερῶν λαβούσῃ· γενομένου δὲ τούτου καὶ τῆς ἀποικίας λαβούσης τέλος, τό τε ἱερὸν ἱδρύσασθαι καὶ τὴν Ἀρισταρχην τιμῆσαι διαφερόντως ἱέρειαν ἀποδείξαντας, ἔν τε ταῖς ἀποίκοις πόλεσι πανταχοῦ τιμᾶν ἐν τοῖς πρώτοις ταύτην τὴν θεὸν καὶ τοῦ ξοάνου τὴν διάθεσιν τὴν αὐτὴν καὶ τἆλλα νόμιμα φυλάττειν τὰ αὐτά, ἅπερ ἐν τῇ μητροπόλει νενόμισται.

[1] Not to be confused with the "Delphian" (Pythian) Apollo. The Delphinian Apollo appears originally to have been a seafaring god who, in the guise of a dolphin, guided ships over the sea (see *Etymologicum Magnum* 255. 18); also Pauly-Wissowa, under Ἀπόλλων Δελφίνιος, p. 47.

[2] Of Artemis.   [3] That is, of Massilia.

[4] Strictly speaking, the "xoana" were the primitive

Moreover, from Scingomagus on you begin to call the country Italy; and the distance from here to Ocelum is twenty-eight miles.

4. Massilia was founded by the Phocaeans, and it is situated on a rocky place. Its harbour lies at the foot of a theatre-like rock which faces south. And not only is the rock itself well fortified, but also the city as a whole, though it is of considerable size. It is on the headland, however, that the Ephesium and also the temple of the Delphinian [1] Apollo are situated. The latter is shared in common by all Ionians, whereas the Ephesium is a temple dedicated solely to the Ephesian Artemis: for when the Phocaeans were setting sail from their homeland an oracle was delivered to them, it is said, to use for their voyage a guide received from the Ephesian Artemis; accordingly, some of them put in at Ephesus and inquired in what way they might procure from the goddess what had been enjoined upon them. Now the goddess, in a dream, it is said, had stood beside Aristarcha, one of the women held in very high honour, and commanded her to sail away with the Phocaeans, taking with her a certain reproduction [2] which was among the sacred images; this done and the colony finally settled, they not only established the temple but also did Aristarcha the exceptional honour of appointing her priestess; further, in the colonial cities [3] the people everywhere do this goddess honours of the first rank, and they preserve the artistic design of the " xoanon " [4] the same, and all the other usages precisely the same as is customary in the mother-city.

wooden images which were supposed originally to have fallen from heaven. Here, as on page 177, " xoanon " is used of a reproduction.

5. Διοικοῦνται δ' ἀριστοκρατικῶς οἱ Μασσαλιῶται πάντων εὐνομώτατα, ἀνδρῶν ἑξακοσίων καταστήσαντες συνέδριον, διὰ βίου ταύτην ἐχόντων τὴν τιμήν, οὓς τιμούχους καλοῦσι. πεντεκαίδεκα δ' εἰσὶ τοῦ συνεδρίου προεστῶτες, τούτοις δὲ τὰ πρόχειρα διοικεῖν δέδοται. πάλιν δὲ τῶν πεντεκαίδεκα προκάθηνται τρεῖς οἱ πλεῖστον ἰσχύοντες, τούτων¹ δὲ τιμοῦχος οὐ γίνεται μὴ τέκνα ἔχων, μηδὲ διὰ τριγονίας ἐκ πολιτῶν γεγονώς. οἱ δὲ νόμοι Ἰωνικοί, πρόκεινται δὲ δημοσίᾳ. χώραν δ' ἔχουσιν ἐλαιόφυτον μὲν καὶ κατάμπελον, σίτῳ δὲ λυπροτέραν διὰ τὴν τραχύτητα, ὥστε πεποιθότες τῇ θαλάττῃ μᾶλλον ἢ τῇ γῇ τὸ πρὸς ναυτιλίας εὐφυὲς εἵλοντο μᾶλλον. ὕστερον μέντοι ταῖς ἀνδραγαθίαις ἴσχυσαν προσλαβεῖν τινα τῶν πέριξ πεδίων ἀπὸ τῆς αὐτῆς δυνάμεως ἀφ' ἧς καὶ τὰς πόλεις ἔκτισαν, ἐπιτειχίσματα τὰς μὲν κατὰ τὴν Ἰβηρίαν τοῖς Ἴβηρσιν, οἷς καὶ τὰ ἱερὰ τῆς Ἐφεσίας Ἀρτέμιδος παρέδοσαν τὰ πάτρια, ὥστε Ἑλληνιστὶ θύειν, τὴν δὲ Ῥόην² Ἀγάθην τοῖς περὶ τὸν ποταμὸν οἰκοῦσι τὸν Ῥοδανὸν βαρβάροις, τὸ δὲ Ταυροέντιον καὶ τὴν Ὀλβίαν καὶ Ἀντίπολιν καὶ Νίκαιαν τῷ τῶν Σαλλύων ἔθνει

C 180

¹ The reading of lm is τούτων δὲ οὐδ' εἷς. Corais reads οὐδείς, inserting δ' after τιμοῦχος. Forbiger, Müller-Dübner, and Meineke read : τούτων δὲ εἷς· τιμοῦχος δ' κ.τ.λ.

² For Ῥόην Casaubon, Corais, and Forbiger read (perhaps rightly) Ῥόδην καί (see Pliny 3. 5).

[1] Aristotle describes and praises the orderliness and moderation of this aristocracy (*Politics* 7. 7. 4 and 8. 6. 2–3). See also Cicero *Pro Flacco* 25. 63.

[2] Literally, "Honour-holders."

5. The government under which the Massiliotes
live is aristocratic, and of all aristocracies theirs is
the best ordered,[1] since they have established an
Assembly of six hundred men, who hold the honour
of that office for life; these they call Timouchoi.[2]
Over the Assembly are set fifteen of its number,
and to these fifteen it is given to carry on the immediate business of the government. And, in turn,
three, holding the chief power, preside over the
fifteen.[3] However, a Timouchos cannot become one
of these three unless he has children or is a descendant
of persons who have been citizens for three gener-
ations. Their laws are Ionic, and are published to
the people. They possess a country which, although
planted with olive-trees and vines, is, on account of
its ruggedness, too poor for grain; so that, trusting
the sea rather than the land, they preferred their
natural fitness for a seafaring life. Later, however,
their valour enabled them to take in some of the
surrounding plains, thanks to the same military
strength by which they founded their cities, I mean
their stronghold-cities, namely, first, those which
they founded in Iberia as strongholds against the
Iberians [4] (they also taught the Iberians the sacred
rites of the Ephesian Artemis, as practised in the
fatherland, so that they sacrifice by the Greek
ritual); secondly, Rhoë Agathe, as a stronghold
against the barbarians who live round about the
River Rhodanus; thirdly, Tauroentium, Olbia, Antipolis, and Nicaea, against the tribe of the Sallyes

---

[3] The later editors, by a slight emendation, add at this
point "and one over the three."
[4] Hemeroscopeium, Emporium and Rhodus (3. 4. 6–8).

καὶ τοῖς Λίγυσι τοῖς τὰς Ἄλπεις οἰκοῦσιν. εἰσὶ δὲ καὶ νεώσοικοι παρ' αὐτοῖς καὶ ὁπλοθήκη· πρότερον δὲ καὶ πλοίων εὐπορία καὶ ὅπλων καὶ ὀργάνων τῶν τε πρὸς τὰς ναυτιλίας χρησίμων καὶ τῶν πρὸς πολιορκίας, ἀφ' ὧν πρός τε τοὺς βαρβάρους ἀντέσχον, καὶ Ῥωμαίους ἐκτήσαντο φίλους, καὶ πολλὰ καὶ αὐτοὶ χρήσιμοι κατέστησαν ἐκείνοις κἀκεῖνοι προσελάβοντο τῆς αὐξήσεως αὐτῶν. Σέξτιος γοῦν ὁ καταλύσας τοὺς Σάλλυας, οὐ πολὺ ἄπωθεν τῆς Μασσαλίας κτίσας πόλιν ὁμώνυμον ἑαυτοῦ τε καὶ τῶν ὑδάτων τῶν θερμῶν, ὧν τινα μεταβεβληκέναι φασὶν εἰς ψυχρά, ἐνταῦθά τε φρουρὰν κατῴκισε Ῥωμαίων, καὶ ἐκ τῆς παραλίας τῆς εἰς τὴν Ἰταλίαν ἀγούσης ἀπὸ Μασσαλίας ἀνέστειλε τοὺς βαρβάρους, οὐ δυναμένων τῶν Μασσαλιωτῶν ἀνείργειν αὐτοὺς τελέως. οὐδ' αὐτὸς δὲ πλέον ἴσχυσεν, ἀλλ' ἢ τοσοῦτον μόνον ὅσον κατὰ μὲν τὰ εὐλίμενα ἀπὸ τῆς θαλάττης ἀπελθεῖν τοὺς βαρβάρους ἐπὶ δώδεκα σταδίους, κατὰ δὲ τοὺς τραχῶνας ἐπὶ ὀκτώ· τὴν δὲ λειφθεῖσαν ὑπ' ἐκείνων τοῖς Μασσαλιώταις παραδέδωκεν. ἀνάκειται δ' ἐν πόλει συχνὰ τῶν ἀκροθινίων, ἃ ἔλαβον καταναυμαχοῦντες ἀεὶ τοὺς ἀμφισβητοῦντας τῆς θαλάττης ἀδίκως. πρότερον μὲν οὖν εὐτύχουν διαφερόντως, περί τε τἆλλα καὶ περὶ τὴν πρὸς Ῥωμαίους φιλίαν, ἧς πολλὰ ἄν τις λάβοι σημεῖα· καὶ δὴ καὶ τὸ ξόανον τῆς Ἀρτέμιδος τῆς ἐν τῷ Ἀυεντίνῳ[1] οἱ Ῥωμαῖοι τὴν αὐτὴν

---

[1] Ἀυεντίνῳ, Wilamowitz, for Ἀβεντίῳ. Corais, Meineke, and others write Ἀβεντίνῳ. Cp. 5. 3. 7.

---

[1] " Aquae Sextiae," now Aix. See 4. 1. 3.
[2] See § 4 (above).

and against those Ligures who live in the Alps.
There are also dry-docks and an armoury among the
Massiliotes.   In earlier times they had a good supply
of ships, as well as of arms and instruments that are
useful for the purposes of navigation and for sieges ;
and thanks to these they not only held out against
the barbarians, but also acquired the Romans as
friends, and many times not only themselves rendered useful service to the Romans, but also were
aided by the Romans in their own aggrandizement.
At any rate, Sextius, who defeated the Sallyes, after
founding not very far from Massilia a city which
bears his own name and that of "the hot waters" [1]
(some of which, they say, have changed to cold
waters), not only settled a garrison of Romans
there, but also drove back the barbarians out of
the seaboard which leads from Massilia into Italy,
since the Massiliotes could not entirely keep them
back.   Yet not even Sextius could effect more
than merely this—that at those parts of the coast
where there were good harbours the barbarians
retired for a distance of only twelve stadia, and
at the rugged parts, only eight.   And the country
thus abandoned by them he has given over to
the Massiliotes.   And in their citadel are set up
great quantities of the first fruits of their victories,
which they captured by defeating in naval battles
those who from time to time unjustly disputed their
claim to the mastery of the sea.   In earlier times,
then, they were exceptionally fortunate, not only
in everything else, but also in their friendship with
the Romans, of which one may detect many signs ;
what is more, the "xoanon" [2] of that Artemis which
is on the Aventine Hill was constructed by the

διάθεσιν ἔχον[1] τῷ παρὰ τοῖς Μασσαλιώταις
ἀνέθεσαν. κατὰ δὲ τὴν Πομπηίου πρὸς Καίσαρα
στάσιν τῷ κρατηθέντι μέρει προσθέμενοι τὴν
πολλὴν τῆς εὐδαιμονίας ἀπέβαλον, ὅμως δ᾿ οὖν
ἴχνη λείπεται τοῦ παλαιοῦ ζήλου παρὰ τοῖς
ἀνθρώποις, καὶ μάλιστα περὶ τὰς ὀργανοποιίας
καὶ τὴν ναυτικὴν παρασκευήν. ἐξημερουμένων
δ᾿ ἀεὶ τῶν ὑπερκειμένων βαρβάρων, καὶ ἀντὶ τοῦ
πολεμεῖν τετραμμένων ἤδη πρὸς πολιτείας καὶ
γεωργίας διὰ τὴν τῶν Ῥωμαίων ἐπικράτειαν, οὔτ᾿
αὐτοῖς ἔτι τούτοις συμβαίνοι ἂν περὶ τὰ λεχθέντα
C 181 τοσαύτη σπουδή. δηλοῖ δὲ τὰ καθεστηκότα νυνί·
πάντες γὰρ οἱ χαρίεντες πρὸς τὸ λέγειν τρέπονται
καὶ φιλοσοφεῖν, ὥσθ᾿ ἡ πόλις μικρὸν μὲν πρότερον
τοῖς βαρβάροις ἀνεῖτο παιδευτήριον, καὶ φιλέλληνας κατεσκεύαζε τοὺς Γαλάτας ὥστε καὶ τὰ
συμβόλαια Ἑλληνιστὶ γράφειν, ἐν δὲ τῷ παρόντι
καὶ τοὺς γνωριμωτάτους Ῥωμαίων πέπεικεν, ἀντὶ
τῆς εἰς Ἀθήνας ἀποδημίας ἐκεῖσε φοιτᾶν, φιλομα-
θεῖς ὄντας. ὁρῶντες δὲ τούτους οἱ Γαλάται καὶ
ἅμα εἰρήνην ἄγοντες, τὴν σχολὴν ἄσμενοι πρὸς
τοὺς τοιούτους διατίθενται βίους οὐ κατ᾿ ἄνδρα
μόνον, ἀλλὰ καὶ δημοσίᾳ· σοφιστὰς γοῦν ὑπο-
δέχονται, τοὺς μὲν ἰδίᾳ, τοὺς δὲ πόλεις κοινῇ
μισθούμενοι, καθάπερ καὶ ἰατρούς. τῆς δὲ λιτό-
τητος τῶν βίων καὶ τῆς σωφροσύνης τῶν Μασσαλιωτῶν οὐκ ἐλάχιστον ἄν τις θείη τοῦτο τεκμήριον·[1]
ἡ γὰρ μεγίστη προὶξ αὐτοῖς ἐστιν ἑκατὸν χρυσοῖ

---

[1] ἔχον, Corais, for ἔχοντες; so Meineke.

[1] "Sophists" in the good sense, who taught wisdom in
speech and action, dicendi faciendique sapientia (Cicero, de
Oratore 3. 16).

Romans on the same artistic design as the "xoanon" which the Massiliotes have. But at the time of Pompey's sedition against Caesar they joined the conquered party and thus threw away the greater part of their prosperity. Nevertheless traces of their ancient zeal are still left among the people, especially in regard to the making of instruments and to the equipment of ships. But since, on account of the overmastery of the Romans, the barbarians who are situated beyond the Massiliotes became more and more subdued as time went on, and instead of carrying on war have already turned to civic life and farming, it may also be the case that the Massiliotes themselves no longer occupy themselves so earnestly with the pursuits aforementioned. Their present state of life makes this clear; for all the men of culture turn to the art of speaking and the study of philosophy; so that the city, although a short time ago it was given over as merely a training-school for the barbarians and was schooling the Galatae to be fond enough of the Greeks to write even their contracts in Greek, at the present time has attracted also the most notable of the Romans, if eager for knowledge, to go to school there instead of making their foreign sojourn at Athens. Seeing these men and at the same time living at peace, the Galatae are glad to adapt their leisure to such modes of life, not only as individuals, but also in a public way; at any rate, they welcome sophists,[1] hiring some at private expense, but others in common, as cities, just as they do physicians. And the following might be set down as not the least proof of the simplicity of the modes of life, and of the self-restraint, of the Massiliotes: the maximum dowry among them is a hundred

καὶ εἰς ἐσθῆτα πέντε καὶ πέντε εἰς χρυσοῦν κόσμον· πλέον δ' οὐκ ἔξεστι. καὶ ὁ Καῖσαρ δὲ καὶ οἱ μετ' ἐκεῖνον ἡγεμόνες πρὸς τὰς ἐν τῷ πολέμῳ γενηθείσας ἁμαρτίας ἐμετρίασαν, μεμνημένοι τῆς φιλίας, καὶ τὴν αὐτονομίαν ἐφύλαξαν, ἣν ἐξ ἀρχῆς εἶχεν ἡ πόλις, ὥστε μὴ ὑπακούειν τῶν εἰς τὴν ἐπαρχίαν[1] πεμπομένων στρατηγῶν μήτε αὐτὴν μήτε τοὺς ὑπηκόους. περὶ μὲν Μασσαλίας ταῦτα.

6. Ἅμα δ' ἥ τε τῶν Σαλύων ὀρεινὴ πρὸς ἄρκτον ἀπὸ τῆς ἑσπέρας κλίνει μᾶλλον καὶ τῆς θαλάττης ἀφίσταται κατὰ μικρόν, καὶ ἡ παραλία παρὰ τὴν ἑσπέραν περινεύει· μικρὸν δ' ἀπὸ τῆς πόλεως τῶν Μασσαλιωτῶν προελθοῦσα ὅσον εἰς ἑκατὸν σταδίους ἐπὶ ἄκραν εὐμεγέθη πλησίον λατομιῶν τινων ἐντεῦθεν ἄρχεται κολποῦσθαι καὶ ποιεῖν τὸν Γαλατικὸν κόλπον πρὸς τὸ Ἀφροδίσιον, τὸ τῆς Πυρήνης ἄκρον· καλοῦσι δ' αὐτὸν[2] καὶ Μασσαλιωτικόν. ἔστι δ' ὁ κόλπος διπλοῦς· ἐν γὰρ τῇ αὐτῇ περιγραφῇ δύο κόλπους ἀφορίζον ἔκκειται τὸ Σήτιον[3] ὄρος, προσλαβὸν καὶ τὴν Βλάσκωνα νῆσον πλησίον ἱδρυμένην· τῶν δὲ κόλπων ὁ μὲν μείζων ἰδίως πάλιν καλεῖται Γαλατικός, εἰς ὃν ἐξερεύγεται τὸ τοῦ Ῥοδανοῦ στόμα, ὁ δ' ἐλάττων ὁ κατὰ Νάρβωνά ἐστι μέχρι Πυρήνης. ἡ μὲν οὖν Νάρβων ὑπέρκειται τῶν τοῦ Ἀτακος ἐκβολῶν καὶ τῆς λίμνης τῆς Ναρβωνίτιδος, μέγιστον ἐμπό-

---

[1] ἐπαρχίαν, Corais, for ὑπαρχίαν; so Meineke.
[2] αὐτόν, Corais, for αὐτό; so the later editors.
[3] Σήτιον, Palmer, for Σίγιον; so Corais and the rest.

---

[1] Roughly, $550.

gold pieces, and five for dress, and five for golden
ornaments; [1] but more than this is not permitted.
Both Caesar and the commanders who succeeded
him, mindful of the former friendship, acted in
moderation with reference to the wrongs done in
the war, and preserved to the city the autonomy
which it had had from the beginning; so that
neither Massilia nor its subjects are subject to the
praetors who are sent to the province.[2] So much
for Massilia.

6. While the mountainous country of the Sallyes
inclines more and more from the west to the north
and retires little by little from the sea, the coastline
bends round to the west; but after extending a
short distance from the city of the Massiliotes, about
a hundred stadia, to a fair-sized promontory near
some stone-quarries, the coastline then begins to
curve inland and to form with the precincts of Aphrodite (that is, the headland of the Pyrenees) the
Galatic Gulf, which is also called the Gulf of Massilia.
The Gulf is double, for, in the same circuit, Mount
Setium,[3] with the help of the Isle of Blascon,[4]
which is situated near by, juts out and thus marks
off two gulfs. Of the two gulfs, the larger, into
which the mouth of the Rhodanus discharges, is
again called, in the proper sense of the term,
"Galatic Gulf"; the smaller is opposite Narbo and
extends as far as the Pyrenees. Now Narbo lies
above the outlets of the Atax and the Lake of Narbonitis, and it is the greatest of the emporiums in

[2] See 4. 2. 2. and footnote 3.
[3] Cape de Cette.
[4] Brescon, a rock opposite Agde, which has been connected
with the mainland to form the port of Agde (Gosselin).

ριον τῶν ταύτῃ, πρὸς δὲ τῷ Ῥοδανῷ πόλις ἐστὶ
καὶ ἐμπόριον οὐ μικρόν, Ἀρελᾶτε· ἴσον δέ πως
διέχει τὰ ἐμπόρια ταῦτα ἀλλήλων τε καὶ τῶν
εἰρημένων ἄκρων, ἡ μὲν Νάρβων τοῦ Ἀφροδισίου,
τὸ δ᾽ Ἀρελᾶτε τῆς Μασσαλίας. ἑκατέρωθεν δὲ
τῆς Νάρβωνος ἄλλοι ποταμοὶ ῥέουσιν οἱ μὲν ἐκ
τῶν Κεμμένων ὀρῶν, οἱ δ᾽ ἐκ τῆς Πυρήνης, πόλεις
ἔχοντες εἰς ἃς ἀνάπλους οὐ πολύς ἐστι μικροῖς
πλοίοις. ἐκ μὲν τῆς Πυρήνης ὅ τε Ῥουσκίνων
καὶ ὁ Ἰλλίβιρρις, πόλιν ἔχων ὁμώνυμον ἑκάτερος
αὐτῶν, τοῦ δὲ Ῥουσκίνωνος καὶ λίμνη πλησίον
ἐστὶ καὶ χωρίον ὕφυδρον μικρὸν ὑπὲρ τῆς θαλάττης, ἁλυκίδων μεστόν, τὸ τοὺς ὀρυκτοὺς κεστρεῖς
ἔχον· δύο γὰρ ἢ τρεῖς ὀρύξαντι πόδας καὶ καθέντι
τριόδοντα εἰς ὕδωρ ἰλυῶδες ἔστι περιπεῖραι τὸν
ἰχθὺν ἀξιόλογον τὸ μέγεθος· τρέφεται δὲ ἀπὸ τῆς
ἰλύος καθάπερ αἱ ἐγχέλυες. οὗτοι μὲν ἐκ τῆς
Πυρήνης ῥέουσιν οἱ ποταμοὶ μεταξὺ Νάρβωνος
καὶ τοῦ Ἀφροδισίου. ἐπὶ θάτερα δὲ[1] μέρη τῆς
Νάρβωνος ἐκ τοῦ Κεμμένου φέρονται πρὸς τὴν
θάλατταν, ἐξ οὗπερ καὶ ὁ Ἄταξ, ὅ τε Ὄρβις[2]
καὶ ὁ Ἄραυρις·[3] τούτων ἐφ᾽ οὗ μὲν Βαίτερα[4]
πόλις ἀσφαλὴς ἵδρυται πλησίον τῆς Νάρβωνος,
ἐφ᾽ οὗ δὲ Ἀγάθη, κτίσμα Μασσαλιωτῶν.

7. Ἐν μὲν οὖν ἔχει παράδοξον ἡ προειρημένη
παραλία, τὸ περὶ τοὺς ὀρυκτοὺς ἰχθῦς, ἕτερον
δὲ μεῖζον τούτου σχεδόν τι, τὸ λεχθησόμενον.
μεταξὺ γὰρ τῆς Μασσαλίας καὶ τῶν ἐκβολῶν
C 182 τοῦ Ῥοδανοῦ πεδίον ἐστὶ τῆς θαλάττης διέχον

---

[1] δέ, before μέρη, Kramer conjectures; Meineke following.
[2] Ὄρβις, Groskurd, for Ὄβρις; later editors following.
[3] Ἄραυρις, Groskurd, for Ῥαύραρις; later editors following.

this country, though there is a city near the Rhodanus which is no small emporium, namely, Arelate. These emporiums are about an equal distance from each other and from the aforesaid headlands—Narbo from the precincts of Aphrodite, and Arelate from Massilia. On either side of Narbo there flow other rivers—some from the Cemmenus Mountains, the others from the Pyrenees—and they have cities to which voyages of no considerable length are made in small ships. From the Pyrenees flow both the Ruscino and the Ilibirris, each of them having a city of like name; and, as for the Ruscino, there is not only a lake near by, but also, a short distance above the sea, a marshy district, full of salt-springs, which contains the "dug mullets"; for if one digs only two or three feet and thrusts his trident down into the muddy water, it is possible to spit a fish that is notable for its size; and it feeds on the mud just as the eels do. These, then, are the rivers which flow from the Pyrenees between Narbo and the precincts of Aphrodite; while on the other side of Narbo there flow to the sea from the Cemmenus (from which the Atax flows) both the Orbis and the Arauris. On the former of these rivers is situated Baetera,⁴ a safe city, near Narbo, and on the other, Agathe, founded by the Massiliotes.

7. Now the aforesaid seaboard has not merely one marvel, namely, that of the "dug mullets," but also another which one might say is greater than that, about which I shall now speak: Between Massilia and the outlets of the Rhodanus there is a plain, circular in shape, which is as far distant from

---

⁴ Βαίτερα, Siebenkees, for Βλίτερα; so, perhaps better, Βαίτερρα, as Meineke reads.

εἰς ἑκατὸν σταδίους, τοσοῦτον δὲ καὶ τὴν διάμετρον, κυκλοτερὲς τὸ σχῆμα· καλεῖται δὲ Λιθῶ-
δες ἀπὸ τοῦ συμβεβηκότος. μεστὸν γάρ ἐστι λίθων χειροπληθῶν, ὑποπεφυκυῖαν ἐχόντων αὐτοῖς
ἄγρωστιν, ἀφ᾽ ἧς ἄφθονοι νομαὶ βοσκήμασίν εἰσιν·
ἐν μέσῳ δ᾽ ὕδατα καὶ ἀλυκίδες ἐνίστανται καὶ
ἅλες. ἅπασα μὲν οὖν καὶ ἡ ὑπερκειμένη χώρα
προσήνεμός ἐστι, διαφερόντως δ᾽ εἰς τὸ πεδίον
τοῦτο τὸ[1] μελαμβόρειον καταιγίζει, πνεῦμα βίαιον
καὶ φρικῶδες· φασὶ γοῦν σύρεσθαι καὶ κυλιν-
δεῖσθαι τῶν λίθων ἐνίους, κατακλᾶσθαι δὲ τοὺς
ἀνθρώπους ἀπὸ τῶν ὀχημάτων καὶ γυμνοῦσθαι
καὶ ὅπλων καὶ ἐσθῆτος ὑπὸ[2] τῆς ἐμπνοῆς. Ἀρι-
στοτέλης μὲν οὖν φησιν ὑπὸ σεισμῶν τῶν καλουμένων βραστῶν ἐκπεσόντας τοὺς λίθους εἰς
τὴν ἐπιφάνειαν συνολισθεῖν εἰς τὰ κοῖλα τῶν
χωρίων. Ποσειδώνιος δὲ λίμνην οὖσαν παγῆναι
μετὰ κλυδασμοῦ, καὶ διὰ τοῦτο εἰς πλείονας
μερισθῆναι λίθους, καθάπερ τοὺς ποταμίους κά-
χληκας καὶ τὰς ψήφους τὰς αἰγιαλίτιδας, ὁμοίως
δὲ καὶ λείους καὶ ἰσομεγέθεις τῇ ὁμοιότητι· καὶ
τὴν αἰτίαν ἀποδεδώκασιν ἀμφότεροι. πιθανὸς μὲν
οὖν ὁ παρ᾽ ἀμφοῖν λόγος· ἀνάγκη γὰρ τοὺς οὕτω

---

[1] τό, Corais inserts ; so Müller-Dübner, and Meineke.
[2] ὑπό, Meineke, for ἀπό.

---

[1] Now the Plaine de la Crau.
[2] So Pliny, 21. 57. And Murray (*Handbook for France*,
vol. 2, p. 154) says that to-day there grows under the stones
on this plain a short sweet herbage which the sheep obtain
by turning over the stones, and that during the winter
months the plain is covered with flocks driven thither from
the French Alps, where they spend the summer.

the sea as a hundred stadia, and is also as much as that in diameter. It is called Stony Plain [1] from the fact that it is full of stones as large as you can hold in your hand, although from beneath the stones there is a growth of wild herbage which affords abundant pasturage for cattle. [2] In the middle of the plain stand water and salt springs, and also lumps of salt. Now although the whole of the country which lies beyond, as well as this, is exposed to the winds, the Black North, a violent and chilly wind, descends upon this plain with exceptional severity; at any rate, it is said that some of the stones are swept and rolled along, and that by the blasts the people are dashed from their vehicles and stripped of both weapons and clothing. Now Aristotle says that the stones, after being vomited to the surface by those earthquakes that are called "Brastae," [3] rolled together into the hollow places of the districts. But Poseidonius says that, since it [4] was a lake, it solidified [5] while the waves were dashing, and because of this was parted into a number of stones—as are the river-rocks and the pebbles on the sea-shore; and by reason of the similarity of origin, the former, like the latter, are both smooth and equal in size. And an account of the cause has been given by both men. Now the argument in both treatises is plausible; for of necessity the stones that have been assembled to-

[3] Aristotle says (*De Mundo* 4) that "those earthquakes are called 'Brastae' which heave up and down at right angles."

[4] The antecedent of "it" in Poseidonius must have been "what is now the stony surface of the plain."

[5] Poseidonius was thinking of both the congealing and petrifying of the waters.

συνεστῶτας λίθους οὐ καθ᾽ ἑαυτοὺς ἢ ἐξ ὑγροῦ
παγέντας μεταβαλεῖν,[1] ἢ[2] ἐκ πετρῶν μεγάλων
C 183 ῥήγματα συνεχῆ λαβουσῶν ἀποκριθῆναι. τὸ μέντοι δυσαπολόγητον Αἰσχύλος καταμαθὼν ἢ παρ᾽
ἄλλου λαβὼν εἰς μῦθον ἐξετόπισε. φησὶ γοῦν
Προμηθεὺς παρ᾽ αὐτῷ, καθηγούμενος Ἡρακλεῖ τῶν
ὁδῶν τῶν ἀπὸ Καυκάσου πρὸς τὰς Ἑσπερίδας·

ἥξεις δὲ Λιγύων εἰς ἀτάρβητον στρατόν,
ἔνθ᾽ οὐ μάχης, σάφ᾽ οἶδα, καὶ θοῦρός περ ὤν,
μέμψει· πέπρωται γάρ σε καὶ βέλη λιπεῖν
ἐνταῦθ᾽· ἑλέσθαι θ᾽ οὔ τιν᾽ ἐκ γαίας λίθον
ἕξεις, ἐπεὶ πᾶς χῶρός ἐστι μαλθακός.
ἰδὼν δ᾽ ἀμηχανοῦντά σε[3] Ζεὺς οἰκτερεῖ,
νεφέλην δ᾽ ὑποσχὼν νιφάδι γογγύλων πέτρων
ὑπόσκιον θήσει χθόν᾽, οἷς ἔπειτα σὺ
βαλὼν[4] διώσει[5] ῥᾳδίως Λίγυν στρατόν·
(*Prometheus Unbound, Fr.* 199, Nauck)

ὥσπερ οὐ κρεῖττον ὄν, φησὶν ὁ Ποσειδώνιος, εἰς
αὐτοὺς τοὺς Λίγυας ἐμβαλεῖν[6] τοὺς λίθους καὶ
καταχῶσαι πάντας ἢ τοσούτων δεόμενον ποιῆσαι
λίθων τὸν Ἡρακλέα. τὸ μὲν οὖν τοσούτων ἀναγκαῖον ἦν, εἴπερ καὶ πρὸς ὄχλον παμπληθῆ·
ὥστε ταύτῃ γε πιθανώτερος ὁ μυθογράφος τοῦ
ἀνασκευάζοντος τὸν μῦθον. ἀλλὰ καὶ τὰ ἄλλα
πεπρῶσθαι φήσας ὁ ποιητὴς οὐκ ἐᾷ μέμφεσθαι

---

[1] μεταβαλεῖν, Corais, for μεταβάλλειν ; so later editors.
[2] ἤ, Corais inserts, later editors following.
[3] σέ, Meineke, for σ᾽ ὁ.
[4] σὺ βαλών, Saumaise, for συμβαλών ; so the editors.
[5] διώσει, Corais, for δηώσει ; so the later editors.
[6] ἐμβαλεῖν, Corais, for ἐμβάλλειν ; so the later editors.

gether in this way cannot separately, one by one, either have changed from liquid to solid or have been detached from great masses of rock that received a succession of fractures. What was difficult to account for, however, Aeschylus, who closely studied the accounts or else received them from another source, removed to the realm of myth. At any rate, Prometheus, in Aeschylus' poem, in detailing to Heracles the route of the roads from the Caucasus to the Hesperides says: "And thou wilt come to the undaunted host of the Ligurians, where thou wilt not complain of battle, I clearly know,—impetuous fighter though thou art; because there it is fated that even thy missiles shall fail thee, and no stone from the ground shalt thou be able to choose, since the whole district is soft ground. But Zeus, seeing thee without means to fight, will have pity upon thee, and, supplying a cloud with a snow-like shower of round stones, will put the soil under cover; and with these stones, thereupon, thou wilt pelt, and easily push thy way through, the Ligurian host."[1] Just as if it were not better, says Poseidonius, for Zeus to have cast the stones upon the Ligures themselves and to have buried the whole host than to represent Heracles as in need of so many stones. Now, as for the number ("so many"), he needed them all if indeed the poet was speaking with reference to a throng that was very numerous; so that in this, at least, the writer of the myth is more plausible than the man who revises the myth. Furthermore, by saying "it is fated," the poet forbids one to find fault in a captious way with anything else in the

---

[1] These verses were quoted by Strabo from the *Prometheus Unbound*, now lost.

φιλαιτίως. καὶ γὰρ ἐν τοῖς περὶ τῆς προνοίας
καὶ τῆς εἱμαρμένης λόγοις εὕροι τις ἂν πολλὰ
τοιαῦτα τῶν ἀνθρωπίνων καὶ τῶν φύσει γινο-
μένων, ὥστ᾽ ἐπ᾽ αὐτῶν φάναι πολὺ κρεῖττον εἶναι
τόδε ἢ τόδε γενέσθαι, οἷον εὔομβρον εἶναι τὴν
Αἴγυπτον, ἀλλὰ μὴ τὴν Αἰθιοπίαν ποτίζειν τὴν
γῆν· καὶ τὸν Πάριν εἰς Σπάρτην πλέοντα ναυαγίῳ
περιπεσεῖν, ἀλλὰ μὴ τὴν Ἑλένην ἁρπάσαντα
δίκας τῖσαι τοῖς ἀδικηθεῖσιν ὕστερον, ἡνίκα τοσοῦτον ἀπειργάσατο φθόρον Ἑλλήνων καὶ βαρ-
βάρων· ὅπερ Εὐριπίδης ἀνήνεγκεν εἰς τὸν Δία·

Ζεὺς γὰρ κακὸν μὲν Τρωσὶ πῆμα δ᾽ Ἑλλάδι
θέλων γενέσθαι ταῦτ᾽ ἐβούλευσεν πατήρ.

(Fr. 1082, Nauck)

8. Περὶ δὲ τῶν τοῦ Ῥοδανοῦ στομάτων Πολύβιος μὲν ἐπιτιμᾷ Τιμαίῳ, φήσας εἶναι μὴ
πεντάστομον, ἀλλὰ δίστομον· Ἀρτεμίδωρος δὲ
τρίστομον λέγει. Μάριος[1] δὲ ὕστερον, ὁρῶν
τυφλόστομον γινόμενον ἐκ τῆς προχώσεως καὶ
δυσείσβολον, καινὴν ἔτεμε διώρυχα, καὶ ταύτῃ
δεξάμενος τὸ πλέον τοῦ ποταμοῦ Μασσαλιώταις
ἔδωκεν ἀριστεῖον κατὰ τὸν πρὸς Ἄμβρωνας καὶ
Τωυγενοὺς πόλεμον· ἐξ οὗ πλοῦτον ἠνέγκαντο
πολύν, τέλη[2] πραττόμενοι τοὺς ἀναπλέοντας καὶ
τοὺς καταγομένους. ὅμως οὖν ἔτι μένει δυσείσ-
πλοα διά τε τὴν λαβρότητα καὶ τὴν πρόσχωσιν
C 184   καὶ τὴν ταπεινότητα τῆς χώρας, ὥστε μὴ καθο-

---

[1] Μάριος, Xylander, for Τίμαιος; so the later editors.
[2] πολύν, τέλη, conjecture of Tyrwhitt, for πολυτελῆ; so
the editors.

passage—"captious," I say, for one might also find
in the discussions on "Providence" and "Predestina-
tion" many instances among the affairs of men and
among the natural occurrences of such a kind that,
in reference to them, one might say that it were
much better for this to have taken place than that;
for example, for Egypt to be well-watered by rains,
rather than that Ethiopia should soak its soil
with water; and for Paris to have met his reversal
by shipwreck on the voyage to Sparta, instead of
later carrying off Helen and paying the penalty to
those whom he had wronged, after he had effected
all that ruin of Greeks and barbarians—a ruin which
Euripides attributed to Zeus: "For Zeus, the father,
willing not only evil for the Trojans but also sorrow
for the Greeks, resolved upon all this."

8. With respect to the mouths of the Rhodanus:
Polybius reproves Timaeus by saying that there are
not five but two; Artemidorus says three; Marius,
later, seeing that, in consequence of the silting,
its mouths were becoming stopped up and difficult
of entrance, cut a new channel, and, upon admitting
the greater part of the river here, presented it to
the Massiliotes as a meed of their valour in the war
against the Ambrones and Toÿgeni; [1] and the wealth
they carried off from this source was considerable,
because they exacted tolls from all who sailed up
and all who sailed down it. Nevertheless, the
mouths still remain difficult of entrance for ships,
not only on account of the impetuosity of the river
and the silting up, but also of the lowness of the

[1] These two peoples joined the Cimbri for the purpose of
invading Italy. With the aid of the Massiliotes, Marius
defeated them at Aix (102 B.C.).

ρᾶσθαι μηδ' ἐγγὺς ἐν ταῖς δυσαερίαις. διόπερ οἱ
Μασσαλιῶται πύργους ἀνέστησαν σημεῖα, ἐξοι-
κειούμενοι πάντα τρόπον τὴν χώραν· καὶ δὴ τῆς
Ἐφεσίας Ἀρτέμιδος κἀνταῦθα ἱδρύσαντο ἱερόν,
χωρίον ἀπολαβόντες ὃ ποιεῖ νῆσον τὰ στόματα
τοῦ ποταμοῦ. ὑπέρκειται δὲ τῶν ἐκβολῶν τοῦ
Ῥοδανοῦ λιμνοθάλαττα· καλοῦσι δὲ Στομαλίμνην,[1]
ὀστράκια δ' ἔχει πάμπολλα καὶ ἄλλως εὐψεῖ.
ταύτην δ' ἔνιοι συγκατηρίθμησαν τοῖς στόμασι
τοῦ Ῥοδανοῦ, καὶ μάλιστα οἱ φήσαντες ἑπτά-
στομον αὐτόν, οὔτε τοῦτ' εὖ λέγοντες οὔτ' ἐκεῖνο·
ὄρος γάρ ἐστι μεταξὺ τὸ διεῖργον ἀπὸ τοῦ ποταμοῦ τὴν λίμνην. ἡ μὲν οὖν ἀπὸ τῆς Πυρήνης ἐπὶ
Μασσαλίαν παραλίαν τοιαύτη καὶ τοσαύτη τις.

9. Ἡ δ' ἐπὶ τὸν Οὐᾶρον ποταμὸν καὶ τοὺς
ταύτῃ Λίγυας τάς τε τῶν Μασσαλιωτῶν ἔχει
πόλεις Ταυροέντιον καὶ Ὀλβίαν καὶ Ἀντίπολιν
καὶ Νίκαιαν καὶ τὸ ναύσταθμον τὸ Καίσαρος τοῦ
Σεβαστοῦ, ὃ καλοῦσι Φόρον Ἰούλιον. ἵδρυται δὲ
τοῦτο μεταξὺ τῆς Ὀλβίας καὶ τῆς Ἀντιπόλεως,
διέχον Μασσαλίας εἰς ἑξακοσίους σταδίους. ὁ
δὲ Οὐᾶρος μέσος ἐστὶ τῆς Ἀντιπόλεως καὶ Νικαίας, τῆς μὲν ὅσον εἴκοσι, τῆς δὲ ἑξήκοντα
σταδίους διέχων, ὥσθ' ἡ Νίκαια τῆς Ἰταλίας
γίνεται κατὰ τὸν νῦν ἀποδεδειγμένον ὅρον, καίπερ οὖσα Μασσαλιωτῶν· ἐπετείχισαν[1] γὰρ τὰ
κτίσματα ταῦτα τοῖς ὑπερκειμένοις βαρβάροις

---

[1] ἐπετείχισαν, Casaubon, for ἐτείχισαν; so the later editors.

[1] Literally, "Mouth-marsh."
[3] The Varus. Cp. 4. 1. 3.

country, so that in foul weather one cannot descry
the land even when close to it. Wherefore the
Massiliotes set up towers as beacons, because they
were in every way making the country their own;
and, in truth, they also established a temple of
the Ephesian Artemis there, after first enclosing a
piece of land which is made an island by the mouths
of the river. Beyond the outlets of the Rhodanus
lies a sea-water marsh; it is called "Stomalimne," [1]
and it has a very great quantity of oysters, and,
besides that, is well supplied with fish. This lake
was by some counted in with the mouths of the
Rhodanus, and particularly by those who said there
were seven mouths, although they were right in
neither the latter nor the former; for there is a
mountain intervening which separates the lake from
the river. This, then, is approximately the nature
and the extent of the seaboard from the Pyrenees
to Massilia.

9. Again, the seaboard which extends from
Massilia to the Varus River and to those Ligures
who live in the region of the river has not only the
following cities of the Massiliotes, namely, Tauroentium, Olbia, Antipolis, and Nicaea, but also that
naval-station of Caesar Augustus which is called
Forum Julium. This naval-station is situated between
Olbia and Antipolis, at a distance of about six
hundred stadia from Massilia. The Varus is between
Antipolis and Nicaea, at a distance of about twenty
stadia from the latter and sixty from the former,
so that, according to what is now the declared
boundary,[2] Nicaea becomes a part of Italy, although
it belongs to the Massiliotes; for the Massiliotes
founded these places as strongholds against those

οἱ Μασσαλιῶται, τήν γε[1] θάλατταν ἐλευθέραν
ἔχειν βουλόμενοι, τῆς χώρας ὑπ' ἐκείνων κρατου-
μένης· ὀρεινὴ γάρ ἐστι καὶ ἐρυμνή, πρὸς μὲν τῇ
Μασσαλίᾳ πλάτος τι μέτριον καταλείπουσα τῶν
ἐπιπέδων χωρίων, προϊόντι δὲ ἐπὶ τὴν ἕω παντάπασιν ἀποθλίβουσα πρὸς τὴν θάλατταν καὶ
μόλις αὐτὴν πορεύσιμον ἐῶσα τὴν ὁδόν. κατέχουσι δὲ τὰ μὲν πρῶτα Σάλλυες, τὰ δὲ τελευταῖα
πρὸς τὴν Ἰταλίαν συνάπτοντες Λίγυες, περὶ ὧν
λεχθήσεται μετὰ ταῦτα. νυνὶ δὲ τοσοῦτον προσθετέον, ὅτι τῆς μὲν Ἀντιπόλεως ἐν τοῖς τῆς
Ναρβωνίτιδος μέρεσι κειμένης, τῆς δὲ Νικαίας
ἐν τοῖς τῆς Ἰταλίας, ἡ μὲν Νίκαια ὑπὸ τοῖς
Μασσαλιώταις μένει καὶ τῆς ἐπαρχίας[2] ἐστίν,
ἡ δ' Ἀντίπολις τῶν Ἰταλιωτίδων ἐξετάζεται,
κριθεῖσα πρὸς τοὺς Μασσαλιώτας καὶ ἐλευθερω-
θεῖσα τῶν παρ' ἐκείνων προσταγμάτων.

10. Πρόκεινται δὲ τῶν στενῶν τούτων ἀπὸ
Μασσαλίας ἀρξαμένοις αἱ Στοιχάδες νῆσοι, τρεῖς
μὲν ἀξιόλογοι, δύο δὲ μικραί· γεωργοῦσι δ' αὐτὰς
Μασσαλιῶται. τὸ δὲ παλαιὸν καὶ φρουρὰν εἶχον,
ἱδρυμένην αὐτόθι πρὸς τὰς τῶν λῃστηρίων ἐφόδους,
C 185 εὐποροῦντες καὶ λιμένων. μετὰ δὲ τὰς Στοιχάδας
ἡ Πλανασία καὶ Λήρων, ἔχουσαι κατοικίας. ἐν
δὲ τῇ Λήρωνι καὶ ἡρῷόν ἐστι τὸ τοῦ Λήρωνος·
κεῖται δ' αὕτη πρὸ τῆς Ἀντιπόλεως. ἄλλα δ'

---

[1] γε, Corais, for τε; so the later editors.
[2] ἐπαρχίας, Corais, for ὑπαρχίας; so the later editors.

---

[1] That is, of Narbonitis (see 4. 1. 3).
[2] An Italiote city was a Greek city in Italy.
[3] Thus called from the Greek "stoichades," "in a row,"—

barbarians who were situated beyond, wishing at
least to keep free the sea, since the land was con-
trolled by the barbarians; for it is mountainous and
also strong for defence, since, although next to
Massilia it leaves a strip of level land of moderate
width, yet as you proceed towards the east it
squeezes the strip off altogether towards the sea,
and scarcely leaves the road itself passable. Now
the first of these districts are occupied by the
Sallyes, but the last by those Ligures whose territory connects with Italy, concerning whom I shall
speak hereafter. But at present I need add only
this, that, although Antipolis is situated among the
parts that belong to Narbonitis, and Nicaea among
those that belong to Italy, Nicaea remains subject
to the Massiliotes and belongs to the Province,[1]
while Antipolis is classed among the Italiote cities,[2]
having been so adjudged in a suit against the
Massiliotes and thereby freed from their orders.

10. Lying off these narrow stretches of coast, if
we begin at Massilia, are the five Stoechades Islands,[3]
three of them of considerable size, but two quite
small; they are tilled by Massiliotes. In early
times the Massiliotes had also a garrison, which
they placed there to meet the onsets of the pirates,
since the islands were well supplied with harbours.
Next, after the Stoechades, are the islands of
Planasia and Lero, which have colonial settlements.
In Lero there is also a hero-temple, namely, that in
honour of Lero; this island lies off Antipolis. And,

a fairly suitable appellation. Pliny (3. 11) applies the name
only to the three large ones, while Pomponius Mela (2. 7)
includes the other islands off the shore from Massilia as far
as the country of the Ligures.

ἐστὶ νησίδια οὐκ ἄξια μνήμης, τὰ μὲν πρὸ τῆς
Μασσαλίας αὐτῆς, τὰ δὲ πρὸ τῆς ἄλλης τῆς
λεχθείσης ἠιόνος. τῶν δὲ λιμένων ὁ μὲν κατὰ
τὸν ναύσταθμον ἀξιόλογος καὶ ὁ τῶν Μασσαλιωτῶν, οἱ δ' ἄλλοι μέτριοι· τούτων δ' ἐστὶ καὶ
ὁ Ὀξύβιος καλούμενος λιμήν, ἐπώνυμος τῶν
Ὀξυβίων Λιγύων. περὶ μὲν τῆς παραλίας ταῦτα
λέγομεν.

11. Τὴν δ' ὑπερκειμένην αὐτῆς χώραν μάλιστα
γεωγραφεῖ τά τε ὄρη τὰ περικείμενα καὶ οἱ ποταμοί, διαφερόντως δὲ ὁ Ῥοδανός, μέγιστός τε ὢν
καὶ πλεῖστον ἀνάπλουν ἔχων, ἐκ πολλῶν πληρούμενος ῥευμάτων· λεκτέον οὖν ἐφεξῆς περὶ τούτων.
ἀπὸ Μασσαλίας τοίνυν ἀρξαμένοις καὶ προϊοῦσιν
ἐπὶ τὴν μεταξὺ χώραν τῶν τε Ἄλπεων καὶ τοῦ
Ῥοδανοῦ, μέχρι μὲν τοῦ Δρουεντία ποταμοῦ
Σάλλυες οἰκοῦσιν ἐπὶ πεντακοσίους σταδίους·
πορθμείῳ δὲ διαβᾶσιν εἰς Καβαλλίωνα πόλιν ἡ
ἐφεξῆς χώρα πᾶσα Καουάρων ἐστὶ μέχρι τῶν τοῦ
Ἴσαρος συμβολῶν πρὸς τὸν Ῥοδανόν· ἐνταῦθα
δὲ καὶ τὸ Κέμμενον συνάπτει πως τῷ Ῥοδανῷ·
μῆκος τὸ μέχρι δεῦρο ἀπὸ τοῦ Δρουεντία σταδίων
ἐστὶν ἑπτακοσίων. οἱ μὲν οὖν Σάλλυες ἐν αὐτοῖς[1]
τά τε πεδία καὶ τὰ ὑπερκείμενα ὄρη κατοικοῦσι,
τῶν δὲ Καουάρων ὑπέρκεινται Οὐοκόντιοί τε καὶ
Τρικόριοι καὶ Ἰκόνιοι καὶ Μέδυλλοι. μεταξὺ δὲ
τοῦ Δρουεντία καὶ τοῦ Ἴσαρος καὶ ἄλλοι ποταμοὶ
ῥέουσιν ἀπὸ τῶν Ἄλπεων ἐπὶ τὸν Ῥοδανόν, δύο

---

[1] αὐτοῖς, Jones, for αὑτοῖς.

[1] South of the Druentia.

besides, there are isles that are not worth mentioning, some off Massilia itself and the others off the rest of the aforesaid shore. As for the harbours, the one that is at the naval-station is of considerable size, and so is that of the Massiliotes, whereas the others are only of moderate size ; among these latter is the harbour that is called Oxybius, so named after the Oxybian Ligures. This is what I have to say about the seaboard.

11. As for the country that lies beyond the seaboard, its geographical limits are, in a general way, traced by the mountains that lie round about it, and also by the rivers—by the Rhodanus River especially, for it not only is the largest but also affords the most navigation inland, since the number of the streams from which it is filled is large. However, I must tell about all these regions in order. If you begin, then, at Massilia, and proceed towards the country that is between the Alps and the Rhodanus : Up to the Druentia River the country is inhabited by the Sallyes for a distance of five hundred stadia ; but if you cross the river by ferry into the city of Caballio, the whole country next thereafter belongs to the Cavari, up to the confluence of the Isar with the Rhodanus ; this is also approximately where the Cemmenus Mountain joins the Rhodanus ; the length of your journey from Druentia up to this place is seven hundred stadia. Now the Sallyes occupy—I mean in their own country [1]— not only the plains but also the mountains that lie above the plains, whereas above the Cavari are situated the Vocontii, Tricorii, Iconii, and Medulli. Between the Druentia and the Isar there are still other rivers which flow from the Alps to the

μὲν οἱ περιρρέοντες πόλιν Καουάρων [1] καὶ Οὐάρων [2] κοινῷ ῥείθρῳ συμβάλλοντες εἰς τὸν Ῥοδανόν,
τρίτος δὲ Σούλγας, ὁ κατὰ Οὔνδαλον πόλιν μισγό-
μενος τῷ Ῥοδανῷ, ὅπου Γναῖος Ἀηνόβαρβος μεγάλῃ μάχῃ πολλὰς ἐτρέψατο Κελτῶν μυριάδας.
εἰσὶ δὲ ἐν τῷ μεταξὺ πόλεις καὶ Αὐενιὼν καὶ
Ἀραυσίων καὶ Ἀερία, τῷ ὄντι, φησὶν Ἀρτεμίδωρος, ἀερία διὰ τὸ ἐφ' ὕψους ἱδρῦσθαι μεγάλου.
ἡ μὲν οὖν ἄλλη πᾶσά ἐστι πεδιὰς καὶ εὔβοτος, ἡ
δ' ἐκ τῆς Ἀερίας εἰς τὴν Δουρίωνα ὑπερθέσεις
ἔχει στενὰς καὶ ὑλώδεις. καθ' ὃ δὲ συμπίπτουσιν
ὁ Ἴσαρ ποταμὸς καὶ ὁ Ῥοδανὸς καὶ τὸ Κέμμενον
ὄρος, Κόϊντος Φάβιος Μάξιμος Αἰμιλιανὸς οὐχ
ὅλαις τρισὶ μυριάσιν εἴκοσι μυριάδας Κελτῶν
κατέκοψε, καὶ ἔστησε τρόπαιον αὐτόθι λευκοῦ
λίθου καὶ νεὼς δύο, τὸν μὲν Ἄρεως, τὸν δ' Ἡρακλέους. ἀπὸ δὲ τοῦ Ἴσαρος εἰς Οὐίενναν τὴν τῶν
Ἀλλοβρίγων μητρόπολιν κειμένην ἐπὶ τῷ Ῥο-
C 186 δανῷ στάδιοί εἰσι τριακόσιοι εἴκοσι. πλησίον

---

[1] Καουάρων, Siebenkees, for Κλαουάρων; so the later editors.
[2] Xylander would omit καὶ Οὐάρων; so Siebenkees, Corais,
Kramer, Forbiger, and Meineke. Groskurd emends to
Καρπένταρον, or Καρπεντάρωνα. Casaubon, comparing Λουερίωνος in 4. 6. 3, conjectures Λουερίωνα.

---

[1] Groskurd, believing with Gosselin that the Ouvèze and
the Mède are the rivers meant by Strabo, emends "and the
Vari" to "Carpenteron"—the "Carpentoracte" (to-day
Carpentras) of Pliny (3. 5). Several scholars (see critical
note above, on this page) omit "and the Vari" altogether.
Ukert (Geogr. 1832, vol. iii, page 138) thinks he recognizes in
"Cavari" and "Vari" the corrupted names of the rivers
now called Rubion and Jabrou, and that the city (which he
thinks has fallen out of the text) is Akousio (mentioned by
Ptolemaeus), to-day Anconne. But Béretta (Les Cités

Rhodanus, namely, two that flow round a city of
the Cavaran Vari,[1] and coming together in a
common stream empty into the Rhodanus; and a
third, the Sulgas, which mingles its waters with the
Rhodanus near the city of Undalum,[2] where in a
great battle Gnaeus Ahenobarbus turned many
myriads of Celti to flight. And there are in the
intervening space [3] the cities of Avenio,[4] Arausio,[5]
and Aeria [6]—"an 'Aeria' in reality," says Artemidorus, "because it is situated on a lofty elevation."
All the country, however, is level and good for
pasturage, except that the stretch from Aeria to
Durio [7] has mountainous passes that are narrow and
wooded. But where the Isar River and the Rhodanus
and the Cemmenus Mountain meet, Quintus Fabius
Maximus Aemilianus, with less than thirty thousand
men all told, cut down two hundred thousand Celti;
and on the spot he set up a trophy of white marble,
and also two temples, one in honour of Ares, the other
in honour of Heracles. From the Isar to Vienna,
the metropolis of the Allobroges, situated on the
Rhodanus, the distance is three hundred and twenty

Mystérieuses de Strabo, pp. 36–44) rightly defends the Greek
text and seems to prove that the city in question was what
is now Bédarrides, at the confluence of the Ouvèze and the
Mède.

  [2] What is now Sorgues, according to Béretta (*op. cit.*
p. 49). The name is also spelled "Vindalum."

  [3] Between the Druentia and the Isar.

  [4] Now Avignon.   [5] Now Orange.

  [6] Béretta (*op. cit.* pp. 50–73) convincingly identifies Aeria
with what is now Carpentras.

  [7] A. Béretta (*op. cit.* 74–100) identifies Durio with what is
now Malaucène. Some scholars emend to "Luerio," a place
referred to in 4. 6. 3, but otherwise unknown, while others,
including Meineke, wrongly emend to Avenio (Avignon).

δ' ὑπέρκειται τῆς Οὐιέννης τὸ Λούγδουνον, ἐφ'
οὗ συμμίσγουσιν ἀλλήλοις ὅ τε Ἄραρ καὶ ὁ
Ῥοδανός· στάδιοι δ' εἰσὶν ἐπ' αὐτὸ πεζῇ μὲν περὶ
διακοσίους διὰ τῆς Ἀλλοβρίγων, ἀνάπλῳ δὲ
μικρῷ πλείους. Ἀλλόβριγες δὲ μυριάσι πολλαῖς
πρότερον μὲν ἐστράτευον, νῦν δὲ γεωργοῦσι τὰ
πεδία καὶ τοὺς αὐλῶνας τοὺς ἐν ταῖς Ἄλπεσι,
καὶ οἱ μὲν ἄλλοι κωμηδὸν ζῶσιν, οἱ δ' ἐπιφανέστατοι τὴν Οὐίενναν ἔχοντες, κώμην πρότερον
οὖσαν, μητρόπολιν δ' ὅμως τοῦ ἔθνους λεγομένην,
κατεσκευάκασι πόλιν. ἵδρυται δ' ἐπὶ τῷ Ῥοδανῷ.
φέρεται δ' ἀπὸ[1] τῶν Ἄλπεων οὗτος πολὺς καὶ
σφοδρός, ὅς γε καὶ διὰ λίμνης ἐξιὼν τῆς Λημέννης[2]
φανερὸν δείκνυσι τὸ ῥεῖθρον ἐπὶ πολλοὺς σταδίους.
κατελθὼν δὲ εἰς τὰ πεδία τῆς χώρας τῆς Ἀλλοβρίγων καὶ Σηγοσιανῶν[3] συμβάλλει τῷ Ἄραρι
κατὰ Λούγδουνον πόλιν τῶν Σηγοσιανῶν.[3] ῥεῖ
δὲ καὶ ὁ Ἄραρ ἐκ τῶν Ἄλπεων, ὁρίζων Σηκοανούς τε καὶ Αἰδούους καὶ Λίγγονας[4] παραλαβὼν
δ' ὕστερον τὸν Δοῦβιν ἐκ τῶν αὐτῶν ὀρῶν φερόμενον πλωτόν, ἐπικρατήσας τῷ ὀνόματι καὶ γενόμενος ἐξ ἀμφοῖν Ἄραρ συμμίσγει τῷ Ῥοδανῷ.
πάλιν δ' ἐπικρατήσας ὁ Ῥοδανὸς εἰς τὴν Οὐίενναν
φέρεται. συμβαίνει δὴ κατ' ἀρχὰς μὲν τοὺς τρεῖς
ποταμοὺς φέρεσθαι πρὸς ἄρκτον, εἶτα πρὸς δύσιν·
εἰς ἓν δ' ἤδη συμπεσὸν[5] ῥεῖθρον πάλιν ἄλλην

[1] ἀπό, Corais, for ἄνω; so the later editors.
[2] Λημέννης, Kramer, for τῆς μεγάλης (cp. 4. 6. 11); so the
later editors.
[3] Σηγοσιανῶν, the editors, for the variants of the MSS.
(see C. Müller Ind. Var. Lect. pp. 962 (154, 32, 33) and 963
(159, 40); also Holmes, Caesar's Conquest of Gaul, p. 848).
[4] Λίγγονας, Corais, for Λιγκασίους; so the editors in general.

stadia. Near Vienna, and beyond it, is situated
Lugdunum, at which the Arar and the Rhodanus
mingle with one another; and the distance to
Lugdunum [1] in stadia is, if you go by foot through
the territory of the Allobroges, about two hundred,
but if by voyage up the river, slightly more than that.
Formerly the Allobroges kept up warfare with many
myriads of men, whereas now they till the plains
and the glens that are in the Alps, and all of them
live in villages, except that the most notable of
them, inhabitants of Vienna (formerly a village, but
called, nevertheless, the "metropolis" of the tribe),
have built it up into a city. It is situated on the
Rhodanus. This river runs from the Alps in great
volume and impetuosity—since on its way out, while
passing through the Lemenna Lake, its stream is
clearly visible for many stadia. And after coming
down into the plains of the country of the Allobroges
and Segusiavi, it meets the Arar at Lugdunum, a
city of the Segusiavi. The Arar, too, flows from
the Alps, since it separates the Sequani from the
Aedui and the Lingones; then, later, taking on the
waters of the Dubis—a navigable river that runs
from the same mountains—it prevails over the Dubis
with its name, and though made up of both mingles
with the Rhodanus as the "Arar." And, in its
turn, the Rhodanus prevails, and runs to Vienna.
So the result is, that at first the three rivers run
northwards, and then westwards; and then, immediately after they have joined together into one

[1] That is, from Vienna, now Vienne.

The people in question are called "Lingones" by other
writers, as well as by Strabo himself (4. 3. 4 and 4. 6. 11).
[5] συμπεσόν, Xylander, for συμπεσών.

καμπὴν λαβὸν νότιον φέρεται τὸ ῥεῦμα μέχρι τῶν
ἐκβολῶν, δεξάμενον καὶ τοὺς ἄλλους ποταμούς,
κἀκεῖθεν ἤδη τὴν λοιπὴν ποιεῖται μέχρι τῆς
θαλάττης ῥύσιν. ἡ μὲν οὖν μεταξὺ τῶν Ἄλπεων
καὶ τοῦ Ῥοδανοῦ τοιαύτη τις.

12. Τὴν δ᾽ ἐπὶ θάτερα μέρη τοῦ ποταμοῦ
Οὐόλκαι νέμονται τὴν πλείστην, οὓς Ἀρηκο-
μίσκους προσαγορεύουσι. τούτων δ᾽ ἐπίνειον ἡ
Νάρβων λέγεται, δικαιότερον δ᾽ ἂν καὶ τῆς ἄλλης
Κελτικῆς λέγοιτο· τοσοῦτον ὑπερβέβληται τῷ
πλήθει τῶν χρωμένων τῷ ἐμπορείῳ. οἱ μὲν οὖν
Οὐόλκαι γειτονεύουσι τῷ Ῥοδανῷ, τοὺς Σάλλυας
ἔχοντες ἀντιπαρήκοντας αὐτοῖς ἐν τῇ περαίᾳ καὶ
τοὺς Καουάρους. ἐπικρατεῖ δὲ τὸ τῶν Καουάρων
ὄνομα καὶ πάντας οὕτως ἤδη προσαγορεύουσι τοὺς
ταύτῃ βαρβάρους, οὐδὲ βαρβάρους ἔτι ὄντας, ἀλλὰ
μετακειμένους τὸ πλέον εἰς τὸν τῶν Ῥωμαίων τύπον
καὶ τῇ γλώττῃ καὶ τοῖς βίοις, τινὰς δὲ καὶ τῇ
πολιτείᾳ. ἄλλα δέ ἐστιν ἄδοξα ἔθνη καὶ μικρά,
παρακείμενα τοῖς Ἀρηκομίσκοις μέχρι Πυρήνης.
μητρόπολις δὲ τῶν Ἀρηκομίσκων ἐστὶ Νέμαυσος,
κατὰ μὲν τὸν ἀλλότριον ὄχλον καὶ τὸν ἐμπορικὸν
πολὺ Νάρβωνος λειπομένη, κατὰ δὲ τὸν πολιτικὸν
ὑπερβάλλουσα· ὑπηκόους γὰρ ἔχει κώμας τέτταρας
καὶ εἴκοσι τῶν ὁμοεθνῶν εὐανδρίᾳ διαφερούσας,
συντελούσας εἰς αὑτήν, ἔχουσα[1] καὶ τὸ καλούμενον
C 187 Λάτιον, ὥστε τοὺς ἀξιωθέντας ἀγορανομίας καὶ

---

[1] ἔχουσα, Corais, for ἐχούσας (ABl), ἔχουσαν (C); so the
later editors.

---

[1] "Jus Latii" (see footnote on "Latins," 3. 2. 15).

bed, the stream again takes another turn and runs a southerly course as far as its outlets (although before this it has received the other rivers), and from there begins to make the remainder of its course as far as the sea. Such, then, is approximately the nature of the country which lies between the Alps and the Rhodanus.

12. As for the country which lies on the other side of the river, most of it is occupied by those Volcae who are called Arecomisci. Narbo is spoken of as the naval-station of these people alone, though it would be fairer to add " and of the rest of Celtica " —so greatly has it surpassed the others in the number of people who use it as a trade-centre. Now, although the Volcae border on the Rhodanus, with the Sallyes and also the Cavari stretching along parallel to them on the opposite side of the river, the name of the Cavari prevails, and people are already calling by that name all the barbarians in that part of the country—no, they are no longer barbarians, but are, for the most part, transformed to the type of the Romans, both in their speech and in their modes of living, and some of them in their civic life as well. Again, situated alongside the Arecomisci as far as the Pyrenees, are other tribes, which are without repute and small. Now the metropolis of the Arecomisci is Nemausus, which, although it comes considerably short of Narbo in its throng of foreigners and of merchants, surpasses Narbo in that of citizens; for it has, subject to its authority, twenty-four villages, which are exceptional in their supply of strong men, of stock like its own, and contribute towards its expenses; and it has also what is called the " Latin right," [1] so that those who

ταμιείας ἐν Νεμαύσῳ ῾Ρωμαίους ὑπάρχειν· διὰ δὲ
τοῦτο οὐδ᾽ ὑπὸ τοῖς προστάγμασι[1] τῶν ἐκ τῆς
῾Ρώμης στρατηγῶν ἐστι τὸ ἔθνος τοῦτο. ἵδρυται δ᾽
ἡ πόλις κατὰ τὴν ὁδὸν τὴν ἐκ τῆς Ἰβηρίας εἰς τὴν
Ἰταλίαν, θέρους μὲν εὔβατον οὖσαν, χειμῶνος δὲ
καὶ ἔαρος πηλώδη καὶ ποταμόκλυστον· τινὰ μὲν
οὖν τῶν ῥευμάτων πορθμείοις περᾶται, τινὰ δὲ
γεφύραις, ταῖς μὲν ξύλων πεποιημέναις, ταῖς δὲ
λίθων. ποιοῦσι δὲ τὰς ἐκ τῶν ὑδάτων δυσκολίας
οἱ χείμαρροι, καὶ μέχρι τοῦ θέρους ἔσθ᾽ ὅτε ἐκ τῶν
Ἄλπεων καταφερόμενοι μετὰ τὴν ἀπότηξιν τῶν
χιόνων. τῆς δ᾽ ὁδοῦ τῆς λεχθείσης ἡ μὲν εὐθὺς ἐπὶ
τὰς Ἄλπεις ἐστί, καθάπερ εἴπομεν, ἡ σύντομος
διὰ Οὐοκοντίων· ἡ δὲ διὰ τῆς παραλίας τῆς Μασσα-
λιωτικῆς καὶ τῆς Λιγυστικῆς μακροτέρα μέν, τὰς
δ᾽ ὑπερθέσεις τὰς εἰς τὴν Ἰταλίαν εὐμαρεστέρας
ἔχει, ταπεινουμένων ἐνταῦθα ἤδη τῶν ὀρῶν. διέχει
δ᾽ ἡ Νέμαυσος τοῦ μὲν ῾Ροδανοῦ περὶ ἑκατὸν σταδίους, καθ᾽ ὃ ἐν τῇ περαίᾳ πολίχνιόν ἐστι Ταρού-
σκων, τῆς δὲ Νάρβωνος ἑπτακοσίους εἴκοσι. πρὸς
δὲ τὸ Κέμμενον ὄρος συνάπτοντες, ἐπιλαμβάνοντες
δὲ καὶ τὸ νότιον πλευρὸν αὐτοῦ μέχρι τῶν ἀκρωτηρίων οἰκοῦσι τῶν τε Οὐολκῶν οἱ Τεκτόσαγες
καλούμενοι καὶ ἄλλοι τινές. περὶ μὲν οὖν τῶν
ἄλλων ἐροῦμεν ὕστερον.

13. Οἱ δὲ Τεκτόσαγες καλούμενοι τῇ Πυρήνῃ
πλησιάζουσιν, ἐφάπτονται δὲ μικρὰ καὶ τοῦ προσαρκτίου πλευροῦ τῶν Κεμμένων, πολύχρυσόν τε

---

[1] προστάγμασι, the reading of o; πράγμασι, ABCl.

---

[1] See 4. 2. 2 and footnote on "autonomous."

have been thought worthy of the offices of aedile and quaestor at Nemausus are by that preferment Roman citizens, and, on account of this fact, this tribe too is not subject to the orders of the praetors who are sent out from Rome.[1] The city is situated on the road that leads from Iberia into Italy, which, although it is easy to travel in summer, is muddy and also flooded by the rivers in winter and spring. Now some of the streams are crossed by ferries, others by bridges—some made of timber, others of stone. But it is the torrents that cause the annoying difficulties that result from the waters, since, after the melting away of the snows, they sometimes rush down from the Alps even till the summer-time. Of the aforesaid road, the branch[2] that leads straight to the Alps is, as I stated, the short cut through the territory of the Vocontii, whereas that through the Massilian and Ligurian seaboard is indeed longer, although the passes it affords over into Italy are easier, since the mountains begin to lower there. The distance of Nemausus from the Rhodanus—reckoning from a point opposite the town of Tarusco, on the other side of the river—is about a hundred stadia; but from Narbo, seven hundred and twenty. Again, in territory that joins the Cemmenus Mountain, and that takes in also the southern side[3] of the mountain as far as its summits, there live that people of the Volcae who are called Tectosages and also certain others. About these others I shall speak later on.

13. The people who are called Tectosages closely approach the Pyrenees, though they also reach over small parts of the northern side of the Cemmenus;

[2] See 4. 1. 2.
[3] To Strabo, the Cemmenus ran east and west.

νέμονται γῆν. ἐοίκασι δὲ καὶ δυναστεῦσαί ποτε καὶ
εὐανδρῆσαι τοσοῦτον, ὥστε στάσεως ἐμπεσούσης
ἐξελάσαι πολὺ πλῆθος ἐξ ἑαυτῶν ἐκ τῆς οἰκείας·
κοινωνῆσαι δὲ τούτοις καὶ ἄλλους ἐξ ἄλλων ἐθνῶν.
τούτων δ' εἶναι καὶ τοὺς κατασχόντας τὴν Φρυγίαν
τὴν ὅμορον τῇ Καππαδοκίᾳ καὶ τοῖς Παφλαγόσι·
τούτου μὲν οὖν ἔχομεν τεκμήριον τοὺς ἔτι καὶ νῦν
λεγομένους Τεκτόσαγας· τριῶν γὰρ ὄντων ἐθνῶν,
ἓν ἐξ αὐτῶν τὸ περὶ Ἄγκυραν πόλιν Τεκτοσάγων
λέγεται, τὰ δὲ λοιπὰ δύο ἐστὶ Τρόκμοι καὶ Τολιστο-
βώγιοι· τούτους δ', ὅτι μὲν ἐκ τῆς Κελτικῆς ἀπωκί-
σθησαν, μηνύει τό γε[1] πρὸς τοὺς Τεκτόσαγας
σύμφυλον, ἐξ ὧν δὲ χωρίων ὡρμήθησαν, οὐκ ἔχομεν
φράζειν· οὐ γὰρ παρειλήφαμεν οἰκοῦντάς τινας
τὰ[2] νυνὶ Τρόκμους ἢ Τολιστοβωγίους ἐκτὸς τῶν
Ἄλπεων οὔτ' ἐν αὐταῖς οὔτ' ἐντός. εἰκὸς δ' ἐκλε-
λοιπέναι διὰ τὰς ἀθρόας ἀπαναστάσεις, καθάπερ
καὶ ἐπ' ἄλλων συμβαίνει πλειόνων· ἐπεὶ καὶ τὸν
ἄλλον Βρέννον τὸν ἐπελθόντα ἐπὶ Δελφοὺς Πραῦσόν
τινές φασιν, οὐδὲ τοὺς Πραύσους δ' ἔχομεν εἰπεῖν,
C 188 ὅπου γῆς ᾤκησαν πρότερον. καὶ τοὺς Τεκτόσαγας
δέ φασι μετασχεῖν τῆς ἐπὶ Δελφοὺς στρατείας,
καὶ τούς τε θησαυροὺς τοὺς εὑρεθέντας παρ' αὐτοῖς

---

[1] γε, Corais, for τε.
[2] τά, Jones, for τήν; the reading of no is τό.

---

[1] Strabo refers to Galatia, a part of Greater Phrygia (12.
8. 1). One of the three Galatian tribes retained the name of
"Tectosages," "from the tribe of that name in Celtica"
(12. 5. 1).

[2] That is, the Gallic Brennus who made an invasion against
Delphi in 278 B.C. with 152,000 infantry and 20,000 cavalry

and the land they occupy is rich in gold. It appears
that at one time they were so powerful and had so
large a stock of strong men that, when a sedition
broke out in their midst, they drove a considerable
number of their own people out of the homeland;
again, that other persons from other tribes made
common lot with these exiles; and that among these
are also those people who have taken possession of
that part of Phrygia which has a common boundary
with Cappadocia and the Paphlagonians.[1] Now as
proof of this we have the people who are still, even
at the present time, called Tectosages; for, since
there are three tribes, one of them—the one that
lives about the city of Ancyra—is called " the tribe
of the Tectosages," while the remaining two are the
Trocmi and the Tolistobogii. As for these latter
peoples, although the fact of their racial kinship with
the Tectosages indicates that they emigrated from
Celtica, I am unable to tell from what districts they
set forth; for I have not learned of any Trocmi
or Tolistobogii who now live beyond the Alps, or
within them, or this side of them. But it is reasonable to suppose that nothing has been left of them
in Celtica on account of their thoroughgoing migrations—just as is the case with several other
peoples. For example, some say that the second
Brennus[2] who made an invasion against Delphi was
a Prausan, but I am unable to say where on earth
the Prausans formerly lived, either. And it is
further said that the Tectosages shared in the
expedition to Delphi; and even the treasures that
were found among them in the city of Tolosa by

(see Pausanias 10. 19); not the Gallic Brennus who a century
before sacked Rome.

ὑπὸ Καιπίωνος[1] τοῦ στρατηγοῦ τῶν Ῥωμαίων ἐν
πόλει Τολώσσῃ τῶν ἐκεῖθεν χρημάτων μέρος εἶναί
φασι, προσθεῖναι δὲ τοὺς ἀνθρώπους καὶ ἐκ τῶν
ἰδίων οἴκων ἀνιεροῦντας καὶ ἐξιλασκομένους τὸν
θεόν· προσαψάμενον δ' αὐτῶν τὸν Καιπίωνα διὰ
τοῦτο ἐν δυστυχήμασι καταστρέψαι τὸν βίον, ὡς
ἱερόσυλον ἐκβληθέντα ὑπὸ τῆς πατρίδος, διαδόχους
δ' ἀπολιπόντα παῖδας, ἃς συνέβη καταπορνευθεί-
σας, ὡς εἴρηκε Τιμαγένης, αἰσχρῶς ἀπολέσθαι.
πιθανώτερος δ' ἐστὶν ὁ Ποσειδωνίου λόγος· τὰ μὲν
γὰρ εὑρεθέντα ἐν τῇ Τολώσσῃ χρήματα μυρίων
που καὶ πεντακισχιλίων ταλάντων γενέσθαι φησί,
τὰ μὲν ἐν σηκοῖς ἀποκείμενα, τὰ δ' ἐν λίμναις
ἱεραῖς, οὐδεμίαν κατασκευὴν ἔχοντα, ἀλλ' ἀργὸν
χρυσίον καὶ ἄργυρον· τὸ δ' ἐν Δελφοῖς ἱερὸν κατ'
ἐκείνους ἤδη τοὺς χρόνους ὑπάρξαι κενὸν τῶν
τοιούτων, σεσυλημένον ὑπὸ τῶν Φωκέων κατὰ τὸν
ἱερὸν πόλεμον· εἰ δὲ καί τι ἐλείφθη, διανείμασθαι
πολλούς· οὐδὲ σωθῆναι δὲ αὐτοὺς εἰκὸς εἰς τὴν
οἰκείαν, ἀθλίως ἀπαλλάξαντας μετὰ τὴν ἐκ Δελφῶν
ἀποχώρησιν καὶ σκεδασθέντας ἄλλους ἐπ' ἄλλα
μέρη κατὰ διχοστασίαν. ἀλλ', ὥσπερ ἐκεῖνός τε
εἴρηκε καὶ ἄλλοι πλείους, ἡ χώρα πολύχρυσος
οὖσα καὶ δεισιδαιμόνων καὶ οὐ πολυτελῶν τοῖς
βίοις πολλαχοῦ τῆς Κελτικῆς ἔσχε θησαυρούς·
μάλιστα δ' αὐτοῖς αἱ λίμναι τὴν ἀσυλίαν παρεῖ-
χον, εἰς ἃς καθίεσαν ἀργύρου ἢ καὶ χρυσοῦ βάρη.
οἱ γοῦν Ῥωμαῖοι κρατήσαντες τῶν τόπων ἀπέδοντο

---

[1] Καιπίωνος, and Καιπίωνα (below), are obvious corrections
for Σκιπίωνος and Σκιπίωνα; so the editors since Xylander.

Caepio, a general of the Romans, were, it is said, a part of the valuables that were taken from Delphi, although the people, in trying to consecrate them and propitiate the god, added thereto out of their personal properties, and it was on account of having laid hands on them that Caepio ended his life in misfortunes—for he was cast out by his native land as a temple-robber, and he left behind as his heirs female children only, who, as it turned out, became prostitutes, as Timagenes has said, and therefore perished in disgrace. However, the account of Poseidonius is more plausible: for he says that the treasure that was found in Tolosa amounted to about fifteen thousand talents (part of it stored away in sacred enclosures, part of it in sacred lakes), unwrought, that is, merely gold and silver bullion; whereas the temple at Delphi was in those times already empty of such treasure, because it had been robbed at the time of the sacred war by the Phocians; but even if something was left, it was divided by many among themselves; neither is it reasonable to suppose that they reached their homeland in safety, since they fared wretchedly after their retreat from Delphi and, because of their dissensions, were scattered, some in one direction, others in another. But, as has been said both by Poseidonius and several others, since the country was rich in gold, and also belonged to people who were god-fearing and not extravagant in their ways of living, it came to have treasures in many places in Celtica; but it was the lakes, most of all, that afforded the treasures their inviolability, into which the people let down heavy masses of silver or even of gold. At all events, the Romans, after they

τὰς λίμνας δημοσίᾳ, καὶ τῶν ὠνησαμένων πολλοὶ
μύλους εὖρον σφυρηλάτους ἀργυροῦς. ἐν δὲ τῇ
Τολώσσῃ καὶ τὸ ἱερὸν ἦν ἅγιον, τιμώμενον σφόδρα
ὑπὸ τῶν περιοίκων, καὶ τὰ χρήματα ἐπλεόνασε
διὰ τοῦτο, πολλῶν ἀνατιθέντων καὶ μηδενὸς προσ-
άπτεσθαι θαρροῦντος.

14. Ἵδρυται δ' ἡ Τολῶσσα κατὰ τὸ στενότατον
τοῦ ἰσθμοῦ τοῦ διείργοντος ἀπὸ τῆς κατὰ Νάρβωνα
θαλάττης τὸν ὠκεανόν, ὅν[1] φησι Ποσειδώνιος
ἐλάττω τῶν τρισχιλίων σταδίων. ἄξιον δ' ἀντὶ
πάντων ἐπισημήνασθαι πάλιν ὅπερ εἴπομεν πρότερον, τὴν ὁμολογίαν τῆς χώρας πρός τε τοὺς
ποταμοὺς καὶ τὴν θάλατταν τήν τ' ἐκτὸς ὁμοίως
καὶ τὴν ἐντός· εὕροι γὰρ ἄν τις ἐπιστήσας οὐκ
ἐλάχιστον μέρος τοῦθ' ὑπάρχον τῆς τῶν τόπων
ἀρετῆς, λέγω δὲ τὸ τὰς χρείας ἐπιπλέκεσθαι τὰς
τοῦ βίου μετὰ ῥᾳστώνης ἅπασι πρὸς ἅπαντας καὶ
C 189 τὰς ὠφελείας ἀνεῖσθαι κοινάς, μάλιστα δὲ νῦν,
ἡνίκα ἄγοντες σχολὴν ἀπὸ τῶν ὅπλων ἐργάζονται
τὴν χώραν ἐπιμελῶς, καὶ τοὺς βίους κατασκευά-
ζονται πολιτικούς. ὥστε ἐπὶ τῶν τοιούτων κἂν
τὸ τῆς προνοίας ἔργον ἐπιμαρτυρεῖσθαί τις ἂν
δόξειεν, οὐχ ὅπως ἔτυχεν, ἀλλ' ὡς ἂν μετὰ λογι-
σμοῦ τινος, διακειμένων τῶν τόπων. ὁ μέν γε
Ῥοδανὸς πολύν τε ἔχει τὸν ἀνάπλουν καὶ μεγάλοις
φορτίοις καὶ ἐπὶ πολλὰ μέρη τῆς χώρας διὰ τὸ

---

[1] ὅν, Xylander, for ὡς; so the later editors.

[1] 4. 1. 2.   [2] The ocean.

mastered the regions, sold the lakes for the public treasury, and many of the buyers found in them hammered mill-stones of silver. And, in Tolosa, the temple too was hallowed, since it was very much revered by the inhabitants of the surrounding country, and on this account the treasures there were excessive, for numerous people had dedicated them and no one dared to lay hands on them.

14. Tolosa is situated on the narrowest part of the isthmus which separates the ocean from the sea that is at Narbo, which isthmus, according to Poseidonius is less than three thousand stadia in width. But it is above all worth while to note again a characteristic of this region which I have spoken of before [1]— the harmonious arrangement of the country with reference, not only to the rivers, but also to the sea, alike both the outer sea [2] and the inner; for one might find, if he set his thoughts upon the matter, that this is not the least factor in the excellence of the regions—I mean the fact that the necessities of life are with ease interchanged by every one with every one else and that the advantages which have arisen therefrom are common to all; but especially so at present, when being at leisure from the weapons of war, the people are tilling the country diligently, and are devising for themselves modes of life that are civil. Therefore, in the cases of this sort, one might believe that there is confirmatory evidence for the workings of Providence, since the regions are laid out, not in a fortuitous way, but as though in accordance with some calculated plan. In the first place, the voyage which the Rhodanus affords inland is a considerable one, even for vessels of great burden, and reaches numerous

τοὺς ἐμπίπτοντας εἰς αὐτὸν ποταμοὺς ὑπάρχειν
πλωτοὺς καὶ διαδέχεσθαι τὸν φόρτον πλεῖστον. ὁ
δ᾽ Ἄραρ ἐκδέχεται καὶ ὁ Δοῦβις ὁ εἰς τοῦτον
ἐμβάλλων, εἶτα πεζεύεται μέχρι τοῦ Σηκοάνα ποταμοῦ, κἀντεῦθεν ἤδη καταφέρεται εἰς τὸν ὠκεανὸν
καὶ τοὺς Ληξοβίους καὶ Καλέτους,¹ ἐκ δὲ τούτων
εἰς τὴν Βρεττανικὴν ἐλάττων ἢ ἡμερήσιος δρόμος
ἐστίν. ἐπεὶ δ᾽ ἐστὶν ὀξὺς καὶ δυσανάπλους ὁ
Ῥοδανός, τινὰ τῶν ἐντεῦθεν φορτίων πεζεύεται
μᾶλλον ταῖς ἁρμαμάξαις, ὅσα εἰς Ἀρουέρνους κομίζεται καὶ τὸν Λείγηρα ποταμόν, καίπερ τοῦ
Ῥοδανοῦ καὶ τούτοις πλησιάζοντος ἐκ μέρους·
ἀλλ᾽ ἡ ὁδὸς πεδιὰς οὖσα καὶ οὐ πολλή, περὶ ὀκτακοσίους σταδίους, ἐπάγεται μὴ χρήσασθαι τῷ
ἀνάπλῳ διὰ τὸ πεζεύεσθαι ῥᾷον· ἐντεῦθεν δ᾽ ὁ
Λείγηρ εὐφυῶς ἐκδέχεται· ῥεῖ δὲ ἐκ τῶν Κεμμένων
εἰς τὸν ὠκεανόν. ἐκ δὲ Νάρβωνος ἀναπλεῖται μὲν
ἐπὶ μικρὸν τῷ Ἄτακι, πεζεύεται δὲ πλέον ἐπὶ τὸν
Γαρούναν ποταμόν, καὶ τοῦθ᾽ ὅσον ὀκτακοσίων ἢ
ἑπτακοσίων σταδίων· ῥεῖ δὲ καὶ ὁ Γαρούνας εἰς
τὸν ὠκεανόν. ταῦτα μὲν ὑπὲρ τῶν νεμομένων τὴν
Ναρβωνῖτιν ἐπικράτειαν λέγομεν, οὓς οἱ πρότερον
Κέλτας ὠνόμαζον· ἀπὸ τούτων δ᾽ οἶμαι καὶ τοὺς
σύμπαντας Γαλάτας Κελτοὺς ὑπὸ τῶν Ἑλλήνων

---

¹ Καλέτους, Xylander, for ὑαδέτους, editors following.

---

[1] The former lived south, the latter north, of the mouth of
the Sequana.

[2] Apparently from the Rhodanus, at its confluence with
the Arar, at Lugdunum (Lyon).

[3] The Rhone for some distance runs as close as thirty miles
to the Loire (Liger) ; the Arvernians lived still farther west.
But there seems to have been no convenient way here to
transfer merchandise to the Loire.

parts of the country, on account of the fact that the
rivers which fall into it are navigable, and in their
turns receive most of the traffic. Secondly, the
Rhodanus is succeeded by the Arar, and by the
Dubis (which empties into the Arar); then the traffic
goes by land as far as the Sequana River; and thence
it begins its voyage down to the ocean, and to the
Lexobii and Caleti;[1] and from these peoples it
is less than a day's run to Britain. But since the
Rhodanus is swift and difficult to sail up, some of
the traffic from here[2] preferably goes by land on the
wagons, that is, all the traffic that is conveyed to the
Arvernians and the Liger River—albeit in a part of
its course the Rhodanus draws close to these also;[3]
still, the fact that the road is level and not long
(about eight hundred stadia)[4] is an inducement
not to use the voyage upstream,[5] since it is easier
to go by land; from here, however, the road is
naturally succeeded by the Liger; and it flows from
the Cemmenus Mountain to the ocean. Thirdly,
from Narbo traffic goes inland for a short distance
by the Atax River, and then a greater distance by
land to the Garumna River; and this latter distance
is about eight hundred or seven hundred stadia.
And the Garumna, too, flows to the ocean. This,
then, is what I have to say about the people who inhabit the dominion of Narbonitis, whom the men of
former times named "Celtae"; and it was from the
Celtae, I think, that the Galatae as a whole were by

---

[4] About the distance from Lyon to Bourbon-Lancy on the
Loire; but it is by no means certain what terminal Strabo
had in mind.

[5] That is, up the Arar, following the first route above-
mentioned to the ocean.

προσαγορευθῆναι, διὰ τὴν ἐπιφάνειαν ἢ καὶ προσ-
λαβόντων πρὸς τοῦτο καὶ τῶν Μασσαλιωτῶν
διὰ τὸ πλησιόχωρον.

II

1. Ἑξῆς δὲ περὶ τῶν Ἀκουιτανῶν λεκτέον καὶ
τῶν προσωρισμένων αὐτοῖς ἐθνῶν τεσσαρεσκαί-
δεκα Γαλατικῶν τῶν μεταξὺ τοῦ Γαρούνα κατοικούντων καὶ τοῦ Λείγηρος, ὧν ἔνια ἐπιλαμβάνει
καὶ τῆς τοῦ Ῥοδανοῦ ποταμίας καὶ τῶν πεδίων
τῶν κατὰ τὴν Ναρβωνῖτιν. ἁπλῶς γὰρ εἰπεῖν,
οἱ Ἀκουιτανοὶ διαφέρουσι τοῦ Γαλατικοῦ φύλου
κατά τε τὰς τῶν σωμάτων κατασκευὰς καὶ κατὰ
τὴν γλῶτταν, ἐοίκασι δὲ μᾶλλον Ἴβηρσιν. ὁρί-
ζονται δὲ τῷ Γαρούνα ποταμῷ, ἐντὸς τούτου καὶ
τῆς Πυρήνης οἰκοῦντες. ἔστι δὲ ἔθνη τῶν Ἀκουιτανῶν πλείω μὲν τῶν εἴκοσι, μικρὰ δὲ καὶ ἄδοξα,
τὰ πολλὰ μὲν παρωκεανιτικά, τὰ δὲ εἰς τὴν
μεσόγαιαν καὶ τὰ ἄκρα τῶν Κεμμένων ὀρῶν μέχρι
Τεκτοσάγων ἀνέχοντα. ἐπειδὴ δὲ μικρὰ μερὶς
C 190 ἦν ἡ τοσαύτη, προσέθεσαν καὶ τὴν μεταξὺ τοῦ
Γαρούνα καὶ τοῦ Λείγηρος. παράλληλοι δέ πώς
εἰσιν οἱ ποταμοὶ τῇ Πυρήνῃ καὶ δύο ποιοῦσι
παραλληλόγραμμα πρὸς αὐτὴν χωρία, ὁριζόμενα
κατὰ τὰς ἄλλας πλευρὰς τῷ τε ὠκεανῷ καὶ τοῖς
Κεμμένοις ὄρεσι· δισχιλίων δ' ὁμοῦ σταδίων
ἐστὶν ὁ πλοῦς ἑκατέρων τῶν ποταμῶν. ἐκβάλλει
δ' ὁ μὲν Γαρούνας τρισὶ ποταμοῖς αὐξηθεὶς εἰς τὸ

---

[1] For the purposes of administration.
[2] Cp. 4. 1. 1.

the Greeks called "Celti"—on account of the fame of the Celtae, or it may also be that the Massiliotes, as well as other Greek neighbours, contributed to this result, on account of their proximity.

II

1. Next, I must discuss the Aquitani, and the tribes which have been included within their boundaries,[1] namely, the fourteen Galatic tribes which inhabit the country between the Garumna and the Liger, some of which reach even to the river-land of the Rhone and to the plains of Narbonitis. ˙For, speaking in a general way, the Aquitani differ from the Galatic race in the build of their bodies as well as in their speech; that is, they are more like the Iberians.[2] Their country is bounded by the Garumna River, since they live between this and the Pyrenees. There are more than twenty tribes of the Aquitani, but they are small and lacking in repute; the majority of the tribes live along the ocean, while the others reach up into the interior and to the summits[3] of the Cemmenus Mountains, as far as the Tectosages. But since a country of this size was only a small division, they[4] added to it the country which is between the Garumna and the Liger. These rivers are approximately parallel to the Pyrenees and form with the Pyrenees two parallelograms, since they are bounded on their other sides by the ocean and the Cemmenus Mountains. And the voyage on either of the rivers is, all told, two thousand stadia. The Garumna, after being increased by the waters of three rivers, dis-

---

[3] Not "extremities" (cp. Τὰ ἄκρα 4. 6. 7).
[4] The Romans.

μεταξὺ Βιτουρίγων τε τῶν Οὐιβίσκων [1] ἐπικαλουμένων καὶ Σαντόνων, ἀμφοτέρων Γαλατικῶν ἐθνῶν· μόνον γὰρ δὴ τὸ τῶν Βιτουρίγων τούτων ἔθνος ἐν τοῖς Ἀκουιτανοῖς ἀλλόφυλον ἵδρυται, καὶ οὐ συντελεῖ αὐτοῖς, ἔχει δὲ ἐμπόριον Βουρδίγαλα ἐπικείμενον λιμνοθαλάττῃ τινί, ἣν ποιοῦσιν αἱ ἐκβολαὶ τοῦ ποταμοῦ. ὁ δὲ Λείγηρ μεταξὺ Πικτόνων τε καὶ Ναμνιτῶν ἐκβάλλει. πρότερον δὲ Κορβιλὼν ὑπῆρχεν ἐμπόριον ἐπὶ τούτῳ τῷ ποταμῷ, περὶ ἧς εἴρηκε Πολύβιος, μνησθεὶς τῶν ὑπὸ Πυθέου μυθολογηθέντων, ὅτι Μασσαλιωτῶν μὲν τῶν συμμιξάντων Σκιπίωνι οὐδεὶς εἶχε λέγειν οὐδὲν μνήμης ἄξιον, ἐρωτηθεὶς ὑπὸ τοῦ Σκιπίωνος περὶ τῆς Βρεττανικῆς, οὐδὲ τῶν ἐκ Νάρβωνος οὐδὲ τῶν ἐκ Κορβιλῶνος, αἵπερ ἦσαν ἄρισται πόλεις τῶν ταύτῃ,[2] Πυθέας δ᾽ ἐθάρρησε τοσαῦτα ψεύσασθαι. τῶν δὲ Σαντόνων πόλις ἐστὶ Μεδιολάνιον. ἔστι δ᾽ ἡ μὲν παρωκεανῖτις τῶν Ἀκουιτανῶν ἀμμώδης ἡ πλείστη καὶ λεπτή, κέγχρῳ τρέφουσα, τοῖς δὲ ἄλλοις καρποῖς ἀφορωτέρα· ἐνταῦθα δ᾽ ἐστὶ καὶ ὁ κόλπος ὁ ποιῶν τὸν ἰσθμὸν πρὸς τὸν ἐν τῇ Ναρβωνίτιδι παραλίᾳ Γαλατικὸν κόλπον, ὁμώνυμος ἐκείνῳ καὶ αὐτός. ἔχουσι δὲ Τάρβελλοι τὸν κόλπον, παρ᾽ οἷς ἐστι τὰ χρυσεῖα σπουδαιότατα πάντων· ἐν γὰρ βόθροις ὀρυχθεῖσιν ἐπὶ μικρὸν εὑρίσκονται καὶ χειροπληθεῖς χρυσίου πλάκες, ἔσθ᾽ ὅτε μικρᾶς ἀποκαθάρσεως δεόμεναι.

[1] Οὐιβίσκων, Xylander, for Ἰόσκων; so Corais, Groskurd, and Forbiger. Ptolemaeus (2. 7. 5) says "Οὐιβίσκοι," and Pliny (4. 33) "Vivisci."

[2] ταύτῃ, Corais, for ταύτης; so the later editors.

charges its waters into the region that is between those Bituriges that are surnamed " Vivisci" and the Santoni—both of them Galatic tribes; for the tribe of these Bituriges is the only tribe of different race that is situated among the Aquitani; and it does not pay tribute to them, though it has an emporium, Burdigala, which is situated on a lagoon that is formed by the outlets of the river. The Liger, however, discharges its waters between the Pictones and the Namnitae. Formerly there was an emporium on this river, called Corbilo, with respect to which Polybius, calling to mind the fabulous stories of Pytheas, has said: "Although no one of all the Massiliotes who conversed with Scipio[1] was able, when questioned by Scipio about Britain, to tell anything worth recording, nor yet any one of the people from Narbo or of those from Corbilo, though these were the best of all the cities in that country, still Pytheas had the hardihood to tell all those falsehoods about Britain." The city of the Santoni, however, is Mediolanium. Now the most of the ocean-coast of the Aquitani is sandy and thin-soiled, thus growing millet, but it is rather unproductive in respect of the other products. Here too is the gulf which, along with that Galatic Gulf which is within the coastline of Narbonitis, forms the isthmus (itself too, like the latter gulf, having the name "Galatic"). The gulf is held by the Tarbelli, in whose land the gold mines are most important of all; for in pits dug only to a slight depth they find slabs of gold as big as the hand can hold, which at times require but little refining; but the rest is gold

---

[1] It is not known to which member of the Cornelian gens Strabo refers; probably Africanus Major.

τὸ δὲ λοιπὸν ψῆγμά ἐστι καὶ βῶλοι, καὶ αὗται
κατεργασίαν οὐ πολλὴν ἔχουσαι. ἡ δὲ μεσόγειος
καὶ ὀρεινὴ βελτίω γῆν ἔχει, πρὸς μὲν τῇ Πυρήνῃ
τὴν τῶν Κωνουενῶν, ὅ[1] ἐστι συγκλύδων,[2] ἐν ᾗ
πόλις Λούγδουνον καὶ τὰ τῶν Ὀνησιῶν[3] θερμὰ
κάλλιστα ποτιμωτάτου ὕδατος· καλὴ δὲ καὶ
ἡ τῶν Αὐσκίων.[4]

2. Τὰ δὲ μεταξὺ τοῦ Γαρούνα καὶ τοῦ Λείγηρος
ἔθνη τὰ προσκείμενα τοῖς Ἀκουιτανοῖς ἐστιν
Ἐλουοὶ μὲν ἀπὸ τοῦ Ῥοδανοῦ τὴν ἀρχὴν ἔχοντες·
Οὐελλάϊοι δὲ μετὰ τούτους, οἳ προσωρίζοντό ποτε
Ἀρουέρνοις, νῦν δὲ τάττονται καθ' ἑαυτούς· εἶτα
Ἀρουέρνοι καὶ Λεμοουίκες[5] καὶ Πετροκόριοι·
πρὸς δὲ τούτοις Νιτιόβριγες καὶ Καδοῦρκοι καὶ
Βιτούριγες οἱ Κοῦβοι καλούμενοι· πρὸς δὲ τῷ
ὠκεανῷ Σάντονοί τε καὶ Πίκτονες, οἱ μὲν τῷ Γα-
ρούνᾳ παροικοῦντες, ὡς εἴπομεν, οἱ δὲ τῷ Λεί-
γηρι. Ῥουτηνοὶ δὲ καὶ Γαβαλεῖς τῇ Ναρβωνίτιδι
πλησιάζουσι. παρὰ μὲν οὖν τοῖς Πετροκορίοις
σιδηρουργεῖά ἐστιν ἀστεῖα καὶ τοῖς Κούβοις
Βιτούριξι, παρὰ δὲ τοῖς Καδούρκοις λινουργίαι,

C 191

---

[1] ὅ, Corais inserts; so the later editors.
[2] For συγκλύδων Corais reads συνηλύδων; Meineke following. But the text is right.
[3] Xylander, comparing Pliny 4. 33, conjectures Μονησίων,
for Ὀνησιῶν.
[4] Αὐσκίων, Xylander, for Ψαυσκίων; so the later editors.
[5] Λεμοουίκες, Xylander, for Λεμοθρίκες; so the later editors.

---

[1] The "Convenae" seem to have been refugees from the
army of Sertorius, whom Pompey generously assembled
together in the territory in question; their city, to which
Strabo refers in this passage, was called "Lugdunum Con-
venarum" (to-day, St. Bertrand de Comminges).

dust and nuggets, the nuggets too requiring no great amount of working. The interior and mountainous country, however, has better soil: first, next to the Pyrenees, the country of the "Convenae" (that is, "assembled rabble"),[1] in which are the city of Lugdunum and the hot springs of the Onesii[2]—most beautiful springs of most potable waters; and, secondly, the country of the Auscii also has good soil.

2. Those tribes between the Garumna and the Liger that belong to Aquitania are, first, the Elui, whose territory begins at the Rhodanus, and then, after them, the Vellavii, who were once included within the boundaries of the Arverni, though they are now ranked as autonomous;[3] then the Arverni, the Lemovices, and the Petrocorii; and, next to these, the Nitiobriges, the Cadurci, and those Bituriges that are called "Cubi";[4] and, next to the ocean, both the Santoni and the Pictones, the former living along the Garumna, as I have said, the latter along the Liger; but the Ruteni and the Gabales closely approach Narbonitis. Now among the Petrocorii there are fine iron-works, and also among the Bituriges Cubi; among the Cadurci, linen

[2] A people otherwise unknown.
[3] Literally "ranked according to themselves." A comparison of 4. 1. 5 (where Strabo speaks specifically of the "autonomy" of the Massiliotes), 4. 1. 12, 4. 6. 4, and the above passage, clearly indicates that the Volcae Arecomisci, the Vellavii, and the Vocontii, were granted a form of autonomy by the Romans—one of the special privileges of that rank being that they were "not subject to the orders of the praetors who are sent out from Rome" (4. 1. 12). Cp. also the government of Messenia under Melanthus (8. 4. 1).
[4] As distinguished from the "Vivisci" (§ 1 above).

παρὰ δὲ τοῖς Ῥουτηνοῖς ἀργυρεῖα· ἔχουσι δ'
ἀργυρεῖα καὶ οἱ Γαβαλεῖς. δεδώκασι δὲ Λάτιον [1]
Ῥωμαῖοι καὶ τῶν Ἀκουιτανῶν τισι, καθάπερ
Αὐσκίοις καὶ Κωνουέναις.

3. Ἀρούερνοι δὲ ἵδρυνται μὲν ἐπὶ τῷ Λείγηρι·
μητρόπολις δ' αὐτῶν ἐστι Νεμωσσὸς ἐπὶ τῷ
ποταμῷ κειμένη. ῥυεὶς δ' οὗτος παρὰ Κήναβον,
τὸ τῶν Καρνούτων ἐμπόριον κατὰ μέσον που τὸν
πλοῦν συνοικούμενον, ἐκβάλλει πρὸς τὸν ὠκεανόν.
τῆς δυνάμεως δὲ τῆς πρότερον Ἀρούερνοι μέγα
τεκμήριον παρέχονται τὸ πολλάκις πολεμῆσαι
πρὸς Ῥωμαίους τοτὲ μὲν μυριάσιν εἴκοσι, πάλιν
δὲ διπλασίαις. τοσαύταις γὰρ πρὸς Καίσαρα
τὸν Θεὸν διηγωνίσαντο μετὰ Οὐερκιγγετόριγος,
πρότερον δὲ καὶ εἴκοσι πρὸς Μάξιμον τὸν Αἰμι-
λιανόν, καὶ πρὸς Δομήτιον δ' ὡσαύτως Ἀηνόβαρβον.
πρὸς μὲν οὖν Καίσαρα περί τε Γεργοουίαν, πόλιν
τῶν Ἀρουέρνων, ἐφ' ὑψηλοῦ ὄρους κειμένην,
συνέστησαν οἱ ἀγῶνες, ἐξ ἧς ἦν ὁ Οὐερκιγγέτοριξ·
καὶ περὶ Ἀλησίαν πόλιν Μανδουβίων,[2] ἔθνους
ὁμόρου τοῖς Ἀρουέρνοις, καὶ ταύτην ἐφ' ὑψηλοῦ
λόφου κειμένην, περιεχομένην δ' ὄρεσι καὶ ποταμοῖς δυσίν, ἐν ᾗ καὶ ἑάλω ὁ ἡγεμὼν καὶ ὁ πόλεμος
τέλος ἔσχε· πρὸς δὲ Μάξιμον Αἰμιλιανὸν κατὰ
τὴν συμβολὴν τοῦ τ' Ἴσαρος καὶ τοῦ Ῥοδανοῦ,

---

[1] Λάτιον, Corais, for Λατίνιον; so the later editors.
[2] Μανδουβίων, Xylander, for Μανδιβούλων; so the later
editors.

---

[1] See § 12 above, and footnote.
[2] "Nemossus" is otherwise unknown. If the name is
correct, it is apparently an earlier name for what was later

factories; among the Ruteni, silver mines; and the
Gabales, also, have silver mines. The Romans have
given the "Latin right"[1] to certain of the Aquitani
just as they have done in the case of the Auscii and
the Convenae.

3. The Arverni are situated on the Liger; their
metropolis is Nemossus,[2] a city situated on the Liger.
This river, after flowing past Cenabum (the emporium
of the Carnutes at about the middle of the voyage,[3]
an emporium that is jointly peopled),[4] discharges its
waters towards the ocean. As for their former power,
the Arverni hold out as a great proof thereof the
fact that they oftentimes warred against the Romans,
at times with two hundred thousand men, and again,
with double that number—with double that number,
for example, when they, with Vercingetorix, struggled
to a finish against the Deified Caesar; and, before
that, also, with two hundred thousand against
Maximus Aemilianus, and also, in like manner,
against Dometius[5] Ahenobarbus. Now the struggles
against Caesar took place near Gergovia (a city of
the Arverni, situated on a high mountain), where
Vercingetorix was born, and also near Alesia (a city
of the Mandubii—a tribe which has a common
boundary with the Arverni—and this city too is
situated on a high hill, although it is surrounded by
mountains and two rivers), in which not only the
commander was captured but the war had its end.
But the struggles against Maximus Aemilianus took
place at the confluence of the Isar and the Rhodanus,

called "Augustonemetum" (now Clermont-Ferrand), the city
of the Arverni mentioned by Ptolemaeus (2. 7. 12).
[3] From Augustonemetum to the outlets of the river.
[4] By both natives and Romans.
[5] More commonly spelled "Domitius."

καθ᾽ ἣν καὶ τὸ Κέμμενον ὄρος πλησιάζει τῷ Ῥο-
δανῷ· πρὸς δὲ Δομήτιον κατωτέρω ἔτι κατὰ τὴν
συμβολὴν τοῦ τε Σούλγα καὶ τοῦ Ῥοδανοῦ. διέ-
τειναν δὲ τὴν ἀρχὴν οἱ Ἀρούερνοι καὶ μέχρι
Νάρβωνος καὶ τῶν ὅρων τῆς Μασσαλιώτιδος,
ἐκράτουν δὲ καὶ τῶν μέχρι Πυρήνης ἐθνῶν καὶ
μέχρι ὠκεανοῦ καὶ Ῥήνου. Βιτυΐτου[1] δέ, τοῦ
πρὸς τὸν Μάξιμον καὶ τὸν Δομήτιον πολεμήσαντος,
ὁ πατὴρ Λουέριος τοσοῦτον πλούτῳ λέγεται καὶ
τρυφῇ διενεγκεῖν, ὥστε ποτὲ ἐπίδειξιν ποιούμενος
τοῖς φίλοις[2] τῆς εὐπορίας ἐπ᾽ ἀπήνης φέρεσθαι
διὰ πεδίου, χρυσοῦ νόμισμα καὶ ἀργύρου δεῦρο
κἀκεῖσε διασπείρων, ὥστε συλλέγειν ἐκείνους
ἀκολουθοῦντας.

III

1. Μετὰ δὲ τὴν Ἀκουιτανὴν μερίδα καὶ τὴν Ναρβωνῖτιν ἡ ἐφεξῆς ἐστι μέχρι τοῦ Ῥήνου παντὸς
ἀπὸ τοῦ Λείγηρος ποταμοῦ καὶ τοῦ Ῥοδανοῦ, καθ᾽
ὃ συνάπτει πρὸς τὸ Λούγδουνον ἀπὸ τῆς πηγῆς
κατενεχθεὶς ὁ Ῥοδανός. ταύτης δὲ τῆς χώρας τὰ
μὲν ἄνω μέρη τὰ πρὸς ταῖς πηγαῖς τῶν ποταμῶν,
τοῦ τε Ῥήνου καὶ τοῦ Ῥοδανοῦ, μέχρι μέσων
C 192   σχεδόν τι τῶν πεδίων ὑπὸ τῷ Λουγδούνῳ τέτα-

---

[1] Βιτυΐτου, Corais, for Βιτίτου; so the later editors.
[2] For φίλοις, Corais, conjectures ὄχλοις; A. Jacob, φύλοις.

---

[1] According to the Greek text, "his followers" would
naturally refer to "his friends." But Athenaeus (4. 37)
quotes Poseidonius, who was probably Strabo's authority for
the incident, as saying, "Luerius, in his effort to win the

where the Cemmenus Mountain approaches closely the Rhodanus; and against Dometius Ahenobarbus, at a place still lower down the Rhodanus, at the confluence of the Sulgas and the Rhodanus. Again, the Arverni not only had extended their empire as far as Narbo and the boundaries of Massiliotis, but they were also masters of the tribes as far as the Pyrenees, and as far as the ocean and the Rhenus. Luerius, the father of the Bituitus who warred against Maximus and Dometius, is said to have been so exceptionally rich and extravagant that once, when making a display of his opulence to his friends, he rode on a carriage through a plain, scattering gold and silver coins here and there, for his followers to pick up.[1]

III

1. The country next in order after the Aquitanian division [2] and Narbonitis [3] reaches as far as the whole of the Rhenus, extending from the Liger River and also from the Rhodanus at the point where the Rhodanus, after it runs down from its source, touches Lugdunum. Now of this country the upper parts that are next to the sources of the rivers (the Rhenus and the Rhodanus), extending as far, approximately, as the centre of the plains, have been classified under

favour of the crowds, rode on a carriage through the plains and scattered gold and silver to the hosts of the Celts which followed him." Corais, by a slight emendation (see critical note on opposite page), conjectures "crowds" for "friends," thus harmonizing the account with that of Athenaeus. The conjecture of A. Jacob, however, of "troops" for "friends" is more plausible, on textual as well as on contextual grounds.

[2] Gallia Aquitanica.   [3] Gallia Narbonensis.

κται, τὰ δὲ λοιπὰ καὶ παρωκεανιτικὰ ὑπ᾽ ἄλλῃ
τέτακται μερίδι, ἣν ἰδίως Βέλγαις προσνέμουσιν·
ἡμεῖς δὲ κοινότερον τὰ καθ᾽ ἕκαστα δηλώσομεν.

2. Αὐτὸ μὲν δὴ τὸ Λούγδουνον, ἐκτισμένον ὑπὸ
λόφῳ κατὰ τὴν συμβολὴν τοῦ τε Ἄραρος τοῦ
ποταμοῦ καὶ τοῦ Ῥοδανοῦ, κατέχουσι Ῥωμαῖοι.
εὐανδρεῖ δὲ μάλιστα τῶν ἄλλων πλὴν Νάρβωνος·
καὶ γὰρ ἐμπορίῳ χρῶνται, καὶ τὸ νόμισμα χαράτ-
τουσιν ἐνταῦθα τό τε ἀργυροῦν καὶ τὸ χρυσοῦν οἱ
τῶν Ῥωμαίων ἡγεμόνες. τό τε ἱερὸν τὸ ἀναδει-
χθὲν ὑπὸ πάντων κοινῇ τῶν Γαλατῶν Καίσαρι
τῷ Σεβαστῷ πρὸ ταύτης ἵδρυται τῆς πόλεως ἐπὶ
τῇ συμβολῇ τῶν ποταμῶν· ἔστι δὲ βωμὸς ἀξιόλογος ἐπιγραφὴν ἔχων τῶν ἐθνῶν ἑξήκοντα τὸν
ἀριθμὸν καὶ εἰκόνες τούτων ἑκάστου μία, καὶ ἄλλος
μέγας.[1] προκάθηται δὲ τοῦ ἔθνους τοῦ Σηγοσιαυῶν[2] ἡ πόλις αὕτη, κειμένου[3] μεταξὺ τοῦ Ῥοδανοῦ
καὶ τοῦ Δούβιος· τὰ δ᾽ ἑξῆς ἔθνη τὰ συντείνοντα
πρὸς τὸν Ῥῆνον, τὰ μὲν ὑπὸ τοῦ Δούβιος ὁρίζεται,
τὰ δ᾽ ὑπὸ τοῦ Ἄραρος. οὗτοι μὲν οὖν, ὡς εἴρηται
πρότερον, ἀπὸ τῶν Ἄλπεων καὶ αὐτοὶ κατενε-
χθέντες, ἔπειτ᾽ εἰς ἓν ῥεῖθρον συμπεσόντες εἰς τὸν
Ῥοδανὸν καταφέρονται· ἄλλος δ᾽ ἐστίν, ὁμοίως ἐν

---

[1] ἄλλος μέγας, C. Müller emends to ἄλλη Σεβαστοῦ;
Meineke reads ἄλλος [:νδριὰς] μέγας.
[2] Σηγοσιαυῶν, the reading of C (see note 3 on p. 198,
and Holmes, *Caesar's Conquest of Gaul*, p. 848).
[3] κειμένου, Xylander, for κειμένη; so the later editors.

---

[1] Gallia Lugdunensis.   [2] Gallia Belgica.
[3] As Strabo has already said, it was not political divisions
(her- the divisions of Lugdunensis and Belgica), but physical
and ethnic distinctions that geographers treated in detail,

Lugdunum;[1] whereas the remaining parts, including the parts along the ocean, have been classified under another division, I mean that division which is specifically assigned to the Belgae.[2] As for me, however, I shall point out the separate parts in a rather general way.[3]

2. Lugdunum itself, then, (a city founded at the foot of a hill at the confluence of the River Arar and the Rhodanus), is occupied by the Romans. And it is the most populous of all the cities of Celtica except Narbo; for not only do people use it as an emporium, but the Roman governors coin their money there, both the silver and the gold. Again, the temple that was dedicated to Caesar Augustus by all the Galatae in common is situated in front of this city at the junction of the rivers. And in it is a note-worthy altar, bearing an inscription of the names of the tribes, sixty in number; and also images from these tribes, one from each tribe, and also another large altar.[4] The city of Lugdunum pre-sides over the tribe of the Segusiavi, which tribe is situated between the Rhodanus and the Dubis. The tribes that come next in order after the Segusiavi, I mean those which together stretch towards the Rhenus, are bounded partly by the Dubis and partly by the Arar. Now these rivers too, as I have said before,[5] first run down from the Alps, and then, falling into one stream, run down into the Rhodanus; and there is still another river, Sequana

since the political divisions made by the Romans varied, and hence were only referred to in a summary way by the geographer (see 4. 1. 1).

[4] C. Müller emends the Greek text to read "and also an image of Augustus"; Meineke, to read "and also a great statue," i. e. of Augustus.   [5] 4. 1. 11.

ταῖς Ἄλπεσι τὰς πηγὰς ἔχων, Σηκοάνας ὄνομα·[1]
ῥεῖ δ᾽ εἰς τὸν ὠκεανόν, παράλληλος τῷ Ῥήνῳ, διὰ
ἔθνους ὁμωνύμου, συνάπτοντος τῷ Ῥήνῳ τὰ πρὸς
ἕω, τὰ δ᾽ εἰς τἀναντία τῷ Ἄραρι, ὅθεν αἱ κάλλισται
ταριχεῖαι τῶν ὑείων κρεῶν εἰς τὴν Ῥώμην κατα-
κομίζονται. μεταξὺ μὲν οὖν τοῦ Δούβιος καὶ τοῦ
Ἄραρος οἰκεῖ τὸ τῶν Αἰδούων ἔθνος, πόλιν ἔχον
Καβυλλῖνον ἐπὶ τῷ Ἄραρι καὶ φρούριον Βίβρακτα.
οἱ δὲ Αἰδούοι καὶ συγγενεῖς Ῥωμαίων ὠνομάζοντο
καὶ πρῶτοι τῶν ταύτῃ προσῆλθον πρὸς τὴν φιλίαν
καὶ συμμαχίαν. πέραν δὲ τοῦ Ἄραρος οἰκοῦσιν
οἱ Σηκοανοί, διάφοροι καὶ τοῖς Ῥωμαίοις ἐκ πολλοῦ
γεγονότες καὶ τοῖς Αἰδούοις· ὅτι πρὸς Γερμανοὺς
προσεχώρουν πολλάκις κατὰ τὰς ἐφόδους αὐτῶν
τὰς ἐπὶ τὴν Ἰταλίαν, καὶ ἐπεδείκνυντό γε οὐ τὴν
τυχοῦσαν δύναμιν, ἀλλὰ καὶ κοινωνοῦντες αὐτοῖς
ἐποίουν μεγάλους, καὶ ἀφιστάμενοι μικρούς· πρὸς
δὲ τοὺς Αἰδούους καὶ διὰ ταῦτα[2] μέν, ἀλλ᾽ ἐπέτεινε τὴν ἔχθραν ἡ τοῦ ποταμοῦ ἔρις τοῦ διείργοντος αὐτούς, ἑκατέρου τοῦ ἔθνους ἴδιον ἀξιοῦντος
εἶναι τὸν Ἄραρα καὶ ἑαυτῷ προσήκειν τὰ διαγω-
γικὰ τέλη. νυνὶ δ᾽ ὑπὸ τοῖς Ῥωμαίοις ἅπαντ᾽ ἐστί.

3. Τὴν δ᾽ ἐπὶ τῷ Ῥήνῳ πρῶτοι τῶν ἁπάντων
οἰκοῦσιν Ἑλουήττιοι,[3] παρ᾽ οἷς εἰσιν αἱ πηγαὶ τοῦ

---

[1] ῥέων, after ὄνομα, Siebenkees deletes; so the later editors.
[2] ταὐτά, Jones, for ταῦτα.
[3] Ἑλουήττιοι, Corais, for Αἰτονάτιοι; so Meineke, Müller-
Dübner, Forbiger, and Tardieu. But Xylander, Casaubon,
and Siebenkees conjecture Ναντουάται. Cp. the first words in
§ 4 following.

by name, which likewise has its sources in the Alps.
It flows into the ocean, however, running parallel to
the Rhenus, through a tribe of like name,[1] whose
country joins the Rhenus in its eastern parts, but in
the opposite parts, the Arar; and it is from their
country that the finest of salted hog-meat is brought
down and shipped to Rome. Now between the
Dubis and the Arar dwells the tribe of the Aedui,
with their city of Cabyllinum, on the Arar, and their
garrison of Bibracte. (The Aedui were not only
called kinsmen of the Romans,[2] but they were also
the first of the peoples in that country to apply for
their friendship and alliance.) But across the Arar
dwell the Sequani, who, for a long time, in fact, had
been at variance with the Romans as well as with the
Aedui. This was because they often joined forces
with the Germans in their attacks upon Italy; aye,
and they demonstrated that theirs was no ordinary
power: they made the Germans strong when they
took part with them and weak when they stood
aloof. As regards the Aedui, not only were the
Sequani at variance with them for the same reasons,
but their hostility was intensified by the strife about
the river that separates them, since each tribe
claimed that the Arar was its private property and
that the transportation tolls belonged to itself. Now,
however, everything is subject to the Romans.

3. As for the country that is on the Rhenus, the
first of all the peoples who live there are the Elvetii,[3]

---

[1] Strabo wrongly thought the Sequana ran through the
country of the Sequani.

[2] Caesar (*De Bello Gallico* 1. 33) says "the Aedui were often
called by the Senate brethren and kinsmen."

[3] Usually spelled "Helvetii."

ποταμοῦ ἐν τῷ ᾽Αδούλᾳ[1] ὄρει. τοῦτο δ᾽ ἐστὶ
μέρος τῶν ῎Αλπεων, ὅθεν καὶ ὁ ᾽Αδούας εἰς τἀναντία μέρη ῥεῖ τὰ πρὸς τὴν ἐντὸς Κελτικὴν καὶ
πληροῖ τὴν Λάριον λίμνην, πρὸς ᾗ ἔκτισται τὸ
Κῶμον, εἶτ᾽ ἐνθένδε εἰς τὸν Πάδον συμβάλλει,
περὶ ὧν ὕστερον ἐροῦμεν. καὶ ὁ ῾Ρῆνος δὲ εἰς ἕλη
C 193 μεγάλα καὶ λίμνην ἀναχεῖται μεγάλην, ἧς ἐφάπτονται καὶ ῾Ραιτοὶ καὶ Οὐινδολικοί, τῶν ᾽Αλπίων
τινὲς καὶ τῶν ὑπεραλπίων. φησὶ δὲ τὸ μῆκος
αὐτοῦ σταδίων ἑξακισχιλίων ᾽Ασίνιος, οὐκ ἔστι
δέ. ἀλλ᾽ ἐπ᾽ εὐθείας μὲν τοῦ ἡμίσους ὀλίγον ἂν
ὑπερβάλλοι, τοῖς δὲ σκολιώμασι καὶ χίλιοι προσ-
τεθέντες ἱκανῶς ἂν ἔχοιεν· καὶ γὰρ ὀξύς ἐστι,
διὰ τοῦτο δὲ καὶ δυσγεφύρωτος, καὶ διὰ πεδίων
ὕπτιος φέρεται τὸ λοιπὸν καταβὰς ἀπὸ τῶν ὀρῶν·
πῶς οὖν οἷόν τε μένειν ὀξὺν καὶ βίαιον, εἰ τῷ
ὑπτιασμῷ προσδοίημεν καὶ σκολιότητας πολλὰς
καὶ μακράς; φησὶ δὲ καὶ δίστομον εἶναι, μεμψά-
μενος τοὺς πλείω λέγοντας. ἐγκυκλοῦνται μὲν δή
τινα χώραν ταῖς σκολιότησι καὶ οὗτος καὶ ὁ Σηκοάνας, οὐ τοσαύτην δέ.[2] ἀμφότεροι δὲ ῥέουσιν ἐπὶ
τὰς ἄρκτους ἀπὸ τῶν νοτίων μερῶν. πρόκειται δ᾽
αὐτῶν ἡ Βρεττανική, τοῦ μὲν ῾Ρήνου καὶ ἐγγύθεν,
ὥστε καθορᾶσθαι τὸ Κάντιον, ὅπερ ἐστὶ τὸ ἐῷον
ἄκρον τῆς νήσου, τοῦ δὲ Σηκοάνα μικρὸν ἀπωτέρω.

---

[1] ᾽Αδούλᾳ, Siebenkees from conj. of Xylander, for Διαδονέλ-
λα; so the later editors.
[2] δέ, Kramer inserts; so Meineke.

in whose territory, on Mount Adula, are the sources
of the river. Mount Adula is a part of the Alps,
and from it flows also the River Addua,[1] in the
opposite direction, that is, towards Cisalpine Celtica,
and fills Lake Larius (near which the city of Comum
has been founded), and then, flowing on from Lake
Larius, contributes its waters to those of the Padus
(matters about which I shall speak later on). The
Rhenus, too, spreads into great marshes and a great
lake, which lake is touched by the territory of both
the Rhaeti and the Vindelici (certain of the peoples
who live in the Alps and also beyond the Alps).
Asinius says that the length of the river is six
thousand stadia, but it is not. In fact, it could only
slightly exceed the half of that in a straight line,
while the addition of one thousand stadia would be
quite sufficient for the windings. For not only is it
swift, and on this account also hard to bridge, but
after its descent from the mountains runs the rest of
the way with even slope through the plains. How,
then, could it remain swift and violent, if to the even
slope of the river we added numerous long windings?
He further says it has only two mouths, after first
finding fault with those who say it has more than
that. So then, both this river and the Sequana
encircle somewhat of territory within their windings,
but not so much as that. Both rivers flow from the
southern parts towards the north; and in front of
them lies Britain, which is near enough to the
Rhenus for Cantium, which is the eastern cape of
the island, to be visible from it, though it is slightly
farther off from the Sequana. Here, too, the Deified

---

[1] But the Addua rises far to the east of Mt. Adula, in
the Rhaetic Alps.

ἐνταῦθα δὲ καὶ τὸ ναυπήγιον συνεστήσατο Καῖσαρ
ὁ Θεὸς πλέων εἰς τὴν Βρεττανικήν. τοῦ δὲ Σηκοάνα τὸ πλεόμενον ὑπὸ τῶν ἐκ τοῦ Ἄραρος δεχο-
μένων τὰ φορτία μικρῷ πλέον ἐστὶν ἢ τὸ τοῦ
Λείγηρος καὶ τὸ τοῦ Γαρούνα· τὸ δὲ ἀπὸ Λουγδούνου μέχρι τοῦ Σηκοάνα ¹ χιλίων σταδίων ἐστίν,
ἔλαττον δ᾽² ἢ διπλάσιον τούτου τὸ³ ἀπὸ τῶν
εἰσβολῶν τοῦ Ῥοδανοῦ μέχρι Λουγδούνου. φασὶ δὲ
καὶ πολυχρύσους τοὺς Ἐλουηττίους μηδὲν μέντοι
ἧττον ἐπὶ λῃστείαν τραπέσθαι, τὰς τῶν Κίμβρων
εὐπορίας ἰδόντας· ἀφανισθῆναι δ᾽ αὐτῶν τὰ δύο
φῦλα, τριῶν ὄντων, κατὰ στρατείας. ὅμως δ᾽ ἐκ τῶν
λοιπῶν⁴ τὸ τῶν ἐπιγόνων πλῆθος ἐδήλωσεν ὁ πρὸς
Καίσαρα τὸν Θεὸν πόλεμος, ἐν ᾧ περὶ τετταράκοντα
μυριάδες σωμάτων διεφθάρησαν, τοὺς δὲ λοιποὺς
σώζεσθαι μεθῆκεν εἰς ὀκτακισχιλίους, ὅπως μὴ τοῖς
Γερμανοῖς ὁμόροις οὖσιν, ἔρημον τὴν χώραν ἀφῇ.

4. Μετὰ δὲ τοὺς Ἐλουηττίους Σηκοανοὶ καὶ
Μεδιοματρικοὶ κατοικοῦσι τὸν Ῥῆνον, ἐν οἷς
ἵδρυται Γερμανικὸν ἔθνος περαιωθὲν ἐκ τῆς οἰκείας,
Τρίβοκχοι. ἐν δὲ τοῖς Σηκοανοῖς ἐστι τὸ ὄρος ὁ
Ἰουράσιος, διορίζει δ᾽ Ἐλουηττίους καὶ Σηκοανούς.
ὑπὲρ οὖν τῶν Ἐλουηττίων καὶ τῶν Σηκοανῶν
Αἰδοῦοι καὶ Λίγγονες οἰκοῦσι πρὸς δύσιν, ὑπὲρ
δὲ τῶν Μεδιοματρικῶν Λεῦκοι καὶ τῶν Λιγγόνων

---

¹ ἤ, before χιλίων, Corais deletes; so Meineke.
² δ᾽, Corais inserts; so Meineke.
³ τό, Corais inserts; so Meineke.
⁴ τόπων (MSS.), after λοιπῶν, Corais suspects; Meineke
deletes.

---

¹ Strabo could not have meant by "Here" the mouth
of the Sequana (which the mere Greek text seems to imply),

Caesar established his navy-yard when he sailed to Britain.[1] The part of the Sequana that is navigated by those who receive the cargoes from the Arar is slightly longer than that of the Liger and that of the Garumna; but the distance from Lugdunum [2] to the Sequana is a thousand stadia, and that from the mouths of the Rhodanus to Lugdunum is less than double this distance. It is said also that the Elvetii, although rich in gold, none the less turned themselves to robbery upon seeing the opulence of the Cimbri; but that on their campaigns two of their tribes (there were three) were obliterated. But still the number of the descendants from what was left of them was shown by their war against the Deified Caesar, in which about four hundred thousand lives were destroyed, although Caesar allowed the rest of them, about eight thousand, to escape, so as not to abandon the country, destitute of inhabitants, to the Germans, whose territory bordered on theirs.

4. After the Elvetii, along the Rhenus, dwell the Sequani and the Mediomatrici, in whose territory are situated the Tribocchi, a Germanic tribe which crossed the river from their homeland. Mount Jura is in the territory of the Sequani; it marks the boundary between the Elvetii and the Sequani. So it is beyond the Elvetii and the Sequani, towards the west, that the Aedui and the Lingones dwell; and beyond the Mediomatrici, that the Leuci and a

much less that of the Rhenus, since Caesar sailed from Portus Itius (see 4. 5. 2 and Caesar *De Bello Gallico* 5. 2) on his second expedition, and almost certainly from there on his first (*De Bello Gallico* 4. 21); and Portus Itius was either Boulogne or Wissant—almost certainly the former. (See Holmes, *Caesar's Conquest of Gaul*, pp. 432-438.)

[2] An overland journey.

τι μέρος. τὰ δὲ μεταξὺ ἔθνη τοῦ τε Λείγηρος καὶ
τοῦ Σηκοάνα ποταμοῦ τὰ πέραν τοῦ Ῥοδανοῦ τε
καὶ τοῦ Ἄραρος παράκειται πρὸς ἄρκτον τοῖς
τε Ἀλλόβριξι καὶ τοῖς περὶ τὸ Λούγδουνον·
τούτων δ' ἐπιφανεστατόν ἐστι τὸ τῶν Ἀρουέρνων
καὶ τὸ τῶν Καρνούτων, δι' ὧν ἀμφοῖν ἐνεχθεὶς
ὁ Λείγηρ εἰς τὸν ὠκεανὸν ἔξεισι. δίαρμα δ' ἐστὶν
εἰς τὴν Βρεττανικὴν ἀπὸ τῶν ποταμῶν τῆς
C 194 Κελτικῆς εἴκοσι καὶ τριακόσιοι στάδιοι· ὑπὸ
γὰρ τὴν ἄμπωτιν ἀφ' ἑσπέρας ἀναχθέντες τῇ
ὑστεραίᾳ περὶ ὀγδόην ὥραν καταίρουσιν εἰς τὴν
νῆσον. μετὰ δὲ τοὺς Μεδιοματρικοὺς καὶ Τρι-
βόκχους παροικοῦσι τὸν Ῥῆνον Τρηούιροι, καθ'
οὓς πεποίηται τὸ ζεῦγμα ὑπὸ τῶν Ῥωμαίων νυνὶ
τῶν στρατηγούντων τὸν Γερμανικὸν πόλεμον.
πέραν δὲ ᾤκουν Οὔβιοι κατὰ τοῦτον τὸν τόπον,
οὓς μετήγαγεν Ἀγρίππας ἑκόντας εἰς τὴν ἐντὸς
τοῦ Ῥήνου. Τρηουίροις δὲ συνεχεῖς Νερούιοι,
καὶ τοῦτο Γερμανικὸν ἔθνος. τελευταῖοι δὲ Με-
νάπιοι πλησίον τῶν ἐκβολῶν ἐφ' ἑκάτερα τοῦ
ποταμοῦ κατοικοῦντες ἕλη καὶ δρυμοὺς οὐχ
ὑψηλῆς, ἀλλὰ πυκνῆς ὕλης καὶ ἀκανθώδους.
κατὰ τούτους δ' ἵδρυνται Σούγαμβροι Γερμανοί.
πάσης δ' ὑπέρκεινται τῆς ποταμίας ταύτης οἱ
Σόηβοι προσαγορευόμενοι Γερμανοὶ καὶ δυνάμει
καὶ πλήθει διαφέροντες τῶν ἄλλων, ὑφ' ὧν οἱ
ἐξελαυνόμενοι κατέφευγον εἰς τὴν ἐντὸς τοῦ Ῥήνου
νυνί· καὶ ἄλλοι δὲ κατ' ἄλλους τόπους δυναστεύ-
ουσι καὶ διαδέχονται τὰ ζώπυρα τοῦ πολέμου,
τῶν πρώτων ἀεὶ καταλυομένων.

---

[1] It is uncertain what campaign or bridge Strabo refers to,
since the time of composition and of revision of Strabo's work
has by no means been settled (see Vol. I, p. 36, footnote 2).

part of the Lingones dwell. But those tribes between the Liger and the Sequana Rivers that are on the far side of the Rhodanus and the Arar are situated side by side, towards the north, with both the Allobroges and the people round Lugdunum; and of these tribes the most conspicuous are those of the Arverni and the Carnutes, through both of whose territories the Liger runs on its way out to the ocean. The passage across to Britain from the rivers of Celtica is three hundred and twenty stadia; for if you put to sea on the ebb-tide at nightfall, you land upon the island about the eighth hour on the following day. After the Mediomatrici and the Tribocchi, along the Rhenus, dwell the Treveri, near whom the bridge has been built by the Roman officers who are now conducting the Germanic war.[1] The Ubii used to live opposite this region, across the Rhenus, though by their own consent they were transferred by Agrippa to the country this side the Rhenus. Next after the Treveri are the Nervii, who are also a Germanic tribe. Last come the Menapii, who dwell on both sides of the river near its mouths, in marshes and woods (not of tall timber, but dense and thorny). It is opposite to these that the Sugambri are situated, a Germanic people. But beyond this whole river-country are those Germans who are called the Suevi and excel all the others in power and numbers (the people driven out by the Suevi in our time have been fleeing for refuge to this side of the Rhenus). And other peoples, also, lord it in different places, and in their turn take up the tinders of war, but the foremost are always put down.[2]

One thinks of the campaigns of Drusus Germanicus (7. 1. 3), of Varus (7. 1. 4), or of Germanicus the Younger (7. 1. 4).

[2] By the Romans, apparently.

5. Τῶν δὲ Τρηουίρων καὶ Νερουίων Σένονες καὶ
Ῥῆμοι πρὸς ἑσπέραν οἰκοῦσιν, ἔτι δ' Ἀτρεβάτιοι
καὶ Ἐβούρωνες· τοῖς Μεναπίοις δ' εἰσὶ συνεχεῖς ἐπὶ
τῇ θαλάττῃ Μορινοὶ καὶ Βελλοάκοι καὶ Ἀμβιανοὶ
καὶ Σουεσσίωνες καὶ Κάλετοι μέχρι τῆς ἐκβολῆς
τοῦ Σηκοάνα ποταμοῦ. ἐμφερὴς δ' ἐστὶ τῇ τῶν
Μεναπίων ἥ τε τῶν Μορινῶν καὶ ἡ τῶν Ἀτρε-
βατίων καὶ Ἐβουρώνων· ὕλη γάρ ἐστιν οὐχ
ὑψηλῶν δένδρων πολλὴ μέν, οὐ τοσαύτη δὲ ὅσην
οἱ συγγραφεῖς εἰρήκασι, τετρακισχιλίων σταδίων,
καλοῦσι δ' αὐτὴν Ἀρδουένναν. κατὰ δὲ τὰς
πολεμικὰς ἐφόδους συμπλέκοντες τὰς τῶν θάμνων
λύγους, βατώδεις οὔσας, ἀπέφραττον[1] τὰς παρόδους. ἔστι δ' ὅπου καὶ σκόλοπας κατέπηττον,
αὐτοὶ δὲ κατέδυνον εἰς τὰ βάθη πανοίκιοι, νησίδια
ἔχοντες ἐν τοῖς ἕλεσι. ἐν μὲν οὖν ταῖς ἐπομβρίαις
ἀσφαλεῖς τὰς καταφυγὰς εἶχον, ἐν δὲ τοῖς αὐχμοῖς
ἡλίσκοντο ῥᾳδίως. νυνὶ δ' ἅπαντες οἱ ἐντὸς
Ῥήνου καθ' ἡσυχίαν ὄντες ὑπακούουσι Ῥωμαίων.
περὶ δὲ τὸν Σηκοάναν ποταμόν εἰσι καὶ οἱ
Παρίσιοι, νῆσον ἔχοντες ἐν τῷ ποταμῷ καὶ πόλιν
Λουκοτοκίαν, καὶ Μέλδοι καὶ Ληξοούιοι, παρωκεανῖται οὗτοι. ἀξιολογώτατον δ' ἐστὶν ἔθνος
τῶν ταύτῃ Ῥῆμοι, καὶ ἡ μητρόπολις αὐτῶν
Δουρικορτόρα μάλιστα συνοικεῖται καὶ δέχεται
τοὺς τῶν Ῥωμαίων ἡγεμόνας.

[1] ἀπέφραττον, Groskurd, for ἀνέφραττον; so the later
editors.

5. West of the Treveri and the Nervii dwell the
Senones and the Remi, and farther on, the Atrebatii
and the Eburones; and after the Menapii, on the
sea, are, in their order, the Morini, the Bellovaci, the
Ambiani, the Suessiones, and the Caleti, as far as
the outlet of the Sequana River. Both the country of
the Morini and that of the Atrebatii and Eburones
resemble that of the Menapii; for much of it, though
not so much as the historians have said (four thousand
stadia), is a forest, consisting of trees that are not
tall; the forest is called Arduenna. At the time of
hostile onsets they used to intertwine the withes of
the brushwood, since the withes were thorny, and
thus block the passage of the enemy.[1] In some
places they also used to fix stakes in the ground—
themselves, with their whole families, slinking away
into the depths of the forest, for they had small
islands in their marshes. Now although the refuge
they took was safe for them in the rainy seasons,
they were easily captured in the dry seasons. But
as it is, all the peoples this side the Rhenus are
living in a state of tranquillity and are submissive
to the Romans. The Parisii live round about the
Sequana River, having an island in the river and a
city called Lucotocia; and so do the Meldi and
the Lexovii—these latter beside the ocean. But the
most noteworthy of all the tribes in this region of
Celtica is that of the Remi; their metropolis,
Duricortora, is most thickly settled and is the city
that entertains the Roman governors.

[1] Caesar (*De Bello Gallico* 2. 17) describes this more fully,
saying that they first cut into saplings and bent them over,
and then intertwined them with brambles and thorns, thus
making wall-like hedges that could neither be penetrated nor
seen through.

IV

1. Μετὰ δὲ τὰ λεχθέντα ἔθνη τὰ λοιπὰ Βελγῶν ἐστιν ἔθνη τῶν παρωκεανιτῶν, ὧν Οὐένετοι μέν εἰσιν οἱ ναυμαχήσαντες πρὸς Καίσαρα· ἕτοιμοι γὰρ ἦσαν κωλύειν τὸν εἰς τὴν Βρεττανικὴν πλοῦν, C 195 χρώμενοι τῷ ἐμπορίῳ. κατεναυμάχησε δὲ ῥᾳδίως, οὐκ ἐμβόλοις χρώμενος (ἦν γὰρ παχέα τὰ ξύλα), ἀλλ' ἀνέμῳ φερομένων ἐπ' αὐτὸν κατέσπων οἱ Ῥωμαῖοι τὰ ἱστία δορυδρεπάνοις· ἦν γὰρ σκύτινα διὰ τὴν βίαν τῶν ἀνέμων· ἁλύσεις δ' ἔτεινον ἀντὶ κάλων. πλατύπυγα δὲ ποιοῦσι καὶ ὑψίπρυμνα καὶ ὑψόπρωρα διὰ τὰς ἀμπώτεις, δρυΐνης ὕλης, ἧς ἐστιν εὐπορία· διόπερ οὐ συνάγουσι τὰς ἁρμονίας τῶν σανίδων, ἀλλ' ἀραιώματα καταλείπουσι· ταῦτα δὲ βρύοις διανάττουσι τοῦ μὴ κατὰ τὰς νεωλκίας καπυροῦσθαι τὴν ὕλην μὴ[1] νοτιζομένην, τοῦ μὲν βρύου νοτιωτέρου ὄντος τῇ φύσει, τῆς δὲ δρυὸς ξηρᾶς καὶ ἀλιποῦς. τούτους οἶμαι τοὺς Οὐενέτους οἰκιστὰς εἶναι τῶν κατὰ τὸν Ἀδρίαν· καὶ γὰρ οἱ ἄλλοι πάντες σχεδόν τι οἱ ἐν τῇ Ἰταλίᾳ Κελτοὶ μετανέστησαν ἐκ τῆς ὑπὲρ τῶν Ἄλπεων γῆς, καθάπερ καὶ οἱ Βόϊοι[2] καὶ Σένονες· διὰ δὲ τὴν ὁμωνυμίαν Παφλαγόνας

---

[1] μὴ, Siebenkees from conj. of Casubon; so the later editors.

[2] Βόϊοι, Xylander, for βίοι; so the later editors.

IV

1. After the aforesaid tribes, the rest are tribes of those Belgae who live on the ocean-coast. Of the Belgae, there are, first, the Veneti who fought the naval battle with Caesar; for they were already prepared to hinder his voyage to Britain, since they were using the emporium there. But he easily defeated them in the naval battle, making no use of ramming (for the beams [1] were thick), but when the Veneti bore upon him with the wind, the Romans hauled down their sails by means of pole-hooks; [2] for, on account of the violence of the winds, the sails were made of leather, and they were hoisted by chains instead of ropes. Because of the ebb-tides, they make their ships with broad bottoms, high sterns, and high prows; they make them of oak (of which they have a plentiful supply), and this is why they do not bring the joints of the planks together but leave gaps; they stuff the gaps full of sea-weed, however, so that the wood may not, for lack of moisture, become dry when the ships are hauled up, because the sea-weed is naturally rather moist, whereas the oak is dry and without fat. It is these Veneti, I think, who settled the colony that is on the Adriatic (for about all the Celti that are in Italy migrated from the transalpine land, just as did the Boii and Senones), although, on account of the like-ness of name, people call them Paphlagonians. [3] I

[1] That is, in the ships of the Veneti. The beams, according to Caesar (*De Bello Gallico* 3. 13), were a foot thick.
[2] "Sharp pointed hooks inserted in, and fastened to, long poles," Caesar says (*loc. cit.*).
[3] Strabo refers to the "Eneti," a Paphlagonian tribe (cp. 1. 3. 2, 1. 3. 21, and 5. 1. 4).

φασὶν αὐτούς. λέγω δ' οὐκ ἰσχυριζόμενος· ἀρκεῖ
γὰρ περὶ τῶν τοιούτων τὸ εἰκός. Ὀσίσμιοι δ'
εἰσίν, οὓς Ὠστιμίους[1] ὀνομάζει Πυθέας, ἐπί τινος
προπεπτωκυίας ἱκανῶς ἄκρας εἰς τὸν ὠκεανὸν
οἰκοῦντες, οὐκ ἐπὶ τοσοῦτον δέ, ἐφ' ὅσον ἐκεῖνός
φησι καὶ οἱ πιστεύσαντες ἐκείνῳ. τῶν δὲ μεταξὺ
ἐθνῶν τοῦ τε Σηκοάνα καὶ τοῦ Λείγηρος οἱ μὲν
τοῖς Σηκοανοῖς, οἱ δὲ τοῖς Ἀρουέρνοις ὁμοροῦσι.

2. Τὸ δὲ σύμπαν φῦλον, ὃ νῦν Γαλλικόν τε
καὶ Γαλατικὸν καλοῦσιν, ἀρειμάνιόν[2] ἐστι καὶ
θυμικόν τε καὶ ταχὺ πρὸς μάχην, ἄλλως δὲ
ἁπλοῦν καὶ οὐ κακόηθες. διὰ δὲ τοῦτο ἐρε-
θισθέντες μὲν ἀθρόοι συνίασι πρὸς τοὺς ἀγῶνας
καὶ φανερῶς καὶ οὐ μετὰ περισκέψεως, ὥστε καὶ
εὐμεταχείριστοι γίνονται τοῖς καταστρατηγεῖν
ἐθέλουσι· καὶ γὰρ ὅτε βούλεται καὶ ὅπου καὶ ἀφ'
ἧς ἔτυχε προφάσεως παροξύνας τις αὐτοὺς ἑτοίμους
ἔσχε πρὸς τὸν κίνδυνον, πλὴν βίας καὶ τόλμης οὐδὲν
ἔχοντας τὸ συναγωνιζόμενον· παραπεισθέντες δὲ
εὐμαρῶς ἐνδιδόασι πρὸς τὸ χρήσιμον, ὥστε καὶ
παιδείας ἅπτεσθαι καὶ λόγων· τῆς δὲ βίας τὸ μὲν
ἐκ τῶν σωμάτων ἐστὶ μεγάλων ὄντων, τὸ δ' ἐκ
τοῦ πλήθους. συνίασι δὲ κατὰ πλῆθος ῥαδίως διὰ
τὸ ἁπλοῦν καὶ αὐθέκαστον, συναγανακτούντων
τοῖς ἀδικεῖσθαι δοκοῦσιν ἀεὶ τῶν πλησίον. νυνὶ
μὲν οὖν ἐν εἰρήνῃ πάντες εἰσὶ δεδουλωμένοι καὶ
ζῶντες κατὰ τὰ προστάγματα τῶν ἑλόντων αὐτοὺς
Ῥωμαίων, ἀλλ' ἐκ τῶν παλαιῶν χρόνων τοῦτο

[1] Ὀσίσμιοι δ' εἰσίν, οὓς Ὠστιμίους, Kramer, from conj. of
Hagenbuch, for οἱ Σίσμιοι δ' εἰσὶν οὓς Τιμίους; so Meineke,
and Forbiger. See text, 1. 4. 5. (Vol. I, p. 238).
[2] ἀρημάνιον is the reading of ABC*l*.

do not speak positively, however, for with reference
to such matters probability suffices.   Secondly, there
are the Osismii (whom Pytheas calls the Ostimii),
who live on a promontory that projects quite far
out into the ocean, though not so far as he and those
who have trusted him say.   But of the tribes that
are between the Sequana and the Liger, some border
on the Sequani, others on the Arverni.

2. The whole race which is now called both
"Gallic" and "Galatic" is war-mad, and both high-
spirited and quick for battle, although otherwise
simple and not ill-mannered.   And therefore, if
roused, they come together all at once for the
struggle, both openly and without circumspection,
so that for those who wish to defeat them by
stratagem they become easy to deal with (in fact,
irritate them when, where, or by what chance pretext you please, and you have them ready to risk
their lives, with nothing to help them in the struggle
but might and daring) ; whereas, if coaxed, they so
easily yield to considerations of utility that they lay
hold, not only of training in general, but of language-
studies as well.[1]   As for their might, it arises partly
from their large physique and partly from their
numbers.   And on account of their trait of simplicity
and straightforwardness they easily come together in
great numbers, because they always share in the
vexation of those of their neighbours whom they
think wronged.   At the present time they are all
at peace, since they have been enslaved and are
living in accordance with the commands of the
Romans who captured them, but it is from the early

[1] Cp. 4. 1. 5.

λαμβάνομεν περὶ αὐτῶν ἔκ τε[1] τῶν μέχρι νῦν
C 196 συμμενόντων παρὰ τοῖς Γερμανοῖς νομίμων. καὶ
γὰρ τῇ φύσει καὶ τοῖς πολιτεύμασιν ἐμφερεῖς εἰσι
καὶ συγγενεῖς ἀλλήλοις οὗτοι, ὅμορόν τε οἰκοῦσι
χώραν, διοριζομένην τῷ Ῥήνῳ ποταμῷ, καὶ παραπλήσια ἔχουσαν τὰ πλεῖστα (ἀρκτικωτέρα δ᾽
ἐστὶν ἡ Γερμανία) κρινομένων τῶν τε νοτίων
μερῶν πρὸς τὰ νότια καὶ τῶν ἀρκτικῶν πρὸς τὰ
ἀρκτικά. διὰ τοῦτο δὲ καὶ τὰς μεταναστάσεις
αὐτῶν ῥᾳδίως ὑπάρχειν συμβαίνει, φερομένων
ἀγεληδὸν καὶ πανστρατιᾷ, μᾶλλον δὲ καὶ[2] πανοι-
κίων ἐξαιρόντων ὅταν ὑπ᾽ ἄλλων ἐκβάλλωνται
κρειττόνων. οἵ τε Ῥωμαῖοι πολὺ ῥᾷον τούτους
ἐχειρώσαντο ἢ τοὺς Ἴβηρας· καὶ γὰρ ἤρξαντο
πρότερον καὶ ἐπαύσαντο ὕστερον ἐκείνοις πολεμοῦντες, τούτους δ᾽ ἐν τῷ μεταξὺ χρόνῳ πάντας
κατέλυσαν, τοὺς ἀνὰ μέσον Ῥήνου καὶ τῶν Πυρηναίων ὀρῶν σύμπαντας. ἀθρόοι γὰρ καὶ κατὰ
πλῆθος ἐμπίπτοντες ἀθρόοι κατελύοντο, οἱ δ᾽
ἐταμίευον καὶ κατεκερμάτιζον τοὺς ἀγῶνας, ἄλλοτε
ἄλλοι καὶ κατ᾽ ἄλλα μέρη λῃστρικῶς πολεμοῦντες.
εἰσὶ μὲν οὖν μαχηταὶ πάντες τῇ φύσει, κρείττους
δ᾽ ἱππόται ἢ πεζοί, καὶ ἔστι Ῥωμαίοις τῆς ἱππείας
ἀρίστη παρὰ τούτων. ἀεὶ δὲ οἱ προσβορρότεροι
καὶ παρωκεανῖται μαχιμώτεροι.

3. Τούτων δὲ τοὺς Βέλγας ἀρίστους φασίν, εἰς

---

[1] τε, after ἐκ, Kramer inserts ; Corais and Meineke insert
καί before ἐκ.
[2] δὲ καί, Corais, for δ᾽ ἐκ ; so the later editors.

---

[1] Namely, the trait of simplicity and straightforwardness.
[2] Cp. 3. 4. 5.   [3] That is, all the Gallic people.
[4] Caesar, for example (De Bello Gallico 1. 1).

times that I am taking this account of them, and also
from the customs that hold fast to this day among
the Germans. For these peoples are not only similar
in respect to their nature and their governments,
but they are also kinsmen to one another; and,
further, they live in country that has a common
boundary, since it is divided by the River Rhenus,
and the most of its regions are similar (though
Germany is more to the north), if the southern
regions be judged with reference to the southern and
also the northern with reference to the northern.
But it is also on account of this trait[1] that their
migrations easily take place, for they move in droves,
army and all, or rather they make off, households and
all, whenever they are cast out by others stronger
than themselves. Again, the Romans conquered
these people much more easily than they did the
Iberians; in fact, the Romans began earlier, and
stopped later, carrying on war with the Iberians,
but in the meantime defeated all these—I mean
all the peoples who live between the Rhenus and
the Pyrenees Mountains. For, since the former
were wont to fall upon their opponents all at once and
in great numbers, they were defeated all at once,
but the latter would husband their resources and
divide their struggles, carrying on war in the manner
of brigands, different men at different times and in
separate divisions.[2] Now although they are all[3]
fighters by nature, they are better as cavalry than
as infantry; and the best cavalry-force the Romans
have comes from these people. However, it is
always those who live more to the north and along
the ocean-coast that are the more warlike

3. Of these people, they say,[4] the Belgae are

πεντεκαίδεκα ἔθνη διῃρημένους, τὰ μεταξὺ τοῦ
Ῥήνου καὶ τοῦ Λείγηρος παροικοῦντα ¹ τὸν ὠκεανόν, ὥστε ² μόνους ἀντέχειν πρὸς τὴν τῶν Γερμανῶν ἔφοδον, Κίμβρων καὶ Τευτόνων. αὐτῶν δὲ
τῶν Βελγῶν Βελλοάκους ἀρίστους φασί, μετὰ δὲ
τούτους Σουεσσίωνας. τῆς δὲ πολυανθρωπίας
σημεῖον· εἰς γὰρ τριάκοντα μυριάδας ἐξετάζεσθαί
φασι τῶν Βελγῶν πρότερον τῶν δυναμένων φέρειν
ὅπλα· εἴρηται δὲ καὶ τὸ τῶν Ἑλουηττίων πλῆθος καὶ τὸ τῶν Ἀρουέρνων καὶ τὸ τῶν συμμάχων,
ἐξ ὧν ἡ πολυανθρωπία φαίνεται καί, ὅπερ εἶπον,
ἡ τῶν γυναικῶν ἀρετὴ πρὸς τὸ τίκτειν καὶ ἐκτρέ-
φειν τοὺς παῖδας. σαγηφοροῦσι δὲ καὶ κομοτρο-
φοῦσι καὶ ἀναξυρίσι χρῶνται περιτεταμέναις,
ἀντὶ δὲ χιτώνων σχιστοὺς χειριδωτοὺς φέρουσι
μέχρις αἰδοίων καὶ γλουτῶν. ἡ δ᾽ ἐρέα τραχεῖα
μέν, ἀκρόμαλλος δέ, ἀφ᾽ ἧς τοὺς δασεῖς σάγους
ἐξυφαίνουσιν, οὓς λαίνας καλοῦσιν· οἱ μέντοι
Ῥωμαῖοι καὶ ἐν τοῖς προσβορροτάτοις ὑποδιφθέρας
τρέφουσι ποίμνας ἱκανῶς ἀστείας ἐρέας. ὁπλι-
σμὸς δὲ σύμμετρος τοῖς τῶν σωμάτων μεγέθεσι,

---

¹ παροικοῦντα, Corais, for παροικοῦντας; so the later editors.
² ὥστε, Xylander, for οὔτε; so the later editors.

---

¹ So in Caesar (*De Bello Gallico* 2. 4), where the Belgae
are credited with being the only people in all Gaul who
prevented the Cimbri and Teutones from entering within
their borders (in the year 103 B.C.).
² Of Gaul as a whole.
³ Strabo follows Caesar (*De Bello Gallico* 2. 4), who got
his information from the Remi, whose figures amount to
306,000. ⁴ 4. 2. 3 and 4. 3. 3.
⁵ 4. 1. 2. ⁶ A kind of coarse cloak.

bravest (who have been divided into fifteen tribes, the tribes that live along the ocean between the Rhenus and the Liger); consequently they alone could hold out against the onset of the Germans— the Cimbri and Teutones.[1] But of the Belgae themselves, they say, the Bellovaci are bravest, and after them the Suessiones. As for the largeness of the population,[2] this is an indication: it is found upon inquiry,[3] they say, that there are as many as three hundred thousand of those Belgae (of former times) who are able to bear arms; and I have already told[4] the number of the Elvetii, and of the Arverni, and of their allies,—from all of which the largeness of the population is manifest, as is also the thing of which I spoke above[5]—the excellence of the women in regard to the bearing and nursing of children. The Gallic people wear the "sagus,"[6] let their hair grow long,[7] and wear tight breeches[8]; instead of tunics[9] they wear slit[10] tunics that have sleeves and reach as far as the private parts and the buttocks. The wool of their sheep, from which they weave the coarse "sagi" (which they[11] call "laenae"), is not only rough, but also flocky at the surface; the Romans, however, even in the most northerly parts[12] raise skin-clothed[13] flocks with wool that is sufficiently fine. The Gallic armour is commensurate with the

---

[7] Hence the Romans often referred to Transalpine Gaul as "Gallia Comata."

[8] The breeches were made of leather (Polybius 2. 30).

[9] That is, ordinary Roman tunics.

[10] At the sides, for the sleeves.

[11] The Romans.   [12] Of Gaul, apparently.

[13] Strabo refers to the custom (still in vogue) of protecting the wool by means of skins tied around the sheep (cp. 12. 3. 13).

μάχαιρα μακρά, παρηρτημένη παρὰ τὸ δεξιὸν
πλευρόν, καὶ θυρεὸς μακρὸς καὶ λόγχαι κατὰ
λόγον καὶ μάδαρις, παλτοῦ τι εἶδος. χρῶνται
δὲ καὶ τόξοις ἔνιοι καὶ σφενδόναις· ἔστι δέ τι καὶ
γρόσφῳ ἐοικὸς ξύλον, ἐκ χειρὸς οὐκ ἐξ ἀγκύλης
ἀφιέμενον, τηλεβολώτερον καὶ βέλους, ᾧ μάλιστα
C 197 καὶ πρὸς τὰς τῶν ὀρνέων χρῶνται θήρας. χαμευ-
νοῦσι δὲ καὶ μέχρι νῦν οἱ πολλοί, καὶ καθεζόμε-
νοι δειπνοῦσιν ἐν στιβάσι. τροφὴ δὲ πλείστη
μετὰ γάλακτος καὶ κρεῶν παντοίων, μάλιστα δὲ
τῶν ὑείων καὶ νέων καὶ ἁλιστῶν. αἱ δ' ὕες καὶ
ἀγραυλοῦσιν, ὕψει τε καὶ ἀλκῇ καὶ τάχει διαφέ-
ρουσαι· κίνδυνος γοῦν ἐστι τῷ ἀήθει προσιόντι,
ὡσαύτως καὶ λύκῳ. τοὺς δ' οἴκους ἐκ σανίδων
καὶ γέρρων ἔχουσι μεγάλους θολοειδεῖς, ὄροφον
πολὺν ἐπιβάλλοντες. οὕτως δ' ἐστὶ δαψιλῆ καὶ
τὰ ποίμνια καὶ τὰ ὑοφόρβια, ὥστε τῶν σάγων
καὶ τῆς ταριχείας ἀφθονίαν μὴ τῇ Ῥώμῃ χορη-
γεῖσθαι μόνον, ἀλλὰ καὶ τοῖς πλείστοις μέρεσι
τῆς Ἰταλίας. ἀριστοκρατικαὶ δ' ἦσαν αἱ πλείους
τῶν πολιτειῶν, ἕνα δ' ἡγεμόνα ἡροῦντο κατ' ἐνιαυτὸν τὸ παλαιόν, ὡς δ' αὕτως εἰς πόλεμον εἷς ὑπὸ
τοῦ πλήθους ἀπεδείκνυτο στρατηγός. νυνὶ δὲ
προσέχουσι τοῖς τῶν Ῥωμαίων προστάγμασι τὸ
πλέον. ἴδιον δὲ τὸ ἐν τοῖς συνεδρίοις συμβαῖνον·
ἐὰν γάρ τις θορυβῇ τὸν λέγοντα καὶ ὑποκρούσῃ,

---

[1] A Celtic word; in Latin, "matara."
[2] "Grosphus" is the Greek word Polybius (6. 22) uses for
a kind of spear used by the Roman "flying troops" ("velites").
"The spear," he says, "has a wooden haft of about two
cubits and is about a finger's breadth in thickness."
[3] In Julius Caesar's day (cp. De Bello Gallico 6. 11).

large size of their bodies: a long sabre, which hangs
along the right side, and a long oblong shield, and
spears in proportion, and a "madaris," [1] a special kind
of javelin. But some of them also use bows and slings.
There is also a certain wooden instrument resembling
the "grosphus" [2] (it is hurled by hand, not by thong,
and ranges even farther than an arrow), which they
use particularly for the purposes of bird-hunting.
Most of them, even to the present time, sleep on
the ground, and eat their meals seated on beds of
straw. Food they have in very great quantities,
along with milk and flesh of all sorts, but particularly
the flesh of hogs, both fresh and salted. Their hogs
run wild, and they are of exceptional height, bold-
ness, and swiftness; at any rate, it is dangerous for
one unfamiliar with their ways to approach them, and
likewise, also, for a wolf. As for their houses, which
are large and dome-shaped, they make them of
planks and wicker, throwing over them quantities
of thatch. And their flocks of sheep and herds of
swine are so very large that they supply an abundance of the "sagi" and the salt-meat, not only to
Rome, but to most parts of Italy as well. The
greater number of their governments used to be
aristocratic [3]—although in the olden time only one
leader was chosen, annually; and so, likewise, for
war, only one man was declared general by the
common people.[4] But now they give heed, for the
most part, to the commands of the Romans. There
is a procedure that takes place in their assemblies
which is peculiar to them: if a man disturbs
the speaker and heckles him, the sergeant-at-arms

---

[4] In Caesar's day (*De Bello Gallico* 6. 13) the common
people were treated almost as slaves and were never consulted.

προσιὼν ὁ ὑπηρέτης, ἐσπασμένος τὸ ξίφος, κελεύει σιγᾶν μετ᾽ ἀπειλῆς· μὴ παυομένου δέ, καὶ δεύτερον καὶ τρίτον ποιεῖ τὸ αὐτό, τελευταῖον δὲ ἀφαιρεῖ τοῦ σάγου τοσοῦτον ὅσον ἄχρηστον ποιῆσαι τὸ λοιπόν. τὸ δὲ περὶ τοὺς ἄνδρας καὶ τὰς γυναῖκας, τὸ διηλλάχθαι τὰ ἔργα ὑπεναντίως τοῖς παρ᾽ ἡμῖν, κοινὸν καὶ πρὸς ἄλλους συχνοὺς τῶν βαρβάρων ἐστί.

4. Παρὰ πᾶσι δ᾽ ὡς ἐπίπαν τρία φῦλα τῶν τιμωμένων διαφερόντως ἐστί, Βάρδοι τε καὶ Οὐάτεις καὶ Δρυΐδαι· Βάρδοι μὲν ὑμνηταὶ καὶ ποιηταί, Οὐάτεις δὲ ἱεροποιοὶ καὶ φυσιολόγοι, Δρυΐδαι δὲ πρὸς τῇ φυσιολογίᾳ καὶ τὴν ἠθικὴν φιλοσοφίαν ἀσκοῦσι· δικαιότατοι δὲ νομίζονται καὶ διὰ τοῦτο πιστεύονται τάς τε ἰδιωτικὰς κρίσεις καὶ τὰς κοινάς, ὥστε καὶ πολέμους διῄτων πρό-τερον καὶ παρατάττεσθαι μέλλοντας ἔπαυον, τὰς δὲ φονικὰς δίκας μάλιστα τούτοις ἐπετέτραπτο δικάζειν. ὅταν τε φορὰ τούτων ᾖ, φορὰν καὶ τῆς χώρας νομίζουσιν ὑπάρχειν. ἀφθάρτους δὲ λέ-γουσι καὶ οὗτοι καὶ ἄλλοι[1] τὰς ψυχὰς καὶ τὸν κόσμον, ἐπικρατήσειν δέ ποτε καὶ πῦρ καὶ ὕδωρ.

---

[1] Meineke, following Corais, wrongly inserts οἱ before ἄλλοι, making οἱ ἄλλοι refer to the Bards and Vates.

---

[1] Cp. Diodorus, 5. 31, and Caesar, De Bello Gallico 6. 13–16.
[2] That is, a big yield of criminals for execution. The Gauls sacrificed criminals to the gods, and when the supply of criminals failed they resorted to the execution even of the innocent (Caesar, De Bello Gallico 6. 16).
[3] For example, the Pythagoreans, as Diodorus Siculus says (5. 28).
[4] One of the cardinal doctrines of the Druids was that of

approaches him with drawn sword, and with a threat commands him to be silent; if he does not stop, the sergeant-at-arms does the same thing a second time, and also a third time, but at last cuts off enough of the man's "sagus" to make it useless for the future. But as for their custom relating to the men and the women (I mean the fact that their tasks have been exchanged, in a manner opposite to what obtains among us), it is one which they share in common with many other barbarian peoples.

4. Among all the Gallic peoples, generally speaking, there are three sets of men who are held in exceptional honour; the Bards, the Vates and the Druids.[1] The Bards are singers and poets; the Vates, diviners and natural philosophers; while the Druids, in addition to natural philosophy, study also moral philosophy. The Druids are considered the most just of men, and on this account they are entrusted with the decision, not only of the private disputes, but of the public disputes as well; so that, in former times, they even arbitrated cases of war and made the opponents stop when they were about to line up for battle, and the murder cases, in particular, had been turned over to them for decision. Further, when there is a big yield from these cases,[2] there is forthcoming a big yield from the land too, as they think. However, not only the Druids, but others as well,[3] say that men's souls, and also the universe, are indestructible,[4] although both fire and water will at some time or other prevail over them.

metempsychosis (Caesar, *De Bello Gallico* 6. 14). See also Diodorus Siculus 5. 28.

5. Τῷ δ' ἁπλῷ καὶ θυμικῷ πολὺ τὸ ἀνόητον
καὶ ἀλαζονικὸν πρόσεστι καὶ τὸ φιλόκοσμον·
χρυσοφοροῦσί τε γάρ, περὶ μὲν τοῖς τραχήλοις
στρεπτὰ ἔχοντες, περὶ δὲ τοῖς βραχίοσι καὶ τοῖς
καρποῖς ψέλια, καὶ τὰς ἐσθῆτας βαπτὰς φοροῦσι
καὶ χρυσοπάστους οἱ ἐν ἀξιώματι. ὑπὸ τῆς
τοιαύτης δὲ κουφότητος ἀφόρητοι μὲν νικῶντες,
ἐκπλαγεῖς δ' ἡττηθέντες ὁρῶνται. πρόσεστι δὲ
τῇ ἀνοίᾳ καὶ τὸ βάρβαρον καὶ τὸ ἔκφυλον ὃ τοῖς
C 198 προσβόροις ἔθνεσι παρακολουθεῖ πλεῖστον, τὸ
ἀπὸ τῆς μάχης ἀπιόντας τὰς κεφαλὰς τῶν πολε-
μίων ἐξάπτειν ἐκ τῶν αὐχένων τῶν ἵππων, κομί-
σαντας δὲ προσπατταλεύειν τὴν θέαν [1] τοῖς προ-
πυλαίοις. φησὶ γοῦν Ποσειδώνιος αὐτὸς ἰδεῖν
ταύτην πολλαχοῦ καὶ τὸ μὲν πρῶτον ἀηδίζεσθαι,[2]
μετὰ δὲ ταῦτα φέρειν πράως διὰ τὴν συνήθειαν.
τὰς δὲ τῶν ἐνδόξων κεφαλὰς κεδροῦντες ἐπεδείκνυον
τοῖς ξένοις, καὶ οὐδὲ πρὸς ἰσοστάσιον χρυσὸν
ἀπολυτροῦν ἠξίουν. καὶ τούτων δ' ἔπαυσαν αὐτοὺς Ῥωμαῖοι, καὶ τῶν κατὰ τὰς θυσίας καὶ
μαντείας ὑπεναντίων [3] τοῖς παρ' ἡμῖν νομίμοις.
ἄνθρωπον δὲ κατεσπεισμένον παίσαντες εἰς νῶτον
μαχαίρᾳ ἐμαντεύοντο ἐκ τοῦ σφαδασμοῦ. ἔθυον
δὲ οὐκ ἄνευ Δρυϊδῶν. καὶ ἄλλα δὲ ἀνθρωποθυσιῶν

---

[1] Meineke transfers τὴν θέαν to a position after ταύτην in
the following sentence; quite unnecessarily.
[2] ἀηδίζεσθαι, Jones. for ἀηθίζεσθαι.
[3] ὑπεναντίων, Casaubon, for ὑπεναντίως; so Corais, and
Meineke.

---

[1] Cp. 4. 4. 2.   [2] Cp. 3. 3. 6 and 11. 4. 7.
[3] Diodorus Siculus (5. 31) says "without a philosopher";

5. In addition to their trait of simplicity and high-spiritedness,[1] that of witlessness and boastfulness is much in evidence, and also that of fondness for ornaments; for they not only wear golden ornaments—both chains round their necks and bracelets round their arms and wrists—but their dignitaries wear garments that are dyed in colours and sprinkled with gold. And by reason of this levity of character they not only look insufferable when victorious, but also scared out of their wits when worsted. Again, in addition to their witlessness, there is also that custom, barbarous and exotic, which attends most of the northern tribes—I mean the fact that when they depart from the battle they hang the heads of their enemies from the necks of their horses, and, when they have brought them home, nail the spectacle to the entrances of their homes. At any rate, Poseidonius says that he himself saw this spectacle in many places, and that, although at first he loathed it, afterwards, through his familiarity with it, he could bear it calmly. The heads of enemies of high repute, however, they used to embalm in cedar-oil and exhibit to strangers, and they would not deign to give them back even for a ransom of an equal weight of gold. But the Romans put a stop to these customs, as well as to all those connected with the sacrifices and divinations that are opposed to our usages. They used to strike a human being, whom they had devoted to death,[2] in the back with a sabre, and then divine from his death-struggle. But they would not sacrifice without the Druids.[3] We are told of still other

Caesar (*De Bello Gallico* 6. 13) says "They" (the Druids) "take care of the sacrifices, public and private."

εἴδη λέγεται. καὶ γὰρ κατετόξευόν τινας καὶ
ἀνεσταύρουν ἐν τοῖς ἱεροῖς καὶ κατασκευάσαντες
κολοσσὸν χόρτου καὶ ξύλων, ἐμβαλόντες εἰς τοῦτον βοσκήματα καὶ θηρία παντοῖα καὶ ἀνθρώπους
ὡλοκαύτουν.

6. Ἐν δὲ τῷ ὠκεανῷ φησιν εἶναι νῆσον μικρὰν
οὐ πάνυ πελαγίαν, προκειμένην τῆς ἐκβολῆς τοῦ
Λείγηρος ποταμοῦ· οἰκεῖν δὲ ταύτην τὰς τῶν
Σαμνιτῶν γυναῖκας, Διονύσῳ κατεχομένας καὶ
ἱλασκομένας τὸν θεὸν τοῦτον τελεταῖς τε καὶ
ἄλλαις ἱεροποιίαις ἐξιλεουμένας· οὐκ ἐπιβαίνειν
δὲ ἄνδρα τῆς νήσου, τὰς δὲ γυναῖκας αὐτὰς πλεού-
σας κοινωνεῖν τοῖς ἀνδράσι καὶ πάλιν ἐπανιέναι.
ἔθος δ' εἶναι κατ' ἐνιαυτὸν ἅπαξ τὸ ἱερὸν ἀποστε-
γάζεσθαι καὶ στεγάζεσθαι πάλιν αὐθημερὸν πρὸ
δύσεως, ἑκάστης φορτίον ἐπιφερούσης· ἧς δ' ἂν
ἐκπέσῃ τὸ φορτίον, διασπᾶσθαι ταύτην ὑπὸ τῶν
ἄλλων· φερούσας[1] δὲ τὰ μέρη περὶ τὸ ἱερὸν μετ'
εὐασμοῦ μὴ παύεσθαι πρότερον πρὶν παύσωνται
τῆς λύττης· ἀεὶ δὲ συμβαίνειν ὥστε τινὰ ἐμπίπτειν τῇ τοῦτο πεισομένῃ.[2] τοῦτο δ' ἔτι μυθωδέ-
στερον εἴρηκεν Ἀρτεμίδωρος τὸ περὶ τοὺς κόρακας
συμβαῖνον. λιμένα γάρ τινα τῆς παρωκεανίτι-
δος ἱστορεῖ Δύο κοράκων ἐπονομαζόμενον, φαίνεσθαι δ' ἐν τούτῳ δύο κόρακας τὴν δεξιὰν πτέρυγα
παράλευκον ἔχοντας· τοὺς οὖν περί τινων ἀμφισ-

---

[1] φερούσας, Xylander, for φερούσης; so the later editors.
[2] τῇ . . . . . πεισομένῃ, Jones, for τὴν . . . . πεισομένην.

---

[1] Caesar (*De Bello Gallico* 6. 16) says : "Others use images
of enormous size, whose members, woven out of twigs, they
fill with living men and set on fire."

kinds of human sacrifices; for example, they would
shoot victims to death with arrows, or impale them
in the temples, or, having devised a colossus of straw
and wood, throw into the colossus cattle and wild
animals of all sorts and human beings, and then
make a burnt-offering of the whole thing.[1]

6. In the ocean, he[2] says, there is a small island,
not very far out to sea, situated off the outlet of the
Liger River; and the island is inhabited by the
women of the Samnitae, and they are possessed by
Dionysus and make this god propitious by appeasing
him with mystic initiations as well as other sacred
performances; and no man sets foot on the island,
although the women themselves, sailing from it,
have intercourse with the men and then return
again. And, he says, it is a custom of theirs once
a year to unroof the temple and roof it again on
the same day before sunset, each woman bringing her
load to add to the roof; but the woman whose load
falls out of her arms is rent to pieces by the rest,
and they carry the pieces round the temple with the
cry of " Ev-ah," [3] and do not cease until their frenzy
ceases; and it is always the case, he says, that some
one jostles the woman who is to suffer this fate.[4]
But the following story which Artemidorus has told
about the case of the crows is still more fabulous:
there is a certain harbour on the ocean-coast, his
story goes, which is surnamed " Two Crows," and
in this harbour are to be seen two crows, with their
right wings somewhat white; so the men who have

---

[2] Poseidonius.

[3] The " Ev-ah " is a joyful hallelujah in honour of Dionysus,
one of whose numerous cult-names is " Evas."

[4] And thus makes the victim, already decided upon
apparently, drop her load of thatch.

βητοῦντας, ἀφικομένους δεῦρο ἐφ' ὑψηλοῦ τόπου
σανίδα θέντας ἐπιβάλλειν ψαιστά, ἑκάτερον
χωρίς· τοὺς δ' ὄρνεις ἐπιπτάντας τὰ μὲν ἐσθίειν,
τὰ δὲ σκορπίζειν· οὗ δ' ἂν σκορπισθῇ τὰ ψαιστά,
ἐκεῖνον νικᾶν. ταῦτα μὲν οὖν μυθωδέστερα λέγει,
περὶ δὲ τῆς Δήμητρος καὶ Κόρης πιστότερα, ὅτι
φησὶν εἶναι νῆσον πρὸς τῇ Βρεττανικῇ καθ' ἣν
ὅμοια τοῖς ἐν Σαμοθρᾴκῃ περὶ τὴν Δήμητραν καὶ
τὴν Κόρην ἱεροποιεῖται. καὶ τοῦτο δὲ τῶν
πιστευομένων ἐστίν, ὅτι ἐν τῇ Κελτικῇ φύεται
δένδρον ὅμοιον συκῇ, καρπὸν δ' ἐκφέρει παραπλή-
C 199 σιον κιοκράνῳ Κορινθιουργεῖ· ἐπιτμηθεὶς δ' οὗτος,
ἀφίησιν ὀπὸν θανάσιμον πρὸς τὰς ἐπιχρίσεις τῶν
βελῶν. καὶ τοῦτο δὲ τῶν θρυλουμένων ἐστίν, ὅτι
πάντες Κελτοὶ φιλόνεικοί [1] τέ εἰσι, καὶ οὐ νομί-
ζεται παρ' αὐτοῖς αἰσχρὸν τὸ τῆς ἀκμῆς ἀφειδεῖν
τοὺς νέους. Ἔφορος δὲ ὑπερβάλλουσάν τε τῷ
μεγέθει λέγει τὴν Κελτικήν, ὥστε ἧσπερ νῦν Ἰβηρίας καλοῦμεν ἐκείνοις τὰ πλεῖστα προσνέμειν
μέχρι Γαδείρων, φιλέλληνάς τε ἀποφαίνει τοὺς
ἀνθρώπους, καὶ πολλὰ ἰδίως λέγει περὶ αὐτῶν οὐκ
ἐοικότα τοῖς νῦν. ἴδιον δὲ καὶ τοῦτο· ἀσκεῖν γὰρ
αὐτοὺς μὴ παχεῖς εἶναι μηδὲ προγάστορας, τὸν δ'
ὑπερβαλλόμενον τῶν νέων τό τῆς ζώνης μέτρον
ζημιοῦσθαι. ταῦτα μὲν περὶ τῆς ὑπὲρ τῶν Ἄλπεων
Κελτικῆς.

---

[1] Meineke reads ἡδονικοί, unwarrantedly, for φιλόνεικοι.
C. Müller suggests as possible φιλομείρακες ; A. Jacob
conjectures φιλόνεοι. See Diodorus Siculus 5. 28 and
5. 32.

---

[1] The Attic name for Persephone (Proserpina).

disputes about certain things come here, put a plank
on an elevated place, and then throw on barley cakes,
each man separately; the birds fly up, eat some of
the barley cakes, scatter the others; and the man
whose barley cakes are scattered wins his dispute.
Now although this story is more fabulous, his story
about Demeter and Core[1] is more credible. He says
that there is an island near Britain on which sacrifices
are performed like those sacrifices in Samothrace that
have to do with Demeter and Core. And the following, too, is one of the things that are believed, namely,
that in Celtica there grows a tree like a fig-tree, and
that it brings forth a fruit similar to a Corinthian-
wrought capital of a column; and that, if an incision
be made, this fruit exudes a sap which, as used
for the smearing of arrows, is deadly. And the
following, too, is one of the things that are repeated
over and over again, namely, that not only are all
Celti fond of strife,[2] but among them it is considered
no disgrace for the young men to be prodigal of their
youthful charms.[3] Ephorus, in his account, makes
Celtica so excessive in its size that he assigns to the
regions of Celtica most of the regions, as far as Gades,
of what we now call Iberia; further, he declares that
the people are fond of the Greeks, and specifies many
things about them that do not fit the facts of to-day.
The following, also, is a thing peculiar to them,
that they endeavour not to grow fat or pot-bellied,
and any young man who exceeds the standard measure
of the girdle is punished. So much for Transalpine
Celtica.

[2] So says Diodorus Siculus (5. 28).
[3] Diodorus Siculus (5. 32) says the same, and more, of this
immorality among the Celts.

V

1. Ἡ δὲ Βρεττανικὴ τρίγωνος μέν ἐστι τῷ σχήματι, παραβέβληται δὲ τὸ μέγιστον αὐτῆς πλευρὸν τῇ Κελτικῇ, τοῦ μήκους οὔθ᾿ ὑπερβάλλον οὔτ᾿ ἐλλεῖπον· ἔστι γὰρ ὅσον τετρακισχιλίων καὶ τριακοσίων ἢ τετρακοσίων σταδίων ἑκάτερον, τό τε Κελτικὸν τὸ ἀπὸ τῶν ἐκβολῶν τοῦ Ῥήνου μέχρι πρὸς τὰ βόρεια τῆς Πυρήνης ἄκρα τὰ κατὰ Ἀκουιτανίαν καὶ τὸ ἀπὸ Καντίου τοῦ καταντικρὺ τῶν ἐκβολῶν τοῦ Ῥήνου, ἑωθινωτάτου σημείου τῆς Βρεττανικῆς, μέχρι πρὸς τὸ ἑσπέριον ἄκρον τῆς νήσου τὸ κατὰ τὴν Ἀκουιτανίαν καὶ τὴν Πυρήνην ἀντικείμενον. τοῦτο μὲν δὴ τοὐλάχιστον διάστημα ἀπὸ τῆς Πυρήνης ἐπὶ τὸν Ῥῆνόν ἐστιν, ἐπεὶ τὸ μέγιστον εἴρηται ὅτι καὶ πεντακισχιλίων σταδίων ἐστίν· ἀλλ᾿ εἰκὸς εἶναί τινα σύννευσιν ἐκ τῆς παραλλήλου θέσεως τῷ ποταμῷ πρὸς τὸ ὄρος, ἀμφοτέρωθεν ἐπιστροφῆς τινος γινομένης κατὰ τὰς πρὸς τὸν ὠκεανὸν ἐσχατιάς.

2. Τέτταρα δ᾿ ἐστὶ διάρματα οἷς χρῶνται συνήθως ἐπὶ τὴν νῆσον ἐκ τῆς ἠπείρου, τὰ ἀπὸ τῶν ἐκβολῶν τῶν ποταμῶν, τοῦ τε Ῥήνου καὶ τοῦ Σηκοάνα καὶ τοῦ Λείγηρος καὶ τοῦ[1] Γαρούνα. τοῖς δ᾿ ἀπὸ τῶν περὶ τὸν Ῥῆνον τόπων ἀναγομένοις οὐκ ἀπ᾿ αὐτῶν τῶν ἐκβολῶν ὁ πλοῦς ἐστιν, ἀλλὰ ἀπὸ τῶν ὁμορούντων τοῖς Μεναπίοις Μορινῶν, παρ᾿ οἷς ἐστι καὶ τὸ Ἴτιον, ᾧ ἐχρήσατο ναυστάθμῳ Καῖσαρ ὁ Θεός, διαίρων εἰς τὴν νῆσον·

---

[1] τοῦ, before Γαρούνα, inserted by all the editors.

[1] Strabo should have made this the shortest side, as Caesar had already done (*De Bello Gallico* 5. 13).

V

1. BRITAIN is triangular in shape; and its longest side [1] stretches parallel to Celtica, neither exceeding nor falling short of the length of Celtica; for each of the two lengths is about four thousand three hundred—or four hundred—stadia: the Celtic length that extends from the outlets of the Rhenus as far as those northern ends of the Pyrenees that are near Aquitania, as also the length that extends from Cantium (which is directly opposite the outlets of the Rhenus), the most easterly point of Britain, as far as that westerly end of the island which lies opposite the Aquitanian Pyrenees. This, of course, is the shortest distance from the Pyrenees to the Rhenus, since, as I have already said,[2] the greatest distance is as much as five thousand stadia; yet it is reasonable to suppose that there is a convergence from the parallel position which the river and the mountains occupy with reference to each other,[3] since at the ends where they approach the ocean there is a curve in both of them.

2. There are only four passages which are habitually used in crossing from the mainland to the island, those which begin at the mouths of the rivers—the Rhenus, the Sequana, the Liger, and the Garumna. However, the people who put to sea from the regions that are near the Rhenus make the voyage, not from the mouths themselves, but from the coast of those Morini who have a common boundary with the Menapii. (On their coast, also, is Itium, which the Deified Caesar used as a naval station when he set sail for the island.[4] He put to sea by

[1] 1. 4. 2 and 2. 5. 28.   [2] 2. 5. 28 and 4. 1. 1.
[4] Cp. 4. 3. 3.

νύκτωρ δ' ἀνήχθη καὶ τῇ ὑστεραίᾳ κατῆρε περὶ
τετάρτην ὥραν, τριακοσίους καὶ εἴκοσι σταδίους
τοῦ διάπλου τελέσας· κατέλαβε δ' ἐν ἀρούραις
τὸν σῖτον. ἔστι δ' ἡ πλείστη τῆς νήσου πεδιὰς
καὶ κατάδρυμος, πολλὰ δὲ καὶ γεώλοφα τῶν
χωρίων ἐστί. φέρει δὲ σῖτον καὶ βοσκήματα καὶ
χρυσὸν καὶ ἄργυρον καὶ σίδηρον. ταῦτα δὴ κομίζεται ἐξ αὐτῆς καὶ δέρματα καὶ ἀνδράποδα καὶ
C 200 κύνες εὐφυεῖς πρὸς τὰς κυνηγεσίας· Κελτοὶ δὲ καὶ
πρὸς τοὺς πολέμους χρῶνται καὶ τούτοις καὶ τοῖς
ἐπιχωρίοις. οἱ δὲ ἄνδρες εὐμηκέστεροι τῶν Κελτῶν εἰσι καὶ ἧσσον ξανθότριχες, χαυνότεροι δὲ
τοῖς σώμασι. σημεῖον δὲ τοῦ μεγέθους· ἀντίπαι-
δας γὰρ εἴδομεν ἡμεῖς ἐν Ῥώμῃ τῶν ὑψηλοτάτων
αὐτόθι ὑπερέχοντας καὶ ἡμιποδίῳ, βλαισοὺς δὲ
καὶ τἄλλα οὐκ εὐγράμμους τῇ συστάσει. τὰ δ'
ἤθη[1] τὰ μὲν ὅμοια τοῖς Κελτοῖς, τὰ δ' ἁπλού-
στερα καὶ βαρβαρώτερα, ὥστ' ἐνίους γάλακτος
εὐποροῦντας μὴ τυροποιεῖν διὰ τὴν ἀπειρίαν,
ἀπείρους δ' εἶναι καὶ κηπείας καὶ ἄλλων γεωργι-
κῶν. δυναστεῖαι δ' εἰσὶ παρ' αὐτοῖς. πρὸς δὲ
τοὺς πολέμους ἀπήναις χρῶνται τὸ πλέον, καθάπερ καὶ τῶν Κελτῶν ἔνιοι. πόλεις δ' αὐτῶν εἰσιν
οἱ δρυμοί· περιφράξαντες γὰρ δένδρεσι κατα-

---

[1] ἤθη, the reading of the MSS., Jones restores (for ἔθη). Cp.
Diodorus Siculus (in reference to the same people): τοῖς
δ' ἤθεσιν ἁπλοῦς εἶναι (5. 21).

---

[1] Cp. the time given in 4. 3. 4. Caesar made his first
voyage to Britain (*op. cit.* 4. 23) between "about the third
watch" (midnight) and "the fourth hour of the day"
(10 A.M.); the second (*op. cit.* 5. 8), between "about sun-

night and landed on the following day about the fourth hour,[1] thus having completed three hundred and twenty stadia[2] in his voyage across; and he found the grain still in the fields.) Most of the island is flat and overgrown with forests, although many of its districts are hilly. It bears grain, cattle, gold, silver, and iron. These things, accordingly, are exported from the island, as also hides, and slaves, and dogs that are by nature suited to the purposes of the chase; the Celti, however, use both these and the native dogs for the purposes of war too. The men of Britain are taller than the Celti, and not so yellow-haired, although their bodies are of looser build. The following is an indication of their size: I myself, in Rome, saw mere lads towering as much as half a foot above the tallest people in the city, although they were bandy-legged and presented no fair lines anywhere else in their figure. Their habits are in part like those of the Celti, but in part more simple and barbaric[3]—so much so that, on account of their inexperience, some of them, although well supplied with milk, make no cheese; and they have no experience in gardening or other agricultural pursuits. And they have powerful chieftains in their country.[4] For the purposes of war they use chariots for the most part, just as some of the Celti do. The forests are their cities; for they fence in a

set" and "about noon," being greatly delayed by unfavourable wind and tide.

[2] That is, forty miles. Caesar (*op. cit.* 5. 2) says "about thirty miles." Cp. 4. 3. 4.

[3] Cp. Caesar *op. cit.* 5. 14 and Diodorus 5. 21.

[4] Diodorus (5 21) says "they have many kings and chieftains, it is said, who are, for the most part, peaceably disposed towards one another."

βεβλημένοις εὐρυχωρῆ κύκλον ἐνταῦθα καὶ αὐτοὶ
καλυβοποιοῦνται καὶ τὰ βοσκήματα κατασταθ-
μεύουσιν, οὐ πρὸς πολὺν χρόνον. ἔπομβροι δ᾽
εἰσὶν οἱ ἀέρες μᾶλλον ἢ νιφετώδεις· ἐν δὲ ταῖς
αἰθρίαις ὁμίχλη κατέχει πολὺν χρόνον, ὥστε δι᾽
ἡμέρας ὅλης ἐπὶ τρεῖς μόνον ἢ τέτταρας ὥρας τὰς
περὶ τὴν μεσημβρίαν ὁρᾶσθαι τὸν ἥλιον· τοῦτο
δὲ κἂν τοῖς Μορινοῖς συμβαίνει, καὶ τοῖς Μεναπίοις καὶ ὅσοι τούτων πλησιόχωροι.

3. Δὶς δὲ διέβη Καῖσαρ εἰς τὴν νῆσον ὁ Θεός,
ἐπανῆλθε δὲ διὰ ταχέων, οὐδὲν μέγα διαπραξά-
μενος οὐδὲ προελθὼν ἐπὶ πολὺ τῆς νήσου, διά τε
τὰς ἐν τοῖς Κελτοῖς γενομένας στάσεις τῶν τε
βαρβάρων καὶ τῶν οἰκείων στρατιωτῶν, καὶ διὰ
τὸ πολλὰ τῶν πλοίων ἀπολέσθαι κατὰ τὴν πανσέ-
ληνον αὔξησιν λαβουσῶν τῶν ἀμπώτεων καὶ τῶν
πλημμυρίδων. δύο μέντοι ἢ τρεῖς νίκας ἐνίκησε
τοὺς Βρεττανούς, καίπερ δύο τάγματα μόνον πε-
ραιώσας τῆς στρατιᾶς, καὶ ἀπήγαγεν ὅμηρά τε
καὶ ἀνδράποδα καὶ τῆς ἄλλης λείας πλῆθος. νυνὶ
μέντοι τῶν δυναστῶν τινες τῶν αὐτόθι πρεσβεύ-
σεσι καὶ θεραπείαις κατασκευασάμενοι τὴν πρὸς
Καίσαρα τὸν Σεβαστὸν φιλίαν, ἀναθήματά τε
ἀνέθηκαν ἐν τῷ Καπετωλίῳ καὶ οἰκείαν σχεδόν τι
παρεσκεύασαν τοῖς Ῥωμαίοις ὅλην τὴν νῆσον·

---

[1] Cp. Caesar op. cit. 5. 21.

[2] It was a question of (1) pasturage and (2) defence against
the enemy.

[3] Caesar (op. cit. 5. 22) says "on account of sudden com-
motions in Gaul," referring to his *second* return to the
continent.

[4] This loss took place before Caesar's *first* return, "on the
day when the moon is wont to make the maximum tides in

spacious circular enclosure with trees which they have felled,[1] and in that enclosure make huts for themselves and also pen up their cattle—not, however, with the purpose of staying a long time.[2] Their weather is more rainy than snowy; and on the days of clear sky fog prevails so long a time that throughout a whole day the sun is to be seen for only three or four hours round about midday. And this is the case also among the Morini and the Menapii and all the neighbours of the latter.

3. The Deified Caesar crossed over to the island twice, although he came back in haste, without accomplishing anything great or proceeding far into the island, not only on account of the quarrels that took place in the land of the Celti, among the barbarians and his own soldiers as well,[3] but also on account of the fact that many of his ships had been lost at the time of the full moon, since the ebb-tides and the flood-tides got their increase at that time.[4] However, he won two or three victories over the Britons, albeit he carried along only two legions of his army; and he brought back hostages, slaves, and quantities of the rest of the booty. At present, however, some of the chieftains there, after procuring the friendship of Caesar Augustus by sending embassies and by paying court to him,[5] have not only dedicated offerings in the Capitolium, but have also managed to make the whole of the island virtually Roman

the ocean" (*op. cit.* 4. 28–29). For Strabo's discussion of these tides, see 3. 5. 8.

[5] Augustus had intended to subjugate Britain, but went no farther than Gaul (Dio Cassius 53. 22). Caesar mentions (*Monumentum Ancyranum*) two British chieftains who came to him as suppliants, " Dumnobellaunua " and " Tim— " (or " Tinc— ").

τέλη τε οὕτως [1] ὑπομένουσι βαρέα τῶν τε εἰσαγο-
μένων εἰς τὴν Κελτικὴν ἐκεῖθεν καὶ τῶν ἐξαγο-
μένων ἐνθένδε (ταῦτα δ' ἐστὶν ἐλεφάντινα ψάλια
καὶ περιαυχένια καὶ λιγγούρια [2] καὶ ὑαλᾶ σκεύη
καὶ ἄλλος ῥῶπος τοιοῦτος) ὥστε μηδὲν δεῖν φρουρᾶς τῆς νήσου· τοὐλάχιστον μὲν γὰρ ἑνὸς τάγματος χρῄζοι ἂν καὶ ἱππικοῦ τινος, ὥστε καὶ φόρους
ἀπάγεσθαι παρ' αὐτῶν, εἰς ἴσον δὲ καθίσταιτ' ἂν [3]
τὸ ἀνάλωμα τῇ στρατιᾷ τοῖς προσφερομένοις χρή-
C 201 μασιν· ἀνάγκη γὰρ μειοῦσθαι τὰ τέλη φόρων
ἐπιβαλλομένων, ἅμα δὲ καὶ κινδύνους ἀπαντᾶν
τινας, βίας ἐπαγομένης.

4. Εἰσὶ δὲ καὶ ἄλλαι περὶ τὴν Βρεττανικὴν
νῆσοι μικραί· μεγάλη δ' ἡ Ἰέρνη πρὸς ἄρκτον
αὐτῇ παραβεβλημένη, πρόμηκες [4] μᾶλλον πλάτος
ἔχουσα. περὶ ἧς οὐδὲν ἔχομεν λέγειν σαφές, πλὴν
ὅτι ἀγριώτεροι τῶν Βρεττανῶν ὑπάρχουσιν οἱ
κατοικοῦντες αὐτήν, ἀνθρωποφάγοι τε [5] ὄντες καὶ
πολυφάγοι, [6] τούς τε πατέρας τελευτήσαντας κατε-
σθίειν ἐν καλῷ τιθέμενοι καὶ φανερῶς μίσγεσθαι
ταῖς τε ἄλλαις γυναιξὶ καὶ μητράσι καὶ ἀδελφαῖς·
καὶ ταῦτα δ' οὕτω λέγομεν, ὡς οὐκ ἔχοντες ἀξιο-

---

[1] οὕτως, Madvig restores, for οὕτως (Xylander's emendation), which is commonly read by the editors since Corais,
except Tozer.

[2] λιγγούρια, for ἀλλυγούρια (cp. 4. 6. 2 λιγγούριον); so the
editors in general.

[3] καθίσταιτ' ἄν, Meineke from conj. of Kramer, for καθίστατο
πᾶν.

[4] πρόμηκες, Jones, for προμήκης; other editors, following
Corais, wrongly insert ἥ after μᾶλλον.

[5] τε, the reading of some of the MSS., instead of δέ.

[6] For πολυφάγοι some of the editors read ποηφάγοι (Epitome
only).

property. Further, they submit so easily to heavy duties, both on the exports from there to Celtica and on the imports from Celtica (these latter are ivory chains and necklaces, and amber-gems[1] and glass vessels and other petty wares of that sort), that there is no need of garrisoning the island; for one legion, at the least, and some cavalry would be required in order to carry off tribute from them, and the expense of the army would offset the tribute-money;[2] in fact, the duties must necessarily be lessened if tribute is imposed, and, at the same time, dangers be encountered, if force is applied.

4. Besides some small islands round about Britain, there is also a large island, Ierne,[3] which stretches parallel to Britain on the north, its breadth being greater than its length.[4] Concerning this island I have nothing certain to tell, except that its inhabitants are more savage[5] than the Britons, since they are man-eaters as well as heavy eaters,[6] and since, further, they count it an honourable thing, when their fathers die, to devour them, and openly to have intercourse, not only with the other women, but also with their mothers and sisters; but I am saying this only with the understanding that I have no trust-

---

[1] "Linguria" (Strabo's word) means gems of red amber, like the red amber ("lingurium" 4. 6. 2) on the coast of Liguria, from which country it gets its name (Ridgeway, *Origin of Currency*, p. 110).

[2] 2. 5. 8.   [3] See 1. 4. 3.

[4] That is, speaking in terms of a rectangle, the *geographical* breadth is longer than the *geographical* length; for *geographical* breadth is measured north and south, and *geographical* length, east and west (see 2. 1. 32). And Strabo's assertion about Ireland is correct.   [5] See 2. 5. 8.

[6] Some of the editors read "herb-eaters" instead of "heavy eaters"—perhaps rightly.

πίστους μάρτυρας (καίτοι τό γε τῆς ἀνθρωποφα-
γίας καὶ Σκυθικὸν εἶναι λέγεται, καὶ ἐν ἀνάγκαις
πολιορκητικαῖς καὶ Κελτοὶ καὶ Ἴβηρες καὶ ἄλλοι
πλείους ποιῆσαι τοῦτο λέγονται).

5. Περὶ δὲ τῆς Θούλης ἔτι μᾶλλον ἀσαφὴς ἡ
ἱστορία διὰ τὸν ἐκτοπισμόν· ταύτην γὰρ τῶν ὀνο-
μαζομένων ἀρκτικωτάτην τιθέασιν. ἃ δ᾽ εἴρηκε
Πυθέας περί τε ταύτης καὶ τῶν ἄλλων τῶν ταύτῃ
τόπων ὅτι μὲν πέπλασται, φανερὸν ἐκ τῶν γνωριζομένων χωρίων· κατέψευσται γὰρ αὐτῶν τὰ
πλεῖστα, ὥσπερ καὶ πρότερον εἴρηται, ὥστε δῆλός
ἐστιν ἐψευσμένος μᾶλλον περὶ τῶν ἐκτετοπι-
σμένων. πρὸς μέντοι τὰ οὐράνια καὶ τὴν μαθημα-
τικὴν θεωρίαν ἂν[1] ἱκανῶς δόξειε κεχρῆσθαι τοῖς
πράγμασι, τοῖς τῇ κατεψυγμένῃ ζώνῃ πλησιάζουσι τὸ τῶν[2] καρπῶν εἶναι τῶν ἡμέρων καὶ
ζῴων τῶν μὲν ἀφορίαν παντελῆ, τῶν δὲ σπάνιν,
κέγχρῳ δὲ καὶ ἄλλοις[3] λαχάνοις καὶ καρποῖς καὶ
ῥίζαις τρέφεσθαι· παρ᾽ οἷς δὲ σῖτος καὶ μέλι γί-

---

[1] ἄν after θεωρίαν, Jones inserts; others insert ἄν after
ἱκανῶς, or read δόξει for δόξειε.
[2] τὸ τῶν, Jones restores; Meineke and others read λέγων;
C. Müller suggests ἱστορῶν.
[3] Meineke and Corais have emended ἄλλοις to ἀγρίοις; C.
Müller conjectures ὤμοις.

---

[1] e.g. when besieged by the Cimbri and Teutones (Caesar,
op. cit. 7. 77).
[2] e.g. when besieged at Numantia by Scipio (Valerius
Maximus 7. 6).
[3] e.g. the city of Potidaea in Greece (Thucydides, 2. 70).
[4] See 1. 4. 2 ff.

worthy witnesses for it; and yet, as for the matter of man-eating, that is said to be a custom of the Scythians also, and, in cases of necessity forced by sieges, the Celti,[1] the Iberians,[2] and several other peoples are said to have practised it.[3]

5. Concerning Thule[4] our historical information is still more uncertain, on account of its outside position;[5] for Thule, of all the countries that are named, is set farthest north. But that the things which Pytheas has told about Thule, as well as the other places in that part of the world, have indeed been fabricated by him, we have clear evidence from the districts that are known to us,[6] for in most cases he has falsified them, as I have already said before,[7] and hence he is obviously more false concerning the districts which have been placed outside the inhabited world. And yet, if judged by the science of the celestial phenomena[8] and by mathematical theory, he might possibly seem to have made adequate use of the facts as regards the people who live close to the frozen zone,[9] when he says that, of the animals and domesticated fruits, there is an utter dearth of some and a scarcity of the others, and that the people live on millet and other herbs, and on fruits and roots; and where there are grain and honey, the people get their

[5] Strabo has insisted (2. 5. 8) that the northern limit of the inhabited world should be placed in Ierne (Ireland), and that therefore Thule falls outside.

[6] Strabo means "from what he has told us about the districts that are known to us" (cp. 1. 4. 3).

[7] 1. 4. 3.   [8] See 1. 1. 15, and footnote 2.

[9] Strabo speaks of "the people who live close to the frozen zone" only for argument's sake; he himself regards such people, as well as those farther north, as non-existent so far as geography is concerned (2. 5. 43).

γνεται, καὶ τὸ πόμα ἐντεῦθεν ἔχειν· τὸν δὲ σῖτον,
ἐπειδὴ τοὺς ἡλίους οὐκ ἔχουσι καθαρούς, ἐν οἴκοις
μεγάλοις κόπτουσι, συγκομισθέντων δεῦρο τῶν
σταχύων· αἱ γὰρ ἅλως ¹ ἄχρηστοι γίνονται διὰ τὸ
ἀνήλιον καὶ τοὺς ὄμβρους.

VI

1. Μετὰ δὲ τὴν ὑπὲρ τῶν Ἄλπεων Κελτικὴν καὶ
τὰ ἔθνη τὰ ἔχοντα τὴν χώραν ταύτην, περὶ αὐτῶν
τῶν Ἄλπεων λεκτέον καὶ τῶν κατοικούντων αὐτάς,
ἔπειτα περὶ τῆς συμπάσης Ἰταλίας, φυλάττουσιν
ἐν τῇ γραφῇ τὴν αὐτὴν τάξιν ἥνπερ δίδωσιν ἡ τῆς
χώρας φύσις. ἄρχονται μὲν οὖν αἱ Ἄλπεις οὐκ
ἀπὸ Μονοίκου λιμένος, ὡς εἰρήκασί τινες, ἀλλ'
ἀπὸ τῶν αὐτῶν χωρίων ἀφ' ὧνπερ καὶ τὰ Ἀπέννινα
ὄρη κατὰ Γένουαν ἐμπόριον Λιγύων καὶ τὰ καλούμενα Σαβάτων Οὔαδα, ὅπερ ἐστὶ τενάγη· τὸ μὲν
C 202 γὰρ Ἀπέννινον ἀπὸ Γενούας, αἱ δὲ Ἄλπεις ἀπὸ
τῶν Σαβάτων ἔχουσι τὴν ἀρχήν· στάδιοι δ' εἰσὶ
μεταξὺ Γενούας καὶ Σαβάτων διακόσιοι πρὸς τοῖς
ἑξήκοντα· μετὰ δὲ τριακοσίους πρὸς τοῖς ἑβδομήκοντα Ἀλβίγγανόν ἐστι πόλισμα, οἱ δ' ἐνοι-
κοῦντες Λίγυες Ἴγγαυνοι καλοῦνται· ἐντεῦθεν δ' εἰς
Μονοίκου λιμένα τετρακόσιοι καὶ ὀγδοήκοντα. ἔν

---

¹ ἅλως, Kramer, for ἄλλως ; so the editors in general.

---

¹ That is, as well as nourishment.
² Obviously a kind of beer, such as "the wheat-beer prepared with honey" and "drunk by the poorer classes" in
Gaul (Athenaeus 4. 36). Diodorus Siculus (5. 26) refers to
this "beverage" of the Gauls, made of "barley" and "mead,"
"what is called beer."

beverage, also,[1] from them.[2] As for the grain, he
says,—since they have no pure sunshine—they pound
it out in large storehouses, after first gathering in
the ears thither;[3] for the threshing floors become
useless because of this lack of sunshine and because
of the rains.

VI

1. AFTER Transalpine Celtica and the tribes which
hold this country, I must tell about the Alps themselves and the people who inhabit them, and then
about the whole of Italy, keeping the same order in
my description as is given me by the nature of the
country. The beginning, then, of the Alps is not at
the Port of Monoecus, as some have told us, but at
the same districts as the beginning of the Apennine
mountains, namely, near Genua, the emporium of the
Ligures, and what is called Vada (that is, " Shoals ")
Sabatorum:[4] for the Apennines begin at Genua, and
the Alps have their beginning at Sabata; and the
distance, in stadia, between Genua and Sabata is
two hundred and sixty; then, after three hundred
and seventy stadia from Sabata, comes the town
of Albingaunum (its inhabitants are called Ligures
Ingauni); and thence, to the Port of Monoecus, four
hundred and eighty stadia. Further, in this last

[3] Diodorus Siculus (5. 21), who, like Strabo, quotes Pytheas
through Poseidonius, makes a similar reference to the Britons,
saying that the Britons "cut off the ears of grain and store
them in houses that are roofed over, and pluck the ears from
day to day. The threshing floors with which Strabo and
Diodorus were familiar were in the open air, *e. g.* in Greece
and Italy.
[4] Also called Vada Sabatia (now Vado).

τε τῷ μεταξὺ πόλις εὐμεγέθης Ἄλβιον Ἰντεμέλιον,
καὶ οἱ κατοικοῦντες Ἰντεμέλιοι. καὶ δὴ καὶ σημεῖον τίθενται τοῦ τὴν ἀρχὴν ἀπὸ τῶν Σαβάτων
εἶναι ταῖς Ἄλπεσι ἐκ τῶν ὀνομάτων τούτων· τὰ
γὰρ Ἄλπια καλεῖσθαι πρότερον Ἄλβια, καθάπερ
καὶ Ἀλπιόνια,¹ καὶ γὰρ νῦν ἔτι τὸ ἐν τοῖς Ἰάποσιν
ὄρος ὑψηλὸν συνάπτον πως τῇ Ὄκρᾳ καὶ ταῖς
Ἄλπεσιν Ἄλβιον λέγεσθαι, ὡς ἂν μέχρι δεῦρο
τῶν Ἄλπεων ἐκτεταμένων.

2. Τῶν οὖν Λιγύων τῶν μὲν ὄντων Ἰγγαύνων,
τῶν δὲ Ἰντεμελίων, εἰκότως τὰς ἐποικίας αὐτῶν
ἐπὶ τῇ θαλάττῃ, τὴν μὲν ὀνομάζεσθαι Ἄλβιον
Ἰντεμέλιον, οἷον Ἄλπιον, τὴν δὲ ἐπιτετμημένως
μᾶλλον Ἀλβίγγαυνον. Πολύβιος δὲ προστίθησι
τοῖς δυσὶ φύλοις τῶν Λιγύων τοῖς λεχθεῖσι τό τε
τῶν Ὀξυβίων καὶ τὸ τῶν Δεκιητῶν. ὅλως δὲ ἡ
παραλία αὕτη πᾶσα μέχρι Τυρρηνίας ἐκ² Μονοίκου λιμένος προσεχής τέ ἐστι καὶ ἀλίμενος πλὴν
βραχέων ὅρμων καὶ ἀγκυροβολίων. ὑπέρκεινται
δὲ οἱ τῶν ὁρῶν ἐξαίσιοι κρημνοί, στενὴν ἀπολεί-
ποντες πρὸς θαλάττῃ πάροδον. κατοικοῦσι δὲ
Λίγυες, ζῶντες ἀπὸ θρεμμάτων τὸ πλέον καὶ γάλακτος καὶ κριθίνου πόματος, νεμόμενοι τά τε
πρὸς θαλάττῃ χωρία καὶ τὸ πλέον τὰ ὄρη. ἔχουσι
δ᾽ ὕλην ἐνταῦθα παμπόλλην ναυπηγήσιμον καὶ
μεγαλόδενδρον ὥστ᾽ ἐνίων τοῦ πάχους τὴν διάμετρον ὀκτὼ ποδῶν εὑρίσκεσθαι· πολλὰ δὲ καὶ τῇ
ποικιλίᾳ τῶν θυίνων οὐκ ἔστι χείρω πρὸς τὰς

¹ Meineke, following Kramer, reads Ἀλπεινά, for Ἀλπιόνια.
² ἐκ, Meineke, for καί.

¹ "Alpionian," is now known only as the name of an
Etrurian *gens*. ² Mt. Velika. Cp. 7. 5. 4.

interval there is a city of fair size, Albium Intemelium, and its occupants are called Intemelii.
And indeed it is on the strength of these names
that writers advance a proof that the Alps begin
at Sabata; for things "Alpian" were formerly
called "Albian," as also things "Alpionian,"[1] and,
in fact, writers add that still to-day the high
mountain[2] among the Iapodes which almost joins
Mount Ocra and the Alps is called "Albius," thus
implying that the Alps have stretched as far as that
mountain.

2. Since, then, the Ligures were partly Ingauni
and partly Intemelii, writers add, it was reasonable
for their settlements on the sea to be named, the
one, Albium (the equivalent of Alpium) Intemelium,
and the other, more concisely, Albingaunum. Polybius, however, adds to the two aforesaid tribes of
the Ligures both that of the Oxybii and that of the
Decietae. Speaking generally, this whole coastline,
from the Port of Monoecus as far as Tyrrhenia, is
not only exposed to the wind but harbourless as well,
except for shallow mooring-places and anchorages.
And lying above it are the enormous beetling cliffs of
the mountains, which leave only a narrow pass next
to the sea. This country is occupied by the Ligures,
who live on sheep, for the most part, and milk, and
a drink made of barley; they pasture their flocks in
the districts next to the sea, but mainly in the
mountains. They have there in very great quantities
timber that is suitable for ship-building, with trees
so large that the diameter of their thickness is sometimes found to be eight feet. And many of these
trees, even in the variegation of the grain, are not

τραπεζοποιίας. ταῦτά τε δὴ κατάγουσιν εἰς τὸ
ἐμπόριον τὴν Γένουαν, καὶ θρέμματα καὶ δέρματα
καὶ μέλι, ἀντιφορτίζονται δὲ ἔλαιον καὶ οἶνον τὸν
ἐκ τῆς Ἰταλίας· ὁ δὲ παρ' αὐτοῖς ὀλίγος ἐστὶ πιτ-
τίτης, αὐστηρός. ἐντεῦθεν δέ εἰσιν οἵ τε[1] γίννοι
λεγόμενοι, ἵπποι τε καὶ ἡμίονοι, καὶ οἱ λιγυστινοί
τε χιτῶνες καὶ σάγοι· πλεονάζει δὲ καὶ τὸ λιγγούριον παρ' αὐτοῖς, ὅ τινες ἤλεκτρον προσαγορεύουσι. στρατεύονται δ' ἱππεῖς μὲν οὐ πάνυ,
ὁπλῖται δὲ ἀγαθοὶ καὶ ἀκροβολισταί· ἀπὸ δὲ τοῦ
χαλκάσπιδας εἶναι τεκμαίρονταί τινες Ἕλληνας
αὐτοὺς εἶναι.

3. Ὁ δὲ τοῦ Μονοίκου λιμὴν ὅρμος ἐστὶν οὐ
μεγάλαις οὐδὲ πολλαῖς ναυσίν, ἔχων ἱερὸν Ἡρακλέους Μονοίκου καλουμένου· ἔοικε δὲ ἀπὸ τοῦ
ὀνόματος καὶ μέχρι δεῦρο διατείνειν ὁ Μασσαλι-
ωτικὸς παράπλους. διέχει δ' Ἀντιπόλεως μικρῷ

---

[1] τε γίννοι, Corais, for γυγήνιοι (ABC), γεγήνιοι (Ald.); so
Groskurd. Meineke and Tozer read only γίννοι, following
Scaliger, and Casaubon.

---

[1] Cp. 17. 3. 4; *Revelation*, 18. 12; Pliny (*Nat. Hist.* 13.
29–31), who discusses at length wood for tables, and tells of
the "mania" of the Romans for large ones of beautiful wood.

[2] Dioscurides (5. 48) gave a formula for the mixture: one
or two ounces of pitch to about six gallons of new wine. It
is the resinated wine still used in Greece.

[3] Aristotle (*Hist. An.* 6. 24) and Pliny (*Nat. Hist.* 8. 69)
define the "ginnus" as the stunted foal of a mare by a mule.
But here the term is simply colloquial for a stunted animal,
whether horse or mule. The Latin word is "hinnus." Cp.
English "ginny" and "flying-jenny."

[4] The sagus was a kind of coarse cloak. Cp. 4. 4. 3.

[5] Literally, "lingurium" (cp. page 259, footnote 1).

[6] "Monoecus" (of which the "Monaco" of to-day is a

inferior to the thyine wood [1] for the purposes of
table-making. These, accordingly, the people bring
down to the emporium of Genua, as well as flocks,
hides and honey, and receive therefor a return-cargo
of olive oil and Italian wine (the little wine they
have in their country is mixed with pitch,[2] and harsh).
And this is the country from which come not only
the so-called "ginni"—both horses and mules,[3]—
but also the Ligurian tunics and "sagi."[4] And
they also have in their country excessive quantities
of amber,[5] which by some is called "electrum."
And although, in their campaigns, they are no good
at all as cavalrymen, they are excellent heavy-armed
soldiers and skirmishers; and, from the fact that they
use bronze shields, some infer that they are Greeks.

3. The Port of Monoecus affords a mooring-place
for no large ships, nor yet for a considerable number;
and it has a temple of Heracles "Monoecus,"[6] as he
is called; and it is reasonable to conjecture from the
name [7] that the coastal voyages of the Massiliotes
reach even as far as the Port of Monoecus.[8] The
distance from the Port of Monoecus to Antipolis is a

corruption) means "the Solitary." The epithet was given
to Heracles, according to Servius (note on the *Aeneid* 6.
829), either because Heracles drove out the inhabitants of
Liguria and remained sole possessor of the land, or because
it was not the custom to associate other divinities with him
in the temples dedicated to him; but according to Prof.
Freeman's suggestion to Tozer (*Selections from Strabo*, p. 138),
the epithet probably refers to the solitary position of the
place, as being the last of the Greek cities on this coast.

[7] The name is Greek.

[6] Strabo means that the Port of Monoecus probably came
under the influence of Massilia. He has already said that
Nicaea, which is only a few miles west of Monoecus, belongs
to Massilia (4. 1. 9).

πλείους ἢ διακοσίους σταδίους. τοὐντεῦθεν δ' ἤδη
C 203 μέχρι Μασσαλίας καὶ μικρὸν προσωτέρω τὸ τῶν
Σαλλύων ἔθνος οἰκεῖ τὰς Ἄλπεις τὰς ὑπερκειμένας καί τινα[1] τῆς αὐτῆς παραλίας ἀναμὶξ
τοῖς Ἕλλησι. καλοῦσι δὲ τοὺς Σάλλυας οἱ μὲν
παλαιοὶ τῶν Ἑλλήνων Λίγυας καὶ τὴν χώραν ἣν
ἔχουσιν οἱ Μασσαλιῶται Λιγυστικήν, οἱ δ'
ὕστερον Κελτολίγυας ὀνομάζουσι, καὶ τὴν μέχρι
Λουερίωνος καὶ τοῦ Ῥοδανοῦ πεδιάδα τούτοις
προσνέμουσιν, ἀφ' ἧς οὐ πεζὴν μόνον, ἀλλὰ καὶ
ἱππικὴν ἔστελλον στρατιάν, εἰς δέκα μέρη δι-
ῃρημένοι. πρώτους δ' ἐχειρώσαντο Ῥωμαῖοι
τούτους τῶν ὑπεραλπίων Κελτῶν, πολὺν χρόνον
πολεμήσαντες καὶ τούτοις καὶ τοῖς Λίγυσιν,
ἀποκεκλεικόσι τὰς εἰς τὴν Ἰβηρίαν παρόδους τὰς
διὰ τῆς παραλίας. καὶ γὰρ καὶ κατὰ γῆν καὶ κατὰ
θάλατταν ἐλῄζοντο καὶ τοσοῦτον ἴσχυον ὥστε
μόλις στρατοπέδοις μεγάλοις πορευτὴν εἶναι τὴν
ὁδόν. ὀγδοηκοστὸν δ' ἔτος πολεμοῦντες διεπράξαντο μόλις ὥστ' ἐπὶ δώδεκα σταδίους τὸ πλάτος
ἀνεῖσθαι τὴν ὁδὸν τοῖς ὁδεύουσι δημοσίᾳ. μετὰ
ταῦτα μέντοι κατέλυσαν ἅπαντας, καὶ διέταξαν
αὐτοὶ τὰς πολιτείας, ἐπιστήσαντες φόρον.[2]

4. Μετὰ δὲ τοὺς Σάλλυας Ἀλβιεῖς καὶ Ἀλ-
βίοικοι καὶ Οὐοκόντιοι νέμονται τὰ προσάρκτια
μέρη τῶν ὀρῶν. παρατείνουσι δὲ οἱ Οὐοκόντιοι

---

[1] τινα, Corais, for τινας; so the later editors.
[2] φόρον, Aldine Ed., for φόβον; so the editors in general,
except Meineke.

---

[1] The Latin form is "Ligures."

little more than two hundred stadia. As for the stretch of country which begins at Antipolis and extends as far as Massilia or a little farther, the tribe of the Sallyes inhabits the Alps that lie above the seaboard and also—promiscuously with the Greeks—certain parts of the same seaboard. But though the early writers of the Greeks call the Sallyes "Ligues," [1] and the country which the Massiliotes hold, "Ligustica," later writers name them "Celto-ligues," and attach to their territory all the level country as far as Luerio and the Rhodanus, the country from which the inhabitants, divided into ten parts, used to send forth an army, not only of infantry, but of cavalry as well. These were the first of the Transalpine Celti that the Romans conquered, though they did so only after carrying on war with both them and the Ligures for a long time—because the latter had barred all the passes leading to Iberia that ran through the seaboard. And, in fact, they kept making raids both by land and sea, and were so powerful that the road was scarcely practicable even for great armies. And it was not until the eightieth year of the war that the Romans succeeded, though only with difficulty, in opening up the road for a breadth [2] of only twelve stadia to those travelling on public business. After this, however, they defeated them all, and, having imposed a tribute upon them, administered the government themselves.

4. After the Sallyes come the Albienses and the Albioeci and the Vocontii, who occupy the northerly parts of the mountains. But the Vocontii, stretching

---

[2] Not from the coastline; we should say that the Romans secured a "right of way."

μέχρι Ἀλλοβρίγων, ἔχοντες αὐλῶνας ἐν βάθει
τῆς ὀρεινῆς ἀξιολόγους καὶ οὐ χείρους ὧν ἔχουσιν
ἐκεῖνοι. Ἀλλόβριγες μὲν οὖν καὶ Λίγυες ὑπὸ
τοῖς στρατηγοῖς τάττονται τοῖς ἀφικνουμένοις εἰς
τὴν Ναρβωνῖτιν, Οὐοκόντιοι δέ, καθάπερ τοὺς
Οὐόλκας ἔφαμεν τοὺς περὶ Νέμαυσον, τάττονται
καθ᾽ αὑτούς. τῶν δὲ μεταξὺ τοῦ Οὐάρου καὶ τῆς
Γενούας Λιγύων οἱ μὲν ἐπὶ τῇ θαλάττῃ τοῖς
Ἰταλιώταις εἰσὶν οἱ αὐτοί, ἐπὶ δὲ τοὺς ὀρεινοὺς
πέμπεταί τις ὕπαρχος τῶν ἱππικῶν ἀνδρῶν,
καθάπερ καὶ ἐπ᾽ ἄλλους τῶν τελέως βαρβάρων.

5. Μετὰ δὲ Οὐοκοντίους Ἰκόνιοι καὶ Τρικόριοι,
καὶ μετ᾽ αὐτοὺς Μέδουλλοι, οἵπερ[1] τὰς ὑψηλο-
τάτας ἔχουσι κορυφάς· τὸ γοῦν ὀρθιώτατον αὐτῶν
ὕψος σταδίων ἑκατὸν ἔχειν φασὶ τὴν ἀνάβασιν,
κἀνθένδε πάλιν τὴν ἐπὶ τοὺς ὅρους τοὺς τῆς
Ἰταλίας κατάβασιν. ἄνω δ᾽ ἔν τισι κοίλοις
χωρίοις λίμνη τε συνίσταται μεγάλη καὶ πηγαὶ
δύο οὐ πολὺ ἄπωθεν ἀλλήλων, ὧν ἐκ μὲν τῆς
ἑτέρας ἐστὶν[2] ὁ Δρουεντίας, ποταμὸς χαραδρώδης
ὃς ἐπὶ τὸν Ῥοδανὸν καταράττει, καὶ ὁ Δουρίας
εἰς τἀναντία· τῷ γὰρ Πάδῳ συμμίσγει, κατενεχθεὶς διὰ Σαλασσῶν εἰς τὴν ἐντὸς τῶν Ἄλπεων
Κελτικήν. ἐκ δὲ τῆς ἑτέρας πολὺ ταπεινότερος

---

[1] οἵπερ, Siebenkees, for ὑπέρ; so the editors.
[2] For ἐστίν Kramer reads εἰσιν; so Groskurd, Meineke, and Müller-Dübner.

---

[1] See 4. 1. 12, and cp. 4. 2. 2 and footnote 3.
[2] i. e., are autonomous with "Latin right" (see 3. 2. 15, 4. 1. 9, 5. 1. 1).
[3] There were two Durias Rivers, namely, the Durias Major (now Dora Baltea) and Durias Minor (now Dora Riparia), both of which emptied into the Padus (Po). The Durias

alongside the others, reach as far as the Allobroges;
they have glens in the depths of their mountainous
country that are of considerable size and not inferior
to those which the Allobroges have. Now the
Allobroges and the Ligures are ranked as subject
to the praetors who come to Narbonitis, but the
Vocontii (as I said of the Volcae who live round
about Nemausus) are ranked as autonomous.[1] Of
the Ligures who live between the Varus River and
Genua, those who live on the sea are the same as
the Italiotes,[2] whereas to the mountaineers a praefect
of equestrian rank is sent—as is done in the case of
other peoples who are perfect barbarians.

5. After the Vocontii come the Iconii and the
Tricorii; and after them the Medulli, who hold the
loftiest peaks. At any rate, the steepest height of
these peaks is said to involve an ascent of a hundred
stadia, and an equal number the descent thence to the
boundaries of Italy. And up in a certain hollowed-
out region stands a large lake, and also two springs
which are not far from one another. One of these
springs is the source of the Druentia, a torrential
river which dashes down towards the Rhodanus, and
also of the Durias, which takes the opposite direction,
since it first courses down through the country of
the Salassi into Cisalpine Celtica and then mingles
with the Padus;[3] while from the other spring there
issues forth, considerably lower than the region

Major passed through the country of the Salassi, who lived
round about Augusta Praetoria Salassorum (now Aosta),
while the Durias Minor rose near the Druentia (Durance)
and emptied into the Padus at what is now Turin, some
twenty miles west of the mouth of the Durias Major. Strabo,
it appears confuses the two rivers, for he is obviously talking
about the Durias Minor.

τούτων τῶν χωρίων ἀναδίδωσιν αὐτὸς ὁ Πάδος,
πολύς τε καὶ ὀξύς, προϊὼν δὲ γίνεται μείζων καὶ
C 204 πρᾳότερος. ἐκ πολλῶν γὰρ λαμβάνει τὴν αὔξησιν
ἐν τοῖς πεδίοις ἤδη γενόμενος καὶ πλατύνεται· τῇ
οὖν διαχύσει περισπᾷ καὶ ἀμβλύνει τὸν ῥοῦν· εἰς
δὲ τὴν Ἀδριατικὴν θάλατταν ἐκπίπτει, μέγιστος
γενόμενος τῶν κατὰ τὴν Εὐρώπην ποταμῶν πλὴν
τοῦ Ἴστρου. ὑπέρκεινται δ' οἱ Μέδουλλοι μάλιστα
τῆς συμβολῆς τοῦ Ἴσαρος πρὸς τὸν Ῥοδανόν.

6. Ἐπὶ δὲ θάτερα μέρη τὰ πρὸς τὴν Ἰταλίαν
κεκλιμένα[1] τῆς λεχθείσης ὀρεινῆς Ταυρινοί τε
οἰκοῦσι Λιγυστικὸν ἔθνος καὶ ἄλλοι Λίγυες.
τούτων δ' ἐστὶ καὶ ἡ τοῦ Δόννου[2] λεγομένη γῆ
καὶ[3] τοῦ Κοττίου. μετὰ δὲ τούτους καὶ τὸν Πάδον
Σαλασσοί· ὑπὲρ δὲ τούτων ἐν ταῖς κορυφαῖς
Κεύτρωνες[4] καὶ Κατόριγες καὶ Οὐάραγροι καὶ
Ναντουᾶται καὶ ἡ Λημέννα λίμνη, δι' ἧς ὁ Ῥοδανός φέρεται, καὶ ἡ πηγὴ τοῦ ποταμοῦ. οὐκ
ἄπωθεν δὲ τούτων οὐδὲ τοῦ Ῥήνου αἱ πηγαί, οὐδ' ὁ
Ἀδούλας τὸ ὄρος, ἐξ οὗ ῥεῖ καὶ ὁ Ῥῆνος ἐπὶ τὰς
ἄρκτους καὶ ὁ Ἀδούας εἰς τἀναντία ἐμβάλλων
εἰς τὴν Λάριον λίμνην τὴν πρὸς τῷ Κώμῳ.
ὑπέρκεινται δὲ τοῦ Κώμου πρὸς τῇ ῥίζῃ τῶν
Ἄλπεων ἱδρυμένου[5] τῇ μὲν Ῥαιτοὶ καὶ Οὐέννωνες
ἐπὶ τὴν ἕω κεκλιμένοι, τῇ δὲ Ληπόντιοι καὶ
Τριδεντῖνοι καὶ Στόνοι καὶ ἄλλα πλείω μικρὰ

---

[1] κεκλιμένα, Xylander, for κεκριμένα ; so the editors.
[2] Δόννου, conj. of Siebenkees, for Ἰδεόννου (Δονάτου marg.
A prim. manu); so the editors in general. See Pauly-
Wissowa, s.v. Donnus, p. 1548.
[3] Casaubon inserts ἡ after καί ; so some of the editors,
including Meineke.   [4] Κεύτρωνες, A. Jacob, for Κέντρωνες.
[5] ἱδρυμένου, Xylander, for ἱδρυμέναι.

above-mentioned, the Padus itself, large and swift, although as it proceeds it becomes larger and more gentle in its flow; for from the time it reaches the plains it is increased from many streams and is thus widened out; and so, because of the spreading out of its waters, the force of its current is dispersed and blunted; then it empties into the Adriatic Sea, becoming the largest of all the rivers in Europe except the Ister. The situation of the Medulli is, to put it in a general way, above the confluence of the Isar and the Rhodanus.

6. Towards the other parts (I mean the parts which slope towards Italy) of the aforesaid mountainous country dwell both the Taurini, a Ligurian tribe, and other Ligures; to these latter belongs what is called the land of Donnus [1] and Cottius.[2] And after these peoples and the Padus [3] come the Salassi; and above them, on the mountain-crests, the Ceutrones, Catoriges, Varagri, Nantuates, Lake Lemenna (through which the Rhodanus courses), and the source of the Rhodanus. And not far from these are also the sources of the Rhenus, and Mount Adula, whence flows not only, towards the north, the Rhenus, but also, in the opposite direction, the Addua, emptying into Lake Larius, which is near Comum. And beyond Comum, which is situated near the base of the Alps, lie, on the one side, with its slope towards the east, the land of the Rhaeti and the Vennones, and, on the other, the land of the Lepontii, Tridentini, Stoni, and several other small

[1] The father of Cottius.   [2] Cp. 4 1. 3.

[3] The words "and the Padus" have perplexed some of the commentators. They are added, apparently, for the purpose of definitely placing all the Salassi *north of* the Padus; the Taurini lived on both sides of the river.

ἔθνη κατέχοντα τὴν Ἰταλίαν ἐν τοῖς πρόσθεν
χρόνοις, ληστρικὰ καὶ ἄπορα· νυνὶ δὲ τὰ μὲν
ἐξέφθαρται, τὰ δ' ἡμέρωται τελέως ὥστε τὰς δι'
αὐτῶν ὑπερβολὰς τοῦ ὄρους, πρότερον οὔσας
ὀλίγας καὶ δυσπεράτους, νυνὶ πολλαχόθεν εἶναι
καὶ ἀσφαλεῖς ἀπὸ τῶν ἀνθρώπων καὶ εὐβάτους,
ὡς ἔνεστι,[1] διὰ τὴν κατασκευήν. προσέθηκε γὰρ
ὁ Σεβαστὸς Καῖσαρ τῇ καταλύσει τῶν ληστῶν
τὴν κατασκευὴν τῶν ὁδῶν, ὅσην οἷόν τ' ἦν· οὐ
γὰρ δυνατὸν πανταχοῦ βιάσασθαι τὴν φύσιν,
διὰ πετρῶν καὶ κρημνῶν ἐξαισίων, τῶν μὲν
ὑπερκειμένων τῆς ὁδοῦ, τῶν δ' ὑποπιπτόντων,
ὥστε καὶ μικρὸν ἐκβάσιν ἄφυκτον εἶναι τὸν
κίνδυνον, εἰς φάραγγας ἀβύσσους τοῦ πτώματος
ὄντος. οὕτω δέ ἐστι στενὴ κατά τινα[2] αὐτοῦ ἡ
ὁδὸς ὥστ' ἴλιγγον φέρειν τοῖς πεζῇ βαδίζουσι
καὶ αὐτοῖς καὶ ὑποζυγίοις τοῖς ἀήθεσι· τὰ δ'
ἐπιχώρια κομίζει τοὺς φόρτους ἀσφαλῶς. οὔτ'
οὖν ταῦτα ἰάσιμα οὔθ' αἱ κατολισθάνουσαι
πλάκες τῶν κρυστάλλων ἄνωθεν ἐξαίσιοι, συν-
οδίαν ὅλην ἀπολαμβάνειν δυνάμεναι καὶ συνεξ-
ωθεῖν εἰς τὰς ὑποπιπτούσας φάραγγας· πολλαὶ γὰρ
ἀλλήλαις ἐπίκεινται πλάκες, πάγων ἐπὶ πάγοις
γενομένων τῆς χιόνος κρυσταλλωδῶν, καὶ τῶν
ἐπιπολῆς ἀεὶ ῥᾳδίως ἀπολυομένων ἀπὸ τῶν ἐντὸς
πρὶν διαλυθῆναι τελέως ἐν τοῖς ἡλίοις.

---

[1] ὡς ἔνεστι, Corais from conj. of Tyrwhitt, for ὧν ἔν ἐστι
(ACl), ὧν ἔνεστι (B) ; so the later editors.
[2] τινα, Kramer, for τι ; so the editors in general.

tribes, brigandish and resourceless, which in former times held the upper hand in Italy; but as it is, some of the tribes have been wholly destroyed, while the others have been so completely subdued that the passes which lead through their territory over the mountain, though formerly few and hard to get through, are now numerous, and safe from harm on the part of the people, and easily passable— so far as human device can make them so. For in addition to his putting down the brigands Augustus Caesar built up the roads as much as he possibly could; for it was not everywhere possible to over-come nature by forcing a way through masses of rock and enormous beetling cliffs, which sometimes lay above the road and sometimes fell away beneath it, and consequently, if one made even a slight misstep out of the road, the peril was one from which there was no escape, since the fall reached to chasms abysmal. And at some places the road there is so narrow that it brings dizziness to all who travel it afoot—not only to men, but also to all beasts of burden that are unfamiliar with it; the native beasts, however, carry the burdens with sureness of foot. Accordingly, these places are beyond remedy; and so are the layers of ice that slide down from above—enormous layers, capable of intercepting a whole caravan or of thrusting them all together into the chasms that yawn below; for there are numerous layers resting one upon another, because there are congelations upon congelations of snow that have become ice-like, and the congela-tions that are on the surface are from time to time easily released from those beneath before they are completely dissolved in the rays of the sun.

C 205   7. Ἡ δὲ τῶν Σαλασσῶν πολλὴ μέν ἐστιν ἐν
αὐλῶνι βαθεῖ, τῶν ὀρῶν ἀμφοτέρων[1] κλειόντων
τὸ χωρίον, μέρος δέ τι αὐτῶν ἀνατείνει καὶ πρὸς
τὰς ὑπερκειμένας κορυφάς. τοῖς οὖν ἐκ τῆς
Ἰταλίας ὑπερτιθεῖσι τὰ ὄρη διὰ τοῦ λεχθέντος
αὐλῶνός ἐστιν ἡ ὁδός. εἶτα σχίζεται δίχα· καὶ ἡ
μὲν διὰ τοῦ Ποινίνου λεγομένου φέρεται, ζεύγεσιν
οὐ βατὴ κατὰ τὰ ἄκρα τῶν Ἄλπεων, ἡ δὲ διὰ
Κεντρώνων[2] δυσμικωτέρα. ἔχει δὲ καὶ χρυσεῖα
ἡ τῶν Σαλασσῶν, ἃ κατεῖχον ἰσχύοντες οἱ Σα-
λασσοὶ πρότερον, καθάπερ καὶ τῶν παρόδων ἦσαν
κύριοι. προσελάμβανε δὲ πλεῖστον εἰς τὴν μεταλ-
λείαν αὐτοῖς ὁ Δουρίας ποταμός, εἰς τὰ χρυσοπλύσια, διόπερ ἐπὶ πολλοὺς τόπους σχίζοντες
εἰς[3] τὰς ἐξοχετείας τὸ ὕδωρ τὸ κοινὸν ῥεῖθρον
ἐξεκένουν. τοῦτο δ᾽ ἐκείνοις μὲν συνέφερε πρὸς
τὴν τοῦ χρυσοῦ θήραν, τοὺς δὲ γεωργοῦντας τὰ
ὑπ᾽ αὐτοῖς πεδία, τῆς ἀρδείας στερουμένους,
ἐλύπει, τοῦ ποταμοῦ δυναμένου ποτίζειν τὴν
χώραν διὰ τὸ ὑπερδέξιον ἔχειν τὸ ῥεῖθρον. ἐκ δὲ
ταύτης τῆς αἰτίας πόλεμοι συνεχεῖς ἦσαν πρὸς
ἀλλήλους ἀμφοτέροις τοῖς ἔθνεσι. κρατησάντων
δὲ Ῥωμαίων, τῶν μὲν χρυσουργείων ἐξέπεσον καὶ
τῆς χώρας οἱ Σαλασσοί, τὰ δ᾽ ὄρη κατέχοντες
ἀκμὴν τὸ ὕδωρ ἐπώλουν τοῖς δημοσιώναις τοῖς
ἐργολαβήσασι τὰ χρυσεῖα· καὶ πρὸς τούτους[4] δ᾽
ἦσαν ἀεὶ διαφοραὶ διὰ τὴν πλεονεξίαν τῶν δημο-

---

[1] For ἀμφοτέρων, Casaubon reads ἀμφοτέρωθεν; so Meineke, and others.
[2] Κευτρώνων, A. Jacob, for Κεντρώνων.
[3] εἰς before τάς, Casaubon inserts; so the editors in general.
[4] τούτους, Xylander, for τούτοις; so the later editors.

7. Most of the country of the Salassi lies in a deep glen, the district being shut in by both mountains, whereas a certain part of their territory stretches up to the mountain-crests that lie above. Accordingly, the road for all who pass over the mountains from Italy runs through the aforesaid glen. Then the road forks; and one fork runs through what is called Poeninus[1] (a road which, for wagons, is impassable near the summits of the Alps), while the other runs more to the west, through the country of the Ceutrones. The country of the Salassi has gold mines also, which in former times, when the Salassi were powerful, they kept possession of, just as they were also masters of the passes. The Durias River was of the greatest aid to them in their mining—I mean in washing the gold; and therefore, in making the water branch off to numerous places, they used to empty the common bed completely. But although this was helpful to the Salassi in their hunt for the gold, it distressed the people who farmed the plains below them, because their country was deprived of irrigation; for, since its bed was on favourable ground higher up, the river could give the country water. And for this reason both tribes were continually at war with each other. But after the Romans got the mastery, the Salassi were thrown out of their gold-works and country too; however, since they still held possession of the mountains, they sold water to the publicans who had contracted to work the gold mines; but on account of the greediness of the publicans[2] the Salassi were always in disagree-

---

[1] That is, through the Pennine Alps, by Mt. Great Bernard.
[2] Cp. the greed of the New Testament publicans (*e. g.* *Luke* 3. 13).

σιωνῶν.[1] οὕτω δὲ συνέβαινε τοὺς στρατηγιῶντας
ἀεὶ τῶν Ῥωμαίων καὶ πεμπομένους ἐπὶ τοὺς
τόπους εὐπορεῖν προφάσεων ἀφ' ὧν πολεμήσουσι.
μέχρι μὲν δὴ τῶν νεωστὶ χρόνων τοτὲ μὲν πο-
λεμούμενοι, τοτὲ δὲ καταλυόμενοι τὸν πρὸς τοὺς
Ῥωμαίους πόλεμον ἴσχυον ὅμως, καὶ πολλὰ κατέ-
βλαπτον τοὺς δι' αὐτῶν ὑπερβάλλοντας τὰ ὄρη
κατὰ τὸ λῃστρικὸν ἔθος· οἵ γε καὶ Δέκιμον Βροῦ-
τον φυγόντα ἐκ Μουτίνης ἐπράξαντο δραχμὴν
κατ' ἄνδρα· Μεσσάλας δὲ πλησίον αὐτῶν χειμα-
δεύων τιμὴν ξύλων κατέβαλε τῶν τε καυσίμων
καὶ τῶν πτελεΐνων ἀκοντισμάτων καὶ τῶν γυμνα-
στικῶν. ἐσύλησαν δέ ποτε καὶ χρήματα Καίσαρος οἱ ἄνδρες οὗτοι καὶ ἐπέβαλον κρημνοὺς
στρατοπέδοις, πρόφασιν ὡς ὁδοποιοῦντες ἢ γεφυ-
ροῦντες ποταμούς. ὕστερον μέντοι κατεστρέψατο
αὐτοὺς ἄρδην ὁ Σεβαστὸς καὶ πάντας ἐλαφυροπώ-
λησε, κομισθέντας εἰς Ἐπορεδίαν, Ῥωμαίων ἀποικίαν, ἣν συνῴκισαν μέν, φρουρὰν εἶναι βουλόμενοι
τοῖς Σαλασσοῖς, ὀλίγον δ' ἀντέχειν ἐδύναντο οἱ
αὐτόθι ἕως ἠφανίσθη τὸ ἔθνος. τῶν μὲν οὖν ἄλλων
σωμάτων τρεῖς μυριάδες ἐξητάσθησαν ἐπὶ τοῖς
C 206 ἑξακισχιλίοις, τῶν δὲ μαχίμων ἀνδρῶν ὀκτακισχί-
λιοι, πάντας δ' ἐπώλησε Τερέντιος Οὐάρρων ὑπὸ

---

[1] δημοσιωνῶν, Xylander, for δημοσίων; so the later editors.

---

[1] 43 B C.

[2] About sixteen American cents, with far greater purchasing power.

[3] Perhaps for "wooden swords" and the like, used in
"sham battles," as described by Polybius 10. 20.

[4] Now Ivrea.

ment with them too. And in this way it resulted
that those of the Romans who from time to time
wished to lead armies and were sent to the regions
in question were well provided with pretexts for
war. Until quite recently, indeed, although at one
time they were being warred upon by the Romans
and at another were trying to bring to an end their
war against the Romans, they were still powerful,
and, in accordance with their custom of brigandage,
inflicted much damage upon those who passed
through their country over the mountains; at any
rate, they exacted even from Decimus Brutus, on
his flight from Mutina,[1] a toll of a drachma[2]
per man; and when Messala was wintering near
their country, he had to pay for wood, cash down,
not only for his fire-wood but also for the elm-wood
used for javelins and the wood used for gymnastic
purposes.[3] And once these men robbed even Caesar
of money and threw crags upon his legions under
the pretext that they were making roads or bridging
rivers. Later on, however, Augustus completely
overthrew them, and sold all of them as booty,
after carrying them to Eporedia,[4] a Roman colony;
and although the Romans had colonised this city[5]
because they wished it to be a garrison against the
Salassi, the people there were able to offer only
slight opposition until the tribe, as such, was
wiped out. Now although the number of the other
persons[6] captured proved to be thirty-six thousand
and, of the fighting men, eight thousand, Terentius
Varro, the general who overthrew them, sold all

[5] Thus making it a "Roman colony." This was done in
100 B.C. by order of the Sibylline Books (Pliny 3. 21).
[6] The non-combatants.

δόρυ, καταστρεψάμενος αὐτοὺς στρατηγός. τρισχιλίους δὲ Ῥωμαίων πέμψας ᾤκισε τὴν πόλιν Αὐγούσταν ὁ Καῖσαρ ἐν ᾧ ἐστρατοπέδευσε χωρίῳ ὁ Οὐάρρων, καὶ νῦν εἰρήνην ἄγει πᾶσα ἡ πλησιόχωρος μέχρι τῶν ἄκρων ὑπερβολῶν τοῦ ὄρους.

8. Ἑξῆς δὲ τὰ πρὸς ἔω μέρη τῶν ὁρῶν καὶ τὰ ἐπιστρέφοντα πρὸς νότον Ῥαιτοὶ καὶ Οὐινδολικοὶ κατέχουσι, συνάπτοντες Ἐλουηττίοις καὶ Βοΐοις· ἐπίκεινται γὰρ τοῖς ἐκείνων πεδίοις. οἱ μὲν οὖν Ῥαιτοὶ μέχρι τῆς Ἰταλίας καθήκουσι τῆς ὑπὲρ Οὐήρωνος καὶ Κώμου (καὶ ὅ γε Ῥαιτικὸς οἶνος, τῶν ἐν τοῖς Ἰταλικοῖς ἐπαινουμένων οὐκ ἀπολείπεσθαι δοκῶν, ἐν ταῖς τούτων ὑπωρείαις γίνεται), διατείνουσι δὲ καὶ μέχρι τῶν χωρίων, δι᾽ ὧν ὁ Ῥῆνος φέρεται· τούτου δ᾽ εἰσὶ τοῦ φύλου καὶ Ληπόντιοι καὶ Καμοῦνοι.[1] οἱ δὲ Οὐινδολικοὶ καὶ Νωρικοὶ τὴν ἐκτὸς παρώρειαν κατέχουσι τὸ πλέον μετὰ Βρεύνων καὶ Γεναύνων,[2] ἤδη τούτων Ἰλλυριῶν. ἅπαντες δ᾽ οὗτοι καὶ τῆς Ἰταλίας τὰ γειτονεύοντα μέρη κατέτρεχον ἀεὶ καὶ τῆς Ἐλουηττίων καὶ Σηκοανῶν καὶ Βοΐων καὶ Γερμανῶν. ἰταμώτατοι δὲ τῶν μὲν Οὐινδολικῶν ἐξητάζοντο Λικάττιοι καὶ Κλαυτηνάτιοι καὶ Οὐέννωνες, τῶν δὲ Ῥαιτῶν Ῥουκάντιοι καὶ Κωτουάντιοι. καὶ οἱ Ἐστίωνες δὲ τῶν Οὐινδολικῶν εἰσι καὶ Βριγάντιοι, καὶ πόλεις αὐτῶν Βριγάντιον καὶ Καμβόδουνον,

---

[1] Καμοῦνοι, Xylander, for Καμοῦλοι; so the later editors.
[2] Βρεύνων and Γεναύνων, Xylander, for Βρέγκων and Τενναύων; so the later editors.

---

[1] The Greek is a translation of the Latin *sub hasta.*
[2] Augusta Praetoria, about 24 B.C.

of them under the spear.[1]   And Caesar sent three
thousand Romans and founded the city of Augusta[2]
in the place where Varro had pitched his camp,
and at the present time peace is kept by all the
neighbouring country as far as the highest parts of
the passes which lead over the mountain.

8. Next, in order, come those parts of the mountains that are towards the east, and those that
bend round towards the south : the Rhaeti and the
Vindelici occupy them, and their territories join
those of the Elvetii and the Boii; for their territories overlook the plains of those peoples.   Now
the Rhaeti reach down as far as that part of Italy
which is above Verona and Comum (moreover, the
" Rhaetic " wine, which has the repute of not being
inferior to the approved wines of the Italic regions,
is made in the foot-hills of the Rhaetic Alps), and
also extend as far as the districts through which
the Rhenus runs; the Lepontii, also, and Camuni,
belong to this stock.   But the Vindelici and Norici
occupy the greater part of the outer side of the
mountain, along with the Breuni and the Genauni,
the two peoples last named being Illyrians.[3]   All
these peoples used to overrun, from time to time,
the neighbouring parts, not only of Italy, but also
of the country of the Elvetii, the Sequani, the Boii
and the Germans.   The Licattii, the Clautenatii,
and the Vennones proved to be the boldest
warriors of all the Vindelici, as did the Rucantii
and the Cotuantii of all the Rhaeti.   The Estiones,
also, belong to the Vindelici, and so do the Brigantii,
and their cities, Brigantium and Cambodunum, and

[3] The Breuni and Genauni were defeated by Drusus in
17 B.C.   Cp. Horace *Carmina* 4. 14. 10 ff.

καὶ ἡ τῶν Λικαττίων ὥσπερ ἀκρόπολις Δαμασία. τῆς δὲ πρὸς τοὺς Ἰταλιώτας τῶν λῃστῶν τούτων χαλεπότητος λέγεταί τι τοιοῦτον, ὡς, ἐπειδὰν ἕλωσι κώμην ἢ πόλιν, οὐ μόνον ἡβηδὸν ἀνδροφονοῦντας, ἀλλὰ καὶ μέχρι τῶν νηπίων προϊόντας τῶν ἀρρένων, καὶ μηδ' ἐνταῦθα παυομένους, ἀλλὰ καὶ τὰς ἐγκύους γυναῖκας κτείνοντας ὅσας φαῖεν οἱ μάντεις ἀρρενοκυεῖν.

9. Μετὰ δὲ τούτους οἱ ἐγγὺς ἤδη τοῦ Ἀδριατικοῦ μυχοῦ καὶ τῶν κατὰ Ἀκυληΐαν τόπων οἰκοῦσι, Νωρικῶν τέ τινες καὶ Κάρνοι· τῶν δὲ Νωρικῶν εἰσι καὶ οἱ Ταυρίσκοι. πάντας δ' ἔπαυσε τῶν ἀνέδην καταδρομῶν Τιβέριος καὶ ὁ ἀδελφὸς αὐτοῦ Δροῦσος θερείᾳ μιᾷ, ὥστ' ἤδη τρίτον καὶ τριακοστὸν ἔτος ἐστὶν ἐξ οὗ καθ' ἡσυχίαν ὄντες ἀπευτακτοῦσι τοὺς φόρους. κατὰ πᾶσαν δὲ τὴν τῶν Ἄλπεων ὀρεινήν ἐστι μὲν καὶ γεώλοφα χωρία καλῶς γεωργεῖσθαι δινάμενα καὶ αὐλῶνες εὖ συνεκτισμένοι, τὸ μέντοι πλέον, καὶ μάλιστα περὶ τὰς κορυφάς, περὶ ὃ δὴ καὶ συνίσταντο οἱ λῃσταί, λυπρὸν καὶ ἄκαρπον διά τε τὰς πάχνας[1] καὶ τὴν τραχύτητα τῆς γῆς. κατὰ σπάνιν οὖν τροφῆς τε καὶ ἄλλην ἐφείδοντο ἔσθ' ὅτε τῶν ἐν C 207 τοῖς πεδίοις, ἵν' ἔχοιεν χορηγούς· ἀντεδίδοσαν δὲ ῥητίνην, πίτταν, δᾷδα, κηρόν, μέλι, τυρόν· τούτων γὰρ εὐπόρουν. ὑπέρκειται δὲ τῶν Κάρνων τὸ

---

[1] πάχνας, Corais, for τέχνας; so the editors in general.

also Damasia, the acropolis, as it were, of the
Licatii. The stories of the severity of these
brigands towards the Italiotes are to this effect:
When they capture a village or city, they not only
murder all males from youths up but they also
go on and kill the male infants, and they do not
stop there either, but also kill all the pregnant
women who their seers say are pregnant with male
children.

9. Directly after these people come the peoples
that dwell near the recess of the Adriatic and the
districts round about Aquileia, namely, the Carni as
well as certain of the Norici; the Taurisci, also,
belong to the Norici. But Tiberius and his brother
Drusus stopped all of them from their riotous in-
cursions by means of a single summer-campaign;
so that now for thirty-three years they have been
in a state of tranquillity and have been paying their
tributes regularly. Now throughout the whole of
the mountainous country of the Alps there are,
indeed, not only hilly districts which admit of good
farming, but also glens which have been well
built up by settlers; the greater part, however,
(and, in particular, in the neighbourhood of the
mountain-crests, where, as we know, the brigands
used to congregate) is wretched and unfruitful, both
on account of the frosts and of the ruggedness of
the soil. It was because of scarcity, therefore, of both
food and other things that they sometimes would
spare the people in the plains, in order that they
might have people to supply their wants; and in
exchange they would give resin, pitch, torch-pine,
wax, honey, and cheese—for with these things they
were well supplied. Above the Carni lies the

Ἀπέννινον[1] ὄρος, λίμνην ἔχον ἐξιεῖσαν εἰς τὸν
*Ἴσαραν[2] ποταμόν, ὃς παραλαβὼν Ἄταγιν
ἄλλον ποταμὸν εἰς τὸν Ἀδρίαν ἐκβάλλει. ἐκ δὲ
τῆς αὐτῆς λίμνης καὶ ἄλλος ποταμὸς εἰς τὸν
Ἴστρον ῥεῖ, καλούμενος Ἀτησινός.[3] καὶ γὰρ ὁ
Ἴστρος τὰς ἀρχὰς ἀπὸ τούτων λαμβάνει τῶν
ὀρῶν, πολυσχιδῶν ὄντων καὶ πολυκεφάλων. μέχρι
μὲν γὰρ δεῦρο ἀπὸ τῆς Λιγυστικῆς συνεχῆ τὰ
ὑψηλὰ τῶν Ἄλπεων διέτεινε καὶ ἑνὸς ὄρους φαντασίαν παρεῖχεν, εἶτ' ἀνεθέντα καὶ ταπεινωθέντα
ἐξαίρεται πάλιν εἰς πλείω μέρη καὶ πλείους
κορυφάς. πρώτη δ' ἐστὶ τούτων ἡ τοῦ Ῥήνου
πέραν καὶ τῆς λίμνης κεκλιμένη πρὸς ἕω ῥάχις

---

[1] For Ἀπέννινον, Casaubon, Groskurd, and Corais read
Ποίνινον; Gosselin conj. Ἄλπιον; C. Müller Οὐεννώνιον.

[2] For *Ἴσαραν probably Ἰσάρκαν or Ἰσάργαν should be
read (C. Müller and A. Jacob); Meineke reads Ἀιησῖνον.

[3] For Ἀτησινός C. Müller conj. Αἶνος, A. Jacob, οὗτος
Αἶνος; Meineke reads Ἰσάρας.

---

[1] By "the Apennine Mountain" (both here and a few
lines below) Strabo cannot mean the Apennine Range.
Whatever the mountain may be, it must lie above both the
Carni and the Vindelici; and, except in a very loose sense,
no one mountain can fulfil both conditions. To emend to
"Poeninus" (the Pennine Alps; see 4. 6. 7), as do Casaubon,
Corais, and others, does not help matters at all. In fact, the
context seems to show that Strabo has in mind the Carnic
(Julian) Alps. But both this and the names of rivers, as
the MSS. stand, are almost hopelessly inconsistent.

[2] But the "Isaras" (Isar) empties into the Ister (Danube),
not the Adrias (Adriatic); and it is in no sense connected with the Atagis. It is altogether probable that
Strabo wrote "Isarkas" (or "Isargas")— that is, the Latin
"Isarcus" (or "Isargus")—which is now the "Eisach."

[3] By "Atagis" (the Greek for the "Adige" of to-day)
Strabo must refer to one or the other of the two source-

Apennine Mountain,[1] which has a lake that issues forth into the River Isaras,[2] which, after having received another river, the Atagis,[3] empties into the Adriatic. But there is also another river, called the Atesinus,[4] which flows into the Ister from the same lake. The Ister too, in fact, takes its beginning in these mountains, for they are split into many parts and have many peaks; that is, from Liguria up to this point, the lofty parts of the Alps run in an unbroken stretch and present the appearance of one mountain, and then break up and diminish in height, and in turn rise again, into more and more parts, and more and more crests. Now the first of these is that ridge, on the far side of the Rhenus and the lake,[5] which

rivers—the Etsch (or Adige) and Eisach—which meet at Botzen, and from there on constitute what is also called the Etsch (or Adige), the Eisach losing its identity. But if Strabo wrote "Isarkas" (Eisach) instead of "Isaras," he made the other source-river its tributary; hence, since it is the "Atagis," and not the Eisach, that traverses the lake (or rather, to-day, three lakes—Reschen See, Mitter See, and Heider See), we may assume that the copyists have exchanged the positions of "Isarkas" and "Atagis" in the Greek text (Groskurd and others read accordingly), or else, what is more likely, Strabo himself confused the two, just as he confused the Durias Major and Durias Minor in 4. 6. 5 (see also footnote).

[4] The "Atesinus" certainly cannot be identified with the "Atesis" (Hülsen so identifies it, *Pauly-Wissowa*, p. 1924) if it empties into the Ister. According to C. Müller (whom A. Jacob follows, *Revue de Philologie* 36, p. 167), the "Atesinus" is the "Aenus" (the Inn); in this case, says Jacob, the "Stille Bach," which has its source very near the lakes traversed by the Etsch, was formerly taken for the source-stream of the Inn.

[5] This ridge is that which traverses Suabia from south to north, east of, and parallel to, the Rhine; "the lake" appears to be Lake Constance.

μετρίως ὑψηλή, ὅπου αἱ τοῦ Ἴστρου πηγαὶ πλησίον Σοήβων καὶ τοῦ Ἑρκυνίου δρυμοῦ. ἄλλαι δ' εἰσὶν ἐπιστρέφουσαι πρὸς τὴν Ἰλλυρίδα καὶ τὸν Ἀδρίαν, ὧν ἐστι τό τε Ἀπέννινον ὄρος τὸ λεχθὲν καὶ τὸ Τοῦλλον καὶ Φλιγαδία, τὰ ὑπερκείμενα τῶν Οὐινδολικῶν, ἐξ ὧν ὁ Δούρας καὶ Κλάνις καὶ ἄλλοι πλείους χαραδρώδεις ποταμοὶ συμβάλλουσιν εἰς τὸ τοῦ Ἴστρου ῥεῖθρον.

10. Καὶ οἱ Ἰάποδες δὲ (ἤδη τοῦτο ἐπίμικτον Ἰλλυριοῖς καὶ Κελτοῖς ἔθνος) περὶ τούτους οἰκοῦσι τοὺς τόπους, καὶ ἡ Ὄκρα πλησίον τούτων ἐστίν. οἱ μὲν οὖν Ἰάποδες, πρότερον εὐανδροῦντες καὶ τοῦ ὄρους ἐφ' ἑκάτερα[1] τὴν οἴκησιν ἔχοντες καὶ τοῖς λῃστηρίοις ἐπικρατοῦντες, ἐκπεπόνηνται τελέως ὑπὸ τοῦ Σεβαστοῦ Καίσαρος καταπολεμηθέντες. πόλεις δ' αὐτῶν Μέτουλον, Ἀρουπῖνοι, Μονήτιον, Οὐένδων.[2] μεθ' οὓς ἡ Σεγεστικὴ πόλις ἐν πεδίῳ, παρ' ἣν ὁ Σαὸς[3] παραρρεῖ ποταμός, ἐκδιδοὺς εἰς τὸν Ἴστρον. κεῖται δὲ ἡ πόλις εὐφυῶς πρὸς τὸν κατὰ τῶν Δακῶν πόλεμον. ἡ δ' Ὄκρα τὸ ταπεινότατον μέρος τῶν Ἄλπεών ἐστι καθ' ὃ συνάπτουσι τοῖς Κάρνοις καὶ δι' οὗ τὰ ἐκ τῆς Ἀκυληΐας φορτία κομίζουσιν ἁρμαμάξαις εἰς τὸν καλούμενον Ναύπορτον,[4] σταδίων ὁδὸν οὐ πολὺ

---

[1] Corais reads ἑκάτερον for ἑκάτερα; so in general the later editors.

[2] Οὐένδων, Corais, for Οὐένδον, comparing Οὐένδων 7. 5. 4.

[3] Σαὸς, Meineke, for Ῥῆνος αὐτός; Xylander and others had read Σαῦος.

[4] Ναύπορτον, Casaubon, for Πάμπορτον; so the editors in general.

---

[1] The Black Forest.   [2] Also spelled "Iapydes."

leans towards the east—a ridge only moderately high, in which, near the Suevi and the Hercynian Forest,[1] are the sources of the Ister. And there are other ridges which bend round towards Illyria and the Adriatic, among which are the Apennine Mountain above-mentioned and also the Tullum and Phligadia, the mountains which lie above the Vindelici, whence flow the Duras and Clanis and several other torrential rivers which join the stream of the Ister.

10. And further, the Iapodes[2] (we now come to this mixed tribe of Illyrii and Celti[3]) dwell round about these regions; and Mount Ocra[4] is near these people. The Iapodes, then, although formerly they were well supplied with strong men and held as their homeland both sides of the mountain[5] and by their business of piracy held sway over these regions, have been vanquished and completely outdone by Augustus Caesar. Their cities are: Metulum, Arupini, Monetium, and Vendo. After the Iapodes comes Segestica, a city in the plain, past which flows the River Saüs,[6] which empties into the Ister. The situation of the city is naturally well-suited for making war against the Daci. The Ocra is the lowest part of the Alps in that region in which the Alps join the country of the Carni, and through which the merchandise from Aquileia is conveyed in wagons to what is called Nauportus (over a road

---

[3] Cp. 7. 5. 2.   [4] Cp. 4. 6. 1.
[5] Strabo is not clear here. He means (1) by "mountain," not "Ocra," but "Albius," and (2) by "both sides" (of the Albius, on which the Iapodes lived), (*a*) the side towards the Pannonii and the Danube, and (*b*) the side towards the Adriatic (see 4. 6. 1 and especially 7. 5. 4).
[6] The Save.

πλειόνων ἢ τετρακοσίων· ἐκεῖθεν δὲ τοῖς ποταμοῖς κατάγεται μέχρι τοῦ Ἴστρου καὶ τῶν ταύτῃ
χωρίων. παραρρεῖ γὰρ δὴ τὸν Ναύπορτον[1] ποταμὸς ἐκ τῆς Ἰλλυρίδος φερόμενος πλωτός, ἐκβάλλει δ᾽ εἰς τὸν Σάον, ὥστ᾽ εὐμαρῶς εἰς τὴν
Σεγεστικὴν κατάγεται καὶ τοὺς Παννονίους καὶ
Ταυρίσκους. συμβάλλει δ᾽ εἰς τὸν Σάον κατὰ τὴν
πόλιν καὶ ὁ Κόλαπις. ἀμφότεροι δ᾽ εἰσὶ πλωτοί,
ῥέουσι δ᾽ ἀπὸ τῶν Ἄλπεων. ἔχουσι δ᾽ αἱ Ἄλπεις
καὶ ἵππους ἀγρίους καὶ βοάς. φησὶ δὲ Πολύβιος
καὶ ἰδιόμορφόν τι γεννᾶσθαι ζῷον ἐν αὐταῖς,
C 208 ἐλαφοειδὲς τὸ σχῆμα πλὴν αὐχένος καὶ τριχώ-
ματος, ταῦτα δ᾽ ἐοικέναι κάπρῳ, ὑπὸ δὲ τῷ γενείῳ
πυρῆνα ἴσχειν ὅσον σπιθαμιαῖον ἀκρόκομον πωλι-
κῆς κέρκου τὸ πάχος.

11. Τῶν δ᾽ ὑπερθέσεων τῶν ἐκ τῆς Ἰταλίας εἰς
τὴν ἔξω Κελτικὴν καὶ τὴν προσάρκτιον ἡ διὰ
Σαλασσῶν ἐστιν ἄγουσα ἐπὶ Λούγδουνον· διττὴ
δ᾽ ἐστίν, ἡ μὲν ἁμαξεύεσθαι δυναμένη διὰ μήκους
πλείονος, ἡ διὰ Κευτρώνων, ἡ δὲ ὀρθία καὶ στενή,
σύντομος δὲ ἡ διὰ τοῦ Ποινίνου. τὸ δὲ Λούγδουνον
ἐν μέσῳ τῆς χώρας ἐστίν, ὥσπερ ἀκρόπολις, διά
τε τὰς συμβολὰς τῶν ποταμῶν καὶ διὰ τὸ ἐγγὺς
εἶναι πᾶσι τοῖς μέρεσι. διόπερ καὶ Ἀγρίππας
ἐντεῦθεν τὰς ὁδοὺς ἔτεμε, τὴν διὰ τῶν Κεμμένων

---

[1] Ναύπορτον, Casaubon, for Πάμπορτον; so the editors in
general. See 7. 5. 2.

---

[1] The Corcoras (Gurk); see 7. 5. 2.
[2] "Taurisci" is probably an error of copyists for
"Scordisci" (see 7. 5. 2).
[3] The Kulpa.   [4] Segestica.

of not much more than four hundred stadia); from here, however, it is carried down by the rivers as far as the Ister and the districts in that part of the country; for there is, in fact, a river [1] which flows past Nauportus; it runs out of Illyria, is navigable, and empties into the Saüs, so that the merchandise is easily carried down to Segestica and the country of the Pannonii and Taurisci.[2] And the Colapis [3] too joins the Saüs near the city; [4] both are navigable and flow from the Alps. The Alps have both cattle and wild horses. Polybius says that there is also produced in the Alps an animal of special form; it is like a deer in shape, except for its neck and growth of hair (in these respects, he says, it resembles a boar), and beneath its chin it has a sac a span long with hair at the tip, the thickness of a colt's tail.[5]

11. Among the passes which lead over from Italy to the outer—or northerly—Celtica, is the one that leads through the country of the Salassi, to Lugdunum; it is a double pass, one branch, that through the Ceutrones, being practicable for wagons through the greater part of its length, while the other, that through the Poeninus, is steep and narrow, but a short cut.[6] Lugdunum is in the centre of the country—an acropolis, as it were, not only because the rivers meet there, but also because it is near all parts of the country. And it was on this account, also, that Agrippa began at Lugdunum when he cut his roads—that which passes through

---

[5] Polybius seems to refer to the European elk (*cervus alces*), which is no longer to be found in the Alps; or possibly to the Alpine ibex (*capra ibex*), which is almost extinct. [6] Cp. 4. 6. 7.

ὁρῶν μέχρι Σαντόνων καὶ τῆς Ἀκουιτανίας, καὶ
τὴν ἐπὶ τὸν Ῥῆνον, καὶ τρίτην τὴν ἐπὶ τὸν ὠκεανόν,
τὴν πρὸς Βελλοάκοις καὶ Ἀμβιανοῖς, τετάρτη δ'
ἐστὶν ἐπὶ τὴν Ναρβωνῖτιν καὶ τὴν Μασσαλι-
ωτικὴν παραλίαν. ἔστι δὲ καὶ ἐν ἀριστερᾷ ἀφεῖσι
τὸ Λούγδουνον καὶ τὴν ὑπερκειμένην χώραν ἐν
αὐτῷ τῷ Ποινίνῳ πάλιν ἐκτροπὴ διαβάντι τὸν
Ῥοδανὸν ἢ τὴν λίμνην τὴν Λημένναν εἰς τὰ Ἐλουηττίων πεδία· κἀντεῦθεν εἰς Σηκοανοὺς ὑπέρθεσις
διὰ τοῦ Ἰόρα ὄρους καὶ εἰς Λίγγωνας· διά τε τούτων ἐπ' ἄμφω, καὶ ἐπὶ τὸν Ῥῆνον καὶ ἐπὶ τὸν
ὠκεανὸν δ ὁδοι σχίζονται.

12. Ἔτι[1] φησὶ Πολύβιος ἐφ' ἑαυτοῦ κατ' Ἀκυληίαν μάλιστα ἐν τοῖς Ταυρίσκοις τοῖς Νωρικοῖς
εὑρεθῆναι χρυσεῖον οὕτως εὐφυὲς ὥστ' ἐπὶ δύο
πόδας ἀποσύραντι τὴν ἐπιπολῆς γῆν εὐθὺς ὀρυ-
κτὸν εὑρίσκεσθαι χρυσόν, τὸ δ' ὄρυγμα μὴ πλειόνων ὑπάρχειν ἢ πεντεκαίδεκα ποδῶν, εἶναι δὲ τοῦ
χρυσοῦ τὸν μὲν αὐτόθεν καθαρόν, κυάμου μέγεθος
ἢ θέρμου, τοῦ ὀγδόου μέρους μόνον ἀφεψηθέντος,
τὸν δὲ δεῖσθαι μὲν χωνείας πλείονος, σφόδρα δὲ
λυσιτελοῦς· συνεργασαμένων δὲ τοῖς βαρβάροις
τῶν Ἰταλιωτῶν ἐν διμήνῳ, παραχρῆμα τὸ χρυσίον

---

[1] Ἔτι, Casaubon, for Ἐπί; so the later editors.

---

[1] The Lake of Geneva, which is traversed by the Rhone.
[2] Strabo's brevity is again confusing. He suddenly shifts
his standpoint from Lugdunum to the Poeninus. He has in
mind two roads: (1) The road which ran through the
Poeninus to the Rhodanus (at the eastern end of Lake
Geneva), crossed the river, circled round the lake, crossed
again at the other end. and then followed the Rhodanus to
Lugdunum; and (2) a road that branched off from the same

the Cemmenus Mountains as far as the Santoni and
Aquitania, and that which leads to the Rhenus, and,
a third, that which leads to the ocean (the one that
runs by the Bellovaci and the Ambiani); and, a
fourth, that which leads to Narbonitis and the
Massilian seaboard. And there is also, again, in
the Poeninus itself (if you leave on your left
Lugdunum and the country that lies above it),
a bye-road which, after you cross the Rhodanus or
Lake Lemenna,[1] leads into the plains of the Helvetii;[2]
and thence there is a pass through the Jura
Mountain over to the country of the Sequani
and also to that of the Lingones; moreover, the
thoroughfares through these countries branch off
both ways—both towards the Rhenus and towards
the ocean.

12. Polybius further says that in his own time
there was found, about opposite Aquileia in the
country of the Noric Taurisci,[3] a gold mine so well-
suited for mining that, if one scraped away the
surface-soil for a depth of only two feet, he found
forthwith dug-gold,[4] and that the diggings were
never deeper than fifteen feet; and he goes on to
say that part of the gold is immediately pure, in
sizes of a bean or a lupine, when only the eighth
part is boiled away, and that although the rest needs
more smelting, the smelting is very profitable; and
that two months after the Italiotes joined them in
working the mine, the price of gold suddenly

at some point north of the lake into the plains of the
Helvetii.   [3] Cp. § 9 above.
[4] Strabo here, as elsewhere (e g. 3. 2. 8–10), carefully
distinguishes between (1) metals that have to be dug up
from beneath the surface-soil, (2) those in the surface-soil
itself, and (3) those washed down by the rivers.

εὐωνότερον γενέσθαι τῷ τρίτῳ μέρει καθ' ὅλην τὴν
Ἰταλίαν, αἰσθομένους δὲ τοὺς Ταυρίσκους μονο-
πωλεῖν ἐκβαλόντας τοὺς συνεργαζομένους. ἀλλὰ
νῦν ἅπαντα τὰ χρυσεῖα ὑπὸ Ῥωμαίοις ἐστί.
κἀνταῦθα δ', ὥσπερ κατὰ τὴν Ἰβηρίαν, φέρουσιν
οἱ ποταμοὶ χρυσοῦ ψῆγμα, πρὸς τῷ ὀρυκτῷ, οὐ
μέντοι τοσοῦτον. ὁ δ' αὐτὸς ἀνὴρ περὶ τοῦ μεγέθους τῶν Ἄλπεων καὶ τοῦ ὕψους λέγων παρα-
βάλλει τὰ ἐν τοῖς Ἕλλησιν ὄρη τὰ μέγιστα, τὸ
Ταΰγετον, τὸ Λύκαιον, Παρνασσόν, Ὄλυμπον,
C 209 Πήλιον, Ὄσσαν· ἐν δὲ Θρᾴκῃ Αἷμον, Ῥοδόπην,
Δούνακα· καί φησιν ὅτι τούτων μὲν ἕκαστον μικροῦ δεῖν αὐθημερὸν εὐζώνοις ἀναβῆναι δυνατόν,
αὐθημερὸν δὲ καὶ περιελθεῖν, τὰς δ' Ἄλπεις οὐδ'
ἂν πεμπταῖος ἀναβαίη τίς· τὸ δὲ μῆκός ἐστι δισχιλίων καὶ διακοσίων σταδίων τὸ παρῆκον παρὰ
τὰ πεδία. τέτταρας δ' ὑπερβάσεις ὀνομάζει μό-
νον· διὰ Λιγύων μὲν τὴν ἔγγιστα τῷ Τυρρηνικῷ
πελάγει, εἶτα τὴν διὰ Ταυρίνων, ἣν Ἀννίβας διῆλ-
θεν, εἶτα τὴν διὰ Σαλασσῶν, τετάρτην δὲ τὴν
διὰ Ῥαιτῶν, ἁπάσας κρημνώδεις. λίμνας δὲ εἶναί
φησιν ἐν τοῖς ὄρεσι πλείους μέν, τρεῖς δὲ μεγάλας·
ὧν ἡ μὲν Βήνακος ἔχει μῆκος πεντακοσίων σταδίων,
πλάτος δὲ τριάκοντα,[1] ἐκρεῖ δὲ ποταμὸς Μίγκιος·

---

[1] BC*l* read πεντήκοντα (ν' instead of λ').

---

[1] Cp. 3. 2. 10.   [2] See 3. 2. 8.   [3] Polybius 2. 14.
[4] The plains of *Italy* (as Polybius says).
[5] Polybius (3. 56) does not say where Hannibal crossed
the Alps, although he says that Hannibal, after crossing the
Alps. "entered the valley of the Padus and the territory of
the Insubres." Both the ancient writers and modern scholars
differ as to where Hannibal crossed. The reader is referred

became a third less throughout the whole of Italy,
but when the Taurisci learned this they cast out
their fellow-workers and carried on a monopoly.
Now, however, all[1] the gold mines are under the
control of the Romans. And here, too, just as in
Iberia,[2] in addition to the dug-gold, gold-dust is
brought down by the rivers—not, however, in such
quantities as there. The same man, in telling about
the size and the height of the Alps, contrasts
with them the greatest mountains among the
Greeks: Taygetus, Lycaeus, Parnassus, Olympus,
Pelion, Ossa; and in Thrace: Haemus, Rhodope,
Dunax; and he says it is possible for people who
are unencumbered to ascend any one of these
mountains on the same day almost, and also to go
around any one of them on the same day, whereas
one cannot ascend the Alps even in five days; and
their length is two thousand two hundred stadia,[3]
that is, their length at the side, along the plains.[4]
But he only names four passes over the mountains:
the pass through the Ligures (the one that is nearest
the Tyrrhenian Sea), then that through the Taurini,
which Hannibal crossed,[5] then that through the
Salassi, and the fourth, that through the Rhaeti,—
all of them precipitous passes. And as for lakes, he
says that there are several in the mountains, but that
only three are large: one of these, Lake Benacus,[6] has
a length of five hundred stadia and a breadth of thirty,[7]
from which flows the Mincius[8] River; the next, Lake

to the article in *Encyc. Brit. s.v.* "Hannibal," by Caspari,
who inclines to the Mt. Genèvre Pass; and to that in Pauly-
Wissowa *Real-Encyc. s.v.* "Hannibal," by Lenschau, who
thinks "probability decidedly favours the Little St.
Bernard." [6] Lago di Garda.
[7] Some MSS. read "fifty." [8] The Mincio.

ἡ δ' ἑξῆς Οὐερβανὸς τετρακοσίων, πλάτος δὲ
στενοτέρα τῆς πρότερον, ἐξίησι δὲ ποταμὸν τὸν
Ἀδούαν· τρίτη δὲ Λάριος [1] μῆκος ἐγγὺς τριακοσίων
σταδίων, πλάτος δὲ τριάκοντα,[2] ποταμὸν δὲ ἐξίησι
μέγαν Τίκινον· πάντες δὲ εἰς τὸν Πάδον συρρέουσι.
τοσαῦτα καὶ περὶ τῶν ὀρῶν ἔχομεν λέγειν τῶν
Ἀλπεινῶν.

[1] The MSS. read Λάριον.
[2] BC*l* read πεντήκοντα (ν' instead of λ').

Verbanus,[1] four hundred in length, and narrower in breadth than the former, which sends forth the River Addua[2]; and, third, Lake Larius,[3] in length nearly three hundred stadia, and in breadth thirty,[4] which sends forth a large river, the Ticinus[5]; and all three rivers flow into the Padus. This, then, is what I have to say about the Alpine Mountains.

[1] Lago Maggiore. [2] The Adda.

[3] Polybius, if correctly quoted, has made the mistake of exchanging the positions of "Larius" and "Verbanus." Certainly Strabo himself knew that it was from Larius (Lago di Como) that the Addua (Adda) flowed (4 3. 3 4. 6. 6, and 5. 1. 6), and he also knew the course of the Ticinus (5. 1. 11). Yet Strabo himself (4. 3. 3) blundered greatly in making the Addua flow from Mt. Adula.

[4] Some MSS. read "fifty." [5] The Ticino.

BOOK V

1. Μετὰ δὲ τὴν ὑπώρειαν τῶν Ἄλπεων ἀρχὴ τῆς νῦν Ἰταλίας. οἱ γὰρ παλαιοὶ τὴν Οἰνωτρίαν ἐκάλουν Ἰταλίαν, ἀπὸ τοῦ Σικελικοῦ πορθμοῦ μέχρι τοῦ Ταραντίνου κόλπου καὶ τοῦ Ποσειδωνιάτου διήκουσαν, ἐπικρατῆσαν δὲ τοὔνομα καὶ μέχρι τῆς ὑπωρείας τῶν Ἄλπεων προὔβη, προσέλαβε δὲ καὶ τῆς Λιγυστικῆς τὰ μέχρι Οὐάρου ποταμοῦ καὶ τῆς ταύτῃ θαλάττης ἀπὸ τῶν ὁρίων τῶν Τυρρηνικῶν καὶ τῆς Ἰστρίας μέχρι Πόλας. εἰκάσαι δ᾽ ἄν τις εὐτυχήσαντας τοὺς πρώτους ὀνομασθέντας Ἰταλοὺς μεταδοῦναι καὶ τοῖς πλησιοχώροις, εἶθ᾽ οὕτως ἐπίδοσιν λαβεῖν μέχρι τῆς Ῥωμαίων ἐπικρατείας. ὀψὲ δέ ποτε ἀφ᾽ οὗ μετέδοσαν Ῥωμαῖοι τοῖς Ἰταλιώταις τὴν ἰσοπολιτείαν, ἔδοξε καὶ τοῖς ἐντὸς Ἄλπεων Γαλάταις καὶ Ἑνετοῖς τὴν αὐτὴν ἀπονεῖμαι τιμήν, προσαγορεῦσαι δὲ καὶ Ἰταλιώτας πάντας καὶ Ῥωμαίους, ἀποικίας τε πολλὰς στεῖλαι, τὰς μὲν πρότερον τὰς δ᾽ ὕστερον, ὧν οὐ ῥάδιον εἰπεῖν ἀμείνους ἑτέρας.

C 210

---

[1] Gulf of Salerno.
[2] "Ligustica" is "Liguria" in the broadest sense (see 4. 6. 3). [3] Gauls.
[4] That is, "Veneti." The spelling in the MSS. is some-

BOOK V

I

1. AFTER the foothills of the Alps comes the beginning of what is now Italy. For the ancients used to call only Oenotria Italy, although it extended from the Strait of Sicily only as far as the Gulfs of Tarentum and Poseidonia,[1] but the name of Italy prevailed and advanced even as far as the foothills of the Alps, and also took in, not only those parts of Ligustica[2] which extend from the boundaries of Tyrrhenia as far as the Varus River and the sea there, but also those parts of Istria which extend as far as Pola. One might guess that it was because of their prosperity that the people who were the first to be named Italians imparted the name to the neighbouring peoples, and then received further increments in this way until the time of the Roman conquest. At some late time or other after the Romans had shared with the Italiotes the equality of civic rights, they decided to allow the same honour both to the Cisalpine Galatae[3] and to the Heneti,[4] and to call all of them Italiotes as well as Romans, and, further, to send forth many colonies amongst them, some earlier and some later, than which it is not easy to call any other set of colonies better.

times "Heneti" (*e. g.* here and in 3. 2. 13), sometimes "Eneti" (*e. g.* in 1. 3. 2 and 1. 3. 21).

2. Ἑνὶ μὲν οὖν σχήματι σύμπασαν τὴν νῦν
Ἰταλίαν οὐ ῥᾴδιον περιλαβεῖν γεωμετρικῶς, καίτοι φασὶν ἄκραν εἶναι τρίγωνον ἐκκειμένην πρὸς
νότον καὶ χειμερινὰς ἀνατολάς, κορυφουμένην δὲ
πρὸς τῷ Σικελικῷ πορθμῷ, βάσιν δ' ἔχουσαν τὰς
Ἄλπεις· συγχωρῆσαι δὲ δεῖ[1] καὶ τῶν πλευρῶν
μίαν, τὴν ἐπὶ τὸν Πορθμὸν τελευτῶσαν, κλυζο-
μένην δὲ ὑπὸ τοῦ Τυρρηνικοῦ πελάγους. τρίγωνον δὲ ἰδίως τὸ εὐθύγραμμον καλεῖται σχῆμα.
ἐνταῦθα δὲ καὶ ἡ βάσις καὶ ἡ πλευρὰ[2] περιφερεῖς
εἰσιν, ὥστε, εἴ φημι δεῖν συγχωρεῖν, περιφερο-
γράμμου σχήματος θετέον καὶ τὴν βάσιν καὶ τὴν
πλευράν, συγχωρητέον δὲ καὶ τὴν λόξωσιν ταύτης
τῆς πλευρᾶς τὴν ἐπὶ τὰς ἀνατολάς. τἆλλα δ' οὐχ
ἱκανῶς εἰρήκασιν, ὑποθέμενοι μίαν πλευρὰν ἀπὸ
τοῦ μυχοῦ τοῦ Ἀδρίου μέχρι τοῦ Πορθμοῦ· πλευρὰν γὰρ λέγομεν τὴν ἀγώνιον γραμμήν, ἀγώνιος
δ' ἐστὶν ὅταν ἢ μὴ συννεύῃ πρὸς ἄλληλα τὰ μέρη,
ἢ μὴ ἐπὶ πολύ. ἡ δὲ ἀπὸ Ἀριμίνου ἐπὶ τὴν ἄκραν
τὴν Ἰαπυγίαν καὶ ἡ ἀπὸ τοῦ Πορθμοῦ ἐπὶ τὴν
αὐτὴν ἄκραν πάμπολύ τι συννεύουσιν. ὁμοίως δ'
ἔχειν οἴομαι καὶ τὴν ἀπὸ τοῦ μυχοῦ τοῦ Ἀδρίου
καὶ τὴν ἀπὸ τῆς Ἰαπυγίας· συμπίπτουσαι γὰρ
ἐπὶ τοὺς περὶ Ἀρίμινον καὶ Ῥαούενναν τόπους
γωνίαν ποιοῦσιν, εἰ δὲ μὴ γωνίαν, περιφέρειάν γε
ἀξιόλογον. ὥστ', εἰ ἄρα, τοῦτ' ἂν εἴη μία πλευρὰ

---

[1] δεῖ, Jones inserts (as in 1. 3. 7, ταῦτα δὲ δεῖ; cp. also
1. 1. 20, ὑποθέσθαι δεῖ). Groskurd, Kramer, Meineke and
others unnecessarily insert συγχωρῆσαι μὲν οὖν δεῖ τὴν βάσιν
before the συγχωρῆσαι of the text.

[2] ἡ βάσις καὶ ἡ πλευρά, Kramer, for αἱ βάσεις καὶ αἱ πλευραί;
so the later editors.

2. Now it is not easy geometrically to outline what is now Italy, as a whole, by means of a single figure, and yet they [1] say it is a triangular promontory extending towards the south and the winter-risings of the sun, with its vertex at the Strait of Sicily, and with the Alps as its base. I must concede also [2] one of the sides, namely, that which ends at the strait and is washed by the Tyrrhenian Sea. But "triangle" is the specific name for the rectilinear figure, whereas in this case both the base and the side are curved, so that, if I say "I must concede," I must put down both the base and the side as belonging to a curved-line figure, and I must concede also the slant of this side, namely, the slant towards the risings. [3] But as for the rest of the description given by these writers, it is inadequate, because they have assumed only a single side extending from the recess of the Adriatic to the strait; for by "side" we mean the line that has no angle, and a line has no angle when its parts either do not converge towards one another or else not much. But the line from Ariminum [4] to the Iapygian Cape [5] and that from the strait to the same cape converge very much. And the same holds true, I think, with the line from the recess of the Adriatic and that from Iapygia; for, meeting in the regions round about Ariminum and Ravenna, they form an angle, or, if not an angle, at least a considerable curve. Hence this stretch might perhaps be one side

[1] Among others, Polybius (2. 14), whose account should be read in this connection.
[2] That is, in addition to the base.
[3] The winter-risings, of course, as previously said.
[4] Now Rimini.
[5] Now Capo di Leuca.

ὁ παράπλους ὁ ἀπὸ τοῦ μυχοῦ ἐπὶ τὴν Ἰαπυγίαν,
οὐκ εὐθεῖα· τὸ δὲ λοιπὸν τὸ ἐνθένδε ἐπὶ τὸν Πορθμὸν ἄλλην ἂν ὑπογράφοι πλευράν, οὐδὲ ταύτην
εὐθεῖαν. οὕτω δὲ τετράπλευρον μᾶλλον ἢ τρί-
πλευρον φαίη τις ἂν τὸ σχῆμα, τρίγωνον δ' οὐδ-
οπωσοῦν, πλὴν εἰ καταχρώμενος. βέλτιον δ'
ὁμολογεῖν ὅτι τῶν ἀγεωμετρήτων σχημάτων οὐκ[1]
εὐπερίγραφος ἡ ἀπόδοσις.

3. Κατὰ μέρος δ' οὕτως εἰπεῖν δυνατόν, ὅτι τῶν
μὲν Ἄλπεων περιφερὴς ἡ ὑπώρειά ἐστι καὶ κολ-
πώδης, τὰ κοῖλα ἔχουσα ἐστραμμένα πρὸς τὴν
C 211   Ἰταλίαν. τοῦ δὲ κόλπου τὰ μὲν μέσα πρὸς τοῖς
Σαλασσοῖς ἐστι, τὰ δ' ἄκρα ἐπιστροφὴν λαμβάνει,
τὰ μὲν μέχρι τῆς Ὄκρας[2] καὶ τοῦ μυχοῦ τοῦ κατὰ
τὸν Ἀδρίαν, τὰ δ' εἰς τὴν Λιγυστικὴν παραλίαν
μέχρι Γενούας, τοῦ τῶν Λιγύων ἐμπορίου, ὅπου τὰ
Ἀπέννινα ὄρη συνάπτει ταῖς Ἄλπεσιν. ὑπόκειται δ' εὐθὺς πεδίον ἀξιόλογον, πάρισόν πως ἔχον
τὸ πλάτος καὶ τὸ μῆκος, σταδίων ἑκατὸν καὶ δισχι-
λίων· τὸ δὲ μεσημβρινὸν αὐτοῦ πλευρὸν κλείεται
τῇ τε τῶν Ἑνετῶν παραλίᾳ καὶ τοῖς Ἀπεννίνοις
ὄρεσι τοῖς περὶ Ἀρίμινον καὶ Ἀγκῶνα καθήκουσι·
ταῦτα γὰρ ἀρξάμενα ἀπὸ τῆς Λιγυστικῆς εἰς τὴν
Τυρρηνίαν ἐμβάλλει, στενὴν παραλίαν ἀπολεί-
ποντα· εἶτ' ἀναχωροῦντα εἰς τὴν μεσόγαιαν κατ'
ὀλίγον, ἐπειδὰν γένηται κατὰ τὴν Πισᾶτιν, ἐπιστρέφει πρὸς ἕω καὶ πρὸς τὸν Ἀδρίαν ἕως τῶν
περὶ Ἀρίμινον καὶ Ἀγκῶνα τόπων, συνάπτοντα
ἐπ' εὐθείας τῇ τῶν Ἑνετῶν παραλίᾳ. ἡ μὲν

---

[1] οὐκ, after σχημάτων, all editors insert, from man. sec. in B.
[2] Ὄκρας, Casaubon, for ἄκρας ; so the later editors.

(I mean the coasting-voyage from the recess to Iapygia), though the side would not be straight; and the rest of the stretch, thence to the strait, might suggest another side, though this side would not be straight, either. In this sense one might call the figure "four-sided" rather than "three-sided," but in no sense whatever a "triangle," except by an abuse of the term. It is better, however, to confess that the representation of non-geometrical figures is not easy to describe.

3. Taking the parts severally, however, we can speak as follows: as for the Alps, their base is curved and gulf-like, with the cavities turned towards Italy; the central parts of the gulf are near the Salassi, while the extremities take a turn, the one as far as Ocra[1] and the recess of the Adriatic, the other to the Ligurian seaboard as far as Genua (the emporium of the Ligures), where the Apennine Mountains join the Alps. But immediately at the base of the Alps there lies a considerable plain, with its length and its breadth about equal, namely, two thousand one hundred stadia; its southern side is shut in both by the seaboard of the Heneti and by those Apennine Mountains which reach down to the neighbourhood of Ariminum and Ancona; for these mountains, after beginning in Liguria, enter Tyrrhenia, leaving only a narrow seaboard, and then, withdrawing into the interior little by little, when they come to be opposite the territory of Pisa, bend towards the east and towards the Adriatic until they reach the regions round about Ariminum and Ancona, there joining in a straight line the seaboard of the Heneti. Cisalpine Celtica,

[1] Mt. Ocra (4. 6. 1 and 4. 6. 10).

οὖν ἐντὸς Ἄλπεων Κελτικὴ τούτοις κλείεται τοῖς
ὅροις, καὶ ἔστι τῆς μὲν παραλίας τὸ μῆκος ὅσον
τριακοσίων σταδίων ἐπὶ τοῖς ἐξακισχιλίοις μετὰ[1]
τῶν ὁρῶν, μικρὸν δ᾽ ἔλαττον τὸ πλάτος τῶν χιλίων.[2]
ἡ λοιπὴ δ᾽ Ἰταλία στενὴ καὶ παραμήκης ἐστί,
κορυφουμένη διχῶς, τῇ μὲν πρὸς τὸν Σικελικὸν
πορθμὸν τῇ δὲ πρὸς τὴν Ἰαπυγίαν· σφιγγομένη
δ᾽ ἑκατέρωθεν, τῇ μὲν ὑπὸ τοῦ Ἀδρίου τῇ δ᾽ ὑπὸ
τοῦ Τυρρηνικοῦ πελάγους. ἔστι δ᾽ ὅμοιον τὸ
σχῆμα τοῦ Ἀδρίου καὶ τὸ μέγεθος τῇ Ἰταλίᾳ τῇ
ἀφοριζομένῃ τοῖς τε Ἀπεννίνοις ὄρεσ. καὶ τῇ θαλάττῃ ἑκατέρᾳ μέχρι τῆς Ἰαπυγίας καὶ τοῦ ἰσθμοῦ
τοῦ κατὰ τὸν Ταραντῖνον καὶ τὸν Ποσειδωνιάτην
κόλπον· τό τε γὰρ πλάτος τὸ μέγιστον ἀμφοῖν
ἐστι περὶ χιλίους καὶ τριακοσίους σταδίους, τὸ δὲ
μῆκος ἔλαττον οὐ πολὺ τῶν ἑξακισχιλίων. ἡ
λοιπὴ δ᾽ ἐστὶν ὅσην κατέχουσι Βρέττιοι καὶ Λευκανῶν τινες. φησὶ δὲ Πολύβιος, πεζῇ μὲν εἶναι
τὴν παραλίαν τὴν ἀπὸ Ἰαπυγίας μέχρι Πορθμοῦ
καὶ τρισχιλίων σταδίων, κλύζεσθαι δ᾽ αὐτὴν τῷ
Σικελικῷ πελάγει, πλέοντι δὲ καὶ πεντακοσίων
δέουσαν. τὰ δὲ Ἀπέννινα ὄρη συνάψαντα τοῖς
περὶ Ἀρίμινον καὶ Ἀγκῶνα τόποις καὶ ἀφορίσαντα

---

[1] μετά, before τῶν ὁρῶν (from man. sec. in B and from ko) ;
so the editors in general.
[2] For χιλίων, Kramer (from conj. of Casaubon) writes
δισχιλίων ; so the later editors.

---

[1] Polybius (2. 14) frankly calls the part of Italy now
discussed by Strabo a "triangle," giving these dimensions :
"The northern side, formed by the Alps, 2200 stadia ; the
southern, formed by the Apennines, 3600 ; the base, the
seaboard of the Adriatic, from Sena to the recess of the gulf,
more than 2500." Strabo, on the other hand, refuses thus

accordingly, is shut in by these boundaries; and
although the length of the seaboard, together with
that of the mountains, is as much as six thousand
three hundred stadia,[1] the breadth is slightly less
than one thousand.[2]   The remainder of Italy, however, is narrow and elongated, terminating in two
heads, one at the Sicilian Strait and the other at
Iapygia; and it is pinched in on both sides, on one
by the Adriatic and on the other by the Tyrrhenian
Sea.   The shape and the size of the Adriatic are
like that part of Italy which is marked off by the
Apennine Mountains and by both seas as far as
Iapygia and that isthmus which is between the
Gulfs of Tarentum and Poseidonia; for the maximum
breadth of each is about one thousand three
hundred stadia, and the length not much less than
six thousand.[3]   The remainder of Italy, however,
is all the country occupied by the Brettii and certain
of the Leucani.   Polybius[4] says that, if you go by foot,
the seaboard from Iapygia to the strait is as much
as three thousand stadia, and that it is washed by
the Sicilian Sea, but that, if you go by sea, it is as
much as five hundred stadia short of that.   The
Apennine Mountains, after joining the regions round
about Ariminum and Ancona, that is, after marking

to misuse the word "triangle," for he conceives of what he
has previously called "the southern side" as curved and
otherwise irregular.
    [2] The editors have emended "one thousand" to "two
thousand," in order to make the figures consistent with
"two thousand one hundred" above. But Strabo is now
thinking, apparently, of the breadth across the *southern*
side (not the *northern* side at the base of the Alps); that is,
the breadth of Celtica Cispadana, for which the one thousand
is a very close estimate.
    [3] Cp. 2. 5. 20.   [4] 34. 11.

τὸ ταύτῃ[1] πλάτος τῆς Ἰταλίας ἀπὸ θαλάττης ἐπὶ θάλατταν ἐπιστροφὴν λαμβάνει πάλιν καὶ τέμνει τὴν χώραν ὅλην ἐπὶ μῆκος. μέχρι μὲν δὴ Πευκετίων καὶ Λευκανῶν οὐ πολὺ ἀφίσταται τοῦ Ἀδρίου, συνάψαντα δὲ Λευκανοῖς ἐπὶ τὴν ἑτέραν θάλατταν ἀποκλίνει μᾶλλον, καὶ λοιπὸν διὰ μέσων τῶν Λευκανῶν καὶ Βρεττίων διεξιόντα τελευτᾷ πρὸς τὴν Λευκόπετραν τῆς Ῥηγίνης καλουμένην. τυπωδῶς μὲν οὖν εἴρηται περὶ τῆς νῦν Ἰταλίας ἁπάσης ταῦτα· πειρασόμεθα δὲ ἀναλαβόντες εἰπεῖν περὶ τῶν καθ' ἕκαστα, καὶ πρῶτον περὶ τῶν ὑπὸ ταῖς Ἄλπεσιν.

C 212   4. Ἔστι δὲ πεδίον σφόδρα εὔδαιμον καὶ γεωλοφίαις εὐκάρποις πεποικιλμένον. διαιρεῖ δ' αὐτὸ μέσον πως ὁ Πάδος, καὶ καλεῖται τὸ μὲν ἐντὸς τοῦ Πάδου, τὸ δὲ πέραν· ἐντὸς μὲν ὅσον ἐστὶ πρὸς τοῖς Ἀπεννίνοις ὄρεσι καὶ τῇ Λιγυστικῇ, πέραν δὲ τὸ λοιπόν. οἰκεῖται δὲ τὸ μὲν ὑπὸ τῶν Λιγυστικῶν ἐθνῶν καὶ τῶν Κελτικῶν, τῶν μὲν ἐν τοῖς ὄρεσιν οἰκούντων τῶν δ' ἐν τοῖς πεδίοις, τὸ δ' ὑπὸ τῶν Κελτῶν καὶ Ἑνετῶν. οἱ μὲν οὖν Κελτοὶ τοῖς ὑπεραλπίοις ὁμοεθνεῖς εἰσι, περὶ δὲ τῶν Ἑνετῶν διττός ἐστι λόγος. οἱ μὲν γὰρ καὶ αὐτούς φασιν εἶναι Κελτῶν ἀποίκους τῶν ὁμωνύμων παρωκεανιτῶν, οἱ δ' ἐκ τοῦ Τρωικοῦ πολέμου μετ' Ἀντήνορος σωθῆναι δεῦρό φασι τῶν ἐκ τῆς Παφλαγονίας

---

[1] ταύτῃ. Corais, for ταύτης; so the later editors.

off the breadth of Italy there from sea to sea, again take a turn, and cut the whole country lengthwise. As far, then, as the territory of the Peucetii and that of the Leucani they do not recede much from the Adriatic, but after joining the territory of the Leucani they bend off more towards the other sea and then, for the rest of the way, passing throughout the centre of the territory of the Leucani and Brettii, end at what is called Leucopetra[1] in the district of Rhegium. Thus much, then, I have said about what is now Italy, as a whole, in a merely rough-outline way, but I shall now go back and try to tell about the several parts in detail; and first about the parts at the base of the Alps.

4. This country is a plain that is very rich in soil and diversified by fruitful hills. The plain is divided almost at its very centre by the Padus; and its parts are called, the one Cispadana, the other Transpadana.[2] Cispadana is all the part that lies next to the Apennine Mountains and Liguria, while Transpadana is the rest. The latter is inhabited by the Ligurian and the Celtic tribes, who live partly in the mountains, partly in the plains, whereas the former is inhabited by the Celti and Heneti. Now these Celti are indeed of the same race as the Transalpine Celti, but concerning the Heneti there are two different accounts: Some say that the Heneti too are colonists of those Celti of like name[3] who live on the ocean-coast; while others say that certain of the Heneti of Paphlagonia[4] escaped hither with Antenor from the Trojan war, and, as testimony

---

[1] Literally, "White Rock"; now Capo dell' Armi.
[2] Gallia Cispadana and Gallia Transpadana.
[3] See 4. 4. 1.   [4] Cp. 3. 2. 13 and 5. 1. 1.

Ἐνετῶν τινας, μαρτύριον δὲ τούτου προφέρονται
τὴν περὶ τὰς ἱπποτροφίας ἐπιμέλειαν, ἣ νῦν μὲν
τελέως ἐκλέλοιπε, πρότερον δ' ἐτιμᾶτο παρ' αὐτοῖς
ἀπὸ τοῦ παλαιοῦ ζήλου τοῦ κατὰ τὰς ἡμιονίτιδας
ἵππους.   τούτου δὲ καὶ Ὅμηρος μέμνηται·

εξ Ἐνετῶν, ὅθεν ἡμιόνων γένος ἀγροτεράων.

(Il. 2. 852)

καὶ Διονύσιος, ὁ τῆς Σικελίας τύραννος, ἐντεῦθεν
τὸ ἱπποτρόφιον συνεστήσατο τῶν ἀθλητῶν ἵππων,
ὥστε καὶ ὄνομα ἐν τοῖς Ἕλλησι γενέσθαι τῆς
Ἐνετικῆς πωλείας καὶ πολὺν χρόνον εὐδοκιμῆσαι
τὸ γένος.

5. Ἅπασα μὲν οὖν ἡ χώρα ποταμοῖς πληθύει
καὶ ἕλεσι, μάλιστα δ' ἡ τῶν Ἐνετῶν· πρόσεστι
δὲ ταύτῃ καὶ τὰ τῆς θαλάττης πάθη. μόνα γὰρ
ταῦτα τὰ μέρη σχεδόν τι τῆς καθ' ἡμᾶς θαλάττης
ὁμοιοπαθεῖ τῷ ὠκεανῷ, καὶ παραπλησίους[1] ἐκείνῳ
ποιεῖται τάς τε ἀμπώτεις καὶ τὰς πλημμυρίδας,
ὑφ' ὧν τὸ πλέον τοῦ πεδίου λιμνοθαλάττης γίνεται
μεστόν. διώρυξι δὲ καὶ ταραχώμασι, καθάπερ ἡ
Κάτω λεγομένη χώρα τῆς Αἰγύπτου, διωχέτευται,
καὶ τὰ μὲν ἀνέψυκται καὶ γεωργεῖται, τὰ δὲ διά-
πλους ἔχει· τῶν δὲ πόλεων αἱ μὲν νησίζουσιν, αἱ
δ' ἐκ μέρους κλύζονται. ὅσαι δὲ ὑπὲρ τῶν ἑλῶν
ἐν τῇ μεσογαίᾳ κεῖνται, τοὺς ἐκ τῶν ποταμῶν ἀνάπλους θαυμαστοὺς ἔχουσι, μάλιστα δ' ὁ Πάδος.
μέγιστός τε γάρ ἐστι καὶ πληροῦται πολλάκις ἔκ
τε ὄμβρων καὶ χιόνων, διαχεόμενος δ' εἰς πολλὰ

[1] παραπλησίους, the reading of the MSS., Jones restores;
against Kramer and the later editors (παραπλησίως).

to this, adduce their devotion to the breeding of
horses—a devotion which now, indeed, has wholly
disappeared, although formerly it was prized among
them, from the fact of their ancient rivalry in
the matter of producing mares for mule-breeding.
Homer, too, recalls this fact : " From the land of
the Heneti, whence the breed of the wild mules."
Again, Dionysius,[1] the tyrant of Sicily, collected his
stud of prize-horses from here, and consequently
not only did the fame of the Henetian foal-breeding
reach the Greeks but the breed itself was held in
high esteem by them for a long time.

5. Now this whole country is filled with rivers and
marshes, but particularly the part that belongs to
the Heneti. And this part, furthermore, is also
affected by the behaviour of the sea ; for here are
almost the only parts of Our Sea that behave like
the ocean, and both the ebb-tides and the flood-tides
produced here are similar to those of the ocean,
since by them the greater part of the plain is made
full of lagoons. But, like what is called Lower
Egypt, it has been intersected by channels and
dikes ; and while some parts have been relieved by
drainage and are being tilled, others afford voyages
across their waters. Of the cities here, some are
wholly island, while others are only partly surrounded by water. As for all the cities that are
situated above the marshes in the interior, the inland
voyages afforded thereto by the rivers are wonderful,
but particularly by the Padus ; for not only is it the
largest of these rivers but it is oftentimes filled by both
the rains and the snow, although, as the result of

---

[1] Dionysius the Elder (430–367 B.C.).

μέρη κατὰ τὰς ἐκβολὰς τυφλὸν τὸ στόμα ποιεῖ καὶ δυσείσβολός ἐστιν. ἡ δ' ἐμπειρία περιγίνεται καὶ τῶν χαλεπωτάτων.

6. Τὸ μὲν οὖν ἀρχαῖον, ὥσπερ ἔφην, ὑπὸ Κελτῶν περιῳκεῖτο τῶν πλείστων ὁ ποταμός. μέγιστα δ' ἦν τῶν Κελτῶν ἔθνη Βοῖοι καὶ Ἴνσουβροι καὶ οἱ τὴν Ῥωμαίων ποτὲ[1] ἐξ ἐφόδου καταλαβόντες Σένονες μετὰ Γαιζατῶν. τούτους μὲν οὖν ἐξέφθειραν ὕστερον τελέως Ῥωμαῖοι, τοὺς δὲ Βοΐους ἐξήλασαν ἐκ τῶν τόπων, μεταστάντες δ' εἰς τοὺς περὶ τὸν Ἴστρον τόπους μετὰ Ταυρίσκων ᾤκουν πολεμοῦντες πρὸς Δακούς, ἕως ἀπώλοντο πανεθνεί· τὴν δὲ χώραν οὖσαν τῆς Ἰλλυρίδος μηλόβοτον τοῖς περιοικοῦσι κατέλιπον. Ἴνσουβροι δὲ καὶ νῦν εἰσί. Μεδιολάνιον δ' ἔσχον μητρόπολιν, πάλαι μὲν κώμην (ἅπαντες γὰρ ᾤκουν κωμηδόν), νῦν δ' ἀξιόλογον πόλιν, πέραν τοῦ Πάδου συνάπτουσάν πως ταῖς Ἄλπεσι. πλησίον δε καὶ Οὐήρων,[2] καὶ αὕτη πόλις μεγάλη. ἐλάττους δὲ τούτων Βριξία καὶ Μαντούα καὶ Ῥήγιον[3] καὶ Κῶμον· αὕτη δ' ἦν μὲν κατοικία μετρία, Πομπήιος δὲ Στράβων ὁ Μάγνου πατὴρ κακωθεῖσαν ὑπὸ τῶν ὑπερκειμένων Ῥαιτῶν συνῴκισεν· εἶτα Γάϊος Σκιπίων τρισχιλίους προσέθηκεν· εἶτα ὁ Θεὸς Καῖσαρ πεντακισχιλίους ἐπισυνῴκισεν, ὧν οἱ

C 213 (margin)

---

[1] For ποτέ, Xylander reads πόλιν; so the other earlier editors; Bernadakis and Vogel approving.

[2] Οὐήρων, Kramer, for Βήρων; so the later editors.

[3] Strabo almost certainly wrote Βέργομον instead of Ῥήγιον (see footnote on opposite page).

---

[1] § 4 above.   [2] That is, near the Alps.

separating into many streams near the outlets, the mouth is choked with mud and hard to enter. But even the greatest difficulties are overcome by experience.

6. In early times, then, as I was saying,[1] the country round about the Padus was inhabited for the most part by the Celti. And the largest tribes of the Celti were the Boii, the Insubri, and those Senones who, along with the Gaezatae, once seized the territory of the Romans at the first assault. These two peoples, it is true, were utterly destroyed by the Romans later on, but the Boii were merely driven out of the regions they occupied; and after migrating to the regions round about the Ister, lived with the Taurisci, and carried on war against the Daci until they perished, tribe and all—and thus they left their country, which was a part of Illyria, to their neighbours as a pasture-ground for sheep. The Insubri, however, are still in existence. They had as metropolis Mediolanium, which, though long ago only a village (for they all used to dwell only in villages), is now a notable city; it is across the Padus, and almost adjoins the Alps. Near by[2] is Verona also (this, too, a large city), and, smaller than these two, the cities of Brixia, Mantua, Regium,[3] and Comum. Comum used to be only a moderate-sized settlement, but, after its ill treatment by the Rhaeti who are situated above it, Pompey Strabo, father of Pompey the Great, settled a Roman colony there; then Gaius Scipio added three thousand colonists; then the Deified Caesar further settled it with five

---

[3] Regium Lepidum. But Strabo is talking about Transpadana, not Cispadana; and hence it is almost certain that he wrote "Bergomum," not "Regium."

πεντακόσιοι τῶν Ἑλλήνων ὑπῆρξαν οἱ ἐπιφανέ-
στατοι· τούτοις δὲ καὶ πολιτείαν ἔδωκε καὶ ἐνέ-
γραψεν αὐτοὺς εἰς τοὺς συνοίκους· οὐ μέντοι
ᾤκησαν αὐτόθι, ἀλλὰ καὶ τοὔνομά γε τῷ κτίσματι
ἐκεῖνοι κατέλιπον· Νεοκωμῖται γὰρ ἐκλήθησαν
ἅπαντες, τοῦτο δὲ μεθερμηνευθὲν Νοβουμκώμουμ
λέγεται. ἐγγὺς δὲ τοῦ χωρίου τούτου λίμνη
Λάριος καλουμένη· πληροῖ δ' αὐτὴν ὁ Ἀδούας
ποταμός· εἶτ' ἐξίησιν εἰς τὸν Πάδον. τὰς δὲ πηγὰς
ἔσχηκεν ἐν τῷ Ἀδούλᾳ ὄρει, ὅπου καὶ ὁ Ῥῆνος.

7. Αὗται μὲν οὖν πολὺ ὑπὲρ τῶν ἑλῶν ᾤκηνται,
πλησίον δὲ τὸ Παταούιον, πασῶν ἀρίστη τῶν
ταύτῃ πόλεων, ἥ γε νεωστὶ λέγεται τιμήσασθαι
πεντακοσίους ἱππικοὺς ἄνδρας, καὶ τὸ παλαιὸν δὲ
ἔστελλε δώδεκα μυριάδας στρατιᾶς. δηλοῖ δὲ καὶ
τὸ πλῆθος τῆς πεμπομένης κατασκευῆς εἰς τὴν
Ῥώμην κατ' ἐμπορίαν, τῶν τε ἄλλων καὶ ἐσθῆτος
παντοδαπῆς, τὴν εὐανδρίαν τῆς πόλεως καὶ τὴν
εὐτεχνίαν. ἔχει δὲ θαλάττης ἀνάπλουν ποταμῷ
διὰ τῶν ἑλῶν φερομένῳ σταδίων πεντήκοντα καὶ
διακοσίων ἐκ λιμένος μεγάλου· καλεῖται δ' ὁ λιμὴν
Μεδόακος ὁμωνύμως τῷ ποταμῷ. ἐν δὲ τοῖς ἕλεσι
μεγίστη μέν ἐστι Ῥαούεννα, ξυλοπαγὴς ὅλη καὶ
διάρρυτος, γεφύραις καὶ πορθμείοις ὁδευομένη.
δέχεται δ' οὐ μικρὸν τῆς θαλάττης μέρος ἐν ταῖς
πλημμυρίσιν, ὥστε καὶ ὑπὸ τούτων καὶ ὑπὸ ποτα-

---

[1] Strabo seems to mean the last census (14 A.D.) in the
reign of Augustus. The number of citizens at this census,
according to the *Monumentum Ancyranum*, was 4,037,000.

thousand, among whom the five hundred Greeks were the most notable; and to these latter he not only gave the rights of citizenship but also enrolled them among the colonists. The Greeks did not, however, take up their abode there, though they at least left to the settlement the name; for the colonists were, as a whole, called " Neo-Comitae " —that is, if interpreted in Latin, " Novum Comum." Near this place is what is called Lake Larius; it is fed by the River Addua. The river then issues forth from the lake into the Padus; it has its original sources, however, in Mount Adula, in which also the Rhenus has its sources.

7. These cities, then, are situated considerably above the marshes; and near them is Patavium, the best of all the cities in that part of the country, since this city by recent census,[1] so it is said, had five hundred knights, and, besides, in ancient times used to send forth an army of one hundred and twenty thousand. And the quantities of manufactured goods which Patavium sends to Rome to market—clothing of all sorts and many other things — show what a goodly store of men it has and how skilled they are in the arts. Patavium offers an inland voyage from the sea by a river which runs through the marshes, two hundred and fifty stadia from a large harbour; the harbour, like the river, is called Medoacus. The largest city in the marshes, however, is Ravenna, a city built entirely of wood[2] and coursed by rivers, and it is provided with thoroughfares by means of bridges and ferries. At the tides the city receives no small portion of the sea, so that, since

---

[2] Possibly Strabo means simply " built on piles " ; but see *Encyc. Brit.* (1911) under " Ravenna," p. 925.

μῶν ἐκκλυζόμενον[1] τὸ βορβορῶδες πᾶν ἰᾶται τὴν
δυσαερίαν. οὕτως γοῦν ὑγιεινὸν ἐξήτασται τὸ
χωρίον ὥστε ἐνταῦθα τοὺς μονομάχους τρέφειν
καὶ γυμνάζειν ἀπέδειξαν οἱ ἡγεμόνες. ἔστι μὲν
οὖν καὶ τοῦτο θαυμαστὸν τῶν ἐνθάδε, τὸ ἐν ἕλει
τοὺς ἀέρας ἀβλαβεῖς εἶναι, καθάπερ καὶ ἐν

C 214 Ἀλεξανδρείᾳ τῇ πρὸς Αἰγύπτῳ τοῦ θέρους ἡ
λίμνη τὴν μοχθηρίαν ἀποβάλλει διὰ τὴν ἀνάβασιν
τοῦ ποταμοῦ καὶ τὸν τῶν τελμάτων ἀφανισμόν,
ἀλλὰ καὶ τὸ περὶ τὴν ἄμπελον πάθος θαυμάζειν
ἄξιον, φύει μὲν γὰρ αὐτὴν τὰ ἕλη καὶ ποιεῖ ταχὺ
καὶ πολὺν ἀποδιδοῦσαν καρπόν, φθείρεται δὲ ἐν
ἔτεσι τέταρσιν ἢ πέντε. ἔστι δὲ καὶ τὸ Ἄλτινον
ἐν ἕλει, παραπλήσιον ἔχον τῇ Ῥαουέννῃ τὴν θέσιν.
μεταξὺ δὲ Βούτριον τῆς Ῥαουέννης πόλισμα καὶ ἡ
Σπίνα, νῦν μὲν κωμίον, πάλαι δὲ Ἑλληνὶς πόλις
ἔνδοξος. θησαυρὸς γοῦν ἐν Δελφοῖς Σπινιτῶν
δείκνυται, καὶ τἆλλα ἱστορεῖται περὶ αὐτῶν, ὡς
θαλασσοκρατησάντων. φασὶ δὲ καὶ ἐπὶ θαλάσσῃ
ὑπάρξαι, νῦν δ᾽ ἐστὶν ἐν μεσογαίᾳ τὸ χωρίον περὶ
ἐνενήκοντα τῆς θαλάσσης σταδίους ἀπέχον. καὶ
ἡ Ῥαούεννα δὲ Θετταλῶν εἴρηται κτίσμα· οὐ
φέροντες δὲ τὰς τῶν Τυρρηνῶν ὕβρεις ἐδέξαντο
ἑκόντες τῶν Ὀμβρικῶν τινας, οἳ καὶ νῦν ἔχουσι
τὴν πόλιν, αὐτοὶ δ᾽ ἀπεχώρησαν ἐπ᾽ οἴκου. αὗται

---

[1] ἐκκλυζόμενον, Corais, for εἰσκλυζόμενον; so the later
editors.

---

[1] Lake Mareotis (now Mariout); see 17. 1. 7.

[2] The remains of numerous treasuries, i. e. small temple-like
treasure-houses, are still to be seen at Delphi. Different
cities, nations, and princes built them as repositories for their
offerings to the god. For an excellent drawing of the sacred

the filth is all washed out by these as well as by the
rivers, the city is relieved of foul air. At any rate,
the place has been found to be so healthful that
the rulers have given orders to feed and train the
gladiators there. Now this is indeed one of the
marvellous things at Ravenna, I mean the fact that
the air in a marsh is harmless (compare the Egyptian
Alexandria, where, in summer, the lake[1] loses its
baneful qualities by reason of the overflow of the Nile
and the disappearance of the standing waters), but
the behaviour of the vine is also a thing fit to marvel
at ; for although the marshes support it and make
it yield fruit quickly and in great quantities, it dies
within four or five years. Altinum too is in a marsh,
for the position it occupies is similar to that of
Ravenna. Between the two cities is Butrium, a town
belonging to Ravenna, and also Spina, which though
now only a small village, long ago was a Greek city
of repute. At any rate, a treasury[2] of the Spinitae is
to be seen at Delphi ; and everything else that history
tells about them shows that they were once masters
of the sea. Moreover, it is said that Spina was once
situated by the sea, although at the present time the
place is in the interior, about ninety stadia distant
from the sea. Furthermore, it has been said that
Ravenna was founded by the Thessalians ; but since
they could not bear the wanton outrages of the
Tyrrhenians, they voluntarily took in some of the
Ombrici,[3] which latter still now hold the city,
whereas the Thessalians themselves returned home.

precinct, showing the result of the French excavations (1892–
1897), see Frazer's *Pausanias*, vol. V, opposite p. 258.

[3] The "Umbri" of Roman history. See end of § 10
following.

μὲν οὖν ἐπὶ πλέον περιέχονται τοῖς ἕλεσιν, ὥστε
καὶ κλύζεσθαι.

8. Ὀπιτέργιον[1] δὲ καὶ Κωνκορδία[2] καὶ Ἀτρία[3]
καὶ Οὐικετία καὶ ἄλλα τοιαῦτα πολισμάτια ἧττον
μὲν ὑπὸ τῶν ἑλῶν ἐνοχλεῖται, μικροῖς δ' ἀνάπλοις
πρὸς τὴν θάλατταν συνῆπται. τὴν δ' Ἀτρίαν
ἐπιφανῆ γενέσθαι πόλιν φασίν, ἀφ' ἧς καὶ τοὔνομα τῷ κόλπῳ γενέσθαι τῷ Ἀδρίᾳ, μικρὰν μετά-
θεσιν λαβόν. Ἀκυληία δ', ἥπερ μάλιστα τῷ
μυχῷ πλησιάζει, κτίσμα μέν ἐστι Ῥωμαίων,
ἐπιτειχισθὲν τοῖς ὑπερκειμένοις βαρβάροις, ἀναπλεῖται δὲ ὁλκάσι κατὰ τὸν Νατίσωνα ποταμὸν
ἐπὶ πλείους ἢ[4] ἑξήκοντα σταδίους. ἀνεῖται δ'
ἐμπόριον[5] τοῖς περὶ τὸν Ἴστρον τῶν Ἰλλυριῶν
ἔθνεσι· κομίζουσι δ' οὗτοι μὲν τὰ ἐκ θαλάττης,
καὶ οἶνον ἐπὶ ξυλίνων πίθων ἁρμαμάξαις ἀνα-
θέντες καὶ ἔλαιον, ἐκεῖνοι δ' ἀνδράποδα καὶ βοσκήματα καὶ δέρματα. ἔξω δ' ἐστὶ τῶν Ἑνετικῶν
ὅρων ἡ Ἀκυληία. διορίζονται δὲ ποταμῷ ῥέοντι
ἀπὸ τῶν Ἀλπίων ὀρῶν, ἀνάπλουν ἔχοντι καὶ
διακοσίων σταδίων ἐπὶ τοῖς χιλίοις εἰς Νωρηίαν

---

[1] Ὀπιτέργιον, Corais, for Ἐπιτέρπιον ; so the later editors.
[2] Κωνκορδία, Siebenkees (from conj. of Cluverius), for ὁρδία;
so the later editors.   [3] Ἀτρία, all editors, for Ἀδρία.
[4] For πλείους ἤ several editors, including Meineke, wrongly
read πλείστους.
[5] After ἐμπόριον Groskurd, Meineke, and others insert τοῖς
τε Ἑνετοῖς καί ; a tempting but unnecessary emendation.

---

[1] The Greek word for "Adriatic" is merely "Adrias."
[2] So Pliny (3. 20).
[3] Pliny (3 22) placed Aquileia fifteen miles from the sea.
The distance to-day to the ruins of the old Aquileia is seven
miles. The Natiso (Natisone) appears to have changed its
lower course since Strabo's time.

These cities, then, are for the most part surrounded by the marshes, and hence subject to inundations.

8. But Opitergium, Concordia, Atria, Vicetia, and other small towns like them are less hemmed in by the marshes, though they are connected with the sea by small waterways. It is said that Atria was once an illustrious city, and that the Adriatic [1] Gulf got its name therefrom, with only a slight change in the spelling.[2] Aquileia, which is nearest of all to the recess of the Gulf, was founded by the Romans as a fortress against the barbarians who were situated above it; and there is an inland voyage thither for merchant-vessels, by way of the River Natiso, for a distance of more than sixty stadia.[3] Aquileia has been given over as an emporium for those tribes of the Illyrians that live near the Ister;[4] the latter load on wagons and carry inland the products of the sea, and wine stored in wooden jars,[5] and also olive-oil, whereas the former[6] get in exchange slaves, cattle, and hides. But Aquileia is outside the boundaries of the Heneti. The boundary between the two peoples is marked by a river flowing from the Alps,[7] which affords an inland voyage of as much as twelve hundred stadia to the city of Noreia,[8] near

---

[4] Cp. 4. 6. 10 and 7. 5. 2.

[5] In 5. 1. 12 Strabo speaks of wooden jars "larger than houses."

[6] By "the former," Strabo refers of course to the inhabitants, not only of Aquileia, but of the various towns (named and unnamed above) about the recess of the Adriatic.

[7] It is impossible to say what river Strabo had in mind, whether the Isonzo, or the Tagliamento, or the Sile, or the Piave, or what; but no river of to-day answers the conditions.

[8] Now Neumarkt, in the duchy of Styria, Austria.

πόλιν, περὶ ἣν Γναῖος Κάρβων συμβαλὼν Κίμ-
βροις οὐδὲν ἔπραξεν. ἔχει δὲ ὁ τόπος οὗτος
χρυσιοπλύσια εὐφυῆ καὶ σιδηρουργεῖα. ἐν αὐτῷ
δὲ τῷ μυχῷ τοῦ Ἀδρίου καὶ ἱερὸν τοῦ Διομήδους
ἐστὶν ἄξιον μνήμης, τὸ Τίμαυον· λιμένα γὰρ ἔχει
καὶ ἄλσος ἐκπρεπὲς καὶ πηγὰς ἑπτὰ ποτίμου [1]
ὕδατος εὐθὺς εἰς τὴν θάλασσαν ἐκπίπτοντος,
πλατεῖ καὶ βαθεῖ ποταμῷ. Πολύβιος δ᾽ εἴρηκε
πλὴν μιᾶς τὰς ἄλλας ἁλμυροῦ ὕδατος, καὶ δὴ καὶ
τοὺς ἐπιχωρίους πηγὴν καὶ μητέρα τῆς θαλάττης
C 215 ὀνομάζειν τὸν τόπον. Ποσειδώνιος δέ φησι ποταμὸν τὸν Τίμαυον ἐκ τῶν ὀρῶν φερόμενον καταπίπτειν εἰς βέρεθρον, εἶθ᾽ ὑπὸ γῆς ἐνεχθέντα περὶ
ἑκατὸν καὶ τριάκοντα σταδίους ἐπὶ τῇ θαλάττῃ
τὴν ἐκβολὴν ποιεῖσθαι.

9. Τῆς δὲ τοῦ Διομήδους δυναστείας περὶ τὴν
θάλατταν ταύτην αἵ τε Διομήδειοι νῆσοι μαρτύρια
καὶ τὰ περὶ Δαυνίους καὶ τὸ Ἄργος τὸ Ἵππιον
ἱστορούμενα· περὶ ὧν ἐροῦμεν ἐφ᾽ ὅσον πρὸς
ἱστορίαν χρήσιμον, τὰ δὲ πολλὰ τῶν μυθευομένων
ἢ κατεψευσμένων ἄλλως ἐᾶν δεῖ, οἷον τὰ περὶ
Φαέθοντα καὶ τὰς Ἡλιάδας τὰς ἀπαιγειρουμένας
περὶ τὸν Ἠριδανὸν τὸν μηδαμοῦ γῆς ὄντα, πλησίον
δὲ τοῦ Πάδου λεγόμενον, καὶ τὰς Ἠλεκτρίδας
νήσους τὰς πρὸ τοῦ Πάδου καὶ μελεαγρίδας ἐν

---

[1] ποτίμου, Xylander, for ποταμίου (as in 5. 4. 5 and 5. 4. 13);
so most of the editors.

---

[1] 113 B.C. Livy (Epit. 63) says "Carbo and his army were
routed."

[2] Strabo is now speaking of "recess" in its most specific
sense—the inmost recess in the general recess of the Adriatic.

[3] The Timavi Fons (now the Timavo).

[4] Now Arpino.   [5] 6. 3. 9

which Gnaeus Carbo clashed to no effect with the
Cimbri.[1] This region has places that are naturally
well-suited to gold-washing, and has also iron-works.
And in the very recess of the Adriatic [2] there is also
a temple of Diomedes that is worth recording, " the
Timavum " ; for it has a harbour, and a magnificent
precinct, and seven fountains of potable waters which
immediately empty into the sea in one broad, deep
river.[3] According to Polybius, all the fountains
except one are of salt water, and, what is more, the
natives call the place the source and mother of the
sea. But Poseidonius says that a river, the Timavus,
runs out of the mountains, falls down into a chasm,
and then, after running underground about a hundred
and thirty stadia, makes its exit near the sea.

9. As for the dominion of Diomedes in the
neighbourhood of this sea, not only the " Islands
of Diomedes " bear witness thereto, but also the
historical accounts of the Daunii and Argos Hippium,[4]
which I shall relate [5] insofar as they may be historic-
ally useful; but I must disregard most of the
mythical or false stories, as, for example, the stories
of Phaethon, and of the Heliades that were changed
into poplar-trees near the Eridanus (the Eridanus
that exists nowhere on earth, although it is spoken of
as near the Padus),[6] and of the Electrides Islands
that lie off the Padus,[7] and of the guinea-fowls on

[6] Cp. the reference to the Attic Eridanus in 9. 1. 19.
[7] In Hesiod (*Fr.* 199 [220], Rzach) Eridanus is the river-
god on the banks of whose river were quantities of amber
("Electrum"). Later on, since amber was found at the
mouth of the Po, the " Amber (Electrides) Islands " were
placed there (see Pliny 3. 30). In Greek mythology Phaethon
was thrown from the chariot of the Sun into Eridanus, and
his sisters (the Heliades) who had yoked the chariot were
metamorphosed into poplars, and their tears into amber.

αὐταῖς· οὐδὲ γὰρ τούτων οὐδέν ἐστιν ἐν τοῖς τόποις. τῷ δὲ Διομήδει παρὰ τοῖς Ἐνετοῖς ἀποδεδειγμέναι τινὲς ἱστοροῦνται τιμαί· καὶ γὰρ θύεται λευκὸς ἵππος αὐτῷ, καὶ δύο ἄλση τὸ μὲν Ἥρας Ἀργείας δείκνυται, τὸ δ᾽ Ἀρτέμιδος Αἰτωλίδος. προσμυθεύουσι δ᾽, ὡς εἰκός, τὸ ἐν τοῖς ἄλσεσι τούτοις ἡμεροῦσθαι τὰ θηρία καὶ λύκοις ἐλάφους συναγελάζεσθαι, προσιόντων δὲ τῶν ἀνθρώπων καὶ καταψώντων ἀνέχεσθαι, τὰ δὲ διωκόμενα ὑπὸ τῶν κυνῶν, ἐπειδὰν καταφύγῃ δεῦρο, μηκέτι διώκεσθαι. φασὶ δέ τινα τῶν πάνυ γνωριζόμενον [1] ὡς εἴη φιλέγγυος καὶ σκωπτόμενον ἐπὶ τούτῳ, παρατυχεῖν κυνηγέταις λύκον ἐν τοῖς δικτύοις ἔχουσιν· εἰπόντων δὲ κατὰ παιδιάν, εἰ ἐγγυᾶται τὸν λύκον, ἐφ᾽ ᾧτε τὰς ζημίας ἃς εἴργασται διαλύσειν, ἀφήσειν αὐτὸν ἐκ τῶν λίνων, ὁμολογῆσαι· ἀφεθέντα δὲ τὸν λύκον ἵππων ἀγέλην ἀπελάσαντα ἀκαυτηριάστων ἱκανὴν προσαγαγεῖν πρὸς τὸν τοῦ φιλεγγύου σταθμόν· τὸν δ᾽ ἀπολαβόντα τὴν χάριν καυτηριάσαι τε τὰς ἵππους λύκον, καὶ κληθῆναι λυκοφόρους, τάχει μᾶλλον ἢ κάλλει διαφερούσας· τοὺς δ᾽ ἀπ᾽ ἐκείνου διαδεξαμένους τό τε καυτήριον φυλάξαι καὶ τοὔνομα τῷ γένει τῶν ἵππων, ἔθος δὲ ποιῆσαι θήλειαν μὴ ἐξαλλοτριοῦν, ἵνα μένοι παρὰ μόνοις τὸ γνήσιον γένος, ἐνδόξου γενομένης ἐνθένδε ἱππείας. νυνὶ δέ, ὥσπερ ἔφαμεν, πᾶσα ἐκλέλοιπεν

---

[1] γνωριζόμενον, Kramer, for γνωριζομένων; so the later editors.

---

[1] Cp. 1. 2. 15, on the addition of mythical elements.

them; for not one of these things is in that region, either. It is an historical fact, however, that among the Heneti certain honours have been decreed to Diomedes; and, indeed, a white horse is still sacrificed to him, and two precincts are still to be seen—one of them sacred to the Argive Hera and the other to the Aetolian Artemis. But some mythical elements, of course, have been added:[1] namely, that in these sacred precincts the wild animals become tame, and deer herd with wolves, and they allow the people to approach and caress them, and any that are being pursued by dogs are no longer pursued when they have taken refuge here. And it is said that one of the prominent men, who was known for his fondness for giving bail for people and was twitted for this, fell in with some hunters who had a wolf in their nets, and, upon their saying in jest that if he would give bail for the wolf, and agree to settle all the damage the wolf should do, they would set the wolf free from the toils, he agreed to the proposal; and the wolf, when set free, drove off a considerable herd of unbranded horses and brought them to the steading of the man who was fond of giving bail; and the man who received the favour not only branded all the mares with a wolf, but also called them the "wolf-breed"—mares exceptional for speed rather than beauty; and his successors kept not only the brand but also the name for the breed of the horses, and made it a custom not to sell a mare to outsiders, in order that the genuine breed might remain in their family alone, since horses of that breed had become famous. But, at the present time, as I was saying,[2] the practice of horse-breeding has wholly disappeared.

[1] § 4 above.

ἡ τοιαύτη ἄσκησις. μετὰ δὲ τὸ Τίμαυον ἡ τῶν
Ἰστρίων ἐστὶ παραλία μέχρι Πόλας, ἡ πρόσκειται
τῇ Ἰταλίᾳ. μεταξὺ δὲ φρούριον Τεργέστε, Ἀκυ-
ληίας διέχον ἑκατὸν καὶ ὀγδοήκοντα σταδίους.
ἡ δὲ Πόλα ἵδρυται μὲν ἐν κόλπῳ λιμενοειδεῖ,
νησίδια ἔχοντι εὔορμα καὶ εὔκαρπα· κτίσμα δ'
ἐστὶν ἀρχαῖον Κόλχων τῶν ἐπὶ τὴν Μήδειαν
C 216 ἐκπεμφθέντων, διαμαρτόντων δὲ τῆς πράξεως καὶ
καταγνόντων ἑαυτῶν φυγήν· τό κεν φυγάδων μὲν
ἐνίσποι Γραϊκός (ὡς Καλλίμαχος εἴρηκεν), ἀτὰρ
κείνων γλῶσσ' ὀνομηνε Πόλας. τὰ μὲν δὴ πέραν
τοῦ Πάδου χωρία οἵ τε Ἑνετοὶ νέμονται καὶ οἱ[1]
μέχρι Πόλας, ὑπὲρ δὲ τῶν Ἑνετῶν Κάρνοι καὶ
Κενομάνοι καὶ Μεδόακοι καὶ Σύμβροι·[2] ὧν οἱ
μὲν πολέμιοι τοῖς Ῥωμαίοις ὑπῆ ξαν, Κενομάνοι
δὲ καὶ Ἑνετοὶ συνεμάχουν κα· πρὸ τῆς Ἀννίβα
στρατείας, ἡνίκα Βοίους καὶ Σύμβρους[2] ἐπολέμουν, καὶ μετὰ ταῦτα.

10. Οἱ δ' ἐντὸς τοῦ Πάδου κατέχουσι μὲν
ἅπασαν ὅσην ἐγκυκλοῦνται τὰ Ἀπέννινα ὄρη
πρὸς τὰ Ἄλπια μέχρι Γενούας καὶ τῶν Σαβάτων.
κατεῖχον δὲ Βοῖοι καὶ Λίγυες καὶ Σένονες καὶ
Γαιζάται τὸ πλέον· τῶν δὲ Βοίων ἐξελαθέντων,

---

[1] After οἱ Kramer inserts Ἴστριοι; so the later editors.
[2] For Σύμβροι and Σύμβρους Corais reads Ἴνσουβροι and
Ἰνσούβρους; and in § 12 following, for Σύμβρων, Ἰνσούβρ ων;
Meineke following. "Ἴνσουβοι," the last word in § 10
following, seems to indicate that the "Symbri" are to be
identified with the "Insubri."

---

[1] See 1. 2. 39, where the quotation is more complete.
[2] The "Symbri" are here twice referred to, and once in

After the Timavum comes the seaboard of the Istrii
as far as Pola, which belongs to Italy. Between the
Timavum and Pola lies the stronghold of Tergeste, at
a distance of one hundred and eighty stadia from
Aquileia. As for Pola, it is situated in a harbour-
like gulf which has isles with good mooring-places
and with fruitful soil; it was founded in early times
by those Colchians who were sent forth in quest of
Medea, but failed in their undertaking and thus
condemned themselves to exile: " which a Greek
would call 'the city of the exiles,'" as Callimachus
has said, " but their tongue hath named it Polae." [1]
The Transpadane districts, then, are occupied both
by the Heneti and by the peoples who extend as far
as Pola; and, above the Heneti, by the Carni, the
Cenomani, the Medoaci, and the Symbri; [2] of these
peoples, some were once enemies of the Romans, but
the Cenomani and the Heneti used to help the
Romans in their battles, not only before the campaign
of Hannibal (I mean when the Romans were making
war upon the Boii and the Symbri), but thereafter as
well.

10. But the Cispadane peoples occupy all that
country which is encircled by the Apennine Mountains
towards the Alps as far as Genua and Sabata. [3] The
greater part of the country used to be occupied
by the Boii, Ligures, Senones, and Gaezatae; but
since the Boii have been driven out, and since both

[1] § 12 following; but such a people is otherwise unknown.
Two of the editors emend in each case to "Insubri."
[2] That is, the arc described by the Apennines, in their
stretch from the region of Ariminum and Ancona as far as
Genua and Vada Sabatorum (cp. 4. 6. 1, 5. 1. 3), together
with the Po, enclose Gallia Cispadana.

ἀφανισθέντων δὲ καὶ τῶν Γαιζατῶν καὶ Σενόνων,
λείπεται τὰ Λιγυστικὰ φῦλα καὶ τῶν Ῥωμαίων
αἱ ἀποικίαι. τοῖς δὲ Ῥωμαίοις ἀναμέμικται καὶ
τὸ τῶν Ὀμβρικῶν φῦλον, ἔστι δ' ὅπου καὶ Τυρ-
ρηνῶν· ταῦτα γὰρ ἄμφω τὰ ἔθνη πρὸ τῆς τῶν
Ῥωμαίων ἐπὶ πλέον αὐξήσεως εἶχέ τινα πρὸς
ἄλληλα περὶ πρωτείων ἅμιλλαν, καὶ μέσον ἔχοντα
τὸν Τίβεριν ποταμὸν ῥᾳδίως ἐπιδιέβαινον ἀλλήλοις. καὶ εἴ πού τινας ἐκστρατείας ἐποιοῦντο ἐπ'
ἄλλους [1] οἱ ἕτεροι, καὶ τοῖς ἑτέροις ἔρις ἦν μὴ
ἀπολείπεσθαι τῆς εἰς τοὺς αὐτοὺς τόπους ἐξόδου·
καὶ δὴ καὶ τῶν Τυρρηνῶν στειλάντων στρατιὰν
εἰς τοὺς περὶ τὸν Πάδον βαρβάρους καὶ πρα-
ξάντων εὖ, ταχὺ δὲ πάλιν ἐκπεσόντων διὰ τὴν
τρυφήν, ἐπεστράτευσαν οἱ ἕτεροι τοῖς ἐκβαλοῦσιν·
εἶτ' ἐκ διαδοχῆς τῶν τόπων ἀμφισβητοῦντες
πολλὰς τῶν κατοικιῶν τὰς μὲν Τυρρηνικὰς
ἐποίησαν, τὰς δ' Ὀμβρικάς, πλείους δὲ τῶν
Ὀμβρικῶν,[2] ἐγγυτέρω γὰρ ἦσαν. οἱ δὲ Ῥωμαῖοι,
παραλαβόντες καὶ πέμψαντες ἐποίκους πολλαχοῦ, συνεφύλαξαν καὶ τὰ τῶν προεποικησάντων
γένη. καὶ νῦν Ῥωμαῖοι μέν εἰσιν ἅπαντες, οὐδὲν
δ' ἧττον Ὄμβροι τέ τινες λέγονται καὶ Τυρρηνοί,
καθάπερ Ἐνετοὶ καὶ Λίγυες καὶ Ἴνσουβροι.

11. Πόλεις δ' εἰσὶν ἐντὸς τοῦ Πάδου καὶ περὶ
τὸν Πάδον ἐπιφανεῖς Πλακεντία μὲν καὶ Κρεμώνη,

---

[1] ἄλλους (the reading of second hand in B.), for ἀλλήλους;
so the editors.

[2] The reading of the MSS. is οἱ ἐγγυτέρω γὰρ ἦσαν, except
that B omits the οἱ. Meineke, following Kramer, reads οἱ
and omits γάρ.

the Gaezatae and the Senones have been annihilated,[1] only the Ligurian tribes and the Roman colonies are left. The Romans, however, have been intermingled with the stock of the Ombrici and also, in some places, with that of the Tyrrheni;[2] for both these tribes, before the general aggrandizement of the Romans, carried on a sort of competition with one another for the primacy, and since they had only the River Tiber between them could easily cross over against one another. And if, as I suppose, one of the two peoples went forth on a campaign against a third people, the other of the two conceived a contentious desire not to fail to make an expedition to the same places; and so, too, when the Tyrrheni had sent forth an army into the midst of the barbarians round about the Padus and had fared well, and then on account of their luxurious living were quickly cast out again, the other of the two made an expedition against those who had cast them out; and then, in turns, disputing over the places, the two, in the case of many of the settlements, made some Tyrrhenian and some Ombrican—the greater number, however, for the Ombrici were nearer. But the Romans, upon taking control and sending settlers to many places, helped to preserve also the stocks of the earlier settlers. And at the present time, although they are all Romans, they are none the less called, some "Ombri," and some "Tyrrheni," as is the case with the Heneti, the Ligures, and the Insubri.

11. There are some famous cities in Cispadana and in the neighbourhood of the Padus: first, Placentia and Cremona, which are very near each other and

---

[1] See 5. 1. 6.   [2] That is, the Etrusci.

πλησιαίταται κατὰ μέσην που τὴν χώραν, μεταξὺ
δὲ τούτων τε καὶ Ἀριμίνου Πάρμα καὶ Μουτίνη
καὶ Βονωνία πλησίον ἤδη Ῥαουέννης, καὶ μικρὰ
πολίσματα ἀνὰ μέσον τούτων, δι᾽ ὧν ἡ εἰς
Ῥώμην ὁδός, Ἄγκαρα,[1] Ῥήγιον Λέπιδον, Μακροὶ[2]
Κάμποι, ὅπου πανήγυρις συντελεῖται κατ᾽ ἔτος,
Κλάτερνα, Φόρον Κορνήλιον· Φαουεντία δὲ καὶ[3]
C 217 Καισήνα πρὸς τῷ Σάπι[4] ποταμῷ καὶ τῷ Ῥου-
βίκωνι ἤδη συνάπτουσι τῷ Ἀριμίνῳ. τὸ δὲ
Ἀρίμινον Ὄμβρων ἐστὶ κατοικία, καθάπερ καὶ
ἡ Ῥαουέννα· δέδεκται δ᾽ ἐποίκους Ῥωμαίους
ἑκατέρα. ἔχει δὲ τὸ Ἀρίμινον λιμένα καὶ ὁμώνυμον
ποταμόν. ἀπὸ δὲ Πλακεντίας εἰς Ἀρίμινον στάδιοι
χίλιοι τριακόσιοι. ὑπὲρ δὲ Πλακεντίας ἐπὶ μὲν
τοὺς ὅρους τῆς Κοττίου γῆς Τίκινον ἐν τριάκοντα
ἓξ μιλίοις πόλις καὶ ὁμώνυμος ὁ παραρρέων
ποταμός, συμβάλλων τῷ Πάδῳ, καὶ Κλαστίδιον
καὶ Δερτὼν[5] καὶ Ἀκουαιστατιέλλαι μικρὸν ἐν
παρόδῳ. ἡ δ᾽ εὐθεῖα εἰς Ὤκελον παρὰ τὸν Πάδον
καὶ τὸν Δουρίαν ποταμόν, βαραθρώδης ἡ πολλή,
πλείους καὶ ἄλλους ἔχουσα ποταμούς, ὧν καὶ τὸν

---

[1] Ἄγκαρα, Meineke, for Ἄκαρα.
[2] Μακροί, Xylander, for Νάκροι; so the later editors.
[3] καὶ Καισήνα, Corais. for καὶ σήνα; so the later editors.
[4] τῷ Σάπι, Meineke, for Ἰσάπι.
[5] Δερτών, Jones, for Δέθων (cp. Δερτών Artemidorus in
Steph. Byz. s.v.); other editors emend to Δέρθων. Ptolemaeus' spelling is Δερτῶνα (3. 1. 31).

---

[1] Via Aemilia.
[2] A prosperous market-town, which got its name from the
Macri Campi ("Lean Plains"), west of Mutina.

are at about the centre of the country; and secondly—
between these two and Ariminum—Parma, Mutina,
and Bononia (once in Bononia you are near Ravenna),
and also some small towns scattered between these
three which also lie on the road [1] to Rome—
I mean Ancara, Regium Lepidum, Macri Campi [2]
where a public festival is held every year, Claterna,
and Forum Cornelium; and then, Faventia and
Caesena, near the River Sapis and the Rubicon,
where, at last, you are on the borders of Ariminum. [3]
Ariminum is a settlement of the Ombri, just as
Ravenna is, although each of them has received
Roman colonists. And Ariminum has a harbour and
a river of like name. [4] From Placentia to Ariminum
the distance is one thousand three hundred stadia.
Beyond Placentia, towards the boundaries of the land
of Cottius, there lies, within a distance of thirty-six
miles from Placentia, the city of Ticinum (and also
the river of like name [5] that flows past it and joins
the Padus), and also, on a road which runs slightly
to one side, there lie Clastidium, Derton [6] and Aquae
Statiellae. But the direct road to Ocelum [7] runs
along the Padus and the River Durias, the greater
part of it over ravines, since, besides these two, it
has several other rivers to cross, among which is the

[3] The Greek of this last clause is too concise to be accurate
and clear, but the order of the words indicates that Strabo's
thought was correct. He thinks of the traveller as first
reaching Faventia (which is some twenty miles from the
Sapis); then Caesena, which is near (on) the Sapis; then the
Rubicon (which is not near Caesena, but some twenty miles
away), which alone borders on the territory of Ariminum.
[4] The Ariminus, now the Marecchia.
[5] The Ticinus, now the Tessin.
[6] Dertona, now Tortona.   [7] Now Avigliana.

Δρουεντίαν, μιλίων ἐστὶ περὶ ἑξήκοντα. ἐντεῦθεν
δὲ ἤδη τὰ Ἄλπια ὄρη καὶ ἡ Κελτική.

Πρὸς δὲ τοῖς ὄρεσι τοῖς ὑπερκειμένοις τῆς
Λούνης ἐστὶ πόλις Λοῦκα· ἔνιοι δὲ κωμηδὸν
οἰκοῦσιν· εὐανδρεῖ δ' ὅμως ἡ χώρα καὶ τὸ στρατιωτικὸν ἐντεῦθεν τὸ πλέον ἐστὶ καὶ τὸ τῶν
ἱππικῶν πλῆθος, ἐξ ὧν καὶ ἡ σύγκλητος λαμβάνει
τὴν σύνταξιν. ἔστι δὲ ἡ Δερτὼν¹ πόλις ἀξιόλογος
κειμένη κατὰ μέσην τὴν ὁδὸν τὴν ἀπὸ Γενούας
εἰς Πλακεντίαν, ἑκατέρας² διέχουσα σταδίους
τετρακοσίους· κατὰ δὲ ταύτην τὴν ὁδὸν καὶ
Ἀκουαιστατιέλλαι, ἀπὸ δὲ Πλακεντίας εἰς μὲν
Ἀρίμινον εἴρηται· εἰς δὲ Ῥαούενναν κατάπλους
τῷ Πάδῳ δυεῖν ἡμερῶν καὶ νυκτῶν. πολὺ δὲ καὶ
τῆς ἐντὸς τοῦ Πάδου κατείχετο ὑπὸ ἑλῶν,
δι' ὧν Ἀννίβας χαλεπῶς διῆλθε, προϊὼν ἐπὶ
Τυρρηνίαν· ἀλλ' ἀνέψυξε τὰ πεδία ὁ Σκαῦρος
διώρυγας πλωτὰς ἀπὸ τοῦ Πάδου μέχρι Πάρμης
ἄγων· κατὰ γὰρ Πλακεντίαν ὁ Τρεβίας συμβάλλων τῷ Πάδῳ καὶ ἔτι πρότερον ἄλλοι πλείους
πληροῦσι πέραν τοῦ μετρίου. οὗτος δὲ ὁ Σκαῦρός
ἐστιν ὁ καὶ τὴν Αἰμιλίαν ὁδὸν στρώσας τὴν διὰ

¹ Δερτών, Jones, for Δέθων (see footnote 5, p. 326).
² ἑκατέρας, Xylander, for ἑκατέρα; so the later editors.

¹ It is hard to believe that Strabo wrote " Druentia " here,
for he has already properly placed the source of the Druentia
beyond Ocelum (see 4. 6. 5 and the footnote). It is not
unlikely that he wrote "Durias" (*i. e.* Durias Major)
instead, for the road in question not only crossed the Durias
Minor, which it followed, but the Durias Major as well.
Otherwise, he is characterizing the road beyond Ocelum when
he is supposed to be discussing merely the stretch from
Ticinum to Ocelum.

Druentia,[1] a distance of about sixty miles.[2] And
this[3] is where the Alps Mountains and Celtica[4]
begin.

Near those mountains which lie above Luna is a
city, Luca, although some of the people here live
only in villages; nevertheless the country has a
goodly store of men, and the greater part of the
soldiery comes from here, and also the majority of
those men of equestrian rank from whom the
Senate recruits its ranks.[5] Derton is a considerable
city, and it is situated about midway of the road
which runs from Genua to Placentia, being four
hundred stadia distant from each; and this is the
road on which Aquae Statiellae is situated. Of the
distance from Placentia to Ariminum I have already
spoken; there is also a voyage thence by the Padus
down to Ravenna which takes two days and nights.
Now a considerable part of Cispadana too used to be
covered by marshes (through which Hannibal, on
his advance against Tyrrhenia, passed only with
difficulty); but Scaurus[6] drained the plains by running navigable canals from the Padus as far as
Parma; for near Placentia the Padus is joined by
the Trebia, as also before that by several other
rivers, and is thus made excessively full. This
Scaurus is the man who constructed the Aemilian

---

[2] Roman miles, of course. But the distance from Ticinum
to Ocelum is about a hundred miles. Sixty miles is a close
estimate for the distance from Ticinum to the Durias Major.
Most of the editors, including Meineke, emend to "one
hundred and sixty."

[3] Ocelum.   [4] That is, Celtica proper.

[5] Meineke suspects this whole sentence and relegates it
to the foot of the page.

[6] M. Aemilius Scaurus, lived 163 to about 89 B.C.

Πισῶν καὶ Λούνης μέχρι Σαβάτων, κἀντεῦθεν
διὰ Δερτῶνος·¹ ἄλλη δ' ἐστὶν Αἰμιλία διαδεχο-
μένη τὴν Φλαμινίαν. συνυπάτευσαν γὰρ ἀλλήλοις
Μάρκος Λέπιδος καὶ Γάϊος Φλαμίνιος· καθελόντες
δὲ Λίγυας, ὁ μὲν τὴν Φλαμινίαν ἔστρωσεν ἐκ
Ῥώμης διὰ Τυρρηνῶν καὶ τῆς Ὀμβρικῆς μέχρι
τῶν περὶ Ἀρίμινον τόπων, ὁ δὲ τὴν ἑξῆς μέχρι
Βονωνίας, κἀκεῖθεν εἰς Ἀκυληίαν παρὰ τὰς ῥίζας
τὰς τῶν Ἄλπεων ἐγκυκλούμενος τὰ ἕλη. ὅριον
δὲ τῆς χώρας ταύτης, ἣν ἐντὸς Κελτικὴν καλοῦμεν, πρὸς τὴν λοιπὴν Ἰταλίαν τό τε Ἀπέννινον
ὄρος τὸ ὑπὲρ τῆς Τυρρηνίας ἀπεδέδεικτο καὶ ὁ
Αἶσις ποταμός, ὕστερον δὲ ὁ Ῥουβίκων, εἰς τὸν
Ἀδρίαν ἐκδιδόντες ἀμφότεροι.

C 218   12. Τῆς δ' ἀρετῆς τῶν τόπων τεκμήριον ἥ τ'
εὐανδρία καὶ τὰ μεγέθη τῶν πόλεων καὶ ὁ πλοῦτος,
οἷς πᾶσιν ὑπερβέβληνται τὴν ἄλλην Ἰταλίαν οἱ
ταύτῃ Ῥωμαῖοι. καὶ γὰρ ἡ γεωργουμένη γῆ πολλοὺς καὶ παντοίους ἐκφέρει καρπούς, καὶ αἱ ὗλαι
τοσαύτην ἔχουσι βάλανον ὥστ' ἐκ τῶν ἐντεῦθεν
ὑοφορβίων ἡ Ῥώμη τρέφεται τὸ πλέον. ἔστι δὲ
καὶ κεγχροφόρος διαφερόντως διὰ τὴν εὐυδρίαν·
τοῦτο δὲ λιμοῦ μέγιστόν ἐστιν ἄκος· πρὸς ἅπαντας
γὰρ καιροὺς ἀέρων ἀντέχει, καὶ οὐδέποτ' ἐπιλεί-

---

¹ Δερτῶνος, Jones, for Δέθωνος (see footnote 5, p. 326).

¹ 187 B.C.

Way which runs through Pisa and Luna as far as
Sabata and thence through Derton; there is
another Aemilian Way, however—I mean the one
which succeeds the Flaminian. For Marcus Lepidus
and Gaius Flaminius were consuls together[1]; and,
upon subjugating the Ligures, the latter constructed
the Flaminian Way[2] from Rome through Tyrrhenia
and Ombrica as far as the regions of Ariminum, and
the former the succeeding road that runs as far as
Bononia, and from there, along the base of the Alps,
thus encircling the marshes, to Aquileia. Now the
boundary of all this country which we call Cisalpine
Celtica—I mean the boundary between it and the
remainder of Italy—was once designated by that
part of the Apennine Mountains which is beyond
Tyrrhenia, and also by the River Aesis, but later on
by the Rubicon; both these rivers empty into the
Adriatic.

12. As for the excellence of the regions, it is
evidenced by their goodly store of men, the size of
the cities and their wealth, in all which respects
the Romans in that part of the world have surpassed the rest of Italy. For not only does the
tilled land bring forth fruits in large quantities and
of all sorts, but the forests have acorns in such
quantities that Rome is fed mainly on the herds of
swine that come from there. And the yield of
millet is also exceptional, since the soil is well-
watered; and millet is the greatest preventive of
famine, since it withstands every unfavourable
weather, and can never fail, even though there be

[2] But from other accounts this Aemilian Way was built by
Gaius Flaminius the Elder in 220 B.C. (see Pauly-Wissowa,
under "Flaminia Via," p. 2493, and "Flaminina," p. 2502).

πειν δύναται, κἂν τοῦ ἄλλου σίτου γένηται σπά
νις. ἔχει δὲ καὶ πιττουργεῖα θαυμαστά. τοῦ δ'
οἴνου τὸ πλῆθος μηνύουσιν οἱ[1] πίθοι· οἱ ξύλινοι
γὰρ μείζους οἴκων εἰσί· προσλαμβάνει δὲ πολὺ ἡ
τῆς πίττης εὐπορία πρὸς τὸ εὐκώνητον. ἐρέαν δὲ
τὴν μὲν μαλακὴν οἱ περὶ Μουτίνην τόποι καὶ τὸν
Σκουλτάνναν ποταμὸν φέρουσι πολὺ πασῶν καλ
λίστην, τὴν δὲ τραχεῖαν ἡ Λιγυστικὴ καὶ ἡ τῶν
Σύμβρων,[2] ἐξ ἧς τὸ πλέον τῆς οἰκίας[3] τῶν Ἰτα
λιωτῶν ἀμπέχεται, τὴν δὲ μέσην οἱ περὶ Πα
ταούιον, ἐξ ἧς οἱ τάπητες οἱ πολυτελεῖς καὶ
γαύσαποι καὶ τὸ τοιοῦτον εἶδος πᾶν, ἀμφίμαλλόν
τε καὶ ἑτερόμαλλον. τὰ δὲ μέταλλα νυνὶ μὲν οὐχ
ὁμοίως ἐνταῦθα σπουδάζεται διὰ τὸ λυσιτελέστερα
ἴσως εἶναι τὰ ἐν τοῖς ὑπεραλπίοις Κελτοῖς καὶ τῇ
Ἰβηρίᾳ, πρότερον δὲ ἐσπουδάζετο, ἐπεὶ καὶ ἐν
Οὐερκέλλοις χρυσωρυχεῖον ἦν. κώμη δ' ἐστὶ
πλησίον Ἰκτουμούλων, καὶ ταύτης[4] κώμης, ἄμφω
δ' εἰσὶ περὶ Πλακεντίαν. αὕτη μὲν δὴ ἡ πρώτη
μερὶς τῆς Ἰταλίας μέχρι δεῦρο περιωδεύσθω.

II.

1. Δευτέρα δὲ λεγέσθω ἡ Λιγυστικὴ ἡ ἐν αὐτοῖς
τοῖς Ἀπεννίνοις ὄρεσι, μεταξὺ ἱδρυμένη τῆς νῦν
λεχθείσης Κελτικῆς καὶ τῆς Τυρρηνίας, οὐδὲν

---

[1] οἱ before πίθοι, Meineke inserts; so Müller-Dübner.
[2] On Σύμβρ ιν, see footnote 2, p. 3 2.
[3] οἰκίας, the reading of all the MSS., Jones restores, for οἰκετείας, the reading of Kramer, Corais, and Meineke.

scarcity of every other grain. The country has
wonderful pitch-works, also; and as for the wine,
the quantity is indicated by the jars, for the wooden
ones are larger than houses; and the good supply
of the pitch helps much towards the excellent
smearing the jars receive. As for wool, the soft
kind is produced by the regions round Mutina and
the River Scultenna (the finest wool of all); the
coarse, by Liguria and the country of the Symbri,
from which the greater part of the households of
the Italiotes are clothed; and the medium, by the
regions round Patavium, from which are made the
expensive carpets and covers and everything of this
kind that is woolly either on both sides or only on
one. But as for the mines, at the present time
they are not being worked here as seriously as
before—perhaps on account of the fact that those
in the country of the Transalpine Celti and in
Iberia are more profitable[1]; formerly, however, they
were seriously worked, for there was a gold mine at
Vercelli too; Vercelli is a village near Ictumuli
(this too a village), and both are near Placentia. So
much, then, for my geographical description of the
First Portion of Italy.

II

1. LET us call the Second Portion that Liguria[2]
which is in the Apennines themselves, situated
between that Celtica which I have just described and
Tyrrhenia. It contains nothing worthy of detailed

[1] See 4. 1. 13, 4. 2 1, 4. 6. 7, and 3. 2. 8.
[2] Literally, "Ligustica" (see 4. 6. 3, and 5. 1. 1).

---

[4] τῆς, after ταύτης, Corais omits; so the later editors.

ἔχουσα περιηγήσεως ἄξιον, πλὴν ὅτι κωμηδὸν
ζῶσι, τραχεῖαν γῆν ἀροῦντες καὶ σκάπτοντες,
μᾶλλον δὲ λατομοῦντες, ὥς φησι Ποσειδώνιος.
Τρίτοι δ' εἰσὶ συνεχεῖς τούτοις οἱ Τυρρηνοί, τὰ
πεδία ἔχοντες τὰ μέχρι τοῦ ποταμοῦ τοῦ Τιβέριδος, κλυζόμενοι τὰ μὲν πρὸς ἔω μάλιστα μέρη τῷ
ποταμῷ μέχρι τῆς ἐκβολῆς αὐτοῦ, κατὰ δὲ θάτερα
τῷ Τυρρηνικῷ καὶ Σαρδῴῳ πελάγει. ῥεῖ δὲ ἐκ
τῶν Ἀπεννίνων ὀρῶν ὁ Τίβερις, πληροῦται δ' ἐκ
πολλῶν ποταμῶν, μέρος μέν τι δι' αὐτῆς φερόμενος τῆς Τυρρηνίας, τὸ δ' ἐφεξῆς διορίζων ἀπ'
αὐτῆς πρῶτον μὲν τὴν Ὀμβρικήν,[1] εἶτα τοὺς Σαβίνους καὶ Λατίνους τοὺς πρὸς τῇ Ῥώμῃ μέχρι τῆς
παραλίας. παραβέβληνται δέ πως τῷ ποταμῷ
μὲν καὶ τοῖς Τυρρηνοῖς κατὰ πλάτος, ἀλλήλοις δὲ
C 219 κατὰ μῆκος· ἀνέχουσι δὲ πρὸς τὰ Ἀπέννινα ὄρη
τὰ πλησιάζοντα τῷ Ἀδρίᾳ πρῶτοι μὲν οἱ Ὀμβρι-
κοί, μετὰ δὲ τούτους Σαβῖνοι, τελευταῖοι δ' οἱ τὴν
Λατίνην ἔχοντες, ἀρξάμενοι πάντες ἀπὸ τοῦ ποταμοῦ. ἡ μὲν οὖν τῶν Λατίνων χώρα μεταξὺ κεῖται
τῆς τε ἀπὸ τῶν Ὠστίων παραλίας μέχρι πόλεως
Σινοέσσης καὶ τῆς Σαβίνης (τὰ δ' Ὤστιά ἐστιν
ἐπίνειον τῆς Ῥώμης, εἰς ὃ ἐκδίδωσιν ὁ Τίβερις
παρ' αὐτὴν ῥυείς), ἐκτείνεται δὲ ἐπὶ μῆκος μέχρι
τῆς Καμπανίας καὶ τῶν Σαυνιτικῶν ὀρῶν· ἡ δὲ
Σαβίνη μεταξὺ τῶν Λατίνων κεῖται καὶ τῶν
Ὀμβρικῶν, ἐκτείνεται δὲ καὶ αὐτὴ πρὸς τὰ Σαυ-
νιτικὰ ὄρη, καὶ μᾶλλον συνάπτει τοῖς Ἀπεννίνοις
τοῖς κατὰ Οὐηστίνους τε καὶ Πελίγνους καὶ

---

[1] Umbria.

description except that the people live only in villages, plowing and digging rough land, or rather, as Poseidonius says, quarrying stones. The Third Portion is contiguous to the Second—I mean the country of the Tyrrheni, who hold the plains that extend as far as the River Tiber and whose country is washed, on its eastern side (generally speaking), by the river as far as its mouth, and on the other side by the Tyrrhenian and Sardinian Sea. But the Tiber flows from the Apennine Mountains, and is fed by many rivers; for a part of its course it runs through Tyrrhenia itself, and in its course thereafter separates from Tyrrhenia, first, Ombrica,[1] then, the country of the Sabini and also that part of Latium which is near Rome and extends as far as the coastline. These three latter lie approximately parallel to the river and Tyrrhenia in their breadth and also to one another in their length; and they reach up to those parts of the Apennine Mountains which closely approach the Adriatic, in this order: first, Ombrica, then, after Ombrica, the country of the Sabini, and, last, Latium,— all of them beginning at the river. Now the country of the Latini lies between the coastline that stretches from Ostia as far as the city of Sinuessa and the country of the Sabini (Ostia is the port-town of the Roman navy— the port into which the Tiber, after flowing past Rome, empties), although it extends lengthwise as far as Campania and the mountains of the Samnitae. But the country of the Sabini lies between that of the Latini and that of the Ombrici, although it too extends to the mountains of the Samnitae, or rather it joins that part of the Apennines which is in the country of the Vestini, the Peligni, and the

335

Μαρσούς· οἱ δ' Ὀμβρικοὶ μέσοι μὲν κεῖνται τῆς τε Σαβίνης καὶ τῆς Τυρρηνίας, μέχρι δ' Ἀριμίνου καὶ Ῥαουέννης προΐασιν[1] ὑπερβάλλοντες τὰ ὄρη. Τυρρηνοὶ δὲ παύονται ὑπ' αὐτοῖς τοῖς ὄρεσι τοῖς περικλείουσιν ἐκ τῆς Λιγυστικῆς εἰς τὸν Ἀδρίαν, ἀπὸ τῆς οἰκείας ἀρξάμενοι θαλάττης καὶ τοῦ Τιβέριδος. τὰ καθ' ἕκαστα δὲ διέξιμεν, ἀπ' αὐτῶν τούτων ἀρξάμενοι.

2. Οἱ Τυρρηνοὶ τοίνυν παρὰ τοῖς Ῥωμαίοις Ἐτροῦσκοι καὶ Τοῦσκοι προσαγορεύονται. οἱ δ' Ἕλληνες οὕτως ὠνόμασαν αὐτοὺς ἀπὸ τοῦ Τυρρηνοῦ τοῦ Ἄτυος, ὥς φασι, τοῦ στείλαντος ἐκ Λυδίας ἐποίκους δεῦρο. ἐπὶ γὰρ λιμοῦ καὶ ἀφορίας ὁ Ἄτυς, εἷς τῶν ἀπογόνων Ἡρακλέους καὶ Ὀμφάλης, δυεῖν παίδων ὄντων, κλήρῳ Λυδὸν μὲν κατέσχε, τῷ δὲ Τυρρηνῷ τὸν πλείω συστήσας λαὸν ἐξέστειλεν. ἐλθὼν δὲ τήν τε χώραν ἀφ' ἑαυτοῦ Τυρρηνίαν ἐκάλεσε, καὶ δώδεκα πόλεις ἔκτισεν, οἰκιστὴν ἐπιστήσας Τάρκωνα, ἀφ' οὗ Ταρκυνία ἡ πόλις, ὃν διὰ τὴν ἐκ παίδων σύνεσιν πολιὸν γεγεννῆσθαι μυθεύουσι. τότε μὲν οὖν ὑφ' ἑνὶ ἡγεμόνι ταττόμενοι μέγα ἴσχυον, χρόνοις δ' ὕστερον διαλυθῆναι τὸ σύστημα εἰκὸς καὶ κατὰ πόλεις διασπασθῆναι βίᾳ τῶν πλησιοχώρων εἴξαντας· οὐ γὰρ ἂν χώραν εὐδαίμονα ἀφέντες τῇ θαλάττῃ κατὰ λῃστείαν ἐπέθεντο, ἄλλοι πρὸς ἄλλα τραπόμενοι πελάγη, ἐπεί, ὅπου γε συμπνεύσαιεν,

---

[1] προΐασιν, Corais, for προσΐασιν ; so the later editors.

[1] Cp. 5. 4. 2.
[2] The Tyrrhenian Sea.
[3] The Greek spelling is "Tarkunia."

Marsi.[1] And the country of the Ombrici lies between the country of the Sabini and Tyrrhenia, although it extends over the mountains as far as Ariminum and Ravenna. And Tyrrhenia, beginning at its proper sea[2] and the Tiber, ceases at the very foot of those mountains which enclose it from Liguria to the Adriatic. I shall treat the several parts, however, in detail, beginning with the Tyrrheni themselves.

2. The Tyrrheni, then, are called among the Romans "Etrusci" and "Tusci." The Greeks, however, so the story goes, named them thus after Tyrrhenus, the son of Atys, who sent forth colonists hither from Lydia: At a time of famine and dearth of crops, Atys, one of the descendants of Heracles and Omphale, having only two children, by a casting of lots detained one of them, Lydus, and, assembling the greater part of the people with the other, Tyrrhenus, sent them forth. And when Tyrrhenus came, he not only called the country Tyrrhenia after himself, but also put Tarco in charge as "coloniser," and founded twelve cities; Tarco, I say, after whom the city of Tarquinia[3] is named, who, on account of his sagacity from boyhood, is said by the myth-tellers to have been born with grey hair. Now at first the Tyrrheni, since they were subject to the orders of only one ruler, were very strong, but in later times, it is reasonable to suppose, their united government was dissolved, and the Tyrrheni, yielding to the violence of their neighbours, were broken up into separate cities; for otherwise they would not have given up a happy land and taken to the sea as pirates, different bands turning to different parts of the high seas; indeed, in all cases where they acted in concert, they were able,

ἱκανοὶ ἦσαν οὐκ ἀμύνασθαι μόνον τοὺς ἐπιχειροῦν
τας αὐτοῖς,[1] ἀλλὰ καὶ ἀντεπιχειρεῖν καὶ μακρὰς
στρατείας ποιεῖσθαι. μετὰ δὲ τὴν τῆς Ῥώμης
κτίσιν Δημάρατος ἀφικνεῖται, λαὸν ἄγων ἐκ Κορίν
θου, καὶ δεξαμένων αὐτὸν Ταρκυνιτῶν γεννᾷ
Λουκούμωνα ἐξ ἐπιχωρίας γυναικός. γενόμενος
δὲ Ἄγκῳ Μαρκίῳ,[2] τῷ βασιλεῖ τῶν Ῥωμαίων,
φίλος ἐβασίλευσεν οὗτος, καὶ μετωνομάσθη Λεύ
C 220 κιος Ταρκύνιος Πρίσκος, ἐκόσμησε δ᾽ οὖν τὴν
Τυρρηνίαν καὶ αὐτὸς καὶ ὁ πατὴρ πρότερον, ὁ
μὲν εὐπορίᾳ δημιουργῶν τῶν συνακολουθησάντων
οἴκοθεν, ὁ δὲ ταῖς ἐκ τῆς Ῥώμης ἀφορμαῖς. λέγε
ται δὲ καὶ ὁ θριαμβικὸς κόσμος καὶ ὑπατικὸς καὶ
ἁπλῶς ὁ τῶν ἀρχόντων ἐκ Ταρκυνίων δεῦρο μετε
νεχθῆναι καὶ ῥάβδοι καὶ πελέκεις καὶ σάλπιγγες
καὶ ἱεροποιίαι καὶ μαντικὴ καὶ μουσικὴ ὅση δημο
σίᾳ χρῶνται Ῥωμαῖοι. τούτου δ᾽ υἱὸς ἦν ὁ δεύτε
ρος Ταρκύνιος, ὁ Σούπερβος, ὅσπερ καὶ τελευταῖος
βασιλεύσας ἐξέπεσε. Πορσίνας δ᾽, ὁ τῶν Κλου
σίνων βασιλεύς, πόλεως Τυρρηνίδος, κατάγειν
αὐτὸν ἐπιχειρήσας δι᾽ ὅπλων, οὐχ οἷός τε ἦν,
καταλυσάμενος τὴν ἔχθραν ἀπῆλθε φίλος μετὰ
τιμῆς καὶ δωρεῶν μεγάλων.

3. Περὶ μὲν τῆς ἐπιφανείας τῶν Τυρρηνῶν ταῦτα
καὶ ἔτι τὰ τοῖς Καιρετανοῖς πραχθέντα· καὶ γὰρ
τοὺς ἑλόντας τὴν Ῥώμην Γαλάτας κατεπολέμησαν,

---

[1] αὐτοῖς, Xylander, for αὐτούς; so the later editors.
[2] Μαρκίῳ, Corais, for Μάρκῳ; so the later editors.

---

[1] Demaratus became the ruler of the city (8 6. 20).
[2] In the legendary history of Rome, Lucumo was made
king by the Senate and people in 615 B.C.

not only to defend themselves against those who attacked them, but also to attack in turn and to make long expeditions. But it was after the founding of Rome that Demaratus arrived, bringing with him a host of people from Corinth; and, since he was received by the Tarquinians,[1] he married a native woman, by whom he begot Lucumo. And since Lucumo had proved a friend to Ancus Marcius, the king of the Romans, he was made king,[2] and his name was changed to Lucius Tarquinius Priscus. Be that as it may, he too adorned Tyrrhenia, as his father had done before him—the father by means of the goodly supply of artisans who had accompanied him from home and the son by means of the resources supplied by Rome. It is further said that the triumphal, and consular, adornment, and, in a word, that of all the rulers, was transferred to Rome from Tarquinii,[3] as also fasces, axes, trumpets, sacrificial rites, divination, and all music publicly used by the Romans. This Tarquinius was the father of the second Tarquinius, the "Superbus," who was the last of the kings and was banished.[4] Porsinas, the king of Clusium,[5] a Tyrrhenian city, undertook to restore him to the throne by force of arms, but was unable to do so, although he broke up the personal enmity against himself and departed as friend, along with honour and large gifts.

3. Thus much for the lustre of the Tyrrheni. And still to be recorded are the achievements of the Caeretani:[6] they defeated in war those Galatae who

---

[3] The same as "Tarquinia," 5. 2. 2.
[4] 509 B.C.   [5] Now Chiusi.
[6] Their city was Caere, one of the twelve founded by Tyrrhenus.

ἀπιοῦσιν ἐπιθέμενοι κατὰ Σαβίνους, καὶ ἃ παρ᾽
ἑκόντων ἔλαβον Ῥωμαίων ἐκεῖνοι λάφυρα ἄκοντας
ἀφείλοντο· πρὸς δὲ τούτοις τοὺς καταφυγόντας
παρ᾽ αὐτοὺς ἐκ τῆς Ῥώμης ἔσωσαν καὶ τὸ ἀθάνα-
τον πῦρ καὶ τὰς τῆς Ἑστίας ἱερείας. οἱ μὲν οὖν
Ῥωμαῖοι διὰ τοὺς τότε φαύλως διοικοῦντας τὴν
πόλιν οὐχ ἱκανῶς ἀπομνημονεῦσαι τὴν χάριν αὐτοῖς δοκοῦσι· πολιτείαν γὰρ δόντες οὐκ ἀνέγραψαν εἰς τοὺς πολίτας, ἀλλὰ καὶ τοὺς ἄλλους τοὺς
μὴ μετέχοντας τῆς ἰσονομίας εἰς τὰς δέλτους ἐξώ-
ριζον τὰς Καιρετανῶν. παρὰ δὲ τοῖς Ἕλλησιν
εὐδοκίμησεν ἡ πόλις αὕτη διά τε ἀνδρείαν καὶ
δικαιοσύνην· τῶν τε γὰρ ληστηρίων ἀπέσχετο,
καίπερ δυναμένη πλεῖστον, καὶ Πυθοῖ τὸν Ἀγυλ-
λαίων καλούμενον ἀνέθηκε θησαυρόν. Ἄγυλλα
γὰρ ὠνομάζετο τὸ πρότερον ἡ νῦν Καιρέα, καὶ
λέγεται Πελασγῶν κτίσμα τῶν ἐκ Θετταλίας ἀφιγ-
μένων· τῶν δὲ Λυδῶν οἵπερ Τυρρηνοὶ μετωνο-
μάσθησαν, ἐπιστρατευσάντων τοῖς Ἀγυλλαίοις,
προσιὼν τῷ τείχει τις ἐπυνθάνετο τοὔνομα τῆς
πόλεως, τῶν δ᾽ ἀπὸ τοῦ τείχους Θετταλῶν τινος
ἀντὶ τοῦ ἀποκρίνασθαι προσαγορεύσαντος αὐτὸν
χαῖρε, δεξάμενοι τὸν οἰωνὸν οἱ Τυρρηνοὶ τοῦτον
ἁλοῦσαν τὴν πόλιν μετωνόμασαν. ἡ δὲ οὕτω
λαμπρὰ καὶ ἐπιφανὴς πόλις νῦν ἴχνη σώζει μόνον,

---

[1] 390 B.C.

[2] That is, the right of suffrage, *ius suffragii*.

[3] Roman citizens themselves, when disfranchised by the
censor, were enrolled in the *Tabulae Caeritum*, and hence the
odium.　　　　[4] Delphi.　　　　[5] See 9. 3. 8.

had captured Rome,[1] having attacked them when
they were in the country of the Sabini on their way
back, and also took away as booty from the Galatae,
against their will, what the Romans had willingly
given them; in addition to this, they saved all who
fled to them for refuge from Rome, and the immortal
fire, and the priestesses of Vesta.   The Romans, it is
true, on account of the bad managers which the city
had at the time, do not seem to have remembered
the favour of the Caeretani with sufficient gratitude,
for, although they gave them the right of citizenship,
they did not enroll them among the citizens, and
even used to relegate all others who had no share in
the equal right[2] to "the Tablets of the Caeretani."[3]
Among the Greeks, however, this city was in good
repute both for bravery and for righteousness; for
it not only abstained from all piracy, although
particularly well fitted therefor, but also set up
at Pytho[4] what is called "the treasury[5] of the
Agyllaei"; for what is now Caerea[6] was formerly
called Agylla, and is said to have been founded by
Pelasgi who had come from Thessaly.   But when
those Lydians whose name was changed to Tyrrheni
marched against the Agyllaei, one of them approached
the wall and inquired what the name of the city was,
and when one of the Thessalians on the wall, instead
of replying to the inquiry, saluted him with a
"Chaere,"[7] the Tyrrheni accepted the omen, and, on
capturing the city, changed its name accordingly.
But the city, once so splendid and illustrious, now
preserves mere traces of its former self; and the hot
springs near by, which are called Caeretanian

[6] The proper Latin spelling was "Caere."
[7] The regular Greek word of salutation.

341

εὐανδρεῖ δ' αὐτῆς μᾶλλον τὰ πλησίον θερμά, ἃ καλοῦσι Καιρετανά, διὰ τοὺς φοιτῶντας θεραπείας χάριν.

4. Τοὺς δὲ Πελασγούς, ὅτι μὲν ἀρχαῖόν τι φῦλον κατὰ τὴν Ἑλλάδα πᾶσαν ἐπεπόλασε[1] καὶ μάλιστα παρὰ τοῖς Αἰολεῦσι τοῖς κατὰ Θετταλίαν, ὁμολογοῦσιν ἅπαντες σχεδόν τι. νομίζειν δέ φησιν Ἔφορος τὸ ἀνέκαθεν Ἀρκάδας ὄντας ἑλέσθαι στρατιωτικὸν βίον, εἰς δὲ τὴν αὐτὴν ἀγωγὴν προτρέποντας πολλοὺς ἅπασι τοῦ ὀνόματος μεταδοῦναι καὶ πολλὴν ἐπιφάνειαν κτήσασθαι καὶ παρὰ τοῖς Ἕλλησι καὶ παρὰ τοῖς ἄλλοις, παρ' ὅσους ποτὲ ἀφιγμένοι τετυχήκασι. καὶ γὰρ τῆς Κρήτης ἔποικοι γεγόνασιν, ὥς φησιν Ὅμηρος· λέγει γοῦν Ὀδυσσεὺς πρὸς Πηνελόπην·

C 221

ἄλλη δ' ἄλλων γλῶσσα μεμιγμένη· ἐν μὲν Ἀχαιοί,
ἐν δ' Ἐτεόκρητες μεγαλήτορες, ἐν δὲ Κύδωνες,
Δωριέες τε τριχάϊκες, δῖοί τε Πελασγοί.

(Od. 19. 175)

καὶ τὸ Πελασγικὸν Ἄργος ἡ Θετταλία λέγεται, τὸ μεταξὺ τῶν ἐκβολῶν τοῦ Πηνειοῦ καὶ τῶν Θερμοπυλῶν ἕως τῆς ὀρεινῆς τῆς κατὰ Πίνδον, διὰ τὸ ἐπάρξαι τῶν τόπων τούτων τοὺς Πελασγούς. τόν τε Δία τὸν Δωδωναῖον αὐτὸς ὁ ποιητὴς ὀνομάζει Πελασγικόν·

Ζεῦ ἄνα, Δωδωναῖε, Πελασγικέ.

(Il. 16. 233)

πολλοὶ δὲ καὶ τὰ Ἠπειρωτικὰ ἔθνη Πελασγικὰ

342

Springs,[1] have a greater population than it has
—because of those who visit the Springs for the
cure.[2]

4. As for the Pelasgi, almost all agree, in the first
place, that some ancient tribe of that name spread
throughout the whole of Greece, and particularly
among the Aeolians of Thessaly. Again, Ephorus
says that he is of the opinion that, since they were
originally Arcadians, they chose a military life, and
that, in converting many peoples to the same mode
of life, they imparted their name to all, and thus
acquired great glory, not only among the Greeks, but
also among all other peoples whithersoever they had
chanced[3] to come. For example, they prove to have
been colonisers of Crete, as Homer says; at any rate,
Odysseus says to Penelope: " But one tongue with
others is mixed; there[4] dwell Achaeans, there
Cretans of the old stock, proud of heart, there
Cydonians, and Dorians too, of waving plumes, and
goodly Pelasgians." And Thessaly is called " the
Pelasgian Argos " (I mean that part of it which lies
between the outlets of the Peneius River and
Thermopylae as far as the mountainous country of
Pindus), on account of the fact that the Pelasgi
extended their rule over these regions. Further, the
Dodonaean Zeus is by the poet himself named
" Pelasgian ": " O Lord Zeus, Dodonaean, Pelasgian."
And many have called also the tribes of Epirus

---

[1] Now, apparently, Bagni del Sasso.   [2] Cp. 5. 2. 9.
[3] Cp. " Pelargi," p. 347.   [4] Crete.

---

[1] For ἐπεπόλασε, Meineke, following E (which also reads
Πελασγοί, φῦλον ἀρχαῖον καὶ κατὰ τὴν Ἑλλάδα πᾶσαν), reads
ἐπιπολάσαν.

εἰρήκασιν, ὡς καὶ μέχρι δεῦρο ἐπαρξάντων· Πελασγούς τε πολλοὺς καὶ τῶν ἡρώων ὀνόματα[1] καλέσαντες, οἱ ὕστερον ἀπ᾽ ἐκείνων πολλὰ τῶν ἐθνῶν ἐπώνυμα πεποιήκασι· καὶ γὰρ τὴν Λέσβον Πελασγίαν εἰρήκασι, καὶ τοῖς ἐν τῇ Τρωάδι Κίλιξιν Ὅμηρος εἴρηκε τοὺς ὁμόρους Πελασγούς·

Ἱππόθοος δ᾽ ἄγε φῦλα Πελασγῶν ἐγχεσιμώρων,
τῶν, οἳ Λάρισαν ἐριβώλακα ναιετάασκον.

(Il. 2. 840)

τῷ δ᾽ Ἐφόρῳ τοῦ[2] ἐξ Ἀρκαδίας εἶναι τὸ φῦλον τοῦτο ἦρξεν Ἡσίοδος. φησὶ γάρ·

υἱεῖς ἐξεγένοντο Λυκάονος ἀντιθέοιο,
ὅν ποτε τίκτε Πελασγός.

(loc. incert.)

Αἰσχύλος δ᾽ ἐκ τοῦ περὶ Μυκήνας Ἄργους φησὶν ἐν Ἱκέτισιν ἢ[3] Δαναΐσι τὸ γένος αὐτῶν. καὶ τὴν Πελοπόννησον δὲ Πελασγίαν φησὶν Ἔφορος κληθῆναι, καὶ Εὐριπίδης δ᾽ ἐν Ἀρχελάῳ φησὶν ὅτι

Δαναὸς ὁ πεντήκοντα θυγατέρων πατὴρ
ἐλθὼν ἐς Ἄργος ᾤκησ᾽[4] Ἰνάχου πόλιν,

---

[1] For ὀνόματα, Groskurd reads ὀνομαστί; Meineke, ὄνομα.

[2] τοῦ, Corais, following no, for τό (ABl), τῷ (C?); so the later editors.

[3] For ἤ, Meineke reads καί.

[4] The reading of the MSS. is ᾤκησιν (Müller-Dübner, Ind. Var. Lect.). All the editors since Xylander, except Corais and Du Theil (who read ᾤκησεν), read ᾤκισ᾽. Jones reads ᾤκησ᾽.

---

[1] Hippothous was the son of "Lethus Pelasgus" (Iliad 2. 843, and 17. 288). In 13. 3. 2 Strabo takes Homer, in the passage above quoted, to mean Larisa Phryconis, the "Larisa near Cyme," which latter is now Lamurtkeui. On "Larisa Phryconis," see 9. 5. 19.

"Pelasgian," because in their opinion the Pelasgi extended their rule even as far as that. And, further, because many of the heroes were called "Pelasgi" by name, the people of later times have, from those heroes, applied the name to many of the tribes; for example, they have called the island of Lesbos "Pelasgia," and Homer has called "Pelasgi" the people that were neighbours to those Cilicians who lived in the Troad: "And Hippothous led the tribes of spear-fighting Pelasgi, those Pelasgi who inhabited deep-soiled Larissa."[1] But Ephorus' authority for the statement that this race originated in Arcadia was Hesiod; for Hesiod says: "And sons were born of god-like Lycaon, who, on a time, was begotten by Pelasgus." Again, Aeschylus, in his *Suppliants*,[2] or else his *Danaan Women*,[3] says that the race of the Pelasgi originated in that Argos which is round about Mycenae.[4] And the Peloponnesus too, according to Ephorus, was called "Pelasgia."[5] And Euripides too, in his *Archelaus*,[6] says: "Danaus, the father of fifty daughters, on coming into Argos,[7] took up his abode in the city of Inachus,[8] and

---

[2] *Hiketides* 16 ff. and 250 ff.

[3] The *Danaan Women* (*Danaides*) is no longer extant.

[4] That is, the *district* of Argos, in which Mycenae as well as the city of Argos were situated (see 8. 6. 5-10).

[5] The Peloponnesus was called "Argos" as well as "Pelasgia" (8. 6. 5).

[6] The *Archelaus* is no longer extant.

[7] Again the *district* of Argos, elsewhere (8. 6. 8) called "Argeia."

[8] The "city of Inachus"—so called from Inachus, the first king of Argos—was the city of Argos. By a slight change in the Greek most of the editors (see note 4 on opposite page) emend "took up his abode in" to "founded," presumably on the ground that Strabo later says "Danaus founded the acropolis" (Argos) "of the Argives" (8. 6. 9).

Πελασγιώτας δ᾽ ὠνομασμένους τὸ πρὶν
Δαναοὺς καλεῖσθαι νόμον ἔθηκ᾽ ἀν᾽ Ἑλλάδα.

(*Fr.* 228, Nauck)

Ἀντικλείδης δὲ πρώτους φησὶν αὐτοὺς τὰ περὶ
Λῆμνον καὶ Ἴμβρον κτίσαι, καὶ δὴ τούτων τινὰς
καὶ μετὰ Τυρρηνοῦ Ἄτυος εἰς τὴν Ἰταλίαν συνᾶ-
ραι. καὶ οἱ τὴν Ἀτθίδα συγγράψαντες ἱστοροῦσι
περὶ τῶν Πελασγῶν, ὡς καὶ Ἀθήνησι γενομένων
τῶν Πελασγῶν,[1] διὰ δὲ τὸ πλανήτας εἶναι καὶ
δίκην ὀρνέων ἐπιφοιτᾶν ἐφ᾽ οὓς ἔτυχε τόπους Πε-
λαργοὺς ὑπὸ τῶν Ἀττικῶν κληθῆναι.

C 222   5. Τῆς δὲ Τυρρηνίας μῆκος μὲν τὸ μέγιστον εἶναί
φασι τὴν παραλίαν ἀπὸ Λούνης μέχρι Ὠστίων
δισχιλίων που καὶ πεντακοσίων σταδίων, πλάτος
δὲ τοῦ ἡμίσους ἔλαττον τὸ πρὸς τοῖς ὄρεσιν. εἰς
μὲν οὖν Πίσας ἀπὸ Λούνης πλείους τῶν τετρακοσίων σταδίων εἰσίν, ἐντεῦθεν δ᾽ εἰς Οὐολατέρρας
διακόσιοι ὀγδοήκοντα, πάλιν δ᾽ ἐνθένδε εἰς Ποπλώνιον διακόσιοι ἑβδομήκοντα, ἐκ δὲ Ποπλωνίου εἰς
Κόσαν ἐγγὺς ὀκτακόσιοι, οἱ δὲ ἑξακόσιοί φασι.
Πολύβιος δ᾽ οὐκ[2] εἶναι τοὺς πάντας χιλίους τρια-

---

[1] Meineke relegates the second τῶν Πελασγῶν to the foot
of the page, perhaps rightly.
[2] Kramer inserts εὖ after οὐκ; so Müller-Dübner. Meineke
emends εἶναι to εὖ καί, perhaps rightly.

---

[1] Androtion, Philochorus, and others; only fragments of
their works remain.
[2] "Atthis" was the old name of Attica, from Atthis, the
daughter of the mythical king Cranaus (Cp. 9. 1. 18).
[3] Cp. 9. 1. 18 and 9. 2. 3.

throughout Greece he laid down a law that all
people hitherto named Pelasgians were to be called
Danaans." And again, Anticleides says that they
were the first to settle the regions round about
Lemnos and Imbros, and indeed that some of these
sailed away to Italy with Tyrrhenus the son of Atys.
And the compilers[1] of the histories of *The Land of
Atthis*[2] give accounts of the Pelasgi, believing that
the Pelasgi were in fact at Athens too,[3] although the
Pelasgi were by the Attic people called "Pelargi,"[4]
the compilers add, because they were wanderers and,
like birds, resorted to those places whither chance
led them.[5]

5. They say that the maximum length of Tyrrhenia—the coastline from Luna as far as Ostia—is
about two thousand five hundred stadia, and its
breadth (I mean its breadth near the mountains[6])
less than half its length. Now from Luna to Pisa
the distance is more than four hundred stadia; and
thence to Volaterrae, two hundred and eighty; and
again, from here to Poplonium, two hundred and
seventy; and from Poplonium to Cosa,[7] nearly eight
hundred, though some say six hundred. Polybius,
however, says the total number of stadia[8] is not so

---

[4] Literally, "Storks."

[5] Cp. 9. 1. 18, where Strabo refers to the Pelasgi as having
"sojourned" at Athens.

[6] "Near the mountains" is very indefinite, but in § 9
following Strabo applies the same phrase to the city of
Arretium, adding that this city "is farthest of all in the
interior." In the present passage, therefore, he clearly means
that the line of greatest breadth runs to the Apennines near
Arretium—which is correct.

[7] Often called "Cossa"; so in § 8 following.

[8] From Luna to Cosa.

κοσίους τριάκοντα λέγει. τούτων δ' ἡ μὲν Λούνα
πόλις ἐστὶ καὶ λιμήν, καλοῦσι δ' οἱ Ἕλληνες Σελήνης λιμένα καὶ πόλιν. ἡ μὲν οὖν πόλις οὐ μεγάλη,
ὁ δὲ λιμὴν μέγιστός τε καὶ κάλλιστος, ἐν αὐτῷ
περιέχων πλείους λιμένας, ἀγχιβαθεῖς πάντας,
οἷον ἂν γένοιτο ὁρμητήριον θαλαττοκρατησάντων
ἀνθρώπων τοσαύτης μὲν θαλάττης, τοσοῦτον δὲ
χρόνον. περικλείεται δ' ὁ λιμὴν ὄρεσιν ὑψηλοῖς,
ἀφ' ὧν τὰ πελάγη κατοπτεύεται καὶ ἡ Σαρδὼ καὶ
τῆς ἠιόνος ἑκατέρωθεν πολὺ μέρος. μέταλλα δὲ
λίθου λευκοῦ τε καὶ ποικίλου γλαυκίζοντος το-
σαῦτά τ' ἐστὶ καὶ τηλικαῦτα, μονολίθους ἐκδι-
δόντα πλάκας καὶ στύλους, ὥστε τὰ πλεῖστα τῶν
ἐκπρεπῶν ἔργων τῶν ἐν τῇ Ῥώμῃ καὶ ταῖς ἄλλαις
πόλεσιν ἐντεῦθεν ἔχειν τὴν χορηγίαν· καὶ γὰρ
εὐεξάγωγός ἐστιν ἡ λίθος, τῶν μετάλλων ὑπερκειμένων τῆς θαλάττης πλησίον, ἐκ δὲ τῆς θαλάττης

---

[1] Strabo postpones his estimates of the remaining distances
(Cosa–Gravisci–Purgi–Ostia), totalling (about) 740 stadia, to
§ 8 following. Following Groskurd, Meineke unwarrantedly
indicates a lacuna in the text immediately after "some say
six hundred," thinking Strabo must have added at that point
the distance from Cosa to Ostia. Thus he makes the figures
of Polybius (whose original statement, unfortunately, is now
lost) apply to the entire distance from Luna to Ostia. But
by measurement on Kiepert's wall-map of Ancient Italy, 1330
stadia proves to be a very close estimate for the distance,
along the coastal-roads from Luna to Cosa.

[2] That is, "Harbour of the Moon" ("Moon-Harbour").
Cp. "Harbour of Menestheus" (3. 1. 9) and "Harbour of
Monoecus" (4. 6. 3), each phrase meaning the city as well
as the harbour. The Gulf of Spezia (its dimensions are
seven miles by three) is one of the finest harbours in the
world. It is the chief station of the Italian navy, and has
at its head a dockyard and arsenal.

much as one thousand three hundred and thirty.[1]
Of these, take first Luna; it is a city and also
a harbour, and the Greeks call the city as well
as the harbour "Harbour of Selene."[2] The city,
indeed, is not large, but the harbour is both very
large and very beautiful, since it includes within
itself several harbours, all of them deep up to the
very shore,—just such a place as would naturally
become the naval base of a people who were masters
of so great a sea for so long a time. And the
harbour is shut in all round by high mountains,
from which the high seas are to be seen, as also
Sardo,[3] and a considerable stretch of the shore on
either side. And the quarries of marble,[4] both white
and mottled bluish-grey marble, are so numerous, and
of such quality (for they yield monolithic slabs and
columns), that the material for most of the superior
works of art[5] in Rome and the rest of the cities are
supplied therefrom;[6] and, indeed, the marble is easy
to export, since the quarries lie above the sea and

[3] Sardinia. Tozer (*Selections*, p. 144) thinks Strabo must
have meant Corsica, since Sardinia is 180 miles distant.

[4] Now the quarries of Carrara.

[5] For specific references to Roman "works of art" in
stone, see 5. 3. 8.

[6] For a full discussion of stones of all kinds, and their
uses at Rome and elsewhere, see the *Natural History* of
Pliny, Book XXXVI. See also W. G. Renwick's *Marble
and Marble Working* (1909), pp. 20 ff. and 69 ff. Dr. J. S.
Flett (*Encyc. Brit.*, s.v. "Marble") says: "Stone from this
district was employed in Rome for architectural purposes in
the time of Augustus, but the finer varieties, adapted to the
needs of the sculptor, were not discovered until some time
later." The best works of Michelangelo and Canova were
executed in Carrara marble; and the best sculptors of to-day
prefer to use this particular marble.

διαδεχομένου τοῦ Τιβέριος τὴν κομιδήν· καὶ τὴν
ξυλείαν τὴν εἰς τὰς οἰκοδομὰς σελμάτων εὐθυτά-
των καὶ εὐμηκεστάτων ἡ Τυρρηνία χορηγεῖ τὴν
πλείστην, τῷ ποταμῷ κατάγουσα ἐκ τῶν ὀρῶν
εὐθύς. μεταξὺ δὲ Λούνης καὶ Πίσης ὁ Μάκρας[1]
ἐστί,[2] ᾧ πέρατι τῆς Τυρρηνίας καὶ τῆς Λιγυστικῆς κέχρηνται τῶν συγγραφέων πολλοί. ἡ δὲ
Πίσα κτίσμα μέν ἐστι τῶν ἐν Πελοποννήσῳ Πισα-
τῶν, οἳ μετὰ Νέστορος ἐπὶ Ἴλιον στρατεύσαντες
κατὰ τὸν ἀνάπλουν[3] ἐπλανήθησαν, οἱ μὲν εἰς τὸ
Μεταπόντιον, οἱ δ' εἰς τὴν Πισᾶτιν, ἅπαντες
Πύλιοι καλούμενοι. δυεῖν δὲ ποταμῶν κεῖται μεταξὺ κατ' αὐτὴν τὴν συμβολήν, Ἄρνου τε καὶ
Αὔσαρος,[4] ὧν ὁ μὲν ἐξ Ἀρρητίου φέρεται πολύς,
οὐχὶ πᾶς, ἀλλὰ τριχῇ σχισθείς, ὁ δ' ἐκ τῶν
Ἀπεννίνων ὀρῶν· συμπεσόντες δ' εἰς ἓν ῥεῖθρον
μετεωρίζουσιν ἀλλήλους ταῖς ἀντικοπαῖς ἐπὶ τοσοῦτον ὥστε τοὺς ἐπὶ τῶν ἠιόνων ἑστῶτας ἀμφοτέρων μηδ' ἕτερον ὑπὸ θατέρου καθορᾶσθαι, ὥστ'
ἀνάγκη δυσανάπλωτα ἐκ θαλάττης εἶναι· στάδιοι
δ' εἰσὶ τοῦ ἀνάπλου περὶ εἴκοσι. μυθεύουσι δ',
ὅτε πρῶτον ἐκ τῶν ὀρῶν οἱ ποταμοὶ κατεφέροντο
οὗτοι, κωλυομένους ὑπὸ τῶν ἐπιχωρίων, μὴ συμπε-

---

[1] Μάκρας, Kramer, for Μάκρης, (cp. Δουρίας, 4. 6. 5); so the
later editors.
[2] χωρίον, after ἐστί, C. Müller deletes (see *Ind. Var. Lect.*
p. 969).
[3] ὄν, after ἀνάπλουν, Xylander deletes; so the later editors.
[4] Αὔσαρος, Cluver, for Αἴσαρος; so most of the editors,
including Meineke.

---

[1] Since the old city of Luna (now in ruins) was some five
miles south of the Macra, and still farther south of the

near it, and since the Tiber in its turn takes up the cargo from the sea and conveys it to Rome. And the wooden material for the buildings, in beams that are very straight and very long, is for the most part supplied by Tyrrhenia, since by means of the river it can be brought down directly from the mountains. Now between Luna[1] and Pisa is the Macras,[2] which many of the historians have used as the boundary between Tyrrhenia and Liguria.[3] As for Pisa, it was founded by those Pisatae who lived in the Peloponnesus, who made the expedition to Ilium with Nestor and on the return voyage went astray, some to Metapontium, and others to the territory of Pisa, though all of them were called Pylians. Pisa is situated between, and at the very confluence of, two rivers, the Arnus and the Ausar, of which the former runs from Arretium, with great quantities of water (not all in one stream, but divided into three streams), and the latter from the Apennine Mountains; and when they unite and form one stream they heave one another up so high by their mutual resistance that two persons standing on the opposite banks cannot even see each other; and hence, necessarily, voyages inland from the sea are difficult to make; the length of the voyage is about twenty stadia. And the following fable is told: when these rivers first began to flow down from the mountains, and their course was being hindered by the natives for fear that they would unite in one

harbour, Strabo must either have meant the harbour, not the city, of Luna, or else have thought the city was situated on the harbour.

[2] The River Macra.

[3] So Pliny, 3. 7 and 3. 8; Livy, 39. 32, 40. 41; Florus, 2. 3. 4.

σόντες εἰς ἓν κατακλύζοιεν τὴν χώραν, ὑποσχέσθαι
C 223 μὴ κατακλύσειν καὶ φυλάξαι τὴν πίστιν. δοκεῖ
δ' ἡ πόλις εὐτυχῆσαί ποτε, καὶ νῦν οὐκ ἀδοξεῖ διά
τε εὐκαρπίαν καὶ τὰ λιθουργεῖα καὶ τὴν ὕλην τὴν
ναυπηγήσιμον, ᾗ τὸ μὲν παλαιὸν ἐχρῶντο πρὸς
τοὺς κατὰ θάλατταν κινδύνους· καὶ γὰρ μαχιμώτεροι Τυρρηνῶν ὑπῆρξαν, καὶ παρώξυναν αὐτοὺς οἱ
Λίγυες, πονηροὶ γείτονες παρὰ πλευρὰν ὄντες·
νῦν δὲ τὸ πλέον εἰς τὰς οἰκοδομὰς ἀναλίσκεται
τὰς ἐν Ῥώμῃ, κἂν ταῖς ἐπαύλεσι, βασίλεια κατασκευαζομένων Περσικά.

6. Τῶν δὲ Οὐολατερρανῶν ἡ μὲν χώρα κλύζεται
τῇ θαλάττῃ, τὸ δὲ κτίσμα ἐν φάραγγι βαθείᾳ·
λόφος ἐστὶν ὑψηλὸς περίκρημνος πάντῃ, τὴν κο-
ρυφὴν ἐπίπεδος, ἐφ' ᾗ ἵδρυται τὸ τεῖχος τῆς πόλεως.
ἡ δ' ἐπ' αὐτὴν ἀνάβασις πεντεκαίδεκα σταδίων
ἐστὶν ἀπὸ τῆς βάσεως, ὀξεῖα πᾶσι καὶ χαλεπή.
ἐνταῦθα συνέστησάν τινες τῶν Τυρρηνῶν καὶ τῶν
προγεγραμμένων ὑπὸ Σύλλα· πληρώσαντες δὲ
τέτταρα τάγματα στρατιᾶς[1] διετῆ χρόνον ἐπο-
λιορκήθησαν, εἶθ' ὑπόσπονδοι παρεχώρησαν τοῦ
τόπου. τὸ δὲ Ποπλώνιον ἐπ' ἄκρας ὑψηλῆς ἵδρυται, κατερρωγυίας εἰς τὴν θάλασσαν καὶ χερρονη-
σιζούσης, πολιορκίαν καὶ αὐτὸ δεδεγμένον περὶ
τοὺς αὐτοὺς καιρούς. τὸ μὲν οὖν πολίχνιον πᾶν
ἔρημόν ἐστι πλὴν τῶν ἱερῶν καὶ κατοικιῶν ὀλίγων,
τὸ δ' ἐπίνειον οἰκεῖται βέλτιον, πρὸς τῇ ῥίζῃ τοῦ

---

[1] στρατιᾶς, Corais, for στρατείας; so the later editors.

[1] The number of men in these battalions is uncertain,
since the Greek word might mean any regular body of

stream and deluge the country, the rivers promised
not to deluge it and kept their pledge. Again,
Pisa is reputed to have been prosperous on a time,
and at the present time it is not without repute, on
account of its fertility, its stone-quarries, and its
timber for ship-building; in ancient times, indeed,
they utilised this latter material to meet the perils
that faced them on the sea (for they were, to begin
with, more warlike than the Tyrrheni, and their
warlike spirit was sharpened by the Ligures, bad
neighbours living at their flank), but at the present
time most of it is being used up on the buildings at
Rome, and also at the villas, now that people are
devising palaces of Persian magnificence.

6. As for the Volaterrani, their country is washed
by the sea and their settlement is in a deep ravine;
in the ravine there is a high hill, which is precipitous
on all sides and flat on the crest, and it is on this
hill that the walls of the city are situated. The
ascent from the base to the crest is fifteen stadia,
an ascent that is sharp all the way up, and difficult
to make. This is where some of the Tyrrheni and
of those who had been proscribed by Sulla assembled;
and, on filling out four battalions,[1] they withstood a
siege for two years, and even then retired from the
place only under a truce. As for Poplonium, it is
situated on a high promontory that makes an abrupt
descent into the sea and forms a peninsula; it too
sustained a siege at about the same time as
Volaterrae. Now although the town is wholly desert
except for the temples and a few dwellings, the
port-town, which has a little harbour and two docks

soldiers (as often), or a maniple (cp. Polybius 6. 24), or even
a legion (cp. Cassius Dio 71. 9).

ὅρους λιμένιον ἔχον καὶ νεωσοίκους δύο· καὶ[1]
δοκεῖ μοι μόνη τῶν Τυρρηνίδων τῶν παλαιῶν
αὕτη πόλεων ἐπ' αὐτῇ τῇ θαλάττῃ ἱδρῦσθαι·
αἴτιον δ' ἐστὶ τὸ τῆς χώρας ἀλίμενον· διόπερ
παντάπασιν ἔφευγον οἱ κτίσται τὴν θάλατταν, ἢ
προεβάλλοντο ἐρύματα πρὸ[2] αὐτῆς, ὥστε μὴ
λάφυρον ἔτοιμον ἐκκεῖ∘θαι τοῖς ἐπιπλεύσασιν.
ἔστι δὲ καὶ θυννοσκοπεῖον ὑπὸ τῇ ἄκρα. κατοπτεύεται δ' ἀπὸ τῆς πόλεως πόρρωθεν μὲν καὶ
μόλις ἡ Σαρδώ, ἐγγυτέρω δ' ἡ Κύρνος, ἑξήκοντά
πως διέχουσα τῆς Σαρδόνος σταδίους, πολὺ δὲ
μᾶλλον τούτων ἡ Αἰθαλία· ἢ[3] προσεχεστέρα τῇ
ἠπείρῳ ἐστίν, ὅσον τριακοσίους διέχουσα σταδίους, ὅσους καὶ τῆς Κύρνου διέχει. ἄριστον δ'
ἀφετήριον τοῦτο τὸ χωρίον ἐστὶν ἐπὶ τὰς τρεῖς τὰς
λεχθείσας νήσους. εἴδομεν δὲ καὶ ταύτας ἡμεῖς,
ἀναβάντες ἐπὶ τὸ Ποπλώνιον, καὶ μέταλλά τινα
ἐν τῇ χώρᾳ ἐκλελειμμένα. εἴδομεν δὲ καὶ τοὺς
ἐργαζομένους τὸν σίδηρον τὸν ἐκ τῆς Αἰθαλίας
κομιζόμενον· οὐ γὰρ δύναται συλλιπαίνεσθαι
καμινευόμενος ἐν τῇ νήσῳ· κομίζεται δ' εὐθὺς ἐκ

---

[1] δύο· καί, Meineke, for δίο καί ; so Müller–Dübner.
[2] Meineke emends πρός to πρό, following Corais.
[3] ἤ, Meineke inserts ; Casaubon, Kramer, and Müller–
Dübner insert γάρ before τῇ.

---

[1] Corsica.   [2] Elba.
[3] Literally, "oiled together"; hence not "melted together" merely (the meaning given by the dictionaries and
the editors in general), or "reduced to iron bars" (Casaubon
and du Theil). Strabo speaks of "iron," not "iron-ore";
and he does not mean to say that *iron-ore* was not *smelted*
at all on the island. Indeed, Diodorus Siculus (5. 13) tells
us in detail how the people there broke up the masses of

at the base of the mountain, is better peopled; and
in my opinion this is the only one of the ancient
Tyrrhenian cities that was situated on the sea itself;
and my reason is the country's lack of harbours—
precisely the reason why the founders would avoid
the sea altogether, or else would throw forward
defences towards the sea, so as not to be exposed,
a ready prey, to any who might sail against them.
Again, beneath the promontory there is a place for
watching the tunny-fish. And in looking down
from the city you can see, albeit from afar and
with difficulty, the island of Sardo, and, nearer, the
island of Cyrnus[1] (about sixty stadia distant from
Sardo), and, much better than these, the island
of Aethalia;[2] Aethalia is closer to the mainland,
since it is distant only about three hundred stadia,
the same as its distance from Cyrnus. This place
is the best point of departure from the mainland
to the three aforesaid islands. I myself saw these
islands when I went up to Poplonium, and also
some mines out in the country that had failed.
And I also saw the people who work the iron that
is brought over from Aethalia; for it cannot be
brought into complete coalescence[3] by heating in
the furnaces on the island; and it is brought over

"iron-rock," and "burnt" and "melted" the pieces in
"ingenious furnaces"; how they divided the resulting mass
into lumps of convenient size, in form similar to large
sponges; and how they sold the lumps to merchants, who
took them over to the various markets on the mainland.
Hence Strabo is thinking primarily of the high temperature
necessary to bring the iron from a brittle and spongy to a
soft and tough texture; but for the lack of wood on the island
(see Beckmann on *Aristot. Mirab.* c. 95) any further working
of the iron there was wholly impracticable. On the kinds
of iron and how to temper it, see Pliny 34. 41.

355

τῶν μετάλλων εἰς τὴν ἤπειρον. τοῦτό τε δὴ
παράδοξον ἡ νῆσος ἔχει καὶ τὸ τὰ ὀρύγματα
ἀναπληροῦσθαι πάλιν τῷ χρόνῳ τὰ μεταλλευ-
C 224 θέντα, καθάπερ τοὺς πλαταμῶνάς φασι τοὺς ἐν
Ῥόδῳ καὶ τὴν ἐν Πάρῳ πέτραν τὴν μάρμαρον καὶ
τὰς ἐν Ἰνδοῖς ἅλας, ἅς φησι Κλείταρχος. οὔτ'οὖν
Ἐρατοσθένης ὀρθῶς ὁ φήσας μὴ καθορᾶσθαι μήτε
τὴν Κύρνον ἐκ τῆς ἠπείρου μήτε τὴν Σαρδόνα, οὔτ'
Ἀρτεμίδωρος ὁ φήσας ἐν χιλίοις εἶναι καὶ διακοσίοις σταδίοις πελαγίας ἀμφοτέρας. καὶ γὰρ εἴ
τισιν, ἡμῖν γε οὐκ ἂν ὑπῆρξαν ὁραταὶ ἢ[1] ἐπὶ
τοσοῦτον, ἐφ' ὅσον σαφεῖς ἑωρῶντο, καὶ μάλιστα
ἡ Κύρνος. ἔστι δὲ κατὰ τὴν Αἰθαλίαν λιμὴν
Ἀργῷος ἀπὸ τῆς Ἀργοῦς, ὥς φασιν· ἐκεῖσε γὰρ
πλεῦσαι τὴν τῆς Κίρκης οἴκησιν ζητοῦντα τὸν
Ἰάσονα, τῆς Μηδείας ἐθελούσης ἰδεῖν τὴν θεάν.[2]
καὶ δὴ καὶ τῶν ἀποστλεγγισμάτων παγέντων ἃ
ἐποίουν οἱ Ἀργοναῦται, διαμένειν ἔτι καὶ νῦν
διαποικίλους τὰς ἐπὶ τῆς ἠιόνος ψήφους. αἱ δὲ
τοιαῦται μυθοποιίαι τεκμήρια τῶν λεγομένων ὑφ'
ἡμῶν εἰσιν, ὅτι οὐ πάντα Ὅμηρος αὐτὸς ἔπλαττεν,
ἀλλ' ἀκούων θρυλουμένων τῶν τοιούτων πολλῶν
αὐτὸς προσετίθει μήκη διαστημάτων καὶ ἐκτοπισ-

---

[1] ἤ, the reading of the MSS., Jones retains ; others delete.
[2] In a letter to Forbiger, Meineke suggested θείαν for θεάν;
and Forbiger so reads.

---

[1] "Immediately from the mines" might imply, of course,
that the particular supply that went to Poplonium was,
according to Strabo, merely ore as dug from the mines.
[2] Aristotle (Mirab. c. 93), speaking of this same island,
says, on the authority of others, that what was once a
copper mine gave out, and that long thereafter iron appeared

immediately from the mines to the mainland.[1]
However, this is not the only remarkable thing
about the island; there is also the fact that the
diggings which have been mined are in time filled
up again,[2] as is said to be the case with the ledges
of rocks in Rhodes, the marble-rock in Paros, and,
according to Cleitarchus, the salt-rock in India.[3]
Neither, then, is Eratosthenes correct, when he says
that neither Cyrnus nor Sardo can be seen from
the mainland, nor Artemidorus, when he says that
both islands lie in the high sea within twelve
hundred stadia; for even supposing they were visible
to some people at that distance, they could not
have been so to me, at least, or else not to the
extent of their being seen clearly, and particularly
Cyrnus. Again, there is at Aethalia a Portus Argous,[4]
from the ship "Argo," as they say; for when Jason,
the story goes, was in quest of the abode of Circe,
because Medea wished to see the goddess,[5] he sailed
to this port; and, what is more, because the scrapings,
which the Argonauts formed when they used their
strigils, became congealed, the pebbles on the shore
remain variegated still to this day. Now mythical
stories of this sort are proofs of what I have been
saying: that Homer was not wont to fabricate
everything on his own account, but, because he heard
many such stories told over and over again, he was
wont on his own account to add to them by lengthen-
ing the distances and making the settings more
remote; and that, just as he threw the setting of

in the same mine—"the iron which is now used by the
inhabitants of Poplonium."
[3] Cp. 15. 1. 30. [4] Porto Ferrajo.
[5] Meineke conjectures that Strabo wrote "aunt" instead
of "goddess"; cp. 1. 2. 10.

μῶν, καὶ καθάπερ τὸν Ὀδυσσέα εἰς τὸν ὠκεανὸν
ἐξέβαλε, παραπλησίως καὶ τὸν Ἰάσονα, γενομένης καὶ τούτῳ πλάνης τινὸς κἀκείνῳ, καθάπερ
καὶ Μενελάῳ. περὶ μὲν οὖν τῆς Αἰθαλίας
τοσαῦτα.

7. Ἡ δὲ Κύρνος ὑπὸ τῶν Ῥωμαίων καλεῖται
Κορσίκα. οἰκεῖται δὲ φαύλως, τραχεῖά τε οὖσα
καὶ τοῖς πλείστοις μέρεσι δύσβατος τελέως, ὥστε
τοὺς κατέχοντας τὰ ὄρη καὶ ἀπὸ λῃστηρίων ζῶν-
τας ἀγριωτέρους εἶναι θηρίων. ὁπόταν γοῦν ὁρμή-
σωσιν οἱ τῶν Ῥωμαίων στρατηγοί, καὶ προσπε-
σόντες τοῖς ἐρύμασι πολὺ πλῆθος ἕλωσι τῶν
ἀνδραπόδων, ὁρᾶν ἔστιν ἐν τῇ Ῥώμῃ καὶ θαυμάζειν ὅσον ἐμφαίνεται τὸ θηριῶδες καὶ τὸ βοσκη-
ματῶδες ἐν αὐτοῖς· ἢ γὰρ οὐχ ὑπομένουσι ζῆν ἢ
ζῶντες ἀπαθείᾳ καὶ ἀναισθησίᾳ τοὺς ὠνησαμένους
ἐπιτρίβουσιν, ὥστε καίπερ τὸ τυχὸν καταβαλοῦ-
σιν ὑπὲρ αὐτῶν ὅμως μεταμέλειν. ἔστι δ᾿ ὅμως
οἰκήσιμά τινα μέρη καὶ πολίσματά που Βλησίνων
τε καὶ Χάραξ καὶ Ἐνικονίαι καὶ Οὐάπανες. μῆκος
δὲ τῆς νήσου φησὶν ὁ χωρογράφος μίλια ἑκατὸν
ἑξήκοντα, πλάτος δὲ ἑβδομήκοντα· Σαρδόνος δὲ
μῆκος διακόσια εἴκοσι, πλάτος δὲ ἐνενήκοντα ὀκτώ.

---

[1] Strabo again comes back to his favourite theme; cp.
1. 2. 9, 1. 2. 38, and 3. 2. 12.

[2] Cp. Pliny, 3. 12(6).

[3] It is impossible to say what "Chorographer" Strabo
refers to here; and in 5. 2. 8, 6. 1. 11, 6. 2. 1 ("The Choro-
graphy"), 6. 2. 11, 6. 3. 10. The fact that the dimensions
are given in Roman miles indicates that he does not allude
to Eratosthenes, or Polybius, or Artemidorus. Casaubon
thinks he means the "Map of Agrippa." Detlefsen (*Ursprung . . . der Erdkarte Agrippas* in *Quellen und Forschungen
zur alten Geschichte und Geographie*, Heft 13, pp. 21, 61 ff.),

358

his Odysseus out into the ocean, so similarly he threw the setting of his Jason there, because a wandering had actually taken place in the life of Jason too as well as in that of Odysseus—just as also in that of Menelaus.[1] So much, then, for the island of Aethalia.

7. But Cyrnus is by the Romans called Corsica. It affords such a poor livelihood—being not only rough but in most of its parts absolutely impracticable for travel—that those who occupy the mountains and live from brigandage are more savage than wild animals. At any rate, whenever the Roman generals have made a sally, and, falling suddenly upon the strongholds, have taken a large number of the people as slaves, you can at Rome see, and marvel at, the extent to which the nature of wild beasts, as also that of battening cattle, is manifested in them; for either they cannot endure to live in captivity, or, if they live, they so irritate their purchasers by their apathy and insensibility, that, even though the purchasers may have paid for them no more than an insignificant sum, nevertheless they repent the purchase. But still there are some habitable parts in the island, and what might be called towns, namely, Blesinon, Charax, Eniconiae and Vapanes.[2] The length of the island, says the Chorographer,[3] is one hundred and sixty miles, and the breadth seventy; but the length of Sardo is two hundred and twenty, and the breadth ninety-eight. According

and Braun (*Ursprung, Einrichtung und Bedeutung der Erdkarte Agrippas, ibid.*, Heft 17, pp. 22–35) practically establish that the "Map of Agrippa" is meant; but see E. Pais, *Ancient Italy*, trans. by Curtis, p. 385, and Sterrett's *Introduction* to the present work, p. xxvi, and Nissen's *Ital. Landeskunde*, I. p. 17.

κατ' ἄλλους δὲ Κύρνου μὲν περίμετρος περὶ τρισχιλίους[1] λέγεται καὶ διακοσίους σταδίους, τῆς δὲ
Σαρδόνος καὶ τετρακισχιλίους. ἔστι δὲ αὐτῆς τὸ
πολὺ μέρος τραχὺ καὶ οὐκ εἰρηναῖον, πολὺ δὲ καὶ
χώραν ἔχον εὐδαίμονα τοῖς πᾶσι, σίτῳ δὲ καὶ διαφερόντως. πόλεις δ' εἰσὶ μὲν πλείους, ἀξιόλογοι δὲ
C 225 Κάραλις καὶ Σοῦλχοι. τῇ δ' ἀρετῇ τῶν τόπων ἀντι-
τάττεταί τις καὶ μοχθηρία· νοσερὰ γὰρ ἡ νῆσος τοῦ
θέρους, καὶ μάλιστα ἐν τοῖς εὐκαρποῦσι χωρίοις·
τὰ δ' αὐτὰ ταῦτα καὶ πορθεῖται συνεχῶς ὑπὸ τῶν
ὀρείων οἳ καλοῦνται Διαγησβεῖς, Ἰολαεῖς πρότερον ὀνομαζόμενοι. λέγεται γὰρ Ἰόλαος ἄγων τῶν
παίδων τινὰς τοῦ Ἡρακλέους ἐλθεῖν δεῦρο καὶ
συνοικῆσαι τοῖς τὴν νῆσον ἔχουσι βαρβάροις
(Τυρρηνοὶ δ' ἦσαν)· ὕστερον δὲ Φοίνικες ἐπεκρά-
τησαν οἱ ἐκ Καρχηδόνος, καὶ μετὰ τούτων Ῥωμαίοις ἐπολέμουν· καταλυθέντων δὲ ἐκείνων, πάνθ'
ὑπὸ Ῥωμαίοις ὑπῆρξε. τέτταρα δ' ἐστὶ τῶν
ὀρείων ἔθνη, Πάρατοι, Σοσσινάτοι, Βάλαροι,
Ἀκώνιτες, ἐν σπηλαίοις οἰκοῦντες, εἰ δέ τινα
ἔχουσι γῆν σπόριμον, οὐδὲ ταύτην ἐπιμελῶς σπεί-
ροντες, ἀλλὰ τὰς[2] τῶν ἐργαζομένων καθαρπά-
ζοντες, τοῦτο μὲν τῶν αὐτόθι, τοῦτο δ' ἐπιπλέ-
οντες τοῖς ἐν τῇ περαίᾳ, Πισάταις μάλιστα. οἱ
δὲ πεμπόμενοι στρατηγοὶ τὰ μὲν ἀντέχουσι, πρὸς
ἃ δ' ἀπαυδῶσιν, ἐπειδὰν μὴ λυσιτελῇ τρέφειν
συνεχῶς ἐν τόποις νοσεροῖς στρατόπεδον, λείπεται

---

[1] τρισχιλίους, the reading of o and in margin of n; ABCl
read χιλίους, although B has β (δισχιλίους) in margin, second
hand.   [2] Cp. τὰς γᾶς, 2. 5. 26.

---

[1] The best MSS. read "one thousand."
[2] A name otherwise unknown.

to others, however, the perimeter of Cyrnus is called about three thousand[1] two hundred stadia, and of Sardo as much as four thousand. The greater part of Sardo is rugged and not at peace, though much of it has also soil that is blessed with all products—especially with grain. As for cities, there are indeed several, but only Caralis and Sulchi are noteworthy. But the excellence of the places is offset by a serious defect, for in summer the island is unhealthful, particularly in the fruitful districts; and it is precisely these districts that are continually ravaged by those mountaineers who are now called Diagesbes;[2] in earlier times, however, their name was Iolaës; for Iolaüs, it is said, came hither, bringing with him some of the children of Heracles, and took up his abode with the barbarians who held the island (the latter were Tyrrheni). Later on, the Phoenicians of Carthage got the mastery over them, and along with them carried on war against the Romans; but upon the defeat of the Phoenicians, everything became subject to the Romans. There are four tribes of the mountaineers, the Parati, the Sossinati, the Balari, and the Aconites, and they live in caverns; but if they do hold a bit of land that is fit for sowing, they do not sow even this diligently; instead, they pillage the lands of the farmers—not only of the farmers on the island, but they actually sail against the people on the opposite coast, the Pisatae in particular. Now the military governors who are sent to the island resist the mountaineers part of the time, but sometimes they grow weary of it—when it is not profitable continuously to maintain a camp in unhealthful places, and then the only thing left for them is to employ

δὴ[1] στρατηγεῖν τέχνας τινάς· καὶ δὴ τηρήσαντες
ἔθος τι τῶν βαρβάρων (πανηγυρίζουσι γὰρ ἐπὶ
πλείους ἡμέρας ἀπὸ τῆς λεηλασίας), ἐπιτίθενται
τότε καὶ χειροῦνται πολλούς. γίνονται δ᾽ ἐνταῦθα οἱ τρίχα φύοντες αἰγείαν ἀντ᾽ ἐρέας κριοί,
καλούμενοι δὲ μούσμωνες, ὧν ταῖς δοραῖς θωρακί-
ζονται. χρῶνται δὲ πέλτῃ καὶ ξιφιδίῳ.

8. Ἀπὸ πάσης δὲ τῆς μεταξὺ Ποπλωνίου καὶ
Πίσης ἱκανῶς αἱ νῆσοι κατοπτεύονται· ἐπιμήκεις
δ᾽ εἰσὶ καὶ παράλληλοι σχεδὸν αἱ τρεῖς, ἐπὶ νότον
καὶ Λιβύην τετραμμέναι· πολὺ μέντοι τῷ μεγέθει
λείπεται τῶν ἄλλων ἡ Αἰθαλία. ἀπό τε τῆς
Λιβύης τὸ ἐγγυτάτω δίαρμά φησιν ὁ χωρογράφος
εἰς τὴν Σαρδὼ μίλια τριακόσια.[2] μετὰ δὲ τὸ
Ποπλώνιον Κόσσαι πόλις μικρὸν ὑπὲρ τῆς θαλάτ-
της· ἔστι δ᾽ ἐν κόλπῳ βουνὸς ὑψηλός, ἐφ᾽ οὗ τὸ
κτίσμα· ὑπόκειται δ᾽ Ἡρακλέους λιμὴν καὶ πλησίον λιμνοθάλαττα καὶ παρὰ τὴν ἄκραν τὴν ὑπὲρ
τοῦ κόλπου θυννοσκοπεῖον. ἀκολουθεῖ γὰρ ὁ θύννος
οὐ τῇ βαλάνῳ μόνον, ἀλλὰ καὶ τῇ πορφύρᾳ παρὰ
γῆν, ἀρξάμενος ἀπὸ τῆς ἔξω θαλάττης μέχρι καὶ
Σικελίας. ἀπὸ δὲ τῶν Κοσσῶν εἰς Ὠστίαν παρα-
πλέουσι πολίχνιά ἐστι Γραουίσκοι καὶ Πύργοι
καὶ Ἄλσιον καὶ Φρεγήνα. εἰς μὲν δὴ Γραουί-
σκους στάδιοι τριακόσιοι, ἐν δὲ τῷ μεταξὺ τόπος

---

[1] δή (the reading of C), Jones, for δέ.
[2] Gosselin and Groskurd believe that Strabo wrote διακόσια;
see note 2 on opposite page.

---

[1] That is, "mouflons" (*Ovis musimon*); see Pliny 8. 75
(49), and 30. 52.

stratagems; and so, having observed a certain custom of the barbarians (who come together after their forays for a general celebration extending over several days), attack them at that time and over-power many of them. Again, Sardo produces the rams that grow goat-hair instead of wool; they are called, however, "musmones," [1] and it is with the hides of these that the people there make their cuirasses. They also use a small leather shield and a small dagger.

8. The islands can be seen clearly enough from any part of the country between Poplonium and Pisa; they are oblong and approximately parallel, all three of them, and they point towards the south and Libya; Aethalia, however, falls considerably short of the others in size. Further, the shortest passage to Sardo from Libya, according to the Chorographer, is three hundred miles.[2] After Pop-lonium comes Cossa, a city slightly above the sea; that is, there is a high hill at the head of a gulf, and the settlement is on this hill; and beneath lies the Harbour of Heracles and near it is a lagoon and, along the promontory that lies above the gulf, a station for observing the tunny-fish; for along the shore the tunny-fish follow not only the acorns but also the purple fish,[3] beginning their course at the outer sea and going even as far as Sicily.[4] As one sails along the coast from Cossa to Ostia one comes to some small towns: Gravisci, Pyrgi, Alsium and Fregena. To Gravisci, then, the distance is three hundred stadia;

---

[2] Strabo probably wrote *two* hundred miles (the distance given by Pliny, 3. 13).

[3] *Purpura murex.*   [4] See 3. 2. 7.

C 226 ἐστὶ καλούμενος Ῥηγισούιλλα· ἱστόρηται δὲ γενέσθαι τοῦτο βασίλειον Μάλεω τοῦ[1] Πελασγοῦ,
ὅν φασι δυναστεύσαντα ἐν τοῖς τόποις μετὰ τῶν
συνοίκων Πελασγῶν ἀπελθεῖν ἐνθένδε εἰς Ἀθήνας·
τούτου δ᾽ εἰσὶ τοῦ φύλου καὶ οἱ τὴν Ἄγυλλαν
κατεσχηκότες. ἀπὸ δὲ Γραουίσκων εἰς Πύργους
μικρὸν ἐλάττους τῶν ἑκατὸν ὀγδοήκοντα, ἔστι δ᾽
ἐπίνειον τῶν Καιρετανῶν ἀπὸ τριάκοντα σταδίων.
ἔχει δὲ Εἰληθυίας ἱερόν, Πελασγῶν ἵδρυμα, πλού-
σιόν ποτε γενόμενον, ἐσύλησε δ᾽ αὐτὸ Διονύσιος ὁ
τῶν Σικελιωτῶν τύραννος κατὰ τὸν πλοῦν τὸν ἐπὶ
Κύρνον. ἀπὸ δὲ τῶν Πύργων εἰς Ὠστίαν διακόσιοι ἑξήκοντα· ἐν δὲ τῷ μεταξὺ τὸ Ἄλσιον καὶ ἡ
Φρεγήνα. περὶ μὲν τῆς παραλίας τῆς Τυρρηνικῆς
ταῦτα.

9. Ἐν δὲ τῇ μεσογαίᾳ πόλεις πρὸς ταῖς εἰρη-
μέναις Ἀρρήτιόν τε καὶ Περουσία καὶ Οὐολσίνιοι
καὶ Σούτριον· πρὸς δὲ ταύταις πολίχναι συχναί,
Βλήρα τε καὶ Φερεντῖνον καὶ Φαλέριοι καὶ Φαλί-
σκον καὶ Νεπήτα καὶ Στατωνία καὶ ἄλλαι πλείους,
αἱ μὲν ἐξ ἀρχῆς συνεστῶσαι, τινὲς δὲ τῶν Ῥωμαίων οἰκισάντων ἢ ταπεινωσάντων, καθάπερ τοὺς
Οὐηίους πολεμήσαντας πολλάκις καὶ τὰς Φιδήνας.
ἔνιοι δ᾽ οὐ Τυρρηνούς φασι τοὺς Φαλερίους, ἀλλὰ
Φαλίσκους, ἴδιον ἔθνος· τινὲς δὲ καὶ τοὺς Φαλί-

---

[1] Μάλεω τοῦ, G. Hermann, for Μαλαιῶ τοῦ; so the later
editors.

---

[1] Cp. §§ 2-4 above.
[2] The goddess of child-birth.
[3] One of the "twelve" Tyrrhenian cities (cp. § 2. above).

and in the interval is a place called Regis Villa. History tells us that this was once the palace of Maleos, the Pelasgian, who, it is said, although he held dominion in the places mentioned, along with the Pelasgi who helped him to colonise them, departed thence to Athens. And this is also the stock to which the people belong who have taken and now hold Agylla.[1] Again, from Gravisci to Pyrgi the distance is a little less than one hundred and eighty stadia; it is the port-town of the Caeretani, thirty stadia away. And Pyrgi has a temple of Eilethyia,[2] an establishment of the Pelasgi; it was once rich, but it was robbed by Dionysius, the tyrant of the Sicilians, on his expedition to Cyrnus. And again, from Pyrgi to Ostia the distance is two hundred and sixty stadia; and in the interval are Alsium and Fregena. Thus much for the coastline of Tyrrhenia.

9. In the interior there are still other cities besides those already mentioned—Arretium, Perusia, Volsinii, and Sutrium; and, besides these, numerous small towns—Blera, Ferentinum, Falerii, Faliscum, Nepeta, Statonia, and several others; some of them are constituted as of old, while others the Romans have colonised, or else have brought low, as they did Veii,[3] which had oftentimes gone to war with them, and as they did Fidenae.[4] Some, however, call the Falerii, not "Tyrrheni," [5] but "Falisci," a special and distinct tribe; again, others call Faliscum a city with

---

It was captured and destroyed by Camillus in 395 B.C. after a siege of ten years. It then remained uninhabited until the end of the Republic; but it was colonised by Julius Caesar and also by Augustus.

[4] See 5. 3. 2; it was situated south of the Tiber.
[5] That is, not "Etruscans."

σκους πόλιν ἰδιόγλωσσον· οἱ δὲ Αἰκουουμφαλί-
σκον¹ λέγουσιν ἐπὶ τῇ Φλαμινίᾳ ὁδῷ κείμενον
μεταξὺ Ὀκρίκλων καὶ Ῥώμης. ὑπὸ δὲ τῷ Σω-
ράκτῳ ὄρει Φερωνία πόλις ἐστίν, ὁμώνυμος ἐπι-
χωρίᾳ τινὶ δαίμονι τιμωμένῃ σφόδρα ὑπὸ τῶν
περιοίκων, ἧς τέμενός ἐστιν ἐν τῷ τόπῳ θαυμαστὴν
ἱεροποιίαν ἔχον· γυμνοῖς γὰρ ποσὶ διεξίασιν ἀνθρα-
κιὰν καὶ σποδιὰν μεγάλην οἱ κατεχόμενοι ὑπὸ τῆς
δαίμονος ταύτης ἀπαθεῖς καὶ συνέρχεται πλῆθος
ἀνθρώπων ἅμα τῆς τε πανηγύρεως χάριν, ἣ συντελεῖται κατ' ἔτος, καὶ τῆς λεχθείσης θέας. μάλιστα δ' ἐστὶν ἐν μεσογαίᾳ τὸ Ἀρρήτιον πρὸς τοῖς
ὄρεσιν· ἀπέχει γοῦν τῆς Ῥώμης χιλίους καὶ διακοσίους σταδίους, τὸ δὲ Κλούσιον ὀκτακοσίους· ἐγγὺς
δὲ τούτων ἐστὶ καὶ ἡ Περουσία. προσλαμβάνουσι δὲ πρὸς τὴν εὐδαιμονίαν τῆς χώρας καὶ λίμναι,
μεγάλαι τε καὶ πολλαὶ οὖσαι· καὶ γὰρ πλέονται
καὶ τρέφουσιν ὄψον πολὺ καὶ τῶν πτηνῶν τὰ
λιμναῖα· τύφη τε καὶ πάπυρος ἀνθήλη τε πολλὴ
κατακομίζεται ποταμοῖς εἰς τὴν Ῥώμην, οὓς ἐκδι-
δόασιν αἱ λίμναι μέχρι τοῦ Τιβέρεως· ὧν ἐστιν
ἥ τε Κιμινία καὶ ἡ περὶ Οὐολσινίους καὶ ἡ περὶ

---

¹ Αἰκουουμφαλίσκον, Meineke, for Οἰακουσυμφαλίσκον.

¹ Literally, "Level Faliscum"; it was situated in the
plains, three miles from the old city.
² A few lines above, Strabo appears to have counted
"Falerii" and "Faliscum" as separate cities ; perhaps by
"Faliscum" he meant "Aequum Faliscum." The old city of
"Falerii" (or "Falerium") was occupied both by the Falerii
(a Tyrrhenian people) and by the Falisci (a people of Sabine
origin, perhaps, with a dialect closely akin to Latin) ; the
latter, however, inhabited a large tract of surrounding
country as well as the city itself The ancient writers
usually distinguished between the people "Falisci" and the

a special language all its own; and others mean by
Faliscum " Aequum Faliscum," [1] which is situated on
the Flaminian Way between Ocricli and Rome.[2]
The city of Feronia is at the foot of Mount Soracte,
with the same name as a certain native goddess, a
goddess greatly honoured by the surrounding peoples;
her sacred precinct is in the place; and it has remarkable ceremonies, for those who are possessed by
this goddess walk with bare feet through a great
heap of embers and ashes without suffering; [3] and a
multitude of people come together at the same time,
for the sake not only of attending the festal assembly,
which is held here every year, but also of seeing the
aforesaid sight. But Arretium, which is near the
mountains, is farthest of all in the interior; at any
rate, it is twelve hundred stadia distant from Rome,
while Clusium is only eight hundred; and Perusia
is near these two. The lakes, too, contribute to the
prosperity of Tyrrhenia, being both large and
numerous; for they are navigable, and also give
food to quantities of fish and to the various marsh-
birds; quantities of cat-tail, too, and papyrus, and
downy plumes of the reed, are transported by rivers
into Rome—rivers which are sent forth by the lakes
as far as the Tiber; and among these are the
Ciminian Lake,[4] the lake near Volsinii,[5] the lake near

city, but the city itself was often called "Falisci" (or
"Faliscum") as well as "Falerii." The site of the old city
is now occupied by Civita Castellana, while that of the new
Roman city, in the plains, is marked by the ruins of a church
called Santa Maria di Falleri; see *Encyc. Brit.* under "Falerii"
(Thomas Ashby) and "Falisci" (R. S. Conway).

[3] Cp. 12. 2. 7, and 15. 3. 14–15; also Pliny 7. 2, and Virgil
11. 785.

[4] Now Lake Vico.   [5] Now Lake Bolsena.

Κλούσιον καὶ ἡ ἐγγυτάτω τῆς Ῥώμης καὶ τῆς
θαλάττης Σαβάτα· ἀπωτάτω δὲ καὶ ἡ[1] πρὸς
Ἀρρητίῳ ἡ Τρασουμέννα, καθ᾽ ἢν αἱ ἐκ τῆς Κελτικῆς εἰς τὴν Τυρρηνίαν ἐκβολαὶ[2] στρατοπέδοις,
αἷσπερ[3] καὶ Ἀννίβας ἐχρήσατο, δυεῖν οὐσῶν,
ταύτης τε καὶ τῆς ἐπ᾽ Ἀριμίνου διὰ τῆς Ὀμβρικῆς. βελτίων μὲν οὖν ἡ ἐπ᾽ Ἀριμίνου· ταπεινοῦ-
C 227 ται γὰρ ἐνταῦθα ἱκανῶς τὰ ὄρη· φρουρουμένων δὲ
τῶν παρόδων τούτων ἐπιμελῶς, ἠναγκάσθη τὴν
χαλεπωτέραν ἑλέσθαι, καὶ ἐκράτησεν ὅμως νικήσας
μάχας μεγάλας Φλαμίνιον. πολλὴ δὲ καὶ
τῶν θερμῶν ὑδάτων ἀφθονία κατὰ τὴν Τυρρηνίαν,
ἃ[4] τῷ πλησίον εἶναι τῆς Ῥώμης οὐχ ἧττον[5]
εὐανδρεῖ τῶν ἐν Βαΐαις, ἃ διωνόμασται πολὺ
πάντων μάλιστα.

10. Τῇ δὲ Τυρρηνίᾳ παραβέβληται κατὰ τὸ
πρὸς ἔω μέρος ἡ Ὀμβρική, τὴν ἀρχὴν ἀπὸ τῶν
Ἀπεννίνων λαβοῦσα, καὶ ἔτι περαιτέρω μέχρι τοῦ
Ἀδρίου. ἀπὸ γὰρ δὴ Ῥαουέννης ἀρξάμενοι κατέ-
χουσιν οὗτοι τὸ πλησίον καὶ ἐφεξῆς Σάρσιναν,
Ἀρίμινον, Σήναν, Καμάρινον.[6] αὐτοῦ δ᾽ ἐστὶ καὶ

---

[1] ἡ, most of the editors bracket, following Kramer;
Meineke emends to δή.
[2] ἐκβολαί, the reading of all MSS., Jones restores. Kramer,
Meineke, Müller-Dübner, and others emend to εἰσβολαί.
[3] αἷσπερ, all editors, for οἷσπερ.
[4] ἃ, Jones inserts; Siebenkees and others insert ἅπερ, following conj. of Casaubon; Müller-Dübner insert τε after τῷ;
Meineke relegates τῷ . . . . . Ῥώμης to foot of page, regarding
it as a gloss.
[5] δ᾽, after ἧττον, Piccolo deletes: Müller-Dübner bracket.
[6] Καμάρινον (from correction in B), Jones for καὶ Μάρινον;
the editors before Kramer read καὶ Καμάρινον.

---

[1] Now Lake Chiusi.   [2] Now Lake Bracciano.

Clusium,[1] and the lake that is nearest Rome and the sea—Lake Sabata.[2] But the lake that is farthest away and that is near Arretium is Trasumenna,[3] near which is the pass by which an army may debouch into Tyrrhenia from Celtica,[4] the very pass which Hannibal used;[5] there are two, however, this one and the one towards Ariminum through Ombrica. Now the one towards Ariminum is better, since the mountains become considerably lower there; and yet, since the defiles on this pass were carefully guarded, Hannibal was forced to choose the more difficult pass, but, for all that, he got control of it, after having conquered Flaminius in great battles. Furthermore, there are abundant hot springs in Tyrrhenia, and, because of the fact that they are near Rome, they have a population not less than the springs at Baiae, which are by far the most widely renowned of all.[6]

10. Alongside Tyrrhenia, on the part toward the east, lies Ombrica;[7] it takes its beginning at the Apennines and extends still farther beyond as far as the Adriatic; for it is at Ravenna[8] that the Ombrici begin, and they occupy the nearby territory and also, in order thereafter, Sarsina, Ariminum, Sena, Camarinum.[9] Here, too, is the Aesis River,

[3] Now Lake Trasimene.   [4] *Cisalpine* Celtica, of course.
[5] Cp. 5. 1. 11.
[6] Cp 5. 2. 3, on the "Caeretanian Springs."
[7] Umbria.   [8] See 5. 1. 11.
[9] The better spelling is "Camerinum." But the MSS. (see note 6 on opposite page) read "and Marinum," which would seem to mean what is now San Marino; but this city appears not to have been founded until after A.D. 300 and its position does not suit the context here. Many of the editors, following Ortel, delete "and Marinum" as being an interpolation.

ὁ Αἶσις ποταμὸς καὶ τὸ Κιγγοῦλον ὄρος καὶ Σεντῖνον καὶ Μέταυρος ποταμὸς καὶ τὸ ἱερὸν τῆς Τύχης. περὶ γὰρ τούτους τοὺς τόπους ἐστὶ τὰ ὅρια τῆς Ἰταλίας τῆς πρότερον καὶ τῆς Κελτικῆς κατὰ τὸ πρὸς τῇ θαλάττῃ ταύτῃ μέρος, καίπερ μετατιθέντων πολλάκις τῶν ἡγεμόνων. πρότερον μέν γε τὸν Αἶσιν ἐποιοῦντο ὅριον, πάλιν δὲ τὸν Ῥουβίκωνα ποταμόν. ἔστι δ' ὁ μὲν Αἶσις μεταξὺ Ἀγκῶνος καὶ Σήνας, ὁ δὲ Ῥουβίκων μεταξὺ Ἀριμίνου καὶ Ῥαουέννης, ἄμφω δ' ἐκπίπτουσιν εἰς τὸν Ἀδρίαν. νυνὶ δὲ συμπάσης τῆς μέχρι Ἄλπεων ἀποδειχθείσης Ἰταλίας, τούτους μὲν τοὺς ὅρους ἐᾶν δεῖ· τὴν δ' Ὀμβρικὴν καθ' αὑτὴν[1] οὐδὲν ἧττον μέχρι καὶ Ῥαουέννης ὁμολογοῦσιν ἅπαντες διατείνειν· οἰκεῖται γὰρ ὑπὸ τούτων. εἰς μὲν δὴ Ἀρίμινον ἐνθένδε περὶ τριακοσίους φασίν, ἐκ δὲ Ἀριμίνου τὴν ἐπὶ Ῥώμης ἰόντι κατὰ τὴν Φλαμινίαν ὁδὸν διὰ τῆς Ὀμβρικῆς ἅπασα ἡ ὁδός ἐστι μέχρι Ὀκρίκλων καὶ τοῦ Τιβέρεως σταδίων πεντήκοντα καὶ τριακοσίων ἐπὶ τοῖς χιλίοις. τοῦτο μὲν δὴ μῆκος, τὸ δὲ πλάτος ἀνώμαλόν ἐστι. πόλεις δ' εἰσὶν αἱ ἐντὸς τῶν Ἀπεννίνων ὀρῶν ἄξιαι λόγου κατ' αὐτὴν μὲν τὴν Φλαμινίαν ὁδὸν οἵ τε Ὀκρίκλοι πρὸς τῷ Τιβέρει καὶ Λαρόλονι[2] καὶ Νάρνα, δι' ἧς ῥεῖ ὁ Νὰρ ποταμός, συμβάλλων τῷ Τιβέρει μικρὸν ὑπὲρ Ὀκρίκλων, πλωτὸς οὐ μεγάλοις σκάφεσιν· εἶτα

---

[1] αὐτήν, Meineke, for ἥν (others read ἑαυτήν).
[2] Λάρολον (B) and λάρονι (l).

---

[1] The Roman name of this city was "Fanum Fortunae."
[2] Cp 5. 1. 11.
[3] "Larolon" is otherwise unknown. It may have been the name of some stream that emptied into the Tiber near

and Mount Cingulum, and Sentinum, and the
Metaurus River, and the Temple of Fortune.[1] Indeed, it is near these places that the boundary
between the Italy of former days and Celtica
passed (I mean the boundary at the part next to
the Adriatic Sea), albeit the boundary has often
been changed by the rulers; at least they formerly
made the Aesis the boundary and then in turn the
Rubicon.[2] The Aesis is between Ancona and Sena,
the Rubicon between Ariminum and Ravenna, and
both empty into the Adriatic. But as it is, now
that the whole of the country as far as the Alps has
been designated Italy, we should disregard these
boundaries, but none the less agree, as is agreed by
all, that Ombrica, properly so-called, extends all the
way to Ravenna; for Ravenna is inhabited by these
people. From Ravenna, then, to Ariminum the
distance is, they say, about three hundred stadia;
and if you travel from Ariminum toward Rome
along the Flaminian Way through Ombrica your
whole journey, as far as Ocricli and the Tiber, is
thirteen hundred and fifty stadia. This, then, is
the length of Ombrica, but the breadth is uneven.
The cities this side the Apennine Mountains that
are worthy of mention are: first, on the Flaminian
Way itself: Ocricli, near the Tiber and Larolon,[3]
and Narna,[4] through which the Nar River flows (it
meets the Tiber a little above Ocricli, and is
navigable, though only for small boats); then,

Ocricli, as Cluvier conjectures. The reading of one manu-
script (see note on the opposite page) means a city by the
name of "Larolum"; but this reading seems more hopeless
than the other.
    [4] That is, Narnia; now Narni.

Κάρσουλοι καὶ Μηουανία, παρ' ἣν ῥεῖ ὁ Τενέας,
καὶ οὗτος ἐλάττοσι σκάφεσι κατάγων ἐπὶ τὸν
Τίβεριν τὰ ἐκ τοῦ πεδίου· καὶ ἄλλαι δ' εἰσὶ κατοικίαι διὰ τὴν ὁδὸν πληθυνόμεναι μᾶλλον ἢ διὰ
πολιτικὸν σύστημα, Φόρον Φλαμίνιον καὶ Νουκερία, ἡ τὰ ξύλινα ἀγγεῖα ἐργαζομένη, καὶ Φόρον
Σεμπρώνιον· ἐν δεξιᾷ δὲ τῆς ὁδοῦ βαδίζοντι ἐκ
τῶν Ὀκρίκλων εἰς Ἀρίμινον Ἰντέραμνά ἐστι καὶ
Σπολήτιον καὶ Αἴσιον καὶ Καμέρτης, ἐν αὐτοῖς
τοῖς ὁρίζουσι τὴν Πικεντίνην ὄρεσι. κατὰ δὲ θάτερα μέρη Ἀμερία τε καὶ Τοῦδερ, εὐερκὴς[1] πόλις,
καὶ Ἰσπέλλον[2] καὶ Ἰγούιον,[3] πλησίον τοῦτο ἤδη
C 228 τῶν ὑπερβολῶν τοῦ ὄρους. ἅπασα δ' εὐδαίμων
ἡ χώρα, μικρῷ δ' ὀρεινοτέρα, ζειᾷ μᾶλλον ἢ πυρῷ
τοὺς ἀνθρώπους τρέφουσα· ὀρεινὴ δὲ καὶ ἡ Σαβίνη
ἐφεξῆς οὖσα ταύτῃ, παραβεβλημένη τὸν αὐτὸν
τρόπον, ὅνπερ αὕτη τῇ Τυρρηνικῇ· καὶ τῆς Λατίνης δὲ ὅσα πλησιάζει τούτοις τε καὶ τοῖς Ἀπεννίνοις ὄρεσι τραχύτερά ἐστιν. ἄρχεται μὲν οὖν
τὰ δύο[4] ἔθνη ταῦτα ἀπὸ τοῦ Τιβέρεως καὶ τῆς
Τυρρηνίας, ἐκτείνεται δὲ ἐπὶ τὰ Ἀπέννινα ὄρη πρὸς
τῷ Ἀδρίᾳ λοξὰ παρεμβάλλοντα, ἡ δὲ Ὀμβρικὴ
καὶ παραλλάττουσα, ὡς εἴρηται, μέχρι τῆς θαλάττης. περὶ μὲν οὖν τῶν Ὀμβρικῶν εἴρηται.

---

[1] εὐερκής, Casaubon, for εὔελκις; so the later editors.
[2] Ἰσπέλλον (as in Ptolemaeus 3. 1. 47), Jones, for Εἰσπέλλον.
[3] Ἰγυίνν, Groskurd, for Ἴτουρον; so the later editors.
[4] δύο, Casaubon, for δέκα; so the later editors.

[1] That is, Carsulae (now Capella San Damiano), not
Carsioli.
[2] That is, Camerinum; the inhabitants of Camerinum
were often called "Camertes," and the name of the people,
as often, is applied to the city itself.

Carsuli,[1] and Mevania, past which flows the Teneas
(this too brings the products of the plain down to
the Tiber on rather small boats); and, besides,
still other settlements, which have become filled up
with people rather on account of the Way itself
than of political organisation; these are Forum
Flaminium, and Nuceria (the place where the
wooden utensils are made), and Forum Sempronium.
Secondly, to the right of the Way, as you travel
from Ocricli to Ariminum, is Interamna, and Spole-
tium, and Aesium, and Camertes [2] (in the very
mountains that mark the boundary of the Picentine
country); [3] and, on the other side of the Way,
Ameria, and Tuder (a well-fortified city), and His-
pellum, and Iguvium, the last-named lying near
the passes that lead over the mountain. Now as a
whole Ombrica is blessed with fertility, though it is
a little too mountainous and nourishes its people
with spelt rather than with wheat. The Sabine
country also, which comes next in order after
Ombrica, is mountainous, and it lies alongside
Ombrica in the same way that Ombrica lies alongside Tyrrhenia; and further, all parts of the Latin
country that are near to these parts and to the
Apennine Mountains are rather rugged. These
two tribes [4] begin, then, at the Tiber and Tyrrhenia,
and extend to that stretch of the Apennine Mountains near the Adriatic which slants slightly inland,[5]
although Ombrica passes on beyond the mountains,
as I have said,[6] as far as the Adriatic. So much,
then, for the Ombrici.

[3] Picenum.   [4] The Ombrici and the Sabini.
[5] The slant begins opposite Ariminum (see 5. 1. 3).
[6] 5. 2. 1.

III

1. Σαβῖνοι δὲ στενὴν οἰκοῦσι χώραν, ἐπὶ μῆκος δὲ διήκουσαν καὶ χιλίων σταδίων ἀπὸ τοῦ Τιβέρεως καὶ Νωμέντου πολίχνης μέχρις Οὐηστίνων. πόλεις δ᾿ ἔχουσιν ὀλίγας καὶ τεταπεινωμένας διὰ τοὺς συνεχεῖς πολέμους, Ἀμίτερνον καὶ Ῥεάτε, ᾧ πλησιάζει κώμη Ἰντεροκρέα καὶ τὰ ἐν Κωτιλίαις[1] ψυχρὰ ὕδατα, ἀφ᾿ ὧν καὶ πίνουσι καὶ ἐγκαθίζοντες θεραπεύονται νόσους. Σαβίνων δ᾿ εἰσὶ καὶ οἱ Φόρουλοι, πέτραι πρὸς ἀπόστασιν μᾶλλον ἢ κατοικίαν εὐφυεῖς. Κύρης δὲ νῦν μὲν κωμίον ἐστίν, ἣν δὲ πόλις ἐπίσημος, ἐξ ἧς ὥρμηντο οἱ τῆς Ῥώμης βασιλεύσαντες, Τίτος Τάτιος καὶ Νουμᾶς Πομπίλιος· ἐντεῦθεν δὲ καὶ Κυρίτας ὀνομάζουσιν οἱ δημηγοροῦντες τοὺς Ῥωμαίους. Τρήβουλά τε καὶ Ἠρητὸν καὶ ἄλλαι κατοικίαι τοιαῦται κῶμαι μᾶλλον ἢ πόλεις ἐξετάζοιντ᾿ ἄν. ἅπασα δ᾿ αὐτῶν ἡ γῆ διαφερόντως ἐλαιόφυτός ἐστι καὶ ἀμπελόφυτος, βάλανόν τε ἐκφέρει πολλήν· σπουδαία δὲ καὶ βοσκήμασι τοῖς τε ἄλλοις, καὶ δὴ τὸ τῶν ἡμιόνων γένος τῶν Ῥεατίνων διωνόμασται θαυμαστῶς. ὡς δ᾿ εἰπεῖν, ἅπασα ἡ Ἰταλία θρεμμάτων τε ἀρίστη τροφὸς καὶ καρπῶν ἐστιν, ἄλλα δ᾿ εἴδη κατὰ ἄλλα μέρη τῶν πρωτείων τυγχάνει. ἔστι δὲ καὶ πα-

---

[1] Κωτιλίαις, Casaubon, for Κωτισκολίαις; so the later editors.

---

[1] The Latin form of the word is Cutiliae.

III

1. The country the Sabini live in is narrow, but taken lengthwise it reaches even a thousand stadia from the Tiber and the little town of Nomentum, as far as the country of the Vestini. They have but few cities and even these have been brought low on account of the continual wars; they are Amiternum, and Reate (near which is the village of Interocrea, and also the cold springs of Cotiliae,[1] where people cure their diseases,[2] not only by drinking from the springs but also by sitting down in them). Foruli[3] too belongs to the Sabini—a rocky elevation naturally suited to the purposes of revolt rather than habitation. As for Cures, it is now only a small village, but it was once a city of significance, since it was the original home of two kings of Rome, Titius Tatius and Numa Pompilius; hence, the title "Curites"[4] by which the public orators address the Romans. Trebula, Eretum, and other such settlements might be ranked as villages rather than cities. As a whole the land of the Sabini is exceptionally well-planted with the olive and the vine, and it also produces acorns in quantities; it is important, also, for its domestic cattle of every kind; and in particular the fame of the Reate-breed of mules is remarkably widespread. In a word, Italy as a whole is an excellent nurse both of young animals and of fruits, although different species in different parts take the first prize. The

[2] Pliny says these waters are drunk as a purgative (31. 32; cp. 31 6).
[3] Now Civita Tommasa.
[4] In Latin, "Quirites."

λαιότατον γένος οἱ Σαβῖνοι καὶ οἱ[1] αὐτόχθονες·
τούτων δ' ἄποικοι Πικεντῖνοί τε καὶ Σαυνῖται, τούτων δὲ Λευκανοί, τούτων δὲ Βρέττιοι· τὴν δ'
ἀρχαιότητα[2] τεκμήριον ἄν τις ποιήσαιτο ἀνδρείας
καὶ τῆς ἄλλης ἀρετῆς[3] ἀφ' ἧς ἀντέσχον μέχρι
πρὸς τὸν παρόντα χρόνον. φησὶ δ' ὁ συγγραφεὺς
Φάβιος Ῥωμαίους αἰσθέσθαι τοῦ πλούτου τότε
πρῶτον, ὅτε τοῦ ἔθνους τούτου κατέστησαν κύριοι.
ἔστρωται δὲ δι' αὐτῶν ἥ τε[4] Σαλαρία ὁδὸς οὐ
πολλὴ οὖσα, εἰς ἣν καὶ ἡ Νωμεντανὴ συμπίπτει
κατὰ Ἡρητόν, τῆς Σαβίνης κώμην ὑπὲρ τοῦ Τιβέρεως κειμένην, ὑπὲρ[5] τῆς αὐτῆς πύλης ἀρχομένη
τῆς Κολλίνης.

2. Ἑξῆς δ' ἡ Λατίνη κεῖται, ἐν ᾗ καὶ ἡ τῶν
Ῥωμαίων πόλις, πολλὰς συνειληφυῖα καὶ τῆς μὴ

[1] οἱ, Meineke deletes.
[2] τὴν δ' ἀρχαιότητα, Groskurd, Kramer, and Müller-Dübner
suspect, thinking Strabo wrote genitive case.
[3] ἀνδρείας . . . ἀρετῆς, Groskurd and Kramer would emend
to acc. case.
[4] τε, Corais stars; Meineke deletes; wrongly.
[5] For ὑπέρ, Corais reads ἀπό; so the later editors. ὑπέρ is
not at all objectionable; it does not deny the fact that the
Via Salaria begins at the gate.

---

[1] See 5. 4. 2.   [2] See 6. 1. 2.
[3] Bruttii.   [4] See 6. 1. 4.
[5] The old-fashioned simplicity and sternness of the Sabine
race was proverbial (see 4. 2. 12, Martial's Epigrams 10. 32,
11. 15, Horace's Odes 3. 6. 38, Epistles 2. 1. 25, Ovid's Meta-
morphoses 14. 797). And because of these qualities they were
by some writers regarded as having originally come from
Laconia (Dionysius Hal., Antiq. Rom., 1. 1, Justinius 20 1).
Others, by emending six words of the text (see critical notes
2 and 3 above) make Strabo say: "And the bravery and

Sabini not only are a very ancient race but are also the indigenous inhabitants (and both the Picentini and the Samnitae are colonists from the Sabini,[1] and the Leucani from the Samnitae,[2] and the Brettii[3] from the Leucani).[4] And the old-fashioned ways of the Sabini might be taken as an evidence of bravery, and of those other excellent qualities which have enabled them to hold out to the present time.[5] Fabius, the historian, says that the Romans realised their wealth for the first time when they became established as masters of this tribe. As for the roads that have been constructed through their country, there is not only the Via Salaria (though it does not run far) but also the Via Nomentana which unites with it at Eretum[6] (a village of the Sabine country, situated beyond the Tiber), though it begins above the same gate, Porta Collina.[7]

2. Next comes the Latin country, in which the city of the Romans is situated, though it now comprises also many cities of what was formerly non-

those other excellent qualities which have enabled them to hold out to the present time might be taken as an evidence of their antiquity."

[6] Augustus extended the highway to the Adriatic in 17 B.C. Strabo seems to avoid applying either "Via Salaria" or "Via Nomentana" to the extension of the road, although obviously he has in mind the entire journey, as "through their country" shows. There seems to be no evidence in the ancient writers for the assumption of Kramer that "Via Salaria" applied to the whole journey; and the clause "though it does not run far," which he believes should be placed after "Via Nomentana," denies it. Here, as often, Strabo's conciseness has caused the commentators no little worry.

[7] The Porta Collina was the gate of the Servian wall at the north-eastern end of the Quirinal.

Λατίνης πρότερον. Αἶκοι γὰρ καὶ Οὐόλσκοι καὶ
Ἕρνικοι Ἀβοριγῖνές τε οἱ περὶ αὐτὴν τὴν Ῥώμην
καὶ Ῥουτοῦλοι οἱ τὴν ἀρχαίαν Ἀρδέαν ἔχοντες
C 229 καὶ ἄλλα συστήματα μείζω καὶ ἐλάττω τὰ περι-
οικοῦντα τοὺς τότε Ῥωμαίους ὑπῆρξαν, ἡνίκα
πρῶτον ἔκτιστο ἡ πόλις· ὧν ἔνια κατὰ κώμας
αὐτονομεῖσθαι συνέβαινεν, ὑπ' οὐδενὶ κοινῷ φύλῳ
τεταγμένα. φασὶ δὲ Αἰνείαν μετὰ τοῦ πατρὸς
Ἀγχίσου καὶ τοῦ παιδὸς Ἀσκανίου κατάραντας
εἰς Λαύρεντον τῆς πλησίον τῶν Ὠστίων καὶ τοῦ
Τιβέρεως ἠιόνος, μικρὸν ὑπὲρ τῆς θαλάττης, ὅσον
ἐν τέτταρσι καὶ εἴκοσι σταδίοις, κτίσαι πόλιν·
ἐπελθόντα δὲ Λατῖνον τὸν τῶν Ἀβοριγίνων βασι-
λέα τῶν οἰκούντων τὸν τόπον τοῦτον ὅπου νῦν ἡ
Ῥώμη ἐστί, συμμάχοις χρήσασθαι τοῖς περὶ τὸν
Αἰνείαν ἐπὶ τοὺς γειτονεύοντας Ῥουτούλους τοὺς
Ἀρδέαν κατέχοντας στάδιοι δ' εἰσὶν ἀπὸ τῆς
Ἀρδέας εἰς τὴν Ῥώμην ἑκατὸν ἑξήκοντα), νικήσαντα δ' ἀπὸ τῆς θυγατρὸς Λαουινίας ἐπώνυμον
κτίσαι πλησίον πολιν· πάλιν δὲ τῶν Ῥουτούλων
συμβαλόντων εἰς μάχην, τὸν μὲν Λατῖνον πεσεῖν,
τὸν δὲ Αἰνείαν νικήσαντα βασιλεῦσαι καὶ Λατίνους καλέσαι τοὺς ὑφ' αὑτῷ. καὶ τούτου δὲ τελευτήσαντος καὶ τοῦ πατρός, τὸν Ἀσκάνιον Ἄλβαν
κτίσαι ἐν τῷ Ἀλβάνῳ ὄρει, διέχοντι τῆς Ῥώμης
τοσοῦτον, ὅσον καὶ ἡ Ἀρδέα. ἐνταῦθα Ῥωμαῖοι
σὺν τοῖς Λατίνοις Διὶ θύουσιν, ἅπασα ἡ συν-
αρχία ἀθροισθεῖσα· τῇ πόλει δ' ἐφίστησιν[1] ἄρ-
χοντα πρὸς τὸν τῆς θυσίας χρόνον τῶν γνωρίμων
τινὰ νέων. ὕστερον δὲ τετρακοσίοις ἔτεσιν ἱστο-

[1] ἐφίστησιν, the reading of the MSS., Jones restores.
Groskurd and the later editors read ἐφιστᾶσιν.

Latin country. For the Aeci,[1] the Volsci, the Hernici, and also the aborigines who lived near Rome itself, the Rutuli who held the old Ardea, and other groups, greater or less, who lived near the Romans of that time, were all in existence when the city was first founded; and some of these groups, since they were ranked under no common tribe, used to be allowed to live autonomously in separate villages. It is said that Aeneas, along with his father Anchises and his son Ascanius, after putting in at Laurentum, which was on the shore near Ostia and the Tiber, founded a city a little above the sea, within about twenty-four stadia from it; and Latinus, the king of the aborigines, who lived in this place where Rome now is, on making them a visit, used Aeneas and his people as allies against the neighbouring Rutuli who occupied Ardea (the distance from Ardea to Rome is one hundred and sixty stadia), and after his victory founded a city near by, naming it after his daughter Lavinia; and when the Rutuli joined battle again, Latinus fell, but Aeneas was victorious, became king, and called his subjects "Latini"; and after the death of both Aeneas and his father Anchises, Ascanius founded Alba on Mount Albanus, which Mount is the same distance from Rome as Ardea. Here the Romans in company with the Latini—I mean the joint assembly of all their magistrates— offered sacrifice to Zeus; and the assembly put one of the young nobles in charge of the city as governor for the time of the sacrifice. But it is four hundred

[1] The proper Latin spelling is "Aequi"; and so Strabo himself spells the word in 5. 3. 4.

STRABO

ρεῖται τὰ περὶ Ἀμόλλιον καὶ τὸν ἀδελφὸν Νουμίτορα, τὰ μὲν μυθώδη, τὰ δ' ἐγγυτέρω πίστεως.
διεδέξαντο μὲν γὰρ τὴν τῆς Ἄλβας ἀρχὴν ἀμφότεροι παρὰ τῶν ἀπογόνων τοῦ Ἀσκανίου, διατεί-
νουσαν μέχρι τοῦ Τιβέρεως· παραγκωνισάμενος
δ' ὁ νεώτερος τὸν πρεσβύτερον ἦρχεν ὁ Ἀμόλλιος,
υἱοῦ δ' ὄντος καὶ θυγατρὸς τῷ Νουμίτορι, τὸν μὲν
ἐν κυνηγίᾳ δολοφονεῖ, τὴν δέ, ἵνα ἄτεκνος διαμείνῃ,
τῆς Ἑστίας ἱέρειαν κατέστησε, παρθενείας χάριν·
καλοῦσι δ' αὐτὴν Ῥέαν Σιλβίαν·[1] εἶτα φθορὰν
φωράσας, διδύμων αὐτῇ παίδων γενομένων, τὴν
μὲν εἶρξεν[2] ἀντὶ τοῦ κτείνειν, χαριζόμενος τἀδελ-
φῷ, τοὺς δ' ἐξέθηκε πρὸς τὸν Τίβεριν κατά τι
πάτριον. μυθεύεται[3] μὲν οὖν ἐξ Ἄρεως γενέσθαι
τοὺς παῖδας, ἐκτεθέντας δ' ὑπὸ λυκαίνης ὁραθῆναι
σκυλακευομένους· Φαυστύλον δέ τινα τῶν περὶ
τὸν τόπον συφορβῶν ἀνελόμενον ἐκθρέψαι (δεῖ δ'
ὑπολαβεῖν τῶν δυνατῶν τινα, ὑπηκόων δὲ τῷ
Ἀμολλίῳ, λαβόντα ἐκθρέψαι), καλέσαι δὲ τὸν μὲν
Ῥωμύλον, τὸν δὲ Ῥῶμον.[4] ἀνδρωθέντας δ' ἐπιθέ-
σθαι τῷ Ἀμολλίῳ καὶ τοῖς παισί, καταλυθέντων
δ' ἐκείνων καὶ τῆς ἀρχῆς εἰς τὸν Νουμίτορα περι-
στάσης, ἀπελθόντας οἴκαδε κτίσαι τὴν Ῥώμην
ἐν τόποις οὐ πρὸς αἵρεσιν μᾶλλον ἢ πρὸς ἀνάγκην

[1] Σιλβίαν, the reading of ABC*l* (so Meineke); the *Epit.* has
Σιλουίαν.
[2] εἶρξεν, Corais, for ἦρξεν; so the later editors.
[3] μυθεύεται, Meineke following Spengel, for μυθεύονται.
[4] Kramer finds the form Ῥέμον in the *Epit.* and so reads;
so Müller-Dübner. But ABC*l* read Ῥῶμον (cp. the reading
Ῥέμον a few lines later on).

years later that the stories about Amollius [1] and his brother Numitor are placed — stories partly fabulous but partly closer to the truth. In the first place, both brothers succeeded to the rule of Alba (which extended as far as the Tiber) from the descendants of Ascanius; but Amollius, the younger, elbowed the elder out and reigned alone; but since Numitor had a son and a daughter, Amollius treacherously murdered the son while on a hunt, and appointed the daughter, in order that she might remain childless, a priestess of Vesta, so as to keep her a virgin (she is called Rhea Silvia); then, on discovering that she had been ruined (for she gave birth to twins), instead of killing her, he merely incarcerated her, to gratify his brother, and exposed the twins on the banks of the Tiber in accordance with an ancestral custom. In mythology, however, we are told that the boys were begotten by Ares, and that after they were exposed people saw them being suckled by a she-wolf; but Faustulus, one of the swineherds near the place, took them up and reared them (but we must assume that it was some influential man, a subject of Amollius, that took them and reared them), and called one Romulus and the other Romus; [2] and upon reaching manhood they attacked Amollius and his sons, and upon the defeat of the latter and the reversion of the rule to Numitor, they went back home and founded Rome —in a place which was suitable more as a matter

---

[1] The Latin spelling is "Amulius."

[2] The best MSS. here read "Romus," not Remus, though the reverse is true in the use of the word later on; yet note that Strabo is now quoting the mythical version of the story.

C 230 ἐπιτηδείοις· οὔτε γὰρ ἐρυμνὸν τὸ ἔδαφος οὔτε χώραν οἰκείαν ἔχον τὴν πέριξ ὅση πόλει πρόσφορος, ἀλλ' οὐδ' ἀνθρώπους τοὺς συνοικήσοντας· οἱ γὰρ ὄντες ᾤκουν καθ' αὑτούς,[1] συνάπτοντές πως[2] τοῖς τεί- χεσι τῆς κτιζομένης πόλεως, οὐδὲ τοῖς 'Αλβανοῖς πάνυ προσέχοντες. Κολλατία δ' ἦν καὶ 'Αντέμναι καὶ Φιδῆναι καὶ Λαβικὸν καὶ ἄλλα τοιαῦτα τότε μὲν πολίχνια, νῦν δὲ κῶμαι, ἢ[3] κτήσεις ἰδιωτῶν, ἀπὸ τριάκοντα ἢ[4] μικρῷ πλειόνων τῆς 'Ρώμης σταδίων. μεταξὺ γοῦν τοῦ πέμπτου καὶ τοῦ ἕκτου λίθου τῶν τὰ μίλια διασημαινόντων τῆς 'Ρώμης καλεῖται τόπος Φῆστοι. τοῦτον δ' ὅριον ἀποφαίνουσι τῆς τότε 'Ρωμαίων γῆς, οἵ θ' ἱερομνήμονες θυσίαν ἐπιτε- λοῦσιν ἐνταῦθά τε καὶ ἐν ἄλλοις τόποις πλείοσιν ὡς ὁρίοις αὐθημερόν, ἣν καλοῦσιν 'Αμβαρουίαν. γενομένης δ' οὖν στάσεώς φασι κατὰ τὴν κτίσιν ἀναιρεθῆναι τὸν 'Ρέμον.[5] μετὰ δὲ τὴν κτίσιν ἀνθρώπους σύγκλυδας ὁ 'Ρωμύλος ἤθροιζεν, ἀπο- δείξας ἄσυλόν τι τέμενος μεταξὺ τῆς ἄκρας καὶ τοῦ Καπετωλίου, τοὺς δ' ἐκεῖ καταφεύγοντας τῶν

---

[1] MS. A is lacking from αὑτούς to τούτοις near end of paragraph 5. 4. 3, a whole quaternion being lost.
[2] πως, Letronne, for πρός ; so the later editors.
[3] ἤ, before κτήσεις, Jones inserts.
[4] τεσσαράκοντα (μ') after ἤ, Corais deletes ; so Meineke.
[5] The reading of BCl is πρένιον ('ρῶμον sec. hand. in B) ; Meineke reads 'Ρῶμον both here and in preceding instance.

---

[1] See 5. 3. 7. [2] See 5. 3. 7. on this point.
[3] Strabo almost certainly means the " Arvales Fratres " ("Field-Brothers"), so-called, according to Varro (De Ling. Lat. 5. 85), from their offering public sacrifices that the fields (arva) may bring forth fruits. The " Arvales Fratres " was a college of twelve priests, which, according to Roman legend (cp. Gellius 7. 7), originated with Romulus himself. The college was still in existence in A.D. 325.

of necessity than of choice;[1] for neither was the site naturally strong, nor did it have enough land of its own in the surrounding territory to meet the requirements of a city,[2] nor yet, indeed, people to join with the Romans as inhabitants; for the people who lived thereabouts were wont to dwell by themselves (though their territory almost joined the walls of the city that was being founded), not even paying any attention to the Albani themselves. And there was Collatia, and Antemnae, and Fidenae, and Labicum, and other such places—then little cities, but now mere villages, or else estates of private citizens—all at a distance from Rome of thirty stadia, or a little more. At any rate, between the fifth and the sixth of those stones which indicate the miles from Rome there is a place called "Festi," and this, it is declared, is a boundary of what was then the Roman territory; and, further, the priests[3] celebrate sacrificial festivals, called "Ambarvia,"[4] on the same day, both there and at several other places, as being boundaries. Be this as it may, a quarrel arose at the time of the founding of the city, and as a result Remus was slain.[5] After the founding Romulus set about collecting a promiscuous rabble by designating as an asylum a sacred precinct between the Arx and the Capitolium,[6] and by declaring citizens all the neighbours who fled

[4] In Latin, "Ambarvalia"; so called from the leading of the sacrificial victims "round the fields." The festival took place May 27, 29 and 30 (Roman calendar).

[5] Cp. Livy 1. 7.

[6] The northern and southern summits, respectively, of the Capitoline Hill. The depression between the two summits (each in early times covered by a grove) was called "Inter Duos Lucos" (cp. Livy 1. 8), and was the traditional site of "The Asylum of Romulus."

ἀστυγειτόνων πολίτας ἀποφαίνων. ἐπιγαμίας δὲ
τούτοις οὐ τυγχάνων ἐπηγγείλατο ἕνα ἀγῶνα ἱπ-
πικὸν τοῦ Ποσειδῶνος ἱερόν, τὸν καὶ νῦν ἐπιτε-
λούμενον. συνελθόντων δὲ πολλῶν, πλείστων δὲ
Σαβίνων, ἐκέλευσε τὰς παρθένους ἁρπάσαι τὰς
ἀφιγμένας τοῖς δεομένοις γάμου· μετιὼν δὲ τὴν
ὕβριν Τίτος Τάτιος δι' ὅπλων, ὁ βασιλεὺς τῶν
Κυριτῶν, ἐπὶ κοινωνίᾳ τῆς ἀρχῆς καὶ πολιτείας[1]
συνέβη πρὸς τὸν Ῥωμύλον· δολοφονηθέντος δ' ἐν
Λαουινίῳ τοῦ Τατίου, μόνος ἦρξεν ἑκόντων τῶν
Κυριτῶν ὁ Ῥωμύλος. μετὰ δὲ τοῦτον διεδέξατο
τὴν ἀρχὴν Νουμᾶς Πομπίλιος, πολίτης τοῦ Τατίου, παρ' ἑκόντων λαβὼν τῶν ὑπηκόων. αὕτη
μὲν οὖν ἡ μάλιστα πιστευομένη τῆς Ῥώμης κτίσις
ἐστίν.

3. Ἄλλη δέ τις προτέρα καὶ μυθώδης, Ἀρκαδι-
κὴν λέγουσα γενέσθαι τὴν ἀποικίαν ὑπ' Εὐάνδρου·
τούτῳ δ' ἐπιξενωθῆναι τὸν Ἡρακλέα, ἐλαύνοντα
τὰς Γηρυόνου βοῦς· πυθόμενον δὲ τῆς μητρὸς
Νικοστράτης τὸν Εὔανδρον (εἶναι δ' αὐτὴν μαντι-
κῆς ἔμπειρον) ὅτι τῷ Ἡρακλεῖ πεπρωμένον ἦν
τελέσαντι τοὺς ἄθλους θεῷ γενέσθαι, φράσαι τε
πρὸς τὸν Ἡρακλέα ταῦτα, καὶ τέμενος ἀναδεῖξαι
καὶ θῦσαι θυσίαν Ἑλληνικήν, ἣν καὶ νῦν ἔτι
φυλάττεσθαι τῷ Ἡρακλεῖ. καὶ ὅ γε Κοίλιος,[2]
ὁ τῶν Ῥωμαίων συγγραφεύς, τοῦτο τίθεται σημεῖον
τοῦ Ἑλληνικὸν εἶναι κτίσμα τὴν Ῥώμην, τὸ παρ'
αὑτῇ τὴν πάτριον θυσίαν Ἑλληνικὴν εἶναι τῷ
Ἡρακλεῖ. καὶ τὴν μητέρα δὲ τοῦ Εὐάνδρου

---

[1] πολιτείας, the *Epit.*, for πολιτείᾳ; so Kramer and later editors.

[2] Κοίλιος, Kramer, for Κύλιος; so the later editors.

thither for refuge. But since he could not obtain the right of intermarriage for these, he announced one horse-race, sacred to Poseidon, the rite that is still to-day performed ; and when numerous people, but mostly Sabini, had assembled, he bade all who wanted a wife to seize the maidens who had come to the race. Titus Tatius, the king of the Curites, went to avenge [1] the outrage by force of arms, but compromised with Romulus on the basis of partnership in the throne and state. But Tatius was treacherously murdered in Lavinium, and then Romulus, with the consent of the Curites, reigned alone. After Romulus, Numa Pompilius, a fellow-citizen of Tatius, succeeded to the throne, receiving it from his subjects by their own choice. This, then, is the best accredited story of the founding of Rome.

3. But there is another one, older and fabulous, in which we are told that Rome was an Arcadian colony and founded by Evander :—When Heracles was driving the cattle of Geryon he was entertained by Evander ; and since Evander had learned from his mother Nicostrate (she was skilled in the art of divination, the story goes) that Heracles was destined to become a god after he had finished his labours, he not only told this to Heracles but also consecrated to him a precinct and offered a sacrifice to him after the Greek ritual, which is still to this day kept up in honour of Heracles. And Coelius himself,[2] the Roman historian, puts this down as proof that Rome was founded by Greeks—the fact that at Rome the hereditary sacrifice to Heracles is after the Greek ritual. And the Romans honour also the

---

[1] Cp. 5. 3. 7.   [2] Lucius Coelius Antipater.

τιμῶσι Ῥωμαῖοι, μίαν τῶν νυμφῶν νομίσαντες,
Καρμέντιν[1] μετονομασθεῖσαν.

4. Οἱ δ᾽ οὖν Λατῖνοι κατ᾽ ἀρχὰς μὲν ἦσαν ὀλίγοι,
καὶ οἱ πλείους οὐ προσεῖχον Ῥωμαίοις· ὕστερον
δὲ καταπλαγέντες τὴν ἀρετὴν τοῦ τε Ῥωμύλου
καὶ τῶν μετ᾽ ἐκεῖνον βασιλέων ὑπήκοοι πάντες
ὑπῆρξαν. καταλυθέντων δὲ τῶν τε Αἰκούων καὶ
τῶν Οὐόλσκων καὶ Ἐρνίκων, ἔτι δὲ πρότερον Ῥουτούλων τε καὶ Ἀβοριγίνων, (πρὸς δὲ τούτοις Ῥαι-
κῶν, καὶ Ἀργυρούσκων δέ τινες καὶ Πρεφέρνων[2])
ἡ τούτων χώρα Λατίνη προσηγόρευται πᾶσα. ἦν
δὲ τῶν Οὐόλσκων τὸ Πωμεντῖνον πεδίον, ὅμορον
τοῖς Λατίνοις, καὶ πόλις Ἀπίολα,[3] ἣν κατέσκαψε
Ταρκύνιος Πρίσκος. Αἴκουοι δὲ γειτονεύονται
μάλιστα τοῖς Κυρίταις, καὶ τούτων δ᾽ ἐκεῖνος τὰς
πόλεις ἐξεπόρθησεν· ὁ δὲ υἱὸς αὐτοῦ τὴν Σούεσσαν
εἷλε τὴν μητρόπολιν τῶν Οὐόλσκων. Ἕρνικοι δὲ
πλησίον ᾤκουν τῷ τε Λανουίῳ[4] καὶ τῇ Ἄλβα καὶ
αὐτῇ τῇ Ῥώμῃ· οὐκ ἄπωθεν δ᾽ οὐδ᾽ Ἀρικία[5] καὶ
Τελλῆναι καὶ Ἄντιον. Ἀλβανοὶ δὲ κατ᾽ ἀρχὰς
μὲν ὡμονόουν τοῖς Ῥωμαίοις, ὁμόγλωσσοί τε ὄντες

---

[1] Corais and Meineke emend Καρμέντιν το Καρμέντην.

[2] πρὸς ... Πρεφέρνων, Kramer, Meineke and other editors
suspect to have crept in from the margin; Meineke relegates
the words to the foot of the page; see notes on opposite
page.

[3] Ἀπίολα Xylander, for Ἐπίολα; so the later editors.

[4] Λανουίῳ, Kramer, for Λαουινίῳ; so the later editors.

[5] Ἀρικία, Xylander, for Ἀρκία; so the later editors.

---

[1] Thus Virgil (8. 336) spells her name; but the usual
spelling was "Carmenta" (cp. Livy 1. 7. and Dionysius, *Antiq.
Rom.* 1. 32).

[2] The "Aeci" of 5. 3. 2.

mother of Evander, regarding her as one of the nymphs, although her name has been changed to Carmentis.[1]

4. Be that as it may, the Latini at the outset were few in number and most of them would pay no attention to the Romans; but later on, struck with amazement at the prowess both of Romulus and of the kings who came after him, they all became subjects. And after the overthrow of the Aequi,[2] of the Volsci, and of the Hernici, and, still before that, of both the Rutuli and the aborigines (and besides these, certain of the Rhaeci,[3] as also of the Argyrusci[4] and the Preferni),[5] the whole country that belonged to these peoples was called Latium. The Pomptine Plain, on the confines of the Latini, and the city of Apiola, which was destroyed by Tarquinius Priscus, used to belong to the Volsci. The Aequi are the nearest neighbours of the Curites; their cities, too, were sacked by Tarquinius Priscus; and his son captured Suessa, the metropolis of the Volsci. The Hernici used to live near Lanuvium, Alba, and Rome itself; and Aricia, also, and Tellenae and Antium were not far away. At the outset the Albani lived in harmony with the Romans, since they spoke the same language and

[3] "Rhaeci," otherwise unknown. is probably a corruption of "Aricini," the inhabitants of Aricia, the city to which Strabo refers in this paragraph and also in 5. 3. 12.

[4] "Argyrusci," otherwise unknown, is probably a corruption of "Aurunci" (cp. Livy 2. 16, 17, 26 and Dionysius, *Antiq. Rom.* 6. 32, 37).

[5] By "Preferni" Strabo almost certainly refers to the Privernates, whose city was Privernum, now in ruins near Piperno.

καὶ Λατῖνοι, βασιλευόμενοι δ᾽ ἑκάτεροι χωρὶς ἐτύγχανον· οὐδὲν δ᾽ ἧττον ἐπιγαμίαι τε ἦσαν πρὸς ἀλλήλους καὶ ἱερὰ κοινὰ τὰ ἐν Ἄλβᾳ καὶ ἄλλα δίκαια πολιτικά· ὕστερον δὲ πολέμου συστάντος ἡ μὲν Ἄλβα κατεσκάφη πλὴν τοῦ ἱεροῦ, οἱ δ᾽ Ἀλβανοὶ πολῖται Ῥωμαίων ἐκρίθησαν. καὶ τῶν ἄλλων δὲ τῶν περιοικίδων πόλεων αἱ μὲν ἀνῃρέθησαν, αἱ δὲ ἐταπεινώθησαν ἀπειθοῦσαι, τινὲς δὲ καὶ ηὐξήθησαν διὰ τὴν εὔνοιαν. νυνὶ μὲν οὖν ἡ παραλία μέχρι πόλεως Σινοέσσης ἀπὸ τῶν Ὠστίων Λατίνη καλεῖται, πρότερον δὲ μέχρι τοῦ Κιρκαίου μόνον ἐσχήκει τὴν ἐπίδοσιν· καὶ τῆς μεσογαίας δὲ πρότερον μὲν οὐ πολλή, ὕστερον δε καὶ μέχρι Καμπανίας διέτεινε καὶ Σαυνιτῶν καὶ Πελίγνων καὶ ἄλλων τῶν τὸ Ἀπέννινον κατοικούντων.

5. Ἄπασα δ᾽ ἐστὶν εὐδαίμων καὶ παμφόρος πλὴν ὀλίγων χωρίων τῶν κατὰ τὴν παραλίαν, ὅσα ἑλώδη καὶ νοσερά, οἷα τὰ τῶν Ἀρδεατῶν καὶ τὰ μεταξὺ Ἀντίου καὶ Λανουίου μέχρι Πωμεντίνου καί τινων τῆς Σητίνης χωρίων καὶ τῆς περὶ Ταρρακίναν καὶ τὸ Κιρκαῖον, ἢ εἴ τινα ὀρεινὰ καὶ πετρώδη· καὶ ταῦτα δ᾽ οὐ τελέως ἀργὰ οὐδ᾽ ἄχρηστα, ἀλλὰ νομὰς παρέχει δαψιλεῖς ἢ ὕλην ἢ καρπούς τινας ἑλείους ἢ πετραίους· τὸ δὲ Καίκουβον, ἑλῶδες ὄν, εὐοινοτάτην ἄμπελον τρέφει, τὴν

---

[1] That is, the tree-climbing vine.

were Latini, and though they were each, as it happened, ruled by kings, separate and apart, none the less they not only had the right of intermarriage with one another, but also held sacrifices—those at Alba—and other political rights in common ; later on, however, war arose between them, with the result that all Alba was destroyed except the temple, and that the Albani were adjudged Roman citizens. As for the other neighbouring cities, some of them too were destroyed, and others humiliated, for their disobedience, while some were made even stronger than they were because of their loyalty. Now at the present time the seaboard is called Latium from Ostia as far as the city of Sinuessa, but in earlier times Latium had extended its seaboard only as far as Circaeum. Further, in earlier times Latium did not include much of the interior, but later on it extended even as far as Campania and the Samnitae and the Peligni and other peoples who inhabit the Apennines.

5. All Latium is blest with fertility and produces everything, except for a few districts that are on the seaboard—I mean all those districts that are marshy and sickly (such as those of the Ardeatae, and those between Antium and Lanuvium as far as the Pomptine Plain, and certain districts in the territory of Setia and the country round about Tarracina and the Circaeum), or any districts that are perhaps mountainous and rocky ; and yet even these are not wholly untilled or useless, but afford rich pasture grounds, or timber, or certain fruits that grow in marshy or rocky ground (the Caecuban Plain, although marshy, supports a vine that produces the best of wine, I mean the tree-vine).[1] The seaboard

δενδρῖτιν. πόλεις δ' ἐπὶ θαλάττῃ μὲν τῶν Λατίνων εἰσὶ τά τε Ὤστια, πόλις ἀλίμενος διὰ τὴν πρόσχωσιν ἣν ὁ Τίβερις παρασκευάζει, πληρούμενος ἐκ πολλῶν ποταμῶν. παρακινδύνως μὲν οὖν ὁρμίζονται μετέωρα ἐν τῷ σάλῳ τὰ ναυκλήρια, τὸ μέντοι λυσιτελὲς νικᾷ· καὶ γὰρ ἡ τῶν ὑπηρετικῶν σκαφῶν εὐπορία τῶν ἐκδεχομένων τὰ φορτία καὶ ἀντιφορτιζόντων ταχὺν ποιεῖ τὸν ἀπόπλουν πρὶν ἢ τοῦ ποταμοῦ ἅψασθαι, ἢ ἐκ μέρους ἀποκουφισθέντα[1] εἰσπλεῖ καὶ ἀνάγεται μέχρι τῆς Ῥώμης, σταδίους ἑκατὸν ἐνενήκοντα. κτίσμα δ' ἐστὶ τὰ Ὤστια Ἄγκου Μαρκίου. αὕτη μὲν ἡ πόλις τοιαύτη. ἑξῆς δ' ἐστὶν Ἄντιον, ἀλίμενος καὶ αὐτὴ πόλις· ἵδρυται δ' ἐπὶ πέτραις, διέχει δὲ τῶν Ὠστίων περὶ διακοσίους ἑξήκοντα σταδίους. νυνὶ μὲν οὖν ἀνεῖται τοῖς ἡγεμόσιν εἰς σχολὴν καὶ ἄνεσιν τῶν πολιτικῶν ὅτε λάβοιεν καιρόν, καὶ διὰ τοῦτο κατῳκοδόμηνται πολυτελεῖς οἰκήσεις ἐν τῇ πόλει συχναὶ πρὸς τὰς τοιαύτας ἐπιδημίας· καὶ πρότερον δὲ ναῦς ἐκέκτηντο καὶ ἐκοινώνουν τῶν ληστηρίων τοῖς Τυρρηνοῖς, καίπερ ἤδη Ῥωμαίοις ὑπακούοντες. διόπερ καὶ Ἀλέξανδρος πρότερον ἐγκαλῶν ἐπέστειλε, καὶ Δημήτριος ὕστερον, τοὺς ἁλόντας τῶν ληστῶν ἀναπέμπων τοῖς Ῥωμαίοις, χαρίζεσθαι μὲν αὐτοῖς ἔφη τὰ σώματα διὰ τὴν πρὸς τοὺς Ἕλληνας συγγένειαν, οὐκ ἀξιοῦν δὲ τοὺς αὐτοὺς ἄνδρας στρατηγεῖν τε ἅμα τῆς Ἰταλίας

_____

[1] ἢ ἐκ μέρους ἀποκουφισθέντα, Jones, for καὶ μέρους ἀποκουφισθέντος.

_____

[1] Demetrius Polioroetes.

cities belonging to the Latini are, first, Ostia: it is harbourless on account of the silting up which is caused by the Tiber, since the Tiber is fed by numerous streams. Now although it is with peril that the merchant-ships anchor far out in the surge, still, the prospect of gain prevails; and in fact the good supply of the tenders which receive the cargoes and bring back cargoes in exchange makes it possible for the ships to sail away quickly before they touch the river, or else, after being partly relieved of their cargoes, they sail into the Tiber and run inland as far as Rome, one hundred and ninety stadia. Ostia was founded by Ancus Marcius. Such, then, is this city of Ostia. Next comes Antium, it also being a harbourless city. It is situated on masses of rock, and is about two hundred and sixty stadia distant from Ostia. Now at the present time Antium is given over to the rulers for their leisure and relief from the cares of state whenever they get the opportunity, and therefore, for the purposes of such sojourns, many very costly residences have been built in the city; but in earlier times the people of Antium used to possess ships and to take part with the Tyrrheni in their acts of piracy, although at that time they were already subjects of the Romans. It is for this reason that Alexander, in earlier times, sent in complaints, and that Demetrius,[1] later on, when he sent back to the Romans what pirates he had captured, said that, although he was doing the Romans the favour of sending back the captives because of the kinship between the Romans and the Greeks, he did not deem it right for men to be sending out bands of pirates at the same time that they were in command of Italy, or to build in

καὶ ληστήρια ἐκπέμπειν, καὶ ἐν μὲν τῇ ἀγορᾷ Διοσ-
κούρων ἱερὸν ἱδρυσαμένους τιμᾶν, οὓς πάντες
Σωτῆρας ὀνομάζουσιν, εἰς δὲ τὴν Ἑλλάδα πέμπειν
τὴν ἐκείνων πατρίδα τοὺς λεηλατήσοντας· ἔπαυσαν δ᾽ αὐτοὺς Ῥωμαῖοι τῆς τοιαύτης ἐπιτηδεύσεως.
ἀνὰ μέσον δὲ τούτων τῶν πόλεών ἐστι τὸ Λαουί-
νιον, ἔχον κοινὸν τῶν Λατίνων ἱερὸν Ἀφροδίτης,
ἐπιμελοῦνται δ᾽ αὐτοῦ διὰ προπόλων[1] Ἀρδεᾶται.
εἶτα Λαύρεντον. ὑπέρκειται δὲ τούτων ἡ Ἀρδέα,
κατοικία Ῥουτούλων ἄνω[2] ἑβδομήκοντα σταδίοις
ἀπὸ τῆς θαλάττης· ἔστι δὲ καὶ ταύτης πλησίον
Ἀφροδίσιον, ὅπου πανηγυρίζουσι Λατῖνοι. Σαυνῖται δ᾽ ἐπόρθησαν τοὺς τόπους καὶ λείπεται μὲν
ἴχνη πόλεων, ἔνδοξα δὲ διὰ τὴν Αἰνείου γέγονεν
ἐπιδημίαν καὶ τὰς ἱεροποιίας ἃς[3] ἐξ ἐκείνων τῶν
χρόνων παραδεδόσθαι φασί.

6. Μετὰ δὲ Ἄντιον τὸ Κιρκαῖόν ἐστιν ἐν διακοσίοις καὶ ἐνενήκοντα σταδίοις ὄρος, νησίζον θαλάττῃ τε καὶ ἔλεσι· φασὶ δὲ καὶ πολύρριζον εἶναι,
τάχα τῷ μύθῳ τῷ περὶ τῆς Κίρκης συνοικειοῦντες.
ἔχει δὲ πολίχνιον καὶ Κίρκης ἱερὸν καὶ Ἀθηνᾶς
βωμόν, δείκνυσθαι δὲ καὶ φιάλην τινά φασιν
Ὀδυσσέως. μεταξὺ δὲ ὅ τε Στόρας ποταμὸς καὶ
ἐπ᾽ αὐτῷ ὕφορμος. ἔπειτα προσεχὴς αἰγιαλὸς
Λιβί, πρὸς αὐτῷ μόνον τῷ Κιρκαίῳ λιμένιον ἔχων.
ὑπέρκειται δ᾽ ἐν τῇ μεσογαίᾳ τὸ Πωμεντῖνον πεδίον. τὴν δὲ συνεχῆ ταύτῃ πρότερον Αὔσονες

---

[1] προπόλων, Corais, for προγόνων; so the late editors.
[2] ἄνω, the reading of the MSS., Jones restores, for ἐν
(Corais and the later editors).
[3] ἅς, Corais inserts after ἱεροποίας; so the later editors.

their Forum a temple in honour of the Dioscuri, and to worship them, whom all call Saviours, and yet at the same time send to Greece people who would plunder the native land of the Dioscuri. And the Romans put a stop to such practices. Midway between these two cities is Lavinium, which has a temple of Aphrodite that is common to all the Latini, though the Ardeatae, through attendants, have the care of it. Then comes Laurentum. And beyond these cities lies Ardea, a settlement of the Rutuli, seventy stadia inland from the sea. Near Ardea too there is a temple of Aphrodite, where the Latini hold religious festivals. But the places were devastated by the Samnitae; and although only traces of cities are left, those traces have become famous because of the sojourn which Aeneas made there and because of those sacred rites which, it is said, have been handed down from those times.

6. After Antium, within a distance of two hundred and ninety stadia, comes Circaeum, a mountain which has the form of an island, because it is surrounded by sea and marshes. They further say that Circaeum is a place that abounds in roots—perhaps because they associate it with the myth about Circe. It has a little city and a temple of Circe and an altar of Athene, and people there show you a sort of bowl which, they say, belonged to Odysseus. Between Antium and Circaeum is the River Storas, and also, near it, an anchoring-place. Then comes a stretch of coast that is exposed to the south-west wind, with no shelter except a little harbour near Circaeum itself. Beyond this coast, in the interior, is the Pomptine Plain. The country that joins this latter was formerly inhabited by the Ausones, who also

C 233 ᾤκουν, οἵπερ καὶ τὴν Καμπανίαν εἶχον. μετὰ δὲ
τούτους Ὄσκοι· καὶ τούτοις δὲ μετῆν τῆς Καμπανίας, νῦν δ' ἅπαντα Λατίνων ἐστὶ μέχρι Σινοέσσης, ὡς εἶπον. ἴδιον δέ τι τοῖς Ὄσκοις καὶ τῷ
τῶν Αὐσόνων ἔθνει συμβέβηκε· τῶν μὲν γὰρ
Ὄσκων ἐκλελοιπότων ἡ διάλεκτος μένει παρὰ
τοῖς Ῥωμαίοις, ὥστε καὶ ποιήματα σκηνοβατεῖ-
σθαι κατά τινα ἀγῶνα πάτριον καὶ μιμολογεῖσθαι,
τῶν δ' Αὐσόνων οὐδ' ἅπαξ οἰκησάντων ἐπὶ τῇ
Σικελικῇ θαλάττῃ, τὸ πέλαγος ὅμως Αὐσόνιον
καλεῖται. ἑξῆς δ' ἐν ἑκατὸν σταδίοις τῷ Κιρκαίῳ
Ταρρακίνα ἐστί, Τραχινὴ καλουμένη πρότερον
ἀπὸ τοῦ συμβεβηκότος. πρόκειται δὲ αὐτῆς μέγα
ἕλος ὃ ποιοῦσι δύο ποταμοί· καλεῖται δ' ὁ μείζων
Αὔφιδος.[1] ἐνταῦθα δὲ συνάπτει τῇ θαλάττῃ πρῶτον ἡ Ἀππία ὁδός, ἐστρωμένη μὲν ἀπὸ τῆς Ῥώμης
μέχρι Βρεντεσίου, πλεῖστον δ' ὁδευομένη· τῶν δ'
ἐπὶ θαλάττῃ πόλεων τούτων ἐφαπτομένη μόνον,
τῆς τε Ταρρακίνης καὶ τῶν ἐφεξῆς, Φορμιῶν μὲν
καὶ Μιντούρνης καὶ Σινοέσσης, καὶ τῶν ἐσχάτων,
Τάραντός τε καὶ Βρεντεσίου. πλησίον δὲ τῆς
Ταρρακίνης βαδίζοντι ἐπὶ τῆς Ῥώμης παραβέβληται τῇ ὁδῷ τῇ Ἀππίᾳ διῶρυξ ἐπὶ πολλοὺς τόπους

---

[1] For Αὔφιδος, Xylander reads Οὔφιος, Casaubon Αὔφεις,
Groskurd Οὔφεις, Meineke Οὔφης ; see note 4 on opposite page.

[1] § 4 above.
[2] The " Atellanae Fabulae " of the Romans (Pauly-Wissowa
s. v. "Atell. Fab.")

held Campania. After these come the Osci; they too had a share in Campania; but now everything belongs to the Latini as far as Sinuessa, as I said.[1] A peculiar thing has taken place in the case of the Osci and the tribe of the Ausones. Although the Osci have disappeared, their dialect still remains among the Romans, so much so that, at the time of a certain traditional competition, poems in that dialect are brought on the stage and recited like mimes;[2] again, although the Ausones never once lived on the Sicilian Sea, still the high sea is called "Ausonian." Next, within one hundred stadia of Circaeum, is Tarracina, which was formerly called "Trachine"[3] from its actual character. In front of Tarracina lies a great marsh, formed by two rivers; the larger one is called Aufidus.[4] It is here that the Appian Way first touches the sea; it has been constructed from Rome as far as Brentesium[5] and is the most travelled of all; but of the cities on the sea it touches only these: Tarracina, and those that come next in order after it, Formiae, Minturnae, and Sinuessa, and those at the end—Taras[6] and Brentesium. Near Tarracina, as you go toward Rome, there is a canal which runs alongside the Appian Way, and is fed at numerous places by waters

[3] Strabo assumed that "Trachine" was derived from the Greek word "trachys" ("rugged"). Cp. Horace, *Sat.* 1. 5. 26: "Impositum saxis late candentibus Anxur" (Tarracina).

[4] If the MSS. are right, Strabo is in error here. He must have meant the Ufens (now Ufente); the other river was the Amasenus (now Amaseno).

[5] One of the old spellings of Brundisium; the other was "Brendesium" (cp Ptolemaeus, 3. 2. 12, and Polybius, 21. 24). "In the language of the Messapii the stag's head is called 'brentesium'" (6. 3. 6); hence the name of the city.

[6] The old name of Tarentum.

πληρουμένη τοῖς ἑλείοις τε καὶ τοῖς ποταμίοις
ὕδασι· πλεῖται δὲ μάλιστα μὲν νύκτωρ, ὥστ᾽
ἐμβάντας ἀφ᾽ ἑσπέρας ἐκβαίνειν πρωίας καὶ βαδί-
ζειν τὸ λοιπὸν τῇ ὁδῷ, ἀλλὰ καὶ μεθ᾽ ἡμέραν·
ρυμουλκεῖ δ᾽ ἡμιόνιον. ἑξῆς δὲ Φορμίαι Λακωνι-
κὸν κτίσμα ἐστίν, Ὁρμίαι λεγόμενον πρότερον διὰ
τὸ εὔορμον. καὶ τὸν μεταξὺ δὲ κόλπον ἐκεῖνοι
Καιέταν¹ ὠνόμασαν, τὰ γὰρ κοῖλα πάντα καιέτας
οἱ Λάκωνες προσαγορεύουσιν· ἔνιοι δ᾽ ἐπώνυμον
τῆς Αἰνείου τροφοῦ τὸν κόλπον φασίν. ἔχει δὲ
μῆκος σταδίων ἑκατὸν ἀρξάμενος ἀπὸ Ταρρακίνης,
μέχρι τῆς ἄκρας τῆς ὁμωνύμου· ἀνέῳγέ τ᾽ ἐνταῦθα
σπήλαια ὑπερμεγέθη, κατοικίας μεγάλας καὶ πολυτελεῖς δεδεγμένα· ἐντεῦθεν δ᾽ ἐπὶ τὰς Φορμίας
τετταράκοντα. ταύτης δ᾽ ἀνὰ μέσον εἰσὶ καὶ
Σινοέσσης αἱ Μιντοῦρναι, σταδίους ἑκατέρας διέχουσαι περὶ ὀγδοήκοντα. διαρρεῖ δὲ Λεῖρις ποταμός, Κλάνις δ᾽ ἐκαλεῖτο πρότερον· φέρεται δ᾽
ἄνωθεν ἐκ τῶν Ἀπεννίνων ὀρῶν καὶ τῆς Οὐηστί-
νης παρὰ Φρεγέλλας κώμην (πρότερον δ᾽ ἦν πόλις
ἔνδοξος), ἐκπίπτει δ᾽ εἰς ἄλσος ἱερὸν τιμώμενον
περιττῶς ὑπὸ τῶν ἐν Μιντούρναις, ὑποκείμενον
τῇ πόλει. τῶν δὲ σπηλαίων ἐν ὄψει μάλιστα
πρόκεινται δύο νῆσοι πελάγιαι, Πανδατερία² τε

¹ Καιέταν, Jones, for Καιδταν (B), Κεάτα (C); cp. καιέτας
following, and also in 8. 5. 7.
² Πανδατερία, Meineke, for Πανδαρία (BC).

---

¹ For an amusing account of this canal-journey, see Horace,
Sat. 1. 5.
² "Anchoring-place."
³ Strabo does not mention the city of "Caieta" (now
Gaëta); the gulf *east* of it was called by the Romans

from the marshes and the rivers. People navigate
the canal, preferably by night (so that if they
embark in the evening they can disembark early
in the morning and go the rest of their journey
by the Way), but they also navigate it by day.
The boat is towed by a mule.[1] Next after Tarracina comes Formiae, founded by the Laconians,
and formerly called "Hormiae" because of its
good "hormos."[2] And those people also named the
intervening gulf "Caietas,"[3] for the Laconians call
all hollow things "Caietas"; but some say the gulf
was named after the nurse of Aeneas.[4] It has a
length of one hundred stadia, beginning at Tarracina
and extending as far as the promontory of like name.[5]
There are wide-open caverns of immense size at
this place, which have been occupied by large and
very costly residences; from here to Formiae the
distance is forty stadia. Midway between Formiae
and Sinuessa is Minturnae, which is about eighty
stadia distant from each. Through Minturnae flows
the River Liris, formerly called the "Clanis." It
runs from the interior, out of the Apennine Mountains and the country of the Vestini, past Fragellae,
a village (it was formerly a famous city), and empties
into a sacred precinct which is much revered by the
people in Minturnae; the precinct is situated below
the city. In the high sea, off the caverns and visible
thence most of the time, are situated two islands,

"Caietanus Sinus." But, as the context shows, "the intervening gulf" means the gulf between Caieta and Tarracina.
For the meaning of the Spartan word "Caietas," see 8. 5. 7.

[4] According to Virgil (*Aeneid*, 7. 2) her name was "Caieta."

[5] That is, the promontory on which the city of Caieta was
situated.

καὶ Ποντία, μικραὶ μέν, οἰκούμεναι δὲ καλῶς, οὐ
πολὺ ἀπ' ἀλλήλων διέχουσαι, τῆς ἠπείρου δὲ
πεντήκοντα ἐπὶ τοῖς διακοσίοις. ἔχεται δὲ τοῦ
Καιέτου[1] κόλπου τὸ Καίκουβον, τούτου δὲ Φοῦν-
δοι, πόλις ἐν τῇ ὁδῷ τῇ Ἀππίᾳ κειμένη. πάντες δ'
C 234 εἰσὶν οἱ τόποι οὗτοι σφόδρα εὔοινοι· ὁ δὲ Καίκουβος
καὶ ὁ Φουνδανὸς καὶ ὁ Σητινὸς τῶν διωνομασμένων
εἰσί, καθάπερ ὁ Φάλερνος καὶ ὁ Ἀλβανὸς καὶ ὁ
Στατανός. ἡ δὲ Σινόεσσα ἐν Καιετάνῳ[2] κόλπῳ
ἵδρυται, ἀφ' οὗ καὶ τοὔνομα· σίνος γὰρ ὁ κόλπος·
πλησίον ἐστὶ δ' αὐτῆς θερμὰ λουτρά, κάλλιστα
ποιοῦντα πρὸς νόσους ἐνίας. αὗται μὲν αἱ ἐπὶ
θαλάττῃ τῶν Λατίνων πόλεις.

7. Ἐν δὲ τῇ μεσογαίᾳ πρώτη μὲν ὑπὲρ τῶν
Ὠστίων ἐστὶν ἡ Ῥώμη, καὶ μόνη γε ἐπὶ τῷ Τιβέρει κεῖται· περὶ ἧς, ὅτι πρὸς ἀνάγκην, οὐ πρὸς
αἵρεσιν ἔκτισται, εἴρηται· προσθετέον δ' ὅτι οὐδ'
οἱ μετὰ ταῦτα προσκτίσαντές τινα μέρη κύριοι τοῦ
βελτίονος ἦσαν, ἀλλ' ἐδούλευον τοῖς προϋποκει-
μένοις. οἱ μέν γε πρῶτοι τὸ Καπιτώλιον καὶ τὸ
Παλάτιον καὶ τὸν Κουιρῖνον λόφον ἐτείχισαν, ὃς
ἦν οὕτως εὐεπίβατος τοῖς ἔξωθεν ὥστ' ἐξ ἐφόδου

---

[1] Καιέτου, Jones, for Κεάτου (BC), Καιάτου (sec. hand in B).
[2] Καιετάνῳ, from conj. of Capps, for the unintelligible
σητάνοις, Σταγανός (BCl), σιτάνῳ (npr). Meineke relegates
σητάνοις to the foot of the page.

---

[1] Cp. 2. 5. 19.
[2] The Greek word for "gulf," "vale."

Pandateria and Pontia,[1] which, though small, are well peopled; they are not far distant from one another, but they are two hundred and fifty stadia from the mainland. The Caecuban Plain borders on the Gulf of Caietas; and next to the plain comes Fundi, situated on the Appian Way. All these places produce exceedingly good wine; indeed, the Caecuban and the Fundanian and the Setinian belong to the class of wines that are widely famed, as is the case with the Falernian and the Alban and the Statanian. Sinuessa is situated in the Caietan "Kolpos,"[2] and hence its name; for "Kolpos" means "Sinus";[3] and near Sinuessa are hot baths, which are most efficacious for certain diseases.[4] These, then, are the cities of the Latini on the sea.

7. In the interior, the first city above Ostia is Rome, and it is the only city that is situated on the Tiber. With regard to this city, I have already said that it was founded there as a matter of necessity, not as a matter of choice;[5] and I must add that even those who afterwards added certain districts to the settlement could not as masters take the better course, but as slaves must needs accommodate themselves to what had already been founded. The first founders walled the Capitolium and the Palatium and the Quirinal Hill, which last was so easy for outsiders

[3] Strabo now refers to the *Roman* "Caietanus Sinus," and not to "the intervening gulf" above-mentioned.

[4] According to Pliny (31. 4), these baths cured barrenness in women and insanity in men. Whether they have disappeared, or are to be identified with the waters at Torre di Bagni, is not known.

[5] 5. 3. 2.

Τίτος Τάτιος εἷλεν, ἐπελθὼν ἡνίκα μετήει τὴν τῶν
ἁρπαγεισῶν παρθένων ὕβριν. Ἄγκος τε [1] Μάρ-
κιος προσλαβὼν τὸ Καίλιον [2] ὄρος καὶ τὸ Ἀβεντῖ-
νον ὄρος καὶ τὸ μεταξὺ τούτων πεδίον, διηρτημένα
καὶ ἀπ᾽ ἀλλήλων καὶ ἀπὸ τῶν προτετειχισμένων,
προσέθηκεν ἀναγκαίως· οὔτε γὰρ οὕτως ἐρυμνοὺς
λόφους ἔξω τείχους ἐᾶσαι τοῖς βουλομένοις ἐπιτειχίσματα καλῶς εἶχεν, οὔθ᾽ ὅλον ἐκπληρῶσαι
τὸν κύκλον ἴσχυσε τὸν μέχρι τοῦ Κουιρίνου.
ἤλεγξε δὲ Σερούιος τὴν ἔκλειψιν, ἀνεπλήρωσε γὰρ
προσθεὶς τόν τε Ἠσκυλῖνον λόφον καὶ τὸν Οὐιμί-
ναλιν. καὶ ταῦτα δ᾽ εὐέφοδα τοῖς ἔξωθέν ἐστι·
διόπερ τάφρον βαθεῖαν ὀρύξαντες εἰς τὸ ἐντὸς
ἐδέξαντο τὴν γῆν, καὶ ἐξέτειναν ὅσον ἐξαστάδιον
χῶμα ἐπὶ τῇ ἐντὸς ὀφρύϊ τῆς τάφρου, καὶ ἐπέβαλον τεῖχος καὶ πύργους ἀπὸ τῆς Κολλίνας
πύλης μέχρι τῆς Ἠσκυλίνας· ὑπὸ μέσῳ δὲ τῷ
χώματι τρίτη ἐστὶ πύλη ὁμώνυμος τῷ Οὐιμινάλι
λόφῳ. τὸ μὲν οὖν ἔρυμα τοιοῦτόν ἐστι τὸ τῆς
πόλεως, ἐρυμάτων ἑτέρων δεόμενον. καί μοι δοκοῦσιν οἱ πρῶτοι τὸν αὐτὸν λαβεῖν διαλογισμὸν
περί τε σφῶν αὐτῶν καὶ περὶ τῶν ὕστερον, διότι
Ῥωμαίοις προσῆκεν οὐκ ἀπὸ τῶν ἐρυμάτων, ἀλλὰ
ἀπὸ τῶν ὅπλων καὶ τῆς οἰκείας ἀρετῆς ἔχειν τὴν
ἀσφάλειαν καὶ τὴν ἄλλην εὐπορίαν, προβλήματα
νομίζοντες οὐ τὰ τείχη τοῖς ἀνδράσιν ἀλλὰ τοὺς
ἄνδρας τοῖς τείχεσι. κατ᾽ ἀρχὰς μὲν οὖν ἀλλο-
τρίας τῆς κύκλῳ χώρας οὔσης ἀγαθῆς τε καὶ

[1] Corais and Meineke emend τε to δέ.
[2] Καίλιον, Corais, for Κέλιον; so the later editors.

---

[1] Cp. 5. 3. 2.   [2] "Porta Viminalis."

to ascend that Titus Tatius took it at the first onset, making his attack at the time when he came to avenge the outrage of the seizure of the maidens.[1] Again, Ancus Marcius took in Mt. Caelium and Mt. Aventine, and the plain between them, which were separated both from one another and from the parts that were already walled, but he did so only from necessity; for, in the first place, it was not a good thing to leave hills that were so well fortified by nature outside the walls for any who wished strongholds against the city, and, secondly, he was unable to fill out the whole circuit of hills as far as the Quirinal. Servius, however, detected the gap, for he filled it out by adding both the Esquiline Hill and the Viminal Hill. But these too are easy for outsiders to attack; and for this reason they dug a deep trench and took the earth to the inner side of the trench, and extended a mound about six stadia on the inner brow of the trench, and built thereon a wall with towers from the Colline Gate to the Esquiline. Below the centre of the mound is a third gate,[2] bearing the same name as the Viminal Hill. Such, then, are the fortifications of the city, though they need a second set of fortifications. And, in my opinion, the first founders took the same course of reasoning both for themselves and for their successors, namely, that it was appropriate for the Romans to depend for their safety and general welfare, not on their fortifications, but on their arms and their own valour, in the belief that it is not walls that protect men but men that protect walls. At the outset, then, since the fertile and extensive country round about them belonged to others,[3] and since the terrain of the

---

[3] Cp. 5. 3. 2 on this point.

πολλῆς, τοῦ δὲ τῆς πόλεως ἐδάφους εὐεπιχειρή-
του, τὸ μακαρισθησόμενον οὐδὲν ἦν τοπικὸν εὐκλή-
ρημα· τῇ δ' ἀρετῇ καὶ τῷ πόνῳ τῆς χώρας οἰκείας

C 235 γενομένης, ἐφάνη συνδρομή τις ἀγαθῶν ἅπασαν
εὐφυΐαν ὑπερβάλλουσα· δι' ἣν ἐπὶ τοσοῦτον αὐξη-
θεῖσα ἡ πόλις ἀντέχει τοῦτο μὲν τροφῇ, τοῦτο δὲ
ξύλοις καὶ λίθοις πρὸς τὰς οἰκοδομίας, ἃς ἀδιαλείπτως[1] ποιοῦσιν αἱ συμπτώσεις καὶ ἐμπρήσεις
καὶ μεταπράσεις, ἀδιάλειπτοι καὶ αὐταὶ οὖσαι·
καὶ γὰρ αἱ μεταπράσεις ἑκούσιοί τινες συμπτώσεις εἰσί, καταβαλλόντων καὶ ἀνοικοδομούντων
πρὸς τὰς ἐπιθυμίας ἕτερα ἐξ ἑτέρων. πρὸς ταῦτ'
οὖν τό τε τῶν μετάλλων πλῆθος καὶ ἡ ὕλη καὶ οἱ
κατακομίζοντες ποταμοὶ θαυμαστὴν παρέχουσι
τὴν ὑποχορηγίαν, πρῶτος μὲν Ἀνίων ἐξ Ἄλβας
ῥέων, τῆς πρὸς Μαρσοῖς Λατίνης πόλεως, καὶ διὰ
τοῦ ὑπ' αὐτῇ πεδίου μέχρι τῆς πρὸς τὸν Τίβεριν
συμβολῆς, ἔπειθ' ὁ Νὰρ καὶ ὁ Τενέας οἱ διὰ τῆς
Ὀμβρικῆς εἰς τὸν αὐτὸν καταφερόμενοι ποταμὸν
τὸν Τίβεριν, διὰ δὲ Τυρρηνίας καὶ τῆς Κλουσίνης
ὁ Κλάνις. ἐπεμελήθη μὲν οὖν ὁ Σεβαστὸς Καῖσαρ
τῶν τοιούτων ἐλαττωμάτων τῆς πόλεως, πρὸς μὲν
τὰς ἐμπρήσεις συντάξας στρατιωτικὸν ἐκ τῶν
ἀπελευθεριωτῶν τὸ βοηθῆσον, πρὸς δὲ τὰς συμ-

---

[1] ἀδιαλείπτως, the reading of the MSS., Jones restores, for
ἀδιαλείπτους (Corais, Müller-Dübner, and Meineke).

[1] Cp. Horace's "diruit, aedificat, mutat" (*Epist.* 1. 1. 100).
[2] Alba Fucens.   [3] In Latin, the "Tinia."

city was so easy to attack, there was nothing fortunate in their position to call for congratulation,
but when by their valour and their toil they had
made the country their own property, there was
obviously a concourse, so to speak, of blessings that
surpassed all natural advantages; and it is because of
this concourse of blessings that the city, although it
has grown to such an extent, holds out in the way it
does, not only in respect to food, but also in respect
to timber and stones for the building of houses,
which goes on unceasingly in consequence of the
collapses and fires and repeated sales (these last, too,
going on unceasingly); and indeed the sales are
intentional collapses, as it were, since the purchasers
keep tearing down the houses and building new ones,
one after another, to suit their wishes.[1] To meet
these requirements, then, the Romans are afforded a
wonderful supply of materials by the large number
of mines, by the timber, and by the rivers which
bring these down : first, the Anio, which flows from
Alba, the Latin city next to the Marsi,[2] through the
plain that is below Alba to its confluence with the
Tiber; and then the Nar and the Teneas,[3] the rivers
which run through Ombrica down to the same river,
the Tiber; and also the Clanis, which, however, runs
down thither through Tyrrhenia and the territory
of Clusium. Now Augustus Caesar concerned himself about such impairments of the city, organising
for protection against fires a militia composed of
freedmen, whose duty it was to render assistance,[4]

[4] The "cohortes vigilum" were a night police and fire
brigade combined, consisting of seven thousand men, or seven
cohorts. They were distributed throughout the city, one
cohort to every two of the fourteen "regiones." See
Suetonius, *Augustus* 25, and Cassius Dio 55. 26.

πτώσεις τὰ ὕψη τῶν καινῶν οἰκοδομημάτων καθε-
λὼν καὶ κωλύσας ἐξαίρειν ποδῶν ἑβδομήκοντα τὸ
πρὸς ταῖς ὁδοῖς ταῖς δημοσίαις. ἀλλ' ὅμως ἐπέ-
λειπεν ἂν ἡ ἐπανόρθωσις, εἰ μὴ τὰ μέταλλα καὶ
ἡ ὕλη καὶ τὸ τῆς πορθμείας εὐμεταχείριστον
ἀντεῖχε.

8. Ταῦτα μὲν οὖν ἡ φύσις τῆς χώρας παρέχεται τὰ εὐτυχήματα τῇ πόλει, προσέθεσαν δὲ
Ῥωμαῖοι καὶ τὰ ἐκ τῆς προνοίας. τῶν γὰρ Ἑλλήνων περὶ τὰς κτίσεις εὐστοχῆσαι μάλιστα
δοξάντων, ὅτι κάλλους ἐστοχάζοντο καὶ ἐρυμνό-
τητος καὶ λιμένων καὶ χώρας εὐφυοῦς, οὗτοι
προὐνόησαν μάλιστα ὧν ὠλιγώρησαν ἐκεῖνοι,
στρώσεως ὁδῶν καὶ ὑδάτων εἰσαγωγῆς καὶ ὑπονόμων τῶν δυναμένων ἐκκλύζειν τὰ λύματα τῆς
πόλεως εἰς τὸν Τίβεριν· ἔστρωσαν δὲ καὶ τὰς
κατὰ τὴν χώραν ὁδούς, προσθέντες ἐκκοπάς τε
λόφων καὶ ἐγχώσεις κοιλάδων, ὥστε τὰς ἁρμα-
μάξας δέχεσθαι πορθμείων φορτία· οἱ δ' ὑπόνο-
μοι συννόμῳ λίθῳ κατακαμφθέντες ὁδοὺς ἁμάξαις
χόρτου πορευτὰς ἐνίας ἀπολελοίπασι. τοσοῦτον
δ' ἐστὶ τὸ εἰσαγώγιμον ὕδωρ διὰ τῶν ὑδραγω-
γείων ὥστε ποταμοὺς διὰ τῆς πόλεως καὶ τῶν
ὑπονόμων ῥεῖν, ἅπασαν δὲ οἰκίαν σχεδὸν δεξαμενὰς καὶ σίφωνας καὶ κρουνοὺς ἔχειν ἀφθόνους,
ὧν πλείστην ἐπιμέλειαν ἐποιήσατο Μάρκος
Ἀγρίππας, πολλοῖς καὶ ἄλλοις ἀναθήμασι κοσμή-

and also to provide against collapses, reducing the heights of the new buildings and forbidding that any structure on the public streets should rise as high as seventy feet; but still his constructive measures would have failed by now were it not that the mines and the timber and the easy means of transportation by water still hold out.

8. So much, then, for the blessings with which nature supplies the city; but the Romans have added still others, which are the result of their foresight; for if the Greeks had the repute of aiming most happily in the founding of cities, in that they aimed at beauty, strength of position, harbours, and productive soil, the Romans had the best foresight in those matters which the Greeks made but little account of, such as the construction of roads and aqueducts, and of sewers that could wash out the filth of the city into the Tiber. Moreover, they have so constructed also the roads which run throughout the country, by adding both cuts through hills and embankments across valleys, that their wagons can carry boat-loads; and the sewers, vaulted with close-fitting stones, have in some places left room enough even for wagons loaded with hay to pass through them.[1] And water is brought into the city through the aqueducts in such quantities that veritable rivers flow through the city and the sewers; and almost every house has cisterns, and service-pipes, and copious fountains—with which Marcus Agrippa concerned himself most, though he also adorned the city with

---

[1] Pliny (36. 24) uses the same figure in describing the dimensions of the sewers constructed by Tarquinius Priscus: (Tarquinius Priscus) amplitudinem cavis eam fecisse proditur ut vehem faeni large onustam transmitteret.

C 236 σας τὴν πόλιν. ὡς δ' εἰπεῖν, οἱ παλαιοὶ μὲν τοῦ
κάλλους τῆς Ῥώμης ὠλιγώρουν, πρὸς ἄλλοις μεί-
ζοσι καὶ ἀναγκαιοτέροις ὄντες· οἱ δ' ὕστερον, καὶ
μάλιστα οἱ νῦν καὶ καθ' ἡμᾶς, οὐδὲ τούτου καθυ-
στέρησαν, ἀλλ' ἀναθημάτων πολλῶν καὶ καλῶν
ἐπλήρωσαν τὴν πόλιν. καὶ γὰρ Πομπήϊος καὶ ὁ
Θεὸς Καῖσαρ καὶ ὁ Σεβαστὸς καὶ οἱ τούτου παῖδες
καὶ οἱ φίλοι καὶ γυνὴ καὶ ἀδελφὴ πᾶσαν ὑπερε-
βάλλοντο σπουδὴν καὶ δαπάνην εἰς τὰς κατα-
σκευάς· τούτων δὲ τὰ πλεῖστα ὁ Μάρτιος ἔχει
κάμπος, πρὸς τῇ φύσει προσλαβὼν καὶ τὸν ἐκ τῆς
προνοίας κόσμον. καὶ γὰρ τὸ μέγεθος τοῦ πεδίου
θαυμαστόν, ἅμα καὶ τὰς ἁρματοδρομίας καὶ τὴν
ἄλλην ἱππασίαν ἀκώλυτον παρέχον[1] τῷ τοσούτῳ
πλήθει τῶν σφαίρᾳ καὶ κρίκῳ καὶ παλαίστρᾳ
γυμναζομένων· καὶ τὰ περικείμενα ἔργα καὶ τὸ
ἔδαφος ποᾶζον δι' ἔτους καὶ τῶν λόφων στεφάναι
τῶν ὑπὲρ τοῦ ποταμοῦ μέχρι τοῦ ῥείθρου σκηνο-
γραφικὴν ὄψιν ἐπιδεικνύμεναι δυσαπάλλακτον
παρέχουσι τὴν θέαν. πλησίον δ' ἐστὶ τοῦ πεδίου
τούτου καὶ ἄλλο πεδίον καὶ στοαὶ κύκλῳ παμπλη-
θεῖς καὶ ἄλση καὶ θέατρα τρία καὶ ἀμφιθέατρον

---

[1] παρέχον, Groskurd, for παρέχων; so the later editors.

---

[1] From the more ancient point of view, as the Greek word
here translated "structures" shows, these structures might
all have been erected as divine offerings; but in later times
the word seems often to have lost this connotation (cp.
W. H. D. Rouse, *Votive Offerings*, p. 273).

[2] See the note above on "structures."

[3] For a list of some of these "friends" of Augustus and
what they built, see Suetonius, *Augustus* 29.

[4] Cp "works of art," 5. 2. 5 and the footnote.

[5] According to Hülsen (*Pauly-Wissowa*, *s.v.* "Agrippae

many other structures.[1] In a word, the early
Romans made but little account of the beauty of
Rome, because they were occupied with other,
greater and more necessary, matters; whereas the
later Romans, and particularly those of to-day and
in my time, have not fallen short in this respect
either—indeed, they have filled the city with many
beautiful structures.[2] In fact, Pompey, the Deified
Caesar, Augustus, his sons and friends,[3] and wife and
sister, have outdone all others in their zeal for buildings and in the expense incurred. The Campus
Martius contains most of these, and thus, in
addition to its natural beauty, it has received still
further adornment as the result of foresight. Indeed, the size of the Campus is remarkable, since it
affords space at the same time and without inter-
ference, not only for the chariot-races and every
other equestrian exercise, but also for all that multitude of people who exercise themselves by ball-
playing, hoop-trundling, and wrestling; and the
works of art[4] situated around the Campus Martius,
and the ground, which is covered with grass
throughout the year, and the crowns of those hills
that are above the river and extend as far as its
bed, which present to the eye the appearance of
a stage-painting—all this, I say, affords a spectacle
that one can hardly draw away from. And near this
campus is still another campus,[5] with colonnades
round about it in very great numbers, and sacred
precincts, and three theatres, and an amphitheatre,

campus ") Strabo refers to the Campus of Agrippa ; but
Tozer (*S lections* p. 154) is in doubt whether Strabo means
this campus or the Campus Flaminius. Both campuses, of
course, formed a part of the Campus Martius.

καὶ ναοὶ πολυτελεῖς καὶ συνεχεῖς ἀλλήλοις, ὡς
πάρεργον ἂν δόξειεν ἀποφαίνειν τὴν ἄλλην πόλιν.
διόπερ ἱεροπρεπέστατον νομίσαντες τοῦτον τὸν
τόπον καὶ τὰ τῶν ἐπιφανεστάτων μνήματα ἐνταῦθα κατεσκεύασαν ἀνδρῶν καὶ γυναικῶν. ἀξιολογώτατον δὲ τὸ Μαυσώλειον καλούμενον, ἐπὶ κρηπῖδος ὑψηλῆς λευκολίθου πρὸς τῷ ποταμῷ χῶμα
μέγα, ἄχρι κορυφῆς τοῖς ἀειθαλέσι τῶν δένδρων
συνηρεφές· ἐπ᾽ ἄκρῳ μὲν οὖν εἰκών ἐστι χαλκῆ
τοῦ Σεβαστοῦ Καίσαρος, ὑπὸ δὲ τῷ χώματι θῆκαί
εἰσιν αὐτοῦ καὶ τῶν συγγενῶν καὶ οἰκείων, ὄπισθεν
δὲ μέγα ἄλσος περιπάτους θαυμαστοὺς ἔχον· ἐν
μέσῳ δὲ τῷ πεδίῳ ὁ τῆς καύστρας αὐτοῦ περί-
βολος, καὶ οὗτος λίθου λευκοῦ, κύκλῳ μὲν περικεί-
μενον ἔχων σιδηροῦν περίφραγμα, ἐντὸς δ᾽ αἰγεί-
ροις κατάφυτος. πάλιν δ᾽ εἴ τις εἰς τὴν ἀγορὰν
παρελθὼν τὴν ἀρχαίαν ἄλλην ἐξ ἄλλης ἴδοι παραβεβλημένην ταύτῃ[1] καὶ βασιλικὰς στοὰς καὶ
ναούς, ἴδοι δὲ καὶ τὸ Καπιτώλιον καὶ τὰ ἐνταῦθα
ἔργα καὶ τὰ ἐν τῷ Παλατίῳ καὶ τῷ τῆς Λιβίας
περιπάτῳ, ῥᾳδίως ἐκλάθοιτ᾽ ἂν τῶν ἔξωθεν.
τοιαύτη μὲν ἡ Ῥώμη.

9. Τῶν δ᾽ ἄλλων τῆς Λατίνης πόλεων τὰς μὲν
ἑτέροις γνωρίσμασι, τὰς δὲ ὁδοῖς ἀφορίσαιτ᾽ ἄν
τις ταῖς γνωριμωτάταις, ὅσαι διὰ τῆς Λατίνης

---

[1] ταύτῃ, Corais, for ταύτην; so the later editors.

---

[1] The remains of this Mausoleum are still to be seen on
the Via de' Pontefici.
[2] Cassius Dio (69. 23) says that the Mausoleum was filled
by the time of Hadrian's death (138 A.D.).
[3] Cp. Suetonius, *Augustus* 100.

and very costly temples, in close succession to one
another, giving you the impression that they are
trying, as it were, to declare the rest of the city
a mere accessory. For this reason, in the belief
that this place was holiest of all, the Romans have
erected in it the tombs of their most illustrious men
and women. The most noteworthy is what is called
the Mausoleum,[1] a great mound near the river on a
lofty foundation of white marble, thickly covered
with ever-green trees to the very summit. Now on
top is a bronze image of Augustus Caesar; beneath
the mound are the tombs of himself and his kinsmen
and intimates;[2] behind the mound is a large sacred
precinct with wonderful promenades; and in the
centre of the Campus is the wall (this too of white
marble) round his crematorium;[3] the wall is surrounded by a circular iron fence and the space within
the wall is planted with black poplars. And again,
if, on passing to the old Forum, you saw one forum
after another ranged along the old one, and basilicas,[4]
and temples, and saw also the Capitolium and the
works of art there and those of the Palatium and
Livia's Promenade, you would easily become oblivious
to everything else outside.[5] Such is Rome.

9. As for the rest of the cities of Latium, their
positions may be defined, some by a different set of
distinctive marks, and others by the best known roads
that have been constructed through Latium; for they

---

[4] Tozer (*Selections*, p. 155) says, "ἄλλην ἐξ ἄλλης refer to
βασιλικὰς στοὰς" and translates, "should see, ranged one
after another on either side of this, both basilicas and temples." But the Greek hardly admits of his interpretation.

[5] For a more detailed account of the public works and
buildings at Rome, the reader is referred to Pliny 36. 24.

ἔστρωνται· ἢ γὰρ ἐπὶ ταύταις ἢ παρὰ ταύταις ἢ
μεταξὺ ἵδρυνται. γνωριμώταται δὲ τῶν ὁδῶν ἥ
τε Ἀππία καὶ ἡ Λατίνη καὶ ἡ Οὐαλερία· ἡ μὲν
C 237   τὰ πρὸς θαλάττῃ[1] ἀφορίζουσα μέρη τῆς Λατίνης
μέχρι Σινοέσσης, ἡ δὲ τὰ πρὸς τῇ Σαβίνῃ μέχρι
Μαρσῶν, μέση δ' αὐτῶν ἡ Λατίνη ἡ συμπίπτουσα
τῇ Ἀππίᾳ κατὰ Κασιλῖνον,[2] πόλιν διέχουσαν
Καπύης ἐννεακαίδεκα σταδίους· ἄρχεται δὲ[3] ἀπὸ
τῆς Ἀππίας, ἐν ἀριστερᾷ ἀπ' αὐτῆς ἐκτρεπομένη
πλησίον Ῥώμης, εἶτα διὰ τοῦ Τουσκλανοῦ ὄρους
ὑπερβᾶσα μεταξὺ Τούσκλου πόλεως καὶ τοῦ
Ἀλβανοῦ ὄρους κάτεισιν ἐπὶ Ἄλγιδον πολίχνιον
καὶ Πικτὰς πανδοχεῖα. εἶτα συμπίπτει καὶ ἡ Λα-
βικανή, ἀρχομένη μὲν ἀπὸ τῆς Ἠσκυλίνης πύλης,
ἀφ' ἧς καὶ ἡ Πραινεστίνη· ἐν ἀριστερᾷ δ' ἀφεῖσα
καὶ ταύτην καὶ τὸ πεδίον τὸ Ἠσκυλῖνον πρόεισιν
ἐπὶ πλείους τῶν ἑκατὸν καὶ εἴκοσι σταδίων, καὶ
πλησιάσασα τῷ Λαβικῷ, παλαιῷ κτίσματι κατε-
σπασμένῳ, κειμένῳ δ' ἐφ' ὕψους, τοῦτο μὲν καὶ
τὸ Τούσκουλον ἐν δεξιοῖς ἀπολείπει, τελευτᾷ δὲ
πρὸς τὰς Πικτὰς καὶ τὴν Λατίνην· διέχει δὲ τῆς
Ῥώμης τὸ χωρίον τοῦτο διακοσίους καὶ δέκα
σταδίους. εἶθ' ἑξῆς μὲν ἐπ' αὐτῆς τῆς Λατίνης
εἰσὶν ἐπίσημοι κατοικίαι καὶ πόλεις Φερέντινον,
Φρουσίνων, παρ' ἣν ὁ Κόσας ῥεῖ ποταμός, Φα-
βρατερία, παρ' ἣν ὁ Τρῆρος ῥεῖ, Ἀκουῖνον, ἢ[4]

---

[1] θαλάττῃ, Jones, for θάλατταν.
[2] Κασιλῖνον, Cluvier, for Κάσινον ; so the editors.
[3] τό, before ἀπό, is deleted by the editors.
[4] ἤ, Jones inserts before μεγάλη ; others bracket the ἐστὶ
after πόλις, or (as Meineke) delete it, or (as Corais) insert δὲ
after Ἀκουῖνον.

are situated either on these roads, or near them, or between them. The best known of the roads are the Appian Way, the Latin Way, and the Valerian Way. The Appian Way marks off, as far as Sinuessa, those parts of Latium that are next to the sea, and the Valerian Way, as far as the Marsi, those parts that are next to the Sabine country; while the Latin Way is between the two—the Way that unites with the Appian Way at Casilinum, a city nineteen stadia distant from Capua. The Latin Way begins, however, at the Appian Way, since near Rome it turns off from it to the left, and then, passing through the Tusculan Mountain, and over it at a point between the city of Tusculum and the Alban Mountain, runs down to the little city of Algidum and the Inns of Pictae;[1] and then it is joined by the Labican Way. This latter begins at the Esquiline Gate, as also does the Praenestine Way, but it leaves both the Praenestine Way and the Esquiline Plain to the left and runs on for more than one hundred and twenty stadia, and, on drawing near to Labicum (a city founded in early times, once situated on an eminence, but now demolished), leaves both it and Tusculum on the right and comes to an end at Pictae and the Latin Way; the distance of this place from Rome is two hundred and ten stadia. Then in order, as you proceed on the Latin Way itself, you come to important settlements and the cities of Ferentinum, Frusino (past which the Cosa[2] flows), Fabrateria (past which the Trerus[3] flows), Aquinum (it is a large city, and

---

[1] " Ad Pictas."
[2] The river is still called " Cosa."
[3] Now the Sacco.

μεγάλη πόλις ἐστί, παρ' ἣν ὁ Μέλπις ῥεῖ ποταμὸς
μέγας, Ἰντεράμνιον,[1] ἐν συμβολῇ δυεῖν ποταμῶν
κείμενον, Λείριός τε καὶ ἑτέρου· Κάσινον καὶ αὕτη
πόλις ἀξιόλογος, ὑστάτη τῶν Λατίνων. τὸ γὰρ
Τέανον τὸ καλούμενον Σιδικῖνον ἐφεξῆς κείμενον
ἐκ τοῦ ἐπιθέτου δηλοῦται διότι τῶν Σιδικίνων ἐστίν.
οὗτοι δὲ Ὄσκοι, Καμπανῶν ἔθνος ἐκλελοιπός,
ὥστε λέγοιτ' ἂν τῆς Καμπανίας καὶ αὕτη, μεγίστη
οὖσα τῶν ἐπὶ τῇ Λατίνῃ πόλεων, καὶ ἡ ἐφεξῆς
ἡ τῶν Καληνῶν, καὶ αὕτη ἀξιόλογος συνάπτουσα
τῷ Κασιλίνῳ.

10. Ἐφ' ἑκάτερα δὲ τῆς Λατίνης ἐν δεξιᾷ μέν
εἰσιν αἱ μεταξὺ αὐτῆς καὶ τῆς Ἀππίας, Σητία τε
καὶ Σιγνία, φέρουσαι οἶνον, ἡ μὲν τῶν πολυτελῶν
ἕνα, ἡ δὲ τὸν σταλτικώτατον κοιλίας, τὸν Σιγνῖνον[2]
λεγόμενον· πρὸ δὲ ταύτης[3] ἐστὶ Πρίβερνον καὶ
Κόρα καὶ Σύεσσα Τραπόντιον[4] τε καὶ Οὐελίτραι
καὶ Ἀλέτριον· ἔτι δὲ Φρεγέλλαι, παρ' ἣν ὁ Λεῖρις
ῥεῖ ὁ εἰς τὰς Μιντούρνας ἐκδιδούς, νῦν μὲν κώμη,
πόλις δέ ποτε γεγονυῖα ἀξιόλογος καὶ τὰς πολλὰς τῶν ἄρτι λεχθεισῶν περιοικίδας[5] πρότερον
ἐσχηκυῖα, αἳ νῦν εἰς αὐτὴν συνέρχονται, ἀγοράς
τε ποιούμεναι καὶ ἱεροποιίας τινάς· κατεσκάφη

---

[1] ὅν, before ἐν, Corais and others bracket ; Meineke rightly
deletes.
[2] Σιγνῖνον, Meineke, for Σίγνιον.
[3] Nearly all the editors, including Müller-Dübner and
Meineke, wrongly emend πρὸ δὲ ταύτης to πρὸς δὲ ταύταις.
[4] For Τραπόντιον, Siebenkees, from conjecture of Cluvier,
reads τῶν Πωμεντίνων, while C. Müller conjectures Καρβέντιον.
[5] περιοικίδας, Groskurd, for περιοικίας ; so the later editors.

---

[1] That is, the last on the Latin Way.
[2] Cales, now Calvi.

past it flows a large river, the Melpis), Interamnium
(which is situated at the confluence of two rivers,
the Liris and another), and Casinum (this too a noteworthy city), which is the last city of Latium;[1] for
what is called Teanum "Sidicinum," which is situated
next in order after Casinum, shows clearly from its
epithet that it belongs to the Sidicini.   These people
are Osci, a tribe of Campani that has disappeared;
and therefore this city might be called a part of
Campania, although it is the largest of the cities on
the Latin Way, as also might the city [2] that comes
next after it, that of the Caleni (this too a noteworthy city), although its territory joins that of
Casilinum.

10. Then take the cities on either side of the
Latin Way.   On the right are those between it and
the Appian Way, namely, Setia and Signia, which
produce wine, the former, one of the costly wines,
and the latter, the best for checking the bowels
(what is called the "Signine" wine).   And farther
on, beyond Signia, is Privernum, and Cora, and
Suessa,[3] and also Trapontium,[4] Velitrae, and Ale-
trium; and besides these, Fregellae (past which the
Liris flows, the river that empties at Minturnae[5]),
which is now merely a village, although it was once
a noteworthy city [6] and formerly held as dependencies
most of the surrounding cities just mentioned (and
at the present time the inhabitants of these cities
meet at Fregellae both to hold markets and to per-
form certain sacred rites), but, having revolted, it was

[3] Suessa Pometia, of which no traces are left.
[4] Trapontium is otherwise unknown, unless it be identified
with Tripontio, a place mentioned only in an inscription of
Trajan.   [5] Cp. 5. 3. 6.   [6] Cp. § 6 above.

δ᾽ ὑπὸ Ῥωμαίων ἀποστᾶσα. πλεῖσται δ᾽ εἰσὶ
καὶ τούτων καὶ τῶν ἐν τῇ Λατίνῃ καὶ τῶν
ἐπέκεινα ἐν τῇ Ἑρνίκων τε καὶ Αἴκων καὶ Οὐόλσκων ἱδρυμέναι, Ῥωμαίων δ᾽ εἰσὶ κτίσματα. ἐν
ἀριστερᾷ δὲ τῆς Λατίνης αἱ μεταξὺ αὐτῆς καὶ
C 238 τῆς Οὐαλερίας, Γάβιοι μὲν ἐν τῇ Πραινεστίνῃ
ὁδῷ κειμένη, λατόμιον ἔχουσα ὑπουργὸν τῇ Ῥώμῃ
μάλιστα τῶν ἄλλων, διέχουσα τὸ ἴσον τῆς
Ῥώμης τε καὶ Πραινέστου, περὶ ἑκατὸν σταδίους.
εἶθ᾽ ἡ Πραίνεστος, περὶ ἧς αὐτίκα ἐροῦμεν· εἶθ᾽
αἱ[1] ἐν τοῖς ὄρεσι τοῖς ὑπὲρ Πραίνεστον, ἥ τε τῶν
Ἑρνίκων πολίχνη Καπίτουλον καὶ Ἀναγνία,
πόλις ἀξιόλογος, καὶ Κερεάτε καὶ Σώρα, παρ᾽
ἣν ὁ Λεῖρις παρεξιὼν εἰς Φρεγέλλας ῥεῖ καὶ
Μιντούρνας· ἔπειτα ἄλλα τινὰ καὶ Οὐέναφρον,
ὅθεν τὸ κάλλιστον ἔλαιον· ἡ μὲν οὖν πόλις ἐφ᾽
ὕψους κεῖται, παραρρεῖ δὲ τὴν τοῦ λόφου ῥίζαν
ὁ Οὐουλτοῦρνος, ὃς καὶ παρὰ τὸ Κασιλῖνον
ἐνεχθεὶς ἐκδίδωσι κατὰ τὴν ὁμώνυμον αὐτῷ
πόλιν. Αἰσερνία δὲ καὶ Ἀλλιφαὶ ἤδη Σαυνι-
τικαὶ πόλεις εἰσίν, ἡ μὲν ἀνῃρημένη κατὰ τὸν
Μαρσικὸν πόλεμον, ἡ δ᾽ ἔτι συμμένουσα.

11. Ἡ Οὐαλερία δ᾽ ἄρχεται μὲν ἀπὸ Τιβούρων,
ἄγει δ᾽ ἐπὶ Μαρσοὺς καὶ Κορφίνιον, τὴν τῶν
Πελίγνων μητρόπολιν. εἰσὶ δ᾽ ἐν αὐτῇ Λατῖναι
πόλεις Οὐαρία[2] τε καὶ Καρσέολοι καὶ Ἄλβα,
πλησίον δὲ καὶ πόλις Κούκουλον. ἐν ὄψει δ᾽ εἰσὶ
τοῖς ἐν Ῥώμῃ Τίβουρά τε καὶ Πραίνεστος καὶ

---

[1] αἱ, the obvious correction of Corais, for ἡ.
[2] Οὐαρία, Kramer from the conj. of Cluvier, for Οὐαλερία;
so the later editors.

demolished by the Romans. Most of these cities, as also of those on the Latin Way and of those on the far side of it, are situated in the country of the Hernici, the Aeci, and the Volsci, though all were founded by the Romans. Again, on the left of the Latin Way are the cities between it and the Valerian Way: first, Gabii, situated on the Praenestine Way, with a rock-quarry that is more serviceable to Rome than any other, and equidistant—about one hundred stadia—from Rome and Praeneste; then Praeneste, about which I shall speak presently; then the cities in those mountains that are above Praeneste: Capitulum, the little city of the Hernici, and Anagnia, a noteworthy city, and Cereate, and Sora (past which the Liris flows as it issues from the mountains and comes to Fregellae and Minturnae [1]); and then certain other places, and Venafrum, whence comes the finest olive-oil. Now the city of Venafrum is situated on an eminence, and past the base of the hill flows the Volturnus River, which runs past Casilinum also and empties into the sea at the city of like name.[2] But when you come to the cities of Aesernia and Allifae you are already in Samnitic territory; the former was destroyed in the Marsic War, while the latter still endures.

11. The Valerian Way has its beginning at Tibur, and leads to the country of the Marsi, and to Corfinium, the metropolis of the Peligni. On the Valerian Way are the following cities of Latium: Varia, Carseoli, and Alba,[3] and also, near by, the city of Cuculum.[4] Tibur, Praeneste, and Tusculum are all visible from Rome. First, Tibur:

---

[1] Cp. 5. 3. 6.   [2] Volturnum.   [3] Alba Fucens.
[4] Now Cucullo, otherwise called Scutolo.

Τοῦσκλον. Τίβουρα μέν, ᾗ¹ τὸ Ἡράκλειον, καὶ
ὁ καταράκτης, ὃν ποιεῖ πλωτὸς ὢν ὁ Ἀνίων, ἀφ'
ὕψους μεγάλου καταπίπτων εἰς φάραγγα βαθεῖαν
καὶ καταλσῆ πρὸς αὐτῇ τῇ πόλει. ἐντεῦθεν δὲ
διέξεισι πεδίον εὐκαρπότατον παρὰ τὰ μέταλλα
τοῦ λίθου τοῦ Τιβουρτίνου καὶ τοῦ ἐν Γαβίοις,
καὶ τοῦ² ἐρυθροῦ λεγομένου, ὥστε τὴν ἐκ τῶν
μετάλλων ἐξαγωγὴν καὶ τὴν πορθμείαν εὐμαρῆ
τελέως εἶναι, τῶν πλείστων ἔργων τῆς Ῥώμης
ἐντεῦθεν κατασκευαζομένων. ἐν δὲ τῷ πεδίῳ
τούτῳ καὶ τὰ Ἄλβουλα καλούμενα ῥεῖ ὕδατα
ψυχρὰ ἐκ πολλῶν πηγῶν, πρὸς ποικίλας νόσους
καὶ πίνουσι καὶ ἐγκαθημένοις ὑγιεινά· τοιαῦτα δὲ καὶ τὰ Λαβανά, οὐκ ἄπωθεν τούτων ἐν
τῇ Νωμεντανῇ καὶ τοῖς περὶ Ἡρητὸν τόποις.
Πραίνεστος δ' ἐστὶν ὅπου τὸ τῆς Τύχης ἱερὸν
ἐπίσημον χρηστηριάζον· ἀμφότεραι δ' αἱ πόλεις
αὗται τῇ αὐτῇ προσιδρυμέναι τυγχάνουσιν ὀρεινῇ,
διέχουσι δ' ἀλλήλων ὅσον σταδίους ἑκατόν, τῆς
δὲ Ῥώμης Πραίνεστος μὲν καὶ διπλάσιον, Τίβουρα
δ' ἔλαττον. φασὶ δ' Ἑλληνίδας ἀμφοτέρας, Πραίνεστον γοῦν Πολυστέφανον καλεῖσθαι πρότερον.

---

¹ Before ᾗ Corais and Meineke insert ἐν; but Müller-
Dübner follow the MSS.
² For καὶ τοῦ Meineke, from conj. of Kramer, reads
τοῦ καί.

---

¹ Cp. 5. 3. 7.
² The Greek word here translated " wooded " suggests a
sacred grove. Strabo obviously refers to the grove that was
sacred to Tiburnus, the founder of Tibur. Cp. Horace, *Odes*
1. 7. 13.
³ Cp. Pliny 36. 48.   ⁴ Cp. § 10 above.

it possesses the temple of Heracles, and also the waterfall formed by the Anio, a navigable river [1] which falls down from a great height into a deep, wooded [2] ravine near the city itself. Thence the river flows out through a very fruitful plain past the quarries of the Tiburtine stone, [3] and of the stone of Gabii, [4] and of what is called " red stone " ; so that the delivery from the quarries and the transportation by water are perfectly easy—most of the works of art [5] at Rome being constructed of stone brought thence. In this plain, also, flow what are called the Albula waters [6]—cold waters from many springs, helpful, both as drinking-water and as baths, in the cure of various diseases; and such, also, are the Labana waters, [7] not far from the former, on the Nomentan Way and in the neighbourhood of Eretum. Secondly, Praeneste: here is the temple of Fortuna, noted for its oracles. [8] Both of these cities are situated near the same mountain range, and they are about one hundred stadia distant from one another; but from Rome Praeneste is as much as double that distance, whereas Tibur is less than double. Both are called Greek cities; [9] in any case Praeneste, they say, was formerly called " Polystephanos." [10]

---

[5] On " works of art," see 5. 2. 5. and footnote.

[6] Now " La Solfatara " (" Sulphur waters ").

[7] Now called " Bagni di Grotta Marozza."

[8] This was probably the largest temple in Italy. " The modern city of Palestrina is almost entirely built on its site and substructions " (Tozer, *Selections*, p. 157).

[9] Horace (*Carmina* 2. 6. 5) speaks of " Tibur, Argeo positum colono."

[10] " Many-wreathed," so called, apparently, from the several terraces. But Pliny (3. 9) says Praeneste was formerly called " Stephane " (Wreath).

ἐρυμνὴ μὲν οὖν ἑκατέρα, πολὺ δ' ἐρυμνοτέρα
Πραίνεστος· ἄκραν[1] γὰρ ἔχει τῆς μὲν πόλεως
ὕπερθεν ὄρος ὑψηλόν, ὄπισθεν δ' ἀπὸ τῆς συνε-
χούσης ὀρεινῆς αὐχένι διεζευγμένον, ὑπεραῖρον
καὶ δυσὶ σταδίοις τούτου πρὸς ὀρθίαν ἀνάβασιν.
C 239 πρὸς δὲ τῇ ἐρυμνότητι καὶ διώρυξι κρυπταῖς
διατέτρηται πανταχόθεν μέχρι τῶν πεδίων, ταῖς
μὲν ὑδρείας χάριν, ταῖς δ' ἐξόδων λαθραίων, ὧν
ἐν μιᾷ Μάριος πολιορκούμενος ἀπέθανε. ταῖς
μὲν οὖν ἄλλαις πόλεσι πλεῖστον τὸ εὐερκὲς πρὸς
ἀγαθοῦ τίθεται, Πραινεστίνοις δὲ συμφορὰ γεγένηται διὰ τὰς Ῥωμαίων στάσεις. καταφεύγουσι
γὰρ ἐκεῖσε οἱ νεωτερίσαντες· ἐκπολιορκηθέντων
δέ, πρὸς τῇ κακώσει τῆς πόλεως καὶ τὴν χώραν
ἀπαλλοτριοῦσθαι συμβαίνει, τῆς αἰτίας μετα-
φερομένης ἐπὶ τοὺς ἀναιτίους. ῥεῖ δὲ διὰ τῆς
χώρας Οὐέρεστις ποταμός. πρὸς ἕω δὲ τῆς Ῥώμης
εἰσὶν αἱ λεχθεῖσαι πόλεις.

12. Ἐνδοτέρω δὲ τῆς κατ' αὐτὰς ὀρεινῆς ἄλλη
ῥάχις ἐστί, μεταξὺ αὐλῶνα καταλείπουσα τὸν

---

[1] ἄκραν, Corais, for ἄκρον; so the later editors.

---

[1] Aix Praenestina; now Castel San Pietro.
[2] "This hill, which is of considerable elevation (being not
less than 2400 feet above the sea, and more than 1200 above
its immediate base), projects like a great buttress or bastion
from the angle of the Apennines towards the Alban Hills"
(Bunbury, *Dict. Geogr.* II, p. 665, quoted by Tozer). See
Encyc. Brit. s.v. "Praeneste" (J. G. Frazer).
[3] On the reservoirs of Praeneste, "hollowed out in the
rock of the mountain," and the water-supply in general, see
Magoffin, *A Study of the Topography of Praeneste*, Johns
Hopkins University Historical Studies, 1908, p. 435.

Now each is well fortified by nature, but Praeneste is much more so, since it has for a citadel [1] a high mountain which not only rises above the city but also in the rear is disjoined from the unbroken mountain range by a neck of land above which it rises as much as two stadia in a perpendicular ascent.[2] And in addition to its natural strength, subterranean passages have been bored through it from all sides as far as the plains—some for water-supply,[3] others for secret exits (it was in one of these that Marius was put to death when he was being besieged). Now although in the case of all other cities, generally speaking, good defences are accounted a blessing, in the case of the Praenestini they have proved to be a misfortune, because of the seditions among the Romans. For all who have attempted a revolution take refuge in Praeneste; and, if forced by a siege to surrender, the inhabitants, in addition to the damage done to their city, meet with the further misfortune that their territory is alienated, the guilt being transferred to the guiltless.[4] The Verestis [5] River flows through the territory in question. The aforesaid cities are to the east of Rome.

12. But still closer to Rome than the mountainous country [6] where these cities lie, there is another ridge, which leaves a valley (the valley near

---

[4] For example, in 198 B.C., when there was an uprising of slaves : in 82 B.C., when the younger Marius made Praeneste his headquarters. And in 63 B.C. Catiline sought to occupy Praeneste for headquarters but his effort was frustrated by the consul (Cicero, *Against Catiline* 1. 8).

[5] The "Verestis" is otherwise unknown.

[6] The Volscian Mountains.

κατὰ Ἄλγιδον, ὑψηλὴ μέχρι τοῦ Ἀλβανοῦ ὄρους.
ἐπὶ ταύτης δὴ τὸ Τοῦσκλον ἵδρυται, πόλις οὐ
φαύλως κατεσκευασμένη· κεκόσμηται δὲ ταῖς
κύκλῳ φυτείαις καὶ οἰκοδομίαις, καὶ μάλιστα
ταῖς ὑποπιπτούσαις ἐπὶ τὸ κατὰ τὴν Ῥώμην
μέρος. τὸ γὰρ Τούσκουλον ἐνταῦθα ἐστὶ λόφος
εὔγεως καὶ εὔυδρος, κορυφούμενος ἠρέμα πολλαχοῦ καὶ δεχόμενος βασιλείων κατασκευὰς
ἐκπρεπεστάτας. συνεχῆ δ᾽ ἐστὶ καὶ τὰ τῷ
Ἀλβανῷ ὄρει ὑποπίπτοντα, τὴν αὐτήν τε ἀρετὴν
ἔχοντα καὶ κατασκευήν. ἐφεξῆς δ᾽ ἐστὶ πεδία,
τὰ μὲν πρὸς τὴν Ῥώμην συνάπτοντα καὶ τὰ
προάστεια αὐτῆς, τὰ δὲ πρὸς τὴν θάλατταν· τὰ
μὲν οὖν πρὸς τὴν θάλατταν ἧττόν ἐστιν ὑγιεινά,
τὰ δὲ ἄλλα εὐάγωγά τε καὶ παραπλησίως
ἐξησκημένα. μετὰ δὲ τὸ Ἀλβαὸν Ἀρικία ἐστὶ
πόλις ἐπὶ τῇ ὁδῷ τῇ Ἀππίᾳ· στάδιοι δ᾽ εἰσὶν
ἐκ τῆς Ῥώμης ἑκατὸν ἑξήκοντα· κοῖλος δ᾽ ἐστὶν ὁ
τόπος, ἔχει δ᾽ ὅμως ἐρυμνὴν ἄκραν. ὑπέρκειται δ᾽
αὐτῆς τὸ μὲν Λανούιον,[1] πόλις Ῥωμαίων, ἐν
δεξιᾷ τῆς Ἀππίας ὁδοῦ, ἀφ᾽ ἧς ἔποπτος ἥ τε
θαλασσά ἐστι καὶ τὸ Ἄντιον, τὸ δ᾽ Ἀρτεμίσιον,
ὃ καλοῦσι Νέμος, ἐκ τοῦ ἐν ἀριστερᾷ μέρους τῆς
ὁδοῦ τοῖς[2] ἐξ Ἀρικίας ἀναβαίνουσιν. τῆς δ᾽
Ἀρικίνης τὸ ἱερὸν λέγουσιν ἀφίδρυμά τι·[3] τῆς

---

[1] Λανούιον. Cluvier. for Λανουΐνιον ; so the later editors.
[2] τοῖς. Siebenkees from conj. of Cluvier, for τῆς ; so
generally the later editors.
[3] The reading ἀναβαίνουσιν . . . . ἀφίδρυμά τι is that
of Groskurd so Meineke and others) for ἀναβαίνουσιν εἰς τὴν
δ᾽ Ἀρικίνην τὸ ἱερόν. λέγουσι δι᾽ ἀφιδρύματα.

---

[1] Mt. Albanus, now Monte Cavo, is the highest summit.
[2] That is, on one's way from Tusculum.

Algidum) between them and is high as far as Mt.
Albanus.[1] It is on this chain that Tusculum is
situated, a city with no mean equipment of buildings ; and it is adorned by the plantings and villas
encircling it, and particularly by those that extend
below the city in the general direction of the
city of Rome ; for here Tusculum is a fertile and
well-watered hill, which in many places rises gently
into crests and admits of magnificently devised royal
palaces. Adjoining this hill are also the foothills
of Mt. Albanus, with the same fertility and the
same kind of palaces. Then, next, come the plains,
some connecting with Rome and its suburbs, and
others with the sea. Now although the plains that
connect with the sea are less healthful, the others
are both pleasant to dwell in and decked out in
similar manner. After Mt. Albanus [2] comes Aricia,
a city on the Appian Way ; it is one hundred and
sixty stadia distant from Rome. Aricia lies in a
hollow, but for all that it has a naturally strong
citadel.[3] Above Aricia lies, first, on the right hand
side of the Appian Way, Lanuvium,[4] a city of the
Romans, from which both the sea and Antium are
visible, and, secondly, to the left of the Way as you
go up from Aricia, the Artemisium, which they call
Nemus.[5] The temple of the Arician,[6] they say, is a

[3] The ancient Aricia lay in the "Vallis Aricina" (now
"Valle Aricciana"), an extinct crater below the modern town
of Ariccia, which latter occupies the site of the ancient
citadel, a steep hill.
[4] "Lavinium," the reading of the MSS., has rightly been
emended to "Lanuvium." "Owing to a curious confusion
between this place and Lavinium, which dates back to the
middle ages, its modern name is 'Civita Lavinia'" (Tozer,
Selections, p. 159).   [5] That is "Nemus Dianae."
[6] *Sc.* "Diana," that is, "Artemis."

Ταυροπόλου· καὶ γὰρ τι βαρβαρικὸν κρατεῖ καὶ
Σκυθικὸν περὶ τὸ ἱερὸν ἔθος. καθίσταται γὰρ
ἱερεὺς ὁ γενηθεὶς αὐτόχειρ τοῦ ἱερωμένου πρότερον δραπέτης ἀνήρ· ξιφήρης οὖν ἐστιν ἀεί,
περισκοπῶν τὰς ἐπιθέσεις, ἕτοιμος ἀμύνεσθαι.
τὸ δ' ἱερὸν ἐν ἄλσει, πρόκειται δὲ λίμνη πελαγί-
ζουσα, κύκλῳ δ' ὀρεινὴ συνεχὴς ὀφρὺς περίκειται
καὶ λίαν¹ ὑψηλὴ καὶ τὸ ἱερὸν καὶ τὸ ὕδωρ
ἀπολαμβάνουσα ἐν κοίλῳ τόπῳ καὶ βαθεῖ. τὰς
μὲν οὖν πηγὰς ὁρᾶν ἐστιν, ἐξ ὧν ἡ λίμνη

O 240 πληροῦται· τούτων δ' ἐστὶν ἡ ² Ἡγερία καλουμένη,
δαίμονός τινος ἐπώνυμος· αἱ δ' ἀπορρύσεις ἐνταῦθα
μὲν ἄδηλοί εἰσιν, ἔξω δὲ δείκνυνται πόρρω πρὸς
τὴν ἐπιφάνειαν ἀνέχουσαι.

13. Πλησίον δ' ἐστὶ τῶν χωρίων τούτων καὶ
Ἀλβανὸν ὄρος πολὺ ὑπερκῦπτον τοῦ Ἀρτεμισίου
καὶ τῶν περὶ αὐτὸ ὀφρύων, καίπερ ὑψηλῶν οὐσῶν
καὶ ὀρθίων ἱκανῶς. ἔχει δὲ καὶ τοῦτο λίμνην
πολὺ μείζω τῆς κατὰ τὸ Ἀρτεμίσιον.³ προσωτέρω
δὲ τούτων αἱ λεχθεῖσαι πρότερον πόλεις τῆς
Λατίνης εἰσί. μάλιστα δ' ἐν μεσογαίᾳ τῶν
Λατίνων πόλεών ἐστιν ἡ Ἄλβα, ὁμοροῦσα

---

¹ λίαν, Corais (who omits καί), for μίαν; so the later
editors.
² ἡ Ἡγερία, Corais, for ἱερεία; so Meineke.
³ ὄρος after Ἀρτεμίσιον, Corais deletes; so generally the
editors, including Meineke.

---

¹ That is, "Artemis Tauropolos"—Artemis in her capacity
as goddess of the Tauri.
² The "Scythian element" referred to is the sacrifice of
strangers by the Tauri, as described, for example, in Euripides' Iphigeneia among the Tauri.
³ Strabo refers to the Lacus Nemorensis (now Lago di

copy of that of the Tauropolos.[1] And in fact a
barbaric, and Scythian,[2] element predominates in
the sacred usages, for the people set up as priest
merely a run-away slave who has slain with his own
hand the man previously consecrated to that office;
accordingly the priest is always armed with a sword,
looking around for the attacks, and ready to defend
himself. The temple is in a sacred grove, and in
front of it is a lake which resembles an open sea,
and round about it in a circle lies an unbroken
and very high mountain-brow, which encloses both
the temple and the water in a place that is
hollow and deep. You can see the springs, it is
true, from which the lake is fed (one of them is
"Egeria," as it is called after a certain deity), but
the outflows at the lake itself are not apparent,
though they are pointed out to you at a distance
outside the hollow, where they rise to the surface.[3]

13. Near these places is also Mt. Albanus, which
rises considerably above the Artemisium and the
mountain-brows round about it, though they too are
high and rather steep. This mountain also has a lake,[4]
much larger than the one at the Artemisium. The
previously mentioned cities of Latium[5] are farther
away[6] than these places. But of all the cities of
Latium, Alba[7] is the farthest in the interior, since

Nemi), an extinct crater three miles in circumference and
over three hundred feet deep. It is now drained by an
artificial emissarium. According to Servius (note on Virgil,
Aeneid 7. 515) it was called by the Latini the "Speculum"
("mirror") of Diana.

[4] Lacus Albanus, now Lago di Albano.
[5] Tibur and Praeneste.
[6] That is, from Rome—the same standpoint as at beginning
of § 9.   [7] Alba Fucens.

Μαρσοῖς· ἵδρυται δ' ἐφ' ὑψηλοῦ πάγου λίμνης[1]
Φουκίνας πλησίον, πελαγίας τὸ μέγεθος· χρῶνται
δ' αὐτῇ μάλιστα μὲν Μαρσοὶ καὶ πάντες οἱ
πλησιόχωροι. φασὶ δ' αὐτὴν καὶ πληροῦσθαί
ποτε μέχρι τῆς ὀρεινῆς καὶ ταπεινοῦσθαι πάλιν,
ὥστ' ἀναψύχειν τοὺς λιμνωθέντας τόπους καὶ
γεωργεῖσθαι παρέχειν, ἤτοι μεταστάσεις τῶν
κατὰ βάθους ὑγρῶν σποράδην καὶ ἀδήλως
γίνονται, πάλιν δ' ἐπισυρρέουσιν, ἢ τελέως
ἐκλείπουσιν αἱ πηγαὶ καὶ πάλιν συνθλίβονται,
καθάπερ ἐπὶ τοῦ Ἀμενάνου συμβαίνειν φασὶ
τοῦ διὰ Κατάνης ῥέοντος· ἐκλείπει γὰρ ἐπὶ πολλὰ
ἔτη καὶ πάλιν ῥεῖ. ἐκ δὲ τῆς Φουκίνας εἶναι τὰς
πηγὰς ἱστοροῦσι τοῦ Μαρκίου ὕδατος τοῦ τὴν
Ῥώμην ποτίζοντος καὶ παρὰ τἆλλα εὐδοκιμοῦντος
ὕδατα. τῇ δὲ Ἄλβᾳ διὰ τὸ ἐν βάθει τῆς χώρας
ἱδρῦσθαι καὶ διὰ τὸ εὐερκὲς ἀντὶ φρουρᾶς ἐχρή-
σαντο πολλάκις Ῥωμαῖοι, τοὺς φυλακῆς δεομένους
ἐνταῦθα καθείργοντες.

---

[1] λίμνης . . . . ., πελαγίας, Meineke, for λίμνη . . . . ,
πελαγία.

---

[1] Lago di Fucino (Celano) was completely drained by
Prince Torlonia, 1855–1869 A.D.
[2] That is, the flowing waters in the depths of the earth
(cp. 3. 5. 7), as distinguished from the "springs" by which
Strabo always means the mouths at the surface of the earth.

it is on the confines of the Marsi; it is situated on a
lofty rock, near Lake Fucinus,[1] which in size is like
an open sea. The lake is used mostly by the Marsi
and all the neighbouring peoples. They say that it
not only fills up sometimes as far as the mountainous
country, but also lowers again enough to permit the
places which have been converted into marshes to
get dry and to be tilled—whether it be that changes
take place, sporadically and in a way that is not
apparent, in the flow of the waters down in the
depths,[2] and that they flow back together again, or
that the springs completely fail and then by pres-
sure are brought together again—as is said to be the
case with the Amenanus, the river that flows through
Catana, for it fails for many years and then flows
again.[3] It is from Lake Fucinus, the story goes,
that the springs of the Aqua Marcia come,[4] which
brings drinking-water to Rome and has the highest
repute as compared with the other waters. Because
of the fact that Alba is situated deep in the interior
of the country, and is also well-walled, the Romans
often used it for a prison, shutting up therein those
who have to be kept under guard.[5]

[3] The result, apparently, of volcanic action in Mt. Aetna
from which it flows.
[4] The "Aqua Marcia" was one of the Roman aqueducts, and
its principal reservoir was near Sublaqueum (now Subiaco).
The story was that the River Pitonius (now Pedogna) rose
in the mountains of the Peligni, flowed through Lake Fucinus
without mingling with its waters, then disappeared in the
earth, and finally came forth as the "Marcian Waters" near
Sublaqueum. Pliny himself (31. 24) believed the story (see
Tozer, *Selections*, p. 162).
[5] For instance, Syphax, King of Numidia (Livy 30. 17),
Perseus, King of Macedonia (Livy 45. 42), and Bituitus,
King of the Arverni (Valerius Max. 9. 6, and Livy *Epit.* 61).

STRABO

IV

1. Ἐπεὶ δ' ἀπὸ τῶν προσαλπίων ἐθνῶν ἀρξάμενοι καὶ τῶν πρὸς αὐτοῖς ὀρῶν τῶν Ἀπεννίνων, ἔπειθ' ὑπερβάντες ταῦτα τὴν ἐντὸς ἐπήλθομεν πᾶσαν ὅση μεταξὺ κεῖται τοῦ Τυρρηνικοῦ πελάγους καὶ τῶν Ἀπεννίνων ὀρῶν τῶν κεκλιμένων πρὸς τὸν Ἀδρίαν μέχρι Σαυνιτῶν καὶ Καμπανῶν, νῦν ἐπανιόντες δηλώσομεν τὰ ἐν τοῖς ὄρεσι τούτοις οἰκοῦντα καὶ ταῖς ὑπωρείαις τῆς τε ἐκτὸς μέχρι τῆς παραλίας τῆς Ἀδριατικῆς καὶ τῆς ἐντός. ἀρκτέον δὲ πάλιν ἀπὸ τῶν Κελτικῶν ὅρων.[1]

2. Ἔστι δ' ἡ Πικεντίνη[2] μετὰ τὰς τῶν Ὀμβρικῶν πόλεις τὰς μεταξὺ Ἀριμίνου καὶ Ἀγκῶνος. ὥρμηνται δ' ἐκ τῆς Σαβίνης οἱ Πικεντῖνοι, δρυοκολάπτου τὴν ὁδὸν ἡγησαμένου τοῖς ἀρχηγέταις, ἀφ' οὗ καὶ τοὔνομα· πῖκον γὰρ τὸν ὄρνιν τοῦτον ὀνομάζουσι, καὶ νομίζουσιν Ἄρεως ἱερόν. οἰκοῦσι δ' ἀπὸ τῶν ὀρῶν ἀρξάμενοι μέχρι τῶν πεδίων καὶ τῆς θαλάττης, ἐπὶ μῆκος ηὐξημένην ἔχοντες μᾶλλον ἢ πλάτος τὴν χώραν, ἀγαθὴν πρὸς ἅπαντα, βελτίω δὲ τοῖς ξυλίνοις καρποῖς ἢ τοῖς σιτικοῖς. ἔστι δ' εὖρος μὲν τὸ ἀπὸ τῶν ὀρῶν ἐπὶ θάλατταν ἀνώμαλον τοῖς διαστήμασι, μῆκος δ' ἀπὸ Αἴσιος ποταμοῦ μέχρι Κάστρου παράπλουν ἔχον σταδίων ὀκτακοσίων. πόλεις δ' Ἀγκὼν μὲν Ἑλληνίς, Συρακουσίων κτίσμα τῶν φυγόντων τὴν Διονυσίου τυραννίδα· κεῖται δ' ἐπ' ἄκρας μὲν

C 241

---

[1] That is, the southern boundaries of Cisalpine Celtica (Gaul); see 5. 1. 3 and 5. 2. 10.
[2] Picenum.

IV

1. I began with the tribes that live next to the Alps, and with that part of the Apennine Mountains which lies next to them, and then, passing over that part, traversed all the country on this side which lies between the Tyrrhenian Sea and that part of the Apennine Mountains which bends towards the Adriatic and stretches to the countries of the Samnitae and the Campani; I shall now, therefore, go back and indicate the tribes that live in these mountains, and also in the foothills both of the country outside the mountains, as far as the Adriatic seaboard, and of the country this side. But I must begin again with the Celtic boundaries.[1]

2. Next after those cities of the Ombrici that are between Ariminum and Ancona comes the Picentine country.[2] The Picentini are originally from the Sabine country, a woodpecker having led the way for their progenitors; and hence their name, for they call this bird " picus," and consider it sacred to Mars. The country they live in begins at the mountains and extends as far as the plains and the sea, thus having increased in length more than breadth; it is good for every use to which it may be put, though better for fruits than for grain. Its breadth—that from the mountains to the sea—taken at the different intervals,[3] is irregular, while its length, by a voyage along the coast from the Aesis River to Castrum, is eight hundred stadia. Its cities are, first, Ancona, a Greek city, founded by the Syracusans who fled from the tyranny of Dionysius; it is situated on a promontory, which by its curve,

[3] That is, at the different cities on the seacoast.

λιμένα ἐμπεριλαμβανούσης τῇ πρὸς τὰς ἄρκτους ἐπιστροφῇ, σφόδρα δ' εὔοινός ἐστι καὶ πυροφόρος.[1] πλησίον δ' αὐτῆς Αὔξουμον πόλις μικρὸν ὑπὲρ τῆς θαλάττης· εἶτα Σεπτέμπεδα καὶ Πνευεντία καὶ Ποτεντία καὶ Φίρμον Πικηνόν· ἐπίνειον δὲ ταύτης Κάστελλον. ἐφεξῆς δὲ τὸ τῆς Κύπρας ἱερόν, Τυρρηνῶν ἵδρυμα καὶ κτίσμα· τὴν δ' Ἥραν ἐκεῖνοι Κύπραν καλοῦσιν· εἶτα Τρουεντῖνος ποταμὸς καὶ πόλις ἐπώνυμος· εἶτα Καστρουνόουμ[2] καὶ ὁ Ματρῖνος ποταμός, ῥέων ἀπὸ τῆς Ἀδριανῶν πόλεως, ἔχων ἐπίνειον τῆς Ἀδρίας ἐπώνυμον ἑαυτοῦ. ἔστι δ' ἐν τῇ μεσογαίᾳ καὶ αὕτη καὶ τὸ Ἄσκλον τὸ Πικηνόν, ἐρυμνότατον χωρίον καὶ[3] ἐφ' ᾧ κεῖται τὸ τεῖχος, καὶ τὰ περικείμενα ὄρη στρατοπέδοις οὐ βάσιμα. ὑπὲρ δὲ τῆς Πικεντίνης Οὐηστῖνοί τε καὶ Μαρσοὶ καὶ Πελίγνοι καὶ Μαρρουκῖνοι καὶ Φρεντανοί, Σαυνιτικὸν ἔθνος, τὴν ὀρεινὴν κατέχουσιν, ἐφαπτόμενοι μικρὰ τῆς θαλάττης. ἔστι δὲ τὰ ἔθνη ταῦτα μικρὰ μέν, ἀνδρικώτατα δὲ καὶ πολλάκις τὴν ἀρετὴν ταύτην ἐπιδεδειγμένα Ῥωμαίοις, πρῶτον μέν, ἡνίκα ἐπολέμουν· δεύτερον δέ, ὅτε συνεστράτευον· τρίτον

---

[1] πυροφόρος, Corais, for εὐπυροφόρος ; see Meineke.

[2] Καστρουνόουμ (Corais, -νόβουμ ; Meineke, -νόουν) Jones, for καὶ τρουνόουμ (see Αἰκουουμ—, 5. 2. 9).

[3] After καὶ Kramer suggests the insertion of διὰ τὸν λόφον. Since Groskurd the editors indicate a lacuna after καί.

---

[1] "Pneuentia" is otherwise unknown ; perhaps Strabo wrote "Pollentia" (see Corais-du Theil-Letronne, Vol. II., p. 236, and Nissen, *Italische Landeskunde*, Vol. II., p. 422.

[2] Castellum Firmanorum, now Porto di Ferno or Porto San Giorgio.

[3] In Latin, "Cuprae Fanum."

towards the north encloses a harbour; and it is
exceedingly productive of wine and wheat. Near
it is the city of Auxumum, which is a short distance
above the sea; then Septempeda, Pneuentia,[1]
Potentia and Firmum Picenum (its port-town is
Castellum).[2] Next in order comes the temple of
Cupra,[3] which was established, and founded as a city,
by the Tyrrheni, who call Hera "Cupra"; then,
the River Truentinus [4] and the city named after it;[5]
then Castrum Novum, and the River Matrinus [6]
(which flows from the city of the Adriani [7]), on
which is Adria's port-town,[8] named after the river.
Not only is Adria in the interior, but also Asculum
Picenum, a place that is well fortified by nature, not
only where the wall is situated—but also the
mountains that lie round about it are impassable
for armies.[9] Beyond the Picentine country are the
Vestini, the Marsi, the Peligni, the Marrucini, and
the Frentani (a Samnitic tribe); they occupy the
mountain-country there, their territory touching
upon the sea for only short stretches. These tribes
are small, it is true, but they are very brave and
oftentimes have exhibited this virtue to the Romans:
first, when they went to war against them; a second
time, when they took the field with them as allies;

[4] Now the Tronto.
[5] Truentum, also called Castrum Truentinum.
[6] Now the Piomba.
[7] Adria, or Hadria.   [8] Matrinum.
[9] The words "not only . . . armies" are awkward in
English as in the Greek, but the meaning is clear enough.
Kramer's guess (see critical note on opposite page) would
yield the following: "not only on account of the hill on
which the wall is situated, but also (on account of) the
mountains that lie round about it, which are impassable for
armies."

δ᾽, ὅτε δεόμενοι τυχεῖν ἐλευθερίας καὶ πολιτείας
μὴ τυγχάνοντες ἀπέστησαν καὶ τὸν Μαρσικὸν
καλούμενον ἐξῆψαν πόλεμον, Κορφίνιον, τῶν
Πελίγνων μητρόπολιν, κοινὴν ἅπασι τοῖς Ἰταλιώταις ἀποδείξαντες πόλιν ἀντὶ τῆς Ῥώμης, ὁρμητήριον τοῦ πολέμου, μετονομασθεῖσαν Ἰταλικήν,
καὶ ἐνταῦθα δὴ[1] τοὺς συνεπομένους ἀθροίσαντες
καὶ χειροτονήσαντες ὑπάτους καὶ στρατηγούς·
δύο δ᾽ ἔτη συνέμειναν ἐν τῷ πολέμῳ, μέχρι
διεπράξαντο τὴν κοινωνίαν περὶ ἧς ἐπολέμουν.
Μαρσικὸν δὲ ὠνόμασαν τὸν πόλεμον ἀπὸ τῶν
ἀρξάντων τῆς ἀποστάσεως, καὶ μάλιστα ἀπὸ
Πομπαιδίου. τὰ μὲν οὖν ἄλλα κωμηδὸν ζῶσιν,
ἔχουσι δὲ καὶ πόλεις ὑπὲρ μὲν τῆς θαλάττης
τό τε Κορφίνιον καὶ Σούλμων[2] καὶ Μαρούιον καὶ
Τεάτε[3] τὴν τῶν Μαρρουκίνων μητρόπολιν. ἐπ᾽
αὐτῇ δὲ τῇ θαλάττῃ τό τε Ἄτερνον, ὅμορον τῇ
Πικεντίνῃ, ὁμώνυμον δὲ τῷ ποταμῷ τῷ διορίζοντι
τήν τε Οὐηστίνην καὶ τὴν Μαρρουκίνην· ῥεῖ γὰρ
ἐκ τῆς Ἀμιτερνίνης, διὰ δὲ Οὐηστίνων, παρα-
λιπὼν ἐν δεξιᾷ τοὺς Μαρρουκίνους ὑπὲρ[4] τῶν
Πελίγνων κειμένους, ζεύγματι περατός. τὸ δὲ
πόλισμα τὸ ἐπώνυμον αὐτοῦ Οὐηστίνων μέν

---

[1] δή, Kramer, for δέ; so the later editors.
[2] Σούλμων, Jones, for Σοῦλμον; Meineke emends to
Σούλμωνα.
[3] Τεάτε, Jones, for Τεγεάτην (C.), Τεαγεάτην (B.); Müller-
Dübner and Meineke read Τεατέαν.
[4] τῷ, after ὑπέρ, the editors omit.

---

[1] But on coins the name is spelled "Italia," not "Italica"
(Pauly-Wissowa, s.v. "Corfinium").

and a third time when, begging for freedom and
political rights without getting them, they revolted
and kindled what is called the Marsic War, for they
proclaimed Corfinium (the metropolis of the Peligni)
the common city for all the Italiotes, instead of
Rome, making it their base of operations for the
war and changing its name to Italica;[1] and here it
was that they mustered all their followers and
elected consuls and praetors.[2] And they persisted
in the war for two years, until they achieved the
partnership for which they went to war. The war
was named "Marsic" after the people who began
the revolt, Pompaedius in particular.[3] Now these
peoples live in villages, generally speaking, but they
also have cities: first, above the sea, Corfinium,
Sulmon, Maruvium, and Teate,[4] the metropolis of
the Marrucini. And, secondly, on the sea itself,
Aternum, which borders on the Picentine country
and is of like name with the river[5] that separates
the Vestine country from the Marrucine; for it flows
from the territory of Amiternum, and through the
Vestine country, leaving on its right that part of
the Marrucine country which lies above the Peligni
(it may be crossed by a pontoon-bridge).[6] But
although the little city[7] that is named after the river

---

[1] They chose two consuls and twelve praetors, in imitation
of the Roman government (see Nissen, *Italische Landskunde*,
Vol. II., p. 448, and also Corais-du Theil-Letronne, Vol. II.,
p. 242.

[3] Pompaedius Silo, the Marsian, was killed in battle in
88 B.C., shortly before the end of the war.

[4] Now Chieti.   [5] The Aternus.

[6] On this bridge, see Nissen, *Italische Landeskunde*, Vol.
II., p. 439.

[7] The same Aternum above-mentioned.

C 242 ἐστι, κοινῷ δ' ἐπινείῳ χρῶνται καὶ οἱ Πελίγνοι
καὶ οἱ Μαρρουκῖνοι· διέχει δὲ τὸ ζεῦγμα τέτταρας
καὶ εἴκοσι σταδίους ἀπὸ Κορφινίου. μετὰ δὲ
Ἄτερνον Ὄρτων, ἐπίνειον Φρεντανῶν, καὶ Βοῦκα,
καὶ αὐτὴ[1] Φρεντανῶν, ὅμορος Τεάνῳ τῷ Ἀπούλῳ.
Ὀρτώνιόν[2] ἐστιν ἐν τοῖς Φρεντάνοις, πέτραι
λῃστρικῶν ἀνθρώπων, οἷς αἱ οἰκήσεις ἀπὸ τῶν
ναυαγίων πήγνυνται· καὶ τἆλλα θηριώδεις εἶναι
λέγονται.[3] μεταξὺ δὲ Ὄρτωνος καὶ Ἀτέρνου ὁ
Σάγρος ποταμὸς ὁρίζων τοὺς Φρεντανοὺς ἀπὸ
τῶν Πελίγνων· ὁ δὲ παράπλους ἀπὸ τῆς Πικεντίνης ἐπὶ τοὺς Ἀπούλους οὓς οἱ Ἕλληνες
Δαυνίους καλοῦσι, σταδίων ἐστὶν ὅσον τετρακοσίων ἐνενήκοντα.

3. Ἑξῆς δὲ μετὰ τὴν Λατίνην ἐστὶν ἥ τε Καμπανία, παρήκουσα τῇ θαλάττῃ, καὶ ὑπὲρ ταύτην
ἡ Σαυνῖτις ἐν μεσογαίᾳ μέχρι Φρεντανῶν καὶ τῶν
Δαυνίων, εἶτ' αὐτοὶ Δαύνιοι καὶ τἆλλα ἔθνη τὰ
μέχρι τοῦ Σικελικοῦ πορθμοῦ. πρῶτον δὲ περὶ
τῆς Καμπανίας ῥητέον. ἔστι δ' ἀπὸ τῆς Σινοέσσης
ἐπὶ μὲν τὴν ἑξῆς παραλίαν κόλπος εὐμεγέθης
μέχρι Μισηνοῦ, κἀκεῖθεν ἄλλος κόλπος πολὺ

---

[1] αὐτή, Groskurd, for αὐτό; so the later editors.
[2] See note 2 below.
[3] λέγονται is not found in the earlier MSS., and only
in *n p*.

---

[1] Apparently what is now Termoli (see Pauly-Wissowa,
s.v., and Nissen, Vol. II., p. 783).
[2] "Ortonium" is otherwise unknown. The text appears
to be corrupt, but all emendations are mere guesses. Meineke
relegates the whole sentence to the foot of the page. We
should have expected Strabo to refer here to the Frento River
as the southern boundary of the country of the Frentani.

belongs to the Vestini, it is used as a common port
both by the Peligni and the Marrucini. The pontoon-
bridge is twenty-four stadia distant from Corfinium.
After Aternum comes Orton, the port-town of the
Frentani, and then Buca[1] (it too belongs to the
Frentani), whose territory borders on that of Teanum
Apulum. Ortonium[2] is in the country of the
Frentani, a cliff-town belonging to pirates, whose
dwellings are pieced together from the wreckage of
ships; and in every other respect they are said to
be a bestial folk. Between Orton and Aternum is
the Sagrus River, which separates the country of the
Frentani from that of the Peligni.[3] The voyage
along the coast from the Picentine country to
the country of those Apuli whom the Greeks
call "Daunii"[4] is about four hundred and ninety
stadia.

3. Next in order after Latium come both Campania,
which stretches along the sea, and, above Campania,
in the interior, the Samnite country,[5] which extends
as far as the country of the Frentani and the Daunii;
then the Daunii themselves, and the rest of the tribes
on to the Sicilian Strait. But I must first speak of
Campania. There is a fair-sized gulf which, beginning
at Sinuessa, extends along the coast next thereafter
as far as Misenum, and also another gulf, much larger
than the first, which begins at Misenum; they call

---

[3] Ptolemaeus (3. 16) wrongly associates the *mouth* of the
Sagrus with the country of the Peligni (cp. Nissen, Vol. II.,
p. 778), for the Sagrus empties between Ortona and Histonium
(not Aternum). Strabo's assertion, however, might be interpreted to mean, not the lower course, but the northerly fork,
of the Sagrus; otherwise he too is in error.
[4] Cp. 5. 1. 9 and 6. 3. 9. [5] Samnium.

μείζων τοῦ προτέρου, καλοῦσι δ' αὐτὸν Κρατῆρα,
ἀπὸ τοῦ Μισηνοῦ μέχρι τοῦ 'Αθηναίου, δυεῖν
ἀκρωτηρίων, κολπούμενον. ὑπὲρ δὲ τούτων τῶν
ἠιόνων Καμπανία πᾶσα ἵδρυται, πεδίον εὐδαιμονέ-
στατον τῶν ἁπάντων· περίκεινται δ' αὐτῷ γεωλοφίαι τε εὔκαρποι καὶ ὄρη τά τε τῶν Σαυνιτῶν
καὶ τὰ τῶν Ὄσκων. 'Αντίοχος μὲν οὖν φησι τὴν
χώραν ταύτην 'Οπικοὺς οἰκῆσαι, τούτους δὲ καὶ
Αὔσονας καλεῖσθαι, Πολύβιος δ' ἐμφαίνει δύο
ἔθνη νομίζων ταῦτα· 'Οπικοὺς γάρ φησι καὶ
Αὔσονας οἰκεῖν τὴν χώραν ταύτην περὶ τὸν
Κρατῆρα. ἄλλοι δὲ λέγουσιν, οἰκούντων 'Οπικῶν
πρότερον καὶ Αὐσόνων, Σιδικίνους [1] κατασχεῖν
ὕστερον Ὄσκων τι ἔθνος, τούτους δ' ὑπὸ Κυμαίων,
ἐκείνους δ' ὑπὸ Τυρρηνῶν ἐκπεσεῖν· διὰ γὰρ τὴν
ἀρετὴν περιμάχητον γενέσθαι τὸ πεδίον· δώδεκα
δὲ πόλεις ἐγκατοικίσαντας τὴν οἷον κεφαλὴν
ὀνομάσαι Καπύην. διὰ δὲ τὴν τρυφὴν εἰς μα-
λακίαν τραπομένους, καθάπερ τῆς περὶ τὸν Πάδον
χώρας ἐξέστησαν, οὕτω καὶ ταύτης παραχωρῆσαι
Σαυνίταις, τούτους δ' ὑπὸ 'Ρωμαίων ἐκπεσεῖν.
τῆς δ' εὐκαρπίας ἐστὶ σημεῖον τὸ σῖτον ἐνταῦθα
γίνεσθαι τὸν κάλλιστον, λέγω δὲ τὸν πύρινον, ἐξ
οὗ καὶ ὁ χόνδρος, κρείττων ὢν πάσης καὶ ὀρύζης
καὶ ἐν ὀλίγῳ σιτικῆς τροφῆς. ἱστορεῖται δ' ἔνια

---

[1] Σιδικίνους, Madvig, and Niese independently, for οἱ δ'
ἐκείνους (see 5. 3. 10). Siebenkees, Corais, Groskurd, and
Müller-Dübner read μετ' ἐκείνους; Kramer conjectures σὺν
ἐκείνοις; Meineke strangely omits the phrase altogether
without comment.

the latter[1] the "Crater,"[2] and the "Crater" forms
a bay between the two capes of Misenum[3] and
Athenaeum.[4]   Above these coasts lies the whole of
Campania; it is the most blest of all plains, and
round about it lie fruitful hills, and the mountains
of the Samnitae and of the Osci.   Antiochus,[5] it is
true, says that the Opici once lived in this country
and that "they are also called Ausones," but Polybius
clearly believes that they are two different tribes, for
he says "the Opici and the Ausones live in this
country round about the Crater."   Again, others
say that, although at first it was inhabited by the
Opici, and also by the Ausones,[6] later on it was
taken by the Sidicini, an Oscan tribe,[7] but the Sidicini were ejected by the Cumaei, and in turn the
Cumaei by the Tyrrheni.   For on account of its
fertility, they continue, the plain became an object
of contention; and the Tyrrheni founded twelve
cities in the country and named their capital city
"Capua";[8] but on account of their luxurious living
they became soft, and consequently, just as they had
been made to get out of the country round about the
Padus,[9] so now they had to yield this country to the
Samnitae; and in turn the Samnitae were ejected
by the Romans.   A proof of the fruitfulness of the
country is that it produces the finest grain—I mean
the wheat from which groats are made, which is
superior, not only to every kind of rice, but also to
almost every kind of grain-food.   It is reported

---

[1] The Gulf of Naples.   [2] Cp. 5. 4. 8.
[3] Now Cape Miseno.
[4] In Latin, Minerva; now Punta della Campanella.
[5] Antiochus Syracusanus, the historian.
[6] See Pauly-Wissowa, *s.v.*   [7] See 5. 3. 9.
[8] Cp. 5. 4. 10.   [9] See 5. 1. 10.

τῶν πεδίων σπείρεσθαι δι᾽ ἔτους δὶς μὲν τῇ ζειᾷ,
C 243 τὸ δὲ τρίτον ἐλύμῳ, τινὰ δὲ καὶ λαχανεύεσθαι τῷ
τετάρτῳ σπόρῳ. καὶ μὴν τὸν οἶνον τὸν κράτιστον
ἐντεῦθεν ἔχουσι Ῥωμαῖοι τὸν Φάλερνον καὶ τὸν
Στατανὸν καὶ Καληνόν· ἤδη δὲ καὶ ὁ Σουρεντῖνος
ἐνάμιλλος καθίσταται τούτοις, νεωστὶ πειρασθεὶς
ὅτι παλαίωσιν δέχεται. ὡς δ᾽ αὕτως εὐέλαιός
ἐστι καὶ πᾶσα ἡ περὶ τὸ Οὐέναφρον, ὅμορον τοῖς
πεδίοις ὄν.

4. Πόλεις δ᾽ ἐπὶ μὲν τῇ θαλάττῃ μετὰ τὴν
Σινόεσσαν Λίτερνον, ὅπου τὸ μνῆμα τὸ Σκιπίωνος
τοῦ πρώτου προσαγορευθέντος Ἀφρικανοῦ· διέ-
τριψε γὰρ ἐνταῦθα τὸ τελευταῖον, ἀφεὶς τὰς
πολιτείας κατ᾽ ἀπέχθειαν τὴν πρός τινας.
παραρρεῖ δὲ ὁμώνυμος τῇ πόλει ποταμός. ὡς δ᾽
αὕτως καὶ Οὐουλτοῦρνος ὁμώνυμός ἐστι τῇ παρ᾽
αὐτὸν πόλει ἐφεξῆς κειμένῃ· ῥεῖ δ᾽ οὗτος διὰ
Οὐενάφρου καὶ τῆς Καμπανίας μέσης. ταύταις
δ᾽ ἐφεξῆς ἐστι Κύμη, Χαλκιδέων καὶ Κυμαίων
παλαιότατον κτίσμα· πασῶν γάρ ἐστι πρεσ-
βυτάτη τῶν τε Σικελικῶν καὶ τῶν Ἰταλιωτίδων.
οἱ δὲ τὸν στόλον ἄγοντες, Ἱπποκλῆς ὁ Κυμαῖος
καὶ Μεγασθένης ὁ Χαλκιδεύς, διωμολογήσαντο
πρὸς σφᾶς αὐτούς, τῶν μὲν[1] ἀποικίαν εἶναι, τῶν
δὲ τὴν ἐπωνυμίαν· ὅθεν νῦν μὲν προσαγορεύεται
Κύμη. κτίσαι δ᾽ αὐτὴν Χαλκιδεῖς δοκοῦσι. πρότερον μὲν οὖν ηὐτύχει· καὶ τὸ Φλεγραῖον καλού-

---

[1] But Meineke, following Corais, inserts τὴν before
ἀποικίαν.

that, in the course of one year, some of the plains
are seeded twice with spelt, the third time with
millet, and others still the fourth time with vege-
tables. And indeed it is from here that the Romans
obtain their best wine, namely, the Falernian, the
Statanian, and the Calenian,[1] though already the
Surrentine wine is taking its place as a rival of
the three, for recent tests show that it admits of
ageing. And so, in the same way, all the country
round about Venafrum, which is on the border
of the plains, is well-supplied with the olive.

4. The cities on the sea after Sinuessa are:
Liternum, where is the tomb of Scipio, the one first
to be called "Africanus"; for he spent his last days
here, giving up the affairs of state, so strong was his
hatred for certain persons. A river[2] of like name
flows by the city. And so, likewise, the Vulturnus
has a name like that of the city[3] which is situated
beside it and which comes next in order after
Sinuessa; this river flows through Venafrum and the
centre of Campania. Next in order after these two
cities comes Cumae,[4] a city founded in most ancient
times by people from Chalcis and Cumae; for it is
the oldest of all the Sicilian and the Italiote cities.
However, the men who led the expedition, Hippocles
of Cumae[5] and Megasthenes of Chalcis, made an
agreement with one another that the city should be
a colony of Chalcis, and a namesake of Cumae; and,
hence, although the city is now called Cumae, it is
reputed to have been founded by the Chalcidians
alone. In earlier times, then, the city was prosperous,
and so was what is called the Phlegraean Plain,

---

[1] Cp. 5 3. 6.   [2] The Liternus.   [3] Vulturnum.
[4] In Greek "Cyme."   [5] The Euboean "Cyme."

μενον πεδίον, ἐν ᾧ τὰ περὶ τοὺς Γίγαντας
μυθεύουσιν, οὐκ ἄλλοθεν, ὡς εἰκός, ἀλλ᾽ ἐκ τοῦ
περιμάχητον τὴν γῆν εἶναι δι᾽ ἀρετήν· ὕστερον
δ᾽ οἱ Καμπανοὶ κύριοι καταστάντες τῆς πόλεως
ὕβρισαν εἰς τοὺς ἀνθρώπους πολλά· καὶ δὴ καὶ
ταῖς γυναιξὶν αὐτῶν συνῴκησαν αὐτοί. ὅμως δ᾽
οὖν ἔτι σῴζεται πολλὰ ἴχνη τοῦ Ἑλληνικοῦ
κόσμου καὶ τῶν νομίμων. ὠνομάσθαι δ᾽ ἔνιοι
Κύμην ἀπὸ τῶν κυμάτων φασί· ῥαχιώδης γὰρ
καὶ προσεχὴς ὁ πλησίον αἰγιαλός. εἰσὶ δὲ καὶ
κητεῖαι[1] παρ᾽ αὐτοῖς ἄρισται. ἐν δὲ τῷ κόλπῳ
τούτῳ καὶ ὕλη τίς ἐστι θαμνώδης, ἐπὶ πολλοὺς
ἐκτεινομένη σταδίους, ἄνυδρος καὶ ἀμμώδης, ἣν
Γαλλιναρίαν ὕλην καλοῦσιν. ἐνταῦθα δὴ λῃστή-
ρια συνεστήσαντο οἱ Πομπηίου Σέξτου ναύαρχοι
καθ᾽ ὃν καιρὸν Σικελίαν ἀπέστησεν ἐκεῖνος.

5. Πλησίον δὲ τῆς Κύμης τὸ Μισηνὸν ἀκρωτήριον καὶ ἐν τῷ μεταξὺ Ἀχερουσία λίμνη, τῆς
θαλάττης ἀνάχυσίς τις τεναγώδης. κάμψαντι δὲ
τὸ Μισηνὸν λιμὴν εὐθὺς ὑπὸ τῇ ἄκρᾳ, καὶ μετὰ
C 244 τοῦτον ἐγκολπίζουσα ἠὼν εἰς βάθος, ἐν ᾗ αἱ
Βαῖαι καὶ τὰ θερμὰ ὕδατα τὰ καὶ πρὸς τρυφὴν
καὶ πρὸς θεραπείαν νόσων ἐπιτήδεια. ταῖς δὲ
Βαίαις συνεχὴς ὅ τε Λοκρῖνος κόλπος καὶ ἐντὸς
τούτου ὁ Ἄορνος, χερρόνησον ποιῶν τὴν ἀπο-
λαμβανομένην μέχρι Μισηνοῦ γῆν ἀπὸ τῆς πλα-

---

[1] κητεῖαι, all editors, for κιττ(ε)ίαι.

which mythology has made the setting of the story of the Giants—for no other reason, it would seem, than that the land, on account of its excellence, was a thing to fight for; but later on, when the Campani became established as masters of the city, they committed numerous outrages against the people in general, and, what is more, cohabited with the wives of the citizens. Nevertheless, many traces of the Greek decorum and usages are still preserved there. But according to some, "Cumae" is named after the "Kumata";[1] for the neighbouring shore is surfy and exposed to the wind. And Cumae also has the best fisheries for the catching of large fish. Moreover, on this gulf there is a forest of scrub trees, extending for many stadia over a waterless and sandy tract, which they call "Silva Gallinaria."[2] Here it was that the admirals of Sextus Pompeius assembled bands of pirates at that critical time when he caused Sicily to revolt.[3]

5. Near Cumae is Cape Misenum, and between them is the Acherusian Lake, a kind of shoal-water estuary of the sea. After you double Cape Misenum you immediately come to a harbour, at the base of the cape, and, after the harbour, to a stretch of coast which runs inland and forms a deeply indented gulf —the coast on which is situated Baiae, and those hot springs that are suited both to the taste of the fastidious and to the cure of disease. Contiguous to Baiae is Gulf Lucrinus,[4] and also, behind this gulf, Gulf Avernus,[5] which forms a peninsula of the land that is cut off as far as Misenum, beginning from the

---

[1] In Greek, "billows."   [2] Poultry-Forest.
[3] Cp. 6. 1. 6.   [4] Now Lake Lucrino.
    [5] Now Lake Averno.

γίας¹ τῆς μεταξὺ Κύμης καὶ αὐτοῦ, λοιπὸς γάρ
ἐστιν ὀλίγων σταδίων ἰσθμὸς διὰ τῆς διώρυγος
ἐπ' αὐτὴν Κύμην, καὶ τὴν πρὸς αὐτῇ² θάλατταν.
ἐμύθευον δ' οἱ πρὸ ἡμῶν ἐν τῷ Ἀόρνῳ τὰ περὶ τὴν
νέκυιαν τὴν Ὁμηρικήν· καὶ δὴ καὶ νεκυομαντεῖον
ἱστοροῦσιν ἐνταῦθα γενέσθαι καὶ Ὀδυσσέα εἰς
τοῦτ' ἀφικέσθαι. ἔστι δ' ὁ μὲν Ἄορνος κόλπος
ἀγχιβαθὴς καὶ ἀρτίστομος, λιμένος καὶ μέγεθος
καὶ φύσιν ἔχων, χρείαν δ' οὐ παρεχόμενος λιμένος
διὰ τὸ προκεῖσθαι τὸν Λοκρῖνον κόλπον προσ-
βραχῆ καὶ πολύν. περικλείεται δ' ὁ Ἄορνος
ὀφρύσιν ὀρθίαις, ὑπερκειμέναις πανταχόθεν πλὴν
τοῦ εἴσπλου, νῦν μὲν ἡμέρως ἐκπεπονημέναις,
πρότερον δὲ συνηρεφέσιν ἀγρίᾳ ὕλῃ μεγαλοδένδρῳ
καὶ ἀβάτῳ, αἱ κατὰ δεισιδαιμονίαν κατάσκιον
ἐποίουν τὸν κόλπον. προσεμύθευον δ' οἱ ἐπιχώ-
ριοι καὶ τοὺς ὄρνεις τοὺς ὑπερπετεῖς γινομένους
καταπίπτειν εἰς τὸ ὕδωρ, φθειρομένους ὑπὸ τῶν

---

¹ πλαγίας, conjecture of C. Müller, and Madvig, for πελαγίας. Corais amends to παραλίας. Meineke relegates τῆς
πελαγίας to the foot of the page.
² αὐτῇ, Corais, for αὐτήν; so Meineke.

---

¹ Agrippa connected Lake Avernus and Lake Lucrinus
with a canal, and Lake Avernus with the port of Cumae
with a tunnel.
² "Necyia" is the title the ancients gave to the eleventh
book of the Odyssey, which tells the story of Odysseus'
descent into Hades and of the magic rites by which the
ghosts of the dead were called up, and also relates the
various conversations in Hades.

transverse line which runs between Cumae and Avernus, for there remains an isthmus only a few stadia broad, that is, reckoning straight through the tunnel to Cumae itself and to the sea next to Cumae.[1] The people prior to my time were wont to make Avernus the setting of the fabulous story of the Homeric "Necyia";[2] and, what is more, writers tell us that there actually was an oracle of the dead here and that Odysseus visited it. Now Gulf Avernus is deep up to the very shore and has a clear outlet;[3] and it has both the size and character of a harbour, although it is useless as a harbour because of the fact that Gulf Lucrinus lies before it and is somewhat shallow as well as considerable in extent. Again, Avernus is enclosed round about by steep hill-brows that rise above it on all sides except where you sail into it (at the present time they have been brought by the toil of man into cultivation, though in former times they were thickly covered with a wild and untrodden forest of large trees); and these hill-brows, because of the superstition of man, used to make the gulf a shadowy place. And the natives used to add the further fable that all birds that fly over it fall down into the water,[4] being killed by the vapours that

[3] Although the Romans called Lucrinus and Avernus "lakes," Strabo calls them "gulfs"—the former a sea-gulf and the latter an inner gulf connecting with the former. The configuration of the country has been greatly changed since Strabo's time, for instance, in 1538 A.D., when what is now Monte Nuova (455 ft.) was upheaved by volcanic eruption, and the area of Lake Lucrinus was much reduced.

[4] Cp. Virgil, *Aeneid* 6. 239 and Lucretius 6. 740. The word "Avernus" means "Birdless."

ἀναφερομένων ἀέρων, καθάπερ ἐν τοῖς Πλουτω-
νίοις. καὶ τοῦτο[1] χωρίον Πλουτώνιόν τι ὑπε-
λάμβανον, καὶ τοὺς Κιμμερίους ἐνταῦθα γενέσθαι.[2]
καὶ εἰσέπλεόν γε οἱ προθυσάμενοι καὶ ἱλασάμενοι[3] τοὺς καταχθονίους δαίμονας, ὄντων τῶν
ὑφηγουμένων τὰ τοιάδε ἱερέων, ἠργολαβηκότων
τὸν τόπον. ἔστι δὲ πηγή τις αὐτόθι ποτίμου[4]
ὕδατος ἐπὶ τῇ θαλάττῃ, τούτου δ' ἀπείχοντο
πάντες, τὸ τῆς Στυγὸς ὕδωρ νομίσαντες· καὶ τὸ
μαντεῖον ἐνταῦθά που ἵδρυται· τόν τε Πυριφλε-
γέθοντα ἐκ τῶν θερμῶν ὑδάτων ἐτεκμαίροντο τῶν
πλησίον καὶ τῆς Ἀχερουσίας. Ἔφορος δὲ τοῖς
Κιμμερίοις προσοικειῶν τὸν τόπον φησὶν αὐτοὺς
ἐν καταγείοις οἰκίαις οἰκεῖν, ἃς καλοῦσιν ἀργίλλας,
καὶ διά τινων ὀρυγμάτων παρ' ἀλλήλους τε φοιτᾶν
καὶ τοὺς ξένους εἰς τὸ μαντεῖον δέχεσθαι, πολὺ
ὑπὸ γῆς ἱδρυμένον· ζῆν δ' ἀπὸ μεταλλείας καὶ
τῶν μαντευομένων, καὶ τοῦ βασιλέως ἀποδείξαντος
αὐτοῖς συντάξεις. εἶναι δὲ τοῖς περὶ τὸ χρηστή-

---

[1] Kramer, Meineke, and Müller-Dübner insert τὸ (in brackets) after τοῦτο.

[2] γενέσθαι, Jones, for λέγεσθαι.

[3] ἱλασάμενοι, Corais, for ἱλασόμενοι; so Meineke, who, however, omits the οἱ after γε.

[4] ποτίμου, Corais (from conj. of Xylander), for ποταμίου (as in 5. 1. 8 and 5. 4. 13.); so Meineke.

---

[1] For example, the "Plutonium" at Hierapolis in Asia Minor (13. 4. 14). The "Plutonia" were precincts where mephitic vapours arose, and they were so called because they were regarded as entrances to the nether world. The cave itself, within the "Plutonium," was called "Charonium" (14. 1. 11 and 14. 1. 44).

[2] See 1. 1. 10 and 1. 2. 9.

rise from it, as in the case of all the Plutonia.[1]   And
people used to suppose that this too was a Plutonian
place and that the Cimmerians[2] had actually been
there.   At any rate, only those who had sacrificed
beforehand and propitiated the nether deities could
sail into Avernus, and priests who held the locality
on lease were there to give directions in all such
matters; and there is a fountain of potable water
at this place, on the sea, but people used to abstain
from it because they regarded it as the water of the
Styx; and the oracle, too, is situated somewhere
near it; and further, the hot springs near by and
Lake Acherusia[3] betokened the River Pyriphlege-
thon.[4]   Again, Ephorus, in the passage where he
claims the locality in question for the Cimmerians,
says: They live in underground houses, which they
call "argillae,"[5] and it is through tunnels that they
visit one another, back and forth, and also admit
strangers to the oracle, which is situated far beneath
the earth; and they live on what they get from
mining, and from those who consult the oracle,[6] and
from the king of the country, who has appointed
to them fixed allowances;[7] and those who live

[3] Now Lake Fusaro.
[4] Literally, "flaming with fire." This river was a tributary
of the Acheron in the nether world.   The River Acheron
(now Phanariotikos), in Epirus, was associated with the
nether world: it disappears in the earth for some distance
and then reappears, losing its waters in the marshy
"Acherusian Lake" before emptying into the Ionian Sea.
[5] "Argillae" apparently means "clay"-dwellings.
[6] That is, as we may infer, on the meat of the sacrificial
victims, in addition to any fees which may have been
charged
[7] Thus acknowledging, according to Ephorus, that the
country belongs to the Cimmerians.

443

ριον [1] ἔθος πάτριον, μηδένα τὸν ἥλιον ὁρᾶν, ἀλλὰ
τῆς νυκτὸς ἔξω πορεύεσθαι τῶν χασμάτων· καὶ
διὰ τοῦτο τὸν ποιητὴν περὶ αὐτῶν εἰπεῖν, ὡς
ἄρα

οὐδέ ποτ' αὐτούς
Ἥλιος φαέθων ἐπιδέρκεται·   (Od. 11. 15)

C 245 ὕστερον δὲ διαφθαρῆναι τοὺς ἀνθρώπους ὑπὸ
βασιλέως τινός, οὐκ ἀποβάντος αὐτῷ τοῦ χρησμοῦ,
τὸ δὲ μαντεῖον ἔτι συμμένειν, μεθεστηκὸς εἰς
ἕτερον τόπον. τοιαῦτα μὲν οἱ πρὸ ἡμῶν ἐμυθο-
λόγουν, νυνὶ δὲ τῆς μὲν ὕλης τῆς περὶ τὸν Ἄορνον
κοπείσης ὑπὸ Ἀγρίππα, τῶν δὲ χωρίων κατοι-
κοδομηθέντων, ἀπὸ δὲ τοῦ Ἀόρνου διώρυγος ὑπο-
νόμου τμηθείσης μέχρι Κύμης, ἅπαντ' ἐκεῖνα
ἐφάνη μῦθος· τοῦ Κοκκηίου τοῦ ποιήσαντος τὴν
διώρυγα ἐκείνην τε καὶ ἐπὶ Νέαν πόλιν ἐκ Δικαιαρχείας ἐπὶ ταῖς Βαίαις ἐπακολουθήσαντός πως
τῷ περὶ τῶν Κιμμερίων ἀρτίως λεχθέντι λόγῳ,
τυχὸν ἴσως καὶ πάτριον νομίσαντος τῷ τόπῳ
τούτῳ δι' ὀρυγμάτων εἶναι τὰς ὁδούς.

6. Ὁ δὲ Λοκρῖνος κόλπος πλατύνεται μέχρι
Βαιῶν, χώματι εἰργόμενος ἀπὸ τῆς ἔξω θαλάττης
ὀκτασταδίῳ τὸ μῆκος, πλάτος δὲ ἁμαξιτοῦ πλα-
τείας, ὅ φασιν Ἡρακλέα διαχῶσαι, τὰς βοῦς
ἐλαύνοντα τὰς Γηρυόνου· δεχόμενον δ' ἐπιπολῆς
τὸ κῦμα τοῖς χειμῶσιν, ὥστε μὴ πεζεύεσθαι
ῥᾳδίως, Ἀγρίππας δὲ ἐπεσκεύασεν. εἴσπλουν δ'
ἔχει πλοίοις ἐλαφροῖς, ἐνορμίσασθαι μὲν ἄχρη-

---

[1] χρηστήριον (ko and mgo) ιor ληστήριον (ABCEl).

[1] L. Cocceius Auctus, an architect and engineer, employed
by Agrippa.

about the oracle have an ancestral custom, that
no one should see the sun, but should go outside
the caverns only during the night; and it is for
this reason that the poet speaks of them as follows:
"And never does the shining sun look upon them";
but later on the Cimmerians were destroyed by a
certain king, because the response of the oracle did
not turn out in his favour; the seat of the oracle,
however, still endures, although it has been removed
to another place. Such, then, are the stories the
people before my time used to tell, but now that
the forest round about Avernus has been cut down
by Agrippa, and the tracts of land have been built
up with houses, and the tunnel has been cut
from Avernus to Cumae, all those stories have
proven to be mere myths; and yet the Cocceius[1]
who made, not only this tunnel, but also the one
from Dicaearchia (near Baiae) to Neapolis, was
pretty well acquainted with the story just now related about the Cimmerians, and it may very well be
that he also deemed it an ancestral custom,[2] for this
region, that its roads should run through tunnels.

6. Gulf Lucrinus broadens out as far as Baiae;
and it is shut off from the outer sea by a mound
eight stadia in length and broad as a wagon-road.
This mound is said to have been brought to com-
pletion by Heracles, when he was driving the cattle
of Geryon. But since it admitted the waves over
its surface in times of storm, so that it could not
easily be traversed on foot, Agrippa built it up
higher. The gulf affords entrance to light boats
only; and, though useless as a place to moor boats,

---

[2] Cocceius was a native of the region in question.

στος, τῶν ὀστρέων δὲ θήραν ἔχων ἀφθονωτάτην. ἔνιοι δὲ τοῦτον αὐτὸν τὴν λίμνην εἶναι τὴν Ἀχερουσίαν φασίν, Ἀρτεμίδωρος δὲ αὐτὸν τὸν Ἄορνον. τὰς δὲ Βαίας ἐπωνύμους εἶναι λέγουσι Βαίου τῶν Ὀδυσσέως ἑταίρων τινός, καὶ τὸ Μισηνόν. ἑξῆς δ᾽ εἰσὶν αἱ περὶ Δικαιαρχείαν ἀκταὶ καὶ αὐτὴ ἡ πόλις. ἦν δὲ πρότερον μὲν ἐπίνειον Κυμαίων ἐπ᾽ ὀφρύος ἱδρυμένον, κατὰ δὲ τὴν Ἀννίβα στρατείαν συνῴκισαν Ῥωμαῖοι καὶ μετωνόμασαν Ποτιόλους ἀπὸ τῶν φρεάτων· οἱ δ᾽ ἀπὸ τῆς δυσωδίας τῶν ὑδάτων, ἦν[1] ἅπαν τὸ χωρίον ἔχει[1] μέχρι Βαιῶν καὶ τῆς Κυμαίας ὅτι θείου πλῆρές ἐστι καὶ πυρὸς καὶ θερμῶν ὑδάτων. τινὲς δὲ καὶ Φλέγραν διὰ τοῦτο τὴν Κυμαίαν νομίζουσι κληθῆναι, καὶ τῶν πεπτωκότων γιγάντων τὰ κεραύνια τραύματα ἀναφέρειν τὰς τοιαύτας προχοὰς τοῦ πυρὸς καὶ τοῦ ὕδατος. ἡ δὲ πόλις ἐμπόριον γεγένηται μέγιστον, χειροποιήτους ἔχουσα ὅρμους διὰ τὴν εὐφυΐαν τῆς ἄμμου· σύμμετρος γάρ ἐστι τῇ τιτάνῳ καὶ κόλλησιν ἰσχυρὰν καὶ πῆξιν λαμβάνει. διόπερ τῇ χάλικι καταμίξαντες τὴν ἀμμοκονίαν προβάλλουσι χώματα εἰς τὴν θάλατταν, καὶ κολποῦσι

---

[1] ἦν, Jones inserts; and, with Holstein, emends ἐκεῖ (before μέχρι) to ἔχει. Meineke inserts γὰρ after ἅπαν and deletes ὅτι (before θείου).

---

[1] That is, after Misenus (see 1. 2. 18).
[2] By Strabo's time the city had expanded a considerable distance along the coast in both directions.
[3] In Latin, "putei."
[4] In Latin, "puteo," "stink."
[5] That is, "Blazing-land," if the etymologists here referred to by Strabo were right. "Phlegra" was also the old name

it affords most abundant catches of oysters. And some say that this gulf itself is Lake Acherusia, while Artemidorus says that Gulf Avernus itself is that lake. But Baiae is said to be named after one of the companions of Odysseus, Baius; and also Misenum.[1] Next in order come the headlands that are in the neighbourhood of Dicaearchia, and then the city itself. In earlier times it was only a port-town of the Cumaeans, situated on the brow of a hill,[2] but at the time of Hannibal's expedition the Romans settled a colony there, and changed its name to Puteoli from the wells [3] there—though some say that it was from the foul smell [4] of the waters, since the whole district, as far as Baiae and Cumae, has a foul smell, because it is full of sulphur and fire and hot waters. And some believe that it is for this reason that the Cumaean country was called "Phlegra," [5] and that it is the wounds of the fallen giants, inflicted by the thunderbolts, that pour forth those streams of fire and water. And the city has become a very great emporium, since it has havens that have been made by the hand of man—a thing made possible by the natural qualities of the sand, for it is in proper proportion to the lime,[6] and takes a firm set and solidity. And therefore, by mixing the sand-ash [7] with the lime, they can run jetties out into the sea and thus make the wide-open shores

of Pallene, the westernmost of the peninsulas of Chalcidice, and a volcanic region. Mythology associates the Giants with both regions (cp. 5. 4. 4).

[6] That is, its constituents are in proper proportion to the constituents of the lime.

[7] This volcanic substance is now called "pozzuolana," or "tuff."

STRABO

τὰς ἀναπεπταμένας ἠιόνας, ὥστ' ἀσφαλῶς ἐνορ-
C 246 μίζεσθαι τὰς μεγίστας ὁλκάδας. ὑπέρκειται δὲ
τῆς πόλεως εὐθὺς ἡ τοῦ Ἡφαίστου ἀγορά, πεδίον
περικεκλειμένον διαπύροις ὀφρύσι, καμινώδεις
ἐχούσαις ἀναπνοὰς πολλαχοῦ καὶ βρωμώδεις [1]
ἱκανῶς· τὸ δὲ πεδίον θείου πλῆρές ἐστι συρτοῦ.

7. Μετὰ δὲ Δικαιαρχίαν ἐστὶ Νεάπολις Κυ-
μαίων· ὕστερον δὲ καὶ Χαλκιδεῖς ἐπῴκησαν καὶ
Πιθηκουσσαίων τινὲς καὶ Ἀθηναίων, ὥστε καὶ
Νεάπολις ἐκλήθη διὰ τοῦτο. ὅπου δείκνυται
μνῆμα τῶν Σειρήνων μιᾶς, Παρθενόπης, καὶ ἀγὼν
συντελεῖται γυμνικὸς κατὰ μαντείαν. ὕστερον δὲ
Καμπανῶν τινας [2] ἐδέξαντο συνοίκους διχοστα-
τήσαντες, καὶ ἠναγκάσθησαν τοῖς ἐχθίστοις ὡς
οἰκειοτάτοις χρήσασθαι, ἐπειδὴ τοὺς οἰκείους ἀλλο-
τρίους ἔσχον. μηνύει δὲ τὰ τῶν δημάρχων ὀνόματα, τὰ μὲν πρῶτα Ἑλληνικὰ ὄντα, τὰ δ' ὕστερα
τοῖς Ἑλληνικοῖς ἀναμὶξ τὰ Καμπανικά. πλεῖστα
δ' ἴχνη τῆς Ἑλληνικῆς ἀγωγῆς ἐνταῦθα σῴζεται,
γυμνάσιά τε καὶ ἐφηβεῖα καὶ φρατρίαι [3] καὶ ὀνόματα Ἑλληνικά, καίπερ ὄντων Ῥωμαίων. νυνὶ δὲ
πεντετηρικὸς ἱερὸς ἀγὼν συντελεῖται παρ' αὐτοῖς,
μουσικός τε καὶ γυμνικὸς ἐπὶ πλείους ἡμέρας,

---

[1] βρωμώδεις, Dindorf, for βρομώδεις; so the editors in
general.
[2] τινας, Xylander, for τινες; so the later editors.
[3] ἐφηβεῖα καὶ φρατρίαι, Siebenkees (from conj. of Tyrwhitt),
for ἐφηβιακὰ φράτρια (Al), ἐφηβειακὰ φρατρία (BC); so the later
editors.

---

[1] In Latin, "Forum Vulcani"; now La Solfatara.
[2] That is, "New City." The older name was "Parthenope" (see 14. 2. 10, and Beloch, *Campanien*, 1890, pp. 29–30).
[3] "Demarch" was the local title of the chief magistrates;

curve into the form of bays, so that the greatest
merchant-ships can moor therein with safety. Immediately above the city lies the Forum of Hephaes-
tus,[1] a plain shut in all round by exceedingly hot
ridges, which in numerous places have fumaroles that
are like chimneys and that have a rather noisome
smell; and the plain is full of drifted sulphur.

7. After Dicaearchia comes Neapolis, a city of
the Cumaeans. At a later time it was re-colonised
by Chalcidians, and also by some Pithecussaeans and
Athenians, and hence, for this reason, was called
Neapolis.[2] A monument of Parthenope, one of the
Sirens, is pointed out in Neapolis, and in accordance
with an oracle a gymnastic contest is celebrated
there. But at a still later time, as the result of a
dissension, they admitted some of the Campani as
fellow-inhabitants, and thus they were forced to
treat their worst enemies as their best friends, now
that they had alienated their proper friends. This
is disclosed by the names of their demarchs, for
the earliest names are Greek only, whereas the
later are Greek mixed with Campanian.[3] And very
many traces of Greek culture are preserved there—
gymnasia, ephebeia,[4] phratriae,[5] and Greek names of
things, although the people are Romans. And at the
present time a sacred contest is celebrated among
them every four years, in music[6] as well as gym-
nastics; it lasts for several days, and vies with the

and apparently several of them held office together (see
Tozer, *Selections*, p. 168, and Beloch, *Campanien*, pp. 31, 45).

[4] Places for *youths* (ephebi) to take exercise.

[5] Beloch (pp. 41–44), from inscriptions of Neapolis, gives
the names of nine different phratriae.

[6] "Music" is here used, apparently, in the broad sense,
including all the arts over which the Muses presided.

ἐνάμιλλος τοῖς ἐπιφανεστάτοις τῶν κατὰ τὴν Ἑλλάδα. ἔστι δὲ καὶ ἐνθάδε διῶρυξ κρυπτή, τοῦ μεταξὺ ὅρους τῆς τε Δικαιαρχείας καὶ τῆς Νεαπόλεως ὑπεργασθέντος ὁμοίως, ὥσπερ ἐπὶ τὴν Κύμην, ὁδοῦ τε ἀνοιχθείσης ἐναντίοις ζεύγεσι πορευτῆς, ἐπὶ πολλοὺς σταδίους· τὰ δὲ φῶτα ἐκ τῆς ἐπιφανείας τοῦ ὅρους, πολλαχόθεν ἐκκοπεισῶν θυρίδων, διὰ βάθους πολλοῦ κατάγεται. ἔχει δὲ καὶ ἡ Νεάπολις θερμῶν ὑδάτων ἐκβολὰς καὶ κατασκευὰς λουτρῶν οὐ χείρους τῶν ἐν Βαίαις, πολὺ δὲ τῷ πλήθει λειπομένας· ἐκεῖ γὰρ ἄλλη πόλις γεγένηται, συνῳκοδομημένων βασιλείων ἄλλων ἐπ' ἄλλοις, οὐκ ἐλάττων τῆς Δικαιαρχείας. ἐπιτείνουσι δὲ τὴν ἐν Νεαπόλει διαγωγὴν τὴν Ἑλληνικὴν οἱ ἐκ τῆς Ῥώμης ἀναχωροῦντες δεῦρο ἡσυχίας χάριν τῶν ἀπὸ παιδείας ἐργασαμένων ἢ καὶ ἄλλων διὰ γῆρας ἢ ἀσθένειαν ποθούντων ἐν ἀνέσει ζῆν. καὶ τῶν Ῥωμαίων δ' ἔνιοι χαίροντες τῷ βίῳ τούτῳ, θεωροῦντες τὸ πλῆθος τῶν ἀπὸ τῆς αὐτῆς ἀγωγῆς ἐπιδημούντων ἀνδρῶν, ἄσμενοι φιλοχωροῦσι καὶ ζῶσιν αὐτόθι.

8. Ἐχόμενον δὲ φρούριόν ἐστιν Ἡράκλειον, ἐκκειμένην εἰς τὴν θάλατταν ἄκραν ἔχον, καταπνεομένην Λιβὶ θαυμαστῶς, ὥσθ' ὑγιεινὴν ποιεῖν

---

[1] Augustus himself attended the contest shortly before his death (Suetonius, *Augustus* 98).

[2] See 5. 4. 5.

[3] See 5. 3. 8 and the footnote (on the size of the sewers at Rome).

most famous of those celebrated in Greece.[1] Here, too, there is a tunnel—the mountain between Dicaearchia and Neapolis having been tunneled like the one leading to Cumae,[2] and a road having been opened up for a distance of many stadia that is wide enough to allow teams going in opposite directions to pass each other.[3] And windows have been cut out at many places, and thus the light of day is brought down from the surface of the mountain along shafts that are of considerable depth.[4] Furthermore, Neapolis has springs of hot water and bathing-establishments that are not inferior to those at Baiae, although it is far short of Baiae in the number of people, for at Baiae, where palace on palace has been built, one after another, a new city has arisen, not inferior to Dicaearchia. And greater vogue is given to the Greek mode of life at Neapolis by the people who withdraw thither from Rome for the sake of rest—I mean the class[5] who have made their livelihood by training the young, or still others who, because of old age or infirmity, long to live in relaxation; and some of the Romans, too, taking delight in this way of living and observing the great number of men of the same culture as themselves sojourning there, gladly fall in love with the place and make it their permanent abode.

8. Next after Neapolis comes the Heracleian Fortress,[6] with a promontory which runs out into the sea and so admirably catches the breezes of the southwest wind that it makes the settlement a

---

[4] But to-day the Grotta di Posilipo has no shafts of light; and Seneca (*Epist.* 57. 1) complains of its darkness and dust. Accordingly, Beloch (p. 84) concludes that Strabo confuses the tunnel in question with that of Cumae.

[5] Strabo means Greeks.   [6] Herculaneum.

C 247 τὴν κατοικίαν. Ὄσκοι δ᾽ εἶχον καὶ ταύτην καὶ τὴν
ἐφεξῆς Πομπαίαν,[1] ἣν παραρρεῖ ὁ Σάρνος ποταμός,
εἶτα Τυρρηνοὶ καὶ Πελασγοί, μετὰ ταῦτα δὲ Σαυνῖ-
ται· καὶ οὗτοι δ᾽ ἐξέπεσον ἐκ τῶν τόπων. Νώλης
δὲ καὶ Νουκερίας καὶ Ἀχερρῶν,[2] ὁμωνύμου κατοικίας τῆς περὶ Κρέμωνα, ἐπίνειόν ἐστιν Πομπαία[3]
παρὰ τῷ Σάρνῳ ποταμῷ καὶ δεχομένῳ τὰ φορτία
καὶ ἐκπέμποντι. ὑπέρκειται δὲ τῶν τόπων τούτων
ὄρος τὸ Οὐεσούιον, ἀγροῖς περιοικούμενον παγκά-
λοις πλὴν τῆς κορυφῆς· αὕτη δ᾽ ἐπίπεδος μὲν πολὺ
μέρος ἐστίν, ἄκαρπος δ᾽ ὅλη, ἐκ δὲ τῆς ὄψεως τε-
φρώδης, καὶ κοιλάδας φαίνει σηραγγώδεις πετρῶν
αἰθαλωδῶν κατὰ τὴν χρόαν, ὡς ἂν ἐκβεβρωμένων
ὑπὸ πυρός· ὥστε[4] τεκμαίροιτ᾽ ἄν τις τὸ χωρίον
τοῦτο καίεσθαι πρότερον καὶ ἔχειν κρατῆρας πυρός,
σβεσθῆναι δ᾽ ἐπιλιπούσης τῆς ὕλης. τάχα δὲ
καὶ τῆς εὐκαρπίας τῆς κύκλῳ τοῦτ᾽ αἴτιον, ὥσπερ
ἐν τῇ Κατάνῃ, φασί, τὸ κατατεφρωθὲν μέρος ἐκ
τῆς σποδοῦ τῆς ἀνενεχθείσης ὑπὸ τοῦ Αἰτναίου
πυρὸς εὐάμπελον τὴν γῆν ἐποίησεν. ἔχει μὲν
γὰρ τὸ λιπαῖνον καὶ τὴν ἐκπυρουμένην βῶλον καὶ

---

[1] Corais emends Πομπαίαν to Πομπηίαν; so Müller-Dübner
and Meineke; see note 1 below.
[2] Ἀχερρῶν, Kramer, for Ἀγχέρων (Al); see Ἀχέρραι, 5. 4. 11.
[3] Πομπαία, Jones, for the corrupt ποιεῖ; others emend to
Πομπηία.
[4] ὥστε, Corais, for ὡς.

---

[1] On "Pompaia," the Oscan name of Pompeii, see Nissen,
Landeskunde II., p. 763, footnote 3.
[2] In Latin, "Acerrae."
[3] "Acerrae," as spelled by Polybius (2. 34).
[4] That is, the "hot ashes" (what we call "volcanic ash,"
a finely powdered lava), now ash-dust.

healthful place to live in. Both this settlement and
the one next after it, Pompaia [1] (past which flows the
River Sarnus), were once held by the Osci; then, by
the Tyrrheni and the Pelasgi; and after that, by the
Samnitae; but they, too, were ejected from the places.
Pompaia, on the River Sarnus—a river which both
takes the cargoes inland and sends them out to sea—
is the port-town of Nola, Nuceria, and Acherrae [2] (a
place with name like that of the settlement [3] near
Cremona). Above these places lies Mt. Vesuvius,
which, save for its summit, has dwellings all round,
on farm-lands that are absolutely beautiful. As for
the summit, a considerable part of it is flat, but all
of it is unfruitful, and looks ash-coloured, and it
shows pore-like cavities in masses of rock that are
soot-coloured on the surface, these masses of rock
looking as though they had been eaten out by fire;
and hence one might infer that in earlier times this
district was on fire and had craters of fire, and then,
because the fuel gave out, was quenched. Perhaps,
too, this is the cause of the fruitfulness of the
country all round the mountain; just as at Catana,
it is said, that part of the country which had been
covered with ash-dust from the hot ashes carried up
into the air by the fire of Aetna made the land suited
to the vine; for it [4] contains the substance that
fattens [5] both the soil which is burnt out and that

[5] Strabo wrongly thought that the volcanic ash itself con-
tained a fatty substance which enriched the soil. The enrich-
ing substance, of course, was the organic matter which
accumulated in the ash-dust during a long period of weather-
ing. In time the ash-dust became ash-soil. In 6. 2. 3 Strabo
quotes Poseidonius as saying that this same part of the
country was covered with volcanic ash "to a considerable
depth."

453

τὴν ἐκφέρουσαν τοὺς καρπούς. πλεονάζουσα μὲν
οὖν τῷ λίπει πρὸς ἐκπύρωσιν ἐπιτηδεία, καθάπερ
ἡ θειώδης πᾶσα, ἐξικμασθεῖσα δὲ καὶ λαβοῦσα
σβέσιν καὶ ἐκτέφρωσιν εἰς καρπογονίαν μετέβαλε.
συνεχὲς δέ ἐστι τῇ Πομπαίᾳ τὸ Συρρεντὸν τῶν
Καμπανῶν, ὅθεν πρόκειται τὸ ᾿Αθήναιον, ὅ τινες
Σειρηνουσσῶν ἀκρωτήριον καλοῦσιν· ἔστι δὲ ἐπ᾿
ἄκρῳ μὲν ᾿Αθηνᾶς ἱερόν, ἵδρυμα ᾿Οδυσσέως. διά-
πλους δ᾿ ἐνθένδε βραχὺς εἰς Καπρέας νῆσον.
κάμψαντι δὲ τὴν ἄκραν νησῖδές εἰσιν ἔρημοι πε-
τρώδεις, ἃς καλοῦσι Σειρῆνας. ἐκ δὲ τοῦ πρὸς
Συρρεντὸν μέρους ἱερόν τι δείκνυται καὶ ἀναθήματα
παλαιὰ τιμώντων τῶν[1] πλησίον τὸν[2] τόπον. μέχρι μὲν δεῦρο ἔχει τέλος ὁ κόλπος ὁ Κρατὴρ προσ-
αγορευόμενος, ἀφοριζόμενος δυσὶν ἀκρωτηρίοις
βλέπουσι πρὸς μεσημβρίαν, τῷ τε Μισηνῷ καὶ
τῷ ᾿Αθηναίῳ. ἅπας δ᾿ ἐστὶ κατεσκευασμένος
τοῦτο μὲν ταῖς πόλεσιν, ἃς ἔφαμεν, τοῦτο δὲ ταῖς
οἰκοδομίαις καὶ φυτείαις, αἱ μεταξὺ συνεχεῖς οὖσαι
μιᾶς πόλεως ὄψιν παρέχονται.

9. Τοῦ μὲν οὖν Μισηνοῦ πρόκειται νῆσος ἡ
Προχύτη, Πιθηκουσσῶν δ᾿ ἔστιν ἀπόσπασμα.
Πιθηκούσσας δ᾿ ᾿Ερετριεῖς ᾤκισαν καὶ Χαλκιδεῖς,

---

[1] τῶν, Kramer, for τόν; so the later editors.
[2] τόν, before τόπον, Corais inserts; so the later editors.

---

[1] Some of the ash-soil, Strabo means, becomes so rich that
it is combustible, and unfit for the vine and different fruits;
but he does not say whether it is later burnt out by volcanic
matter, or by some accidental or human agency. The burning
out of excessively rich soil was at one time not an uncommon
practice in England and Germany (F. H. Storer, *Agriculture*,
7th. ed., Vol. III., pp. 188 ff.). The English company now

which produces the fruits;[1] so then, when it[2] acquired plenty of fat, it was suited to burning out, as is the case with all sulphur-like substances, and then when it had been evaporated[3] and quenched[4] and reduced to ash-dust, it passed into a state of fruitfulness. Next after Pompaia comes Surrentum, a city of the Campani, whence the Athenaeum[5] juts forth into the sea, which some call the Cape of the Sirenussae. There is a sanctuary of Athene, built by Odysseus, on the tip of the Cape. It is only a short voyage from here across to the island of Capreae; and after doubling the cape you come to desert, rocky isles, which are called the Sirens. On the side of the Cape toward Surrentum people show you a kind of temple, and offerings dedicated there long ago, because the people in the neighbourhood hold the place in honour. Here, then, the gulf that is called the "Crater"[6] comes to an end, being marked off by two capes that face the south, namely, Misenum and Athenaeum. And the whole of the gulf is garnished, in part by the cities which I have just mentioned, and in part by the residences and plantations, which, since they intervene in unbroken succession, present the appearance of a single city.

9. The island of Prochyta lies off Cape Misenum, and it is a fragment broken off of Pithecussae.[7] Pithecussae was once settled by Eretrians and also

operating in the region of Lake Copais in Boeotia burns out the soil before putting it in cultivation.

[2] That is, the ash-dust, now ash-soil.

[3] As often, Strabo is unduly concise. He means: "when the ash-soil had taken fire, and the excess fat had been driven out by the fire."

[4] In natural course, and by rain.   [5] Cp. 1. 2. 12.

[6] Cp. 5. 4. 3.   [7] But cp. 1. 3. 19.

εὐτυχήσαντες δι᾽ εὐκαρπίαν καὶ διὰ τὰ χρυσεῖα
ἐξέλιπον τὴν νῆσον κατὰ στάσιν, ὕστερον δὲ καὶ
ὑπὸ σεισμῶν ἐξελαθέντες καὶ ἀναφυσημάτων
πυρὸς καὶ θαλάττης καὶ θερμῶν ὑδάτων· ἔχει γὰρ
C 248   τοιαύτας ὑποφορὰς¹ ἡ νῆσος, ὑφ᾽ ὧν καὶ οἱ πεμ-
φθέντες παρὰ Ἱέρωνος τοῦ τυράννου τῶν Συρακουσίων ἐξέλιπον τὸ κατασκευασθὲν ὑφ᾽ ἑαυτῶν
τεῖχος καὶ τὴν νῆσον· ἐπελθόντες δὲ Νεαπολῖται
κατέσχον. ἐντεῦθεν καὶ ὁ μῦθος, ὅτι φασὶ τὸν
Τυφῶνα ὑποκεῖσθαι τῇ νήσῳ ταύτῃ, στρεφομένου
δὲ τὰς φλόγας ἀναφυσᾶσθαι καὶ τὰ ὕδατα, ἔστι δ᾽
ὅτε καὶ νησῖδας ἐχούσας ζέον ὕδωρ. πιθανώτερον
δὲ Πίνδαρος εἴρηκεν ἐκ τῶν φαινομένων ὁρμηθείς·
ὅτι πᾶς ὁ πόρος οὗτος, ἀπὸ τῆς Κυμαίας ἀρξάμενος
μέχρι τῆς Σικελίας, διάπυρός ἐστι, καὶ κατὰ βάθους ἔχει κοιλίας τινὰς εἰς ἓν συναπτούσας πρός
τε ἀλλήλας² καὶ πρὸς τὴν ἤπειρον. διόπερ ἥ τε
Αἴτνη τοιαύτην ἔχειν δείκνυται φύσιν, οἵαν ἱστοροῦσιν ἅπαντες, καὶ αἱ τῶν Λιπαραίων νῆσοι καὶ
τὰ περὶ τὴν Δικαιαρχείαν καὶ Νεάπολιν καὶ
Βαΐας χωρία καὶ αἱ Πιθηκοῦσσαι. ταῦτ᾽ οὖν δια-
νοηθεὶς τῷ παντὶ τόπῳ τούτῳ φησὶν ὑποκεῖσθαι
τὸν Τυφῶνα·

                                        νῦν γε μὰν
    ταί θ᾽ ὑπὲρ Κύμας ἁλιερκέες ὄχθαι
    Σικελία τ᾽ αὐτοῦ πιέζει στέρνα λαχνάεντα.
                                        (Pyth. 1. 33)

¹ ὑποφοράς (AC?), Jones restores; instead of ἀποφοράς.
² ἀλλήλας, Xylander, for Ἕλληνας; so the later editors.

¹ Strabo's conciseness (if the MSS. are correct) leaves the
passage obscure as to whether (1) both peoples left together
because of a quarrel with other inhabitants, and later on
returned, only to be driven out by the earthquakes (about

Chalcidians, who, although they had prospered there on account of the fruitfulness of the soil and on account of the gold mines, forsook the island[1] as the result of a quarrel; later on they were also driven out of the island by earthquakes, and by eruptions of fire, sea, and hot waters; for the island has "fistulas" of this sort, and it was these that caused also the people sent thither by Hiero the tyrant of Syracuse to forsake the island and the fortress they had erected there; and then the Neapolitans came over and took possession. Hence, also, the myth according to which Typhon lies beneath this island, and when he turns his body the flames and the waters, and sometimes even small islands containing boiling water, spout forth. But what Pindar says is more plausible, since he starts with the actual phenomena; for this whole channel, beginning at the Cumaean country and extending as far as Sicily, is full of fire, and has caverns deep down in the earth that form a single whole, connecting not only with one another but also with the mainland; and therefore, not only Aetna clearly has such a character as it is reported by all to have, but also the Lipari Islands, and the districts round about Dicaearchia, Neapolis, and Baiae, and the island of Pithecussae. This, I say, is Pindar's thought when he says that Typhon lies beneath this whole region: "Now, however, both Sicily and the sea-fenced cliffs beyond Cumae press hard upon his shaggy breast." And

500 B C.), or (2) left separately, first, the Chalcidians, because of a quarrel between the two, and, later on, the Eretrians, because of the earthquakes, or (3) part of each left at first, and the rest later on ; but the first interpretation seems more likely. Livy (8. 22), without mentioning the Eretrians, ascribes the founding of Cumae to the Chalcidians who had previously settled " Aenaria and Pithecussa."

καὶ Τίμαιος δὲ περὶ τῶν Πιθηκουσσῶν φησιν ὑπὸ τῶν παλαιῶν πολλὰ παραδοξολογεῖσθαι, μικρὸν δὲ πρὸ ἑαυτοῦ τὸν Ἐπωπέα[1] λόφ,ν ἐν μέσῃ τῇ νήσῳ τιναγέντα[2] ὑπὸ σεισμῶν ἀναβαλεῖν πῦρ καὶ τὸ μεταξὺ αὐτοῦ καὶ τῆς θαλάττης ἐξῶσαι πάλιν ἐπὶ τὸ πέλαγος, τὸ δὲ ἐκτεφρωθὲν τῆς γῆς, μετεωρισμὸν λαβόν, κατασκῆψαι πάλιν τυφωνο- ειδῶς εἰς τὴν νῆσον, καὶ ἐπὶ τρεῖς τὴν θάλατταν ἀναχωρῆσαι σταδίους, ἀναχωρήσασαν δὲ μετ' οὐ πολὺ ὑποστρέψαι καὶ τῇ παλιρροίᾳ κατακλύσαι τὴν νῆσον, καὶ γενέσθαι σβέσιν τοῦ ἐν αὐτῇ πυρός, ἀπὸ δὲ τοῦ ἤχου τοὺς ἐν τῇ ἠπείρῳ φυγεῖν ἐκ τῆς παραλίας εἰς τὴν Καμπανίαν. δοκεῖ δὲ τὰ θερμὰ ὕδατα ἐνταῦθα θεραπεύειν τοὺς λιθιῶντας. αἱ δὲ Καπρέαι δύο πολίχνας εἶχον τὸ παλαιόν, ὕστερον δὲ μίαν. Νεαπολῖται δὲ καὶ ταύτην κατέσχον, πολέμῳ δὲ ἀποβαλόντες τὰς Πιθηκούσσας ἀπέ- λαβον πάλιν, δόντος αὐτοῖς Καίσαρος τοῦ Σε- βαστοῦ, τὰς δὲ Καπρέας ἴδιον ποιησαμένου κτῆμα[3] καὶ κατοικοδομήσαντος. αἱ μὲν οὖν παράλιοι πόλεις τῶν Καμπανῶν καὶ αἱ προκείμεναι νῆσοι τοιαῦται.

10. Ἐν δὲ τῇ μεσογαίᾳ Καπύη μέν ἐστιν ἡ μη- τρόπολις, κεφαλὴ τῷ ὄντι κατὰ τὴν ἐτυμότητα τοῦ ὀνόματος, τὰ γὰρ ἄλλα πολίχνια νομίζοιτ' ἂν κατὰ τὴν σύγκρισιν πλὴν Τεάνου Σιδικίνου, καὶ γὰρ αὕτη ἀξιόλογος. κεῖται δ' ἐπὶ τῇ ὁδῷ τῇ Ἀππίᾳ αὐτή τε καὶ αἱ[4] τῶν ἄλλων ἐπὶ Βρεντέσιον

C 249

---

[1] Ἐπωπέα, du Theil, for Ἐπωμέα ; so the later editors.
[2] τιναγέντα is the reading of B ; παγέντα, of A, corrected in some later MSS. to ῥαγέντα, which may be right.
[3] κτῆμα, Corais, for κτίσμα; so the later editors.

Timaeus, also, says that many marvellous things are
told by the ancients about Pithecussae, and that
only shortly before his own time the hill called
Epopeus, in the centre of the island, on being shaken
by earthquakes, cast forth fire and shoved the part
between it and the sea back to the open sea; and
the part of the land that had been burned to ashes,
on being lifted high in the air, crashed down again
upon the island like a whirlwind; and the sea
retreated for three stadia, but not long after retreating turned back and with its reverse current deluged
the island; and, consequently, the fire in the island
was quenched, but the noise was such that the people
on the mainland fled from the coast into Campania.
The hot springs in the island are thought to cure
those who have gall-stones. Capreae had two small
towns in ancient times, though later on only one.
The Neapolitans took possession of this island too;
and although they lost Pithecussae in war, they got
it back again, Augustus Caesar giving it to them,
though he appropriated Capreae to himself personally
and erected buildings on it. Such, then, are the seaboard cities of Campania and the islands that lie off it.

10. In the interior, take first Capua: It is the
capital city—a "capital" in reality, as the etymology
of its name implies,[1] for in comparison with it all the
rest might be regarded as only small towns, except
Teanum Sidicinum, which is indeed a noteworthy
city. It, too,[2] lies on the Appian Way, and so do
the three cities which, among the rest, lead from it[3]

---

[1] Cp. 5. 4. 3. [2] As well as Capua.
[3] That is, from Capua.

---

[4] αἱ, after καί, Corais deletes, inserting αἱ after ἄλλων
(Meineke and Müller-Dübner following.)

ἄγουσαι ἀπ' αὐτῆς, Καλατία[1] καὶ Καύδιον[2] καὶ
Βενεουεντόν· ἐπὶ δὲ Ῥώμης Κασίλινον ἵδρυται ἐπὶ
τῷ Οὐουλτούρνῳ ποταμῷ, ἐν ᾗ πολιορκούμενοι
Πραινεστίνων ἄνδρες τετταράκοντα καὶ πεντακόσιοι πρὸς ἀκμάζοντα Ἀννίβαν ἐπὶ τοσοῦτον
ἀντέσχον, ὥσθ' ὑπὸ λιμοῦ διακοσίων δραχμῶν
πραθέντος μεδίμνου,[3] ὁ μὲν πωλήσας ἀπέθανεν,
ἐσώθη δ' ὁ πριάμενος. ἰδὼν δ' αὐτοὺς πλησίον
τοῦ τείχους σπείροντας γογγύλην ἐθαύμαζεν, ὡς
ἔοικεν, ὁ Ἀννίβας τῆς μακροθυμίας, εἰ ἐλπίζοιεν
τέως[4] ἀνθέξειν ἕως τελεσφορήσειεν ἡ γογγύλη· καὶ
δὴ περιγενέσθαι πάντας φασὶ πλὴν ἀνδρῶν ὀλίγων
τῶν ἢ λιμῷ διαλυθέντων ἢ ἐν ταῖς μάχαις.

11. Πρὸς δὲ ταῖς ῥηθείσαις ἔτι καὶ αὗται Καμ-
παναὶ πόλεις εἰσίν, ὧν ἐμνήσθημεν πρότερον,
Κάλης[5] τε καὶ Τέανον Σιδικῖνον, ἃς διορίζουσιν
αἱ δύο Τύχαι ἐφ' ἑκάτερα ἱδρυμέναι τῆς Λατίνης
ὁδοῦ. καὶ ἔτι Σουεσσοῦλα καὶ Ἀτέλλα καὶ Νῶλα
καὶ Νουκερία καὶ Ἀχέρραι καὶ Ἀβέλλα καὶ ἄλλαι ἔτι ἐλάττους τούτων κατοικίαι, ὧν ἐνίας Σαυ-
νίτιδάς φασιν εἶναι. Σαυνῖται δὲ πρότερον μὲν
καὶ μέχρι τῆς Λατίνης τῆς περὶ Ἀρδέαν ἐξοδίας

---

[1] Καλατία, Kramer, for Καλατερία; so the later editors.
[2] Καύδιον, Corais, for Καλύδιον; so the later editors.
[3] For μεδίμνου (the reading of all MSS.), Corais, Meineke
and others read μνᾶς (following the conj. of Casaubon).
[4] τέως, Corais, for ὡς; so the later editors.
[5] Κάλης, Kramer, for Κάλκη; so the later editors.

---

[1] See 5. 3. 6 and footnote.
[2] From Capua, not from Teanum Sidicinum.

to Brentesium,[1] namely, Calatia, Caudium, and Beneventum.   But Casilinum is situated towards Rome,[2] on the River Vulturnus; it was here that five hundred and forty of the Praenestini held out against Hannibal—then at the height of his strength —for so long that, by reason of famine, a "medimnus"[3] was sold for two hundred "drachmae,"[4] and the man who sold it died of hunger, whereas the man who bought it escaped with his life.   And when Hannibal saw them sowing turnips near the wall, he wondered, and with reason, at their long-suffering—that they expected to hold out long enough for the turnips to get ripe; and in fact they all survived, it is said, except a few who perished either because of hunger or in the battles.

11. But in addition to the cities aforesaid, the following (to which I have adverted before) are also Campanian cities—Cales[5] and Teanum Sidicinum, whose territories are separated by the two temples of Fortune situated on either side of the Latin Way; and so are Suessula, Atella, Nola, Nuceria, Acherrae, Abella, and other settlements (some of which are said to be Samnite) that are still smaller than these.   As for the Samnitae: In earlier times they made expeditions even as far as that part of the Latin country which is about Ardea,

---

[3] About a bushel and a half (of grain). But, following Casaubon, all the editors except Groskurd emend "medimnus" to "rat," to agree with the story of Pliny (8. 82), Valerius Maximus (7. 6), and Frontinus (*Stra'egemata* 4. 5. 20).   And it seems almost certain that Strabo so wrote.

[4] In Latin, " denarii"; that is, about forty dollars; but with far greater purchasing power than now.   The three writers quoted in the preceding footnote say "two hundred denarii."   [5] 5. 3. 9.

ποιούμενοι, μετὰ δὲ ταῦτα αὐτὴν τὴν Καμπανίαν
πορθοῦντες πολλὴν ἐκέκτηντο δύναμιν· καὶ γὰρ
ἄλλως δεσποτικῶς ἄρχεσθαι μεμαθηκότες ταχὺ
ὑπούργουν τοῖς προστάγμασι. νυνὶ δ᾽ ἐκπεπόνηνται τελέως ὑπό τε ἄλλων καὶ τὸ τελευταῖον ὑπὸ
Σύλλα τοῦ μοναρχήσαντος Ῥωμαίων· ὃς ἐπειδὴ
πολλαῖς μάχαις καταλύσας τὴν τῶν Ἰταλιωτῶν
ἐπανάστασιν, τούτους σχεδόν τι μόνους συμμέ-
νοντας ἑώρα καὶ ὁμοίως ὁμοροῦντας,[1] ὥστε καὶ ἐπ᾽
αὐτὴν τὴν Ῥώμην ἐλθεῖν, συνέστη πρὸ τοῦ τείχους
αὐτοῖς, καὶ τοὺς μὲν ἐν τῇ μάχῃ κατέκοψε, κελεύ-
σας μὴ ζωγρεῖν, τοὺς δὲ ῥίψαντας τὰ ὅπλα, περὶ
τρισχιλίους ἄνδρας ἢ τετρακισχιλίους φασίν, εἰς
τὴν δημοσίαν ἔπαυλιν τὴν ἐν τῷ Κάμπῳ κατα-
γαγὼν εἶρξε· τρισὶ δὲ ὕστερον ἡμέραις ἐπιπέμψας
στρατιώτας ἅπαντας ἀπέσφαξε, προγραφάς τε
ποιούμενος οὐκ ἐπαύσατο πρὶν ἢ πάντας τοὺς ἐν
ὀνόματι Σαυνιτῶν διέφθειρεν ἢ ἐκ τῆς Ἰταλίας
ἐξέβαλε· πρὸς δὲ τοὺς αἰτιωμένους τὴν ἐπὶ τοσοῦτον ὀργὴν ἔφη καταμαθεῖν ἐκ τῆς πείρας ὡς οὐδέ-
ποτ᾽ ἂν εἰρήνην ἀγάγοι Ῥωμαίων οὐδὲ εἷς ἕως ἂν
συμμένωσι καθ᾽ ἑαυτοὺς Σαυνῖται. καὶ γάρ τοι
νυνὶ κῶμαι γεγόνασιν αἱ πόλεις, ἔνιαι δ᾽ ἐκλελοί-
C 250 πασι τελέως, Βοιανόν, Αἰσερνία, Πάννα, Τελεσία
συνεχὴς Οὐενάφρῳ, καὶ ἄλλαι τοιαῦται, ὧν οὐδεμίαν ἄξιον ἡγεῖσθαι πόλιν· ἡμεῖς δ᾽ ἐπέξιμεν μέχρι
τοῦ μετρίου διὰ τὴν τῆς Ἰταλίας δόξαν καὶ δύ-

---

[1] ὁμοίως ὁμοροῦντας may be corrupt. Meineke reads ὁμοίως
ὁρμῶντας.

and then, after that, ravaged Campania itself, and therefore they must have possessed considerable power (indeed, the Campani, since they were already schooled in the obedience of other despots, quickly submitted to the new commands); but now they have been completely worn out—first by others and last of all by Sulla, who became dictator of the Romans; for when, on putting down the insurrection of the Italiotes by many battles, he saw that the Samnitae, almost alone, were holding together and, in like manner as before, were on the border, ready actually to march against Rome itself, he joined battle with them before the walls; and some of them he cut down in the battle (for he had ordered that none be taken alive), while the rest, who had flung down their arms (about three or four thousand men, it is said) he brought down to the Villa Publica in the Campus Martius and imprisoned; three days later, however, he let soldiers loose upon them and thus slaughtered them all; and further, he would not stop making proscriptions until either he had destroyed all Samnitae of importance or banished them from Italy. And to those who found fault with him for such excessive wrath he said he had realised from experience that not a Roman could ever live in peace so long as the Samnitae held together as a separate people. And verily their cities have now come to be mere villages (though some have utterly vanished), I mean Bovianum, Aesernia, Panna, Telesia (close to Venafrum), and others like them. No one of these deserves to be regarded as a city, but I, for my part, am thus going into detail, within due bounds, because of the glory and power of Italy. Bene-

ναμιν. Βενεουεντὸν δ' ὅμως συνέστηκεν εὖ καὶ
Οὐενουσία.

12. Περὶ δὲ Σαυνιτῶν καὶ τοιοῦτός τις λόγος
φέρεται, διότι πολεμοῦντες Σαβῖνοι πολὺν χρόνον
πρὸς τοὺς Ὀμβρικοὺς εὔξαντο, καθάπερ τῶν Ἑλλήνων τινές, τὰ γενόμενα τῷ ἔτει τούτῳ καθιερῶσαι, νικήσαντες δὲ τῶν γενομένων τὰ μὲν κατέ-
θυσαν, τὰ δὲ καθιέρωσαν· ἀφορίας δὲ γενηθείσης,
εἶπέ τις ὡς ἐχρῆν καθιερῶσαι καὶ τὰ τέκνα. οἱ
δ' ἐποίησαν τοῦτο καὶ τοὺς γενομένους τότε παῖδας
Ἄρεως ἐπεφήμισαν, ἀνδρωθέντας δ' ἔστειλαν εἰς
ἀποικίαν, ἡγήσατο δὲ ταῦρος· ἐν δὲ τῇ τῶν Ὀπι-
κῶν κατευνασθέντος (ἐτύγχανον δὲ κωμηδὸν ζῶντες), ἐκβαλόντες ἐκείνους ἱδρύθησαν αὐτόθι καὶ
τὸν ταῦρον ἐσφαγίασαν τῷ Ἄρει τῷ δόντι αὐτὸν
ἡγεμόνα κατὰ τὴν τῶν μάντεων ἀπόφασιν. εἰκὸς
δὲ διὰ τοῦτο καὶ Σαβέλλους αὐτοὺς ὑποκοριστικῶς
ἀπὸ τῶν γονέων προσαγορευθῆναι, Σαμνίτας δ'
ἀπ' ἄλλης αἰτίας, οὓς οἱ Ἕλληνες Σαυνίτας λέγουσι. τινὲς δὲ καὶ Λάκωνας συνοίκους αὐτοῖς
γενέσθαι φασὶ καὶ διὰ τοῦτο καὶ φιλέλληνας ὑπάρξαι, τινὰς δὲ καὶ Πιτανάτας καλεῖσθαι. δοκεῖ δὲ
καὶ Ταραντίνων πλάσμα τοῦτ' εἶναι, κολακευόντων
ὁμόρους καὶ μέγα δυναμένους ἀνθρώπους καὶ ἅμα
ἐξοικειουμένων, οἵ γε καὶ ὀκτὼ μυριάδας ἔστελλόν

---

[1] The Greek word here translated "nickname" often
means simply a "diminutive." In that case, Strabo means
by "Sabelli" merely "Little Sabini"; but since the people
in question are "Sons of War," he seems to allude also to
the Latin "bellum."　　　　[2] Cp. Pliny 3. 17.

ventum, however, has held up very well, and so
has Venusia.

12. Concerning the Samnitae there is another
story current to this effect: The Sabini, since they
had long been at war with the Ombrici, vowed
(just as some of the Greeks do) to dedicate everything that was produced that year; and, on winning
the victory, they partly sacrificed and partly dedicated
all that was produced; then a dearth ensued, and
some one said that they ought to have dedicated
the babies too; this they did, and devoted to Mars
all the children born that year; and these children,
when grown to manhood, they sent away as colonists,
and a bull led the way; and when the bull lay down
to rest in the land of the Opici (who, as it chanced,
were living only in villages), the Sabini ejected them
and settled on the spot, and, in accordance with the
utterance of their seers, slaughtered the bull as a
sacrifice to Mars who had given it for a guide. It
is reasonable to suppose therefore that their name
"Sabelli" is a nickname derived from the name of
their forefathers,[1] while their name "Samnitae"
(the Greeks say "Saunitae") is due to a different
cause.[2] Some say, moreover, that a colony of Laconians joined the Samnitae, and that for this reason
the Samnitae actually became philhellenes, and that
some of them were even called "Pitanatae."[3] But
it is thought that the Tarantini simply fabricated
this, to flatter, and at the same time to win the
friendship of, a powerful people on their borders;
because, on a time, the Samnitae were wont to send
forth an army of as many as eighty thousand infantry

[3] That is, as though from Pitane, in Laconia, or as though
members of a Spartan clan by that name.

ποτε τῆς πεζῆς στρατιᾶς, ἱππέας δ' ὀκτακισχιλίους. φασὶ δὲ νόμον [1] εἶναι παρὰ τοῖς Σαυνίταις
καλὸν καὶ προτρεπτικὸν πρὸς ἀρετήν· οὐ γὰρ
ἔξεστι διδόναι τὰς θυγατέρας οἷς ἂν ἐθέλωσιν,
ἀλλὰ κρίνεσθαι κατ' ἔτος δέκα μὲν παρθένους
δέκα δὲ τῶν νέων, τοὺς ἀρίστους καὶ τὰς ἀρίστας·
τούτων τῷ πρώτῳ τὴν πρώτην δίδοσθαι, τῷ δευ-
τέρῳ τὴν δευτέραν καὶ ἑξῆς οὕτως· ἐὰν δ' ὁ λαβὼν
τὸ γέρας μεταβαλόμενος γένηται πονηρός, ἀτιμά-
ζουσι καὶ ἀφαιροῦνται τὴν δοθεῖσαν. ἑξῆς δ'
εἰσὶν Ἱρπῖνοι, καὐτοὶ Σαυνῖται· τοὔνομα δ' ἔσχον
ἀπὸ τοῦ ἡγησαμένου λύκου τῆς ἀποικίας· ἵρπον
γὰρ καλοῦσιν οἱ Σαυνῖται τὸν λύκον· συνάπτουσι
δὲ Λευκανοῖς τοῖς μεσογαίοις. περὶ μὲν Σαυνιτῶν
ταῦτα.

13. Καμπανοῖς δὲ συνέβη διὰ τὴν τῆς χώρας
εὐδαιμονίαν ἐπ' ἴσον ἀγαθῶν ἀπολαῦσαι καὶ κα-
κῶν. ἐπὶ τοσοῦτον γὰρ ἐξετρύφησαν [2] ὥστ' ἐπὶ
δεῖπνον ἐκάλουν πρὸς ζεύγη μονομάχων, ὁρίζοντες
ἀριθμὸν κατὰ τὴν τῶν δείπνων [3] ἀξίαν. Ἀννίβα
C 251 δ' ἐξ ἐνδόσεως λαβόντος αὐτούς, δεξάμενοι χειμα-
δίοις τὴν στρατιὰν οὕτως ἐξεθήλυναν ταῖς ἡδοναῖς
ὥσθ' ὁ Ἀννίβας ἔφη νικῶν κινδυνεύειν ἐπὶ τοῖς
ἐχθροῖς γενέσθαι, γυναῖκας ἀντὶ τῶν ἀνδρῶν τοὺς
στρατιώτας ἀπολαβών. Ῥωμαῖοι δὲ κρατήσαντες
πολλοῖς κακοῖς ἐσωφρόνισαν αὐτούς, ὕστατα δὲ

---

[1] νόμον, all editors, for μόνον.
[2] ἐξετρύφησαν, Meineke, for εὖ ἐτρύφησαν.
[3] Kramer emends δεῖπνον to συνδείπνων; so Müller-Dübner
and Meineke; perhaps rightly.

---

[1] Some of the editors emend the text to read " by the rank
of their guests."

and eight thousand cavalry. And they say that among the Samnitae there is a law which is indeed honourable and conducive to noble qualities; for they are not permitted to give their daughters in marriage to whom they wish, but every year ten virgins and ten young men, the noblest of each sex, are selected, and, of these, the first choice of the virgins is given to the first choice of the young men, and the second to the second, and so on to the end; but if the young man who wins the meed of honour changes and turns out bad, they disgrace him and take away from him the woman given him. Next after the Samnitae come the Hirpini, and they too are Samnitae; they got their name from the wolf that led the way for their colony (for "hirpus" is what the Samnitae call the wolf); and their territory adjoins that of those Leucani who live in the interior. So much, then, for the Samnitae.

13. As for the Campani, it was their lot, because of the fertility of their country, to enjoy in equal degree both evil things and good. For they were so extravagant that they would invite gladiators, in pairs, to dinner, regulating the number by the importance of the dinners;[1] and when, on their instant submission to Hannibal, they received his army into winter-quarters, the soldiers became so effeminate because of the pleasures afforded them that Hannibal said that, although victor, he was in danger of falling into the hands of his foes, because the soldiers he had got back were not his men, but only women. But when the Romans got the mastery, they brought them to their senses by many severe lessons, and, last of all, portioned out to Roman

καὶ κατεκληρούχησαν τὴν γῆν. νυνὶ μέντοι μετ᾽
εὐπραγίας διάγουσι τοῖς ἐποίκοις ὁμονοήσαντες
καὶ τὸ ἀξίωμα φυλάττουσι τὸ ἀρχαῖον καὶ τῷ
μεγέθει τῆς πόλεως καὶ κατ᾽ εὐανδρίαν. μετὰ δὲ
τὴν Καμπανίαν καὶ τὴν Σαυνῖτιν μέχρι Φρεντανῶν ἐπὶ μὲν τῇ Τυρρηνικῇ θαλάττῃ τὸ τῶν Πικεντίνων ἔθνος οἰκεῖ, μικρὸν ἀπόσπασμα τῶν ἐν τῷ
Ἀδρίᾳ Πικεντίνων, ὑπὸ Ῥωμαίων μετῳκισμένον
εἰς τὸν Ποσειδωνιάτην κόλπον, ὃς νῦν Παιστανὸς
καλεῖται, καὶ ἡ πόλις ἡ Ποσειδωνία Παιστός, ἐν
μέσῳ τῷ κόλπῳ κειμένη. Συβαρῖται μὲν οὖν ἐπὶ
θαλάττῃ τεῖχος ἔθεντο, οἱ δ᾽ οἰκισθέντες ἀνωτέρω
μετέστησαν, ὕστερον δὲ Λευκανοὶ μὲν ἐκείνους,
Ῥωμαῖοι δὲ Λευκανοὺς ἀφείλοντο τὴν πόλιν. ποιεῖ
δ᾽ αὐτὴν ἐπίνοσον ποταμὸς πλησίον εἰς ἕλη ἀναχεόμενος.[1] μεταξὺ δὲ τῶν Σειρηνουσσῶν καὶ τῆς
Ποσειδωνίας Μαρκῖνα, Τυρρηνῶν κτίσμα οἰκού-
μενον ὑπὸ Σαυνιτῶν. ἐντεῦθεν εἰς Πομπαίαν διὰ
Νουκερίας οὐ πλειόνων ἑκατὸν καὶ εἴκοσι σταδίων
ἐστὶν ὁ ἰσθμός. διήκουσι δ᾽ οἱ Πίκεντες μέχρι
τοῦ Σιλάριδος ποταμοῦ τοῦ ὁρίζοντος ἀπὸ ταύτης

---

[1] Συβαρῖται . . . ἀναχεόμενος is transposed by Meineke (as
suggested by Du Theil, Groskurd, Kramer, and C. Müller)
to a position after ἡ Ποσειδωνία in 6. 1. 1.

---

[1] Strabo says elsewhere (5. 4. 2) that the Frentani were a
"Samnitic tribe," but he has preferred to discuss the two
peoples and their countries separately (see also 5. 4. 3).

[2] Hereafter Strabo will call this tribe "Picentes" (cp. the
Latin terms).

[3] This was merely a fortified trading-post. It was near
what the Romans called "Portus Alburnus" (see Nissen,
Landeskunde, Vol. II., p. 892).

[4] About one-half of a mile inland, to the site of Poseidonia.

settlers a part of the land. Now, however, they are living in prosperity, being of one mind with the new settlers, and they preserve their old-time reputation, in respect to both the size of their city and the high quality of its men. After Campania, and the Samnite country (as far as the Frentani[1]), on the Tyrrhenian Sea dwells the tribe of the Picentini,[2] a small offshoot of those Picentini who dwell on the Adriatic, which has been transplanted by the Romans to the Poseidonian Gulf; this gulf is now called the Paestan Gulf; and the city of Poseidonia, which is situated in the centre of the gulf, is now called Paestus. The Sybaritae, it is true, had erected fortifications on the sea,[3] but the settlers removed them farther inland;[4] later on, however, the Leucani took the city away from the Sybaritae, and, in turn, the Romans took it away from the Leucani. But the city is rendered unhealthy by a river that spreads out into marshes in the neighbourhood.[5] Between the Sirenussae and Poseidonia lies Marcina, a city founded by the Tyrrheni and now inhabited by Samnitae. From here to Pompaia, by way of Nuceria, the distance across the isthmus is not more than one hundred and twenty stadia. The country of the Picentes extends as far as the River Silaris, which

[5] Meineke, following the suggestion of Du Theil, transposes the Greek for "The Sybaritae . . . neighbourhood" to a position after the first sentence in Book VI, assuming that the Greek as it stands makes Poseidonia a city of the Picentini. But the words in question seem to be merely a digression ; and in that case "the settlers" now referred to are not to be confused with the "transplanted" Picentini, whose city was Picentia. The river in question is now represented by the "Fosso Capo dei Fiumi" and the marshes near it.

STRABO

τῆς χώρας τὴν ἀρχαιαν Καμπανίαν·[1] ἐφ' οὗ τοῦτ'
ἴδιον ἱστοροῦσιν περὶ τοῦ ὕδατος[2] ὄντος ποτίμου,[3]
τὸ καθιέμενον εἰς αὐτὸ φυτὸν ἀπολιθοῦσθαι φυλάτ-
τοι· τὴν χρόαν καὶ τὴν μορφήν. τῶν δὲ Πικέντων
ὑπῆρχε μητρόπολις Πικεντία, νυνὶ δὲ κωμηδὸν
ζῶσιν ἀπωσθέντες ὑπὸ Ῥωμαίων διὰ τὴν πρὸς
Ἀννίβαν κοινωνίαν· ἀντὶ δὲ στρατείας ἡμεροδρο-
μεῖν καὶ γρ‸μματοφορεῖν ἀπεδείχθησαν ἐν τῷ
τότε δημοσίᾳ, καθάπερ καὶ Λευκανοὶ καὶ Βρέττιοι
κατὰ τὰς αὐτὰς αἰτίας· ἐπετείχισαν δ' αὐτοῖς
Σάλερνον Ῥωμαῖοι φρουρᾶς χάριν μικρὸν ὑπὲρ
τῆς θαλάττης· εἰσὶ δ' ἀπὸ Σειρηνουσσῶν ἐπὶ
Σίλαριν στάδιοι διακόσιοι ἑξήκοντα.

[1] For Καμπανίαν (the reading of the MSS. except C, which
reads Καινίαν) Meineke and others read 'Ιταλίαν. See C. Müller,
Ind. Var. Lect., p 974).

[2] τοῦ. after ὕδατος, Meineke omits.

[3] ποτίμου, the editors in general, for ποταμίου (cp. same
emendation in 5. 1. 8 and 5. 4. 5).

separates the old Campania from this country.[1] In
regard to this river, writers report the following
as a special characteristic, that although its water
is potable, any plant that is let down into it turns
to stone, though it keeps its colour and its shape.[2]
Picentia first belonged to the Picentes, as metropolis,
but at the present time they live only in villages,
having been driven away by the Romans because
they had made common cause with Hannibal. And
instead of doing military service, they were at that
time appointed to serve the State as couriers and
letter-carriers (as were also, for the same reasons,
both the Leucani and the Brettii); and for the sake
of keeping watch over the Picentes the Romans
fortified Salernum against them, a city situated only
a short distance above the sea. The distance from
the Sirenussae to the Silaris is two hundred and
sixty stadia.

[1] The later editors emend "Campania" to "Italy" (cp.
5. 1. 1). But it seems far more likely that Strabo wrote
(or else had in mind) the words " Lucania and " before " the
Silaris River." In this case " this country " means Lucania.
Indeed, Strabo says in the succeeding paragraph (6. 1. 1)
that Lucania begins at Silaris. And he has already defined
the seaboard of the Campania of his own time as beginning
at Sinuessa, and ending at Surrentum and the Cape of
Minerva (see 5 2. 1, 5. 3. 4, 5. 4. 3, and 5. 4. 8–9).
[2] So Pliny (2. 106) and Silius Italicus (8. 581).

A PARTIAL DICTIONARY OF PROPER NAMES [1]

A

Acherrae, 453, 461

Addua River, 227, 273, 295, 313

Adriatic, the, 273, 283, 301, 303, 305, 319, 331, 427, 469

Adula, Mt., 227, 273, 313

Aedua, the, 199, 225, 229

Aeneas, Trojan founder of Rome, 379, 393, 397

Aequi (Aeci), the, 379, 387, 415

Aeschylus (525–456 B.C.), the tragic poet; quoted concerning the Stony Plain, 187; on the Pelasgi, 345

Aesis River, 331, 369, 371

Aetna, Mt., 453, 457

Afranius, one of Pompey's generals, 99

Agrippa, Marcus Vipsanius (consul 37, 28, 27, B.C.); his transfer of the Ubii across the Rhenus, 231; built roads from Lugdunum, 289; his adornment of Rome, 405; cut down forest about Avernus, 445

Ahenobarbus, Gnaeus Dometius (consul 122 B.C.); routed the Celti, 197, 219

Alba, 379, 381, 387, 403, 423

Albanus, Mt., 379, 411, 421, 423

Alexander the Great (356–323 B.C.); set up altars as limits of his Indian Expedition, 139; his complaints against the pirates of Antium, 391

Allobroges, the, 197, 199, 231, 271

Alps, the, 263, 265, 283, 289, 293, 299, 303, 329, 427

Amollius (Amulius), legendary King of Rome, 381

Anacreon of Teos (b. about 560 B.C., 59; the great lyric poet, of whose works only fragments remain

Anas River, 11, 19

Ancona, 303, 305, 371, 427

Ancus Marcius, legendary King of Rome, 339, 391, 401

Anio River, 403, 417

Anticleides of Athens, 347 (lived about the time of Alexander the Great), author, among other works, of the *Returns* of Greeks from their mythical expeditions

Antiochus of Syracuse (fl. about 420 B.C.), author of a *History of Sicily* and *The Colonising of Italy*, of which only fragments are extant; on the Opici and Ausones, 435

Antipolis, 171, 175, 191, 267

Antium, 387, 389, 391, 393, 421

Antony, Marcus, the triumvir, 23

Apennine Mountains, 263, 285, 287, 303, 305, 307, 323, 333, 335, 351, 373, 389, 397, 427

Appian Way, 395, 399, 411, 413, 421, 459

Aquae Sextiae, 171, 177 ,

Aquileia, 283, 287, 291, 317, 323, 331

Aquitani, the, 163, 213

Aquitania, 253, 291

Arar River, 199, 211, 223, 225, 229

Ardea, 379, 393

Ariminum, 301, 303, 305, 327, 329, 369, 371

Aristarcha, the priestess of Artemis, 173

Aristotle of Stagira (see *Dictionary* in vol. i.), on the cause of the tides, 67; on the stones of Stony Plain, 185

Arretium, 351, 365, 367

Artabrians (Arotrebians), 69, 71, 157

A PARTIAL DICTIONARY OF PROPER NAMES

Carpetanians, the, 65, 103

Carteia, whither Gnaeus Pompey fled, 23; identified with Tartessus, 59

Casilinum, 411, 413, 415

Castalo, 25, 97; its mined lead, 47; a powerful city, 65

Cavari, the, 195, 201

Celtae, the, 163, 211

Celti, the, 197, 235, 251, 255, 261, 307, 311, 333

Celtiberia, 101, 105

Celtiberians, the, 87, 103, 105, 109, 123

Celtica (*see* Transalpine and Cisalpine), four parts of, 169; size of, 251, 253; its exports and imports, 259

Cemmenus Mountain, 163, 195, 203, 211, 213, 291

Cimbri, the, 241, 319

Cisalpine Celtica, 227, 271, 303, 331, 371

Cispadana, 307, 323, 325, 329

Cleitarchus, who accompanied Alexander the Great on his Asiatic expedition; on the salt-rock in India, 357

Clusium, 367, 403

Coelius, Lucius Antipater (b. about 175 B.C.), the Roman historian, 385

Corduba, founded by Marcellus (in his third consulship, 152 B.C.), 21, 23

Corsica (*see* Cyrnus)

Cosa (Cossa), 347, 363

Cottius, 171, 273, 327; king of several Ligurian tribes in the Cottian Alps, but submitted to Augustus, who gave him the title of Praefect, whereupon he built roads over the Alps, and in 8 B.C. erected at Segusio (now Susa), in honour of Augustus, a triumphal arch which is still to be seen

Crassus, Publius Licinius (consul 97 B.C.); his visit to the Cassiterides Islands, 159

Crates of Mallus (see *Dictionary* in vol. i); his use of Homer as basis of scientific investigations, 85

Cumae, 437, 439, 447, 451

Cuneus, country adjacent to Sacred Cape, 7

Cyrnus (Corsica), 355, 359, 361

D

Daci, the, 287, 311

Demetrius of Phalerum (b. about 350 B.C.), pupil of Theophrastus, philosopher, statesman, orator, historian, and author of numerous works on various subjects; on the Attic silver mines, 43

Demetrius Poliorcetes (337–283 B.C.); his complaints against the pirates of Antium, 391

Dicaearchia, 445, 447, 451, 457

Dicaearchus of Messene in Sicily (see *Dictionary* in vol. i.), on the Pillars of Heracles, 137

Dionysius the Elder (430–367 B.C.); his stud of prize-horses, 309; robbed temple of Eilethyia, 365; his tyranny, 427

Dionysus, imitated by Alexander in the erection of altars, 139, 141; Samnitae women possessed by, 249

Dometius Ahenobarbus (*see* Ahenobarbus)

Druentia River, 171, 195, 271, 329

Druids, the, 245, 247

Drusus Germanicus (consul 9 B.C.), brother of Tiberius Caesar; his campaign against the Carni and Norici, 283

Dubis River, 199, 211, 223, 225

Durias River, 271, 277, 327

Durius River, 65, 69, 101

E

Ebusus, island of, 91, 125

Edetanians, the, 81, 103, 105

Elvetii, the, 225, 229, 281, 291

Ephorus (see *Dictionary* in vol. i.), 7; his account of Celtica, 251; on the Pelasgi, 343, 345; on the Cimmerians, 443

Eratosthenes of Cyrene (see *Dictionary* in vol. i.), on Tartessis, 49; on Tarraco's roadstead, 91; on the Pillars of Heracles, 137; on the distance of Cyrnus and Sardo from mainland, 357

Erytheia, 49, 133

Euripides (480–406 B.C.), the tragic poet; attributes the ruin of Greeks and barbarians to Zeus, 189; on the Pelasgians, 345

475

A PARTIAL DICTIONARY OF PROPER NAMES

477

A PARTIAL DICTIONARY OF PROPER NAMES

A PARTIAL DICTIONARY OF PROPER NAMES

Q

Quintus Fabius Maximus Aemilianus Allobrogicus (consul 121 B.C.); cut down 200,000 Celti, 197, 219

R

Ravenna, 301, 313, 327, 329, 369, 371

Rhaeti, the, 227, 273, 281, 293, 311

Rhenus River, 163, 221, 223, 225, 227, 229, 233, 239, 253, 273, 281, 291, 313

Rhodanus River, 167, 175, 183, 189, 191, 195, 197, 199, 209, 211, 217, 221, 223, 229, 269, 271, 273, 291

Rome, 379, 381, 391, 399, 409

Romulus, traditional founder of Rome, 381, 387

Rubicon River, 327, 331, 371

Rutuli, the, 379, 387, 393

S

Sabine country, the, 373, 377, 411, 427

Sabini, the, 335, 375, 465

Sacred Cape, 5, 7, 11, 49, 61

Salassi, the, 271, 273, 277, 289, 293, 303

Sallyes, 169, 175, 181, 193, 195, 201, 269

Samnitae, the, 377, 389, 393, 427, 435, 461, 463, 465

Samnium (Samnite country), 433, 469

Santoni, the, 215, 217, 291

Sardo (Sardinia), 349, 355, 359, 361, 363

Scaurus, M. Aemilius (163–about 89 B.C.), conducted canals from the Padus to Parma, 329

Scipio Africanus Major (consul 205–194 B.C.); his tomb at Liternum, 437

Scipio, Caius (identity unknown), added 3000 colonists to Comum, 311

Segusiavi, 199, 223

Seleucus the Chaldean astronomer, on the regularity and irregularity of the tides, 153

Senones, the, 233, 235, 311, 323

Sequana River, 211, 223, 227, 229, 253

Sequani, the, 199, 225, 229, 281, 293

Sertorius (fl. about 90 B.C.), was praetor 83 B.C., was later invited by the Lusitanians to become their commander, and as such held at bay all Roman generals, but was assassinated by certain of his own officers in 72 B.C.; his mastery in Iberia, 87; his last battles, 99; his war in Iaccetania against Pompey, 101; his war with Metellus, 103

Servius Tullius, legendary King of Rome, 401

Sextius, Titus, one of Caesar's legates in Gaul and at the time of Caesar's death (44 B.C.) governor of the province of Numidia; defeated the Sallyes and founded Aquae Sextiae (now Aix), 177

Sicily, 439, 457

Sicily, Strait of, 299, 301, 433

Sidicini, the, 413, 435

Silaris River, 469, 471

Sinuessa, 389, 395, 411, 433, 437

Spinitae, the; their treasury at Delphi, 315

Stesichorus (see *Dictionary* in vol. i.), on the neat-herd of Geryon, 49

Stoechades Island, 193

Sucro River, 89, 105

Suessa, metropolis of the Volsci, 387, 413

Suessiones, the, 233, 241

Suevi, the, 231, 287

Sulla (138–78 B.C.), 353, 463

T

Tagus River, 11, 25, 61, 65, 67, 103

Tarentum (Taras), 395

Tarentum, Gulf of, 299, 305

Tarquinius Priscus, King of Rome, 387

Tarquinius Superbus, 339

Tarracina, 389, 395

Tarraco, 91, 95, 99, 123

Tartessus, river and city, 49; associated with Tartarus, 51, 53; identified with Carteia, 59

Tarusco, 171, 203

Taurini, the, 273, 293

Teanum Sidicinum, 413, 459, 461

Tectosages, 203, 213

Teneas (Tinia) River, 373, 403

Thule (the island reported by Pytheas), 261

479

A PARTIAL DICTIONARY OF PROPER NAMES

MAPS

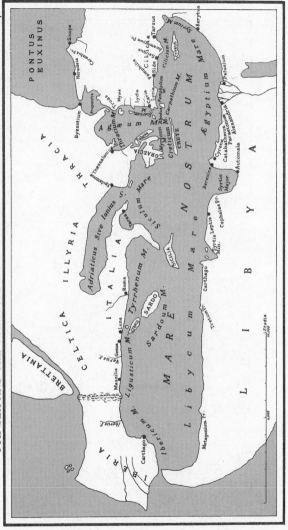

OUR SEA AND THE SURROUNDING COUNTRIES ACCORDING TO STRABO

Map II

Artabrorum Portus

Nerium Pr.

ARTABRI sivo
CELTICI AROTREBÆ

CANTA

Melsus F.

ASTURES

HISPANI

Saesurugis

Intercatia

Pallantia

Baenis
Minius F.

Belion

Durius F.

VACCÆI

CE

NI

VETTONES

CARP

Vacua F.

Mundas F.

LUSITANI

HISPANIA

Tagus F.

Moron

Olysipo

Salacia

Augusta Emerita

Anas F.

BÆTURIA

Sisapo

Oria

ULTERIOR

Pax Augusta

B Æ

TURDETANI

Baetis F.

Castulo

Obulco

Mentis

meces

Obulco

TURDULI

CUNEUS

Ossonoba

TARTESSUS

Ebura

Asia

Hispalis

Herculis I.?

TARTE
SIS

BASTULI

Mael

Carteia

Malaca

Caepionis Turris

Gades I.

Stadia

100   500

**IBERIA
(HISPANIA)**

FRETUM COLUMNARUM   M. A F

Map III.

GALLICUS
SINUS

Oeaso

VASCONES

SINUS
GALLICUS

CERRETANI

ACCETANI

Trapaea Pompeii
Templum Veneris
Pyrenaeae
Emporium

Caesar

Osca

ILERGETES

Augusta

Ilerda

NDIGETES

BARTOLAETAE

ILEABILIS

Celsa

LEETANI

Veteres

unta

Dertosa

Tarraco

Oleastrum

XES

Iberus F.

Jbriga

Chersonesus

BALEARES sive GYMNESIÆ Iae

Saguntum

Pollentia
Palma

I. MINOR

Egelasta

I. MAJOR

Sucro

Sucro F.

EBUSUS I.

EBUSUS
PITYUSSÆ Iae
OPHIUSSA I.

Hemeroscopeium

Alone

Carthago Nova

MARE

HISPANICUM

Nerium Pr.

M A R E

Tagus F.
Anas F.
Baetis F.

Iberus

Sucro F.
Carthago Nova
Stadia

Gades

SKETCH
OF
IBERIA
ACCORDING TO
STRABO

BYCUM

BRETTANIA

CANTIUM PR.

FRETUM BRETAN

320

Itium

MOR

ATRE

AMBIANI

CALETI

LEXOVII

BELLOVACI

Sequana F.

GI

GABÆUM PR.

BELG

PARISII

VENETI

B

Cenabum

NAMNITÆ

Liger F.

CARNUTES

PICTONES

BITURIGES

CUB

GA

Garumna F.

LEMOVICES

Mediolanum

Z

Nemoss

SANTONI

A

PETROCORII

BITURIGES

NITIOBRIGES

Burdigala

CADURCI

SINUS
GALLICUS

AQUITANI

TARBELLI TARUSATES

RUT

Allobii

VOLC

Tolosa

VO

Aquae

CONVENÆ

Onesio: um

Lugdunum

N

A

C

P

E
N

Illiber

M

Stadia

100   300

CELTICA
(GALLIA)

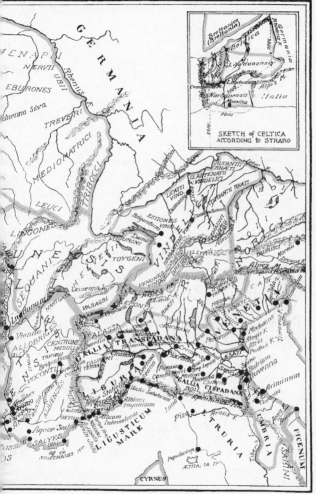

Map IV.

SKETCH of CELTICA
ACCORDING to STRABO

EDWARD STANFORD, LTD., LONDON